LOVE
SEX
DEATH&
WORDS

LOVE SEX DEATH & WORDS

SURPRISING TALES FROM A YEAR IN LITERATURE

JOHN SUTHERLAND & STEPHEN FENDER

ICON BOOKS

Published in the UK in 2010 by
Icon Books Ltd, Omnibus Business Centre,
39–41 North Road, London N7 9DP
email: info@iconbooks.co.uk
www.iconbooks.co.uk

Sold in the UK, Europe, South Africa and Asia
by Faber & Faber Ltd, Bloomsbury House,
74–77 Great Russell Street,
London WC1B 3DA or their agents

Distributed in the UK, Europe, South Africa and Asia
by TBS Ltd, TBS Distribution Centre, Colchester Road,
Frating Green, Colchester CO7 7DW

Published in Australia in 2010
by Allen & Unwin Pty Ltd,
PO Box 8500, 83 Alexander Street,
Crows Nest, NSW 2065

Distributed in Canada by
Penguin Books Canada,
90 Eglinton Avenue East, Suite 700,
Toronto, Ontario M4P 2YE

ISBN: 978-184831-164-0

Typeset in Adobe Garamond Pro by Marie Doherty

Printed and bound in the UK by
CPI Mackays, Chatham ME5 8TD

Contents

CONTENTS

CONTENTS

About the authors

John Sutherland is Lord Northcliffe Professor Emeritus at University College London. He has taught at Edinburgh University, UCL, and the California Institute of Technology. He has two honorary doctorates (Surrey and Leicester Universities) for 'services to literary criticism'. A Fellow of the Royal Society of Literature, he is also President of the Society of Indexers, and was Chair of the Man-Booker Prize panel, 2005.

Stephen Fender was born in San Francisco, and educated at Stanford and the Universities of Wales and Manchester. He has taught English and American literature at the University of Edinburgh, University College London and Sussex University, where he was Professor of American Studies from 1985 to 2001, and founding Director of the Graduate Research Centre in the Humanities. He has also taught in the USA at Santa Clara, Williams and Dartmouth Colleges, and while at UCL he designed and taught MA-level courses at the Institute for US Studies, London. At present he is an Honorary Professor of English at UCL.

Acknowledgements

Stephen Fender would like to thank Winifred Campbell, Brian Oatley, Peter Nicholls, Janet Pressley, Anna Ranson, and Jennifer Wall for their ideas and comments.

Preface

2 July

2010 On this day, as the authors of this book put their heads together to write their preface (traditionally the last thing to be written), Beryl Bainbridge died. She was well on in years and was known to be frail. The obituaries were all in stock and up to date. They appeared, some of them, the same day – virtually before the novelist's body had cooled.

Bainbridge was much loved – one of the 'national teddy-bear' authors, along with her NW1 neighbour, Alan Bennett. The other image that attached to her was that of perpetual bridesmaid. She was forever being shortlisted, or touted, for the Booker Prize, the UK's major award in fiction, but never quite won it. The British love a good loser, and none was a more gracious loser than Beryl.

The anecdotes about her were, many of them, chestnuts, but still relished because she was so liked. She was expelled from school at fourteen as a 'corrupting influence', having lost her virginity to a German POW called Franz the year before. Her subsequent life, which included a walk-on part in *Coronation Street*, was rackety. As the *Guardian* obituarist, Janet Watts, records:

> One day her elderly former mother-in-law appeared at the front door, took a loaded gun from her handbag and fired. Beryl foiled that attack, and the episode appears in *The Bottle Factory Outing*, which won the *Guardian* fiction prize.

One of us – John Sutherland – also lives in Camden, where Bainbridge, now a 'dame', used to take a shortcut in front of where he lives. Her lungs were ruined by years of smoking and she would often take a minute or two's wheezing rest on a doorstep with a street drunk called Tom, with whom, she said, she discussed such things as W.B. Yeats's late poetry.

It was a remarkable life. But – prepared as the world was for it – no one knew precisely when it would end. Her death was a wholly random event. She herself confidently expected to die in her 71st year (the age her mother and grandmother passed away) and made a touching

TV programme, *Beryl's Last Year*, a kind of Ignatian meditation on her own end. She was, as it happened, wrong – surviving, as she did, three more years.

Life (and death) are – unless you are facing execution like Gary Gilmore (see our entry for 17 January) – random events. Literature itself comprises nothing but a mass of randomness. If a novel, or poem, is rejected early on, a major writer may never happen. Any author's life is full of accidents, tosses of the coin that can fall either way up – one leading to literary creation, the other to silence. What if Dickens *had* been killed in the Staplehurst crash (see our entry for 9 June)?

For our convenience we package literature into syllabuses, curricula, canons, genres, Dewey Decimal Sectors. But literature is vast, growing (ever faster) and inherently miscellaneous. This book, using a calendrical frame, is a tribute to that miscellaneity. Anything can happen anywhere anytime. As can 'nothing', as Philip Larkin sagely reminds us.

The authors have between them a hundred years of scholarship, teaching and conversing about literature (often between themselves). What they know is like two crammed attics – full of interesting junk. But that junk is worth having. The world of books, they believe, is something forever to be explored, never comprehensively mapped. As you read this book, diurnal entry by diurnal entry, stop and try to predict (without peeking) what is going to happen on the next day. Chances are you won't be anywhere close.

Stephen Fender, a pioneer of American Studies in the UK (and an expatriate American) is responsible for many, but not all, of the New World entries. John Sutherland, a Victorianist by speciality, is responsible for many, but not all, in that period.

1 January

Peter Pan: *eternal boy, eternal copyright*

1988 The copyright history of James Barrie's most famous creation, *Peter Pan*, is vexed – and legally unique.

The origin of the character was in stories Barrie told to the children of one of his friends. One of them was called Peter. The image of Pan – thanks to cultish 1890s literary paganism – was current in the Edwardian period (the mischievous goaty-god makes an entry, for example, into another favourite children's book of the period, *The Wind in the Willows*).

At the time Barrie was best known as a novelist. His contemporaries would have predicted that his reputation with posterity would rest on such works as *Auld Licht Idylls*, or *The Little Minister*. These are out of print nowadays and largely forgotten, while *Peter Pan*, thanks to the Christmas pantomime, is set to fly on till the crack of doom.

The character was first introduced in Barrie's 1902 novel for adults, *The Little White Bird*. The play (aimed at children, principally) *Peter Pan, or The Boy Who Wouldn't Grow Up* had its premiere in London on 27 December 1904. The novel *Peter Pan in Kensington Gardens* was spun off as a follow-up to the play in 1906. Barrie then adapted the play into another novel, *Peter and Wendy* (usually shortened to *Peter Pan*), in 1911. In 1929 Barrie, who had no children of his own, donated the work, and all the Peter Pan revenues, to the Great Ormond Street Hospital for Children, in London.

These differing initiation dates, originating conceptions and ownership issues have caused copyright confusion (as has the fact that there is, in Anglo-American law, no copyright in ideas, scenarios or characters – only in the verbal forms in which they are expressed).

Further confusion has arisen in the decades since Barrie's death, in 1937. The work, popularised by such (copyright licensed) adaptations as Walt Disney's in 1953, has been a major source of revenue for the hospital. The normal term of copyright in the UK is 50 years post mortem, which meant that *Peter Pan* entered the public domain at the end of 1987.

It then re-entered copyright protection with the EU 'harmony' regulations of 1995, which extended copyright to 70 years post mortem. This was done largely to compensate German literary estates, which had lost out on international copyright revenue during the Second

World War. Along with *Mein Kampf* (whose copyright had expired in 1995) *Peter Pan* was given a new lease of copyright life until 2007, when – in the normal course of events – it would have popped back into the public domain on the 70th anniversary of Barrie's death.

This process, however, was forestalled by a measure introduced by the Labour government in 1998 (interested in keeping a healthy income stream into the NHS). This extraordinary amendment to the law affecting intellectual property:

> conferred on trustees for the benefit of the Hospital for Sick Children, Great Ormond Street, London, a right to a royalty in respect of the public performance, commercial publication, broadcasting or inclusion in a cable programme service of the play 'Peter Pan' by Sir James Matthew Barrie, or of any adaptation of that work, notwithstanding that copyright in the work expired on 31 December 1987.

The situation (particularly in the US) is tangled and has led to serial litigation. But in essence the situation is simple. Peter, the perpetual boy, has – from 1 January 1988 onwards – perpetual copyright. For ever and ever, amen.

2 January

The SS Commodore *sinks off the coast of Florida, leaving Stephen Crane adrift in an open boat*

1897 Leaving Jacksonville, Florida, for Cuba, the ship struck a sandbar that damaged the hull and started a leak in the boiler room. When the pumps failed she settled in the water and finally sank some sixteen miles offshore. Aboard was Stephen Crane, poet and novelist, renowned author of *Maggie, a Girl of the Streets* (1893) and *The Red Badge of Courage* (1895). When the crew took to the lifeboats, Crane found himself in a ten-foot dinghy along with the injured ship's captain, its cook and an engine-room oiler.

What followed was his best-remembered short story, 'The Open Boat', which he would publish in *Scribner's Magazine* just four months later. The narrative is freighted with portentous, third-person irony to reflect the seriousness of the men's situation. Only the oiler Billie is named; the others are just 'the correspondent' (Crane's stand-in), 'the captain' and 'the cook'.

'None of them knew the color of the sky', as the famous opening words have it. Crane is good on contrasting points of view. 'Viewed from a balcony, the whole thing would doubtlessly have been weirdly picturesque', but what the men see are the huge waves that threaten to swamp them if not kept a close eye on. They know the colour of those all right.

The men support each other, taking turns at the oars without complaint, doing their best to steer in the heaving seas. But set against the fellowship of comrades is the indifference of nature. They catch sight of land but it's out of reach. 'If I am going to be drowned – if I am going to be drowned – if I am going to be drowned, why in the name of the seven mad gods who rule the sea, was I allowed to come thus far and contemplate sand and trees?' Nature's answer to this question – as to all others – is a 'high cold star on a winter's night'. Finally they get ashore, but only after the dinghy has capsized in the surf, forcing the men to swim for it. Billie is drowned. The nameless ones survive.

The truth fell short of this elemental struggle between nature and humanity. In real life the *Commodore*, not much larger than an inshore trawler, had been loaded to the gunwales with munitions for the Cuban insurrection against Spain. Crane had been sent along as a reporter for the Bacheller-Johnson newspaper syndicate to get the story. The whole adventure took just a day and a night. Just four days after the *Commodore* went down, Stephen Crane was back in the arms of his new girlfriend, a brothel madam named Cora Taylor whom he had met in Jacksonville before leaving for Cuba.

3 January

Construction begins on the Brooklyn Bridge, long-standing icon of American modernism

1870 It took thirteen years to build, but when it was done it spanned more than a mile over the East River between Manhattan and Brooklyn, then the longest suspension bridge in the world and the first to be held up by filaments of steel wire.

Even before the bridge was started, the idea of crossing that stretch of water had fascinated the poet Walt Whitman as an image of links between work and home, between fellow voyagers, even between the poet and his future readers. This is from 'Crossing Brooklyn Ferry' (1860):

> I too saw the reflection of the summer night in the water,
> Had my eyes dazzled by the shimmering track of beams,
> Looked at the fine centrifugal spokes of light round the shape
>   of my head in the water,
> Looked on the haze on the hills southward and south westward,
> Looked on the vapor as it flew in fleeces tinged with violet.

But it took the bridge to bring technology into the optimistic future vision, in the aesthetics of the machine age. Precisionist painters like Charles Sheeler, Joseph Stella and George Ault rendered factories, sky-scrapers and grain elevators almost cubistically – as simplified planes of light and colour. In two paintings by Stella and a film photographed by Sheeler and Paul Stand (*Manhatta*, 1920) the Bridge is imaged head-on, its suspension cables focusing on the arches of its pillars.

Not just painting but poetry too had to accommodate the com-monplace present – and especially modern industrial technology. 'For unless poetry can absorb the machine,' Hart Crane wrote in 1929, it will have 'failed of its full contemporary function.' Crane's ambitious sequence *The Bridge* (1930) both begins and ends with the Brooklyn Bridge, imagining it as the first link westwards and backwards in time to an American past to be recuperated for use in the present.

> O sleepless as the river under thee,
> Vaulting the sea, the prairies' dreaming sod,
> Unto us lowliest sometime sweep, descend
> And of the curveship lend a myth to God.

4 January

The death of T.S. Eliot

1965 No British poet's death was more momentous (particularly among his fellow poets) than that of T.S. Eliot on this day. It was his stature as a patron, as much as a practitioner, which rendered his death the end of a literary period.

In his private journal, Ted Hughes (all of whose major works had been published by Faber, of which Eliot was senior editor) recorded that the death was

> like a crack over the head. I've so tangled him in my thoughts, dreamt of him so clearly and unambiguously. At once I feel windswept, unsafe. He was in my mind constantly, like a rather over-watchful, over-powerful father. And now he has gone.

In the genuinely windswept wastes of Siberia, where he was in exile, Josef Brodsky wrote, on 12 January, the elegy 'Verses on the Death of T.S. Eliot'. It begins (translated from the Russian): 'He died at start of year, in January' and clearly evokes Auden's poem on the death of Yeats.

A continent away, in the *Sewanee Review*, Allen Tate wrote, with Dantean flourishes:

> It was only several days later that I *understood* that T.S. Eliot was dead. One dies every day one's own death, but one cannot imagine the death of the man who was *il maestro di color che sanno** – or, since he was an artist and not after his young manhood a philosopher: *il maestro di color che scrivonno.*†

Those who were not poets were less poetic in their response. Groucho Marx wrote in a letter:

> I was saddened by the death of T.S. Eliot. My wife and I had dinner at his home a few months ago and I realized then that he was not long for this world. He was a nice man, the best epitaph any man can have.

---

* 'The master of men who know.' (Dante, *Inferno*, Canto IV, describing Aristotle.)
† 'The master of men who write.'

The authors of this book were junior lecturers at Edinburgh University in 1965. On hearing the news of Eliot's death, a less excited colleague remarked: 'Then I don't suppose he'll be turning again.'

5 January

Dumas fights a duel

1825 It's not an easy statistic to gather but, given the nature of his plots (musketeers and Counts of Monte Cristo), no novelist features more duels in his fiction, nor features them more climactically, than Alexandre Dumas (*père*).

The twenty-year-old Dumas came to Paris with the restoration of the monarchy in 1822. It would be seven years before he made his name as a writer (of plays, initially), and twenty years before, with the D'Artagnan romances, he would become the most popular writer of fiction in France – specialising in the clash of swords (although the plot of *The Three Musketeers* hinges, initially, on duels being banned). Initially he worked at the Palais Royal, in the office of the Duc D'Orléans.

In his memoirs Dumas recalls fighting a duel. It began over a game of billiards when one of the company chose to be sarcastic about the dandyish Dumas's dress. The affair was arranged by the seconds, with the normal rituals, for 5 January – traditionally they were fought at dawn. Dumas was the challenger.

Pistols were initially the chosen weapon. In the event it was changed to swords. The site was a snow-swept quarry. Dumas's opponent slept in, however, and the date was pushed back to the sixth and the place changed to Montmartre. The event quickly descended into farce as quarry workers (who left their beds earlier than the high-born duellists) gathered to watch the fun and Dumas's sword proved, on the routine measurement of rapiers, to be shorter than his adversary's. Nor were things helped by Dumas's adversary experiencing difficulty (having forgotten his braces) in keeping his trousers up. There was a serious likelihood of his expiring in his underpants. Both of them were somewhat less skilled in swordplay than Edmond Dantès.

Honour was satisfied when Dumas drew blood by nicking his opponent in the shoulder. Duels were always more glamorous in Dumas's later fiction and doubly so in the innumerable stage and movie versions of it.

6 January

The Feast of Fools and the end of the world

1482 No novel opens with a more precise calendrical reference than Victor Hugo's *The Hunchback of Notre Dame* (the melodramatic translation of the author's more neutral *Notre Dame de Paris*):

> Three hundred and forty-eight years, six months, and nineteen days ago to-day, the Parisians awoke to the sound of all the bells in the triple circuit of the city, the university, and the town ringing a full peal. The sixth of January, 1482, is not, however, a day of which history has preserved the memory.

Fiction has preserved it. The day, we learn, is notable to the citizens of Hugo's Paris as the 'double solemnity, united from time immemorial, of the Epiphany and the Feast of Fools'. On this day the lay populace elect their 'Pope of Fools'. On 6 January 1482 the street vote goes to the bell-ringer of Notre Dame – principally because of his hilarious physical deformity. He is a living satire less of the Pontiff than of humanity itself:

> His whole person was a grimace. A huge head, bristling with red hair; between his shoulders an enormous hump, a counterpart perceptible in front; a system of thighs and legs so strangely astray that they could touch each other only at the knees, and, viewed from the front, resembled the crescents of two scythes joined by the handles; large feet, monstrous hands; and, with all this deformity, an indescribable and redoubtable air of vigour, agility, and courage, – strange exception to the eternal rule which wills that force as well as beauty shall be the result of harmony. Such was the pope whom the fools had just chosen for themselves.

Is this the image of God? Quasimodo's grotesque anatomy and indomitable willpower have become folkloric: as much for Charles Laughton's classic depiction in the 1939 film as for Hugo's 1831 novel.

There is another significance to the date than the street festival. Hugo sees 1482 as an epochal literary moment. The point is made by 'the sworn bookseller of the university, Master Andry Musnier' in conversation with 'the furrier of the king's robes, Master Gilles Lecornu':

> 'I tell you, sir, that the end of the world has come. No-one has ever beheld such outbreaks among the students! It is the accursed inventions of this century that are ruining everything, – artilleries, bombards, and, above all, *printing*, that other German pest. No more manuscripts, no more books! printing will kill bookselling. It is the end of the world that is drawing nigh.'

By 'no more books' he means the end of the manuscript codex. Printing will, Musnier foresees, also be the end of monarchy and its lovely hierarchies. And the end of cathedrals – the 'script' of old France. After books there will be no more Notre Dames.

Who then (historically) is the villain of *Notre Dame de Paris*? Not the hunchback but Gutenberg. The novel eerily prophesies contemporary 21st-century jeremiads about the death of the book with the arrival of such newfangled things as Gutenberg.org (see 1 December) and the Kindle e-reader. The end of another world draws nigh.

7 January

John Berryman follows his paternal destiny

1972 John Berryman, the American poet, was born John Allyn Smith Jr. His father, John Allyn Smith Sr., committed suicide when young John was twelve. He took the surname of his mother's second husband. After a long battle with alcoholism, Berryman seemed to have come to terms with his addiction in 1970 – writing a memoir, *Recovery*, recording the fact. Having been clean and sober for a year and a half, during which time a daughter was born to him and his wife, he followed his father's example and killed himself.

The event is vividly recorded by his biographer, Paul Mariani. It was a Friday and Berryman had passed an unsettled night. He told his wife he was going to his office at the University of Minneapolis, where he had a teaching appointment. It was bitterly cold:

> Instead of going to his office, he walked out onto the upper level of the Washington Avenue Bridge … Three quarters of the way across, he stopped and stared down. A hundred feet below and to his right rode the river: narrow, gray, and half frozen … He climbed onto the chest-high metal railing and balanced himself. Several students inside the walkway stopped what they were doing when they saw him and stared in disbelief. He made a gesture as if waving, but he did not look back … Three seconds later his body exploded against the knoll, recoiled from the earth, then rolled gently down the incline. The campus police were the first to arrive and found a package of [Tareyton cigarettes], some change, and a blank check with the name Berryman on it.

8 January

Villon escapes the rope, and is never heard of again

1463 Little is known of Francois Villon's life (even his surname is uncertain – it may have been a nickname with an etymological connection with 'villain'). Although he graduated from the University of Paris his later career was that of thief, vagabond and rogue. He was also (more memorably) one of the greatest vernacular poets of the French medieval period.

His most famous line, 'où sont les neiges d'antan?' (translated by Dante Gabriel Rossetti as 'Where are the snows of yesteryear?') has become proverbial. It sums up the mordant wit of his balladry.

After a street quarrel in June 1455 – one of many recorded in court documents – Villon was arrested, tortured and condemned to be hanged. It was the occasion of his most famous poem, 'Ballad of the Gibbet' ('Ballade des Pendus'):

> Brothers and men that shall after us be,
> Let not your hearts be hard to us:

For pitying this our misery
Ye shall find God the more piteous.
Look on us six that are hanging thus,
And for the flesh that so much we cherished
How it is eaten of birds and perished,
And ashes and dust fill our bones' place,
Mock not at us that so feeble be,
But pray God pardon us out of His grace.

The pardon came not from God, but the court. On 5 January 1463 the sentence was commuted, on appeal, to banishment from Paris for ten years. A full pardon was denied on the grounds of his 'wicked life'.

Banishment involved the sentence being read out, publicly, in front of the gallows which Villon had cheated and apostrophised. Villon tossed off a couple of witty *ballades* of gratitude to the *parlement* which had commuted his sentence.

He left Paris on the 8th of the month. 'After January 1463,' his biographer Michael Freeman writes in *The Villain's Tale* (the author's name is as apt as the title) 'we lose all trace of Francois Villon.'

9 January

Deconstruction deconstructed?

1988 If deconstruction, as a dominant Anglo-American literary theory, was constructed on 21 October 1966 (see the entry for that date), it was profoundly shaken on 9 January 1988 with Jon Wiener's article in *The Nation* ('Deconstructing de Man').

Wiener was indebted to a young Belgian scholar, Ortwin de Graef. De Graef (initially a disciple, and a graduate student doing a thesis on Paul de Man, the leading exponent of the new critical school) had turned up some 170 articles written by de Man during the Nazi occupation of Belgium – most of them for the country's leading newspaper, *Le Soir* (known, during this sad period, as *Le Soir volé* – 'the stolen *Le Soir*'). They were mainly hack work, but a handful offered clear evidence of party-line anti-Semitism, notably a piece published on 4 March 1941, 'The Jews in Contemporary Literature', which concluded:

A solution to the Jewish problem that would lead to the creation of a Jewish colony isolated from Europe would not have, for the literary life of the West, regrettable consequences. It would lose, in all, some personalities of mediocre worth and would continue, as in the past, to develop according to its higher laws of evolution.

Even if he did not know the 'solution' his current employers had in mind, de Man, it was pointed out, could not but have noticed the current persecution of Belgian Jews who, at this date, were banned from professional employment (not least writing for *Le Soir*) and branded with yellow stars. Was the deconstruction enterprise an attempt by de Man to erase his past, render it meaningless so as to soothe a nagging conscience? There was much ingenious psychobiography on the topic.

In the wake of de Graef's revelations, and their follow-up reverberations in the Anglo-American press, other skeletons were hauled out of the deceased de Man's cupboard: bigamy, lying to immigration officials, allowing it to be thought he had been involved with the Belgian resistance.

Deconstruction was not, as a critical procedure, destroyed by the revelation of de Man's wartime publications and alleged malfeasance. But it was substantially deconstructed.

10 January

In Philadelphia, Thomas Paine publishes a pamphlet that will change the world

1776 Today it's hard to imagine a published essay changing history. However stirring the argument, however profoundly researched, the article in the magazine or morning paper will leave the world pretty well unchanged. But Thomas Paine lived in a period in which the 'media' were not the newspapers, television and the internet, but the printed word and the word from the pulpit – itself often distributed in print after the first hearing.

Born in Thetford, Norfolk and radicalised in Lewes, Sussex, where he organised the local excise men, Paine was persuaded by Benjamin Franklin to emigrate to Philadelphia. There he was quickly caught up in the arguments for and against American independence from Great Britain.

Yet despite two decades of polemic, protests and petitions, not to mention skirmishes like the Boston Massacre, the Boston Tea Party and the opening of actual hostilities in 1775, when the 'shot heard round the world' forced a party of British soldiers to retreat from Concord, Massachusetts, through Lexington back to Boston, to be harried by colonial militias all the way – despite all this, only a third of the delegates to the Continental Congress at the beginning of 1776 were in favour of severing ties with the mother country.

Then came Tom Paine's *Common Sense*, 48 treasonable, incendiary pages, calling for an end to compromise and a decisive break from Britain. The pamphlet was an instant sensation, selling 120,000 copies in the first three months. 'Given that America had only two million free citizens at the time,' writes Brendan O'Neill, 'that is the equivalent of an American author selling 15 million books in three months today.'*

By the end of the year *Common Sense* had sold half a million copies and gone through 23 editions. These masses of ordinary readers forced the authorities to change their minds, from those delegates to the Congress to General George Washington, who would soon lead the American Continental Army into battle against Great Britain, funded in part by the royalties from *Common Sense*.

How did Paine do it? He appealed to people's common understanding of 'nature', a concept repeated frequently in the pamphlet. It was against the nature of geography for a small island to govern a continent. Men and women are born equal by nature, therefore it was unnatural for one man to rule others in perpetuity, especially when he had not earned his position, but merely inherited it.

Above all, knowing his audience to be made up largely of dissenting Protestants, he borrowed the non-conformist language used by radicals like Gerrard Winstanley and the 17th-century Diggers, or 'True Levellers' (see 10 October). 'Government by kings was first introduced into the world by the *Heathens*', he wrote, 'from whom the children of Israel copied the custom. It was the most prosperous invention the *Devil* ever set on foot for the promotion of *idolatry*.' (Italics added.)

Those words in italics were hot buttons in Digger rhetoric. So were the terms Paine used to dismiss the notion that Britain was the

---

* Brendan O'Neill, 'Who Was Thomas Paine?', BBC News magazine, 8 June 2009: http://news.bbc.co.uk/2/hi/uk_news/magazine/8089115.stm

mother country. All 'the more shame upon her conduct,' he parried, 'even brutes do not devour their young'. But in any case, 'the phrase PARENT OR MOTHER COUNTRY hath been *jesuitically* adopted by the King and his *parasites*, with a low *papistical* design of gaining an unfair bias on the *credulous* weakness of our minds'.

In fact even more than nature, it was the credulity and idolatry that many Protestants supposed to be so characteristic of Roman Catholicism that underpinned Paine's strictures against compromise with Great Britain. Hence his devastating satire on the notion that the divine right of British kings to rule over their subject peoples had somehow descended unimpeded and undiluted from William the Conqueror:

> A French bastard landing with an armed Banditti and establishing himself king of England against the consent of the natives, is in plain terms a very paltry rascally original. It certainly hath no divinity in it. However it is needless to spend much time in exposing the folly of hereditary right; if there are any so weak as to believe it, let them promiscuously worship the Ass and the Lion, and welcome. I shall neither copy their humility, nor disturb their devotion.

11 January

Lorna Sage dies as her memoir triumphs

2001 Few important books have been published in a closer race with the undertaker than Lorna Sage's *Bad Blood*. Her best-selling personal memoir (the procreator of what, in more debased form, would become a genre of so-called 'misery memoirs') was published in October 2000.

Bad Blood went on to win the Whitbread Prize in the first week of January 2001. Sage died a few days later. She described what writing *Bad Blood* meant to her (and illustrated the remarkable vividness of her literary style) in an article in the *Guardian*, shortly before her death:

> Starting a memoir, you open a door on to the past. The moment *Bad Blood* became real to me was when, in my mind's eye, I saw just which door, and who was leading the way:

'Grandfather's skirts would flap in the wind along the church-yard path and I would hang on.'

I am still pleased with the book's first words, though I had no idea what I was letting myself in for. My bitter, theatrical vicar-grandfather, stagnating in the remote rural parish of Hanmer in North Wales for his sins (women and drink, mostly), was my reference point, my black flag on the map of the past, my arrow pointing – 'You were here', this is where you begin.*

A chronic sufferer from terminal emphysema, Sage knew, while writing the memoir, that this was also where she would end.

The life recorded in *Bad Blood* is remarkable, but in its way typical of the meritocratic opportunities opened in the second half of the 20th century by the Butler Education Act, and the Robbins expansion of the universities in the 1960s.

She was born Lorna Stockton in rural Shropshire on 13 January 1943. Her father, a peacetime haulage contractor, was serving in the army. Her mother was the daughter of an Anglican clergyman. Neither Lorna's mother nor her grandmother had been happy with their marriage partner. The Stockton family lived in a council house after her vicar grandfather retired from his living.

While still at her girls' high (i.e. grammar) school, Lorna met, married and had a child by Victor Sage. She was a mother at sixteen. Despite the obvious handicaps, she made it to Durham University, graduating in 1966 with a first-class degree in English (as did her husband, Vic). She never – as would soon become necessary for an academic career – did a PhD, but got an assistant lectureship at a 'new university', the University of East Anglia, in Norwich, where she would spend the remainder of her working life (her husband also landed a job in the department).

Sage became an authority on modern women's literature, and a prominent reviewer in national newspapers, magazines and on cultural TV programmes. Her marriage to Sage was dissolved in 1974, and she remarried five years later.

Bad Blood is a voyage of introspection. Sage locates the fluid of the title – and her extraordinary drive to succeed in life – in her grandfather (who died when she was nine): 'I ... acquired from grandpa

---

* *Guardian*, 12 January 2001.

vanity, ambition and discontent along with literacy. I didn't know my place.'

12 January

Agatha Christie, the queen of mystery, and Dame of the British Empire, dies

1976 One of the larger mysteries about the 'queen of mystery' is why – of all the crime novelists who have put pen to paper – she should be the most overwhelmingly popular. A devotee website set up in 2008 plausibly asserts: 'Agatha Christie remains the most popular novelist in history with over two billion of her books sold at a conservative estimate.'*

Christie's tentacles spread worldwide, and magma deep. On 24 May 2009, Iranian authorities reported that a woman serial killer (un-named) had killed some six victims. A doped glass of fruit juice was her weapon of choice. The murderess confessed that she had picked up her poisoning techniques from 'the novels of Agatha Christie'.

The Iranian fan was not the first to use the queen of crime's toxic expertise. The mass poisoner Graham Young (memorialised in the 1995 film *The Young Poisoner's Handbook*) was inspired to use his toxin of choice, the 'undetectable' and lethal thallium, by Agatha Christie's 1961 novel *The Pale Horse*. Young was dubbed 'the teacup murderer' by the tabloid press – the friendly 'cuppa' being his preferred way of administering thallium to his luckless victims. He committed suicide in prison: poison unknown.

Christie was famously good on poisons. During the First World War, and newly married, she worked as a voluntary nurse at Torquay Hospital and was put in charge of the dispensary. Here it was that she gained her formidable expertise about dangerous drugs.

The largest mystery in Christie's life will never be solved. 1926 was the critical year in her life. Her mother died. Her marriage, to the ne'er-do-well Archie Christie, broke down. Archie, she learned, had been flagrantly unfaithful. On 6 December 1926 British newspapers carried screaming headlines about Mrs Christie's mysterious disappearance.

---

* www.agathachristie.com

A car with articles of her clothing had been found abandoned. A nation-wide woman-hunt was mounted. Rivers were dragged.

Eleven days later she was discovered serenely taking tea in a hotel at Harrogate, registered under the name of Archie's mistress. The unconvincing explanation given out to the world was that she had suffered an attack of 'amnesia'. Christie never revealed (nor would allow to be discussed in her presence) what happened, or what she had intended, during those eleven days in May.

Despite long-running tax problems, Christie, the 'queen of crime', was, in her later years, a wealthy and honoured woman of letters (and, on the strength of her late-life marriage to the archaeologist Sir Max Mallowan, happily married the second time round). She was awarded a CBE in 1956 and was made a Dame of the British Empire in 1971. She died on this day in 1976. Her tombstone at Cholsey in Berkshire is inscribed 'Agatha Christie the writer'.

13 January

Truth on the march

1898 What history calls 'the Dreyfus affair' began in 1894 when it was discovered that French military secrets about artillery dispositions were being passed to the Germans. Since the Franco-Prussian war, relations between the countries had been tense. Suspicion fell on a French officer of Jewish origin, Alfred Dreyfus. He was arrested on 15 October 1894, stripped of his captain's rank (the epaulets ritually torn from his uniform) and sentenced by court martial, in camera, to life imprisonment on Devil's Island.

Two years later the real culprit was identified, Major Ferdinand Walsin Esterhazy. To save military embarrassment, it was covered up and Dreyfus left to rot in French Guiana. The story leaked out. To the allegations of rank injustice were added those of institutional anti-Semitism. Dreyfus's case became a 'cause'. It was raised to white heat by the acquittal, after inquiry, of Esterhazy.

This it was that provoked, on 13 January 1898, Emile Zola's 4,000-word open letter, addressed to the president of France, in the newspaper *L'Aurore*, headlined '*J'accuse!*'. Two hundred thousand copies of the newspaper were sold that day. '*La verité est en marche et rien ne l'arrêtera*' ('truth is on the march and nothing can stop it'), proclaimed the novelist-turned-campaigner.

The authorities had every intention of stopping it. A fortnight later Zola was put on trial for criminal libel (the libel was to have alleged that Esterhazy's tribunal was knowingly complicit in corruption). Zola's trial dragged on for two weeks, with ugly mobs – some shouting anti-Semitic slogans – outside.

Zola was convicted and sentenced to the maximum punishment allowed by law, a year's imprisonment. He fled to England, where there was considerable sympathy for Dreyfus, living there for a year. In September 1899, Dreyfus was finally pardoned. Zola returned, but was financially ruined and exhausted. He died in 1902, in mysterious circumstances (he was asphyxiated by a defective chimney – anti-Dreyfusards were suspected by many).

Full military reparation did not come for Dreyfus until 1906, when, at a full-dress parade, he was promoted to major and returned to service in the artillery. He attended the ceremony to install Zola's ashes in the Panthéon in 1908, at which he was wounded by a gunshot from a journalist and would-be assassin, Louis Gregori.

14 January

A.S. Byatt fights for her local

2001 The connection between literature and the public house is honourable. The first great vernacular poem in the language, Chaucer's *Canterbury Tales*, opens in a Southwark hostelry, the Tabard. Inspirational as its conviviality is in some cases, pubs – and the booze they serve – are sometimes inimical to the production of literature. The inebriated muse rarely produces masterpieces. Probably more good poetry was lost than conceived in the Wagon and Horses, known as the 'Glue Pot' because once you went in you were stuck all day, where the BBC poets – Dylan Thomas, Louis MacNeice, Roy Campbell, W.R. Rodgers – liked to drink their day away.

On the whole, though, authors are solidly behind their local. On this day it was reported that the Booker-winning novelist Dame Antonia Byatt had joined battle against the Archbishops of Canterbury and York in support of hers.

The Minster school, which trained the choir of Lincoln Cathedral, had acquired the adjoining site on Lindum Hill, on which was situated Lincoln's oldest pub, the Adam and Eve – named after mankind's first sinners – a nicely ironic tavern sign. Having bought the property from the brewery which owned it, the Church Schools Company (whose patrons are the country's two archbishops) intended to take over the pub's gardens for its own purposes, de-license the listed building and convert the shell of what was once the pub into a student hostel. No more cakes and ale at the *Adam and Eve*.

A.S. Byatt learned about this desecration (it could hardly, in the circumstances, be called 'sacrilege') from the American film star Gwyneth Paltrow, who had starred in the recent film adaptation of *Possession* (1990). The *Adam and Eve* had been a location for scenes in the movie.

Dame Antonia, whose novel was set around Lincoln, and who had been brought up herself not far away, made her views publicly known: 'I would be very upset if the pub closed. I have known it since I was a child. In places like Lincoln, where there isn't much left, it really ought to be left alone.'

Happily, the Adam and Eve pub survived. It supports (under a medallion of the city's most famous literary personage, Alfred Lord Tennyson) the annual Lincoln Beer Festival.

15 January

The youngest novelist in English literature dies, aged 89

1972 Margaret Mary Julia Ashford, nicknamed by her family 'Daisy', was born in 1881 and brought up in Lewes, Sussex, among a prosperous and numerous Catholic family. As a nine-year-old girl she wrote novels after tea and before bedtime (a strict six o'clock) for the delectation of her father, a civil servant in the War Office. A readership of one. He copied the stories out for her, in a more legible adult hand, but retaining her turns of phrase and orthography. Given the size of the Ashford brood, Daisy clearly won more than her fair share of paternal attention.

Before she could put pen to paper she dictated to her father her first story, *The Life of Father McSwiney*, which she composed aged four.

Daisy's mature oeuvre includes *The Hangman's Daughter*, *Where Love Lies Deepest*, and the novel on which her fame rests, *The Young Visiters*.

This last work was published in 1919 by Chatto and Windus as a curiosity, with an introduction by J.M. Barrie, who – manuscript in hand – vouched for the bona fides of the 'nine-year-old authoress' and that the work was 'unaided'.

The Chatto editor in charge of the project, Frank Swinnerton (himself a novelist), interviewed the now fortyish author before giving it the go-ahead. Miss Ashford daringly asked Swinnerton for as much as £10. Chatto came through, voluntarily, with £500 and eventually paid thousands more. As the *Daily Mail* recorded, one half of London was laughing over *The Young Visiters* in 1919. The other half was impatiently waiting for the next edition to be printed, so they could get hold of the work that everyone else was in fits about.

Miss Ashford wrote nothing more after going to board at a convent school aged thirteen, in Haywards Heath. Fiction was put away with other childish things. She married a farmer, ran a hotel and had children of her own. Doubtless she told a rattling good bedtime story. Her identity as the authentic author of a work that was often considered a fake because it was so good was confirmed, at the end of a long and useful life, on 15 January 1972, in a *Times* obituary.

The flavour of the romance is given in the first paragraph:

Mr Salteena was an elderly man of 42 and was fond of asking peaple to stay with him. He had quite a young girl staying with him of 17 named Ethel Monticue. Mr Salteena had dark short hair and mustache and wiskers which were very black and twisty. He was middle sized and he had very pale blue eyes. He had a pale brown suit but on Sundays he had a black one and he had a topper every day as he thorght it more becoming. Ethel Monticue had fair hair done on the top and blue eyes. She had a blue velvit frock which had grown rarther short in the sleeves. She had a black straw hat and kid gloves.

Ethel is also given to 'sneery' looks when things do not go quite her way. Happy to say, everything does go her way and all ends happily other than for Mr Salteena. But at a superannuated 42, what could the old codger expect?

16 January

Samuel Clemens, aged fifteen, publishes his first story in his hometown paper, the Hannibal, Missouri Western Union, *edited by his older brother*

1851 Humorous sketches were a staple of the American popular press at the time. They kept people reading, and, since they were usually undated, could be slotted in whenever a filler was needed. Samuel Clemens wrote over 350 of them wherever he worked as a journeyman printer, and later reporter – in St Louis, Chicago, New York, Philadelphia, San Francisco and Carson City, Nevada.

His first was a short piece of about 150 words, headed 'A Gallant Fireman'. In it, a fire breaks out next door but one to the *Union* printing house, forcing Clemens and his workmates to consider moving their material out of the way, in case the fire should spread. In the process, 'our gallant *devil* [printer's apprentice] … immediately gathered the broom, an old mallet, the wash pan and a dirty towel … rushed out of the office and deposited his precious burden some ten squares off'.

Trouble was, he was 'of a *snailish* disposition, even in his quickest moments', so the fire had been put out before he got back. On returning, 'thinking he had immortalized himself, [he] threw his giant frame in a tragic attitude, and exclaimed, with an eloquent expression: "If that thar fire hadn't bin put out, thar'd a' bin the greatest *confirmation* of the age."'

Alright, maybe compared to Mozart, who wrote his first *opera* when he was eleven years old, Clemens was no prodigy. But the sketch does contain important clues to the later work of the man who would become Mark Twain. Here the author is already deriving humour from accents as indicators of social level, and from elevated rhetoric – especially when it misses the mark, as in 'confirmation' for 'conflagration'.

It also shows just how deeply interwoven with newspapers Clemens was. The story didn't just appear in a newspaper; it's also about one. And so were a number of his later sketches – those written in Nevada, for example, where local reporters, especially those of rival papers, often form the target of good-natured jokes.

Clemens himself started out as a printer's devil, when he went to work for the Hannibal *Gazette* at the age of twelve. The editors of the *Early Tales and Sketches* think he not only wrote 'A Gallant Fireman', but set it up in type as well.* From the beginning his involvement with publishing was underpinned by the physical process itself. And if laboriously hand-setting a stick of type teaches you anything beyond the craft itself, it's the virtue of brevity.

17 January

Gary Gilmore is executed by firing squad in Salt Lake City, Utah, ending nearly a decade's moratorium on the death penalty in the US

1977 In the 1960s people in the USA began to question the fairness and efficacy of the death penalty. It was racially biased, with African-Americans – 12 per cent of the population – making up 54 per cent of those executed. It was arbitrary, with some states invoking the punishment for rape and other offences as well as murder. By 1967 an informal moratorium was in place pending a definitive judgment by the Supreme Court.

When it came in 1972, *Furman v. Georgia* didn't really decide the issue. The majority of Supreme Court justices ruled that the death penalty constituted a 'cruel and unusual punishment' in violation of the eighth amendment of the Constitution, but only two of them declared the penalty to be unconstitutional in all instances. The main burden of the judgement hit out at the arbitrary nature of offences punishable by death, and the racial bias of the penalty. The states were ordered to bring their statutes in line so as to reflect these concerns.

Gilmore was the ideal way back into the death penalty. First, he was white. Second, he had been convicted of shooting a motel manager in Provo, Utah, on 20 July 1976, and (though the second case never came to court) a gas station attendant on the day before. Third, he wanted to die, rejecting all attempts of anti-death-sentence groups to have the sentence commuted, and attempting suicide three times while awaiting his execution.

He was killed by firing squad at 8.07 in the morning on this day. Lacking a regular room for firing squads, the prison used its abandoned cannery instead. Gilmore's last words were 'Let's do it'.

---

* E.M. Branch, Robert Hirst and Harriet Smith (eds), *The Works of Mark Twain*, Vol. 15, *Early Tales & Sketches*, Berkeley: University of California Press, 1979, pp. 5–6.

And the literary consequences? One was very short, a T-shirt sporting the murderer's three last words. The other, weighing in at 1,024 pages, was the Pulitzer-Prize-winning *The Executioner's Song* (1980), arguably the American novelist and journalist Norman Mailer's best book. As though struck by the unfamiliar reality of Gilmore's story, Mailer abandoned his usual self-referential, rococo style, in favour of a moving, documentary insight – based on interviews, letters and court records – into a complex personality and a momentous event.

18 January

Imagists, ex-Rhymers and aesthetes dine on roast peacock at Wilfred Scawen Blunt's stud farm

1914 It was Ezra Pound's idea. From 1913 to 1916 he shared the six-room Stone Cottage in Sussex with W.B. Yeats, serving as the elder poet's secretary. One day Pound suggested that they do something to mark the 74th birthday of Wilfred Scawen Blunt, the revered poet of love and nature, and campaigner against British imperialism in Egypt and India.

Yeats and Pound rounded up some poetic allies – the former drawing Victor Gustave Plarr and Thomas Sturge Moore from the old London-based Rhymers' Club that he had founded, the latter inviting fellow imagists Frederic Manning, F.S. Flint and Richard Aldington. According to Yeats' biographer Roy Foster, all seven travelled down on this day to Blunt's stud farm in Horsham in a car hired for £5, carrying their poems of homage in 'a stone casket carved with a recumbent figure by Gaudier-Brzeska' (the sculptor was another of Pound's enthusiasms).

Despite the cold, the occasion went off well. 'The meal included a roast peacock, allegedly at WBY's request', Foster adds. Blunt himself 'responded to his lionization with a slightly crusty amusement. He claimed he had never really been a poet, had only ever written verse "when I was rather down on my luck and made mistakes either in love or politics or some other branch of active life", and preferred to be celebrated as a horse breeder'.*

---

* R.F. Foster, *W.B. Yeats: A Life*, Vol. 1, *The Apprentice Mage*, Oxford: Oxford University Press, 1997, p. 509.

A few mundane questions remain. How did they all fit in the car? Since £5 is worth over £400 in today's money, it may have been a very big car. And where did they find the peacock? Not at the local butchers, surely.

In any case, it's a good story in which everyone plays out according to form: Yeats exotic, Pound generous and Blunt – well, blunt. Do poets have so much fun nowadays?

19 January

The Irish author Christopher Nolan wins the Whitbread Prize

1988 Compared to his namesake, the Anglo-American film director of *Insomnia*, *Batman Begins* and *The Prestige* (2002, 2005 and 2006), this Christopher Nolan was born under a darker star. Deprived of oxygen for two hours at birth, he came into the world with cerebral palsy, paralysed apart from his head and eyes. Forty-three years later he died. A statement released by his family a day later said: 'Following the ingestion of some food into his airways yesterday, oxygen deprivation returned to take the life it had damaged more than 40 years ago.'

But in between, what a life. He couldn't speak, but his loving parents sensed the clever, talented personality within. His father used to read to him – excerpts from Joyce's *Ulysses* and poetry. When he was eleven, Christopher was prescribed Baclofen, a muscle relaxant that calmed the worst spasmodic movements of the condition, and increased his control over his head and neck. With what he called a 'unicorn stick' fixed to his head, he learned to poke the keys of a special computer, but it could take twelve hours to write a page, and his mother had to cradle his head while he did it.

At last his thoughts and feelings could reach the outside world. In his first letter to his aunt and uncle, he wrote: 'I bet you never thought you would be hearing from me!' The words came out like water from a burst dam. In fact that's what he called his first book, a much acclaimed collection of poetry called *Dam-Burst of Dreams*, published when he was just fifteen.

More followed – *Torchlight and Lazer Beams* (1988), a play written with Dublin theatre director Michael Scott, a novel called *The Banyan Tree* (1999) – but the book that won the Whitbread was *Under the Eye of the Clock*, his autobiographical study written in the free-indirect style – that is, in the third person inside the head of a character – who was in this case an alter ego of the author himself named Joseph Meehan.

Everyone goes through torments of anxiety and embarrassment trying to make friends in an unfamiliar environment. Most suppress or forget the experience; few write about it. Nolan's disability licensed him to voice, and enjoined his readers to pay attention to, those primal fears, and perhaps be reminded of their own. Here is Joseph on his first day in a new school:

> Sally forward Joseph Meehan called an inner nested notion and gently heeding he damn-well forward sallied. Zoo-caged, he cracked the communication barrier by schooling hamfisted facial muscles to naturally smile on cue ...

He's both inside and outside the spectacle, feeling it subjectively, seeing it objectively. But self-pitying it's not.

20 January

The European Union enjoys itself

1972 Friedrich Schiller's lyric poem, *An die Freude* (usually translated as 'Ode to Joy'), was written in 1785. German Romanticism theorised itself earlier than its English counterpart and the 'Ode to Joy' celebrated what would be an important idea in the movement internationally (see, for example, Wordsworth's fine sonnet 'Surprised by Joy'). *An die Freude*, however, simply does not translate into English as anything other than high-sounding doggerel, viz:

Tochter aus Elysium	Daughter of Elysium
Wir betreten feuertrunken,	We enter, fire-imbibed,
Himmlische, dein Heiligtum.	Heavenly, thy sanctuary.

Octosyllabics rarely work in English poetry. Nor do the compounds ('fire-imbibed'!) which come naturally to an agglutinative language like German.

Schiller's 'Ode to Joy' would have seemed destined to remain locked in its original German, but for the fact that, 40 years later, Beethoven made it the grand finale to his Ninth Symphony. As such it became the most famous Romantic poem in the world.

In recognition of the poem's universality, and its supra-national abstractness (none of those worrying chauvinisms to be found in 'God Save the Queen', the Marseillaise or – most horribly – 'Deutschland, Deutschland über Alles'), the Ode to Joy, as set to music by Beethoven, was adopted by the Council of Europe as the European Community's anthem from 20 January 1972 onwards. The EU, as it would become, was officially joyful.

The dignity of the anthem was, however, somewhat tarnished when, in 1974, the rebel state of Rhodesia – having unilaterally declared independence and white supremacy – ran a contest for a new national anthem. The winner was Mary Bloom, a South African, with a defiant lyric set to Beethoven's chorale:

> Rise O voices of Rhodesia,
> God may we thy bounty share,
> Give us strength to face all danger,
> And where challenge is, to dare.

For the Labour UK government of the time – desperate to end the Rhodesian crisis – it was deeply embarrassing as Europeans, albeit reluctant Europeans, to stand to attention in Brussels or Strasbourg to what was the battle-song of those disloyal white settlers ('kith and kin', as they called themselves). No joy in that.

21 January

George Moore, the 'English Zola', dies

1933 Moore was born in 1852 in County Mayo, Ireland, the son of a wealthy Catholic Liberal MP and stable owner (a background which features prominently in Moore's best-known and finest novel, *Esther Waters* (1894)). His father died ('of political frustration', allegedly) and Moore – already committed to a bohemian life in Paris – came into 12,000 acres of prime Irish property and an income for life. In Paris

Moore was absorbed by the new aesthetic doctrines of Impressionism and Naturalism. His hoped-for career as an artist came to nothing.

He returned to Britain and made London his base in 1879. His first novel, *A Modern Lover* (1883), the story of a young artist in London, was a frank homage to 'Zola and his odious school', as the *Spectator* put it. The hero, Lewis Seymour, callously betrays the three women who sacrifice their virtue to him. *A Mummer's Wife* (1883) opened new areas of sexual frankness for the Victorian novel and established Moore as a rebel against the kind of bourgeois decency represented, pre-eminently, by Mudie's 'select' circulating library, which banned the novel.

Moore was deeply affected by the misfortunes of his publisher, Henry Vizetelly. In 1884–5, Vizetelly published five translations of Zola's fiction, including *Nana* and *L'Assommoir*. He continued introducing a shocked British public to the French novelist until 1888, when a translation of *La Terre* finally incensed the authorities to legal action. Vizetelly pleaded guilty to publishing obscene articles and was fined £100. In 1889, he republished his Zola titles, slightly expurgated by his son Ernest. Again Henry Vizetelly was tried at the Old Bailey and sentenced to three months' imprisonment. He was 69, and in poor health. His firm collapsed and he died four years later.

Moore supported Vizetelly and continued to emulate Zola. He crusaded, with some success, against the moral hegemony of the lending libraries and what Henry James called 'the tyranny of the young reader'. Literature, Moore believed, should have the right to bring the occasional blush to a maiden's cheek. He lived long enough, dying on 21 January 1933, to read *Lady Chatterley's Lover*.

22 January

Anthony Powell's great dance begins

1951 The first paragraph of *A Question of Upbringing* (published on this day), the opening volume of Powell's twelve-volume *Dance to the Music of Time* sequence, begins with a London road-mending, in winter. Nothing is happening:

> The men at work at the corner of the street had made a kind of
> camp for themselves, where, marked out by tripods hung with

hurricane lamps, an abyss in the road led down to a network of subterranean drain-pipes.

The description meanders on for another 200 words, ending: 'The grey, undecided flakes continued to come down, though not heavily, while a harsh odour, bitter and gaseous, penetrated the air. The day was drawing in.'

Where, the reader wonders, is all this going? Nowhere very quickly, it's safe to assume, like the hole in the road. But the effect is instantly hypnotic. No writer in English is more the master of the slow tempos of life than Powell.

Anthony Powell was born the only child of a distinguished soldier and a mother some fifteen years older than her husband. He was officer class; she had her roots in the land-owning classes of England. Somewhat perversely, he grew up prouder of his Welshness than his Englishness (his surname, he ordained, should be pronounced to rhyme with 'Noel' and not 'towel').

At Eton he fell in with Henry Green and Cyril Connolly and at Oxford (Balliol) with Evelyn Waugh, as one of what would later be called the Brideshead Generation. One of Powell's critics wittily retitled his great work 'A dance to the Eton Boating Song'.

Powell left Oxford (although in one sense he never did) with the de rigueur 'gentleman's third in history and drifted to London, as if drawn by a magnet'. 'I am a metropolitan man', he once said of himself. He joined the publisher Duckworth (his father had 'friends' who arranged it). One of his early signings was Evelyn Waugh, whose *Decline and Fall* would influence his own work. *Afternoon Men* came out under the Duckworth imprint in 1931, to be followed in quick succession by *From a View to a Death* (1933) and *Venusberg* (1932).

In late December 1934 (always his favourite month – he liked the gloom) Powell married Lady Violet Georgiana Pakenham, a scion of the English Catholic aristocracy. The couple would have two sons.

On the outbreak of war, he gave up writing for the duration. After a false start in the infantry Powell found his niche in 'intelligence', working as a liaison officer with expatriate allies from occupied countries in Europe. He was demobilised in 1945 with the rank of major, a chestful of decorations and a sense of vague remorse that he had had such a cushy war. And, as he said, a very 'boring' one.

In 1948 Powell fell, as he always did, into a comfortable berth as the *Times Literary Supplement*'s fiction review editor. In 1950, he inherited a fortune from an uncle he barely knew. Money, too, always seemed to fall his way. It enabled him to move into a fine country house, The Chantry, in Somerset. Another bequest, when his father died in 1959, insulated him against the inconveniences of post-war austerity. Financial security also enabled him to embark on his grand project, *A Dance to the Music of Time*, and to take his time doing it.

The sequence was launched in 1951 – the year of the Festival of Britain which, in his prelude to his own grand project, *The Sword of Honour* trilogy, Waugh portrayed as the end of English civilisation. Under his series-hero's less jaundiced, but equally gloomy, eye Powell surveys 50 years of England. The viewpoint is conservative, like Waugh's, but less angrily so. Powell rarely put people's backs up. 'Tony is the only Tory I have ever liked', said George Orwell – someone who elsewhere repudiated everything Powell's class stood for.

Alongside *Dance*, which was completed in 1975, Powell kept private journals which, when published in 1982, revealed an increasingly bilious temperament. His last novel was *The Fisher King* (1985). He turned down a knighthood – even though it was offered by a Conservative administration. It would, probably, have looked paltry alongside his wife's lineage. Or perhaps too Widmerpoolian. He left over £1.5 million on his death and a fictional sequence to rival Balzac's.

23 January

After the failure of his stage play, Guy Domville, *Henry James resolves to 'take up my own old pen again'*

1895 The episode has become legendary: James, shamed as a dramatist, returns to his proper profession as a prose stylist to produce his late, great novels. In 2004 the story dominated two (good) novelised biographies of Henry James. Colm Tóibín's *The Master* leads with it, and it forms the climax of David Lodge's *Author, Author*.

Daringly for such a complex prose stylist famous for his competing points of view, Henry James had tried his hand at a play, *Guy Domville*, about a man caught in a love triangle while trying to renounce the active life for the priesthood.

James stayed away from the opening, preferring a neighbouring premiere instead, that of Oscar Wilde's *An Ideal Husband*. He thought it dreadful – clumsy, feeble and vulgar – but the audience adored it.

What would such a crowd make of *Guy Domville*? He set off to find out, just as his play was finishing. Greeting him backstage at the Victorian Theatre, actor-manager George Alexander dragged him onstage to take the author's plaudits.

At first James took the audience's tumult for approval. He was rudely disabused. They were jeering, not cheering – louder and more abusively as the author's face rose from his bow of appreciation. 'The worst part was now' – Tóibín has imagined it – 'when he could not conceal the expression on his own face, the look of panic he could not prevent.'

Yet the biographer and critic Richard Ellmann has added a few nuances to the old tale of unmitigated disaster. The next evening James sat through a full performance, which the audience treated respectfully. Critics like William Archer, H.G. Wells and George Bernard Shaw liked it, and it did run for five weeks. Despite the firm resolution entered in his notebook on this day, he wrote another play afterwards – *Summersoft*, at the instigation of the actress Ellen Terry, though she never produced it – in which Ellmann detects distinct echoes of Wildean dialogue.*

Meanwhile, Alexander was busy working on a new production for the Victorian. Its name? *The Importance of Being Earnest*.

24 January

Arthur Miller and Marilyn Monroe are divorced in Ciudad Juarez, Mexico

1961 'Egghead weds Hourglass', ran the 1956 headline in *Variety*. The American papers couldn't get over the unlikely marriage of sex and the intellect (in those days the playwright was commonly called an 'intellectual' in the popular prints). But Miller himself acknowledged the link between his feelings for Monroe and if not his mental powers, then at least his creativity. As he wrote in his autobiography, *Timebends* (1987):

---

* Richard Ellmann, 'James Amongst the Aesthetes', in John R. Bradley (ed.), *Henry James and Homo-Erotic Desire*, London: Macmillan; New York: St Martin's, 1999, pp. 25–44, 40–1.

Flying homeward, her scent still on my hands ... I could, after all, lose myself in sensuality. This novel secret entered me like a radiating force, and I welcomed it as a sort of proof that I would write again.

They had met when Miller went to Hollywood to make a film about crooked labour leaders on the Brooklyn waterfront, only to drop out of the project when told by the studio chief of Columbia Pictures to change the villains from the mob to wicked communists. The project was later re-aligned as *On the Waterfront* (1954).

His resistance to the anti-communist film script, the production of *The Crucible* (1953 – see 1 March) and his enlarged public profile brought Miller to the attention of the House Un-American Activities Committee (HUAC). While the HUAC investigations were proceeding, studio executives urged Monroe to dump Miller, but she refused. Subpoenaed in 1956, he was convicted of contempt when he refused to 'name names'.

It was all about publicity. In *Timebends* Miller recalls the HUAC chairman, Francis E. Walter, offering to cancel Miller's subpoena provided he could be photographed shaking hands with Miller's new wife.

What went wrong? We'll never have her side of the story now. His is set out in *Timebends*, which can be exciting about the power of their early love, honest and harrowing about their break-up, but keeps coming adrift in group-therapy phrases like 'I knew I must flee or walk into a doom beyond all knowing'.

Why or how it happened, most film people agree that the marriage was in a pretty rough state by the time they came to make *The Misfits* (John Huston, 1961), a script (ironically) that Miller had written as a Valentine gift to his wife. It was not only the marriage that perished. The Nevada sun and the stress of production combined to fray the nerves of actors and crew alike. Huston drank a lot and sometimes fell asleep on set. Monroe was drinking too, and taking sleeping pills. Two days after filming finished Clark Gable suffered a heart attack, dying ten days after that. A year and a half later Marilyn Monroe herself would die of an overdose; whether it was intentional or not has never been established.

For Miller one of the few good things to come out of the *Misfits* experience (apart from the film itself, which isn't half bad) was Inge Morath, a Magnum photographer covering the movie. She and Miller married in 1962, remaining happily together until her death in 2002.

25 January

Rabbie Burns: whisky, literature and lassies

1759 Burns is the only author in the English language to have an annual revel – or booze-up – dedicated to him by name. Not that he is the only toper to be found in the annals of literature. One could, as plausibly, have a Ben Jonson Night (after a particularly heavy evening, one of the 'Tribe of Ben' would be assigned to take their chief home in a wheelbarrow); a Dylan Thomas Night (Thomas came up with the drinker's favourite epigram: 'An alcoholic is someone you don't like who drinks as much as you do'); or an Ernest Hemingway Night (Hemingway it was who uttered the drinker's favourite maxim: 'A man does not exist until he is drunk').

Burns Night (commonly known as 'Burns Supper' by those who celebrate it) takes place only three weeks after that other massive Scottish drinking session, Hogmanay. 25 January is Burns' birthday. The first celebratory events, in his native Ayrshire, took place on his death-day – 21 July. But so long are the Scottish summer days, and so demanding work in the briefly arable fields, that July pushed the nocturnal conviviality uncomfortably far into the night. It was switched to midwinter.

Hogmanay is an 'open' revel. In the cities of Scotland (as all over the world, where the Christian calendar rules) there are street parties. All shutters are lifted. In Scotland, every door is opened for the 'first footing' by some dark-haired stranger. One of the more comical cultural spectacles of the first minutes of the New Year is watching non-Scots (and, indeed, many natives) bellowing out Burns' most famous anthem, with no more idea of what

And we'll take a right guid willie-waught,
For auld lang syne.

means than if the poet had written in Sanskrit. Willie-waught?

Burns Supper, by contrast, is a closed or 'club' event – restricted to knowledgeable members (particularly Scots of the diaspora, who form nostalgic Caledonian societies), and highly ritualised. It is also, in Scotland, a Lowland, not a Highland event – and most enthusiastically commemorated in Burns' western region.

A haggis soaked in whisky is piped in ceremonially and apostrophised, in mock reverence, as the company stands:

Fair fa' your honest, sonsie face,
Great chieftain o' the puddin-race!
Aboon them a' ye tak your place,
Painch, tripe, or thairm:
Weel are ye wordy o' a grace
As lang's my arm.

Toasts are drunk – loyally to the monarch (the Lowlands, contrary to what is vulgarly believed by non-Scots, did not join those bare-arsed Celts in their mad 1715 and 1745 rebellions against the Crown) and lasciviously to the 'Lassies'. Burns was as famous a wencher as he was a carouser. Wheelbarrows are normally called around one o'clock on the 26th.

As a British writer (in addition to his dialect poetry he wrote verse in the King's English – without much applause) Burns is the most famous 'peasant poet' in the language. But what is his language? 'Lallans' [lowland Scots dialect]. Poets of a radical persuasion (notably Hugh MacDiarmid) – who have co-opted Burns as a fellow Anglophobic republican – have made attempts to restore Scottish poetry to the pure, Burnsian fount of the native tongue and have failed. As devolution, and possible independence, reshapes the country's destiny Lallans may yet assert itself as the *lingua Caledonia*.

26 January

James Frey confesses his fact is fiction, and wins twice over

2006 The most spectacular *mea culpa* in literature took place on this date, before an audience of some 50 million.

Oprah Winfrey's Book Club (*OBC*) had been launched ten years earlier, in September 1996. It was spun off from the hugely popular TV talk show hosted by the African-American (former film star) 'personality'. 'I want to get the country reading again', Oprah declared by way of explanation.

There was predictable scorn from those who believed the country (or at least their part of it) had never stopped reading and needed no encouragement from a mere celebrity. As Jonathan Yardley, in the *Washington Post*, sneered: 'I watched it once and nearly gagged on all the treacle and psychobabble.' (5 November 2001)

The book trade did not sneer. Oprah's inaugural selection, Jacquelyn Mitchard's *Deep End of the Ocean* (a novel that had not set the Potomac on fire), sold close on a million copies overnight and shot to the top of the *New York Times* bestseller list. The 'Oprah Effect', as it was labelled, proved to be the most potent advertising agent in the history of books. Every selection on *OBC* picked up between half a million and a million sales – irrespective of genre or quality.

Why? Not because Oprah claimed to be a literary critic but because the reading public trusted her (as they rarely do literary critics). Her most loyal audience were women of middle age, watching in their homes – traditionally a core book readership. Where Oprah led they would follow.

There was a clear tendency to Oprah's selections (in which she had a guiding hand). She, and her advisers, manifested high-mindedness, a liking for 'self-help' books, and a strong 'home-team' rooting for African-American writers. Toni Morrison, for example, got no fewer than four picks in ten years (Oprah also bought the film rights to *Beloved*).

Ted Striphas, in his 2009 monograph *The Late Age of Print*, sees *OBC* as symptomatic of the changing cultural landscape in the 21st century, specifically that most fraught of marriages – TV and the Printed Page.

In 1951, at a time when there were around 12 million television sets in the US, Ray Bradbury's *Fahrenheit 451* pictured the spread of TV as the death of the book – which, henceforth, would be preserved only by a fanatically literate underground sect. *OBC* proved just the opposite. TV could actually expand the readership for books.

The most sensational of the *OBC* shows took place following Oprah's endorsement of James Frey's 'drunkalogue', *A Million Little Pieces*, in September 2005. The Oprah Effect boosted Frey's (alleged) memoir of his descent into alcoholic hell and back into the number 1 slot on the *New York Times* bestseller list. It was, to date, *OBC*'s biggest-selling title. Oprah made Frey rich.

On 8 January 2006 the exposé website thesmokinggun.com publicised, in facsimile, Frey's criminal record sheet and revealed that the book was, at best, a tissue of gross exaggeration and, at worst, fabrication.

Frey was hauled back on to the *Oprah* talk show, in front of a now-hostile live audience, on 26 January. Why, the 'Empress of Empathy' (Maureen Dowd's description) asked, did Frey lie? 'I feel duped', she said (as the audience cheered), 'but more importantly, I feel that you betrayed millions of readers' (louder cheers, mixed with boos).

Frey, stumblingly, claimed that the 'essence' of the book was true. It was the Blanche Dubois defence: 'In my heart I never lied.' This would be his line in the months that followed. His publisher, Random House, took a more cautious line. They offered full refunds to anyone who honestly felt they had been misled as to the authenticity of *A Million Little Pieces*.

The event prompted a debate about 'memoirist's licence', in which Frey continued to argue that 'truth' should not be hampered by what actually happened. Most of the contributors to the debate were unaware of the fact that they were waltzing around issues dealt with as the Mimesis paradox in Aristotle's *Poetics*, a couple of thousand years before.

Some US libraries nervously reclassified *A Million Little Pieces* as fiction. The *New York Times*, after some dithering, continued to enter it in the 'Fiction Bestsellers' list. It had a new lease of life there. The Oprah Effect, even when accompanied by a damning critical verdict, worked yet again. There is, as book people like to say, no such thing as bad publicity.

27 January

The US Congress sets up an Indian Territory in what is now Oklahoma

1825 It was the territory for which Huck Finn would 'light out' when he got tired of being 'sivilized'. Freedom for him, maybe, but not for the Native Americans living in the south and south-east of the continent whom the government planned to dump there. In 1830, President Andrew Jackson's Indian Removal Bill would force the Choctaw, Seminole, Creek, Chickasaw and Cherokee tribes to leave their homelands for the Indian Territory, in order to make room for white settlers in Florida, Alabama, Georgia and the Carolinas. This brutal policy, pursued over the next eight years, displaced some 46,000 natives from their homes. Along the forced migration that came to be called the 'Trail of Tears' many died of cold, hunger and illness.

For Washington Irving, though, Indian removal registered very differently. In 1832 (see 7 June) he returned home from seventeen years living and writing in Europe, where he had established his reputation with books like *The Sketch Book* (1819–20), *Bracebridge Hall* (1822) and *The Conquest of Granada* (1829). In his preface to *The Sketch Book* Irving had claimed that the American scene, for all the sublimity of its landscape, nevertheless lacked the 'storied and poetical association' to be found in the 'masterpieces of art', the 'ancient and local custom' – even the 'very ruins' of Europe.

By now, though, Fenimore Cooper had begun to show that the country offered plenty of history and custom for the novelist to draw on – in the Revolutionary War (on land and at sea), and above all in the romance of the disappearing Native Americans. So when a friend of Irving's, an Indian Commissioner called Henry Ellsworth, invited him to accompany one of the forced migrations moving west late in 1832, the novelist jumped at the chance. 'I should have an opportunity of seeing the remnants of those great Indian tribes,' he wrote to his brother, 'which are now about to disappear as independent nations' – and prove he could write about America, he might have added.

The result of his experience, *A Tour on the Prairies* (1835), is the most exotic account of the American West to be produced by an American writer: 'tour' says it all. Sunlight through trees reminded him of gothic cathedrals; the Indians, 'stately fellows' with 'fine Roman countenances', looked 'like figures of monumental bronze' – safely reified into classical artefacts.

'We send our youth abroad to grow luxurious and effeminate in Europe,' Irving comments (now rejecting his own trajectory), when a 'tour on the prairies would be more likely to produce that manliness, simplicity, and self-dependence most in union with our political institutions.' So for all his exoticism, he didn't cut himself off from the history going on around him, but joined the expansionist flow. As the Native Americans vanished from the scene, the West would become an arena in which to test American manhood. The theme would be taken up and magnified by Francis Parkman, Owen Wister and Theodore Roosevelt (see 15 February, 29 June and 4 August), then given the final scholarly imprimatur in Frederick Jackson Turner's 'The Significance of the Frontier in American History' (1893).

28 January

Horace Walpole coins the word 'serendipity'

1754 Son of Robert Walpole, the powerful Whig politician who invented for himself the post of Prime Minister, Horace was the popular writer who invented the gothic novel. The gothic tale often pretended to be a 'translation' of a long-lost manuscript relating the hauntings and horrors of a medieval castle, abbey or country house.

Walpole's prototype of the genre, *The Castle of Otranto*, came out in 1764, and purported to be *Translated by William Marshal, Gent. From the Original Italian of Onuphrio Muralto, Canon of the Church of St. Nicholas at Otranto*. When in a preface to the third edition Walpole acknowledged his authorship, he promptly lost much of his critical support and started a debate on whether fiction should be 'romantic' – that is, fanciful – or true to life.

As a contribution to thought, however, that was nothing compared to his coining the word 'serendipity'. Serendipity is the chance discovery of something fortunate when you're looking for something else. The concept has proved crucial to scientific thought and policy. Roy J. Plunket, for example, discovered Teflon when he was searching for a gas to be used in refrigeration. The British scientist William Ramsay first isolated the element helium, which he named after the Greek god of the sun, because while looking for argon he noticed an unknown gas with a yellow line seen in the spectrum of the sun. Alexander Fleming came across penicillin when he returned from holiday to find that some cultures of bacteria that he had left behind had been killed by *penicillium* mould that had accidentally got into the Petri dishes. And so on.

Walpole himself described serendipity as 'accidental sagacity'. As he explained in a letter written on this day, he got the word from 'a silly tale called "The Three Princes of Serendip" [the old Arabic name for present-day Sri Lanka], who were always making discoveries ... of things which they were not in quest of: for instance, one of them discovered that a camel blind of the right eye had travelled the same road lately, because the grass was eaten only on the left side, where it was worse than on the right'.

Scientists are always coming up with new words for their new discoveries. In fact the enormous vocabulary of English owes a lot to the English-speaking nations' pre-eminence in science (see 10 June). Hence radar (for **ra**dio **d**etection **a**nd **r**anging), laser (**l**ight **a**mplification by stimulated emission of radiation) and X-ray – itself a serendipitous discovery by Wilhelm Roentgen while investigating cathode ray tubes.

Wordsmiths they may be, but authors are less prolific with neologisms. Of course there are exceptions. Shakespeare, who sometimes seems to have given us words for half our imaginings, came up with 'puke', 'gossip', 'swagger', 'unreal', 'critic' and many more. But a lot of his verbal inventions are really old words in new combinations or grammatical uses, like 'blood-stained', or 'blanket' as a verb.

Lewis Carroll's poem 'Jabberwocky' in *Through the Looking Glass, and What Alice Found There* (1871) is often cited as a treasure house of neologisms. But of the 24 new words there (all patiently glossed to Alice by Humpty Dumpty, who can 'explain all the poems that were ever invented – and a good many that haven't been invented just yet'), only 'chortled' has survived into common usage.

More recently Martin Amis seemed to be transforming the language of transatlantic public relations in his brilliant *Money: A Suicide Note* (1984). For a while people really did go around London talking of 'rug-rethinks' for haircuts and 'blastfurters' for hot dogs. But it didn't last.

No, it was Horace Walpole who did the business. He invented a word that the philosophy of thought really needed, and that has therefore entered most of the world's languages more or less unchanged.

29 January

The death of George III elegised and satirised

1819 Few deaths of monarchs have inspired a poem as fine, or a poem as mediocre, as that of George III.

On this day the Poet Laureate, Robert Southey, as part of his official duty, commemorated the passing of the king (in truth long gone in age, madness and total incompetence) with an effusion in hexameters – the least British of prosodies – entitled 'The Vision of Judgement'. It pictured the deceased king welcomed into heaven, by an appropriately deferential angelic host. The implication was that he would reign there, as he had on earth.

The poem took a year to publish and in the preface Southey made the mistake of attacking Byron (without actually naming him) as the leader of the 'Satanic School' of poetry. There would be no welcome in heaven for the author of *Don Juan*, it was implied. The other place awaited.

Byron penned a rapid response, subtly retitled 'A Vision of Judgment' (i.e. with an indefinite pronoun and differently spelled 'Judgment' – a cataloguer's nightmare). The poem was written in flowing ottava rima, Byron's favourite verse form.

In the preface, Byron contemptuously pointed to Southey's earlier composition of the verse play *Wat Tyler*, with its celebration of regicide, adding:

> If Mr Southey had not rushed in where he had no business, and where he never was before, and never will be again, the following poem would not have been written. It is not impossible that it may be as good as his own, seeing that it cannot, by any species of stupidity, natural or acquired, be *worse*. The gross flattery, the dull impudence, the renegado intolerance, and impious cant, of the poem by the author of *Wat Tyler* are something so stupendous as to form the sublime of himself – containing the quintessence of his own attributes.

The poem itself is a majestic denunciation of the most useless of England's kings – a title for which George III's successor, Byron's 'fat friend' (i.e. the Prince Regent, later George IV), is a close contender:

> ... of all
> The fools who flocked to swell or see the show,
> Who cared about the corpse? The funeral
> Made the attraction, and the black the woe,
> There throbbed not there a thought which
> pierced the pall;
> And when the gorgeous coffin was laid low,
> It seemed the mockery of hell to fold
> The rottenness of eighty years in gold.

30 January

*King Charles I of England is beheaded. A fortnight later John
Milton will risk his life to defend the act in a pamphlet*

1649 Better known today to students of English as the author of
Paradise Lost (1667), John Milton was also a radical political activist
and an opponent of inherited power and privilege – a republican in
a monarchical age. He believed that natural law overrode the divine
right of kings, and his politics were based on the idea, developed by
the Dutch political theorist Hugo Grotius (1583–45), that monarchs
ruled according to an implied contract between free individuals and
their ruler, in which the people agreed to obey in return for peace and
security of person and property under law.

Kings who broke this contract – those, for instance, who governed for themselves alone or for a clique instead of the common
good – could be deprived of their power and replaced. That's exactly
what Parliament thought Charles I had done, and they fought and
financed six years of bitter civil warfare to prove it. By the beginning
of December 1648, the Parliamentary army's victory was complete and
the king was in prison.

But having fought and defeated him – indeed, as Milton argued,
tried often enough to kill him in the field – some parliamentarians
drew back from the prospect of trying the king for treason, deposing
him and executing him if found guilty. Some of these foot-draggers
were royalists; the majority belonged to the Presbyterian branch of the
Protestant cause.

On 6 December, Colonel Thomas Pride put a brutal end to the
debate by leading troops into the House of Commons to eject the tem-
porisers. The rest, who came to be known as the 'Rump Parliament',
quickly got on with the business of trying the king. A commission
they set up found him guilty, deposed him and put him to death on
30 January. Milton almost certainly witnessed the public beheading of
the monarch.

The Tenure of Kings and Magistrates, Milton's polemic published
only a fortnight after the king's death, targets not the royalists – a lost
cause so far as he was concerned – but those backsliding Presbyterians.
In this, it might be said, he gives an early sign of the factionalism that
would eventually undo Cromwell's Republic.

What was the point, he argued, of waging war on the king, then refusing the logical outcome of that rebellion? In a sense they had already killed the king, in that they had deprived him of his official status – that second 'body' beyond the personal that bestowed monarchical authority.

Milton's pamphlet attempted to persuade not only by its logic but also by a special kind of rhetoric that one might call ligature syntax. Here's how it works:

> Others, who have been fiercest against their Prince, under the notion of a Tyrant, and no meane indenciaries of the Warre against him, when God out of his providence and high disposal hath delivered him into the hand of their brethren, on a suddaine and in a new garb of Allegiance, which their doings have long since cancell'd, they plead for him, pity him, extol him, protest against those that talk of bringing him to the tryall of Justice, which is the sword of God, superior to all mortall things, in whose hand soever by apparent signs his testified wil is to put it.

If you parse, or diagram, this sentence, the main clause consists of a subject – 'Others' – and a predicate of four parallel verbs – 'plead … pity … extol … protest'. All the rest is syntactically subordinate, serving to modify the main clause in one way or another. The relative clauses 'who … Prince' and 'no meane … him' are adjectival descriptors of those 'Others'. 'When … brethren' is adverbial, telling when. So is 'on a suddaine … Allegiance', telling both when and how. The adjectival clause 'which … cancell'd' moves a further step down the ladder of subordination, modifying 'Allegiance', which is already serving as a modifier. On that same lower level is the clause 'That talk … Justice', which modifies 'those' (who would proceed with the trial).

Then, going even further down the ladder – to rungs three, four, five and (believe it or not) six below the main clause – Milton slips in the dagger. The 'tryall' is described as one 'of Justice', which in turn is modified by 'sword', and that again by 'of God', which is finally modified by the parallel clauses 'superior … things' and 'in whose hand … to put it'.

To put it in terms of information, what was the big news that Milton was trying to convey? That it was God's justice to kill the king. Only he couldn't presume to say so directly; instead he had to bury the message deep in the bowels of one of the most complex English sentences ever published.

Anyway, it did the business – at least insofar as it got Milton a job in Cromwell's government. In March of that year they appointed him Secretary for Foreign Tongues – in effect, their propagandist, or (in modern terms) spin doctor. His first job was to answer the highly effective *Eikon Basilike* (*Sacred Image of the King*), a miscellany – purporting to be written by the imprisoned Charles himself – of diary entries, pious reflections on the institution of monarchy and prayers for his enemies. Milton's riposte, *Eikonoklastes* (*The Image Breaker*), did little to counter the effect of this masterpiece of royalist propaganda.

More successful – though for obvious reasons hardly a bestseller in his native country – was his answer (in Latin) to *Defensio Regia, pro Carlo I*, by Salmasius (Claude Saumaise, the French classical scholar). Milton's *Defensio pro populo Anglicano* (1651) asked the European proponents of monarchy what business it was of theirs how the English worked out their own political destiny.

Other treatises followed, and *defensios* to even more absurd continental attacks, but they all wound up on the bonfire after the fall of the republican Commonwealth and the death of Cromwell. In the autumn of 1659 Milton himself was put in prison. His punishment might have been a lengthy stay there – or worse – had it not been for the intervention of his secretary, the metaphysical poet Andrew Marvell, by now an MP. By 30 May 1660, the Stuarts were back in the driving seat in the form of Charles II, newly 'restored' to the throne. Milton, now blind, got on with *Paradise Lost*.

31 January

Louis Asa-Asa tells how he was captured in Africa and sold there six times before a storm forced his landing in Cornwall

1831 Louis Asa-Asa's story, or 'The Negro Boy's Narrative' as the title had it, was published on this day as a short addendum to the far more substantial *History of Mary Prince*, but it added the dimension, normally lacking in slave narratives, of the subject's treatment within his native country before ever boarding ship for Europe, the West Indies or the United States.

Prince's story, the first by a woman slave to be published in England, had traced her life from her birth to slave parents in Bermuda, through her sale to four masters, to her arrival and life in England as a servant. There, after a series of disagreements with her master and mistress, she was thrown out of the house. Through her connection with the Moravian Church she met the abolitionist Thomas Pringle, who arranged for her story to be taken down by Susanna Strickland, later to become one of Canada's literary founding mothers (see 21 August).

Shortly before the *History of Mary Prince* went to press, Pringle was given Asa-Asa's narrative, as dictated to a friend and fellow abolitionist, George Stephen. Asa-Asa had fetched up in England when a French slaver on which he was imprisoned lost its bearings in a storm and sought refuge in St Ives, Cornwall. His story was transcribed, according to Pringle, in 'as nearly as possible the narrator's words, with only such correction as was necessary to connect the story, and render it grammatical'.

Asa-Asa's narrative tells how his village in Sierra Leone was terrorised repeatedly by a tribe he calls the Adinyés, who would burn buildings, killing some people and marching others off to be sold as slaves: 'They took away brothers and sisters and husbands and wives.' When they caught Louis and about twenty others, they marched them to the sea, forcing them to 'carry chickens and meat for [their] food'. One man, who was too ill to carry his rations, they 'ran ... through the body with a sword'.

When they got to the sea – another departure from the typical slave's story – they weren't put on an ocean-going slaver right away, but taken around in a small boat to be sold and re-sold repeatedly. Louis himself 'was sold six times over, sometimes for money, sometimes for cloth, and sometimes for a gun'. It was half a year before he saw 'the white people' who would chain him side by side with others aboard the slave ship, to endure the foul conditions of the middle passage.

But it was a French slave ship that carried Louis Asa-Asa away. The British had abolished the slave trade in 1807, after two decades of campaigning by William Wilberforce, Charles Fox, Lord Grenville and others. And it was Africans who had done the initial buying and selling of human beings.

1 February

The New York Review of Books *is first published*

1963 It all began with a newspaper strike that shut down the major New York papers from December 1962 until the end of March of the following year. Among the casualties was the *New York Times Book Review*, issued every Sunday as a magazine supplement to the mother paper. The *Review* had been running since 1896, covering between twenty and 30 new books per week in judiciously measured prose.

In the *NYTBR*'s temporary absence a group of like-minded literary friends saw their chance to start up another kind of review altogether. They included Barbara Epstein, a senior editor at Doubleday's, her husband Jason, then a vice president at Random House and America's version of Allen Lane (see 22 May), and Elizabeth Hardwick, author of a famous attack on the 'sweet, bland commendations' of contemporary book reviewing.

The *New York Review of Books* actually hit the streets some three weeks after its publication date, 1 February. It looked different. It *felt* different. Mimicking a mass-circulation paper, with its rough newsprint in tabloid format, yet with very special headline type fetched from Holland, it already looked, as the novelist Tom Wolfe was soon to put it, like 'the chief theoretical organ of radical chic'.

But the real difference was in the editorial strategy. Robert Silvers and Barbara Epstein set out from the start to review books in their contemporary political context, and to allow authors to take as long as they wanted to do so. So whereas the *NYTBR* might have reviewed around 1,250 books a year, and the *Times Literary Supplement* around 2,600, the *NYRB*, with its generous word limits and fortnightly timetable, would struggle to reach 400.

Besides, not all the essays were based on books. During the Vietnam War I.F. Stone, the veteran Washington investigative journalist, used the transcript of a hearing before the Senate Committee on Foreign Relations (available from the Government Printing Office, price 30¢) as a peg on which to hang an eight-page attack on L.B. Johnson's use of the Gulf of Tonkin incident as a pretext for widening the conflict. In Mary McCarthy's case it wasn't a book she reviewed but a situation; she travelled to Vietnam and used her experiences as her text on which to base a three-part critique of American policy there.

Since the sixties the paper's adversarial stance has become even firmer, if anything. Reaganomics, the administration of George W. Bush and the role of the Supreme Court in hoisting him into the White House, the second Iraq war and its dreadful aftermath, even the inadequacy of the American press in letting all this go by with minimal scrutiny – all have come in for the paper's well informed, analytically acute contempt.

Of course those on the American right, including some formerly liberal New York intellectuals who ought to know better, have repeatedly accused the *NYRB* of being un-American. They think it should review books, not spout politics. But in truth the paper has always worked to a venerable – if latterly forgotten – tradition: that of the 19th-century quarterly magazines on both sides of the Atlantic like the *Edinburgh*, the *Quarterly*, the *Westminster* and the *North American*. These too invited gifted writers to hang long, opinionated essays on slender pegs, and were very partisan indeed.

In pursuit of such conditions, good writers have flocked to the *NYRB* like swallows to a barn. As a recent *Guardian* editorial put it: 'It has published Auden, Updike, Sontag, Roth, Arendt, Mailer, Vidal, Bellow, Lowell, Capote and – oh well, everyone.'* And besides, it has the most intriguing classified ads in the business – as accurate an insight into the socio-cultural environment as any Woody Allen film:

> MWF [that's Married White Female], attractive, intelligent, humorous, articulate, and sexy, seeks a local collaborator in the form of a tall man with similar qualities to hang out with. Married or single, 45–65. Hair (preferably on head), height, and brains preferred.

> REFINED/LOVELY MANHATTANITE, 5'5" seeks well-educated, principled NYC male, 60–69, widowed or divorced only, Jewish (not religious), nonsmoker. Serious-minded only.

---

* Editorial, *Guardian*, 25 October 2008.

2 February

Long Day's Journey into Night's *long road to performance*

1956 This was a notable year for theatre (see 12 May), the year in which British theatre broke the fetters of old-fogeydom with *Look Back in Anger*. John Osborne was, however, not the only playwright looking back that year. Improbably, Eugene O'Neill's searingly retrospective play, *Long Day's Journey into Night*, saw its first performance at the Royal Dramatic Theatre in Stockholm, Sweden, on 2 February 1956. O'Neill was three years dead (which did not prevent a posthumous Pulitzer Prize for *Long Day's Journey*).

In the play O'Neill depicts the cauldron-like family situation in which he was brought up: notably a skinflint, former-matinee-idol father (James Tyrone), who is willing to let his tubercular son, Edmund, die rather than spend money he can easily afford. Completing the Tyrone family are an alcoholic elder son, Jamie (who may have deliberately killed a younger son of the family, Eugene, in the cradle), and a morphiniste mother. The action covers one typical tortured day in the Tyrone household in 1912 on the New England coast, fog-horns booming their melancholy obbligato, as the Tyrone family drench themselves in whisky, narcotics and mutual recrimination.

O'Neill completed the work in 1941 and dedicated the manuscript to his (third) wife, Carlotta, with the inscription:

For Carlotta, on our 12th Wedding Anniversary

Dearest: I give you the original script of this play of old sorrow, written in tears and blood. A sadly inappropriate gift, it would seem, for a day celebrating happiness. But you will understand. I mean it as a tribute to your love and tenderness which gave me the faith in love that enabled me to face my dead at last and write this play – write it with deep pity and understanding and forgiveness for all the four haunted Tyrones.

These twelve years, Beloved One, have been a Journey into Light – into love. You know my gratitude. And my love!

GENE
Tao House
July 22, 1941

The manuscript was then locked up in the vault of his publisher, Random House, with the instruction that it was not to be published or performed until 25 years after the playwright's death. Carlotta, however, donated the copyright to Yale University, who authorised its performance and publication a mere three years after O'Neill's death. His wish that the first performance should be in Sweden, the country which had given him the Nobel Prize for Literature in 1936, was, unlike the date restriction, observed.

3 February

The Reverend George Crabbe dies in Trowbridge, far from his family and roots in East Anglia, leaving many volumes of unpublished poems behind him

1832 Samuel Johnson, who helped Crabbe by suggesting a few emendations to his poetic sequence *The Village* (1783), got it about right. According to Boswell, he admired the work 'for its sentiments as to the false notions of rustic happiness and virtue'. Or to put it another way, because it wasn't Oliver Goldsmith's *The Deserted Village* (1770), of which the following gives a flavour:

> Sweet Auburn! loveliest village of the plain,
> Where health and plenty cheered the labouring swain

That word 'swain' gives it away; this is a pastoral vision of the countryside, written by a city boy. (The word would recur ironically in *The Village*, where the 'swains', denied a livelihood on the land, have become smugglers.) By contrast to Goldsmith, George Crabbe was born poor in Suffolk and though no labourer, his training as a doctor and clergyman taught him to pay close attention to the realities of life around him.

He could see for himself that although the countryside abounded in 'fruitful fields' and 'numerous flocks', the country poor got little of it for themselves, let alone enjoyed 'health and plenty'. In addition, he picked up a sharp sense of class difference from his three years as chaplain at Belvoir Castle, where the Duke of Rutland treated him kindly, encouraging his poetry, but the servants made fun of him as a rude provincial trying to rise above his station.

But Crabbe's most astute perception was that sentimentality goes along with – in fact, is usually diagnostic of – cruelty. 'Peter Grimes' in *The Borough* (1810) traces the decline of a violent fisherman into homicide and madness through an almost documentarily objective point of view. Rather than attempt any suppositions about Grimes' motives and other thought processes, the narrative works through his social and physical environment.

Grimes buys a series of boys from London workhouses to help out on his boat. He beats them, half starves them – in effect kills them through neglect and brutality. To all this the villagers pay scant attention until the third boy appears, 'of manners soft and mild', who the seamen's wives fancy to be:

> Of gentle blood, some noble sinner's son,
> Who had, belike, deceived some humble maid,
> Whom he had first seduced, and then betray'd—

When this one goes missing, the town pays proper attention, and 'the mayor himself with tone severe replied,— / "Henceforth with thee shall never boy abide"'. Losing his livelihood pushes Grimes over the edge. When he appears raving mad in the village, the people treat him as a Bedlam exhibit:

> 'Look! Look!' they cried; 'his limbs with horror shake,
> And as he grinds his teeth, what noise they make!'

Then Benjamin Britten re-imported the sentimentality in bucketloads, when his opera of the same name (1945) turned the protagonist into a misunderstood pederast.

4 February

Rupert Brooke goes off to his corner of a foreign field

1915 'Their name liveth for evermore' say the monuments to the fallen of the First World War. None more so than the name of Rupert

Brooke. When war broke out in August 1914, Brooke, at 27, had some reputation as a literary critic (principally for his work on Jacobean drama) and as a poet associated with the Bloomsbury Group – whose liberal-humanist values he shared.

His tepid pre-war Georgian literary style is exemplified in his second-best-known poem, 'The Old Vicarage, Grantchester' (the current owner, Jeffrey Archer, is doubtless forever asked if there is 'honey still for tea').

Brooke was strikingly good-looking, bisexual and well-connected: a particular friend was Edward Marsh, one of the principal patrons of early 20th-century verse. It was through Marsh, via Winston Churchill (then first lord of the admiralty) that Brooke was commissioned into the Royal Naval Volunteer Reserve on this day.

Brooke's war sonnets, later published in the volume *1914: and Other Poems* (and dashed off in December of that year) are most famous for the gallantly death-anticipating 'The Soldier':

If I should die, think only this of me:
That there's some corner of a foreign field
That is for ever England.
There shall be
In that rich earth a richer dust concealed;
A dust whom England bore, shaped, made aware,
Gave, once, her flowers to love, her ways to roam,
A body of England's, breathing English air,
Washed by the rivers, blest by suns of home.

Brooke was, of course, a sailor. But the notion of corpses rotting at sea was not poetic. His vessel left port on 28 February 1915 for what would be a battle at Gallipoli (one of Churchill's less happy strategic initiatives). En route, on a hospital ship on 23 April, Brooke died of a mosquito bite turned septic. His corpse was landed and summarily buried in a foreign field, at Kyros in Greece.

Brooke's patriotic poems were too useful as propaganda not to be exploited on the home front. On Easter Sunday 1915 (22 March), Dean Inge read 'The Soldier' from the pulpit of St Paul's Cathedral. 'The enthusiasm of a pure and elevated patriotism has never found a nobler expression', Inge added, by way of comment.

The poet was then still living but would shortly be dead.

Winston Churchill wrote his obituary in *The Times*, hailing him as 'one of England's noblest sons'.

1914: and Other Poems was published in May 1915, and reprinted, it is estimated, every two months during the course of the war as foreign fields overflowed with the rich dust of British troops.

5 February

Longmans digs in for a very long stay

1797 British publishing has always been dynastic in its character. This has been its strength, and the means by which its strongest elements have survived in a business little better than gambling on the public's notoriously fickle taste in reading matter.

The most venerable 'houses' in the history of the book in Britain, Oxford University Press and Cambridge University Press, can both of them claim half a millennium's existence – and dispute among themselves which was actually, by a few years, the first in the field.

The longest-surviving commercial house is Longmans. In the 17th century the family were successful Bristol soap-makers. Thomas Longman (1699–1755), the patriarch of the publishing firm, was born in Bristol, and was sent by his family, aged seventeen, to be an articled apprentice in the London book trade. He exchanged soap for ink.

Following the financial securities brought in by the Queen Anne copyright act of 1710, print products enjoyed a boom during this period. Having served his time and learned his business, Thomas borrowed money (over £2,000 – a huge sum at the time) from the family's Bristol coffers to set up his own house at the 'Sign of The Ship' (which would be the firm's emblem), near Paternoster Row, the home of the British book trade (see also 29 December).

Thomas was not a publisher in the modern sense, but a 'bookseller'. He traded in books – both their production and their retailing. But, since he was childless, there was no expectation that the name Longman would survive four centuries as an imprint.

On his death, the firm passed into the proprietorship of his nephew, another Thomas Longman (1730–97). He had twelve children, and the family interest was continued. But not with any great flair or trade prominence. It was with this Thomas Longman's death, on 5 February 1797, that the company's root was finally planted.

Thomas's eldest son – inevitably another Thomas Longman (1771– 1842) – made the firm a publishing powerhouse. The age, with industrialisation, urbanisation, increased literacy and modern transport systems, was propitious for the book trade. Longman III (so to call him) imaginatively expanded into papermaking and printing. But, as the historian Asa Briggs records in his history of the firm: 'The basis of the house's strength was capital. Thomas Norton Longman had left nearly £200,000 in 1842, when he died accidentally after falling from his horse on his way back from Paternoster Row to his house in Hampstead.'

This Thomas Longman was the first of the family to enter Parliament. Among other things, publishing was now clearly a 'profession for gentlemen'.

Longman would continue as a family dynasty – and as the most eminent imprint in the London publishing community – until the early 1970s, when it was swallowed into the maw of the Viking-Penguin-Pearson multinational combine. The age of family publishing had passed.

6 February

Raymond Chandler publishes his first novel-length detective fiction, The Big Sleep, *at the advanced age of 51*

1939 Chandler's *The Big Sleep*, and the 'Philip Marlowe PI' series it initiated, are high points in the 'hard-boiled' crime fiction genre. More significantly, they served to raise that genre from the pulpy soup in which it was spawned to 'Literature'. Chandler was plausibly considered for a Nobel Prize and – given the 1938 winner (Pearl S. Buck) – might well have graced that award. Certainly, Chandler's Marlowe series have lasted longer in reader popularity than Buck's trilogy about 20th-century China, which kicked off with *The Good Earth* in 1931. It was filmed – Oscar-winningly – in the same year as *The Big Sleep*.

Chandler came to writing fiction late in life, with career failures dragging behind him. The child of a broken family, he was educated (as he was proud to advertise) at an English public school – Dulwich. He was knocked about in the First World War fighting with the Canadian army, and – before taking to literature – had failed in the California oil industry. Not easy to do at that period, when you could start a gusher in the Long Beach fields with a pickaxe. Given his problems with alcohol in the 1930s, it would have been very wise to steer clear of Ray with a pickaxe in his hand.

Always dominated by his mother, and sexually timid, he married the day after his mother died. His wife, Cissie, was decades older than he. As an acquaintance tartly noted, the new Mrs Chandler was 50 years old, looked 40 and dressed twenty. But she helped Ray dry out, and start a redemptive late career in crime fiction.

He was assisted by the market for high-class, hard-boiled detective fiction created by *Black Mask* magazine. The journal had been founded in 1920 by H.L. Mencken and his partner, George Jean Nathan, who sold it after a year to be run by various editors until the dominating Captain Joseph T. 'Cap' Shaw took over. Shaw was a former bayonet instructor and a theorist on the subject of the detective story. He demanded from his contributors a clear, uncluttered style and storyline, and he 'Hammettised' the magazine. Dashiell Hammett published the first of his 'Continental Op' stories in *Black Mask* in October 1922. Erle Stanley Gardner published his first story in the magazine in 1923 and Raymond Chandler published his first short story in *Black Mask* in 1933. Thereafter he served an apprenticeship with a string of short pieces revolving around various precursors of Philip Marlowe.

The Big Sleep introduces the 38-year-old PI as 'a shop soiled Sir Galahad' taking on the corruption of the southern Californian 'old money' elite (a caste Chandler knew well from his oilman days). *The Big Sleep* – which does not have an easily followed plot – was filmed by Howard Hawks, starring Humphrey Bogart as Marlowe, in 1946. Famously, the director wired the novelist asking him to explain the significance of the murdered chauffeur, only to be told that Chandler himself did not know the answer.

7 February

Madame Bovary *in the dock*

1857 1857 is the *annus mirabilis* for students of obscenity. In Britain the first formal legislation on the offence (the Obscene Publications Act, known as 'Lord Campbell's Act') was enacted in that year. In

France, there were three high-profile trials in 1857: against Flaubert's *Madame Bovary*, against Baudelaire's poems *Les Fleurs du Mal*, and (more forgettably, despite its runaway popularity at the time) Eugène Sue's *Les Mystères du Peuple*.

The newly introduced law in Britain and the French prosecutions defined two quite distinct ideas about the means by which dangerous books (worse than cyanide or prussic acid, according to Lord Campbell) should be controlled by the well-meaning state.

The Anglo-Saxon approach, soon adopted in the US, took as its defining criterion that obscenity was to be defined by its inherent tendency to 'deprave and corrupt' (this test was officially clarified as a handy slogan in the judge Sir Alexander Cockburn's definition of obscenity in 1868).

Especially, that is, works with the tendency to deprave and corrupt the vulnerable 'young'. Would it, in Dickens' sarcastic formulation, bring a blush to a maiden's cheek? If so, it was offensive and could be proceeded against. In fact the vagueness of the definition (how did one measure 'depravity'?) induced a spirit of excessive caution and self-censorship in the book trade. British publishing became institutionally timid for a hundred years.

In France, as established in the courts in the same year, 1857, the criterion was *outrage aux bonnes moeurs* – public indecency. The question asked in France had nothing to do with mademoiselle's cheeks. Did a work, by its encouragement to moral disorder, threaten the stability of the state?

After its serialisation in *La Revue de Paris* between October 1856 and December 1856, *Madame Bovary* was prosecuted as a threat to public order and religion and duly cleared on that score on 7 February 1857. Refined descriptions of adultery, it was determined, offered no risk to the republic. Inevitably the novel went on to be a best-seller.

The difference between the French and Anglo-Saxon regulations led to markedly different literary cultures. Zola, for example, was a heroic author in France and a purveyor of filth in Britain. The publisher of his translated works, Henry Vizetelly (see 21 January), was imprisoned for depraving the English public with Zolaism – he had, *The Times* said, thrown a vial of acid in the face of the great British public.

This dualism attained its absurd height in the 20th century when a whole succession of English literary 'classics' (e.g. *Ulysses*, Henry Miller's '*Tropics*', *Lady Chatterley's Lover*, *Lolita*, *Naked Lunch*) could be published only in Paris.

The anomaly was belatedly cleared up by reform of the obscenity law in the US in 1959 and in the UK a year later.

8 February

The Pickwick Papers *are launched and almost sink*

1836 On this date the up-and-coming London publishers (with a long way still to come in the book trade) Chapman and Hall invited Charles Dickens to write the text ('letterpress'), under the pseudonym 'Boz', for a random series of sporting papers (called in the trade 'Nimrod' publications, after the great hunter in the Bible).

The project was centred, initially, on the illustrations of the well known Robert Seymour, who had a line in 'Sporting Sketches'. Dickens was a wholly unknown journalist in his early twenties. The only original aspect about the 'Pickwick Papers', as they were to be called, was that Chapman and Hall decided they should be published monthly, in one 'gathering' (32 pages), with an 'advertiser' (paper wrappers, with two or three pages of ads), costing 1 shilling (a considerable amount of money in 1836), with two engravings on steel by Seymour (these, it was expected, could be extracted and framed).

There was nothing new about the part-issue of books in 'fascicles' like this. The practice goes back to the 17th century and was a handy way of spreading costs for impecunious readers. What was new was that Chapman and Hall's monthly issue of their papers on 'magazine day' (the last Friday of the month) was designed to sell the 'parts' like a journal – taking advantage of the new railway distribution system emerging across the country.

The first instalment of *The Posthumous Papers of the Pickwick Club* began to appear in April. It was not a success. Sales sank as low as 400 – well below break-even point. From the start there was friction – effectively a power struggle – between Dickens (who wanted more 'story') and his senior partner (who felt it was 'his' venture). There was a particularly fierce quarrel on the night of 19 April. The following day, Seymour shot himself. Dickens promptly took charge and was responsible, in a month or so, for appointing the congenial illustrator who would work with (effectively 'for') him through much of his later career – Hablot K. Browne, who took on the matching nom de plume,

'Phiz', in witness of his subordinate role. As Dickens went on to pull in thousands of pounds over the next few years, Browne slaved away at £5 for a full-page illustration.

Now effectively a novel – not a loose gathering of sporting papers – organised around the magnificent comic creation of Samuel Pickwick, the series went on to enjoy huge success, selling up to 40,000 copies a month. Dickens went on to become the Shakespeare of Victorian fiction and very rich. Behind every great fortune, says Balzac, lies a crime. So friends of Robert Seymour felt about 'the Great Inimitable'. Friends of Dickens answer that great careers in literature require some steel: something with which the young Boz (and the older Dickens) was amply supplied.

9 February

Frank O'Hara sees a headline that Lana Turner has 'collapsed' and immediately writes a poem

1962 The whole poem reads:

Lana Turner has collapsed!
I was trotting along and suddenly
it started raining and snowing
and you said it was hailing
but hailing hits you on the head
hard so it was really snowing and
raining and I was in such a hurry
to meet you but the traffic
was acting exactly like the sky
and suddenly I see a headline
LANA TURNER HAS COLLAPSED!
there is no snow in Hollywood
there is no rain in California
I have been to lots of parties
and acted perfectly disgraceful
but I never actually collapsed
oh Lana Turner we love you get up

This is one of O'Hara's *Lunch Poems*, so called because they evoke chance encounters while the poet is on his lunch break from his job at the Museum of Modern Art, New York. To add to the sense of casualness, the poem does away with punctuation marks (apart from the exclamation points after 'collapsed'), to good comic effect in the last line, especially. The lines often run on (as in 'hits you on the head / hard') and lack the usual capital letters at their start.

Characters appear without the formality of an introduction (who is 'you'?), and the poem's plot seems to be governed by the quotidian – the weather, newspaper headlines and random thoughts – to all of which the aimless act of 'trotting along' keeps the narrative consciousness open.

Unkind critics have referred to the *Lunch Poems* as O'Hara's 'I-do-this-I-do-that' poems, but not everything is what it seems. This one was actually written on the Staten Island ferry, which means that although the poem may have been composed in a hurry (the ferry takes less than half an hour to cross between Manhattan and Richmond), its apparently immediate elements, like the traffic, meeting 'you', arguing about the weather, or even seeing a headline about Lana Turner, aren't really as 'there' as they seem.

In other words, there's nothing self-revelatory about the poem. O'Hara hated the confessional style, as exemplified in Robert Lowell's *Life Studies* (1959) and in the work of Anne Sexton and Sylvia Plath. Referring to Lowell's 'Skunk Hour', he told Edward Lucie-Smith: 'I don't think that anyone has to get themselves to go and watch lovers in a parking lot necking in order to write a poem, and I don't see why it's admirable to feel guilty about it. They should feel guilty.'*

By contrast to 'Skunk Hour', 'Lana Turner' is a poem of surfaces. The words don't refer to deep psychological states so much as play against or interrogate each other, so that, for example, the word 'collapsed' registers not anything that happened to Lana Turner (fainted? fell into a drunken stupor? died of a heart attack?) but the clichéd use of the word in newspaper headlines.

---

* 'Edward Lucie-Smith: An Interview with Frank O'Hara', in Frank O'Hara (ed. Donald Allen), *Standing Still and Walking in New York*, San Francisco: Grey Fox Press, 1983, p. 13.

10 February

The king of the cuckolds dies

1837 No poet of the Romantic movement can claim to have died as romantically as Alexander Pushkin. In 1829, aged 30, he fell in love with a beautiful sixteen-year-old girl, Natalya Nikolayevna Goncharova. They married two years later. The glamorous couple moved in Moscow's high society and were seen at every grand ball.

Pushkin was famous as the author of *Eugene Onegin* (completing its serial publication in 1832, with a clear depiction of Natalya as 'Tatyana') but – like other poets – not rich. Natalya was, gossip informed him and the world, conducting an affair with Baron Georges d'Anthès, whom the Pushkins had met in 1834. D'Anthès was a dashing Frenchman who had come to Russia and joined the tsar's army. He began taking an interest in Natalya in 1835.

In 1836 Pushkin received a poison pen letter informing him that he had been elected to the 'The Serene Order of Cuckolds'. It may have been baseless. D'Anthès had, by now, married Natalya's sister. But Pushkin was determined to follow the script laid down in *Eugene Onegin*, where Lensky provokes the hero to a duel over Tatyana.

Pushkin would prove unluckier than Onegin. Despite furious efforts to prevent it, the duel, with pistols, took place on 27 January 1837. D'Anthès fired first and wounded Pushkin. Pushkin then fired, and winged his opponent. Pushkin was, it transpired, fatally hurt. He died, lingeringly, on 10 February.

His death was the occasion of extraordinary public mourning which – since he was a proclaimed critic of the government – caused alarm. By the tsar's order (the potentate had also, at one point, eyed the beautiful Natalya), Pushkin was buried out of the way, and discreetly, at a monastery. D'Anthès was expelled from Russia and lived a long life, dying in 1895. According to the *New York Times*, reporting the event in 1837, 'every patriotic Russian will spit on the ground on hearing the name of d'Anthès'.

11 February

Sylvia Plath commits suicide, in the coldest winter in England for fifteen years

1963 Only those (like the present authors) who lived through the winters of 1947 and 1963 can know not how cold they were (much less so, in terms of degrees, than winters in Plath's native Boston) but how wretchedly ill-equipped British heating, plumbing and transport was for the unseasonably freezing weather. It was a bad time.

The weather doubtless exacerbated Plath's suicidal depression; but there were other factors. She had long suffered self-destructive impulses. She attempted suicide at least twice in college and her first (and only) published novel, *The Bell Jar* (by 'Victoria Lucas', published a month before her death), replays that period of her life. In the months leading up to her death when she wrote her most famous poems, a number of them revolved around the theme of suicide. Notably 'Lady Lazarus', with its laconically morbid opening lines: 'Dying / is an art, like everything else. / I do it exceptionally well.' Her physician had been trying to find her a place in a psychiatric unit for weeks. But the NHS was no more efficient that winter than British central heating.

Her tempestuous marriage to the poet Ted Hughes was the trigger for her suicide. He had abandoned her, and their two children, for Assia Wevill, the wife of the Canadian poet David Wevill. Plath had moved to a flat in 23 Fitzroy Road, a house where W.B. Yeats had once lived.

Early in the morning of 11 February, Plath put milk and bread in the children's room, broke their window (to let in air), went down to the kitchen, sealed the doors with wet towels, turned on the gas in the oven and waited to die. Her friend and active promoter of her poetry, Al Alvarez, who had seen her shortly before, speculates that it may have been initially at least a half-hearted suicide attempt – a cry for help. If so, it failed. Her dead body was found some hours later.

She was buried five days later in the Hughes family cemetery at Heptonstall. The headstone, which identifies her as 'Sylvia Hughes', has been regularly vandalised. Plath's death, it is not coincidental to note, occurred in the period that the National Organization of Women was formed, 28 June 1966. Her suicide has, for many women, taken on symbolic meaning.

After Plath's death, Hughes lived with Assia Wevill. She committed suicide – in exactly the same way as Plath – on 23 March 1969, killing their child as well. Hughes remarried in 1970, and died of cancer in 1998. On 16 March 2009, Hughes and Plath's son, Nicholas, killed himself.

12 February

Alexander Solzhenitsyn is stripped of his Soviet citizenship

1974 Few novelists' lives in the 20th century have been as eventful as Solzhenitsyn's. He was born into a prosperous and intellectual (but less than aristocratic) family a year after the 1917 revolution. He studied maths and philosophy at Moscow University and was, at this stage of his life, a communist patriot. In the Great Patriotic War against Germany he saw active service and rose to the rank of captain in the artillery.

In February 1945, a few weeks before victory, he was arrested for injudiciously sarcastic comments about Stalin in a letter to a friend. After the usual brutal interrogation in the Lubyanka prison, he was sentenced to eight years in a labour camp. This provided the experience for his first published novel (unpublishable when written – but circulated in samizdat), *One Day in the Life of Ivan Denisovich*. Having served his sentence he was sent into internal exile (routine for political prisoners) in Kazakhstan. There he was diagnosed with stomach cancer. This supplied the experience for *Cancer Ward* (published in 1967 in the USSR and banned the following year) – an allegory of totalitarian life in Stalinist Russia. By now Solzhenitsyn had renounced Marxism for his idiosyncratically forged brand of Christianity – although he remained throughout his life, even in exile, a staunch Russian patriot.

In 1956, with the Khrushchevian 'thaw', he was permitted to return to Moscow. The Russian premier also authorised the belated publication of *Ivan Denisovich* in the journal *Novy Mir* in 1962. Solzhenitsyn's later works were less to the authorities' taste, after Khrushchev's fall from power in 1964. He was not allowed to collect the Nobel Prize awarded to him in 1970. He was rendered an 'unperson', dismissed from the Writers' Union, and his house raided for his work in progress, the massive denunciation of Stalinist terror that was *The Gulag Archipelago*.

When portions of this work were published in Paris, Solzhenitsyn was arrested on 12 February 1974 and charged with treason. He was exiled the following day. He took up residence in the United States, where he was an inveterate critic of the Soviet regime – exiling him was a mistake of epic proportions. He made a triumphant return to his homeland in 1994 after the fall of the USSR and died in 2008, a survivor both of cancer and of communism.

13 February

Allied air forces firebomb Dresden

1945 On the night of 13 February 1945, three months before the end of the Second World War, the author Kurt Vonnegut was a POW sheltering in an underground animal slaughterhouse during the devastating fire-bombing of Dresden. He survived. Thousands didn't. Dresden was thought wrongly by its inhabitants, and by the large numbers of refugees fleeing the Russian advance, to be an 'open city' and the 'safest air-raid shelter in Germany'. It wasn't, Churchill decreed (arguably to show the USSR some Allied muscle).

On the same night Billy Pilgrim, the hero of Vonnegut's novel *Slaughterhouse-Five*, is a POW in the same shelter as Vonnegut during the devastating fire-bombing of Dresden. He too survives. But he goes crazy.

Vonnegut published many accounts of his Dresden experience. The following is from an interview in 1974:

> I was present in the greatest massacre in European history, which was the destruction of Dresden by fire-bombing ... The American and British air forces together killed 135,000 people in two hours. This is a world's record. It's never been done faster, not in the Battle of Britain or Hiroshima. (In order to qualify as a massacre you have to kill *real* fast.) But I was there, and there was no news about it in the American papers, it was so embarrassing.

RAF estimates later downscaled the civilian casualties to 35,000. This figure has been disputed (notably by the right-wing historian David

Irving, who goes for a number almost twice Vonnegut's 135,000).
Thirty-five thousand, of course, is not a figure to which one would
attach the word 'mere'. But it undercuts, if one wants to do a Bertram
Rumfoord (the gung-ho military historian in *Slaughterhouse-Five*),
Vonnegut's allegation that Dresden was a worse massacre than
Hiroshima – something that he was insisting up to a few months
before his death in 2007.

Fiction, like history, has been generally silent about Dresden.
Vonnegut himself had almost insuperable difficulty writing his
'Dresden novel'. He had to forge an entirely new 'schizophrenic' technique, weaving realism, science-fiction schlock (little green men from
Tralfamadore) and slapstick social comedy into a startlingly innovative
pattern. The novel's composition accompanied a catastrophic crisis in
the author's family life (his marriage broke up and his son developed
schizophrenia). *Slaughterhouse-Five* was finally published, to huge
acclaim, in 1969. Nonetheless, for all the praise he received, Vonnegut
went to his grave angry (in his ironic way) that posterity would not recognise the firebombing of Dresden for the war crime he always maintained it was.

14 February

Salman Rushdie goes to ground

1989 Salman Rushdie's *The Satanic Verses* was published in September
1988. It received perplexed reviews in the London literary press –
where it was widely seen as something of a disappointment from the
author of the Booker Prize-winning *Midnight's Children*. No (London)
reviewer found the novel offensive.

Offence was taken in Saudi Arabia (whose moral guardians had had
longstanding suspicions about Rushdie). The novel caught fire – literally – on 14 January, when a thousand Muslim protesters marched
through Bradford with a copy of *The Satanic Verses* tied to a stake. The
book was ritually burned. The media had been forewarned and cameras were present in force.*

---

* The incineration may be viewed on: http://www.guardian.co.uk/commentisfree/video/2009/
feb/11/satanic-verses-rushdie-fatwa-khomeini

Book-burning is always telegenic and CNN picked up the event. There ensued riots in the Indian subcontinent. In Iran (which had current political resentments against the UK), on 14 February, the Ayatollah Khomeini issued a fatwa against the British author Rushdie and his British publishers (Penguin) for *The Satanic Verses*. Any devout assassin was guaranteed entry to paradise and a multi-million-dollar reward for ridding the world of the literary apostate and blasphemer (as Rushdie was proscribed).

In his later novel *The Ground Beneath her Feet* (2000), written in series of safe houses under the protection of Britain's Special Branch, Rushdie labels the fatwa a 'Valentine card', echoing Jean Cocteau's ironic comment that harsh criticisms of literature are the love letters of disappointed suitors. He would need to take refuge (initially under the government of 'Mrs Torcher' – satirised in *The Satanic Verses*) for a decade and a half.

The principal ground of offence perceived by Islamists in *The Satanic Verses* is commonly misunderstood. It was not merely the use of the abusive occidental name 'Mahound' for the Prophet, nor his (alleged) lecherousness. It was the novel's contention that the Koran was not the immutably received word of God, but – effectively – fiction (embellished by the Prophet's secretary, 'Salman the Persian'). That it is, effectively, a wonderful work of fiction, God's Novel.

Predictably, the furore made Rushdie's novel (still as impenetrable to the majority of Western readers as *Finnegans Wake*) a bestseller. Nothing gets a book going so successfully as flames licking around its covers (in front of the cameras, of course).

15 February

Francis Parkman launches The Oregon Trail

1849 *The Oregon Trail* grew out of a 'summer's journey out of bounds' that Parkman made to the American West in 1846, of which he kept a journal. On this day the book was published, just in time for the Forty-Niner market of adventurers going to California in search of gold.

Parkman was another of those well-bred, well-educated easterners – like Theodore Roosevelt and Owen Wister (see 4 August and 29 June) – for whom the West was a rite of passage to American manhood. In the book this theme is heightened by three points of reference, none of which is important in the original journal.

One is a group of English tourists whom Parkman and his party meet on the trail, who carry with them enough ammunition for a regiment, and a redundancy of 'spare rifles and fowling pieces, ropes and harnesses' – not to mention 'telescopes and portable compasses' and their personal baggage. Of course they 'broke the axle-tree of their wagon', bringing 'the whole cumbrous machine lumbering into the bed of a brook!' Oddly, in the journal it's Parkman's wagon that breaks its axle-tree, but here it has to happen to the English to show how encumbered the Old World is by precedent.

Then there are the natives. Parkman couldn't make up his mind whether they represented a complex traditional culture, or no culture at all. Of one Oglala Sioux 'warrior' he first describes him with a 'statue-like form limbed like an Apollo of bronze' and then lying 'there in the sun before our tent, kicking his heels in the air and cracking jokes with his brother'.

Finally the issue of the author's health, barely mentioned in the journal, becomes a recurring concern in the book – until one morning when, feeling a renewed 'strength and elasticity of limb', he climbs a mountain and stepping 'forth into the light' sees the 'pale blue prairie ... stretching to the farthest horizon'. This prospect sets the West in perspective – not just visual but moral and intellectual too. It's the real climax of *The Oregon Trail*, because it's when the neophyte becomes the initiate.

16 February

The Thirties are over. Belatedly

2009 'We *were* the 1930s', boasted Stephen Spender. If so, the decade ended with the death of Edward Upward on this day, six decades later. Although he was not included in Roy Campbell's satirical collective name 'MacSpaunday' (Louis Macneice, Spender, W.H. Auden and Cecil Day Lewis) Upward was, through his connection and collaborative writing efforts with Christopher Isherwood, one of what Spender called 'the gang' (unironically – it was the era of Prohibition and Al Capone). As Spender wrote to one of the gang's outriders, the publisher John Lehman, in 1931:

> There are four or five friends who work together, although they are not all known to each other. They are W.H. Auden, Christopher Isherwood, Edward Upward and I ... Whatever one of us does in writing, travelling or taking jobs is a kind of exploration which may be taken up by the others.

Unlike the others Spender mentions (and John Lehman), Upward was not gay. He married, very happily, in 1936. Unlike his fellow gangsters, Upward took up a career as a public school teacher, sticking at it for the whole length of his career (Spender and Auden dabbled, but found the classroom uncongenial). And Upward, a card-carrying member of the Communist party after 1932, brought a Marxist stringency to the 'gang'. A contemporary of Isherwood's at Cambridge, Upward wrote with him a series of squibs and satires set in the imaginary village of Mortmere.

Despite loyal attempts by his fellow gangsters to promote his fiction, Upward's novels (half of which came out in the last fifteen years of his life) were all politely received but made no great impact. He resigned from the Communist party (which he regarded as having become soft in its ideology) in 1948. Widowed, and having outlived all his fellow gangsters, he lived out the last decades of his life on the Isle of Wight, a living monument to the Thirties which – like MacSpaunday – he never really left.

17 February

John Sadleir, the greatest financial swindler (to that date) in British commercial history, commits suicide by poison on Hampstead Heath

1856 No financial crook has inspired better literature than John Sadleir (1813–56). The Irish-born (distantly related through his father to Shakespeare), Catholic and Clongowes College-educated Sadleir began life as a lawyer with his brother William in Dublin. In 1839 – a period of wild railway speculation – he and another brother, James, founded the Tipperary Joint Stock Bank. It expanded rapidly. In 1846,

Sadleir moved to London. He was now wealthy, and set up house, magnificently, in Gloucester Square. He joined the best clubs, the Reform and White's. He rode to hounds and kept a stable of hunters. He did not marry – although he had liaisons of a fashionable kind.

It was the railway boom which buoyed him up. He took shares in many speculative ventures, and sat on boards of the innumerable companies spawned by the mania. He also became chairman of the London and County Joint Stock Bank, which had 60 branches and 20,000 accounts.

By 1847, he was grand enough to be elected to Parliament, for Carlow. Five years later, his brother James and three cousins joined him in the House. They were active in the prosecution of Catholic emancipation, as part of the 'papal brigade'. It was the period of the so-called 'papal aggression' – the setting-up of a Catholic hierarchy in Britain.

Sadleir over-extended himself, and neglected his primary business. By February 1856 his bank was insolvent, largely owing to Sadleir's personal overdraft of £288,000. He was driven to fraud and wild financial gambles, in a desperate attempt to keep afloat. He ran up debts of £1.5 million for the banks over which he had power – an unimaginably large figure at the time.

In the face of inevitable disgrace and criminal prosecution he disposed of himself with prussic acid on the night of 17 February 1856, on Hampstead Heath, near Jack Straw's Castle, the tavern. He is buried in an unmarked grave in Highgate cemetery.

There had never been a financier as spectacularly criminal as Sadleir. He inspired a string of wicked fictional 'Napoleons of the City': Merdle in Dickens's *Little Dorrit* (1857); Davenport Dunn in Charles Lever's 1858 novel of that name; Jabez Morth in Mary Elizabeth Braddon's *Trail of the Serpent* (1861); and Augustus Melmotte in Anthony Trollope's *The Way We Live Now* (1875).

One can almost forgive Sadleir the thousands of ruined widows and children for passages, such as the following, which his malefactions inspired:

Mr Merdle was immensely rich; a man of prodigious enterprise; a Midas without the ears, who turned all he touched to gold. He was in everything good, from banking to building. He was in Parliament, of course. He was in the City, necessarily. He was Chairman of this, Trustee of that, President of the other. The weightiest of men had said to projectors, 'Now, what name have you got? Have you got Merdle?' And, the reply being in the negative, had said, 'Then I won't look at you.'

18 February

Mark Twain's Huckleberry Finn *is published in the US, delayed by an obscene engraving*

1885 The American edition came out over two months after appearing in England and Canada, because an unknown engraver in the American publishers, Charles L. Webster Company, had added an erect penis to the picture of Silas Phelps on the penultimate page of Chapter XXXII. The pictures in all copies had to be cut out by hand and replaced by a new printing of the original plate.

The joke would prove prophetic of the book's reception; along with great approbation, it has attracted 100 years of objections to its language. Libraries, including the otherwise liberal Free Public Library in progressive Concord, Massachusetts, would ban the book as 'obscene' – not in the sense of sexually explicit, but in the older sense of not fit for public performance. More recently the book has been criticised for its racial discourse, in particular Huck's frequent use of the word 'nigger'.

The reason why the Concord library called the characters' dialogue 'rough, coarse and inelegant' is that they were the first in American fiction to talk as real people actually spoke. Before *Huckleberry Finn* characters said things like: 'Faith, Sir, I have much inclination to indulge the man, if it should only be to let him behold the firm countenance we maintain.'

That comes from James Fenimore Cooper's *The Last of the Mohicans* (1826). As Mark Twain himself commented of Cooper's dialogue, 'To believe that such talk really ever came out of people's mouths would be to believe that there was a time when time was of no value to a person who thought he had something to say; when it was the custom to spread a two-minute remark out to ten; when a man's mouth was a rolling-mill, and busied itself all day long in turning four-foot pigs of thought into thirty-foot bars of conversational railroad iron by attenuation.'

19 February

Ezra Pound's The Pisan Cantos *wins the first-ever Bollingen Prize for poetry*

1949 The award caused a critical storm that spread to the popular press, raising once again (as had the trial of Oscar Wilde – see 25 May) that old question of whether aesthetics is a kind of morality. In other words, does art have a system of morality that can be kept separate from life?

Ezra Pound, the archetypal Anglo-American modernist, was the author of works ranging in size from the early imagist 'In a Station of the Metro' (a poem not much longer than its title), through the cultural critique of *Hugh Selwyn Mauberly* (1920) to the monumental *The Cantos* (1922 onwards, unfinished at his death in 1972, at which point he had reached number 120). He was also a generous patron to many artistic contemporaries and midwife to T.S. Eliot's *The Waste Land*.

From 1924 he lived in Italy. When the Fascists took power, he became an ardent admirer of Mussolini, writing to him from time to time, and even meeting him once in 1933 when he presented the Duce with a copy of his first 30 *Cantos*. Hugely delighted with the encounter, Pound would recall it in *Canto 41*:

'Ma questo,'
Said the Boss, 'è divertente.'*
Catching the point before the aesthetes had got there;

With so much goodwill about, it was natural that Pound would want to support the Italian side in the war against the Allies. Pound hated the war anyway, so he wrote articles for the Italian papers denouncing it as a Jewish bankers' conspiracy. Between 1941 and 1943 he also made well over 100 broadcasts on Rome Radio attacking the war. They were in English, colloquial in tone, spoken in a kind of folksy accent and clearly aimed at Americans (including soldiers on active service) in an attempt to get them to question their nation's war effort against the Axis.†

---

* 'But this ... is amusing.'
† The full text of the broadcasts can be found in Leonard W. Doob (ed.), *Ezra Pound Speaking: Radio Speeches of World War II*, Westport, CT: Greenwood Press, 1978.

As the Allies completed their dangerous conquest of Italy, Pound was arrested by Italian partisans and handed over to the US authorities. On 24 May 1945 he was incarcerated in a US Army 'Detention Training Camp' (DTC) on the Via Aurelia just north of Pisa, where he was kept in an open cage for almost a month, before being allowed a tent.

It was here that Pound wrote most of *Cantos* 74 to 84, the so-called *Pisan Cantos.* They are indeed different from the other *Cantos* – more reflective, less declamatory; quoting from conversations in his personal past more than from the writings of philosophers and politicians; immensely attentive to nature near and far, from a green baby grass-hopper swinging on a blade of grass to the snow on the marble of the Carrara mountains to the north-east of the DTC.

On his return to the States Pound was charged with treason, but was judged unfit to plead because of his mental condition, and committed to St Elizabeth's Hospital in Washington, DC. There he was the centre of something of a salon, visited by poets like Elizabeth Bishop, Robert Lowell and William Carlos Williams, and a cadre of younger men keen to learn more about his ideas about economic history. Meanwhile, publication of *The Pisan Cantos* in 1948 aroused a great deal of interest – so much so that the Fellows of American Letters at the Library of Congress decided to award the volume the first-ever Bollingen Foundation poetry award on this day in 1949.

Then all hell broke loose. 'Pound, in Mental Clinic, Wins Prize for Poetry Penned in Treason Cell', thundered the Sunday *New York Times.* Scarcely less alarming was Robert Hillyer in *The Saturday Review of Literature* ('Treason's Strange Fruit'), for whom *The Pisan Cantos* were a vehicle for 'Fascism, anti-Semitism' and 'contempt for America'. It was all down to a conspiracy made up of T.S. Eliot and other friends of Pound, together with the 'New Critics' whose doctrine disallowed the truth value of a work of art, focusing instead on its inherent worth as an aesthetic object – a 'Well-Wrought Urn', to borrow New Critic Cleanth Brooks' title of 1947.

Eighty-four writers and critics, including e.e. cummings and Lionel Trilling, wrote to *The Saturday Review* to counter Hillyer's attack. The magazine declined to print their letter.

Congressmen like Jacob K. Javits of New York and James T. Patterson of Connecticut addressed the House, and read Hillyer's essay into the Congressional record. The Congressional Joint Committee on the Library of Congress resolved that no more literary prizes should be granted under the Library's auspices.

There was some truth in Hillyer's analysis, daft as it may sound at this distance. If not a conspiracy, then the Bollingen award was certainly the result of a remarkable likeness of critical orientation among the Fellows – most of whom, like T.S. Eliot, W.H. Auden, Mark Van Doren and Conrad Aiken, were friends of Alan Tate, the Library's consultant in poetry, who had appointed them.

It was left to a later historian to point out the irony that during the Cold War, 'most Americans would have felt more at home with Soviet "Realist" premises, which demanded a subordination of art to politically defined mass needs, than with a seemingly incomprehensible aesthetic theory originating in T.S. Eliot's obscure complaints about a "dissociation of sensibility"'.*

The British had a more direct approach to problems like these. When they finally got their hands on another expatriate American broadcasting treason from an enemy country, William Joyce (aka 'Lord Haw-Haw'), they strung him up without delay or ceremony. As *Private Eye* would put it, 'it's the only language they understand'.

20 February

F.T. Marinetti publishes the Futurist Manifesto on the front page of Le Figaro, *Paris*

1909 'We had stayed up all night, my friends and I, under hanging mosque lamps with domes of filigreed brass, domes starred like our spirits, shining like them with the prisoned radiance of electric hearts.' Then, a call to action: '"Let's go!" I said. "Friends, away! Let's go! Mythology and the Mystic Ideal are defeated at last. We're about to see the Centaur's birth and, soon after, the first flight of Angels!"'

No sooner were the words out of Marinetti's mouth than they raced on in their car, 'hurling watchdogs against doorsteps, curling them under our burning tires like collars under a flatiron' until made to swerve by two cyclists 'shaking their fists, wobbling like two equally convincing but nevertheless contradictory arguments' until the car winds up in a ditch, its wheels in the air:

---

* Frank A. Ninko, *The Diplomacy of Ideas: US Foreign Policy and Cultural Relations, 1938–1951*, New York: Cambridge University Press, 1981.

O maternal ditch, almost full of muddy water! Fair factory drain! I gulped down your nourishing sludge; and I remembered the blessed black breast of my Sudanese nurse ... When I came up – torn, filthy, and stinking – from under the capsized car, I felt the white-hot iron of joy deliciously pass through my heart!

So much for the preamble – the movement's birth and baptism, so to speak. As for the manifesto itself, it contained eleven paragraphs hymning 'the beauty of speed' imaged in 'a racing car whose hood is adorned with great pipes' and whose driver 'hurls the lance of his spirit across the Earth, along the circle of its orbit'. Paragraphs five and six promised a violent, radical and intentionally misogynist programme:

5.   We will glorify war – the world's only hygiene – militarism, patriotism, the destructive gesture of freedom-bringers, beautiful ideas worth dying for, and scorn for woman.

6.   We will destroy the museums, libraries, academies of every kind, will fight moralism, feminism, every opportunistic or utilitarian cowardice.

It was absurd, extreme – deliberately so (the Futurists could be self-mocking as well as self-advertising). What did it all mean in practice? In painting, urban scenes in which nature and artifice – trees, sky, houses, buses – blended into each other, through a 'divisionist' medium of dots, stripes and planes of colour. In poetry, forced analogies between nature and the machine (not unlike metaphysical conceits), that perennial modernist chimera, the 'abolition of syntax' so as to 'free' the word (*parole in libertà* was both the theme and the method of Marinetti's own concrete poem *Zang Tumb Tumb*, which appeared in instalments between 1912 and 1914).

Did Futurism leave a legacy? Fragments of its mood and method could be found in Surrealism, Dada and the vorticism of *Blast* (see 2 July). But none would survive the First World War, which it no longer seemed so witty to 'glorify' as 'the world's only hygiene'.

21 February

Dead, but not yet buried

2005 Guillermo Cabrera Infante was born in Cuba in 1929. He was the eldest son of parents who founded the Cuban Communist party. Their politics led, inevitably, to friction with the authorities (Cuba was, effectively, a US possession – following its liberation from Spain – and a Yankee playground). Guillermo's parents were imprisoned in 1936. On their release the family went to live in Havana: the location that meant most to their son for the rest of his life.

Cabrera Infante enrolled as a medical student at the University of Havana in 1949, but promptly switched to journalism. Films were always a passion for him and he published on them enthusiastically and perceptively in the 1950s. He had proclaimed dissident views and, like his parents, spent some time in prison for pieces the authorities found offensive. Prohibited from writing under his own name, he adopted a pseudonym ('G. Cain' – after the Biblical outcast) and continued annoying the Batista regime.

When Fidel Castro took over the country in 1959 Cabrera Infante was, initially, a staunch supporter of the socialist revolution. The new authorities liked him as well. He was awarded a position of authority in the newly established state film institute, and an editorial position on the cultural supplement of the party's newspaper, *Revolución*. He divorced his first wife and remarried during this period and in 1960 published his first volume of fiction, *Así en la paz como en la guerra* (*As in Times of Peace, So in Times of War*).

He was, however, already chafing at the party's censorship of artistic expression. In 1962, he accepted a diplomatic position in Belgium where he could express himself unfettered. Here it was that he wrote *Tres tristes tigres* (1967; *Three Trapped Tigers*) – an exercise in Joycean verbal wit, set in Havana (his Dublin) before the revolution. It won an array of international prizes.

In 1965 Cabrera Infante finally resolved on exile from a country he loved, but could no longer – under Castro – live in (although, until his death, he would write about it obsessively, particularly Havana). After Franco's Spain denied him residency he moved to England, becoming a citizen in 1979, the country's first Cuban novelist.

In England he published novels and wrote screenplays and film reviews (his English was as proficient as that of any native speaker), and published a celebration of the cigar, *Holy Smoke* (1985). Cuba had, by now, long disowned him as a traitor to the country and his books were banned on the island. However, some Cubans saw him as the country's greatest living novelist. His last years in England were depressed and unhappy. Castro, it seemed, would live for ever.

Cabrera died on 21 February 2005 of MRSA, while being treated in a London hospital for a fractured hip. He had requested, in the event of his death, that his ashes be kept unburied until – after Castro and his regime were gone – they could be interred in Cuba. They remain unburied.

22 February

Coetzee's Gulliverism

2007 Literature is in its essence national property – 'English Literature', 'American Literature', 'French Literature'. In *Pictures of an Institution*, Randall Jarrell imagines a small South American country whose 'great author' is called Gomez. The inhabitants think of Shakespeare as 'the English Gomez'. When Saul Bellow asked (there is some doubt that he ever did), 'Who is the Zulu Tolstoy?', he was making a chauvinistic point about nationalism as much as any point about literature. In other words, that great nations (alone) have great authors.

J.M. Coetzee is indisputably a great author. Who owns him? It is a tricky question. He was born into an Afrikaans family, but one which spoke principally English (there was also a dash of Polish in his background). He was brought up and educated in South Africa (a phase of his life chronicled in his fictionalised memoir, *Boyhood*). Arguably the Zulus, after Mandela, could mount a claim on the basis of country of residence.

In his early twenties, unwilling to live under apartheid, Coetzee moved to London where, having studied maths and English as a university student, he was one of the first generation of IBM computer programmers (this phase of his life is chronicled in *Youth*).

Coetzee moved on to America in 1965, where he studied and later taught English at university level. He applied to be naturalised in the US, but was rejected by the Immigration and Naturalization Service for having taken part in violent anti-Vietnam protests. Coetzee returned to South Africa in 1971, to take up a university post in Cape Town. On his retirement in 2002, he migrated to Australia. In 2006, he became an Australian citizen.

All these national locations, and affiliations, find reflection in Coetzee's fiction – both geographically and thematically. But 'nation', one suspects, means less to Coetzee – one of the most enigmatic writers of his time – than 'species'. He seems, like Gulliver at the end of his travels, to have decided that his true kinship is with animal-, not human-kind.

In a series of books, articles and speeches from the mid-1990s onwards Coetzee proclaimed his zoophilia. In his 2003 novel *Esther Costello* he put into the lead character the belief that humans' factory-style husbandry of animals was not merely the equivalent of the Jewish Holocaust but – in terms of numbers and the fact that it is ongoing – much worse. In a novel this opinion could be attributed to the fanaticism of a fictional character: no more the author's personal views than are Savonarola's extremities in George Eliot's novel, *Romola*.

But on 22 February 2007, in a lecture to the 'Voiceless' animal protection society in Sydney, Coetzee proclaimed as his personal belief 'the Holocaust on your breakfast plate' (as satirical journalists called it):

> The transformation of animals into production units dates back to the late 19th century, and since that time we have already had one warning on the grandest scale that there is something deeply, cosmically wrong with regarding and treating fellow beings as mere units of any kind. This warning came so loud and clear that one would have thought it impossible to ignore. It came when in the mid-20th century a group of powerful and bloody-minded men in Germany hit on the idea of adapting the methods of the industrial stockyard, as pioneered and perfected in Chicago, to the slaughter – or what they preferred to call the processing – of human beings.
>
> Of course we cried out in horror when we found out what they had been up to. We cried: What a terrible crime, to treat human beings like cattle! If we had only known beforehand! But our cry should more accurately have been: What a terrible crime, to treat human beings like units in an industrial process! And that cry should have had a postscript: What a terrible crime, come to think of it – a crime against nature – to treat any living being like a unit in an industrial process!

In the 1960s (the period in which the novelist entered adulthood) the cry had been 'one race – the human race'. For Coetzee, in the years of his maturity it is 'one species, the animal species'.

23 February

The print run begins of the Gutenberg Bible, in Mainz, Germany

1455 Recently we have all been through a step change in the sharing of information like that experienced by Europeans of the 15th and 16th centuries. Ours is the internet; theirs was the invention of printing with movable alphabetical type.

First came writing, though at first that didn't advance literature so much as state bureaucracy. Early papyri and clay tablets were inventories, receipts, lists of payment in beer to manual workers, at a time when imaginative literature like epics and lyric poems were sung or spoken from memory.

Another great leap forward was the codex – the book as we know it, with lots of pages bound together along one edge. This had two advantages over the scroll: you could write on both sides of the page, and (much more important) the reader could flick to different parts of the text much more quickly – like moving from videotapes to DVDs.

But books had to be either written by hand or printed from elaborately carved woodblocks, which limited their distribution to the elites of church and state. Printing using type that could be set up, used for multiple copies, then distributed and ultimately used again for another text introduced mass production to the mix.

What Gutenberg did was to take a wine press, add a padded flat surface to the bottom of the screw, and below that a 'chase' or frame in which to clamp the type and its spacers. The type was inked with a roller, paper or vellum placed over it, and the upper surface screwed down. Trained as a goldsmith, Gutenberg knew what alloy would make the type able to withstand repeated use. He also worked out that ink based on oil rather than water would stick better to the type.

Gutenberg's idea to print the whole of St Jerome's Latin translation of the Old and New Testaments was itself a radical step, since most worshippers in a Catholic service would know the Bible only through the missal – a sort of anthology of scripture with certain selected texts to be read out on a particular day. Though his massive Bible remained expensive, within a little over half a century printing had spread to over 2,000 cities in Europe, and had got much cheaper. When Bibles became affordable, people could gain direct access to God's word without the mediation of the parish priest – the fundamental principle of the Reformation.

To speed the process reformers like Martin Luther and John Calvin could now publish their sermons and religious tracts more cheaply. Before long came political pamphlets, newspapers, street ballads – even (eventually) imaginative literature. As print capitalism spread, so more and more people wanted to learn how to read. The process of enlightenment was reciprocal. 'We change our tools', as Jeff Bezos, CEO of Amazon.com, has said of the internet, 'and then our tools change us.'

24 February

The Theatre Royal, Drury Lane, burns down, prompting a laconic quip from its newly ruined owner

1809 It wasn't the first Drury Lane theatre, nor the first to burn. A theatre has stood on Bridges Street (now Catherine Street) in Covent Garden, backing onto Drury Lane, since 1663, three years after the Restoration cancelled the Puritan ban on public performance. The first escaped the Great Fire of 1666, but burned to the ground six years later. Its successor, designed by Christopher Wren, was home to the great actor-manager David Garrick and his famous 24 Shakespeare performances. On leaving the stage in 1776, Garrick sold his shares in the theatre to the Irish dramatist Richard Brinsley Sheridan, who used it to premiere both his enormous success (and perennial favourite) *The School for Scandal* (1777) and *The Critic* (1779).

In time the Wren building, even as refurbished by the Adam brothers (with Robert providing a handsome classical façade on the Bridges Street side) fell into such disrepair that it had to be knocked down. Sheridan put £80,000 of his personal fortune, including the earnings from his comedies of manners, into an ambitious new project capable of seating 3,600 on the ground floor and in six tiers of galleries supported by iron columns. The producers found it increasingly difficult to fill this cavern with ordinary, 'legitimate' theatre, so they staged plays that created their effect with spectacular display rather than well-turned verbal exchanges. One such spectacle featured a river flowing into a lake large enough to row a boat on.

Despite an iron safety curtain that was supposed to prevent it, the third theatre caught fire on 24 February 1809, and by late afternoon was burning furiously. Sheridan, who was also the Member of Parliament for Sheffield, could see the glow from the House of Commons, then in session. 'A motion was made to adjourn,' according to the *Annual Register* for that year, 'but Mr Sheridan said, with great calmness, "that whatever might be the extent of the private calamity, he hoped it would not interfere with the public business of the country".'

Finally he and 'many of his friends' left for the scene, only to confirm the bad news. The theatre was insured, but for far less than it would cost to rebuild it. Rumour has it that he went into a nearby tavern, ordered a drink and proceeded to sip it slowly (another version has him out on the street, glass in hand). When asked how he could remain so calm while his fortune was going up in flames, he replied: 'A man may surely take a glass of wine by his own fireside.'

25 February

The other Naipaul dies. Prematurely

1985 Shiva(dhar Srivinasa) Naipaul was born in 1945 in Port of Spain, Trinidad. He was one of two sons of the distinguished Trinidadian journalist Seepersad Naipaul, who died when Shiva was seven. His brother V.S. ['Vidia'] Naipaul was twelve years Shiva's senior and more influenced by his father. The Naipauls were Indian by origin and their ancestors had come to the Caribbean in the 19th century as indentured labourers. Both the Naipaul sons were emotionally torn between Indian heritage and West Indian upbringing.

Shiva Naipaul had the best school education (with a strong English flavour to it) the island could offer and like his brother before him won a scholarship to study at the University of Oxford. He enrolled for a variety of subjects, none of them with any success. He graduated with a gentleman's third (in Chinese) in 1968. He had married the year before. It was a year of social upheaval and a period of emotional confusion for Naipaul. As the *Oxford Dictionary of National Biography*

(*ODNB*) records:

> He never truly felt at home anywhere; and so began a rootless and dislocated existence starting in Britain in 1964 where not 'being straightforwardly Indian or straightforwardly West Indian' was a confusion that the rest of the world could not deal with.

It was additionally awkward having a novelist brother who had already won himself a distinguished name. Nonetheless, Shiva was determined to write fiction himself. He settled in London and, in 1970, published a novel set in the West Indies, *Fireflies*. Comparisons with Vidia's *A House for Mr Biswas* were inevitable, and not always to Shiva's advantage. *Fireflies* nonetheless won prizes and laid the way for another Trinidadian novel, *The Chip-Chip Gatherers*, which won the Whitbread Prize for that year, 1974.

Naipaul then went silent as an author of fiction for ten years, restricting himself to some short stories and travel writing. The tone of his published work was increasingly bleak and sardonic. It was at its bleakest with his chronicle of the Jonestown massacre, *Black and White* (1980). A third novel, *A Hot Country*, was published in 1983 for a fiction readership which had largely forgotten him, if not his surname.

Naipaul was poised on the brink of a major career when, wholly unexpectedly, he died of a thrombosis, shortly after his 40th birthday, on 25 February 1985. The *Spectator*, a magazine for which he had written over the years (and on which his wife worked), established a prize in his honour. It is, of course, routinely mistaken for an award honouring the achievements of the other, Nobel-winning, Naipaul.

Geoffrey Wheatcroft, who wrote the above *ODNB* entry, has written elsewhere reflecting on Shiva's alleged misanthropy:

> It's impossible not to wonder how he would have developed … Vidia has been garlanded with the highest honours, knighthood to Nobel prize, but it would be an exaggeration to say that, while he has grown as a great writer, he has also mellowed into a great liberal philanthropist, and I doubt if Shiva would have done so either. V.S. Naipaul's sharp critique of Islam is looking rather perceptive at present, but there is no use pretending that he is full of warm sympathy for the Third World, and nor was Shiva.*

---

* *Spectator*, 13 August 2005.

26 February

In Paris, Ernest Hemingway receives two cables from New York accepting his manuscript of In Our Time

1925 In Paris during the twenties Hemingway taught Ezra Pound how to box, and Pound taught him to distrust adjectives. Or at least that's how the novelist remembered it in *A Moveable Feast* (1964). Certainly Pound's imagism – the concrete image standing alone, without modification or explanation, to evoke an emotional response in the reader – is a key into Hemingway's famously plain style.

That style made its debut in *In Our Time* (1925), a collection of short stories, each prefaced by a short inter-chapter seldom more than a page long. In some stories Nick Adams features as a sort of alter ego for Hemingway himself – whether in youth, as in 'Indian Camp', in which Nick watches his doctor father deliver a Native American baby, or as a war veteran in 'Cross Country Snow', in which Nick and George regret having to leave the Swiss Alps to return to the States.

Its inter-chapters were the real innovation, though. Here is part of one:

> They shot the six cabinet ministers at half-past six in the morning against the wall of a hospital. There were pools of water in the courtyard. It rained hard. All the shutters of the hospital were nailed shut. One of the ministers was sick with typhoid. Two soldiers carried him downstairs and out into the rain. They tried to hold him up against the wall but he sat down in a puddle of water.

The short declarative sentences, free of dependent clauses; the documentary edge to the precise time of day; the concrete details like the pools of water – all work to establish that off-hand tone so typical of Hemingway's prose. Hard boiled it may be, yet it's hardly without feeling, what with that sombre irony of the hospital backdrop: the caring institution with its shutters 'nailed shut'.

The most daring thing about the passage is what might be called its pseudo-reference. What cabinet ministers? Who are the 'they' who shot them? What's the occasion? The definite article 'the' implies that readers know the context, but of course we don't. But then we don't need to; it's an atmospheric sketch, not a history – nor, for that matter, a conventional novel – and it's very Hemingway.

27 February

Poet meets drummer

1972 The distinguished journalist Nicholas Tomalin reported for the *Sunday Times* on the lavish party held by the Burtons, to commemorate Elizabeth Taylor's 40th birthday. She and Richard were joined at the time in one of their serial marriages. The event was held in Hungary, where Burton was making the monumental flop (as it turned out) *Bluebeard's Castle*.

Everyone who was anyone (Brando, Frankie Howerd, Michael Caine) was invited – the Burtons picking up travel and hotel expenses. Stephen Spender knew Richard Burton through mutual Oxford University friends (notably Nevill Coghill). On meeting the actor in 1982, at the Gritti Palace, Venice, Spender found him as 'friendly, quiet, curiously assured, as I've always found him – so much in contrast with his drunken public image'.

For the 1972 birthday party, only one air ticket was provided per guest. Stephen found himself a little lonely, but struck up conversation with Ringo Starr. As Tomalin records:

> They chatted for 10 minutes and, as they drifted apart, Spender suggested it might be nice to meet again in London. 'What did yous [*sic*] say your name was?' Ringo asked. 'Stephen Spender,' said Stephen Spender. 'Yes, well, Stephen, just you telephone the Apple recording company in London and tell them we've met, that your name is Stephen Spender and I said you should ring. And do make it clear it was at Elizabeth's party we met.'

The anecdote must, of course, have originated with Spender and indicates why, throughout his life, he was regarded as one of the most amusing dinner-party guests in literary London.

28 February

F.R. Leavis demolishes C.P. Snow

1962 C.P. Snow began revolving his thesis about the 'two cultures' that were impeding the progress of modern Britain as early as 1956, in an article in the *New Statesman*. The thesis was elaborated in a talk delivered on 7 May 1959 in Cambridge, subsequently published as *The Two Cultures and the Scientific Revolution*.

There were, Snow argued, 'New Men' and 'Old Men'. The first knew Shakespeare but were stumped by the Second Law of Thermodynamics: the others vice versa. There was, he implied, one man who effortlessly bridged the two. There should be more Snows.

The two-culture thesis was influential and adopted as holy writ in the sixth-forms of Britain. Congenial as it was with liberal education-ists, it provoked ferocious refutation from the leading literary critic of the time, F.R. Leavis.

In an answering lecture, delivered at Cambridge on 28 February 1962, Leavis, much the more effective polemicist, denied any such cul-tural split. He mocked the pontifical tone of Snow's argument which, as he bitingly observed, only genius could justify: but, then, who could imagine genius using such a tone? As for Tolstoyan pretension:

> Snow is, of course, a – no, I can't say that; he isn't: Snow thinks of himself as a novelist … his incapacity as a novelist is … total … as a novelist he doesn't exist; he doesn't begin to exist … Not only is he not a genius … he is intellectually as undistinguished as it is possible to be.

Snow's reputation among the discriminating few, and his *amour propre*, never recovered. With the public at large his reputation was unaffected. Sixth-formers still read and disgorge it.

29 February

Gay's 'Newgate Pastoral' will do

1728 John Gay's *The Beggar's Opera* (known as a 'Newgate Pastoral') was produced at Lincoln's Inn Fields (along with Drury Lane, one of the two principal playhouses in London) on 29 February 1728. It was a tense occasion for the playwright and his fellow members of the Scriblerus Club (Alexander Pope, for example), who were among the audience. The work was, as the *Daily Journal* described, a 'new English opera in a manner *entirely* new'. The novelty was stage dialogue interspersed with ballads (to musical accompaniment). *The Beggar's Opera* was satirical – Swiftian, almost, in its critique of the English criminal justice system. It daringly attacked the leading politician of the day, Robert Walpole (as Bob Booty); and it ran entirely against the accepted norms and conventions of Italian opera. Colley Cibber, the proprietor at Drury Lane, had played safe by turning Gay's offering down.

The work opens in Peachum's house, in which the thief-taker cheerfully outlines his nihilistic philosophy of life:

> Through all the Employments of Life
> Each Neighbour abuses his Brother;
> Whore and Rogue they call Husband and Wife:
> All Professions be-rogue one another:
> The Priest calls the Lawyer a Cheat,
> The Lawyer be-knaves the Divine:
> And the Statesman, because he's so great,
> Thinks his Trade as honest as mine.

At the end of the first act (of three) on the first night there was complete silence. The absence of applause was not, however, evidence of audience displeasure but head-scratching uncertainty as to how to react to this spectacle of roguery, thievery and whoredom. When the curtain descended on the third act, the clapping was thunderous. Pope realised that his friend had triumphed when he overheard the Duke of Argyle exclaim, in his adjoining box: 'It will do.'

It did very well for Gay, running as it did for 62 nights (with every third night a benefit for the playwright – who was estimated to have made some £600 from the first run). On the strength of the play's success the manager of Lincoln's Inn Fields, John Rich, was able to construct a fine new establishment (the Theatre Royal, Covent Garden), the forerunner of today's Royal Opera House. Bertolt Brecht paid Gay the sincerest flattery by imitating his work as *Drei Groschen Oper* (*Threepenny Opera*) with music by Kurt Weill.

1 March

The witch trials open in Ingersoll's Tavern, Salem Village, Massachusetts

1692 At first only three women were charged. Over the rest of that spring and summer, as the confusion and hysteria grew and the examinations were moved to the meeting house, 55 men and women would 'confess' to witchcraft. Over 150 would be imprisoned, nineteen hanged, and Giles Corey, aged 81, pressed to death under a platform loaded with stones.

The panic was fed by underlying anxiety about whether the colony's royal charter would be renewed, combined with fear that the devil was actively and secretly undermining the pious community. The effects of his work were plain to see: a number of adolescent girls were falling about convulsed into grotesque postures, complaining of invisible bites and pinches on their arms and legs.

Who had done the devil's work? As always in witch scares, suspicion fell on older women, many widowed or single, marginal to the town. One by one they were accused. Since they bore no marks of their wickedness, the court had no way of determining their guilt apart from forcing confessions through leading questions:

> Sarah Goode what evil Spirit have you familiarity with?
> None …
> Why do you hurt these children?
> I doe not hurt them. I scorn it.
> Who doe you imploy then to do it?
> I imploy no body.
> What creature do you imploy then?

And so on. No wonder Arthur Miller was so fascinated with the Salem trials. His play *The Crucible* (1953) kept the language and characters of the original, but the audience knew it was really about the House Un-American Activities Committee (HUAC), another 'court' that could subpoena witnesses, deny them the right to cross-examine others testifying against them, try to brow-beat them into admitting to invisible abuses, then charge them with contempt if they refused to confess.

On 18 August 1955, HUAC questioned the folk-singer Pete Seeger on his performances for alleged communist-front cultural organisations:

MR TAVENNER: [...] I have before me a photostatic copy of the June 20, 1947, issue of the *Daily Worker*, [in which] ... appears this advertisement: 'Tonight—Bronx, hear Peter Seeger and his guitar, at Allerton Section housewarming.' May I ask you whether or not the Allerton Section was a section of the Communist Party? ...

MR SEEGER: I am not going to answer any questions as to my association, my philosophical or religious beliefs or my political beliefs, or how I voted in any election, or any of these private affairs. I think these are very improper questions for any American to be asked, especially under such compulsion as this ...*

Because he refused to plead the Fifth Amendment of the Constitution, which allows witnesses to refuse to testify if their testimony would incriminate them, Pete Seeger's failure to answer landed him in jail for a year for contempt of Congress.

2 March

Lucky Jim *is conceived*

1948 Kingsley Amis and Philip Larkin forged their friendship as undergraduates at Oxford (their drunken nights are commemorated in Larkin's poem, 'Dockery and Son') and confirmed the relationship with a lifelong, immensely comic (and often scatological) correspondence. On 2 March 1948, Amis wrote to his chum Larkin, now a junior librarian at the University College of Leicester, to say:

I will arrive in Lester [*sic*] at lunch time on Friday [5 March], precise details by card or wire to follow. Will u meet me at the station or what? Inform by card *where*. Hasta vista.

It was Amis's first visit to Leicester. He himself was in Oxford, collecting a degree, but about to apply (successfully) for a junior lectureship at Swansea. Neither man (first-class degrees both of them, from a *real*

---

* http://www.peteseeger.net/HUAC.htm

university) had much regard for red-brick. Both were writing, ambitiously. Larkin had already done a couple of novels. Amis was thrashing around, looking for a subject. In the 2 March letter he thinks he may have got a lead from the ghost stories of M.R. James (much later this would emerge as his fantasy of alcoholic haunting, *The Green Man*, 1969).

Larkin picked up Amis at Leicester station and walked with him to his 'digs' in Dixon Drive, which he shared, glumly, with 'a dough-faced physicist co-lodger'. The library opened on Saturday morning and required Larkin's attendance. The two men walked to the university, located opposite the municipal cemetery (later immortalised in Larkin's poem 'Toads Revisited'). The buildings were a decommissioned Victorian lunatic asylum. Even by the standards of that municipal architecture it was not a distinguished edifice.

Larkin parked Amis in the Senior Common Room while he went off to work. As Amis recalled: 'I looked around a couple of times and said to myself, "Christ, somebody ought to do something with this".'

Something was done, after much confabulation with Larkin, with Amis's first novel, the story of Lucky Jim Dixon and his trials at the converted lunatic asylum university.

3 March

The Birth of a Nation *is released: literature meets film*

1915 Having established itself in Hollywood (to escape copyright complications about camera technology on the east coast, and to take advantage of California's never-ending sunshine), the movie industry eagerly sought material to film. They found it in popular fiction. At first (as with camera technology) they plundered, reaping where they had not sown.

The formal relationship between screen and printed page was inaugurated – controversially – on 15 April 1914 when D.W. Griffith closed a deal to buy the rights to Thomas Dixon's *The Clansman* (Griffith's employees, reports Wyn Craig Wade in *The Fiery Cross*, 'thought their boss had gone mad'). Griffith began shooting the movie in California on 4 July – meaningful date.

Dixon (1864–1946) was born, during the Civil War, in North Carolina, one of five children of a Baptist minister. Before the war the Dixon family was rich. After the war they found themselves plunged in abject poverty, down there with the 'darkies' they had always lorded it over. It had a (de)formative effect on the growing Thomas.

During these hard years his father (also Thomas Dixon) rode with the Ku Klux Klan and became a senior member, or 'Wizard', as did other disaffected members of his family. The KKK, an underground movement, was formed by veterans of the Confederate Army to assert white supremacy (by violence if necessary) against reforms imposed by the victorious North and the hated Republican party. It established a surrogate aristocracy for an unfairly (as they thought) degraded master-class.

A clever boy, Thomas went to Johns Hopkins on a full scholarship, qualifying as a lawyer in 1886. One of his contemporaries at Hopkins, and a personal friend, was the future president, Woodrow Wilson.

Dixon was elected to the North Carolina legislature in 1885 but resigned a year later to enter the Baptist ministry. He was a wildly popular 'lyceum lecturer' and gave dramatic sermons to admiring congregations as far north as New York and Boston.

Dixon's career in fiction began with his seeing a stage performance of *Uncle Tom's Cabin*, which inflamed his dormant KKK sentiments. He resolved to strike back with *romans à these* arguing the southern cause, notably *The Clansman* (1905), which sold 40,000 copies in its first ten days of publication.

The narrative opens with victory for the Union being shouted through the streets of Washington. Young, beautiful and 'fair' Elsie Stoneman has nursed back to health a young Rebel officer, Ben Cameron, who will face the firing squad when he recovers for the crime of fighting behind enemy lines as a 'guerrilla'. Elsie goes to Lincoln and successfully pleads in person for Ben's life. The fatherly president gladly grants a pardon. He goes on to explain that his aim for the United States has never been negro emancipation, perish the thought, but repatriation of the former slaves to Africa: 'I can conceive of no greater calamity than the assimilation of the Negro into our social and political life as our equal.' 'Mulatto citizenship' is an abomination.

Elsie and Ben duly marry and return to his native South Carolina, only to discover that 'the white man's day is done'. A band of blacks gang-rape Ben's former love, the 'belle' Marion Lenoir, and her mother. Unable to live with the shame, the ladies commit suicide. The Klan avenges them. Bloodily. The 'Fiery Cross' burns everywhere. The white-sheeted riders restore justice and (for the uppity blacks) condign retribution. The novel's last words are: 'Civilization has been saved, and the South redeemed from shame.'

Immortality was bestowed on *The Clansman* when D.W. Griffith took it as the source for his epochal film, *The Birth of a Nation*. Dixon was the first novelist ever to receive 'subsidiary rights' ($2,000) for a film adaptation of his work. After a successful sneak preview in Los Angeles, Griffith prepared for the major release in New York. The newly formed National Association for the Advancement of Colored People (NAACP) mounted a series of legal protests, on the grounds of racial defamation.

Dixon – by now a veteran in racist polemic – wrote to his college friend Woodrow Wilson on 3 February 1915. The president, he suggested, might like to look at this crowning achievement of the burgeoning American film industry. On 18 February 1915 there was a private showing of the movie in the East Room of the White House for Wilson, his wife and daughters. Dixon and Griffith were present. The president was impressed: 'It is like writing history with lightning', he said.

All legal challenges overcome, the film was released in New York (at a massive $2 a ticket) on 3 March, at the aptly named Liberty Theater. Men and women (many wearing antebellum fancy dress) packed out the opening evening.

The Birth of a Nation – which closely follows the plot of *The Clansman* – is regarded as a classic of American film. And also, alas, an everlasting blemish on American race relations.

4 March

Kidnapped by Native Americans, Mary Rowlandson is carried dry-shod over the Baquaug River, which proves an impassable barrier to the English army pursuing them

1676 First published in 1682, Mary Rowlandson's account of her *Captivity and Restoration* ran through fourteen further editions by the end of the 17th century. Clearly the theme of an innocent captured by alien forces had a powerful effect on American readers. In time, dozens more captivity stories would follow, in which the kidnappers could be

Jesuit priests, or Romans enslaving Jews (in the case of *Ben Hur*, 1880), or even a British officer, as in Susanna Rowson's sentimental romance *Charlotte Temple* (1791), the most popular work of fiction in America until *Uncle Tom's Cabin*.

But in Rowlandson's narrative there is a further layer of spiritual autobiography. She scrutinises each twist and turn of her captivity for signs of what it portends for her own salvation. So when 'many hundreds' of what she calls the 'heathen' manage to cross the river 'bag and baggage' – 'some sick, some lame', including 'squaws' with 'papooses at their backs' – she naturally expects the pursuing English army to follow on pretty smartish. But they don't. 'On that very day', she writes, 'came the English army after them to this river, and saw the smoke of their wigwams, and yet this river put a stop to them.'

Rowlandson was disappointed not just because the English failed to save her, but also because of what the episode portended. After all, she knew her Old Testament. It was God's chosen people who crossed the Red Sea dry-shod, and the heathen Egyptian army that got swallowed up in the converging waters. Something was wrong here. The best she can offer by way of interpretation is: 'We were not ready for so great a mercy as victory and deliverance.' And by 'we' she means not just the captives but also their would-be rescuers.

5 March

Shakespeare comes to America. Very slowly

1750 There is dispute as to where and when the first Shakespeare was performed in the American colonies – much of the confusion arising from the difficulty of distinguishing between amateur and professional performance.

The first permanent playhouse was built in Williamsburg, Virginia in 1716. It is hard to believe that some Shakespeare productions did not grace its boards. An amateur performance of *Romeo and Juliet* is recorded as having taken place there on 23 March 1730.

The first professional performance of a Shakespeare play is commonly assumed to have taken place on 5 March 1750, when the scratch Murray and Kean troupe performed *Richard III* in New York. Louis Hallam's wholly professional 'Company of Comedians' performed *The*

Merchant of Venice at Williamsburg in 1752, which is taken by the *Cambridge Guide to American Theatre* as the true starting point.

What is clear is that theatre – and specifically Shakespearian theatre – was slow to take hold in the Colonies. Two reasons are put forward: the strong residual antagonism of Puritanism, which regarded the theatre as a sink of iniquity; and republican resistance to England's national poet (the anti-monarchical *Richard III* might have appealed on that ground).

Puritan hostility was probably the stronger factor (there is, for example, no volume of Shakespeare in the 1682 Harvard Library catalogue, compiled by Cotton Mather). Lingering Puritanism also inhibited the growth of any native theatre culture. The first professional performance in America of a play by an American playwright was as late as 1767 (Thomas Godfrey's *The Prince of Parthia* – until well into the 19th century, the company of American dramatists is as wholly undistinguished as Godfrey).

Hostility to the stage climaxed in the period immediately preceding the Revolution. The first Continental Congress, held on 20 October 1774, banned:

> every species of extravagance and dissipation, especially all horse-racing, and all kinds of gaming, cock fighting, exhibitions of shows, plays, and other expensive diversions and entertainments.

No American cakes and ale. But not, thankfully, for long.

6 March

Poe meets Dickens. Ravens fly

1842 In histories of detective fiction, two primal texts are routinely cited. One is the short story, 'The Murders in the Rue Morgue', by Edgar Allan Poe, first published in *Graham's Magazine* on 20 April 1841. In this 'tale of ratiocination' ('detective story' had not yet been coined as a literary term) the French sleuth, Auguste Dupin (based on the real-life Eugène François Vidocq), is confronted by the archetypal 'locked room' mystery. Two women are discovered, mutilated and brutally murdered. But their apartment in the rue Morgue is wholly sealed. How did the murderer gain ingress and egress? The culprit, it emerges (improbably, but with impeccable logic), was an acrobatic, fenestrating, orang-utan.

In England, Dickens is credited with the first detective in fiction, if not the first detective novel (that credit usually goes to his protégé, Wilkie Collins), with Inspector Bucket in *Bleak House* (based on Dickens's admired 'thief taker', Inspector Field, of the newly-formed Scotland Yard). *Bleak House* was published serially, from March 1852 to September 1853.

Fascinatingly, Dickens met Poe on the English novelist's first visit to America. The occasion is recorded in a letter from Dickens, dated 6 March 1842. It is clear that the two of them had been corresponding on the finer points of their art:

> My Dear Sir, — I shall be very glad to see you whenever you will do me the favour to call. I think I am more likely to be in the way between half-past eleven and twelve, than at any other time. I have glanced over the books you have been so kind as to send me, and more particularly at the papers to which you called my attention. I have the greater pleasure in expressing my desire to see you on this account. Apropos of the 'construction' of [William Godwin's] *Caleb Williams*, do you know that Godwin wrote it backwards, – the last volume first, – and that when he had produced the hunting down of Caleb, and the catastrophe, he waited for months, casting about for a means of accounting for what he had done ?
>
> Faithfully yours always, Charles Dickens

It would seem the two writers met the following day, or shortly thereafter.

Caleb Williams is also credited by some partisans as the proto-detective story. But what is most interesting in Dickens's letter is his mention of the backwards construction trick. This is elaborated in Matthew Pearl's 2009 novel, *The Last Dickens*, in which it is fantasised that somewhere Dickens, following Godwin's example, wrote down the ending of his tantalisingly incomplete last work, *The Mystery of Edwin Drood*. Cunning detective work uncovers it (in Pearl's novel, that is).

What conversation the two writers had is, sadly, unrecorded. But it is likely that Dickens ('Great Inimitable' that he was) took some inspiration for *Bleak House* from his admired American counterpart. Even more likely is that when Poe published his most famous poem, 'The Raven', on 29 January 1845 he owed the idea of the ominous bird to *Barnaby Rudge*'s Grip. Poe had reviewed Dickens's novel, enthusiastically, in *Graham's Magazine* on its publication in 1841, taking particular note of the symbolic bird.

7 March

Alice B. Toklas dies at 89, 21 years after the death of her companion, Gertrude Stein

1967 It was a lovely spring day in Paris. When he called before noon on Gertrude Stein at her legendary flat at 27 rue de Fleurus, the maid gave Ernest Hemingway a glass of *eau-de-vie*. 'The colorless alcohol felt good on my tongue', he recalled in *A Moveable Feast* (1964), his memoir of life in Paris in the 1920s, 'and it was still in my mouth when I heard someone speaking to Miss Stein as I have never heard one person speak to another; never, anywhere, ever':

> Then Miss Stein's voice came pleading and begging, saying, 'Don't, pussy. Don't. Don't, please don't. I'll do anything, pussy, but please don't do it. Please don't. Please don't, pussy.'

He made his excuses and left without seeing the great woman again, and that, as he put it, was 'The way it ended with Miss Stein'. They had been friends, had respected each other's work. He knew Alice B. Toklas as Gertrude Stein's 'companion'. Can this really have been the first time he realised that she was also her lover? Or was it the shock of such an august figure being humiliated that ended their friendship – out of embarrassment, as it were? But then, as she once told him: 'Hemingway, after all you are ninety percent Rotarian.'

That last comment is reported in *The Autobiography of Alice B. Toklas* (1933), written by Stein, not Toklas. Toklas's real autobiography is spread out over two works – *The Alice B. Toklas Cookbook* (1954), which is only partly a cookbook since it contains as many personal reminiscences as it does recipes, and *What is Remembered* (1963), a moving memoir of their life together and the people they knew –

soberly written, informative, and testimony to a deep mutual love, whatever occasional spats might have erupted along the way.

The books are shot through with ironic gaps between publicity, reputation and literary value. The cookbook is one of the best-selling cookbooks ever, mainly due to a much-celebrated recipe for 'Haschich [*sic*] Fudge', which wasn't even Toklas's own, but given to her by a friend. *The Autobiography of Alice B. Toklas* was a great commercial success. Though predictably disliked by Hemingway, it was actually a clever narrative manoeuvre, in that it tried to relate events as Toklas would have told them. Meanwhile, Stein's own most original narrative experiments – *Three Lives* (1909), the ground-breakingly modernist *Tender Buttons* (1914), and the monumental *The Making of Americans* (1925) – have gone largely unread. Big mistake.

8 March

The author of The Wind in the Willows *is born*

1859 The author of *The Wind in the Willows* – that archetypally English idyll – was, in biographical fact, a Scot. Kenneth Grahame was born into the Edinburgh professional classes. But the solid family framework around him dissolved almost immediately. His mother died of fever, giving birth to her fourth child, before Kenneth was six. His barrister father fell into alcoholism and died alone in France. He never communicated with his children, who were left to the care of an extended family.

There are no fathers, no mothers, no wives, no siblings in the animal world of *The Wind in the Willows*. After public school in Oxford (a city he adored) there arrived the great sorrow of Grahame's life. He did not 'go up' to the university. His guardian uncle determined that the boy must do something useful. It was, according to his biographer, 'the most crushing blow that Grahame suffered, perhaps in his whole life'. It's a strange notion of catastrophe; but real enough for Grahame. Paradise was now forever lost.

Kenneth was installed, by patronage, into the cogs and wheels of the Bank of England. In this great machine he would work, mechanically, for 30 years. Although Oxford had been denied him, Grahame imbibed the university's 1890s Paterian-Wildean decadence. Gem-like flames licked, decorously, around his ankles. He bought into Great-God-Pan-worshipping 'neo-paganism', a cult that, guardedly, promulgated all those Hellenic practices that Victorian England frowned on – not least after the savage Labouchere amendment of 1885 making 'gross indecency' a crime.

By day a dutiful *fonctionnaire* in the Bank, by night Grahame roamed Soho, a bohemian. Literary introductions furnished him an entry into John Lane's *Yellow Book*. His first volume of collected pieces, *Pagan Papers* (1893), carried a frontispiece by Aubrey Beardsley. A green carnation could not have been more emblematic.

The papers were well received. Grahame (all the while slaving by day at the Bank) followed up two years later with another series, delicately recapturing childhood experiences: *The Golden Age*.

In the same year, 1895, disaster struck with the Wilde trials. Prudently, Grahame married in 1899. The marriage proved a disaster, although it put to rest any suspicions about his private life. He was 40, his wife, Elspeth, in her late thirties. Sex was discontinued as soon as begun. It produced one son. It was to young Alastair, as bedtime entertainment, that *The Wind in the Willows* was conceived and eventually published in 1908.

In the book Grahame pictures an ideal ménage: women do not come into it. In their 'digs', like Holmes and Watson, Ratty and Moley are two chaps living together: it's a Darby and Darby situation. No Joans need apply. The story, as the author insisted, was 'clean of the clash of sex'.

Grahame wrote nothing of significance after *The Wind in the Willows* and his later life was chronically wretched. It is recorded by his biographer that he changed his underwear once a year. He died in 1932 and left his estate to the Bodleian Library, as homage to the university he had never attended.

9 March

Rand's religion: the almighty dollar

1982 If there were an award for the most influential bad novelist in literary history, Ayn Rand would, one suspects, be a strong contender. Alisa Rosenbaum was born, Russian Jewish, in St Petersburg in 1905.

It was a bad year to be Jewish, with pogroms everywhere. 1917 was a bad year to be Russian, and Alisa fled the newly established USSR in 1925 to live in the US. An astonishingly enterprising woman, she settled in Hollywood to become a screenwriter (in a language not her own, and a society of which she knew very little, and a medium that had only just discovered 'talkies'). She changed her name to Ayn Rand, married, and made a decent living for herself in a business (films) not easy to thrive in.

Rand's career took its definitive turn in 1932 with the anti-Soviet screenplay, *Red Pawn*. Thereafter her drama and (after 1943, with *The Fountainhead*) her fiction was ferociously pro-capitalist. She was, it was later said, a 'hob-nailed Reagan'. Gordon ('Greed is good') Gecko was a pinko alongside Ayn.

Rand formulated her views into a philosophy she called 'Objectivism', founded on a belief in 'Rational Selfishness'. She propagated her views in her massive novel, *Atlas Shrugged*, published in 1957. The novel revolves around the idea of the wealth-creators (i.e. moguls, magnates, and millionaires) of the US imitating their workers, trade unionising, and going on strike. The capitalistic Atlas shrugs off the burden of making himself rich, and the mass of the population descends into the dystopian chaos they have brought on themselves with their irrational demand that the state look after them. The moral, as one disaffected blogger ('uncyclopedia') puts it, is that 'Poor People Are Lazy Assholes'.

Despite scathing reviews, *Atlas Shrugged* made the *New York Times* bestseller list. More importantly, it recruited disciples to Rand's political views. These views were expounded in the narrative and, in manifesto form, in a long appendix (ostensibly a radio address). In it the hero (Rand's spokesperson), John Galt, exalts selfishness and excoriates (socialistic) selflessness. 'Your acceptance of the code of selflessness', he informs the American public:

> has made you fear the man who has a dollar less than you because it makes you feel that that dollar is rightfully his. You hate the man with a dollar more than you because the dollar he's keeping is rightfully yours. Your code has made it impossible to know when to give and when to grab.

It is the working classes who are the 'exploiters' (grabbers). Galt's philosophy can be summed up in his personal insignia, the dollar sign, '$'. Rand herself affected jewellery emblazoned with the same sacred $. When, aged 77, she died on this day in 1982, she was buried in the

Kensico cemetery, Valhalla, New York. Alongside the casket was a six-foot-tall floral display in the shape of the dollar sign.

Rand has always been a controversial figure. Posthumously much of the controversy centred on Alan Greenspan, who, as chairman of the Federal Reserve, effectively ran the American economy from 1987 to 2006. Greenspan was a confessed disciple of Rand's in his younger years and attended the 1982 funeral. Was he, with the levers of power in his hand, putting into practice her principles – had the US, under his management, become 'Aynerica' with the motto, 'In the Dollar we trust'? The still loyal band of Objectivists are divided on the question, many thinking he was weak-kneed (as Ayn would never have been) in his acquiescence to the 'mixed economy'.

10 March

The first two Cantos of Byron's Childe Harold *are published; Walter Scott sensibly turns to writing novels*

1812 The morning of 10 March was when Byron, aged 23, 'awoke and found himself famous'. On the day before that, the age's most famous poet had been Walter Scott – author of *The Lay of the Last Minstrel, Marmion* and, most spectacularly, *The Lady of the Lake* (the poem that invented the Scottish tourist industry).

The shrewdest of authors, Scott appreciated, as he said, that 'Byron bet [i.e. beat] me'. He could not rival the author of *Childe Harold* when it came to popular verse narrative. So, pragmatist that he was, the Wizard of the North turned to prose narrative.

Legend (energetically promoted by the author himself) had it that Scott had as early as 1805 'thrown together' some seven opening chapters of what would later become *Waverley*. He'd tinkered with it but could not excite his publishers or himself with a historical romance set at the time of the 1745 uprising. And, anyway, his poetry – which he could write at conversational speed – was earning him thousands of pounds. Young Byron changed all that.

There then occurred the famous episode of the 'old writing desk' – one of the hoarier myths of 19th-century literature. On giving up the ur-*Waverley* in 1805, Scott (allegedly) had tossed the manuscript (i.e. the opening chapters) into a writing desk drawer. On taking up residence in his grand new house at Abbotsford (built lavishly to his own specifications), new and more elegant furniture was required for his study. The old writing desk was thrown into an attic. The yellowing manuscript was 'entirely forgotten' and 'mislaid for several years'.

Fate, in the shape of uncaught salmon (Abbotsford's grounds had the Tweed running through them), intervened. In autumn 1813, as Scott recalled: 'I happened to want some fishing tackle for the use of a guest [John Richardson, a fanatical angler] when it occurred to me to search the old writing desk in which I used to keep articles of that nature. I got access to it with some difficulty; and in looking for lines and flies, the long-lost manuscript presented itself. I immediately set to work to complete it according to my original purpose.'

The 'readiest writer' of his time (as Carlyle called him), Scott dashed off *Waverley* in a few weeks and the novel was published (anonymously) in three volumes on 7 July 1814. Its runaway success, and that of a dozen other bestsellers by 'the author of *Waverley*' (Scott did not admit authorship until 1826), tilted the field of literary endeavour towards fiction for a century or more. Scott had made the form not merely respectable but, as Henry James (in another context) put it, *discutible*.

Scholarly research has exploded the 'old writing desk' genesis. *Waverley*'s manuscript suggests that Scott initially set to work on the project in 1810, not 1805, and never threw his work-in-progress away into some forgotten drawer. Readers have, in general, always preferred the myth – as, indeed, they have always preferred Scott's romantic account of the '45 over historical accounts.

11 March

Following the defeat of the French in Egypt, the British army presents the Rosetta Stone to the Society of Antiquaries in London

1802 The Rosetta Stone, so called because it was discovered in the Egyptian port of Rosetta or Rashid, is one of the most popular exhibits at the British Museum, where it has been kept for over two centuries. From a few feet away it's not much to look at – a lump of dark grey granite measuring 3 feet 9 inches high and 2 feet 4½ inches wide. It's what's on it that makes it remarkable. The same message is given three times over: in Greek; in the Egyptian demotic, or vernacular; and in hieroglyphics, or the sacred writing used by the priestly caste.

Before French army engineer Captain Pierre-François Bouchard discovered the stele in the summer of 1799, modern knowledge of hieroglyphics was limited to a few fragments. Now here was a sizeable chunk of a language known to everyone with a liberal education – between 1,600 and 1,700 words in the English translation of the Greek – enough to unlock a wide variety of the puzzling symbols.

What was found – by the English physicist Thomas Young and the French scholar Jean-François Champollion, perhaps the greatest natural linguist of his generation – was that the hieroglyphics worked in two ways: phonetically and as pictograms. The picture writing was clear enough: the outline of an ibis stood for an ibis. But it could be read abstractly too, as when a crescent could stand for the moon and also a month, or the diagram of a reed and tablet, for writing or even a scribe. The phonetic hieroglyphs worked synthetically, each element contributing a sound based on the name of the thing pictured, which, added to the other 'letters' in the 'word', gave the sound (not the picture) of the thing or concept represented.

How exciting was the message, once deciphered? Alas, not very. It dates from 196 BC, the first anniversary of the coronation of the thirteen-year-old Ptolemy V. It's bulked out with flattery along the lines of 'O King, live for ever', in which is embedded a priestly decree thanking the king for his favours shown, in such a way as almost to imply he'd better keep up the good work:

> King Ptolemy, the ever-living, beloved by Ptah, the god Manifest and Gracious, the son of King Ptolemy and Queen Arsinoë, the Parent-loving gods, has done many benefactions to the temples and to those who dwell in them, and also to all those subject to his rule, being from the beginning a god born of a god and a goddess.

The benediction in return for a benefaction gets down to particulars, with reference to the revenues both of silver and of grain bestowed on the temples, in return for which 'the gods have rewarded him with health, victory, power, and all other good things, his sovereignty to continue to him and his children for ever' – so long as he keeps the moolah coming.

12 March

The author of the nation's anthems is born in Covent Garden, London

1710 Anthems – whether national or not – often come of unexpected antecedents. 'La Marseillaise' was set to a tune from Mozart's Piano Concerto no. 25, by a royalist who narrowly escaped the guillotine. 'The Star-Spangled Banner', a poem about the American flag surviving a night's bombardment by the British navy, was set to a popular English drinking song. The origins of 'God Save the King/Queen' are lost in history, with the words echoed in a Biblical salutation and an old Royal Navy oath inviting the response 'Long to reign over us', and the tune popping up in medieval plainsong, a 1619 keyboard piece by John Bull, and a Scottish carol, 'Remember O Thou Man'.

Where it all came together, oddly enough, was in the post-Restoration metropolitan theatre. In 1745, *The Gentleman's Magazine* published 'a new song set for two voices', 'God Save our Lord the King', 'as sung at both playhouses', the Theatre Royal, Drury Lane, and Covent Garden. The catalyst was the landing in Scotland of James Francis Edward Stewart in pursuit of the Jacobite claim to the British throne, and his defeat of George II at the Battle of Prestonpans on 21 September 1745. In London, players, managers and audiences alike thrilled to Thomas Arne's setting of the anthem at Drury Lane (see 24 February).

Arne, born on this day in 1710, had cut his teeth on the music for a masque first performed for Frederick of Hanover, Prince of Wales, son of George II, at his country house, Cliveden, in 1740. Entitled *Arthur*, the spectacle rested on a preposterous analogy between King Arthur and Frederick, both reposing in their rural retreats ready to sally forth and restore the nation to 'liberty, virtue and honour'. The high point of the performance was the first outing given to 'Rule Britannia', with lyrics by David Mallet and James Thomson. Later, Arne expanded the music of the piece, turning the masque into a full-blown oratorio, to be performed first in Dublin and then again at Drury Lane.

Why was it that 'God Save the King' and 'Rule Britannia', drawing on obscure traditional sources, first emerged as patriotic songs during the 1740s? Was it because the experience of being ruled and threatened by foreign monarchs concentrated the country's collective mind on its national identity? And why should those solemn anthems have first been voiced in the metropolitan theatre – and that of a distinctly 'light' variety? Perhaps at the Last Night of the Proms, when the groundlings dress up in funny costumes, blow hooters and shout 'Rule Britannia', they are not engaged in some postmodern parody, but behaving squarely within the tradition of the song's performance.

13 March

A play is anathematised, a movement is born

1891 Ibsen had written his play *Ghosts* in 1881. Although the 'pox' figures often enough in Renaissance and 18th-century literature, Ibsen's work was the first time that syphilis had been realistically – horrifically – depicted on the British stage. The British stage was not ready in 1881. It was ten years before, to evade the heavy hand of the Lord Chamberlain's censorship, a 'members only' performance was mounted in London, on 13 March 1891.

This was a period when venereal disease was a major public concern (particularly its debilitating effect on the armed services), and legislation – the notorious 'Contagious Diseases Act', introduced in 1864 – permitted the forcible incarceration of women diagnosed diseased (but not men). The Act had been repealed, amid controversy, in 1886.

The attack on *Ghosts* was led by the *Daily Telegraph* drama critic, Clement Scott, who declared it (in a much echoed diatribe): 'An open drain; a loathsome sore unbandaged; a dirty act done publicly; a lazarhouse with all its doors and windows open … absolutely loathsome and fetid … Crapulous stuff.' Not the kind of thing that theatres proclaim on their pavement placards. Scott went on to anathematise *Hedda Gabler* as a display of 'appalling selfishness' (a strange, but typically moralistic, objection).

Scott (1841–1904) embodied the core of West End theatre conventionalism. He had been the leading drama critic in England for going on 30 years, and had been on the *Telegraph* since 1871. A convert to Roman Catholicism, he routinely took a stern moral line on what he reviewed. He was plausibly suspected of having too close a connection with actor-managers – notably Henry Irving and Beerbohm Tree (Scott was married to the sister of George Du Maurier, the dramatic adaptation of whose *Trilby* made Tree's fortune). Accusations of his being too close to what he was supposed to offer objective judgement on, and receiving what amounted to bribes, led to a libel trial in 1882 (which Scott won) and a cloud of suspicion that was never dispersed. Scott, it may be said, had no interest – intellectual or financial – in the old theatrical order being shaken.

Shaken it was. 'Ibsenism' (under the manifesto of G.B. Shaw's *Quintessence of Ibsenism*), and the leadership of William Archer, became a movement that eventually brought the English theatre into the 20th century. Scott was not in post to see the turn of the millennium. In 1897 he was fired from the *Daily Telegraph* for having declared in an interview that the acting profession led, inevitably, to immorality among actresses. And, presumably, lots of VD.

14 March

Mrs Beeton, arbiter of household management, is born

1836 For more than 140 years Isabella Beeton laid down the law on how to manage servants and cook for minor royalty in her perennial, though much revised, *Book of Household Management*, still being given routinely as a wedding present right up to the end of the last century. The first edition covered the full hierarchy of household staff, from the housekeeper, who should 'rise early, and see that all the domestics are duly performing their work', through the butler, to 'wait upon the family' at meals, 'assisted by the footman', to the coachman, groom and stable boy.

Then there was advice on how to throw a grand dinner party, on what 'legal memoranda' to keep about the house, on how to make up inexpensive prescriptions at home for common ailments, even how to bleed a patient struck with 'the strong kind of apoplexy' when a surgeon wasn't available – and recipes, recipes, recipes: over 900 pages of them. Recipes for fish, fowl, game, calf, veal, pork and 'common hog', lamb and mutton, vegetables, breads and sweets of all kinds: desserts from puddings to pastries took up six chapters.

For all that, you need to forget what you thought you knew about Isabella Mary Beeton. She was not a stuffy, middle-aged Victorian housewife; for that matter, the book itself is not the guide to social mores in the Victorian era that it's often claimed to be, since almost no one – least of all its author – really lived like that.

The real Mrs Beeton was an intelligent journalist with her eye on the main chance, married to a publisher. They lived in a semi-detached house in Pinner, attended by one maid (a virtually universal complement of labour even in lower-middle-class homes before the Second World War) and a part-time gardener. Together they would commute to work on the train, at a time when married, middle-class women didn't do that – he to manage the publishing business, she to edit and write for the various women's magazines financed by the fortune he had made on a pirated edition of *Uncle Tom's Cabin* (see 20 March).

She was prone to miscarriages. Of her three live births, the first died at three months, the second at three years, and the third killed her – of puerperal fever – at the age of 28. On this evidence, and having been granted access to her papers, her biographer Kathryn Hughes has worked out that she almost certainly suffered from syphilis, contracted by her husband from prostitutes and communicated to her on her wedding night.*

Her death was kept a secret for as long as possible, says Hughes. The publishers of her immensely successful book didn't want her readers to know that the woman they turned to for advice on everything from a chesty cough to a light sponge cake had failed to create a nurturing domestic environment for herself.

15 March

The Ides of March: Julius Caesar is assassinated

44 BC When he enters the Capitol on that fateful morning, Shakespeare's Caesar meets the soothsayer who had warned him to 'Beware the Ides of March'. 'The Ides of March are come', he quips. 'Aye, Caesar; but not gone.'

This encounter comes straight from Plutarch's *Life of Caesar*, as do the portents the night before the murder: thunder and lightning, Calpurnia's bad dreams, the augurers failing to find a heart in the sacrificed beast (Plutarch's list runs on to include 'multitudes of men all on fire').

---

* Kathryn Hughes, 'The sickly Mrs Beeton', *The Times*, 8 October 2005.

So what does Shakespeare add to the historical account? He takes a series of events, already 'dramatic' in the newspaper sense, and shapes them into real drama. Caesar is killed in the Capitol, rather than the Theatre of Pompey. The assassination, the competing speeches in the Forum by Brutus and Mark Antony (missing in Plutarch), and the reading of Caesar's will all take place on the Ides of March, whereas the murder, the funeral and the will are spread out between 15 and 20 March in Plutarch.

It's those great speeches that schoolchildren used to have to memorise, and for the good reason that – despite all the portents – they determine the characters' fortunes thereafter. Brutus (a much more 'honourable man' in the play than in its source) painfully sets out his dilemma: 'Not that I loved Caesar less, but that I loved Rome more.'

Antony cloaks his true intentions from the outset, saying that he 'comes to bury Caesar, not to praise him', then – harping on the phrase 'honourable man' with increasing sarcasm – proceeds to play the crowd, refusing to read Caesar's will, moving them to pity and rage at the sight of the corpse, then calling them back to hear the will after all, when they start off on their tour of mayhem. In all, Antony gets 135 lines to Brutus's 47 (in the last seven of which he is politely introducing Antony to the crowd). It isn't fair, but it's politics. 'Now let it work', says Antony. 'Mischief, thou art afoot. / Take thou what course thou wilt!'

A curious footnote on the date. When Caesar's own reform of the Roman calendar came into force, the Ides of March fell on the 14th, not the 15th of the month.

16 March

Lytton Strachey declines to do battle

1916 The Military Service Act of this year meant that even male Britons as unlikely as Lytton Strachey were eligible to serve in the forces. Strachey was duly summoned to an 'Advisory Committee' on 7 March, where he stated his conscientious objection. It was not, he insisted, a religious objection, but 'moral'. He firmly believed this war to be 'profoundly evil'. The committee made no judgement, but referred his case to a tribunal at Hampstead Town Hall on 16 March.

The hearing took place at 5.00pm and was public. Attending were prominent members of the Bloomsbury Group, of which Strachey was a luminary, and his sisters.

Strachey placed a 'light blue air cushion' on the bench before seating himself, and spread a rug across his knees. The examination then began (the following description is from Michael Holroyd, Strachey's biographer). The military representative on the committee began by asking:

> 'I understand, Mr Strachey, that you are a conscientious objector to all wars?'
>
> 'Oh, no', came the piercing high-pitched reply, 'not at all. Only this one'.
>
> 'Then tell me, Mr Strachey, what you would do if you saw a German soldier attempting to rape your sister?'
>
> Lytton turned and forlornly regarded each of his sisters in turn. Then he confronted the Board once more and answered with gravity:
>
> 'I should try and interpose my own body'.

Unsurprisingly, the Board were not amused, and the question of exemption was adjourned until Strachey had undergone medical examination. The doctors confirmed that he was wholly unfit.

Strachey found the experience rather thrilling. As he said: 'For a few moments I realised what it was like to *be* one of the lower classes.' It was not, however, an experience that he took any care to repeat.

17 March

Marx waxes literary over the Crimean War

1854 Of all the Marxists, the most literary – in taste and breadth of reading – was Karl Marx himself. Had he not made his name in economics he might well rank as a literary critic of some note. Not one to keep his learning in separate compartments, Marx mustered a barrage of literary allusion to vent, in the *New York Daily Tribune*, 17 March 1854, his disgust at the War Debate in the British Parliament of that week, committing the country to join with imperial France against

Russia in the Crimea:

A singularity of English tragedy, so repulsive to French feelings that Voltaire used to call Shakespeare a drunken savage, is its peculiar mixture of the sublime and the base, the terrible and the ridiculous, the heroic and the burlesque. But nowhere does Shakespeare devolve upon the clown the task of speaking the prologue of a heroic drama. This invention was reserved for the Coalition Ministry. My Lord Aberdeen has performed, if not the English Clown, at least the Italian Pantaloon. All great historical movements appear, to the superficial observer, finally to subside into farce, or at least the common-place. But to commence with this is a feature peculiar alone to the tragedy entitled, War with Russia, the prologue of which was recited on Friday evening in both Houses of Parliament, where the Ministry's address in answer to the Minister's message was simultaneously discussed and unanimously adopted, to be handed over to the Queen yesterday afternoon, sitting upon her throne in Buckingham Palace.

Marx (who had been in England for only five years, and whose reverence for Shakespeare had been acquired in his native Germany) had complex views on the Crimean War. He was impressed by the solidarity (particularly among the British working classes). He loathed tsarist Russia, and was – with reservations – in favour of anything that might do it damage. As the war progressed, he noted the cooling of the bourgeoisie's enthusiasm 'as it began to affect their purse'. In the end, it all came down to capital.

18 March

Philip Massinger joins the eminent literary company in Southwark Cathedral

1640 Outside Poets' Corner in Westminster Abbey the most glorious gathering of the literary dead is to be found in the louche South Bank premises of Southwark Cathedral. There are literary monuments (plaques and windows) to John Bunyan, Lancelot Andrewes, Samuel Johnson, John Gower, Geoffrey Chaucer. And, of course,

Shakespeare, whose brother Edmund is buried there. Also buried there is Shakespeare's collaborator, John Fletcher, and a rival dramatist of his later years, Philip Massinger (interred on this date). Had Shakespeare himself died in one of the regular plagues of the early 17th century he too would, it is certain, have found his resting place here – a few hundred yards as it was from the Globe.

Massinger deserves to be better known than he is. He was born in 1583 in Salisbury, the son of a landed MP and fellow of Merton College, Oxford. Little is known of Philip Massinger's life – it is uncertain, for example, whether he was married or widowed in his adult years.

It is known that he was at St Alban Hall, Oxford in the early years of the 17th century, and at least one source records that he was distracted from his studies by a passion for poetry, romances and drama. He left without a degree, around the time of his father's death in 1603. It is speculated that thereafter he was, for a while, an actor or 'player'.

He was evidently financially distressed in the years that followed. In 1613 he is found, with fellow playwrights Nathan Field and Robert Daborne, writing from the Clink debtors' prison (another few hundred yards from the theatres and Southwark Cathedral), asking a theatrical manager acquaintance for £5.

As with Shakespeare (who was retired to Stratford during the years of Massinger's fame as a dramatist), Massinger's relationship with the Catholic Church is uncertain. It was a difficult time to have too pronounced a faith. Internal evidence of his drama suggests that he was cognisant with Catholicism, and he had relatives who had been recusants.

During the years of his main activity as a playwright (the second decade of the 17th century) Massinger fell into the common practice of collaborative authorship (with Fletcher, notably), something that has led to problems for scholars trying to distinguish various hands. His favoured genre – much to the taste of theatregoers of the period, evidently – was the tragicomedy.

After 1620, Massinger left the company he had been with for several years (the King's Men) and wrote a number of single-handed works, notably his best-known and most-revived play, the comedy *A New Way to Pay Old Debts* (1625) – one of the earliest and most effective satires on mercantilism and the corruptions of early capitalism, in the magnificent character Sir Giles Overreach.

Massinger seems to have been relatively well off at this period of his career. Various bits and pieces can be picked up about his professional life (mainly through quarrels with fellow authors) over the next fifteen years. But he is one of those major figures in English literature whose biography, as we know it, could be written on the back of a postage stamp. He died in March 1640 in a house in the South Bank theatre district. It is recorded that 'he went to bed well, and dyed suddenly – but not of the plague'. He was buried on 18 March, at the cost of £2 (Massinger not being a parishioner), by one account in the same grave as John Fletcher. His last collaboration.

19 March

As Philip Roth turns 74, his alter ego begins to feel his age

2007 It was some time around – or shortly before – his 74th birthday that Philip Roth decided to dispense with his alter ego – not kill him off, because you never know when he'll come in handy again – but at least stop using him as a stand-in for his own anxieties, fantasies, obsessions and paranoia. *Exit Ghost*, which came out later that year and deftly takes its title from a stage direction in *Macbeth*, is supposed to be our last sight of Nathan Zuckerman, who first strode the boards in Roth's *The Ghost Writer* (1979).

Latterly – as in *American Pastoral* (1997), *I Married a Communist* (1998) and *The Human Stain* (2000) – Roth had taken to using Zuckerman as a (never quite neutral) narrator of stories whose interest lay beyond him. But in *Exit Ghost* Zuckerman returns to the centre; the book is about him – just as were *The Ghost Writer*, *Zuckerman Unbound* (1981) and *The Anatomy Lesson* (1983).

Those books can best be understood as Roth's ways of dealing with the reaction to his smash hit, *Portnoy's Complaint* (1969), another American good-bad boy story (see 16 July), about an adolescent's raging hormones struggling against the taboos of a Jewish upbringing in Newark, New Jersey. Amid high praise, the book also came in for a lot of criticism for its satire on Jewish social aspirations and matriarchal family politics.

Through Zuckerman in *The Ghost Writer* Roth could unmake his recent notoriety and sudden fame to revert to a version of his younger self, the earnest, high-minded author of a handful of short stories, who idolises the reclusive E.I. Lonoff as a father to his talent, and fantasises that Amy Bellette, the great author's mysterious young mistress, is Anne Frank, somehow preserved from the Holocaust, who – when she marries him, as of course she must – will absolve him from imputations of anti-Semitism. The whole construction is so improbable, and in such bad taste (while also being so very funny), that of course it had to be the work of Zuckerman's fevered imagination, not Roth's. *Zuckerman Unbound* deals directly with the post-*Portnoy* furore, by liberating a degree of comically excessive bad temper in Zuckerman from which a more discreet Roth might want to hold back.

Half a century on, and if Roth feels his age, he wants Zuckerman to be its outward show. Still impotent and incontinent from an old prostatectomy, Zuckerman returns to New York for medical treatment to stop the leakage. Arranging to swap his house in the Berkshires (not unlike Lonoff's of long ago) with a young couple who write, he falls in love with the woman, returning to his hotel, until they vacate their apartment, to write a one-act drama called 'He and She', to the backdrop of Strauss's *Four Last Songs*. He has already run into Amy Bellette, now impoverished, emaciated and dying of brain cancer. Meanwhile, a brash young Harvard man called Kliman from (God forbid) Los Angeles is hot on the trail of a long-suppressed sexual secret involving the long-deceased Lonoff. Cheerful it's not, if mordantly funny in parts. For Zuckerman (and Roth?) the worst *memento mori* is not the impotence and incontinence but the thought that a Kilman may come after him/them one day.

20 March

After being serialised over 40 weeks in an abolitionist periodical, Uncle Tom's Cabin *comes out as a book*

1852 Ten years after it came out, on meeting the book's author, Harriet Beecher Stowe, President Abraham Lincoln is supposed to have said: 'So this is the little lady who made this big war.' Historians now doubt the literal truth of that anecdote, but its larger truth is undeniable. In its first year alone the book sold 300,000 copies, and after a dip in sales, went on to become the best-selling novel of the 19th century, clocking up figures second only to the Bible. And if it didn't cause the

Civil War, it did more to convert people of the northern states to the abolitionist cause than a million speeches by single-issue campaigners.

Tom is a loyal slave with high Christian principles. Sold down the river by gentle but financially distressed owners, he saves the life of little Eva, whose father, the wealthy plantation-owner Augustine St Clare, buys Tom in gratitude as his own household slave. When Eva dies and her father is accidentally killed, Tom is auctioned to the wicked Simon Legree, a brutal, drunken planter who eventually has Tom flogged to death.

The book's power lies in its Dickensian blend of a strong moral message wrapped in situations stirring the readers' sentiments. Chapter V, in which Tom's original owners discuss the conflict between their loyalty to their slaves and their need for money, is worthy of Dickens at his best. Mrs Shelby objects more to the boorish manners of the slave trader than to what he's come to do, and next morning, after a guiltily sleepless night, still complains when her personal servant doesn't answer her call.

Uncle Tom's Cabin has been blamed for introducing or perpetrating a number of black stereotypes, like the genial matriarch Mammy the cook and the pickaninny child Topsy, who just 'growed'. And throughout the civil rights movements of the second half of the 20th century, 'Uncle Tom' was a byword for the compliant negro. Yet without him and the novel bearing his name, black progress might have started from much further behind.

21 March

Thomas Cranmer, author of the Book of Common Prayer, *is burned at the stake for heresy in St Giles, Oxford*

1556 He had been Henry VIII's Archbishop of Canterbury, a conscientious Protestant who worked out the arguments and tactics to support the annulment of the king's marriage with Catherine of Aragon, and then the doctrinal and liturgical consequences of the split with Rome that followed. Under the evangelical regency of Henry's son, the boy king Edward VI, Cranmer strengthened Protestant reforms in the English church, consolidating its identity as well as his own position.

Then the young king died of tuberculosis at the age of only fifteen. With the succession of Mary Tudor, it was pay-back time for the Catholics. Mary recognised the supremacy of the Pope, married Charles V of Spain in order to cut her Protestant half-sister Elizabeth out of the succession, repealed Edward's religious laws, and had 284 Protestant reformers burned at the stake – among them Thomas Cranmer.

In his *Actes and Monuments* (1563), better known as *Foxe's Book of Martyrs*, that great chronicler of the Marian persecutions, John Foxe, tells the moving story of Cranmer's last days. 'Both English and Spanish divines had many conferences with him', after which he 'signed a recantation of all his former opinions'. This abject humiliation cut little ice with the queen, who (in Foxe's brilliant formulation) 'was resolved to sacrifice him to her resentments'.

Cranmer was expected to broadcast his backsliding. Instead he recanted his recantation, 'refusing' the Pope as 'Christ's enemy and Antichrist' and reaffirming his doctrinal and liturgical beliefs. He was brought to the stake at the bottom of St Giles street, bound with a chain, and, as 'the fire began to burn near him, he stretched forth into the flames his right hand which had signed his recantation, and there held it so steadfastly, that the people might see it burned to a coal before his body was touched'.

Yet his imprint on the Anglican Church has lasted to this day, not least his elegant solution to the furious debate over transubstantiation – the Catholic belief that Christ was really and corporally present in the Eucharist, and the extreme Protestant view that the bread and wine were symbolic only. Cranmer's solution was that Christ's body was indeed present in the consecrated elements, but spiritually rather than bodily.

Because of its clean, compact expression of complex ideas, Cranmer's *Book of Common Prayer* (BCP) of 1549 has infiltrated English literature almost as much as has the Bible. Its prose has proved impossible to modernise without lapsing into absurdity. For example, the petition to Christ in the BCP 'Gloria' goes:

> O Lord God, Lamb of God, son of the father, that takest away the sins of the world, have mercy upon us: thou that takest away the sins of the world, receive our prayer. Thou that sittest at the right hand of God the father, have mercy upon us.

Which the latest modernisation of the BCP, *Common Worship* (2000), renders as:

Lord Jesus Christ, only Son of the Father, Lord God, Lamb of God, you take away the sin of the world: have mercy on us; you are seated at the right hand of the Father: receive our prayer.

You can see that the modernisers are trying to make the petition more 'relevant' to the 21st century – and especially to the 'youth' of our era. So out go the old-fashioned 'thees' and 'thous' and their appropriate verb endings. Fair enough. But also effaced are the relative clauses – presumably on the grounds that subordination makes the prayer too hard to grasp. As a result, Jesus Christ, who already knows that He takes away the sins of the world and is seated on the right hand of God, is told these things, as though in a newsflash. This is the clinching proof of Cranmer's verbal power: to unpick it is to turn it into baby talk.

22 March

Goethe's last words – and the other last words

1832 If Heine's are the wittiest last words of a German man of letters (see 27 November), the most exalted are those of Johann Wolfgang von Goethe. As recorded by his faithful biographer Johann Peter Eckermann (author of *Conversations with Goethe*), they were 'Mehr Licht! Mehr licht!' ('More light! More light!') As a child of the enlightenment, the leader of *Sturm und Drang*, a major philosopher as well as a toweringly great writer, they make a fitting epitaph.

There have, however, been contradictions to this most perfect of valedictions. It is suggested that what Goethe actually said was: 'Open the second shutter, so that more light may come in' (some versions have 'second blind' – the exact domestic layout of Goethe's death chamber is not recorded). The central element is there ('more light') but the instruction is anything but lofty. Banal even. More so in the original German: 'Macht doch den zweiten Fensterladen in der Stube auch auf, damit mehr Licht hereinkomme.'

Another account has it that his last words were intimately tender to his daughter-in-law: 'Come, my little daughter, and give me your little paw.' It's nice to think of him entering eternity, hand in hand, with her.

Other accounts have 'little woman' and even 'little wife' (the German 'Frau' translates either way).

23 March

Sexual intercourse has begun – or has it?

1963 Philip Larkin's opening lines from 'Annus Mirabilis' are (along with 'They fuck you up, your mum and dad') his most quoted:

> Sexual intercourse began
> In nineteen sixty-three
> (Which was rather late for me) –
> Between the end of the *Chatterley* ban
> And the Beatles' first LP.

The chronology is both precise and vague. And, for all its ubiquity in dictionaries of quotation, ultimately meaningless – at least historically.

D.H. Lawrence's novel, *Lady Chatterley's Lover*, banned in the UK ever since its first (offshore) publication in 1928, was acquitted at the Old Bailey on 10 November 1960. The Beatles' first LP – *Love, Love Me Do* – was released on 22 March 1963 (Larkin was jazz critic of the *Daily Telegraph* between 1961 and 1967, and was up with discography).

The title, 'Annus Mirabilis', signals the 'wonderful year' (not three-year 'era'), 1963, to be when sexual intercourse began. And given the precise terminal date of the Beatles' LP, it must be the first three months of 1963. Or, more likely, these months were when a number of trends crested.

One trend was the pill. The contraceptive Enovid was licensed in the UK in 1961. For women, it meant that they – not their untrust-worthily condomed partner – controlled their fertility. This 'empowerment' coincided with the birth of the women's movement, whose primal moment was 19 February 1963, when Betty Friedan's *The Feminine Mystique* was published and, immediately after, NOW (the National Organisation of Women) was formed.

For men, the pill meant sex without fear – or, more often, responsibility. The result was an orgiastic release of pre- and extra-marital sex. What Larkin expresses in 'Annus Mirabilis' (published in 1967) is something akin to Lear's disgusted:

> The wren goes to 't, and the small gilded fly
> Does lecher in my sight. Let copulation thrive.

The mournful parenthesis, '(Which was rather late for me)', could be read as suggesting that Larkin himself had missed the boat sexually, having been born in 1922, and was now too old to swing along with the swinging sixties. It would be a misreading.

Larkin had his first serious sexual relationship with seventeen-year-old student Ruth Bowman, in 1945 (he was some seven years older, and already embarked on his career as a librarian). The relationship lasted three years. In 1950, he began what was to be the longest relationship of his life, with Monica Jones (a lecturer at Leicester University). While involved with her, he had a string of other sexual relationships, sometimes conducting three at the same time. Philip Larkin is, it is worth noting, the only major poet in the English language whom we know (from eyewitness report) to have had a large penis.

24 March

Nietzsche's typewriting course ends

1882 Mark Twain asserts, in 1905, in his essay 'The First Typing Machine', that the first such writer/typewriter was none other than Mark Twain:

> I will now claim – until dispossessed – that I was the first person in the world to apply the type-machine to literature. That book must have been *The Adventures of Tom Sawyer*.

As Darren Wershler-Henry points out in his 'fragmented history of typewriting', *The Iron Whim*, this may be what Huck Finn would call a bit of a 'stretcher'. The evidence of the literary remains indicates that it was not *Sawyer* (1876) but the much later *Life on the Mississippi* (1883). This later date puts Twain in second place, some months behind another famous name.

'Hurrah! The machine has arrived at my house', wrote Friedrich Nietzsche in a postcard to his sister on 11 February 1882. For the sum of 375 marks the philosopher had acquired a Hansen 'writing ball', or 'Schreibkugel'. Hansen was a Swedish pastor and teacher of deaf-mutes. He intended his invention as an aid for these unfortunates, not German philosophers. Nietzsche wrestled with his new device for the following few weeks. One sample of his typewriting survives (in German):

THE WRITING BALL IS A THING LIKE ME: MADE OF
   IRON
YET EASILY TWISTED ON JOURNEYS.
PATIENCE AND TACT ARE REQUIRED IN
   ABUNDANCE,
AS WELL AS FINE FINGERS, TO USE US.

Thus typed Zarathustra. He did not have fingers sufficiently fine, or the necessary patience and tact, Nietzsche eventually decided. Malling Hausen, in his study of the episode, *Nietzsche's Writing Ball*, records that on 24 March 1882 the experiment ended. Nietzsche's fingers could not stand it.

There is speculation that – disappointing as the experience with the writing ball was – it had an influence on the 'telegraphic' or 'fragmentary' style of Nietzsche's later philosophical writing. No effect on Twain's fiction has ever been discerned.

25 March

The Annunciation and Good Friday fall on the same day; John Donne doesn't know whether to feast or fast

1608 The Feast of the Annunciation has always been fixed on 25 March. Until 1752, England and its colonies used to mark the new year from that date too. Easter, on the other hand, is a moveable feast – it falls on the first Sunday after the full moon following the spring equinox – so Good Friday slides back and forth on the calendar, forever yoked to Easter.

Every once in a while the two dates coincide. It doesn't happen all that often – it last occurred in 2005 and will again in 2016 – and when it does, it sets people to thinking. Beginnings, endings; conception, death; God become man (and suffering and dying as a man) – and all reconciled within the overarching divine narrative working itself out in time on earth. What a theme for metaphysical poets, 'catching the sense at two removes', as George Herbert (who was one himself) chided the school of Donne in his poem 'Jordan (I)'.

Donne himself rose to the witty prompt when the two occasions coincided, when he wrote 'Upon the Annunciation and Passion falling upon one day, 1608'. 'My soule eats twice', he marvels, 'Christ hither and away'. On 'this doubtfull day / Of feast or fast, Christ came, and went away'. For Mary, this 'abridgement of Christ's story' is beyond comprehension: 'At once a Sonne is promised her, and gone; / Gabriell gives Christ to her, He her to John; / Not fully a mother, Shee's in Orbitie [mourning]'.

The poem is a meditation, leading Donne (or his devout voice) to the conclusion that 'Death and conception in mankinde is one'. It's a lesson he will lay up in his 'Soule', 'And in my life retaile it every day'.

26 March

Modernist meets Anthroposophist

1911 On this day Franz Kafka attended a lecture by Rudolf Steiner in Berlin. It was, on the face of it, an epic collision of contemporary philosophy and of modernist literature. Kafka, aged 27, was already well into his (very private) writing career and had, in 1910, begun to keep a diary. Steiner (1861–1925), like Kafka a citizen of the Austro-Hungarian empire by upbringing, had carved out a (very public) religio-philosophical doctrine he termed 'Anthroposophy'. His *Outline of Esoteric Science* had recently been published. Steiner was then embarked on building a palace of art (bringing together music, painting, drama, dance, architecture and literature) called the Goetheanum. His enthusiastic, quasi-spiritualist ideas would leave a lasting imprint on European education. It's not clear that they had any lasting effect on Franz Kafka.

Kafka attended the lecture less as a potential convert than as a novelist, *observing* rather than listening; merely *seeing* what Steiner was doing, as if he (Kafka) were at a theatre rather than a lecture. He recorded his observations in his diary:

> Rhetorical effect: relaxed discussion of the objections of opponents, the listener is amazed by this strong opposition, further development and enlivening of these objections, the listener falls into worry, sinks entirely into these objections as if there were nothing else, now the listener takes a response to be impossible and is more than satisfied with a fleeting description of the possibility of defence.
>
> This rhetorical effect corresponds, incidentally, to the commandment of the devotional spirit. – Continual gazing on the surface of one's extended hand. – Leaving out the final point. In general the spoken sentence begins at the speaker with its great capital letter, in its course bends as far as it can out to the listeners, and turns back to the speaker with the final point. But if the final point is left out, then the sentence, no longer held, blows directly onto the listener with the entire breath.

Were ever the semaphorics of a lecture better caught?

27 March

The Vicar of Wakefield *is published, never to go out of print*

1766 It was on this day, and in this year, that the archetypal 'sentimental' novel in English literature was published, in two volumes, at 6s apiece, by the Paternoster Row printer, F. Newbery. The work was immediately successful, has never been out of print, and was much imitated (it still is: the popular TV serial, *The Vicar of Dibley*, is a distant offspring). The year of publication has, however, always been somewhat mysterious.

It is known that Oliver Goldsmith completed the work at least four years earlier. It was Samuel Johnson, Goldsmith's patron, who urged him (along with the gift of a guinea) to publish the work when the notoriously improvident author declared himself in acute financial distress (his usual condition). His landlady was threatening him with debtors' prison. When he went round to see Goldsmith, Johnson found that his guinea had been expended on a bottle of Madeira (a suitably expensive tipple – no gin for Oliver). Johnson replaced the cork in the bottle, and began to 'talk to him about the means he might be extricated':

> He then told me he had a novel ready for the press, which he produced to me. I looked into it and saw its merit; told the land-lady I should soon return; and, having gone to a bookseller, sold it for sixty pounds. I brought Goldsmith the money, and he dis-charged his rent, not without rating his landlady in a high tone for having used him so ill.

Johnson was a friend in need if not the astutest of literary agents. The sale ranks with Milton's £10 for *Paradise Lost* as one of the worst deals in literary history.

Money is, as it happens, at the heart of the novel's plot. Dr Primrose is a country vicar. He outlines his benign philosophy of life in the opening sentences:

> I was ever of opinion, that the honest man who married and brought up a large family, did more service than he who contin-ued single, and only talked of population. From this motive, I had scarce taken orders a year before I began to think seriously of matrimony, and chose my wife as she did her wedding gown, not for a fine glossy surface but such qualities as would wear well.

Mrs Primrose not only wears, but bears well. They have six children ('the offspring of temperance', Dr Primrose is in haste to assure us) and the family lives comfortably, if modestly, off the father's invested wealth. His £35 a year stipend would not keep his church mice in crumbs. Disaster hits when his little fortune is lost through the mal-feasance of a City merchant (who leaves 'not a shilling in the pound' for his investors). Job-like tribulation ensues. Adversity serves not to destroy, but to ennoble further the hero and his family.

The gentle comedy of Goldsmith's novel, and its uplifting faith in the essential goodness of human nature, has charmed readers of every subsequent generation.

28 March

Isaac Rosenberg sends his last poem to Edward Marsh

1918 Isaac Rosenberg was born to a Jewish family that had recently emigrated to England from Lithuania, fleeing the tsar's pogroms. The Rosenbergs moved, shortly before his birth, to London's East End.

Isaac left school at fourteen to become an apprentice engraver. His family had fallen on hard times. He hated the work and continued his education – at great personal difficulty – at the University of London's night school, Birkbeck College. Rosenberg had already displayed remarkable talent – artistic and literary. He studied intermittently at the Slade School, published his first volume of poetry in 1912, and had his first artwork exhibition in 1914.

He was also chronically invalid. His lungs were bad (TB, and other pulmonary ailments, were running at epidemic levels in the East End). Physically, he was a tiny 5 feet 3 inches.

These disqualifications, what with the trenches' insatiable appetite for new blood as the Great War entered its most furious stage, did not trouble the nation's recruiting sergeants. His country needed him. Despite deep-held pacifist beliefs (and a very German name) Rosenberg volunteered, and was sent to the front in 1915. He remained a private – declining any promotion, even to a lowly NCO rank. He was killed, in hand-to-hand combat, on April Fools' Day in 1918. He had, a couple of days earlier, sent what would be his last poem to his friend and patron, Edward Marsh. Due to delays in getting correspondence from the trenches, the poem was not posted until 2 April, by the poet's dead hand. Entitled 'Through These Pale Cold Days', the poem combines a powerful sense of impending death with an awareness of his racial heritage:

Through these pale cold days
What dark faces burn
Out of three thousand years,
And their wild eyes yearn,

While underneath their brows
Like waifs their spirits grope
For the pools of Hebron again —
For Lebanon's summer slope.

They leave these blond still days
In dust behind their tread
They see with living eyes
How long they have been dead.

Rosenberg's body was never identified among the other corpses, although a headstone was erected for him, with a Star of David on it and the inscription: 'Artist and Poet'.

29 March

Brave New World *is liberated in Australia*

1933 Aldous Huxley began writing *Brave New World* (as it was to be entitled) two years before it was published in 1932. It was a conscious change of style for him and a deliberate bid for popularity, using, as it did, the styles and conventions of science fiction.

It had higher purposes. He explained to his schoolmaster father, Leonard, on 24 August 1931 that the work was designed to satirise 'the appallingness of Utopia' – with specific darts directed against the doctrines of Freud, the Pavlovian educational systems currently advocated by behaviourists, and the commercial practices of Henry Ford (whose English Fordopolis was founded in Dagenham in 1928). But the seed of the work, he informed his father, was 'the production of children in bottles' – ectogenesis.

Huxley was the most magpie-eclectic of thinkers. The 'bottled baby' idea was not his, but was picked up from the bio-mathematician J.B.S. Haldane, in a paper read to the Heretic Society, Cambridge, on 4 February 1923. Entitled 'Daedalus: or Science and the Future', it forecast, in pseudo-documentary style, the social repercussions of the advance of life-science over the next decades:

It was in 1951 that Dupont and Schwarz produced the first ectogenetic child. As early as 1901 Heape had transferred embryo rabbits from one female to another, in 1925 Haldane had grown embryonic rats in serum for ten days, but had failed to carry the process to its conclusion, and it was not till 1946 that Clark succeeded with the pig, using Kehlmann's solution

117

as medium. Dupont and Schwarz obtained a fresh ovary from a woman who was the victim of an aeroplane accident, and kept it living in their medium for five years. They obtained several eggs from it and fertilized them successfully, but the problem of nutrition and support of the embryo was more difficult, and was only solved in the fourth year. Now that the technique is fully developed, we can take an ovary from a woman, and keep it growing in a suitable fluid for as long as twenty years, producing a fresh ovum each month, of which 90 per cent can be fertilized, and the embryos grown successfully for nine months, and then brought out into the air … France was the first country to adopt ectogenesis officially, and by 1968 was producing 60,000 children annually by this method.

As Haldane foresaw, and Huxley imaginatively described, bottled babies would erode the traditional nuclear family structure and render sexual intercourse a means of pure carnal pleasure. A never-ending orgy. In fact, Haldane was ten years out in his prophecy. It was the contraceptive pill, in the early sixties, that brought about this drastic change in social life and sexual behaviour.

Sexual liberation was an uneasy subject for the authorities in 1932. *Brave New World* was banned in a number of countries – notably, with much huffing and puffing, in Australia. The ban was lifted on 29 March 1933. *The Times* drily noted: 'It certainly has given the book an immense amount of gratuitous advertising.' Not that Huxley's witty dystopia needed it. The book remains his most popular, is widely prescribed in schools (even in Australasia) and will doubtless sell until AD 2540 (632 AF, i.e. 'After Ford'), the year in which the action is set.

30 March

John Cheever ('Chekhov of the Suburbs') makes the front cover of Time *magazine*

1964 John Cheever was born in New England, of 'good stock'. His father was a shoe salesman, an early casualty of the Great Depression. Slump meant a rackety childhood. He grew up, around Boston, disliking his bossy mother and despising his drunken father.

As a boy he received a bad education at a good school – Thayer Academy. He was expelled in the twelfth grade on grounds (as he variously fictionalised it in later life) of either sexual delinquency, smoking, or poor classroom performance. He serenely turned his disgrace into a short story, and submitted it to Malcolm Cowley at the *New Republic*. Amazingly, the magazine published 'Expelled' in October 1930. He was in print, in a national magazine, at eighteen. What did it feel like? he was asked in later life. 'Eighty-seven dollars', he replied.

College was out of the question (he would, however, in later years claim to be a Harvard man). It was Cowley (also Scott Fitzgerald's literary adviser) who instructed Cheever to cultivate the short story and the *New Yorker* as his principal outlet. Harold Ross's magazine would be what Cheever called his 'lifeboat'. A price was paid. Throughout life, there would be the recurrent criticism (to which the author, in his gloomier moments, subscribed) that beneath the smart gloss of his writing there was no more 'substance' than in a Charles Addams cartoon.

After a brief spell with the Federal Writers' Project, whose proletarian zeal appalled him (too much 'substance' by far), Cheever married in 1941. Why? 'Because I didn't want to sleep alone any more', he would blandly reply in later life. His bed-partner, Mary Winternitz, was of Yale patrician stock (with a dash of Jewish). A talented woman, she deserves commemoration as probably the most tolerant spouse in literary history.

Like other healthy males of his age, Cheever was drafted. He was judged not to be officer material and was transferred into the signal corps and a cushy home posting that allowed him time to write voluminously, drink copiously and dabble with his closet homosexuality. 'If I followed my instincts', he confided in his journal, 'I would be strangled by some hairy sailor in a public urinal'. He prudently suppressed his instincts.

His first collection was published in 1943, while he was still in khaki. After the war the Cheevers (now parents) joined the middle-class, white-flight migration to the suburbs of New York in the early 1950s. At Scarborough, (the 'Shady Hill' of his stories) Cheever would find his richest material. In 1961 the family moved to Ossining. His neighbours, who saw their images satirically rendered in his fiction, regarded him as their 'skunk in the woodpile'. The world outside hailed him as 'the Chekhov of the suburbs'. Cheever taught some creative writing classes at the nearby penitentiary, Sing Sing, the hardest of America's 'joints'. The rough homosexuality of the jail fascinated him.

'I want a life of impossible simplicity', Cheever wrote. Alcohol, uncertain sexuality, and infidelity did not simplify things. In 1975 he touched bottom and sobered up, with the help of AA. In recovery he at last allowed himself to become guiltlessly homosexual. He could never, however, quite eradicate the uneasiness that his writing was less important 'than ironing shirts in a Chinese laundry'.

Money and awards showered on him in his later years. In March 1964 he even made the front page of *Time* magazine. It was in recovery, and at the top of the world, that he produced the novel *Falconer* – set not in the New York suburbs, but Sing Sing.

After his death, from kidney cancer, Cheever left his journal to be published. The last entry reads: 'I have climbed from a bed on the second floor to reach this typewriter. This was an achievement.' He was, his son Benjamin records, 'a writer almost before he was a man'.

31 March

Titanic *poetry*

1909 On this day in Belfast, the keel was laid down in Harland & Wolff shipyard number 401 for the vessel that would be named the *Titanic*.

The largest passenger steamship ever built by man, the White Star Line's flagship would also, it was fondly expected, cross the Atlantic at blue-ribbon-winning speed, offering unprecedented levels of luxury (in first class) and comfort (in steerage).

On its maiden voyage, on 14 April 1912, the *Titanic*, popularly believed unsinkable, struck an iceberg. The provision of lifeboats was inadequate and the launching of them botched. 1,517 of the 2,223 souls on board perished.

The *Titanic* was not merely a technological achievement but expressed, poetically, that quality the ancients called *hubris*. The name itself hinted that there might be something dangerously prideful. In Keats's poem, *Hyperion*, the Titans are the giant race of gods who are displaced by the smaller, smarter, classier Olympians. Size is not enough.

The sinking of the *Titanic* provoked what Aristotle, in his treatise on tragedy, called 'pity and fear' on both sides of the Atlantic – and reams of poetry expressing those emotions. By general agreement the best poem inspired by the event was Thomas Hardy's 'The Convergence of the Twain' (1915). For the sage of Wessex the sinking of the *Titanic* was a clear demonstration of the essential 'irony' of the human condition.

VI

Well: while was fashioning
This creature of cleaving wing,
The Immanent Will that stirs and urges everything

VII

Prepared a sinister mate
For her – so gaily great –
A Shape of Ice, for the time fat and dissociate.

VIII

And as the smart ship grew
In stature, grace, and hue
In shadowy silent distance grew the Iceberg too.

IX

Alien they seemed to be:
No mortal eye could see
The intimate welding of their later history.

There is less consensus as to what is the worst poem to be inspired by the sinking of the *Titanic*. A majority vote goes to the Australian poet, Christopher Thomas Nixon, who was quick off the mark in the last weeks of 1912 with 'The Passing of the *Titanic* (Sic transit gloria mundi)'. Of epic length, it opens:

Through deep-sea gates of famed Southampton's bay,
    A mammoth liner swings in churning slide
Her regal tread ridged opaline gulfs asway,
    And gauntlet flings to chance, wind, shoal and tide.
Ark wonderful! Palatial town marine,
Invention's flower, rose-peak of skill-wrought plan;
The jewelled crown of Art the wizard, seen
    Since Noah's trade in Shinar's land began.

It does not improve over the following 150 lines.

Less lofty was the popular song of 1912, 'My Sweetheart Went Down with the Ship':

My Sweetheart went down with the ship,
Down to an ocean grave,
One of the heroes who gave his life,
The women and children to save,
Gone but not forgotten,
Tho' the big ship rolled and dipt'
He went to sleep in the ocean deep,
My Sweetheart went down with the ship.

The Oscar-winning 1997 film *Titanic* inspired another tidal wave of verse, much of it by schoolchildren as classwork. Many anthologies' worth can be found on the web.

1 April

Scientifiction blasts off

1926 Science fiction has been traced as far back in literature as Aesop and deep beyond that into pre-literary myth. As a modern fictional genre it was given its form by one patriarchal figure, and one magazine: Hugo Gernsback and *Amazing Stories*.

Gernsback (1884–1967) was born in Luxembourg and emigrated to the US in 1905. A pioneer of radio and TV technology (and an inventor), he defined what would be known as 'science fiction' (he coined the term – after an unhappy flirtation with 'scientifiction', which never really caught on). In Gernsback's definition, it was factually hard – not what H.G. Wells called 'scientific romance'. Gernsback's favourite explanation was the equation:

$$science + fiction = science\ fiction$$

Gernsback's most famous contribution to the genre was the similarly algebraically entitled *Ralph 124C 41+*, first published in 1911 (the title is acronymic, like the modern bumper sticker, or texting: 'one to foresee for one'). Essentially it was a tutorial on the author's beloved new technology. Some of his foreseeings, such as planes travelling at the speed of sound, hit the mark. Others, such as Meteoro-Towers (weather control stations) are, alas, still SF.

The first issue of *Amazing Stories* contained items by Verne, Wells and Poe. It cost 25¢ and was printed on pulp paper, with a coloured cover illustration (earth being hit by a Saturnian planet) by Frank R. Paul – later to become a leading SF illustrator. The first issue came out on 10 March 1926, with a cover date of 1 April, which enabled it to stay on drugstore racks for six rather than four weeks.

Within a year, the magazine recruited a readership of 100,000. It was less successful in recruiting top-rate contributors, largely because of Gernsback's parsimony. It was not until the 1950s, in other hands (Gernsback surrendered editorship in 1929), that *Amazing Stories* began featuring the likes of Ray Bradbury, Robert Heinlein and Arthur C. Clarke.

The significance of *Amazing Stories* was its being the first all-SF magazine, and its laying down clearly the literary space the genre would colonise. Gernsback created the genre that others would fill.

2 April

*Alexis de Tocqueville sets sail from Le Havre to examine
the American prison system*

1831 Ever since 1790, when American prisons had pioneered the layout of cells flanking a central corridor, the segregation of prisoners by
age, sex and gravity of crime, and the solitary confinement system,
Europeans had wondered whether they could learn anything useful
about their own ways of locking people up. So in 1831 the French government sent Alexis de Tocqueville and Gustave de Beaumont to investigate the American penal system. Eleven years later, Charles Dickens
would set off on the same quest.

Dickens would find American jails oppressive. De Tocqueville
admired them – as he would many other things about America. In the
event, both authors would range well beyond prisons, into the physical, political, economic and social geography of the country: Dickens
in his acutely observant (though often biased) *American Notes* (1842)
and his picaresque satire *Martin Chuzzlewit* (1833–4); de Tocqueville
in the magisterial *Democracy in America* (two volumes, 1835, 1840),
still the foundation text for students of the American scene.

Here was democracy at work, thought de Tocqueville. Most governments claim to be acting on behalf of 'the people', but in America the
sovereignty of the people was a working principle 'recognized by the
customs and proclaimed by the laws'. Here, 'every man works to earn a
living. … Labor is held in honor'. Because land was free or cheap to the
immigrant willing to work hard, European-style economic and social
elites based on hereditary land-ownership were thin on the ground.

But 'natural' elites of the virtuous or intellectually superior also fell
victims to the levelling spirit, he thought. And the down-side of the
free-land promise was a tendency to restless movement ever westward,
without pause to develop what had been settled. 'In the United States
a man builds a house in which to spend his old age', he writes, 'and he
sells it before the roof is on; he plants a garden and lets it just as the
trees are coming into bearing.'

He recalls exploring an island in the middle of a lake in upstate New
York, 'one of those delightful solitudes of the New World', in which
– to his surprise – he uncovers the traces of a settler's log cabin. 'The
logs … had sprouted afresh … and his cabin was transformed into a

bower.' Confronted with this emblem of death in life, of old age in the New World, 'I exclaimed with sadness: "Are ruins, then, already here?"'

3 April

Mr Pooter decides to keep a diary

1892 George and Weedon Grossmith's *Diary of a Nobody* was first published serially in *Punch* in 1891, and following its huge success in those pages, as a book the following year. The 'nobody' of the title is Charles Pooter, who works in a City office as a clerk under Mr Perkupp. He lives in a rented villa, The Laurels, Brickfield Terrace, Holloway, with his wife Carrie. And it is on taking possession of his Englishman's Castle that he resolves to keep a diary. The first entry is businesslike:

April 3
Tradesmen called for custom, and I promised Farmerson, the ironmonger, to give him a turn if I wanted any nails or tools. By-the-by, that reminds me there is no key to our bedroom door, and the bells must be seen to. The parlour bell is broken, and the front door rings up in the servant's bedroom, which is ridiculous. Dear friend Gowing dropped in, but wouldn't stay, saying there was an infernal smell of paint.

The diary goes on to recount Mr Pooter's Lilliputian daily adventures at work and his social life (in which the biggest event is an invitation to the Mansion House ball). Pooter's son, Lupin, is a source of distress. He gets engaged to a highly unsuitable girl. He joins his father to work for Perkupp, and is discharged. All ends well, however, with Pooter able to buy his own house at last, a consummation recorded as 'the happiest day of my life'. The Grossmiths' charming work was immensely popular and inspired a whole genre of pseudo-diaristic successors, and a new word for the English dictionary-makers, 'Pooterism'. It does not translate well.

4 April

Winston Smith begins his diary

1984 The opening sentence of *Nineteen Eighty-four* is (with that of Jane Austen's *Pride and Prejudice* and Tolstoy's *Anna Karenina*) one of the most famous in literature.

> It was bright cold day in April, and the clocks were striking thirteen.

The allusions are clear and traditional. April, from Chaucer's 'showres soote', is the month of annual rebirth. But Orwell is more in line with Eliot's *Waste Land*:

> APRIL is the cruellest month, breeding
> Lilacs out of the dead land, mixing
> Memory and desire, stirring
> Dull roots with spring rain.

No spring crueller than 1984 in Oceania.

We later learn that the 'bright cold day' of the opening sentence is 4 April 1984. The hero, Citizen Winston Smith, a member of the Outer Party (and a *Times* journalist, whose task is to destroy news unwelcome to the Inner Party), has begun a diary. If found out, it will mean death, but he deludes himself that he has the scarcest thing in 1984, a private place.

Keeping a journal, or diary, or chronicle was – for Orwell – a defining act. It established one's selfhood and one's self-control. As he lay suffocating to death in University College Hospital he kept his terrors at bay by simply writing, as accurately as he could, the things around him in his sick room. Winston Smith's keeping a diary is the first step to his becoming Winston Smith, rather than Citizen 6079 Smith W.

The diary (literally 'daybook'), however, poses an intractable problem:

> April 4th, 1984
> He sat back. A sense of complete helplessness had descended on him. To begin with, he did not know with any certainty that this was 1984. It must be round about that date, since he was fairly

sure that his age was thirty-nine, and he believed that he had been born in 1944 or 1945; but it was never possible nowadays to pin down any date within a year or two.

A world without dates induces that collective schizophrenia (melted reality) on which totalitarianism depends. Orwell should really have entitled his novel *Nineteen Eighty-four(?)*. But of cruel April we are sure. The only historically significant event recorded for 4 April 1984 is President Ronald Reagan's call for the abolition of chemical weapons.

5 April

Pocahontas marries John Rolfe in Jamestown, Virginia

1614 As a daughter of Powhatan, a prominent Algonquin chief when the English first settled Virginia in 1608, Pocahontas was part of one of the great founding myths of the New World – not to mention the star of countless popular prints and a 1995 Disney film.

It was the dashing and hot-tempered Captain John Smith, president of the English colony, who put her at the centre of the first-ever American narrative. His monumental *The General History of Virginia*, published long after the event in 1624, tells how Pocahontas saved his life after her father had captured him and sentenced him to death by having his brains beaten out against a large rock:

> Pocahontas, the Kings dearest daughter, when no entreaty [to spare Smith's life] could prevaile, got his head in her armes, and laid her owne upon his to save him from death: whereat the Emperour was contented he should live.

This promotes Pocahontas to a role far beyond her appearance in Smith's first account of the adventure (see 14 May). If it really happened like this, it might have been some kind of initiation ceremony that Smith interpreted as threat and salvation. An earlier episode in his adventures, in which he claimed to have been released from a Turkish jail by his lover, the Pasha's wife, might have guided his thinking on Pocahontas's intervention.

But then stories about heroes rescued by exotic native girls who have fallen in love with them are the stuff of balladry too, as in 'Lord Bateman', in which a young man of high degree captured in Turkey is allowed to escape by the jailer's daughter.*

Putting the episode, as he does, at the very climax of his personal narrative in Virginia, Smith produces a Renaissance pageant in which a European prince conquers and colonises the wild men of the New World. The other English settlers would reinforce this imperial theme by persuading Pocahontas to be baptised, then married in a Christian ceremony to a young plantation-owner and speculator in tobacco, John Rolfe.

Later Americans would incorporate Pocahontas into the country's founding story. Inside the rotunda, the Capitol building in Washington is decorated with monumental paintings of Columbus landing in the New World and the British General Cornwallis surrendering to the Americans at Yorktown. Alongside these images is Pocahontas, being baptised by a bishop in an improbably grand colonnaded hall.

John Rolfe and 'Rebecca', as she was now called after her baptism, had one son. In 1616 they sailed for England, where she became something of an exotic curiosity and was presented at court. On their way back to Virginia in March 1617, Pocahontas/Rebecca fell ill with smallpox and died. She was buried in an unmarked grave at Gravesend.

6 April

Francis Petrarch catches his first sight of Laura, and will go on to write 366 sonnets about his love for her

1327 Francesco Petrarca was a learned humanist, a priest, a great collector and reviver of the Latin classics, a poet, an essayist and a diarist to match St Augustine. Together with the *Decameron* (1353), by his friend Giovanni Boccaccio, and Dante's *The Divine Comedy* (1308–21), Petrarch's sonnets, the *Canzoniere*, form one of the three pillars of the modern Italian language.

---

* The ballad is no. 53 in the catalogue of Francis James Child, the professor of Medieval and Renaissance English Literature at Harvard: see his *English and Scottish Popular Ballads*; or consult the more accessible collection by Bronson (1959), Vol. 1, pp. 409–65.

How did he come to write them? The story goes that while in church to observe Good Friday, he first saw a woman named Laura, and fell instantly in love with her. He had recently relinquished his vocation as a priest, but she was married; so the very perfection of physical, moral and spiritual beauty which the poet celebrated in her would prevent her granting his desire.

This predicament was different from the troubadours' old convention of courtly love, in which the young man falls for his *seigneur*'s wife, and the two enjoy a clandestine affair. So it needed a new rhetoric to express the genuinely irreconcilable polarities of desire and possibility: classical images of endless suffering (Sisyphus eternally pushing his rock up the hill, only to have it fall back every time); expressions of antithesis, like the Petrarchan trademark oxymorons (icy fire, living death, bitter sweetness); and figures of military advance and retreat.

'Amor, che nel pensier mio vive e regna', for example, is a miniature allegory of his love, that normally lives and reigns in his mind and heart, suddenly declaring itself by advancing to his face and planting its war banner there. At such effrontery the lady, who teaches him to love and suffer, and demands that reason, shame and reverence reign in his passion, rejects his advances. At which point Love, weeping and trembling, abandons his enterprise and doesn't appear again. Then, as usual, the final three lines of the sestet poses the puzzle:

Che poss'io far, temendo il mio signore
se non star seco infin a l'ora estreme?
Ché bel fa chi ben amando more.*

The puzzle here lies in the productive ambiguity. Does 'my lord fearing' mean 'considering my lord is so frightened', or 'fearing [i.e. respecting] my lord [as a good feudal subject should]'? However Laura behaves, the poet will be true to his lord/love because it's been given a fright and because he owes it allegiance. So he will die loving well, or die well, loving, because he is loyal to the emotion – more so than to the lady.

Petrarch more or less invented the sonnet in its quintessentially dialectic form, providing all Europe with a framework for exploring conflicts of all sorts – not only in the paradoxical emotions of romantic love, but also in politics, in work, in friendships, in day-to-day events, in life and death themselves.

---

* 'What can I do, my lord fearing / except stand with him through his dangerous hour? / What a good end he makes who dies loving well.'

7 April

Edith Wharton entertains Morton Fullerton to dinner. Later that night she will write in her diary: 'Non vi leggemmo avante'

1908 'Is it your idea, then, that I should live with you as your mistress?', asks Ellen Olenska of Newland Archer in Wharton's *The Age of Innocence* (1920), 'since I can't be your wife?'

'I want – I want somehow to get away with you into a world where words like that – categories like that – won't exist.'

'Oh, my dear', answers Ellen (who's been around a bit), 'where is that country? Have you ever been there? … I know so many who've tried to find it, and believe me … it wasn't all that different from the old world they'd left, but only rather smaller, and dingier, and more promiscuous.'

That was there and that was then – upper-class New York in the 1870s – a world of snobbery, scheming and hypocrisy in which there is about as much innocence as there is mirth in *The House of Mirth* (1905). But in Paris in 1908 Edith Wharton had fallen in love, and was on the brink of a passionate, adulterous affair. The Italian comes from Dante's *Inferno*, Canto 5: the affair of Paolo and Francesca, who, while reading a romance of courtly love, kiss and – on that day – 'read no further'.

By that time Wharton was an established author who spent part of each year in Paris, married unhappily to a man twelve years her senior, the increasingly unstable Teddy. Morton Fullerton was a cultivated bisexual American adventurer, a veteran of many affairs, and a correspondent in Paris for the London *Times*. He knew everyone from Verlaine and Walter Berry to Oscar Wilde and Henry James, who had used him as the model for Merton Densher in *The Wings of the Dove* (1902).

They shared interests – in literature, the theatre, travel and gossip – as much as they did a bed. Indeed, their sexual encounters, however revelatory to Edith (in June 1908, she wrote to him: 'You woke me from a long lethargy'), had to be arranged to fit in with Teddy's trips away, otherwise taking place mainly in hotels. By 1910 Fullerton had cooled on their relationship. Perhaps he feared being involved in her forthcoming divorce from Teddy.

So how does this bear on that encounter between Ellen and Newland, imagined and articulated a decade afterwards? Was Wharton relieved that she, by contrast, had broken free of that old social prison, or did she reflect that her new life, though certainly not 'smaller and dingier', was, after all, 'more promiscuous'?

8 April

Henry James writes of an idea for a novel that will 'show that I can write an American story'

1883 'The scene of the story', wrote Henry James in his notebook – that rich repository of observations, anecdotes, gossip and creative ideas that fed into so many of his novels and short fiction – 'is laid in Boston and its neighborhood'. 'It relates an episode connected with the so-called "woman's movement".' The heroine was to be beautiful, 'a very clever and "gifted" young woman, … [the] daughter of old abolitionists, spiritualists, transcendentalists, etc.', a fluent public speaker, able to win 'large audiences' to her cause.

The tone is dismissive – the quotation marks make that clear, even without the 'etc.' after the various 'isms' that (to James's mind) had so plagued Boston. But he complicates the issue by bringing onto the scene another woman, this time from a 'rich, exclusive, conservative family', someone without 'talent for appearing in public', who has 'conceived a passionate admiration for our young girl' and 'dreams that the two can work together to "revolutionize the condition of women"'.

Enter the fly in the ointment, though, in the shape of a handsome young man, just returned from ten years in the West, who falls for the beautiful orator while sharing none of her ambitions. He proposes marriage, on condition that she give up her 'mission'. The long struggle – between the two women, and in the mind of the younger between her ideals and attraction to the man – finally ends in 'various vicissitudes, with her letting everything go, breaking forever with her friend, in a terrible final interview'.

No prizes for guessing that James was plotting out what would become *The Bostonians* – not least because the novel, first serialised in *The Century* from February to February, 1885–6, would follow the sketch so closely in both story and characters, in the shape of Verena Tarrant, Olive Chancellor and Basil Ransom. The one crucial difference, though, is that James decided to have Ransom come, not from the West, but from the South. His was a slave-holding family, and he had fought in the Civil War. This makes him a much greater threat to Olive – coming very much from the other side of the abolitionist campaign, yet also mature and (and Olive has to admit) seasoned by loss and danger.

The Bostonians may (unusually for James) have been set in America, but it did little to allay the contempt of such as Theodore Roosevelt (see 29 June), who would continue to dismiss James as an effete turncoat.

9 April

Dylan gets a Pulitzer

2008 The Pulitzer is America's oldest and most prestigious prize for literature, art and music. On 9 April 2008, Bob Dylan joined Ernest Hemingway, William Faulkner and Saul Bellow as one of its laureates. The award drew even more attention than for those eminent writers. He had, newspapers declared, 'made music history by becoming the first rock musician to be awarded the Pulitzer Prize'.

But Dylan was not, of course, merely a rock star. He was a great writer. The point was made by the Pulitzer Prize administrator, Sig Gissler: 'this award reflects the efforts of the Pulitzer board to broaden the scope of the music prize, and encompass the full range of excellence in American music. It also recognises Mr Dylan's lyrical compositions of extraordinary poetic power.' The lyre, of course, is the instrumental ancestor of the guitar. Possibly Homer accompanied himself on one.

That Robert Zimmerman regarded himself as primarily a poet is evident from the name he adopted as a public performer, taken from the Welsh bard, Dylan Thomas. The public recognition of Bob Dylan as a major poet can be credited to the efforts of one of the leading literary critics of the 20th century, Christopher Ricks.

As early as the 1960s, Ricks was making the point on the BBC's Third Programme. It was then widely seen as a mild donnish eccentricity, or perhaps an ill-advised attempt to play Professor Trendhound. Over the years, as his albums went multiple platinum, Ricks continued to give Dylan respectful attention, and critical respect for Dylan as a literary troubadour for his age grew proportionally.

In 2004, Ricks published a 500-page exegetical work, *Dylan's Vision of Sin*, which placed the singer's lyrics within large theological and literary frameworks. Dylan's lyrics, Ricks insisted (as he had been insisting for 40 years), 'have entered the realm of the enduring'. He was, Ricks said (in interviews promoting his 2004 book), 'on the same level as Milton, Keats and Tennyson' (on all of whom Ricks had written authoritative monographs).

Dylan was not, Ricks maintained, 'an obscene howling hobo', as some would like to see him: 'a lot of his songs are full of intelligent witty resourceful references to people like Verlaine and Rimbaud, and to Shakespeare and to Ezra Pound and T.S. Eliot. I don't know why people think that he doesn't know anything about those people.'

Ricks's Dylanology was, plausibly, responsible for the singer's being awarded an honorary doctorate in 2004 from St Andrews University, and the Pulitzer four years later. Who knows, perhaps the Nobel is in the future. If so, Ricks should be on the podium in Stockholm as well.

Oddly, it seems that Dylan and his most eminent exegeticist met only once, in 1999. As Ricks recalled in an interview:

> Five years ago he played a concert here at [Boston] university and I had no hand in arranging it; I was told about it rather late and could have killed the organizers. Shortly before the concert I received word to come backstage, so my wife and I went half an hour before the show. And Dylan said: 'Mr Ricks, we meet at last.' My reply was: 'Have you read any good books lately?'

They went on to discuss Shakespeare's *Richard III*.

10 April

Revolution averted – without too much trouble

1848 Known in Europe as the 'decade of revolution', the British label is 'the hungry forties'. The nearest the country came to national insurrection was the great demonstration, for the third presentation of the 'Chartist Petition', on 10 April 1848. The six 'points' of the Charter were:

Annual general elections
Universal manhood suffrage
Secret ballot
Abolition of property qualifications of MPs
Payment of MPs
Equal electoral districts and redistribution of seats

(All except the first were introduced as reforms over the next hundred years.)

The Chartists organised a 'monster rally' for 10 April on Kennington Common – across the river from Westminster. It was claimed that the petition contained 5,706,000 signatures. When examined by the Clerks of the House, only two million were counted – some of them, such as that of 'Victoria Regina', clearly fraudulent.

Ever since their formation, nine years earlier, the Chartists had been split between 'moral forcers' and 'physical forcers'. The 1848 demonstration was dedicated to moral force.

10 April proved to be a fine sunny day. Some 50,000 were in attendance (the Chartists claimed 500,000, the government 15,000). Many were unemployed, many 'hungry', all desperate for reform.

There was fiery oratory from the 'Lion of Freedom', Feargus O'Connor, the radical MP, demagogue, and proprietor of the *Northern Star* newspaper. Addressing the massed crowd as 'My Children', O'Connor declared:

> I have now for a quarter of a century been mixed up with the democratic movement – in Ireland since 1822, and in England from the year 1833. I have always, in and out of Parliament, contended for your rights, and I have received more than 100 letters, telling me not to come here today, or my life would be sacrificed. My answer was, that I would rather be stabbed in the heart than abstain from being in my place. And my children, for you are my children, and I am only your father and bailiff; but I am your fond father and your unpaid bailiff.
>
> My breath is nearly gone, and I will only say, when I desert you may desert me. You have by your conduct today more than repaid me for all I have done for you, and I will go on conquering until you have the land and the People's Charter becomes the law of the land.

The petition was duly taken to Parliament in three hansom cabs (stickered with slogans such as 'the Voice of the People is the voice of God'). The authorities had banned any procession – which they expected would be the prelude to a riot (as had happened in industrial areas of the kingdom). Troops and police were astutely placed on the bridges across the Thames. Over 100,000 special constables had been recruited.

Truncheons and muskets were not needed. The event went off peacefully – and pointlessly. The petition was contemptuously refused, and Chartism, as a political force, petered out. A couple of years later, O'Connor died of terminal syphilis – in his madness he made a fool of himself in Parliament. Nonetheless, 40,000 mourners attended his burial.

Karl Marx's and Friedrich Engels's *Communist Manifesto* had appeared earlier in 1848; the failure of the petition confirmed their scorn for 'moral force'. The Kennington Common Chartist event is commemorated, centrally, in two great Victorian novels: Mrs Gaskell's *Mary Barton* (1848) and Charles Kingsley's *Alton Locke* (1850). Disraeli's 'Young England' trilogy (particularly *Sybil*, 1845) reflects his keen interest – and some sympathy – for the Chartist programme, parts of which he incorporated into his 1867 Reform Act.

11 April

Frankenstein's Volcano begins to subside

1815 1816 is known, in European history, as 'the year without a summer'. The missing season was caused by the eruption the previous year, far away in Indonesia, of Mount Tambora. It began on 5 April 1815 and climaxed with three massive explosions on 10 April. They hit seven on the Volcanic Explosivity Index – making it the largest such event in a thousand years. Debris in the atmosphere formed a year-long dark mantle over the earth. It meant wonderful sunsets, but obstructed the daily sunlight required for crop ripening. Famine, and bread riots, swept through northern Europe. Switzerland was particularly badly affected.

It happened that a distinguished party of literary people were holidaying in that country in June 1816, at the Villa Diodati alongside Lake Geneva. (The villa had literary associations: Milton once stayed there, which clearly impressed one of the 1816 guests.) They comprised: Lord Byron and his current mistress; Percy Bysshe Shelley and the eighteen-year-old he had left his wife and children for, Mary Wollstonecraft Godwin (soon to add the surname 'Shelley' to that illustrious literary pedigree); and Byron's personal doctor, John Polidori.

The dismal weather precluded excursions. Confined to the villa, and tiring of the few German 'tales of terror' on the library shelves, the company resolved on a competition to see which of them could write the best spine-tingler. Shelley's spine soon proved inadequate to the task, as an entry in Polidori's diary, for 18 June, testifies:

> L[ord] B[yron] repeated some verses of Coleridge's *Christabel*, of the witch's breast; when silence ensued, and Shelley, suddenly shrieking and putting his hands to his head, ran out of the room with a candle. Threw water in his face, and after gave him ether. He was looking at Mrs S[helley], and suddenly thought of a woman he had heard of who had eyes instead of nipples, which, taking hold of his mind, horrified him.

(The relevant lines from 'Christabel' describe the witch Geraldine, whom the heroine has rashly invited into her castle:

> Beneath the lamp the lady bowed,
> And slowly rolled her eyes around;
> Then drawing in her breath aloud,
> Like one that shuddered, she unbound
> The cincture from beneath her breast:
> Her silken robe, and inner vest,
> Dropt to her feet, and full in view,
> Behold! her bosom, and half her side—
> A sight to dream of, not to tell!
> O shield her! shield sweet Christabel!)

Shelley's partner Mary, despite her youth, was made of sterner stuff and came up with *Frankenstein: The Modern Prometheus* (the tale, when published, had an epigraph from Milton, whose epic *Paradise Lost* was an acknowledged source). Byron, ever the narcissist, toyed with a blood-sucking, irresistibly handsome, immortal aristocrat. His sketch was picked up by Polidori and used as inspiration for his short story, *The Vampyre*.

Thus were two of the most profitable franchises in popular fiction (the McDonald's and Burger King of Horror, one might say) established. It's an ill wind (or volcano) that blows no literary good. Tambora is popularly known as 'Frankenstein's Volcano'.

12 April

As forces of the Confederate States of America bombard Fort Sumter, the American Civil War begins

1861 The attack on the Union fort in Charleston Harbor, South Carolina, would convulse the country in a four-year conflict that would change America profoundly and for ever. Slavery would be abolished in the South, the North pushed into rapid industrialisation. Because the technology of weaponry (like the repeating rifle) outran tactics and adequate medical care, more Americans would lose their lives in the Civil War than in all other American wars put together.

These were events as cataclysmic – if not more so – as the Napoleonic wars that raged across Europe in the early 19th century. But where were the great works of fiction proportionate to this monumental conflict? Where was the American *The Charterhouse of Parma* (1839), or *Les Misérables* (1862), or *Vanity Fair* (1853)? Above all, where was America's *War and Peace* (1869)? Like Sherlock Holmes's dog that didn't bark in the night, the American literary voice signified by its silence.

It wasn't for lack of novelists. By mid-century the American renaissance was in full swing, with Hawthorne, Melville and others producing their major work. Henry James, apparently kept out of the conflict by an 'obscure hurt', might nevertheless have found his imagination piqued when his brother Wilky nearly lost his life in the suicidal assault on Fort Wagner by Colonel Shaw's black 54th Regiment – but it was not to be (see 18 July). Of course, there was *Uncle Tom's Cabin* (1852), which, though it might have helped to start the war (see 20 March), wasn't about it.

By contrast, Ambrose Bierce went through the whole war, including the horrific Battle of Shiloh, fighting bravely and getting shot in the head, but his literary expression of the experience is limited to a few sharply observed short stories, of which 'Incident at Owl Creek' is now the best remembered – probably for its surprise ending. As for later work, Stephen Crane's *The Red Badge of Courage* (1895) survives as a poignant study in the psychology of fear on the battlefield, but hardly as a match for *War and Peace*, which 'made [it] … seem like the brilliant imagining of a sick boy who had never seen war', as Hemingway commented in *A Moveable Feast* (1964).

Maybe we're looking in the wrong place, though. Maybe big, turbulent democracies reflect their national trauma, not so much in fiction, as in more demotic prose – say, in the work of journalists like Frederick L. Olmsted, or the writings of generals Grant, Sherman and Robert E. Lee – above all, in the powerful speeches of Abraham Lincoln. How do you weigh the Gettysburg Address against *War and Peace*? Depends on the kind of scales you use.

13 April

'Houston, we have a problem'

1970 Along with Neil Armstrong's famously fumbled 'one small step' and Gene Kranz's 'failure is not an option', this is the best-remembered quote from the 1960s Apollo moonshot expeditions.

The dean of SF authors, Arthur C. Clarke, claimed authorship of the phrase, as co-writer on Stanley Kubrick's 1968 film, *2001: A Space Odyssey*. Clarke it was who came up with the line in which HAL 900 breaks into a TV transmission in which Dave Bowman (*Discovery*'s commander) is listening to his family on earth celebrate his birthday in space with a cosy chorus of 'Happy Birthday'. There follows the exchange:

> HAL: Sorry to interrupt the festivities, Dave, but I think we've got a problem.
> BOWMAN: What is it, Hal?
> HAL: My F.P.C. shows an impending failure of the antenna orientation unit.

This has been almost universally misremembered as: 'Sorry to interrupt the festivities [Dave], but *we have a problem*.' It's a memorable understatement – 'litotes', as grammarians call it. *Discovery*'s mission is doomed.

Virgil 'Gus' Grissom (one of the three astronauts burned to death in their space capsule on 27 January 1967) had actually used the 'we have a problem' trope in a radio transmission as early as 1961. After 1968, the Apollo astronauts were clearly steeped in Kubrick's movie, which flatteringly portrayed their quest as Homeric, heroic and quintessentially American.

The most famous recycling of Clarke's 'we've got a problem' occurred during the Apollo 13 (ominous number) mission, launched on 11 April 1970, under the command of James A. Lovell, to make the third moon landing. Their command module was named *Odyssey*, in honour of Clarke's epic.

Two days later, speeding towards their lunar landing, some 200,000 miles from earth, an oxygen tank exploded. The crew had just dispatched a TV broadcast that used, as its musical theme, the *Also sprach Zarathustra* motif that opened the film.

Lovell then made his famous 'Houston, we have a problem' transmission. Except he didn't. It was a fellow crew-member, Jack Swigert, who said: 'OK Houston, we've had a problem here.' It was followed by Lovell echoing the observation with: 'Houston, we've had a problem.'

Life, as Oscar Wilde said, imitates art. In the Oscar-winning 1995 film of the aborted mission, Jim Lovell (played by Tom Hanks) is given the talismanic 'Houston, we have a problem'. That's how people will always want to remember it.

14 April

Roy Campbell punches Stephen Spender on the nose

1949 The ebullient South African poet Roy Campbell was a lifelong foe to the group of 1930s writers he regarded as 'pink pansies'. They were, in his robust view, communist sympathisers in the Spanish Civil War (Campbell had fought for Franco); scrimshankers and draft-dodgers in the Second World War (Campbell, although over-age, had joined up and served as an NCO; Auden and Isherwood had taken off for America in 1939, Day-Lewis got a cushy berth in the Ministry of Information, Spender became a fireman-poet); and – worst of all – sexual inverts.

Campbell learned that Spender was going to give a reading of his poetry in the crypt of the Ethical Church in Bayswater on the evening of 14 April. He resolved to go along – fortifying himself with a heroic intake of beer before doing so. As his biographer, Peter Alexander, records, Campbell and his friends stood at the back of the hall

> while a large soprano sang *lieder* to warm up the audience, until Spender was introduced. He stepped up to the podium and began to speak. At once Campbell lurched into action. 'I wish to protest on behalf of the Sergeants' Mess of the King's African Rifles', he bellowed, in his best parade-ground voice, stumping down the aisle with his knotty stick. The audience, dumb, swivelled its collective head to watch his progress. Yelling curses at Spender, Campbell threw open a door which he imagined led on to the stage and limped inside to find himself in a passage leading to the lavatory.

He finally made it on stage, and 'leaning on his stick, swung a clumsy right-handed blow that connected lightly with Spender's nose, which promptly began to bleed'. The hall exploded into uproar at what was, surely, the most exciting poetry reading for some time.

When it was suggested that the police be called, Spender declined, with the mild observation: 'He is a great poet, he is a great poet. We must try to understand.' Writing the next day to John Hayward (T.S. Eliot's flatmate), Spender was wryly amused:

> He came up to me and hit me in the face with an honest sergeant's fist before he was dragged away. He went away shouting 'What's more, he's a fucking lesbian'. After this I read my poems, which were well received.

15 April

The Dust Bowl gets its name and the Great Depression gets its dominant image

1935 Following droughts worsening year on year, dust storms had begun to plague the American south-west from 1932, increasing in size and frequency all the time. The really big one came on 'Black Sunday', 14 April 1935. The storm struck Dodge City, Kansas, then moved across the high plains of Texas and New Mexico. People lost their way within feet of where they were trying to go. Livestock and wildlife became blinded and ran around in circles, finally dying from dust ingestion.

Black Sunday gave the Dust Bowl its name. The next day Robert Geiger, an Associated Press reporter travelling through the stricken area, sent a dispatch back to the *Washington Evening Star* referring to 'life in the dust bowl of the continent'.

Soon the phrase was humming across the AP wires to papers all across the country. Within weeks, even a sober professor of agricultural economics was writing of 'vast clouds of dust ris[ing] and roll[ing] across the Great Plains, obscuring the lives of people, blighting homes, hampering traffic, drifting eastwards to New York and westwards to California'.*

Inspired by this account, Pare Lorentz got to work on his documentary film for F.D. Roosevelt's New Deal government, *The Plow That Broke the Plains* (1936), powerfully picturing the dust smothering the farmsteads of Oklahoma, and the farmers heading west to escape it. The film argued that careless ploughing had loosened the topsoil, allowing drought and wind to do the rest.

When it came to still pictures, it was the government photographer Dorothea Lange who caught the mood, with her shots of families marooned by the sides of roads in broken-down cars, and above all in her portrait of the 'Migrant Mother', sheltering from the rain in a lean-to, her children cowering in around her.

And the literary spin-off? John Steinbeck's *The Grapes of Wrath* (1939), of course, the story of the Joads, forced to flee Oklahoma for California, then coming apart as one after another member of the family dies, deserts or lights out ahead of the cops.

---

* Paul Schuster Taylor and Dorothea Lange, 'Again the Covered Wagon', *Survey Graphic*, Vol. 24, No. 7 (July 1935), p. 348.

In truth, the so-called Okies had been heading west since shortly after the turn of the century – more of them between 1910 and 1930 than during the whole of the Depression. Hard times on south-western farms owed more to collapsing markets for wheat, corn and cotton after the First World War than to drought and dust.

In any case, the legendary dust storms fell far short of the vast range suggested in *The Plow That Broke the Plains*, afflicting mainly Kansas and Colorado, brushing past Texas and Oklahoma only at the panhandles where the two states meet.

For all that, though the Depression struck mainly at the factories and businesses of America, it's the stories and pictures of the Okies and the Dust Bowl that came to represent the experience as a whole. In 1998 the Post Office issued a 32¢ stamp with 'Migrant Mother' on it. 'America survives the depression', it said.

16 April

Britain's first novelist (and first woman novelist) dies

1689 Aphra Behn currently holds the title of Britain's first novelist – although there remain chauvinists who would back Daniel Defoe. But had she never written a word of fiction, Behn would still have ranked as one of the most remarkable women of her century.

'Eaffrey' Johnson was born in 1640 near Canterbury. What scant evidence there is suggests that her father was a 'barber'. Among other things, these intimate attenders to the male person were first ports of call for those with venereal problems. In return for services rendered, the Johnsons received favours from powerful local families. It was thus, one assumes, that Eaffrey's father, the barber, was appointed in 1663/4 Lieutenant General of Surinam, a British colonial possession. The Civil War had (temporarily) disturbed the usual power, patronage and privilege circuits. And Surinam was hardly a plum posting – even for a governor with a royal commission in one hand and a shaving bowl in the other.

The colony was located where Guyana now is, between the Orinoco and Amazon rivers (a stream, as Behn charmingly notes, 'almost as large as the Thames'). It was not far from where Robinson Crusoe is shipwrecked at exactly the same period of time that Miss Eaffrey was there – if indeed she was. Slaves from Africa worked the plantations. These 'black cattle' were notoriously ill-treated. It was a black man's hell, and a white man's grave.

Thus it proved for Aphra's father, who evidently died there. Did his daughter accompany him to Surinam? The question vexes readers of Behn's primal novel *Oroonoko*. It seems, from the ostentatious accuracy of her local description and the introduction of actual historical figures, that she indeed knew the place first-hand. Sceptics argue that she was no more there than Defoe was eye-witness to the Plague Year.

It seems (again, the details are hazy) that in her mid-twenties Aphra Johnson married a trader – possibly in slaves – called Hans Behn. He was Dutch or German and apparently died (in the plague?) or absconded, shortly after their marriage. Aphra may even have invented him to render herself a 'respectable' widow.

Whether or not the shady European spouse existed, Mrs Behn (as she hereafter inscribed herself) knew Europe at first hand. In 1666 war broke out between England and Holland. Now in her late twenties, Aphra (codename 'Aphora') served as a spy, for the newly returned Charles II, in Antwerp. The 'she spy' did good work. Legend, apocryphal alas, has it she warned her country of the Dutch navy's incursion up the Thames in 1667. But Aphora did not profit from her service to the nation: 1668 found her in debtor's prison. From 17th-century 007 to Moll Flanders.

She came in from the cold with her first play, *The Forced Marriage*, in 1670. Actresses ('Mrs Bracegirdle', et al.) had broken the old 'boys only' convention – so why not go a step higher and write the things? Particularly if you could do it as wittily – and king-pleasingly – as Mrs Behn. One of her comedies, *The Feign'd Courtezans*, is dedicated to Nell Gwynn. Behn would market more profitable fare than oranges to her monarch and his retinue.

Late in what would be a short life, Aphra Behn turned to fiction, of which *Oroonoko*, published in 1688, is judged her masterpiece. The London theatre, with the monarchy again in bloody dispute, was in recession. And Behn, it is known, was hard up: and, in her forties, 'friends' may have been harder to come by.

In the 'True Story' as the title proclaims itself (the term 'novel' was yet to be invented), an African prince, Oroonoko, along with his wife Imoinda, has been transported to Surinam from West Africa to labour in the plantations. His history is 'set down' by this anonymous young Englishwoman, the daughter of the newly appointed deputy governor, who has just died.

The narrator is struck by the couple's native dignity. Their beauty is anything but native. Oroonoko (renamed 'Caesar' by his captors) has straight hair and 'Roman', not negroid, features. He is less a noble savage, a hundred years *avant la lettre*, than a noble, *tout court*. Oroonoko is no common slave. He kills two tigers and has a closely described battle with an electric ('benumbing') eel. When Imoinda becomes pregnant, Oroonoko is determined that his son shall not be born into slavery. He organises an uprising, and is cheated into surrendering on the point of victory.

Realising it is the end, Oroonoko cuts off Imoinda's face, after he has cut her throat, so no one will see her beauty again. He disembowels himself, but is sewn up by surgeons to be executed, sadistically, for the delectation of a white rabble. Behn's Royal Slave, calmly puffing away at his pipe as his genitals are cut off, is even more stoic, at the moment of regicide, than the Royal Captive, Charles I.

As Virginia Woolf instructs, the enlightened of her gender should 'let flowers fall upon the tomb of Aphra Behn, for it was she who earned them the right to speak their minds'.

17 April

'Holy Thursday', William Blake's 'Song of Experience'

1794 'Holy Thursday', or Maundy Thursday, which fell on this date in 1794, commemorates the day of the Last Supper. Throughout the history of the church it has been marked by archbishops and monarchs giving alms to the poor – even washing their feet, as Jesus did those of his disciples on that night.

The short poems collected in William Blake's *Songs of Innocence* (1789) and *Songs of Innocence and of Experience* (1794) juxtapose (as he put it) 'two contrary states of the human soul'. So the 'Introduction' to the first is largely innocent of declarative verbs, using gerunds and imperatives like 'Piping', 'pipe', 'Sing' and 'write'. The message moves only gradually into articulacy, from the wordless tune, through 'songs of happy cheer', only finally to writing – and even that 'stain[s] the water clear'.

By contrast the 'Introduction' to the latter is the 'voice of the bard! / Who Present, Past & Future sees, whose ears have heard / The Holy

Word / That walk'd among the ancient trees' – and so on down through three further levels of relative clause. It's a voice that speaks of wisdom, but also authority: subordination in politics as well as syntax.

There's a 'Holy Thursday' in both *Innocence* and *Experience*, both about the orphans of the foundling hospital making their annual procession to St Paul's Cathedral. The first is seen through innocent eyes, the verse child-like, the scene rendered through surface phenomena only:

'Twas on a Holy Thursday, their innocent faces clean,
The children walking two and two in red and blue and green,
Grey headed beadles walk'd before with wands as white as
    snow;
Till into the high dome of Paul's they like Thames' waters flow.

By contrast, the second 'Holy Thursday' is analytical, introducing the contexts of economics, politics and morality:

Is this a holy thing to see
In a rich and fruitful land,
Babes reduced to misery,
Fed with cold and usurous hand?

And whereas the children in the first poem 'raise to heaven the voice of song' like a 'mighty wind', those in *Experience* utter only a 'trembling cry':

Can it be a song of joy?
And so many children poor?
It is a land of poverty!

And that poverty is not just the absence of riches, but poverty of intellect and wit, hope and aspiration too.

18 April

Paul Revere gallops through the night from Boston to Lexington,
Massachusetts, to warn patriots that the British are coming

1775 Paul Revere was a Boston engraver and silversmith (his work is so highly prized now that it's found mainly in museums and very wealthy families) who had been involved in revolutionary politics from the 1760s. After the British closed the port of Boston in 1774 and quartered large numbers of their troops there, he began to work as an intelligencer and messenger for the patriot cause.

In April 1775, it became clear that the British were planning a move, probably to seize a cache of rebel arms in Concord. If so, the colonial militias and irregulars would have to be warned. When the British marched westwards, how would they go – directly across the Charles River or via the longer land route south, then west? When it was clear that they were going via the river, Revere and William Dawes rode off at speed for Lexington and (if possible) Concord. In case they were captured, Revere had instructed the sexton of the Old North Church, Boston to hang one lantern in the steeple if the occupying army were going by land, two if over the water.

Thus alerted, patriot militias from Charlestown westwards were ready for the British regulars, ambushing them at Lexington and finally repulsing them at the old North Bridge, Concord, where the 'shot heard round the world' began the Revolutionary War.

Though overtaken by the urgent events of the revolution, Revere's adventure came back into prominence 60 years later, when America's most popular poet, Henry Wadsworth Longfellow, author of 'Evangeline' and *The Song of Hiawatha* – not to mention reams of translations and shorter occasional lyrics – made it the subject of his 'Paul Revere's Ride':

> Listen my children and you shall hear
> Of the midnight ride of Paul Revere,
> On the eighteenth of April, in Seventy-five;
> Hardly a man is now alive
> Who remembers that famous day and year.

Generations of American schoolchildren had to learn these lines by heart. Although they could almost have been a source for William

McGonagall's immortal tribute to the Tay Bridge disaster nineteen years later (see 28 December), the poem improves after this, even if it credits Revere alone with the midnight gallop and has him getting all the way to Concord, which he didn't reach because the British caught him at Lexington and took away his horse.

19 April

Samuel Johnson publishes Rasselas, *his conte philosophique, written in one week to pay for his mother's funeral*

1759 Samuel Johnson – the 'Great Cham' – was, in one of his minor parts, a novelist. In 1759 his 90-year-old mother was dying. His father had gone to his reward in 1731. To cover the expense of his mother's last days, Johnson wrote, in the evenings of one week, *The History of Rasselas, Prince of Abissinia.*

The *ingénu* hero leaves the comfort of his palace in Ethiopia to range the world, seeking the secret of a happy life. He is accompanied by his sister and a philosopher, Imlac (alias Samuel Johnson). There is, Rasselas discovers, no happiness to be found. Life is, as Johnson said elsewhere, a condition in which much is to be endured and little enjoyed. 'Patience is all' with Christian patience.

Few novelists, one imagines, could produce the statutory happy-ever-after with the Dead March from *Saul* playing, incessantly, in their ears and their mother's corpse genteelly decomposing at the undertaker's.

Rasselas is no page-turner – sermons on the human condition seldom are. But it is a valuably informative novel about novels. It brought Johnson £100 and £25 for a prompt second edition. In terms of hourly rate, for a week's scribbling, it was the best money of his writing career.

None but a blockhead, Johnson said, writes for anything but money. Fifty such tales a year (giving himself a fortnight's annual holiday) would have yielded the total of £6,250: a princely sum.

But having no more parents to inter he wrote no more fiction. The fact was, Johnson regarded such work as unworthy. He registered the existence and popularity of the genre in his 1750 essay, 'The Modern Novel' (Johnson coined that compound). But his personal view is summed up in his uncompromising dismissal of Sterne's great novel:

'Nothing odd will last – *Tristram Shandy* did not last.' He was wrong, of course. *Rasselas*, too, has lasted.

20 April

Amiel comes home in triumph

1848 One of the books on Tolstoy's bedside table, frequently consulted, was the *Intimate Journal* of Henri-Frédéric Amiel (1821–81). A favourite book among late Victorians, selections of the journal were translated from the French and published by Mrs Humphry Ward in 1882. For her, Amiel was primarily a poet. It was the lyricism of his thought that distinguished the journal. For Tolstoy, it was 'sincerity' that marked the author of the *Intimate Journal*.

A Swiss, Amiel studied philosophy in Berlin and Paris. In April 1848 he returned to Geneva, just 28 years old, where he was regarded as a prodigy of intellect and sagacity. He was appointed professor of aesthetics at the University of Geneva and a few years later took up the chair of moral philosophy.

Amiel jubilated, lyrically, in his journal entry for the day of his triumphant homecoming to Switzerland:

> GENEVA, April 20, 1848. It is six years to-day since I last left Geneva. How many journeys, how many impressions, observations, thoughts, how many forms of men and things have since then passed before me and in me! The last seven years have been the most important of my life: they have been the novitiate of my intelligence, the initiation of my being into being.
>
> Three snowstorms this afternoon. Poor blossoming plumtrees and peach-trees! What a difference from six years ago, when the cherry-trees, adorned in their green spring dress and laden with their bridal flowers, smiled at my departure along the Vaudois fields, and the lilacs of Burgundy threw great gusts of perfume into my face!

Amiel's doctrine found little sympathy with some of the sterner British critics – notably Matthew Arnold, Mrs Ward's uncle, who reviewed her translation, and its laudatory introduction, harshly. It was Amiel's

'Buddhist' passivity that principally offended Arnold. It was not manly stoicism, but 'feminine' spinelessness. Amiel expresses the passivity that offended Arnold clearly enough, in an early entry of 3 May 1849:

> I have never felt any inward assurance of genius, or any presentiment of glory or of happiness. I have never seen myself in imagination great or famous, or even a husband, a father, an influential citizen. This indifference to the future, this absolute self-distrust, are, no doubt, to be taken as signs. What dreams I have are all vague and indefinite; I ought not to live, for I am now scarcely capable of living. Recognize your place; let the living live; and you, gather together your thoughts, leave behind you a legacy of feeling and ideas; you will be most useful so. Renounce yourself, accept the cup given you, with its honey and its gall, as it comes. Bring God down into your heart. Embalm your soul in Him now, make within you a temple for the Holy Spirit, be diligent in good works, make others happier and better. Put personal ambition away from you, and then you will find consolation in living or in dying, whatever may happen to you.

The sexual and personal loneliness, and the career disappointments, of Amiel's life were sharpened by the horrific suffering of his last seven years. He wrote the final entries in his journal slowly suffocating. Critics see it as a prime example of 'pathographesis' – writing inspired by illness. Amiel's last entry, for 19 April 1881, reads:

> A terrible sense of oppression. My flesh and my heart fail me. 'Que vivre est difficile, ô mon coeur fatigué.'

Dying, too, was difficult. Few, however, have recorded it as sensitively as Amiel – something that evidently appealed to the creator of Ivan Ilyich.

21 April

Jane Carlyle's dubious post-mortem

1866 Popular literary lore has it that Thomas and Jane Welsh Carlyle's wedding night in 1826 was as total a debacle as that of John and Effie Ruskin in 1848. (Effie, in pursuance of annulment on grounds of non-consummation, recorded Ruskin saying '*that he had imagined women were quite different to what he saw I was*, and that the reason he did not make me his Wife was because he was disgusted with my person [on] the first evening 10th April'. There are those who have questioned whether Ruskin was indeed affronted by pubic hair, whether he was impotent, or whether there were other factors. So too with the Carlyles' wedding night.)

There are two main sources for the Carlyle wedding night. One was Jane's *confidante*, the novelist Geraldine Jewsbury. The Carlyles' honeymoon (so to call it) was spent in a small house on the edge of Edinburgh, 21 Comely Bank. It is not a beautiful quarter of that otherwise beautiful city. According to Jewsbury, on the first morning of marriage, as Jane later confided, Carlyle spent the morning furiously tearing up flowers in the garden. The symbolism was obvious.

The other source was the incorrigible literary rogue, Frank Harris. Harris claimed to have had an unbuttoned smoking-room conversation with the eminent physician, Sir Richard Quain, who had examined Jane in late life and having made an internal investigation of her was led to expostulate, in amazement: 'Why! You're virgo intacta.' Thereafter Jane (the most modest of women, as Sir Richard was among the most discreet and respectable of doctors) reportedly confided that on the wedding night Thomas, beneath the sheets, 'had done things to himself – jiggling like'.

Sir Richard (as Harris claimed) understood perfectly: 'the poor devil in a blue funk was frigging himself.' Quain's alleged remarks were elaborated, in later years, in a version circulated by gossip that had Jane's lifelong hymeneal intactness established when her corpse was taken to London's St George's Hospital, after her death on 21 April 1866, and subjected to a post-mortem.

One of Carlyle's doughtiest defenders, Sir James Crichton-Browne, followed up these claims (Harris's is, prima facie, preposterous) in 1903, with some enterprising legwork. 21 Comely Bank, he established, had no garden and since the wedding took place on 17 October, there would be no flowers to tear up. Case closed.

Sir Richard Quain was unavailable for interview. But Crichton-Browne discovered the attending house surgeon at St George's Hospital on the date in question, a Dr Ridge-Jones, and established that there was no examination made, nor any coroner's inquest on Mrs Carlyle's body. Case closed.

22 April

In Household Words, *the weekly periodical he 'conducts',*
Charles Dickens publishes 'Ground in the Mill' alongside the
fourth number of Hard Times

1854 Between 1802 and 1961 the British Parliament passed no fewer than fourteen Acts aimed at the well-being of factory workers. By 1844 the fifth of these was still pretty permissive by today's health and safety standards. Children as young as nine could work up to nine hours per day, so long as they had a lunch break. Machinery had to be fenced in. All accidents had to be reported to a surgeon – but only if fatal.

So why, ten years later, was Dickens able to write, in his article 'Ground in the Mill', of 'a factory girl ... immediately seized by the merciless machine that digs its shaft into her pinafore and hoists her up, tears out her left arm at the shoulder joint, breaks her right arm, and beats her on the head'? And of many other horrific accidents – doing for 'one hundred and six lives, one hundred and forty-two hands or arms ... [and] one thousand, three hundred and forty bones' since the passing of the 1844 Factory Act?

Because deputations of mill-owners had petitioned the government to soften the fencing provisions – limiting them to seven feet high and leaving the overhead horizontal shafts exposed. So a boy tending a shaft belt could 'be suddenly snapped up by it, whirled around a hundred and twenty times in a minute, and at each revolution knocked against the ceiling till his bones are almost reduced to powder'.

When the owners' pleas for legislative mercy failed, they fell back on threats. In *Hard Times*, the owners claimed they were 'ruined' when factory inspectors 'considered it doubtful whether they were quite justified in chopping people up with their machinery', and that rather than submit to regulation and inspection (like present-day investment bankers threatening to take their 'expertise' elsewhere) they would 'sooner pitch [their] property into the Atlantic'.

'However ... [they] were so patriotic after all, that they never had pitched their property into Atlantic yet, but, on the contrary, had been kind enough to take mighty good care of it.'

23 April

Death of Poets Day

1616, 1695, 1740, 1850, 1889, 1915, 1936 etc. Two of the few surviving facts about Shakespeare's life are that he was born and died on the same day of the year – 23 April 1564 and 23 April 1616. And since Shakespeare was also the greatest English writer – in the country as in the language – it's even more satisfying (if a bit spooky) to recall that 23 April is also the day when England's patron saint, St George, is commemorated.

So is some great literary historian in the sky controlling the births and deaths of creative writers? Sometimes it seems so. Take Shakespeare's death day. On the same day in the same year, Spain's greatest poet and novelist, Miguel Cervantes, also breathed his last. And (although he was no poet, but instead a gifted historian) so did El Inca Garcilaso de la Vega, son of a *conquistador* and an Inca princess, whose *La Florida del Inca* (1605) and *Comentarios Reales de los Incas* (1609) did so much to advance European understanding of the Native Americans.

It doesn't stop there. Henry Vaughan, the Welsh metaphysical poet, also died on Death of Poets Day, 1695. So did Thomas Tickell in 1740, Joseph Addison's protégé, who wrote reams of heroic couplets on such topics as 'On the Prospects of Peace' and 'To a Lady Before Marriage'. And, more notably, William Wordsworth, in 1850. Not to mention Rupert Brooke in 1915, on board ship with the British Mediterranean Expeditionary Force on his way to fight at Gallipoli – dead of an infected mosquito bite.

That's not the end of it. Brooke's fateful year was bracketed by Jules Barbary d'Aurevilly's (1889) and Teresa de la Parra's (1936). He was an innovative novelist of hidden motives and complex social contradictions, an inspiration to Henry James, as well as the practical supporter of Stendhal, Flaubert and Baudelaire. She was the Venezuelan novelist, author of the frankly titled *Iphigenia: Diary of a young lady who wrote because she was bored* (1924).

So struck were UNESCO on the Shakespeare–Cervantes connection that they proclaimed 23 April as 'The International Day of the Book'. Unfortunately, that's one parallel death scene that doesn't hold up. Shakespeare didn't die in Stratford at the moment Cervantes expired in Madrid – or even close to it. Cervantes (and Garcilaso) died in the old Julian calendar, Shakespeare by the reformed Gregorian, in which 23 April came ten days later. Same date, different days.

24 April

A terrible beauty is born

1916 Ezra Pound came into W.B. Yeats's life in 1913, in London. For the next three years they were constantly in each other's company – Pound always the mentor, Yeats the pupil. The influence of Pound drastically revised Yeats's view of Ireland, which swivelled over these years from Romantic to anti-Romantic. The shift is aggressively proclaimed in his poem 'September 1913', with its refrain:

Romantic Ireland's dead and gone,
It's with O'Leary in the grave.

Politics replaced *Schwärmerei*. There would be no more 'Lake Isle of Innisfree'. Yeats was now an 'engaged' poet. But what, in the maelstrom of world war and the 1916 Easter Uprising ('Revolution' some called it), did 'engagement' mean?

The Uprising was the more difficult of the two crises. While England was preoccupied with fighting the Germans in France, a band of Irish Nationalists decided that this would be the moment at which to mount a coup and seize independence for their country. The symbolism (Easter being the moment of spiritual rebirth in the Christian calendar) and the quixotic heroism would resound through Irish history eternally. But as a coup, it was a disastrous flop.

The Uprising began on the morning of Easter Monday, 24 April, with a street demonstration by some 1,000 Dubliners. At their head, a commando of rebels set out to capture and take over the major build-ings in the capital: principally the Dublin General Post Office.

It was pure romanticism. And it failed, utterly. The rebels had rifles, the British occupiers had much heavier armament – and knew, having been at war for two years, how to use it. The British garrison quickly mustered and moved in massive strength against the rebels ('criminals', as they were proclaimed). Ruthlessness was ordered: the government, in London, regarded it as a stab in the back while the British Isles (which included Ireland) were in a desperate fight to the death with Germany.

No quarter was given. Martial law was declared and the counter-attack began. Artillery was used, mercilessly. A gunboat was floated along the Liffey river. The collateral damage was huge. But in a couple of days, the rebellion was effectively squashed. The leaders of the rebel-lion were shown no mercy. They were tried in secret by a military court and sentenced to death, the executions announced only after they had been summarily carried out.

Militarily, it was a blinding success for the British. But the huge civilian casualties (over 1,000 non-combatants were killed), the wan-ton destruction of some of the most beautiful parts of the city, and the cruelty of the punishment did what the rebels themselves had been unable to do. The Irish independence movement was, hereafter, his-torically unstoppable. It would happen five years later.

This is Yeats's poetic meditation on that bloody event, offered in his poem 'Easter 1916' – a meditation as simple in its expression, and complex in its resonance, as its title. It opens:

I have met them at close of day
Coming with vivid faces
From counter or desk among grey
Eighteenth-century houses.
I have passed with a nod of the head
Or polite meaningless words,
Or have lingered awhile and said
Polite meaningless words,
And thought before I had done
Of a mocking tale or a gibe
To please a companion
Around the fire at the club,
Being certain that they and I
But lived where motley is worn:

All changed, changed utterly:
A terrible beauty is born.

What is Yeats saying here? That his inactivity – as an intellectual, artist observer of the scene – is culpable, or the proper response of a commonsensical ideologue to these head-in-the-air 'clownish' (motleyed) idealists? Is he, like Stephen Daedalus's God (in Joyce's 1916 novel, *A Portrait of the Artist as a Young Man*), above it all, like a superior being paring his fingernails while below him frogs and mice go at their little wars?

Were these men fools, or patriotic heroes? If the latter, what did that make William Butler Yeats? The poem (completed in September 1916, while the events were still white hot, but in military perspective) continues, reviewing the actions of the rebels, and the inaction of men and women of Yeats's kind. It ends with a salute to the heroes of the uprising, a chilling refrain, and an unanswered, perhaps unanswerable, question:

We know their dream; enough
To know they dreamed and are dead;
And what if excess of love
Bewildered them till they died? [...]
[All] Are changed, changed utterly:
A terrible beauty is born.
Things were simpler on the Lake Isle than in Dublin in Easter 1916.

25 April

The novel is invented, but its inventor has no name for it

1719 There are a number of candidates for the title of 'first novel in English'. Most convincing is Daniel Defoe's *Robinson Crusoe*, published on this day.

Defoe's life was extraordinarily full of event and of literary achievement. He was a great pamphleteer, a government spy, and the father of English journalism. Born around 1660 (the year of the Restoration), he lived in turbulent and dangerous times. More so as he was a dissenter and had a foreign-sounding name (never a good thing in England:

Crusoe's father prudently changed his name from 'Kreutzer'). As chronicled below (see 31 July), Defoe on one occasion found himself in the stocks for things he had written that were, alas, too clever for the dolts who misread them.

He lived a long life, dying in his early seventies in 1731. He was never well off, and downright impoverished by creditors in his last years. And it was in these last years, aged nearly 60 (a fact that the authors of this volume find very cheering), that he can be said to have invented the English novel – or, at the very least, to have helped establish it as the dominant literary form it would become.

The word 'novel' literally means 'new thing', and it is the one dominant literary form whose genesis, and progenitor, we can plausibly claim to know and date. Literary evolution is as fascinating as the evolution of any other species. Why, then, did the novel come into existence at this particular point in historical time, and why in this particular place – England (London, specifically) at the beginning of the 18th century?

A number of answers have been suggested, in addition to Defoe's pre-eminent genius and originality of mind. The rise of the novel coincides, it has been noted, with the rise of capitalism in its modern form. Robinson Crusoe, colonising his island, is *Homo economicus* – the epitome of mercantilism (he even sells Man Friday). The novel – the 'bourgeois epic' as it has been called – coincides with a related event, the rise of the middle class (along with parliamentary democracy).

These are very much after-the-historical-event explanations. It is clear that although Defoe knew what he was doing, neither he nor the booksellers who produced *Robinson Crusoe* could put a name to their fascinating 'novelty'. So extra copies of the title page would be run off, and pinned, or pegged, up on rope-lines as advertisements – hence the intrusion of what we would call a 'blurb':

THE LIFE AND STRANGE SURPRIZING ADVENTURES
OF ROBINSON CRUSOE, Of YORK, MARINER:

Who lived Eight and Twenty Years, all alone in an un-inhabited
Island on the Coast of AMERICA, near the Mouth of the
Great River of OROONOQUE;

Having been cast on Shore by Shipwreck, where-in all the Men
perished but himself.

WITH
An Account how he was at last as strangely deliver'd by
PYRATES.

Written by Himself.

LONDON:
Printed for W. TAYLOR at the *Ship* in *Pater-Noster-Row.*
MDCCXIX.

Any prospective purchaser idly casting an eye over this in the yard outside St Paul's Cathedral (i.e. the 'Row', where booksellers congregated) would assume he was being offered something on the lines of Alexander Selkirk's authentic memoir of being shipwrecked on a desert island (Selkirk's experiences were later published as the 'Life and Adventures of the *Real* Robinson Crusoe').

There is nothing on the Defoe–Taylor title page to indicate that this is fiction – and the ascription 'Written by Himself' is downright misleading. There was, happily for literature, no Trades Description Act to prosecute the vendor in 1719.

For all its misleadingness, the title page goes to the essence of what Defoe is doing, and what the novel is: 'Lies like truth' – as Leslie Stephen called *Robinson Crusoe.* Many contemporaries were taken in, and assumed *Robinson Crusoe* to be 'genuine'. That, one might fancify, is the ultimate sales test for a novel. So good a fiction that the unknowing will take it as fact.

26 April

*George Herbert is inducted as rector of the parish of
Fugglestone-cum-Bemerton, near Salisbury*

1630 It doesn't sound very exciting, but this date marks the point at which one of the best lyricists in the English language turned his back on the secular rewards of politics and high academia in search of his true calling: religion and poetry. In Herbert's case the two vocations were inseparable.

Herbert had it all: brains, money, an influential family. His education took him through Westminster School, through Trinity College, Cambridge, to a university readership in rhetoric and the post of University Orator. This didn't just mean going around giving speeches, but writing official letters to dignitaries, as well as greeting them when they visited Cambridge – always in Latin.

One of the dignitaries in question turned out to be King James I, who was so impressed with the rhetorical flourishes in Herbert's Latin that he encouraged him to frequent the court and stand as Member of Parliament for Montgomeryshire, his home county. When the king died in 1625 and his royal patronage evaporated, Herbert returned to a long-standing intention to study divinity and enter the church.

At Bemerton he was a model parish priest, raising money to repair the church, bringing the sacraments to the infirm, providing clothing for the poor. In his 'Life of George Herbert' Izaak Walton recalls how, while walking to Salisbury, Herbert came across 'a poor man with a poorer horse' that had fallen over with its load. The good parson immediately threw off his 'canonical coat' to help the man to unload the horse, get it up, then reload it, leaving the man with the injunction, 'that if he loved himself, he should be merciful to his beast'.

Herbert lived just three years as rector of Bemerton, until he was carried off by tuberculosis. In that same year, 1633, his collection *The Temple* was published. Only then did it become clear just how much sacred verse he had written in his short tenure in the parish, and how good it was. Take 'The Agonie', a meditation on Sin and Love as emblematised in the Crucifixion:

> Who knows not love, let him assay,
> And taste that juice which, on the crosse, a pike
> Did set again abroach; then let him say
>   If ever he did taste the like.
> Love is that liquour sweet and most divine,
> Which my God feels as bloud, but I as wine.

It could take paragraphs to analyse the subtle poetics here: the run-on between lines 2 and 3; the meaningful rhymes between 'assay' and 'say', 'divine' and 'wine'; and the clever interweaving of Christ's blood and the sacrament of the Eucharist. But the real marvel is how *English* the stanza is – and this from the great Latin rhetorician in another, more secular life. Clearly, for Herbert, leaving the court for his core faith meant dispensing with the Latinism brought in with Norman-conquest French and going back to the roots of his native language – its Anglo-Saxon origins.

27 April

Encounter's CIA connection revealed

1966 On 27 April the *New York Times*, in the course of a series of articles on American intelligence, reported (without any mincing of words) that 'the CIA has supported anti-communist but liberal organisations such as the Congress for Cultural Freedom and some of their newspapers and magazines. *Encounter* magazine was for a long time, though it is not now, one of the indirect beneficiaries of CIA funds.'

The revelation triggered the biggest scandal in higher journalism of the post-war era. *Encounter* had been founded in 1953 as a joint Anglo-American initiative. It was devised, from the first, as an attempt to capture the intellectual high ground from Marxist thinkers (Sartre, Gramsci, et al.).

The magazine was published in the UK, although from the outset it had a dual British–American editorship. The first editorial coupling was the English poet Stephen Spender (who had recently renounced his youthful communism in the book *The God that Failed*) and the American political commentator (later the father of neo-conservatism) Irving Kristol. Kristol was succeeded, five years later, by his compatriot (and fellow neo-con) Melvin Lasky.

Funding for *Encounter* (never profitable) was from the Congress for Cultural Freedom (CCF), based in Paris and Geneva. The cash, allegedly, came from a philanthropic source, the Fairfield Foundation, funded by the millionaire Julius ('Junkie') Fleischmann – enriched by the manufacture of margarine. In point of fact, the CIA was secretly the paymaster.

From the first there were suspicions. Despite being on friendly relations with Spender, E.M. Forster, T.S. Eliot and William Empson declined to contribute to the literary pages for which Spender was principally responsible. It was, as Eliot said, the American 'auspices' that made them reluctant. Empson came right out with it and accused Spender of being a lackey of American imperialism, which led to glasses of wine being thrown at parties (his suit was so stained, Empson said, that it would not show).

Spender, co-editor for fourteen years, maintained plausibly that he did not know about the CIA connection. Letters indicate that he was consistently lied to on the question of who was paying the piper. Kristol also claimed that he did not know, and in later life threatened to sue anyone who said he did. The question was raised again, after lawsuits were no longer a risk, with his death in 2009. Melvin Lasky was widely believed to be a CIA agent in place, although it has never been proved.

When the *New York Times* story broke, Spender was merely a 'corresponding editor', teaching at the time in America. His editorial position on *Encounter* had been taken over by Frank Kermode. Surviving correspondence proves that Kermode knew absolutely nothing about the CIA connection and had been lied to (notably by Lasky).

A terrific row ensued, in which much dirty washing relating to the American and British secret services was made public. The magazine carried on, in sadly damaged form, under the sole editorship of Lasky. The CCF was disbanded. In a sense they had won their battle.

Argument continues as to whether *Encounter*, which published some of the most distinguished higher journalism of its time, was – when all is considered – a good or bad thing. Was that journalism soiled by its remote connection with America's spooks?

28 April

The British bestseller list arrives (belatedly)

1974 It was on this date, and in the *Sunday Times* 'Review' section, as it then was, that the UK's first 'definitive weekly bestseller list' was published. Keeping a finger in this way on the nation's reading pulse had been routine in the United States since the 1890s. Americans loved their bestseller lists.

The UK loathed them. Why? Because they were, as Dickens's Mr Podsnap would say, 'un-English'. Foreign even. The 'trade' wanted nothing to do with them. Books, traditionalists believed, did not *compete* against each other. There were no winners and losers in the world of print. Judging a book not by its *quality*, but by the *quantity* it happened to sell, was sheer Yankee philistinism. Un-English!

The *Sunday Times* resolved to change things. It was the right time to do so. The early 1970s was an era of change – much of it painful. The IRA were blowing up everything that didn't have a shamrock painted on it. 'Who governs Britain?' asked Ted Heath, plaintively, from his bunker in Downing Street. No answer was forthcoming. There was a three-day week, rolling energy cuts, double-digit inflation. Times Newspapers, which had dared to embrace technological processes marginally more advanced than William Caxton's, was at war with the print unions.

Amid this turmoil, the *Sunday Times* bestseller list was born. Harold Evans (an arrant Americanophile) had been appointed editor with a new-broom remit. Photo-composition (as it was then called) was one swish of the broom. With another swish, Evans appointed computer whiz Peter Harland as his right-hand man in charge of 'New Technology'. On appointment in 1973, Harland was charged with setting up a books bestseller list.

Publishers were implacably hostile. Harland was obliged to work from the retail end, laboriously monitoring weekly sales in some 300 bookshops, with elaborate checks to prevent the corrupt practices that infected the music industry's pop charts. Crunching the numbers, in the few hours available weekly, was a formidable challenge.

The *Observer* got wind of what Harland was up to, and in an attempt to spike its rival's guns, promptly bought rights to the impressionistic fortnightly listing distributed with *Gee's Booksellers' Newsletter*. So as not to be pipped at the post, Harland and Evans rushed their first list out on 28 April 1974. The pros and cons of bestsellerism were argued, furiously, for weeks thereafter.

The *Observer* (which to this day remains cool about lists) dropped its fortnightly charts in January 1975, citing 'lack of variety' and the banality of 'all those television based books'. The *Sunday Times* list, meanwhile, went from strength to strength. Harland, on leaving the paper a few years later, founded Bookwatch, one of today's most trusted data-gatherers.

In fiction, the top-selling hardback titles in 1974, as the *Sunday Times* recorded, were Frederick Forsyth's *The Dogs of War* and Agatha Christie's *Poirot's Early Cases*. In paperback fiction, the runaway bestseller was Richard Adams's *Watership Down*. In the April 1974 list, Iris Murdoch made an appearance, for a week or two, with *The Sacred and Profane Love Machine* (one suspects that book-buyers confused it Jacqueline Susann's *The Love Machine*: a very different kettle of fish).

29 April

The Interesting Narrative of the Life of Olaudah Equiano
is published: fact or fiction?

1789 Olaudah Equiano, the 'black Ben Franklin', is the first notable author of African extraction in Western literature. The moot point is whether it is English or American (or – arguably – 'colonial') literature.

Equiano, later known as Gustavus Vassa, was, he claimed, born around 1745 in what is now the Ibo ('Essaka', as he calls it) region of Nigeria. It was then a part of the Abyssinian empire. Equiano's father was, he records, a village elder. He was also a slave-owner, but, his son hastens to add, a very *humane* slave-owner.

By his own account, Equiano was brought up in a condition of Edenic simplicity, a world away from the invasions, wars and revolutions that were upheaving Europe, the Indian subcontinent, and North America during the second half the 18th century.

Aged around eleven, his African paradise was lost. Equiano was kidnapped while playing innocently with his sister, and carried off to slavery. Initially, like his father's slaves, his masters were African. But he was sold on to the traders at the coast. Here it was that he first came into contact with white people. It inspires one of the more vivid sections in his autobiography. They strike him as monsters. These pale devils, with their 'red faces and loose hair' must be cannibals, he assumes: they will eat him.

The description of the middle passage of his life is the most affecting, and horrifying, in Equiano's published memoirs. His later career, vivid as it is on the page, can be briefly summarised. Sold on a number of times, he was transported to Barbados, where he was judged too physically slight for labour in the sugar plantations. He eventually found himself in the colony of Virginia, where he was bought by a Royal Navy officer, renamed Gustavus Vassa, and – as a personal valet – humanely treated.

Equiano endeared himself by loyal service both to his master and, as a sailor on board ship, to the Crown. In England he was, still a teenager, sent to school to learn how to read and write. Equiano also became a devout Christian, persuading his master to let him be baptised in 1759 – so that he might go to heaven.

He might be free up there. But not, for a few years yet, down here. Poor 'Gustavus' was sold on again. He was now a valuable property – a literate, numerate, well-spoken slave. As such he was eventually bought by a Quaker merchant in Philadelphia and put to work as an inventory clerk, on a tiny salary. Equiano eventually saved up the £40 required to buy his freedom.

The great day in his life was 10 July 1766, when he became a free man.

After manumission, he prudently took up residence in England and went into trade himself for a few years (including black gold, or slaves) before allying himself with the British abolitionist movement, whose figurehead he became. He gave heart-rending speeches, preached, and married an Englishwoman in 1795. In 1789, with the help of noble patrons, he published *The Interesting Narrative of the Life of Olaudah Equiano, or Gustavus Vassa, the African.*

The last phase of Equiano's life was, evidently, happy but is largely unrecorded. There were two daughters to his marriage, his wife died in 1796 and he followed her a year later, aged (probably) 52. It's not known where he was buried – although he left a sizeable amount to his daughters.

Equiano's interesting narrative was widely circulated in the abolition movement, as eyewitness evidence of the realities of slavery. So it was accepted for centuries. But a few years ago, scholars – notably Vincent Carretta – found convincing evidence (specifically a baptismal certificate and a ship's muster roll) that Equiano had been born in South Carolina. He was American.

This, if true (and it seems currently incontrovertible), means that the most vivid African and slave-ship sections of the book – its heart – must be invention. Fictional.

30 April

The United States buys the entire Middle West from the French for $15 million, more than doubling the size of the country. Fenimore Cooper has his doubts

1803 'The letter that bought a continent', as they called the Louisiana Purchase Treaty, was signed on this day in Paris – and it did turn the United States into a continental power with the stroke of a pen. Oddly enough, though, territorial aggrandisement was the least of President

Thomas Jefferson's motives in doing the deal. He was more interested in securing the port of New Orleans. All that ideology about the 'manifest destiny' of the Americans to expand to the Pacific would come later.

Later, even, than James Fenimore Cooper's 'Leatherstocking Tales', a series of five prose fictions tracing the European settlement of America, the equivalent of those medieval romance sequences involving Roland, or King Arthur or Sir Gawain. 'Leatherstocking' is one of several epithets that his Native American admirers apply to Nathaniel (Natty) Bumppo, the transcendent figure in all five of the tales, because of his deerskin leggings. Natty appears in other books of the series under different sobriquets, like 'Deerslayer', 'Pathfinder' and 'Hawkeye', depending on his age and the story's setting.

The five books were written and published in the order: *The Pioneers* (1823), *The Last of the Mohicans* (1826), *The Prairie* (1827), *The Pathfinder* (1840), and *The Deerslayer* (1841). Their order in the overriding plot of the series is: *Deerslayer, Mohicans, Pathfinder, Pioneers,* and *Prairie.* The grand survey runs from the 1740s through to 1804, just a year after the Louisiana Purchase. So the sequence takes its readers from the disorderly struggles between European powers – and between shifting groups of 'white' man and 'red' – over the still unsettled frontier lying just west of New York and New England, through to the settlement of Templeton, where in *The Pioneers* the old aristocratic (and Indian) use of the land is confronted by the claims of the new townspeople – finally to run out in *The Prairie.*

The Prairie is far from optimistic about the coming expansion into the new territory. The story opens in an atmosphere of death and degeneration. 'The harvest of our first year of possession had long been passed', says the narrator in Chapter 1, 'and the fading foliage of a few scattered trees was already beginning to exhibit the hues and tints of autumn'. Now the American landscape has passed through its spring and summer, and the hunters of bear and deer have become hunters of bees. Natty still has his faithful carbine by his side, but he now traps beaver. He will die, aged 90, at the end of the book.

This time the Natives are not defeated by brave men in close combat, but sold by foreign governments 6,000 miles away. '"And where were the chiefs of the Pawnee Loups when this bargain was made?" suddenly demanded the youthful warrior. … "Is a nation to be sold like a skin of beaver?" "Right enough, right enough [answers Natty helplessly], and where were truth and honesty also. But might is right according to the fashions of the 'arth; and what the strong choose to do, the weak must call justice.'"

And as the settlers stream onto the prairie, he says to Paul Hover and Captain Duncan Middleton: "'What the world of America is coming to and where the machinations and inventions of its people are to have an end, the Lord only knows. How much has the beauty of the wilderness been deformed in two short lives! ... and I, miserable and worn out as I seem, have lived to see it all.'"

1 May

The nine-year-old Dante Alighieri first meets the eight-year-old Beatrice Portinari when his father takes him to their family home for a May Day party

1274 As Dante tells the story in chapter XXIV of *La Vita Nuova* (1295), his autobiographical quest for spiritual perfection through his idealised love of Beatrice, they met only once again. While out walking in Florence, the poet feels the dormant spirit of love suddenly wake in his heart. Then he sees Love himself afar off, who approaches and says laughing, 'Try to show me some respect'. At that point he sees Beatrice approaching, accompanied by the Lady Vanna, of whom Love says: 'She is the spring, but the other must be called Love, since she resembles me so much':

> Io mi senti' svegliar dentro a lo core
> Un spirito amoroso che dormia:
> E poi vidi venir da lungi Amore
> Allegro sì, che appena il conoscia,
> Dicendo: 'Or pensa pur di farmi onore';
> E 'n ciascuna parola sua ridia.
> E poco stando meco il mio segnore,
> Guardando in quella parte onde venia,
> Io vidi monna Vanna e monna Bice
> Venire inver lo loco là 'v'io era,
> L'una appresso de l'altra maraviglia;
> E sì come la mente mi ridice,
> Amor mi disse: 'Quell'è Primavera,
> E quell'ha nome Amor, sì mi somiglia.'*

The scene would be painted by Henry Holiday (1839–1927), the English Pre-Raphaelite. Three women stroll along the banks of the Arno. Of the two in front, Vanna is in red and Beatrice in white, while

---

* I felt awaken within my heart / A loving spirit that had slept there. / And then I saw Love coming from a distance, / So happy, who as soon as I recognised him, / Said: 'Do you really think you can honour me?' / And he laughed as he spoke each word. / And while my Lord stood with me a little while, / Watching the place he came from, / I saw Lady Vanna and Lady Bice [Beatrice's nickname within the family] / Approaching the place where I stood, / One marvel surpassing another, / And as my memory keeps repeating, / Love said to me: 'The first of these is Spring, / And the other bears the name of Love, since she resembles me.'

Dante stands astonished at the corner of a bridge, clutching his heart. But whereas the artist presents the poet as stricken by the sight of Beatrice, Dante's point is that the emotion precedes the object. His imagination wouldn't have invoked the god of love had not his own 'loving spirit' come awake within him, and he doesn't see Beatrice until having already agreed to honour Love as his feudal lord.

In 'real life' Beatrice married a banker in 1287, and died three years later at the age of 24. Dante's love for her was not the sort to lead to marriage, with 'a boy for you and a girl for me'. He had a wife and children. Beatrice was something else, even more rarefied than Petrarch's Laura (see 6 April), a demi-goddess at the extreme, most worshipful end of the courtly love spectrum.

Which is why she takes over from Vergil as Dante's guide in the last four Cantos of 'Purgatorio' and the whole of 'Paradiso', leading him through the nine celestial spheres of heaven in *The Divine Comedy*.

2 May

An unnoticed revolution in books

1966 There are many industry-transforming events in the evolution of the book. Printing (the manuscript codex book existed centuries before Gutenberg) is one. The Queen Anne copyright law of 1710 another. The papier-mâché stereotype process in the early 19th century a third. Computer typesetting and offset printing in the 1970s a fourth. One such event, however, tends to slip by unnoticed.

On this day, Professor E. Gordon Foster of the London School of Economics published a pilot study, commissioned by the Publishers' Association, which concluded that 'there is a clear need for the introduction of standard numbering, and substantial benefits will accrue to all parties therefrom'.

It struck a chord. As Ted Striphas records in his monograph, *The Late Age of Print* (2009): 'Within a year sixteen hundred British publishers agreed to the new coding system, dubbed the Standard Book Number (SBN).' America (led by the Library of Congress, charged with catalogue control of the national book supply and archive) 'similarly longed for a precise universally recognized coding system'. The ISBN (international SBN) was introduced in 1967.

As Striphas explains: 'It should be emphasised that the ISBN isn't merely a glorified stock number. Rather, it's a carefully conceived, highly significant, and mathematically exact *code* that contains detailed information about the identity of each book.'

Together with the machine-readable barcode (Universal Product Code, UPC), which allowed EPOS (electronic point-of-sale system), introduced ten years later, the ISBN rationalised the book industry globally. It represented a new lease of life for walk-in stores (which could now minimise stock-holding wastage and delivery times) and made possible electronic bookstores such as Amazon. If the traditional book has a future, it is thanks to two acronyms largely invisible to the average consumer (ISBN, UPC). There is safety, as always, in numbers.

3 May

Chekhov's last visit to Moscow

1904 If there is an iconically Russian moment in Chekhov's drama, it is Irina's last, emotional utterance at the end of the second act of *Three Sisters*: 'To Moscow! To Moscow! To Moscow!'

Dying of TB, the dramatist made his escape from Yalta ('Siberia', as he called it – despite the climatic clemency) on 3 May 1904. He arrived in Moscow in leafy spring. Soon after arrival, his doctors (like most of the best Russian physicians, Germans) advised a further trip, to the health resort of Badenweiler (near the less exclusive Baden-Baden) in the Black Forest. The terminally ill Chekhov was packed onto yet another train, for yet another interminable journey. He took his last farewell from Moscow on 3 June.

Chekhov and his wife arrived at the German spa on 9 June. He died three weeks later. His last letter was to his mother:

Dearest Mama,

I send you greetings. My health is improving and I should think that I will be completely better in a week. I like it here. It's quiet and warm, there is a lot of sunshine but it's not too hot. Olga [his wife] bows to you and sends her love. My respects to Masha,

Vanya and everyone else. I bow deeply before you and kiss your hand. I wrote to Masha yesterday.

Your Anton

Rosamund Bartlett (in *Chekhov: Scenes from a Life*) describes the scene of his death:

Chekhov spent his last day playing patience, and died in the early hours of a warm July night, in the presence of his wife, Dr Schwoerer, and the student Leve Rabenek. It had been the first time he had actually asked for a doctor and Olga had dispatched Rabenek to run down the road to Schwoerer's house and ask him to come. Events then moved rapidly and Chekhov died immediately after downing the glass of champagne prescribed by Schwoerer.

This was 2 July. His body was dispatched back to Moscow and buried in the Novodevichy Cemetery a week later. He was, in a sense, home.

4 May

Sherlock Holmes dies at the Reichenbach Falls

1891 Arthur Conan-Doyle (as Arthur Doyle snootily relabelled himself in later life) wanted, in 1891, to kill Holmes even more desperately than the detective's arch-foe, Professor Moriarty. Sherlock Holmes, Doyle complained, 'takes my mind from better things'.

Holmes originated, famously, in one of Doyle's tutors at Edinburgh's School of Medicine, Professor Joseph Bell. (*Professor* Moriarty – the virtuoso of the binomial theory – is, as critics note, Holmes's dark self; it is significant that the two of them should eventually perish 'locked in each other's arms'.)

Professor Bell was famous for 'reading' symptoms and deducing a patient's background as soon as he or she set foot in his surgery. Holmes does the same trick often enough at 221b Baker Street, to the amazement of an anything but Bell-like Dr Watson ('the idiot friend', as Julian Symons calls the detective's dumb accomplice).

In the mid-1880s, Doyle – in his mid-twenties, and a none too successful doctor in Southsea – toyed with the idea of some stories centred on an amateur sleuth, 'J. Sherrinford Holmes', who would employ Bell's deductive techniques to solve crimes. The outcome was the Sherlock Holmes novella, *A Study in Scarlet* (1887). No top-drawer publisher would take it, and it was eventually serialised in a magazine edited by Mrs Beeton's husband (see 14 March).

Holmes attained mass popularity when the editor of George Newnes's newly-founded *Strand Magazine* made Holmes a main selling item. The editor, Herbert Greenhough Smith, apprehended that 'here was the greatest short story writer since Edgar Allan Poe'. These Sherlock Holmes stories were devised to correct 'the great defect' in current detective fiction, lack of logic. They were illustrated by Sidney Paget, who supplied the detective with his famous deerstalker and aquiline profile. A new 'Holmes' could double the *Strand*'s circulation to half a million. A franchise was born.

The formulaic stories were, Doyle came to believe, beneath him. In *The Final Problem*, the famous hand-to-hand fight to the death was staged on a fearful ledge by the majestic Reichenbach Falls, above Meiringen in Switzerland.

Watson does not witness the struggle, but reconstructs it from footprints, Holmes's 'alpine-stock', 'small silver cigarette case', and a note left on the fatal grassy ledge above the 'dreadful cauldron of swirling water and seething foam [where] will lie for all time the most dangerous criminal and the foremost champion of the law of their generation'.

'All time' proved premature. Doyle was not allowed to kill his golden goose. It was too golden. Under the lure of cash (particularly dollars), Holmes was exhumed in 1901 and 1905 and innumerably thereafter in what became a veritable industry. Moriarty too was brought back to life in a trilogy by the 20th-century popular writer John Gardner (1926–2007).

The funicular station at the base of the mountain leading to the falls has a memorial plaque dedicated to the 'most famous detective in the world … At this fearful place, Sherlock Holmes vanquished Professor Moriarty, on 4 May 1891.' Or not.

5 May

John Scopes is charged with teaching evolution in a Tennessee school

1925 Billed as 'the trial of the century', the Scopes trial started out as a publicity stunt. The Tennessee state legislature had passed a law prohibiting the teaching in public (state) schools of 'any theory that denies the story of the Divine Creation of man as taught in the Bible'. Wishing to put their town on the map, a committee of local business-men in Dayton, Tennessee convinced John Scopes, a local teacher, to stand in a case to test the law.

Scopes was the school's football coach, but had stood in for its science teacher while he was ill. He couldn't remember whether he had actually covered evolution on the few days he had taught the class, but told the group: 'If you can prove that I've taught evolution and that I can qualify as a defendant, then I'll be willing to stand trial.'

In 1925 the State of Tennessee duly obliged, taking Scopes to court for having broken the law. Dubbed 'the monkey trial' by the Baltimore *Sun*'s astringent columnist H.L. Mencken, the court case astonished and amused the nation, not least because each side attracted such illustrious advocates. The prosecution was spearheaded by the fundamentalist preacher and former progressive Democratic candidate for president, William Jennings Bryan. Leading the defence was Clarence Darrow, distinguished civil libertarian and America's most brilliant trial lawyer of the time, fresh from his successful defence of thrill killers Leopold and Loeb.

Darrow and Scopes lost their case, but not before an unprecedented legal manoeuvre in which Darrow called Bryan to the witness stand to answer a number of searching questions into the literal truth of the Bible. For instance, did Joshua really stop the sun in its tracks for a whole day? What would have been the effect on the earth, had he managed it? A year later the state repealed the law, perhaps considering that they had had enough publicity on that score.

Thirty years later the trial inspired a workmanlike, amusing and in places moving play, *Inherit the Wind* (1955), meant by its authors, Jerome Lawrence and Robert E. Lee, to highlight the red scare then being promoted by the House Un-American Activities Committee, and by Joseph McCarthy's Senate Subcommittee on Investigations.

After two years on Broadway, the play was revived twice, in 1996 and 2007. In 2009 the Old Vic in London staged it to full houses and standing ovations, with Kevin Spacey and David Troughton superb as the Darrow and Bryan figures. The powerful movie (1960) starred Frederick March as Bryan and Spencer Tracy as Darrow.

In *Epperson vs. Arkansas* (1968) the Supreme Court ruled that bans on teaching of evolution were unconstitutional, under the Bill of Rights, which protects free speech and prohibits the establishment of religion, yet it seems that bigotry resurfaces in sufficient new (or warmed-up old) guises to keep *Inherit the Wind* in business.

6 May

The Washington office of the Federal Writers' Project writes to the south-eastern region to praise their life history of ex-slave Betty Cofer

1937 Ever since Mayhew's *London Labour and the London Poor* (1851), oral histories had been associated with the underprivileged, the relatively powerless, those whose political and cultural voices had been silenced or suppressed by the establishment. In America no group fitted this description better than African-American slaves.

The Popular Fronters and progressives of the New Deal, who had opposed lynching, promoted black voting rights and encouraged an interracial union movement, felt a kind of white collective guilt about slavery. So when the Federal Writers' Project (FWP) set out to collect American life stories (see 27 July), ex-slaves were a top priority. To add to the urgency, time was running out. By the second half of the 1930s no African-American who had once been a slave could have been under 70 years of age.

Trouble was, the progressives in Washington couldn't collect the data themselves. For that they had to rely on fieldworkers – many in the South – who had their own biases, among which were a need to pretend that the Civil War and Emancipation hadn't really made much difference. This is how Mary A. Hicks introduced her interview with ex-slave Betty Cofer in North Carolina:

Here, in 1856, was born a negro girl, Betty, to a slave mother. Here, today, under the friendly protection of this same Jones family, surrounded by her sons and her son's sons, lives this same Betty in her own little weather-stained cottage. Encircling her house are lilacs, althea, and flowering trees that soften the bleak outlines of unpainted out-buildings. A varied collection of old-fashioned plants and flowers crowd the neatly swept dooryard. A friendly German-shepherd puppy rouses from his nap on the sunny porch to greet visitors enthusiastically.

That syntactical parallelism, 'Here ... Here ...' sets the frame for time-less continuity. Betty's cottage may be 'little' and 'weather-stained', and her 'unpainted out-buildings' 'bleak' in outline, but they are redeemed by her continuing cultivation of the values with which she was imbued in her antebellum existence, as symbolised by the various 'old-fashioned plants and flowers' that soften the outlines of her otherwise harsh life after Emancipation.

You might expect the national office to be less than happy with this sanitised account of slavery days. Not at all. They loved it. In a letter to Edwin Björkman, state director for North Carolina, in May 1937, associate director of the FWP in Washington, George Cronyn wrote: 'Mr Lomax and I found the story of Aunt Betty Cofer of great inter-est and well told. It has a rich human flavor and presents an authentic picture of the period.'

'Mr Lomax' was John A. Lomax, a musicologist and pioneering collector of (especially black) folk songs. Though nowhere near as lib-eral as his son John, he had written to state directors warning against ex-slave narratives that were nothing more than 'a commentary on the benevolent institution of slavery'. So his approval of the Betty Cofer piece remains a mystery.

Maybe white folklorists, however racially liberal and open to dis-interested inquiry into black cultural practice, could not escape their own cultural conditioning. Condescension to the African-American may simply have been too ingrained, perhaps derived from *Gone With the Wind* (1936) and Ulrich B. Phillips's standard history, *American Negro Slavery* (1918), in which the institution was explained in terms of the African-American's genetic and cultural backwardness.

7 May

Even though Richard Wright has broken with the Communist party, the FBI Director memoes the New York office to keep a Security Index Card on the African-American author

1945 Born on a plantation in 1908, the son of a share-cropper who abandoned the family soon after his birth, Wright went through a troubled upbringing and interrupted education in Mississippi before moving to Chicago in 1927, later finding work on the Federal Writers' Project (see 27 July). He joined the Communist party in 1933, after attending meetings at the local John Reed Club in order to make literary contacts.

Anyone familiar with *Native Son* (1940), in which the novel's protagonist gets driven around Chicago by two wealthy white communist slummers, would know that Richard Wright's feelings towards the American Communist party were a far cry from simple adulation. In real-life Chicago (and later in New York) he found race and politics often to be at cross purposes. He often felt condescended to by the whites in the party, while the blacks denounced him as a bourgeois intellectual.

Wright left the party in 1942, but didn't make the rift public until 1944, when he published an essay over two issues of *The Atlantic Monthly*, in which he argued that – both home and abroad – communist persecution of its supposed opponents was more subtle and merciless than white persecution of black in the American South.

The FBI, which had long targeted Wright as a dangerous radical, added a photostat of the *Atlantic* essay to his file. At first the New York office considered calling him in for interview, intending to turn him as an informer against the local party, but then they changed their minds, since (as the Special Agent in Charge wrote to J. Edgar Hoover) Wright's decision was motivated by 'the Communist Party's failure to be sufficiently radical and militant with respect to the advancement of the Negro'.

Hoover approved New York's decision. 'In view of the militant attitude of the subject toward the Negro problem … you should submit a recommendation for the preparation of a Security Index Card in this case.'* What that meant was the FBI would continue to regard Wright as an enemy of the people.

---

* SAC (Special Agent in Charge), New York City, to Director, FBI, 26 February 1945; John Edgar Hoover to SAC, New York, 7 May 1945. http://foia.fbi.gov/rnwright/rnwright1a.pdf, 67c.

A year later, Wright left the United States for Paris. He would never return to his native country.

8 May

Nobbled

1962 Most novelists have their rituals. Few have been as obsessively ritual about the dates of starting, delivering, and publishing their work as Dick Francis.

Francis was born in Pembrokeshire in 1920 of semi-gentrified stock. His father was a prosperous dealer in horseflesh, and the child grew up surrounded by the beasts that would be the most important thing in his life. Infant Dick won his first race aged eight, and left school at fifteen, intending to be a jockey. A sudden growth and weight spurt in his teens meant that his chosen line would be 'jump', not 'flat' – the sport of kings and midgets. Francis may have been an unusual child in wanting to grow up but not to grow.

Of military-service age when war broke out, Francis volunteered for the cavalry but was recruited into the RAF – first as a non-commissioned engine-fitter and then, after much pestering on his part, as a pilot. He got his wings, and his pips, in 1944. In his autobiography, he says that he was actively involved in the Dambuster raid. Since that heroic event took place in 1943, he was not – unless as a civilian stowaway. In fact his war service was disappointingly uneventful.

Not, it must be said, from any lack of personal pluck. The career he chose on leaving the service in 1947 meant at least one bone-breaking fall a season and bruises all the way. On his marriage, in the same year, 1947, the groom's right arm was in a sling. Francis would break his collar bone nine times in his riding career – a recurrent injury that eventually drove him out of the sport.

His wife Mary was a graduate in modern languages, a teacher and a woman of extraordinary energy (even after a bout of polio in 1949) and of volubly right-wing views. There would be two children to the marriage. 1947 was a good year in every way for Francis, with sixteen wins and the woman of his life.

Francis was always reckoned in the top ten of his profession, and as champion jockey in 1953–4 he rode for the Queen Mother. But a year later Francis's life, as he liked to say, 'ended'. Everything else would be afterlife. It was a dramatic final act. In the 1955 Grand National, riding for the QM and leading the field by many lengths, Francis's horse, Devon, mysteriously collapsed only yards short of the finishing line. Francis had never won the National, the peak of a jump-jockey's career. His disappointment was bitter.

Was Devon nobbled? Perhaps; it's a recurrent theme in Francis's thrillers. But the most likely explanation seems to have been a gigantic fart that was so explosive as to prostrate the unluckily flatulent beast.

Francis retired, having ridden 2,305 races and 345 winners. In his retirement he turned to authorship. His first racing-world thriller, *Dead Cert*, came out in 1962. He would thereafter, until 2001, produce one a year.

According to the novelist himself, he was no Henry James: 'I start at Chapter 1, page 1, and plod on to THE END.' Starting gates and finishing lines made him comfortable. His invariable practice was to begin a new book on New Year's Day, and deliver the MS to Michael Joseph on 8 May for publication in September.

According to Julian Symons (the critic who made crime fiction critically respectable), 'Francis has been overpraised'. One of the more famous overpraisers is Philip Larkin, who declared Francis 'always 20 times more readable than the average Booker entry'. Francis was also a favourite with Kingsley Amis, Queen Elizabeth II, and, of course, his employer, her mum.

Dick and Mary Francis, both broken in body, retired to Florida in their last years. Graham Lord's flagrantly 'unauthorised' biography, published in 1999, alleged outright that Mary ghosted every one of the 'Dick Francis' novels. According to Lord, she confirmed his thesis, telling him that her authorship was suppressed in order to preserve the 'taut … masculine' feel of the works.

9 May

Everyman's publisher dies; Everyman books live on

1926 Joseph Mallaby Dent was born in 1849 in Darlington, the tenth child of a house-painter. Having been apprenticed as a printer – in which trade he showed little skill – young Joseph went to London in

1867, where he set up shop in the book business (principally book-binding, at which he had much skill).

Dent was moderately prosperous, but in 1887 his property burned down and, in his rebuilt premises, he launched Dent & Co. in 1888. In the 1890s, he established himself as one of the more energetic of the new generation of British publishers. By this stage he had already raised the standards of the binding and illustration of popular books. In this decade, Dent put out the 40-volume 'Temple Shakespeare', edited by Israel Gollancz, with title-pages illustrated by Walter Crane, at one shilling a volume. As Jonathan Rose records in his *Oxford Dictionary of National Biography* essay on Dent, 'the series was to sell 5 million copies over the next forty years'.

Always passionate about cheap series reprints (especially of fiction – he was, from childhood, a passionate lover of Scott), Dent, in collaboration with Ernest Rhys, established the Everyman Library in 1906. The first volume was Boswell's *Life of Samuel Johnson*, which Dent had first come across, aged 15, in a chapel mutual improvement society.

The Universal Education Act of 1870 had brought into play a whole new constituency of readers – most of them unable to afford the high price of new books or of commercial library subscription. The initial aim of the Everyman project was to put, and keep, in print 1,000 of the classic works of world literature, at one shilling a volume (150 were published in the first year; the thousandth title did not see the light of print until 1956). It was Rhys who proposed the epigraph, published on the flyleaf of every volume (from the medieval morality play, *Everyman*):

Everyman, I will go with thee
and be thy guide,
In thy most need to go
by thy side.

Particular attention was paid to the bindings and endpapers of J.M. Dent books – he was among the first London publishers to have an instantly recognisable 'house style'. Despite the superior production, and the low cost, the series was phenomenally successful. Dent was obliged to build a new printing house (the Temple Press) to meet demand.

As Rose records:

Dent has been criticized for his over-reverent, conservative, petit bourgeois tastes in literature. (He always pronounced it *litter-chah*, his employee Frank Swinnerton recalled.) Since the early Everyman volumes were reprints of out-of-copyright texts, they inevitably represented the standard canon of Greek, Roman, English, American, and western European classics. By 1956 the firm's editorial director admitted that many of the Victorian war-horses had already become anachronisms. With puritanical fastidiousness, Dent blocked the admission of Tobias Smollett and Moll Flanders to Everyman's Library. Yet in other respects the series was remarkably inclusive, embracing the Russian classics, the great books of India, and an impressive range of female novelists. (Dent himself wrote the introduction to Elizabeth Gaskell's *Cranford*, one of his personal favourites.) A Liberal nonconformist, Dent was inspired by an almost religious mission to bring culture to the masses.

By the time of Dent's death, on 9 May 1926, 20 million Everyman volumes had been sold. The series, after many mutations, survives.

10 May

Bibliocaust

1933 Just six weeks after the Nazis achieved a majority in the parliament and Hitler assumed the chancellorship, loyal student associations combined to organise the first public book-burnings of what would become the Third Reich, in the Opernplatz in Berlin's Unter den Linden Strasse. The aim of the exercise was symbolic rather than in any way methodically censorious.

The SA (Ernst Röhm's brown-shirted stormtroopers) supplied a guard of honour; brass bands played. It was night, and the students entered as a torchlit parade. The event was choreographed and photographed by the newly formed Ministry of Propaganda. A large scaffold was erected for the incineration itself, which was ritually performed. Representative students would advance towards the flame to intone their *Feuersprüche* – fire oath – before casting the anathematised 'un-German' volume into the flames. The whole event was presided over by Josef Goebbels (himself a novelist).

After the burning of the Reichstag (27 February 1933), the May book-burning was imitated in university cities over the whole of Germany. It demonstrated, forcibly, the control over the mind of the country that the new government (still for the moment nominally democratic – the Nazis had been voted into power) would enforce. Works regarded as Marxist or decadent ('*Asphaltliteratur*') or by Jewish writers were methodically targeted. Heine was everywhere burned. Even statues to him were pulled down.

The images of what the book historian Matthew Fishburn calls the 'Bibliocaust' were publicised in newspapers and newscasts across the world. In Britain, protest solidified as the 'Library of the Burned Books', an association under the international presidency of H.G. Wells, Romain Rolland, Heinrich Mann and Lion Feuchtwanger (all notable 'burnees'). An exhibition of the 'Burned Books' was put on display in Paris in May 1934. As their literature proclaimed:

> Among the books which were burned or suppressed in Germany were such classics as the entire works of Heinrich Heine, and various writings by Lessing, Voltaire, Einstein and Freud. Further the novels of such modern authors as Heinrich Mann, E.M. Remarque, Lion Feuchtwanger, and Jacob Wassermann and the historical works of Emil Ludwig and Mehring were also destroyed.

In the longer term the Nazi Bibliocaust had the perverse (for the book-burners) effect of liberalising the British and American book world – as a demonstration of democratic liberty. Judge Woolsey's ruling in the US in 1934 that Joyce's *Ulysses* was not obscene and the uninhibited publication of the work by The Bodley Head in the UK in 1936 can plausibly be seen as responses to Nazi censorship.

More dramatic was the ostentatious display and wide circulation of James Murphy's translation of *Mein Kampf* (*My Struggle*) in the mid- to late 1930s. Hitler's book received a sales boost in the UK after the outbreak of war and was at one point, in 1941, listed as a bestseller. Its production was halted not by any action of the authorities but by a Luftwaffe raid on the publisher, Hutchinson, in early 1942, which destroyed the stereo plates. It is not recorded whether the bombs in question were high explosive or incendiary.

11 May

Faulkner's Go Down, Moses is published

1942 Originally appearing as *Go Down, Moses, and other Stories*, the book would be described more accurately as a novel in seven movements. Spanning roughly 70 years from just before the Civil War to 1940, the stories trace the life of Isaac (Ike) McCaslin. A central narrative strand is Ike's initiation into the mysteries of hunting by Sam Fathers, son of a Native American father and slave mother. In the two chapters, 'The Old People' and 'The Bear' (often read and studied apart as Faulkner's most admired short story), Ike learns not just how to hunt, but to respect the wilderness as a spiritual as well as physical place.

The book's title comes from another kind of spiritual:

Go down, Moses,
Way down in Egypt land,
Tell old Pharaoh,
Let my people go.

So a crucial element in the book's historical register is the blacks' emancipation from slavery, while remaining in effect captive to that form of indentured servitude called share-cropping. The whites are similarly resistant to change in their attitude to the blacks. They no longer treat them as animals, but maintain a paternalistic stance towards them, amounting almost to condescension.

The irony underlying all this superiority is that Lucius Quintus Carothers, the original McCaslin, had an alliance with a slave woman that produced an alternative offspring to his white family. Yet not even Lucius's great, great, great grandson (and Ike's cousin) Roth Edmunds can escape the fateful legacy of racial bias. Until he is seven, he plays, eats and even sleeps with his black relative Henry Beauchamp:

Then one day the old curse of his fathers, the old haughty ancestral pride based not on any value but on an accident of geography, stemmed not from courage and honor but from wrong and shame, descended to him.

12 May

As Kenneth Tynan lauds Look Back in Anger *in the Sunday*
Observer, *a 'small miracle in British culture' ensues*

1956 The first performance of John Osborne's play took place at
the Royal Court theatre, Sloane Square, under the auspices of the
newly formed English Stage Society. Their inaugural plays were, like
Osborne's, aggressively anti-English.

Look Back in Anger is a foundation text (along with Colin Wilson's
The Outsider and Kingsley Amis's *Lucky Jim*) of the so-called 'Angry
Young Man' movement (the phrase is attributed to Harold Hobson,
then theatre critic on the *Sunday Times*).

The play's core is a savage denunciation of middle-class England –
principally via the dissident, twenty-something hero, Jimmy Porter.
Osborne anatomises him in the opening stage direction:

> He is a disconcerting mixture of sincerity and cheerful malice, of
> tenderness and freebooting cruelty; restless, importunate, full of
> pride, a combination which alienates the sensitive and insensi-
> tive alike.

Jimmy is searingly intelligent, the (drop-out) product of a 'university
which is not even redbrick, but white tile'. Proletarian by self-assertion,
he is something of a cultural snob – liking only traditional jazz, 9d
Sunday newspapers (i.e. the *Observer*) and good books. Less 'discon-
certing' than – in the preferred American phrase (as immortalised in
James Dean's *Rebel without a Cause* (1955)) – 'crazy mixed up'.

The challenging task of capturing Osborne's explosive ingredients
was entrusted, on the first run, to Kenneth Haigh; two years later
Richard Burton played Jimmy on film, to an audience of millions.

Literary movements typically require a helpful push from the critical establishment to give them shape and impetus. The critical reception of *Look Back in Anger* was largely confused and nervous. *Waiting
for Godot*, produced the year before, had earlier rattled the London
theatrical press out of its comfortable stock responses.

Typical was Philip Hope-Wallace in the *Manchester Guardian* who
labelled *Look Back in Anger* 'a strongly felt but rather muddled first
drama', and Patrick Gibbs in the *Daily Telegraph* who thought it 'a work
of some power, uncertainly directed'. The uncertainty (and, arguably,

the muddle) was among the critics. *The Times* (grandly anonymous) thundered negatively: 'his first play has passages of good violent writing, but its total gesture is altogether inadequate.'

Osborne's gesture, of course, was two fingers to everything *The Times* stood for.

One critic – in the same twenties age group as Porter and Osborne – had no uncertainty. Already hailed as the most powerful theatre critic since George Bernard Shaw, Kenneth Tynan lauded the play uncompromisingly in the *Observer* (12 May). Astor's paper was Porter's Sunday reading. In 1956 – virtually alone in Fleet Street – it condemned Anthony Eden's Suez adventure; indifferent to the circulation loss that its lack of 'patriotism' incurred.

Tynan began by recalling Somerset Maugham's comment on the dramatis personae of Amis's *Lucky Jim*: 'they are scum.' He then went on to assert: '*Look Back in Anger* presents post-war youth as it really is.' More importantly, Tynan saw in Porter not just a 'character' but a portent. Porterism was a movement on the move:

> The Porters of our time deplore the tyranny of 'good taste' and refuse to accept 'emotional' as a term of abuse; they are classless, and they are also leaderless. Mr Osborne is their first spokesman in the English theatre.

There were, Tynan calculated with mocking pseudo-precision, some 6,733,000 Porters in Britain: 'that is the number of people in this country between twenty and thirty.' Tynan himself was in that army: 'I doubt if I could love anyone who did not wish to see *Look Back in Anger*. It is the best young play of the decade.'

13 May

De Quincey writes to Wordsworth

1803 If there were an award for the most successful fan letter in English literature, it should go to Thomas de Quincey, later famous as the author of the classic Romantic memoir, *Confessions of an English Opium-Eater* (1822).

Born in 1785, De Quincey's upbringing was chaotic and wholly unpromising. Precocious but neurotic, he ran away from school and, at the age of eighteen, near starvation in London, he penned a letter to Wordsworth – a writer whom, on the strength of the *Lyrical Ballads*, he regarded as a god. On 13 May 1803, he drafted the letter to Wordsworth in his diary. It began:

> What I am going to say, I know, would seem strange to most men: and to most men therefore I would *not* say it; but to you I will, because your feelings do not follow the current of the world. From the time when I first saw the 'Lyrical Ballads' I made a resolution to obtain (if I could) the friendship of their author.

It was an extraordinarily brash letter from a young nobody to a great somebody. De Quincey probably thought so himself, and did not dispatch the letter for some weeks. 'Gradually', as De Quincey's biographer, Robert Morrison, records:

> he rewrote it, and finally, on the afternoon of 31 May, he completed an augmented and, in parts, thoroughly revised version. Copied and sealed by twenty minutes before 4 o'clock, Thomas took it straight to the post office and mailed it to Wordsworth care of his publisher Longman in Paternoster Row, London.

'What claim', he wrote, 'can I urge to a fellowship such as yours … beaming (as it does) with genius so wild and so magnificent? I dare not say that I too have some spark of that heavenly fire which blazes there.'

There was no reply for two months. The familiar fate of all such letters. But it had been held up in the publisher's office. Wordsworth did not receive it until 27 July and wrote back almost the same day, saying: 'I am already kindly disposed to you.'

It was the foundation of the most important relationship in De Quincey's life. A few years later he, too, would settle in Dove Cottage, Grasmere (the other poet's home), living and writing there for a decade. It was here, in the heart of the literary Lake District, that he addicted himself to the drug that he describes so lyrically (and at times so gothically) in his most famous work.

14 May

John Smith lands in Virginia

1607 Other English adventurers had tried to gain a foothold in the New World, but none had succeeded. Now three shiploads of settlers dropped anchor around 40 miles up the James River, Virginia. This time the English had come for good.

With them was a former pirate and mercenary soldier who had arrived with his spoils back in London just in the nick of time to sign up for the Virginia adventure. He was John Smith, whose experience, love of action, and independent means recommended him to the London backers of the Virginia Company. Less fond of him were his social betters on the voyage. They took his strong-minded decisiveness for mutiny, and had him confined below decks for much of the trip.

Imagine their chagrin, then, when they opened their sealed orders on landing to find that the Company had appointed Smith to sit on the council of the plantation. So effective was he as a leader that he was elected its president the following year.

Now he is remembered for how he wrote about the experience. Like *Mourt's Relation* (see 15 November), Smith's *True Relation* of the settlement (1608) was a booster's tract, full of the natural plenty of the new country, and the tractability of the natives. Exploring the Chickahominy River, they are greeted by 'the people in all places kindely intreating us, daunsing and feasting us with strawberries, Mulberries, Bread, Fish, and other their Countrie provisions whereof we had plenty'. It's like the ending of a Shakespeare comedy.

And Instead of being held captive by Powhatan and his warlike tribe, as in his later, formal history of the settlement, *The General History of Virginia* (1624), Smith is a guest, feasted with 'great Platters of sundrie Victuals', while exchanging information with the chief on the geography of their respective territories.

Without the captivity, of course, there can be no dramatic intervention of Pocahontas (see 5 April). In the *True Relation* she is 'a child of tenne yeares old' of great 'wit and spirit', who rather than saving his life, had been sent by her father to plead for the release of some natives held captive at the English fort.

15 May

Amazon's stream strengthens to flood force

1997 On this day Amazon.com (AMZN) was first quoted on the NASDAQ. The firm was founded by the 30-year-old Jeff Bezos in 1994. A graduate of Princeton (Phi Beta Kappa), his background was in finance and computers, not books. Bezos started the company, as young Silicon Valley pioneers traditionally did, in his garage. Presumptuously, he called it 'Amazon' after the largest stream in the world.

Spurning San Francisco, the heart of the new online industry, he went further north up the coast to Seattle. Here he set up not the first, but what would soon become the biggest, web-bookstore: Amazon.com.

Bezos's Amazon came on stream in 1995, at the same time that the home-based desktop computer became widely internet-connectable. Amazon soon diversified from books to a multi-product electronic-order/postal-supply retail business, combining old and new technologies. By cutting out the middleman bookshop, it allowed the purchaser to order from a millions-strong catalogue with large discounts. Efficient stock control was a further edge that the webstore had over the walk-in store.

After some bumpy years (the dot.com bomb rocked it) in which shares dropped as low as $1.50 from the initial $18 at the NASDAQ launch, the company's value has grown inexorably. Bezos always maintained that he was in for the very long haul and warned investors to stay away if they did not want to stick with him. By 1999, he was *Time* magazine's 'Person of the Year'.

On 31 December 2008, Amazon was entered on the S&P 100 index, as one of the elite corps of American business enterprises. The following year, 2009, saw the launch of its Kindle reader – a delivery system that, it was expected, would cut out the need for physical delivery of book products. Given Bezos's record, it would be a reasonable bet that he will succeed, making himself in the process the most influential bookman since Gutenberg.

16 May

Burgess reviews Burgess (favourably)

1963 The most famous writer to review his own works behind a protective mask of anonymity was Walter Scott, who gave a lengthy and favourable notice to his first series of *Tales of my Landlord* in the January 1817 issue of the *Quarterly Review* (the Tory journal that Scott himself had set up, with John Murray, in opposition to Archibald Constable's *Edinburgh Review*).

Later in the century Walt Whitman shamelessly (and again anonymously) puffed his first volume, *Leaves of Grass*, in 1855. As late as 1876, in an anonymous article in the *New Jersey Post* (26 January), Whitman was still promoting Whitman to an insufficiently appreciative American readership and editors who mistreated his genius with, as Whitman believed, 'determined denial, disgust and scorn'.

In the 20th century the most flamboyant self-reviewer was Anthony Burgess. In the early stages of his literary career Burgess picked up work as a reviewer for the *Yorkshire Post* – a paper that then had influential literary pages. Burgess's first novels appeared under the pseudonym 'Joseph Kell'.

Unaware of the relationship, the *Post's* literary editor gave Burgess Kell's *Inside Mr Enderby* to review. Burgess, who loved literary mischief, duly produced a sagacious review, published on 16 May 1963. Mr Kell, he blandly informed his readers (with a double meaning that only he appreciated), was 'a quiet and cunning novelist'. Readers, however, should be warned:

> *Inside Mr Enderby* is, in many ways, a dirty book. It is full of bowel blasts and flatulent borborygms, emetic meals … and halitosis … those of my readers with tender stomachs are advised to leave it alone.

In the context of post-*Chatterley* 'liberation' such warnings were, of course, an incitement to buy. Dirty books were in vogue.

Burgess's editor was not amused by the jape and Burgess–Kell was sacked. In a 1992 essay, 'Confessions of the Hack Trade', and in late-life interviews, Burgess justified his deceit with allusions to Walter Scott, Swift's self-lacerating 'Verses on the Death of Dr Swift', and the persuasive argument that the author of a novel 'knows its faults better than any casual reader'.

It is suspected that the so-called 'reviews' invited on Amazon.com have revived, to epidemic proportions, the practice of self-puffery – the vast bulk of it infinitely less witty than Burgess on Kell.

17 May

Héloise is buried alongside Abelard in the cemetery at the nunnery that he had built for her

1164 It is Europe's oldest tale of romantic love. The theologian Peter Abelard (1079–1142) had set up a school of philosophy on the Left Bank of the Seine, opposite the cathedral school of Notre Dame de Paris. One of his students, over twenty years his junior, was the gifted, beautiful Héloise (1101–64), whose care and education had been supervised by her doting uncle Fulbert, a canon of the cathedral.

Of course they fell in love. She got pregnant. As so often with academic couples, their child naming was eccentric. They called their baby Astrolabe, after the last word in astronomical technology, recently introduced from Spain. When her guardian found out, he was furious, but after Abelard begged his forgiveness, and his permission to marry Héloise, Uncle Fulbert relented.

They did marry, but entirely against Héloise's wishes. She argued that the publicity that the marriage would give to their affair would deprive Abelard of his job, and the world of a great teacher and philosopher. Leaving Astrolabe with Abelard's sister, she went to stay in the convent at Argenteuil, north-west of Paris.

Then things took a really nasty turn. Suspecting that Abelard had abandoned his niece, Fulbert conspired with his kinsmen to break into Abelard's lodgings and (as the victim himself put it circumspectly) 'cut off those parts of my body with which I had done that which was the cause of their sorrow'. Now Abelard too retired from the world, taking refuge in the Abbey of Saint Denis, where he became a monk. Later he would return to teaching (and intense theological controversy), but that's another story.

These events entered literature in a remarkable series of five long letters they exchanged after their separation, in which she reiterates her passionate longing for him while chafing at the cloisters, and he admits his inability to forget her, though imploring her to turn to God in her distress.

The narrative of their affair started nothing less than a whole new literary fashion, the convention of romantic love. The second part of *The Romance of the Rose* (Jean de Meun, 1275), that classic of courtly love, picks up her objections to marriage, radically altering them to the accusation that the institution forces sex on the wife through the 'mastership' of the husband, rather than through spontaneous mutual passion, thus giving Chaucer the idea for his Wife of Bath in *The Canterbury Tales* (some time after 1380).

François Villon worked Héloise into his 'Where are the snows of yesteryear' lament, his 'Ballade des Dames du Temps Jadis' (1533; see 8 January):

> Où est la très sage Helloïs,
> Pour qui fut chastré et puis moyne
> Pierre Esbaillart [Abelard] à Saint-Denis? …
> Mais où sont les neiges d'antan?*

Their story caught the imagination even of such an austere moralist as Alexander Pope. His 'Eloisa to Abelard' (1716) picks up Jean de Meun's theme, allocating over twenty (out of 366) decasyllabic lines to her complaint against marriage: rather than wife, she says, 'make me mistress to the man I love'.

Meanwhile, back in real life, Abelard's only further contact with Héloise had been when he managed to establish her as Prioress of the Oratory of the Paraclete, which he had founded north-west of Troyes. On his death his remains were carried there, to be watched over by his lover until she too joined him in the tomb.

---

* 'Where is the very wise Héloise, / For whom was castrated and then made a monk / Pierre Esbaillart [Abelard] in Saint Denis? … / But where are the snows of yesteryear?'

18 May

Proust, Joyce, Picasso, Stravinsky and Diaghilev sit down to the modernist dinner from hell

1922 It was modernism's *annus mirabilis* – *Ulysses*, *The Waste Land* and *Jacob's Room* published; *À la recherche du temps perdu* finally brought to its conclusion. Minor tremors included the first night of Stravinsky's ballet *Le Renard*, performed by Diaghilev's Ballets Russes in Paris, and the ambitious dinner party that followed.

It was the brainchild of Sydney and Violet Schiff, a wealthy British couple living in Paris at the time. The idea was to celebrate the ballet, but also to bring together the notables of modernist writing and painting who had yet to meet. This meant Stravinsky and Diaghilev, of course, but also Erik Satie, Picasso, the shy James Joyce and the (by now) extremely retiring Marcel Proust, together with a back-up cast of assorted aristocrats, writers, painters, musicians and Bloomsbury's own Clive Bell.*

Anxious anticipation of the grand occasion seems to have prompted some over-preparation: Joyce arrived drunk and later slumped over the dinner table asleep. Proust had been so daunted at the thought of the dinner that he downed a dose of adrenalin that scorched his throat and kept him complaining about pain in his stomach for most of the evening.

Conversation between the greats didn't go as planned. Proust told Stravinsky how much he admired Beethoven. Stravinsky, anxiously anticipating the first reviews of his ballet, retorted, 'I detest Beethoven', and turned away. Later in the evening Proust asked a now-revived Joyce, 'Do you like truffles?' Joyce answered, 'Yes I do.'

But what else did the Schiffs expect? What do geniuses 'say' anyway, outside their work? Even now, literary festivals are premised on the belief that if you kidnap authors for an hour or two, you'll capture some of the magic of their creativity. But the audience's curiosity (and hence the author's answers) is usually limited to issues of mechanics and scheduling, like 'What time of day do you start writing, and for how long?' When artists talk not to their public but to other artists, competitiveness makes them defensive, and talk strays even further from the works themselves.

---

* Richard Davenport Hines, *A Night at the Majestic: Proust and the Great Modernist Dinner Party*, London: Faber & Faber, 2006.

19 May

Mounted settlers from surrounding towns attack the natives at Peskeompskut; language poet Susan Howe scrambles the history

1676 The Indians had gathered at Peskeompskut, at the falls on the Connecticut River, near present-day Montague, Massachusetts, to fish, trade and plan raids against the surrounding English settlements. At dawn on 19 May Captain William Turner led 160 English soldiers to attack the camp, killing over 200 natives (mainly women and children, though earlier histories omit this fact) and setting fire to their wigwams.

But when a native band from a nearby camp got to hear of the massacre, they moved in on the English to cut off their escape route, killing 37 soldiers and wounding others. Eventually the rest got back to safety, apart from the Reverend Hope Atherton and seven or eight others. These men got lost, holding out for three or four days in the woods until hunger forced them to surrender to the Indians. But the natives tied straw around them, set it alight and made them run until consumed by fire. Only Atherton was spared, because (as a contemporary report put it) when 'a little man with a black coat and without a hat came toward [the natives] they were afraid and ran away, thinking it was the Englishman's God'.

This is the 'background', much of it provided by Susan Howe herself, to her postmodern treatment of the events in 'Hope Atherton's Wanderings', in her *Singularities* (1990). Here is how the 'poem' goes in part:

Prest try to set after grandmother
Revived by and laid down left by ...

Clog nutmeg abt noon
Scraping cano muzzell
Foot path sand and so
Gravel rubbish vandal
Horse flesh ryal table
Sand enemys flood sun
Danielle Warnare Servt
Turner Dalls Fight us
Next wearer April One

In fact many of these words – though not in this order – are taken from a 19th-century history of the frontier settlement of Deerfield by George Sheldon, and describe the flight of another fugitive from the Falls Fight, one Jonathan Wells. Here is part of it with the relevant words italicised:

> J.W. was glad to leave him, lest he sh^d be a *clog* or hindrance to him. Mr W. grew faint, & once when ye Indians *prest* him, he was near fainting away, but by eating a *nutmeg* (which his *grandmother* gave him on going out) he was *revived*.

Wounded in the leg, he crosses a stream using his musket as a crutch, but for fear of wetting the lock, puts the *muzzell* end into the water instead, which, filled with so much *gravel* and *sand*, renders the gun useless when the natives come at him across the river in a *cano*. And so on.

So Howe offers one 'background' narrative to contextualise her poem, but actually raids another, hidden source that she doesn't want her readers to know about – unlike Pound or Williams, for example (see 19 February, 4 and 13 July), who wanted their fragments like these to tease the reader into looking up their sources. But Howe's sources have none of that exemplary status. They are not 'a shrine and a monument' but time-bound, patriarchal texts resting on the assumption that it was the 'manifest destiny' of white Europeans to bring order to the wilderness. They cry out for deconstruction. Howe goes one better by dismantling them as well, concentrating on the sounds and rhythms of the words while preventing them from forming any coherent narrative at all.

They named the falls after Captain Turner, who led the murderous, incompetent raid in the first place.

20 May

W.H. Auden becomes an American citizen

1946 Despite the false promise of the Munich Agreement, many British people sensed towards the end of 1938 that war with Germany was on its way. So when in the New Year of 1939 W.H. Auden and his friend Christopher Isherwood sailed for New York on board the steamer *Champlain*, it looked to many as though they were fleeing their threatened homeland for a (then) neutral country where they'd be safe.

Evelyn Waugh's reaction that Auden fled to the US 'at the first squeak of an air-raid warning' was typical of the poet's enemies.* Even friends like Stephen Spender reproached him for giving up the 'struggle'.† Spender, part-Jewish and therefore with more to fear from a successful German invasion, would stay behind and fight the Blitz as a fireman.

Auden thought England was provincial, that its political and aesthetic culture had declined along with its industry. America was no promised land for him, but at least New York, where he planned to settle, was cosmopolitan, in touch with the rest of the world. 'An artist ought either to live where he has live roots or where he has no roots at all', he told Louis MacNeice in 1940.‡

Of course he was welcomed by the New York literary community. Before long he was giving lectures and writing for the *New Yorker*. In the autumn of 1939 he had moved to Brooklyn, begun to attend services at the local Episcopal church, and taken up with a Brooklyn boy, Chester Kallman.§

By the end of the war it was clear that Auden's work had changed direction. He himself had repudiated much of his earlier work – particularly the communist invocations of history like 'Spain 1937' – and had re-established his Christian faith. But back in England all signs of an increasing conservatism were put down to his formal change of citizenship. Now the line of attack wasn't his cowardice and treachery. What preoccupied a younger generation of English critics was the depletion of energy and loss of focus in the poet's work following his emigration.

So John Wain claimed that the characteristically trenchant 'Auden line' had been smashed by his 'renunciation of English nationalism', while Philip Larkin lamented the loss of Auden's 'dominant and ubiquitous unease' when he absconded to America. 'At one stroke', Larkin proclaimed, 'he lost his key subject and emotion – Europe and the fear

---

* Richard Davenport-Hines, *Auden*, London: Minerva, 1996, p. 180.
† Stan Smith, 'Introduction', *The Cambridge Companion to W.H. Auden*, Cambridge University Press, 2004, p. 6.
‡ Cited in Davenport-Hines, *Auden*, p. 180.
§ Brad Lockwood, 'Remembering W. H. Auden', *Brooklyn Daily Eagle*, 29 September 2009.

of war – and abandoned his audience together with their common dialect and concerns.'*

21 May

Henry Pye is appointed Poet Laureate

1790 Henry James Pye (1745–1813) was made the king's poet on the death of his predecessor in the post, Thomas Warton. Neither is memorable. But of all the 22 poets who have held the post, Pye is routinely cited as the prime example of the mediocrity associated with the laureateship – versifying flunkey to the monarch. He is, along with Thomas Shadwell and William McGonagall, famous for his sublime badness. A sad kind of immortality.

When offered the laureate's post on Pye's death in 1813 Walter Scott was advised to turn it down by his patron, the Duke of Buccleuch, because 'it will stick to you like court [adhesive] plaister'. Scott took the advice and nominated Robert Southey – who went on to become the most ridiculed of laureates for his poem on the death of George III, 'A Vision of Judgment'. Its sole virtue was to inspire one the great (republican) satires, Byron's 'A Vision of Judgement'.

Pye's was – as laureateships have traditionally been – a political appointment. He was a friend to William Pitt, whose Whiggish-Toryish principles he shared. With revolution raging in France, a 'safe' laureate was desirable. The two greatest poets of the age – Robert Burns (radical, 'low', and Scottish) and William Cowper (barely sane) – were non-runners.

It was on Pye's retiring from Parliament, in 1790, that he was given the consolatory appointment. He had prepared himself for it, years before, with a sycophantically loyal ode 'On the Birth of the Prince of Wales' (the poem headed his major collection, *Poems on Various Subjects*, 1787) . Birthday poems were the principal task of the laureate and Pye did his worst in the genre.

Pye's major achievement in the office of laureate was to abolish the annual 'tierce of Canary wine' (or 'butt of sack') that traditionally went with the post. He had it commuted to a cash remuneration of £27 to supplement the £100 honorarium. The payment continued well

---

* Cited in Smith, 'Introduction', p. 7.

into the 20th century, although for nostalgic reasons the wine was also sometimes provided, ex gratia.

As a poet, Pye's major effort as laureate was an epic on the greatest of English kings, *Alfred* (1801). Appearing as it did at the same period as Coleridge and Wordsworth's *Lyrical Ballads*, it gives a fair demonstration of Pye's merits as a poet. The following is his description of Alfred burning the cakes:

> The objects round him, like the viewless air,
> Pass o'er his mind, nor leave an image there;
> Hence oft, with flippant tongue, the busy dame
> The reckless stranger's apathy would blame,
> Who, careless, let the flame those viands waste,
> His ready hunger ne'er refused to taste.
> Ah! little deeming that her pensive guest,
> High majesty, and higher worth, possess'd:
> Or that her voice presumptuous dared to chide
> Alfred, her country's sovereign, and its pride.

Pye's *Aerophorion* (1794) is, it is claimed, 'the first poem in English to celebrate hot-air ballooning'. Hot air would seem to be somehow appropriate.

22 May

Allen Lane launches Penguin Books

1935 The UK's first mass-market paperbacks were launched as Penguin Books (under the Bodley Head imprint) on this date. The first batch of ten were:

Ariel: a Shelley Romance – André Maurois
A Farewell to Arms – Ernest Hemingway
Poet's Pub – Eric Linklater
Madame Claire – Susan Ertz
The Unpleasantness at the Bellona Club – Dorothy L. Sayers
The Mysterious Affair at Styles – Agatha Christie
Twenty-Five – Beverley Nichols

William – E.H. Young
Gone to Earth – Mary Webb
Carnival – Compton Mackenzie

After a quickly aborted experiment with Woolworth's 3d and 6d department stores, Lane's stylish reprints (drawing on the talents of typogra-
phers and designers such as Eric Gill and Stanley Morison) established
themselves in conventional bookshop outlets. Penguins were, from the
first, paperbacks that sold like hardbacks, and in many cases were an
even more respectable imprint. For an author to be 'Penguined' was a
mark of high merit.

Allen Lane learned his publishing with his uncle John Lane (whose
surname he adopted), whose house put out the work of many of the
most distinguished writers of the late Victorian and Edwardian period
– most famously, perhaps, Oscar Wilde (who returned the compliment
by naming the suave butler in *The Importance of Being Earnest* 'Lane').
Allen Lane, in his early thirties at the time, claimed to have had the
inspiration for his paperback pocket books while standing on the platform of Exeter station, having just visited Agatha Christie and having
nothing to read.

Lane eschewed pictorial covers throughout his long career as Britain's
leading paperback publisher. He thought them vulgar. In America the
mass-market paperback pioneer was Robert de Graff, who launched
his 'Pocket Books' in 1939. His strategy was less to embed his product
in the traditional bookstore than to circumvent that outlet entirely. De
Graff's 25¢ Pocket Books were essentially 'drugstore' paperbacks. They
had eye-catching illustrated covers, newsprint-quality paper, and, typically, slapdash typography. They were designed to retail less like books
(items of civilised furniture) than short-life magazines. And not, necessarily, the more respectable kind of magazine.

23 May

John Banville throws a spanner in Ian McEwan's works

2005 There are no prizes for the most devastating review ever published. Were there one, the winner for this year (and arguably for the
first decade of the 21st century) would be that published on this day.

When Ian McEwan's novel *Saturday* was released in early summer 2005, the reviewers, British and American, fell over themselves to throw superlatives at it. 'Few literary events are today met with as much enthusiasm', crooned the *Boston Globe*, 'as the publication of a McEwan novel. *Saturday*, a brilliant and graceful hymn to the contented contemporary man, will be greeted with cheers.'

Quick to join in the cheering was the *Daily Telegraph* ('This is a rich book, sensuous and thoughtful'), the *New York Times* ('it's clear that with this volume, Mr McEwan has not only produced one of the most powerful pieces of post-9/11 fiction yet published, but also fulfilled that very primal mission of the novel: to show how we – a privileged few of us, anyway – live today'), the *Guardian* ('One of the most oblique but also most serious contributions to the post-9/11, post-Iraq war literature, it succeeds in ridiculing on every page the view of its hero that fiction is useless to the modern world'), and the *Spectator* ('*Saturday* is an exemplary novel, engrossing and sustained. It is undoubtedly McEwan's best'). Even the normally crusty *London Review of Books*, like the ranks of Tuscany, could scarce forbear to cheer (if somewhat sniffily):

> The customarily firm forward march of the narrative works surprisingly well with the more spaced-out requirements of a day-in-the-life story, and at its best the combination of precision and lyricism is very effective.

Praise indeed.

Saturday is, as the above reviewer notes, a circadian novel – like *Mrs Dalloway* and *Ulysses*. The Day in Question is 15 February 2003. On that day, across the world, there were demonstrations in protest against the imminent invasion of Iraq. That in London, organised by the Stop the War Coalition, was massive. Estimates of protestor attendance (overwhelmingly peaceful) ranged as high as two million.

McEwan's narrative follows 24 hours in the life of a brain surgeon, Henry Perowne, who lives in Fitzroy Square and carries out his operations at University College Hospital, 200 yards away across Tottenham Court Road. On Saturdays he plays squash in a gym at adjoining Huntley Street, and on this day he intends to pick up some smoked salmon in nearby Marylebone High Street, for a dinner party in the evening. His day is interrupted by the mustering of the demonstrators in Gower Street (by the hospital) and by a street accident that leads to home invasion. The hero is ambivalent about the rights and wrongs of the coming war.

Saturday looked set to win the Man-Booker prize for 2005. There was not a bad word to be found against it in the opinion-forming prints. Its progress to triumph in October (when the Prize is awarded) was, however, stalled (at least in popular opinion) by a devastating review of the book by fellow novelist John Banville, in the *New York Review of Books*, in May. After a devastatingly sarcastic summary of the narrative, Banville concluded:

> *Saturday* is a dismayingly bad book. The numerous set pieces – brain operations, squash game, the encounters with Baxter, etc. – are hinged together with the subtlety of a child's Erector Set. The characters too, for all the nuzzling and cuddling and punching and manhandling in which they are made to indulge, drift in their separate spheres, together but never touching, like the dim stars of a lost galaxy.

There were protests (not least from the chair of the Man-Booker committee, who wrote a letter contradicting Banville's estimate). Ironically, *Saturday* did not win the Man-Booker that year. John Banville's *The Sea* did.

24 May

Guy Burgess tries to telephone W.H. Auden just before defecting to Moscow

1951 Auden was passing through London on his way from New York to Ischia, where he and his lover, the American poet and librettist Chester Kallman, shared a house. While staying with Natasha and Stephen Spender in St John's Wood, he was called on the phone by Guy Burgess, ex-Eton, ex-Cambridge, ex-MI6 and (just about to be) ex-Foreign Office. Auden was out.

The next day Burgess called again. Once again, Auden was out. On returning, having 'evidently dined well', according to Spender's biographer (and one of this book's authors), he was asked if he would

return the call. '"Do I have to?" Auden drawled: "he's always drunk".'[*]
By this time Burgess was on his way out of the country. Having telegraphed a message to his mother that he was off on a Mediterranean
holiday, he and Donald Maclean boarded a cross-channel steamer at
Southampton. Both men were defecting to the Soviet Union.

As a younger man, Auden had liked to think of himself as a sort of
spy – poetry itself, he thought, was like espionage, transporting ideas
across borders – but why would the cleverest and most dangerous real-
life spy of the Cold War era try twice to reach him before leaving the
country for good?

Richard Davenport-Hines, who tells this story in his biography of
Auden, conjectures that because of 'his dislike of English liberalism',
Auden 'apparently had the same emblematic importance to Burgess
as for thousands of other men of their generation'. Sexual orientation
came into the equation too. 'This affair provoked fears that national
security was threatened by "crypto homosexuals"', writes Davenport-
Hines, 'and the Home Secretary and other officials instituted a campaign of arrests ... which amounted to a sexual witch-hunt and ruined
many lives in the 1950s.'

Auden and the Spenders didn't escape so neatly. Both were plagued
by the press, once the story of Burgess's phone calls had got out –
Spender claiming (as late as 10 June) that he found it 'very difficult'
to believe Burgess a Soviet spy, and Auden investigated, even back in
Ischia, by the local *carabinieri*.[†]

25 May

*Oscar Wilde is convicted of gross indecency and sentenced to
two years' hard labour*

1895 The downfall of Oscar Wilde began with a spelling mistake.
On 18 February 1895 the Marquess of Queensberry – boxing legisla-
tor, bully, and near-madman – left a calling card at the writer's club,
addressed to him as a 'posing somdomite'. Wilde had been conducting
a flagrantly public affair with the Marquess's son, Bosie.

---

[*] John Sutherland, *Stephen Spender: The Authorized Biography*, London and New York:
Viking, 2004, p. 360.
[†] Richard Davenport-Hines, *Auden*, London: Minerva, 1995, p. 276.

The card was, technically, a public declaration. Wilde, disastrously, chose to take offence and – idealistically – to strike a blow for the love that dared not speak its name (but could spell it correctly). He brought a charge against the Marquess for criminal libel.

The trial began on 3 April 1895. Wilde fenced brilliantly with the leading defence lawyer of the day, Edward Carson. It was as witty a performance as in his current West End comedy, *The Importance of Being Earnest*. But wit, paradox and epigram can wilt in the heavy atmosphere of court. Asked if he had kissed a certain young male servant, Wilde retorted that he had not, adding: 'He was a particularly *plain* boy.' He got his laugh, and lost his case.

A warrant was issued for Wilde's arrest immediately after the collapse of the criminal libel trial. He was arrested at the Cadogan Hotel. It inspired Betjeman's comic-pathetic poem:

> A thump, and a murmur of voices—
>   ('Oh why must they make such a din?')
> As the door of the bedroom swung open
>   And TWO PLAIN CLOTHES POLICEMEN came in:
> 'Mr Woilde, we 'ave come for tew take yew
>   Where felons and criminals dwell:
> We must ask yew tew leave with us quoietly
>   For this *is* the Cadogan Hotel.'

On 25 May, Wilde was sentenced to two years' hard labour for 'gross indecency' (sex with rent boys, principally). The provision in the law under which he was convicted had been passed through Parliament in 1885 by Henry Labouchère, an admirer of the playwright.

26 May

Born: iconographer of the Great Depression

1895 When Dorothea Lange abandoned studio photography for documentary work, she became the most literary of photographers – in both her method and her influence. In 1935 she teamed up with – then married – the Berkeley agricultural economist Paul Schuster Taylor. Their reports on the miserable living conditions of farm migrants in

California during the Depression would prompt the government to provide 'sanitary camps' for the Okies, give Pare Lorentz the idea for *The Plow That Broke the Plains* (1936), involve John Steinbeck in their campaign (see 5 October), and inspire *The Grapes of Wrath* (1939).

For Lange, the caption was almost as important as the photo. Once asked whether a picture should be left to speak for itself, she denied wanting to tell the viewer what to look for, but saw no reason not to offer relevant background. The caption 'Winter in New England' would be redundant to a winter scene in New England, 'but you could say, "this part of the country is … losing its population", or "People are leaving this part of the United States which was really the cradle of democratic principles"'. In other words 'background' was alright so long as it supplied a pessimistic historical generalisation.

Lange's photo captions in her and Taylor's field reports were highly evocative, almost poetic at times. In fact the narrow margins of her notebook break the lines up so that they look like an early poem by William Carlos Williams. To her question, 'Are you making a living?', one migrant in a Marysville, California, shanty town answered:

Oh, we're getting along
As good as us draggin'
Around people can expect
If you call it a livin'—

And following her inset description, 'Rag houses / Split open garbage cans', another added:

'ex service man raised decent like I was
raised by my father, No rag
houses then. I can't make it'—

This was powerful stuff, even without the pictures, but it had the force of portraying her subjects as victims of natural forces. This bias was strongest in her photograph of a Madonna-like woman cradling three children in a makeshift tent – the so-called 'Migrant Mother' – since reproduced over 10,000 times, and now an icon of the Depression as a whole.

This time she didn't wait for a quote, but used a succession of captions to sketch in her own 'background'. This was a mother of 'seven hungry children', she wrote, 'destitute in a pea pickers camp' after the crop failed in Nipomo, California. One caption affirmed that 'These people had just sold their tent to buy food', another that they had sold the tyres from their car.

None of this was true. Recent research has uncovered that, far from being a passive victim, the mother was a local organiser for the radical Cannery and Agricultural Industrial Workers' Union. On the day the picture was taken, her husband and two older boys had taken the radiator off their Hudson car to get it repaired at a local garage. So they hadn't had to sell the car tyres, and they hadn't sold their tent, and they weren't stuck in Nipomo. The next morning the family took off for Watsonville, 140 miles to the north along Highway 101, to work in the lettuce fields.

27 May

Cromwell returns, bloodily, from Ireland to be greeted, ironically, by Andrew Marvell

1650 Few war criminals have inspired great poems. Adolf Hitler, for example, inspired what must surely be the worst song lyrics ever: 'Adolf Hitlers Lieblingsblume ist das schlichte Edelweiss' ('Adolf Hitler's favourite flower is the simple Edelweiss' – Julie Andrews's as well, ironically, in the anti-Hitlerian *Sound of Music*).

After winning the Civil War in England, Cromwell – now Lord Protector – embarked on a campaign of conquest in Ireland, using his victorious, battled-trained army and its fearsomely advanced artillery.

The aim was to reduce Ireland to the status of a docile colony, dominated in course of time by a transplanted ruler class (the Ascendancy). For centuries after, Ireland would be what Gladstone called it, 'the thorn in England's side'.

Over 600,000 people – some 40 per cent of the Irish population – are estimated to have perished as a result of the three-year conflict. Notably brutal was the massacre of civilians at Drogheda in 1649. With Ireland subdued, Cromwell returned to England, making land on 27 May 1650. In honour of the event, the poet Andrew Marvell penned 'An Horatian Ode Upon Cromwell's Return From Ireland'. Marvell's loyalty had switched from the king to the Commonwealth, and the poem is supremely ambiguous. It opens:

The forward Youth that would appear
Must now forsake his Muses dear,
Nor in the Shadows sing
His Numbers languishing.

'Tis time to leave the Books in dust,
And oyl th'unused Armours rust:
Removing from the Wall
The Corslet of the Hall.

So restless Cromwell could not cease
In the inglorious Arts of Peace,
But through adventrous War
Urged his active Star.

And, like the three-fork'd Lightning, first
Breaking the Clouds where it was nurst,
Did through his own Side
His fiery way divide.

For 'tis all one to Courage high,
The Emulous or Enemy;
And with such, to inclose
Is more than to oppose.

Then burning through the Air he went,
And Pallaces and Temples rent ...

Is this praise (comparing Cromwell to the spear that mortified Christ, and the destroyer of 'Temples')? Is it awe? Or is it subtly veiled criticism? Being literature it can, of course, be all three. Cromwell's reaction to the poem is not recorded.

28 May

The first Hay Festival

1988 In Britain, literary festivals tended, until the late 20th century, to be both local and parochial – the kinds of things that took place in church halls. By the turn of the century, they had become big business, with between 150 and 200 major events attracting tens of thousands of visitors, commercial sponsorship, and strong interest from the book trade.

The Cheltenham Literary Festival began, in a small way, in 1949, as the offshoot of a longer-running (since 1926) arts festival. It claims to be the 'longest running festival of its kind' in the world. Cheltenham, a favoured spa resort, has a proud literary heritage (there are plaques to the two laureates, Tennyson and Cecil Day-Lewis, and other notables visible on the town's fine 18th-century architecture).

Hay-on-Wye (Y Gelli Gandryll) is a much less obvious site for a major literary festival. The village is perched, uneasily, on the English–Welsh border, a universe away from the London literary world. Hay lost its railway connection in 1963, dooming it to Brigadoon status. The population is under 2,000.

Nonetheless, in the early 1970s, Hay became the world's first 'book town'. This was largely the initiative of the bibliophile Richard Booth, who had retired to Hay in 1961 to open a second-hand bookshop – more in the nature of a warehouse, as it turned out. Booth's store was advertised as the largest of its kind anywhere, and attracted a stream of book-lovers to Hay. Booth's motto was: 'You buy books from all over the world and your customers come from all over the world.' Some 40 other bookshops (one for every 30-odd residents) sprang up to cater for these customers.

On 1 April 1977, Booth declared Hay an 'independent kingdom' and appointed himself its monarch. As intended, the stunt attracted huge publicity. In 1988 two locals, Norman Florence and his son Peter Florence, launched Hay's literary festival. They did so with the £23,000 winnings that Norman had picked up playing poker.

The first Hay-on-Wye Literary Festival ran from 28–31 May. There were 35 events. Around 1,200 people (many village people) attended. Highlights were a one-man show on Wilfred Owen by Peter Florence (then an actor) and readings by Carol Ann Duffy and Arnold Wesker. Payments at Hay, for all but stellar performers, have traditionally been in kind – usually wine, donated by some well-intentioned local merchant.

The essence of the festival from the beginning was to bring writers and their public together. Over the years, Peter Florence took over as director. Attendance had swelled to an estimated 80,000 (with 120,000 ticket sales) by the 20th anniversary festival in 2007.

It had, by this point, become a powerful engine to sell books as much as to cultivate the intimacies of literary community. At the 2007 event, Bill Clinton (no passed-on bottle of plonk for him, but a reputed £100,000) called the Hay Festival a 'Woodstock for the mind'. He was there, tramping through the mud, to promote his (allegedly ghosted) autobiography.

Margaret Drabble – who had been one of the pioneer visitors in 1988 – complained to one of the festival sponsors, the *Independent* newspaper, vowing that 2007 would be her 'last Hay':

> It's a pity. The whole thing has become a celebrity festival, not an author's festival. Of course there are some very fine writers there this year. But the whole thing of festivals has become about book sales and marketing, nothing to do with meeting readers. They argue that if they're selling your book then you don't get a fee. But I like to get a fee unless I choose to be a patron or a friend which I am to one or two small festivals. I don't want £100K and I don't see why Bill Clinton did, and he's not an author.

Back to the church hall, in other words.

29 May

H.G. Wells publishes his first (timeless) 'scientific romance'

1895 H.G. Wells's career took its distinctive turn when, aged eighteen, he won a government scholarship to the Normal School of Science in Kensington, and was released from the dreary prospect of working as a counter-jumper in a drapery emporium (a period of his life commemorated in his cockney comedy, *Kipps*).

At the NSC, young Wells ('Bertie') came under the influence of T.H. Huxley – 'Darwin's bulldog'. *The Origin of Species* (published seven years before Wells was born) became the young Wells's bible. Wells did not, however, excel in his classes. He was too preoccupied with writing in the student journal: notably an early version of *The Time Machine* called, unsexily, *The Chronic Argonauts*.

Had he worked at his lessons, Wells would probably have become a middlingly successful scientist. But where his genius (as opposed to his talent) lay was in absorbing the scientific discoveries currently being thrown up and imaginatively repackaging them for the unscientific masses.

What form should that package take? Wells was initially unsure. *The Time Machine* began as a series of plodding explanatory essays. But he soon realised that audiences prefer stories to lectures. Thus his career, and its hundred books, began.

Time travel had been a favourite motif of imaginative literature long before the youthful Wells's chronic fantasies. The weak point in the scenario, however, was how you actually get into the future, or the past. A favourite technique was that of Bunyan, in *The Pilgrim's Progress*: 'I dreamed a Dream'. Two imaginative works that influenced *The Time Machine* use this device: Edward Bellamy's *Looking Backward* (1889) and William Morris's *News from Nowhere* (1890). Both have protagonists who fall asleep and, like Rip van Winkle, mysteriously wake up in the far future.

Morris and Bellamy were proto-socialists, and congenial to young Wells. But there was something fundamentally lame in the dream-vision gimmick. Another early title for his story was 'The Time Traveller'. But finally he settled on *The Time Machine*. The mechanics of the story were all-important.

What, precisely, is the machine? Wells does not give a detailed description, other than that it has a saddle and a triangular frame, and some mysterious crystals propelling it. Clearly it is a version of the bicycle.

A bicycle capable of whizzing along the fourth dimension is as implausible as Doc Brown's flux-capacitor-boosted De Lorean DMC-12 in the *Back to the Future* movie series (one of the innumerable offspring of *The Time Machine*). But Wells's bejewelled roadster makes the point that, if we ever do cross the time-barrier, technology – not slumber – will get us there. On his journey into the future, the traveller has adventures in 702581, at which point in time humanity has bifurcated (as some feared it had in the 1890s) into ultra-aesthetic, Wildean-decadent Eloi, and fearsomely proletarian Morlocks. The traveller makes two trips even further into the future, and witnesses the imminent heat death of the solar system.

The two direct inspirations for *The Time Machine* were, firstly, an article by Simon Newcomb (which the traveller mentions in his initial exposition to his friends) published in *Nature*, 1894. Newcomb, one of the country's leading mathematicians, argued that, 'as a perfectly legitimate exercise of thought', we should admit the possibility of objects existing in a fourth dimension – time. Wells undertook just such an exercise.

The other scientific validation of his story for Wells was a lecture by T.H. Huxley in the same year, 1894, in which the author's mentor made the supremely pessimistic point that 'our globe has been in a state of fusion, and, like the sun, is gradually cooling down ... the time will come when evolution will mean an adaptation to universal winter, and all forms of life will die out ... if for millions of years our globe has taken the upward road, yet some time the summit will be reached and the downward road will be commenced.'

After serialisation, *The Time Machine* was published by Heinemann on 29 May 1895 (around the period that Wilde was being martyrised by the Morlock-philistines). The book has been in print ever since.

30 May

Dramatist Christopher Marlowe is murdered in Deptford, London: assassination or drunken brawl?

1595 He was stabbed through the eye in a tavern. Was he killed for his outrageous lifestyle? Assassinated as a state spy gone rogue? Or, more prosaically, was he just the victim of a drunken brawl over a 'trull'? The issue is still undecided to this day. He was 29.

Seen by many as Shakespeare's closest rival, Christopher Marlowe may be said to have invented the English history play with *Edward II* (first performed some time before 1594), which examined the conflict between private favour and the public responsibilities of kingship. Before that, his *Tamburlaine the Great* (first performed, 1587) had explored the amorality of power, while *The Jew of Malta* (1592) dramatised the struggle between a vengeful Jew and greedy, hypocritical Christians, and *Dr Faustus* (1594) questioned how far a man could go to reinvent himself beyond the confines of good and evil as conventionally understood.

Which is to say that Marlowe's plays tested the boundaries of conventional moral thinking, especially about the pleasures of winning and wielding power, and the relative weakness of those who would redress its wrongs.

But the notoriety of his plays was nothing compared to the scandal of Marlowe's life. Encouraged by his own outrageous self-advertising, his contemporaries invented him as a bad-boy in the convention of the Romantics, long before that literary and philosophical movement was dreamt of. Rumour had it that he was an atheist. He was almost certainly homosexual. 'All they that love not tobacco and boys are fools', he is famously supposed to have said.

Today no one really knows what to believe about his life, so literary theory has taken over, assigning Marlowe's notoriety to that tradition of licensed misrule allowed on the South Bank, safely across the river from London, and site of the city's theatres, brothels and bear-baiting arenas.

Licensed misrule serves, by contrast, to define the social and political norms of the establishment. To add to the mystery, recent scholarship suggests that Marlowe may have been borrowed from his studies at Cambridge to act as a spy posing as a Catholic to entrap other Catholics plotting against the Elizabethan settlement.* If this is correct, we may never know 'what side of the law he was on', whether his death was plotted or merely chaotic.

31 May

Evelyn Waugh looks on as No. 3 Commando blow up a tree for Lord Glasgow

1942 Did the serio-comedy of Apthorpe's exploding thunder-box in Waugh's *Men at Arms* (1952) have any source in reality? A letter the author wrote to his wife Laura on this day offers a clue. Waugh was stationed at Largs, Ayrshire, near Lord Glasgow's estate, with No. 3 Commando, commanded by John Durnford-Slater. Some of them

---

* See Park Honan, *Christopher Marlowe: Poet and Spy*, New York: Oxford University Press, 2005.

(not Waugh) had just returned from a raid on the Lofoten Islands. Now they were cooling their heels.

Let the author himself take over the narrative. The precision of his diction and syntax (the punctuation alone rewards close scrutiny), his comic timing and his skill at saving the best for last, as in a good joke, make it clear why Waugh has qualified as the 20th century's best English stylist:

> So No. 3 Cmdo were very anxious to be chums with Lord Glasgow so they offered to blow up an old tree stump for him and he was very grateful and he said dont spoil the plantation of young trees near it because that is the apple of my eye and they said no of course not we can blow a tree down so that it falls on a sixpence and Lord Glasgow said goodness you are clever and he asked them all to luncheon for the great explosion. So Col. Durnford-Slater, D.S.O. said to his subaltern, have you put enough explosive in the tree. Yes, sir, 75 lbs. Is that enough? Yes sir I worked it out by mathematics it is exactly right. Well better put a bit more. Very good sir. …
>
> So soon the[y] let the fuse and waited for the explosion and presently the tree, instead of falling quietly sideways, rose 50 feet into the air taking with it ½ acre of soil and the whole of the young plantation.
>
> And the subaltern said Sir I made a mistake, it should have been 7½ pounds not 75.
>
> Lord Glasgow was so upset he walked in dead silence back to his castle and when they came to the turn of the drive in sight of his castle what should they find but that every pane of glass in the building was broken.
>
> So Lord Glasgow gave a little cry & ran to hide his emotion in the lavatory and there when he pulled the plug the entire ceiling, loosened by the explosion, fell on his head.

1 June

Sydney Smith defends his style as the model English clergyman

1820 'The Chancellor is quite right about political sermons', he wrote to his friend, the Whig peer Lord Holland, 'and in this I have erred; but I have a right to preach on general principles of toleration and the fault is not mine if the congregation apply my doctrines to passing events.' These 'passing events' included the abolition of the slave trade and the issue of Catholic emancipation. He was for both.

Thus the Reverend Sydney Smith, the essayist, reformer, farmer and popular lecturer on moral philosophy, the man who thought up the *Edinburgh Review*, and the man who asked: 'In the four quarters of the globe, who reads an American book?' Here, though, he was holding his fire; he loathed the reactionary chancellor, John Scott (later Earl of Eldon), whom he would later describe as 'a cunning canting old Rogue'.

Smith loved London, where his best (and best-connected) friends lived – loved its gossip and good conversation – but when the Residence Act of 1808 made his living in Foston-le-Clay, in Yorkshire, conditional on his actually living there (instead of sending a curate to fill his place), he made the best of it, spending £4,000 on refurbishing the house and farm buildings where there had been no resident clergyman for 150 years, and (as he wrote in this same letter) playing 'my part in the usual manner, as doctor, justice, road-maker, pacifist, preacher, farmer, neighbor, and diner-out'.

'If I can mend my fortunes', he added, 'I shall be very glad; if I cannot, I shall be not be very sorry.' Later he would go through the same process at the other end of the country, in Combe Florey, Somerset: doctoring, preaching, farming and rebuilding the rectory, just 200 yards away from the house in which Evelyn Waugh was later to spend the last decade of his life.

2 June

Thomas Hardy is born, dies, and is reborn

1840 Thomas Hardy, the chronicler of Wessex, was born on this day, the son of a stonemason, Thomas Hardy Sr., in a thatched artisan's cottage (commemorated in Hardy's teenage poem, 'Domicilium') some three miles from Dorchester ('Casterbridge' in the later novels). He was the first child, born five months after his parents' wedding – 'prematurely', as the polite fiction was.

He may well have been legitimately premature. On its birth the puny infant was observed to be still-born. The body was put aside for Christian disposal. It was the quick-witted midwife, Lizzie Downton (clearly not a nurse of the Sairey Gamp school), who detected a noise from the child and rescued it from premature burial.

Hardy was struck by the 'irony' of his birth, death, rebirth. Premature, still-born babies feature in his fiction (notably Tess's offspring 'Sorrow') and in one of the most bitter of his poems, 'In the Cemetery':

'You see those mothers squabbling there?'
Remarks the man of the cemetery.
'One says in tears, "'Tis mine lies here!"
Another, "Nay, mine, you Pharisee!"
Another, "How dare you move my flowers
And put your own on this grave of ours!"
But all their children were laid therein
At different times, like sprats in a tin.

'And then the main drain had to cross,
And we moved the lot some nights ago,
And packed them away in the general foss
With hundreds more. But their folks don't know,
And as well cry over a new-laid drain
As anything else, to ease your pain!'

Hardy is commemorated by a tablet in Westminster Abbey (where his bodily ashes were interred) and in his local churchyard at Stinsford (where his heart is interred).

There is, alas, no memorial to the midwife Lizzie Downton – one of the great forgotten donors to Victorian literature.

3 June

Enoch's melancholy return

1997 The wittiest fantasia on the 'decadent' *fin de siècle* is Max Beerbohm's short story, 'Enoch Soames: A Memory of the Eighteen-nineties'. A doomed poet (doomed less by genius and debauchery than utter mediocrity), steeped in absinthe and feeble depravity, Enoch sells his soul to the devil. He does so in return for a diabolic passport that will enable him to visit the Round Reading Room of the British Museum, 100 years after his death, to relish what he is confident will be posthumous fame, on the basis of his slim volumes *Negations* and *Fungoids*. His soul is a small price to pay. The narrator (Beerbohm himself) gives a sample of Enoch's verse, commemorating his Faustian pact:

NOCTURNE

Round and round the shutter'd Square
I strolled with the Devil's arm in mine.
No sound but the scrape of his hoofs was there
And the ring of his laughter and mine.
We had drunk black wine.

I scream'd, 'I will race you, Master!'
'What matter,' he shriek'd, 'to-night
Which of us runs the faster?
There is nothing to fear to-night
In the foul moon's light!'

Then I look'd him in the eyes
And I laugh'd full shrill at the lie he told
And the gnawing fear he would fain disguise.
It was true, what I'd time and again been told:
He was old – old.

Not much has changed in the library, AD 1997, Enoch discovers, when he makes his trip into the future. It's a bit like H.G. Wells's far future in *The Time Machine*: egg-hairless people, all wearing woollen 'sanitary' uniforms and as indistinguishable from each other as battery chicks.

Enoch's time-trip turns out disastrously. After a desperate scour of the catalogues, the only reference to himself he can discover is on page 234 of '*Inglish Littracher 1890–1900* bi T.K. Nupton, publishd bi th Stait, 1992', where he reads that:

> a riter ov th time, naimed Max Beerbohm, hoo woz stil alive in th twentith senchri, rote a stauri in wich e pautraid an immajnari karrakter kauld 'Enoch Soames' – a thurd-rait poit hoo beleevz imself a grate jeneus an maix a bargin with th Devvl in auder ter no wot posterriti thinx ov im! It iz a sumwot labud sattire, but not without vallu az showing hou seriusli the yung men ov th aiteen-ninetiz took themselvz.

Enoch Soames, that is, survives as a fictional character in 'Enoch Soames'. Trapped in the text: Jacques Derrida could not invent it.

Enoch Soames Day, 3 June 1997, was celebrated in the magnificent Round Reading Room – where Karl Marx, George Bernard Shaw, and innumerable Soamesian literary forgettables had worked, but neglected to make any deal with the Prince of Darkness for their return. Soames himself was eagerly looked for, but did not appear. He would, as the story predicts, have recognised the magnificently unchanged structure: the brainpan of the nation, as Thackeray called it.

A year later, that structure ceased to exist when, in June 1998, the new St Pancras site opened and the old 'RRR' was converted into a tourist canteen and souvenir boutique area. Some cynics alleged (and most Soamesians would like to think) that the removal was deliberately delayed – so that the luckless Enoch would not land in a building site. There was enough disappointment awaiting him without that.

4 June

Perón becomes president. Borges becomes an inspector of chickens

1946 The 47-year-old Jorge Luis Borges was, by this date, internationally famous and widely read abroad. His own background was cosmopolitan. Born in Buenos Aires, the son of a well-off and cultivated lawyer, Jorge was educated in Switzerland and Spain. English was spoken, alongside Spanish, in his family (throughout his life, Borges had a fierce love of Anglo-Saxon literature).

Borges returned to Argentina in his early twenties. Already a published poet (of the 'Ultraist' modernist school), he took up day-work in Buenos Aires as a cataloguer in the national library system (an image of which would recur in his later 'fictions' – see, e.g., 'The Library of Babel', 1941). Already Borges's eyes were failing. It was a family weakness, and had blinded his father.

On 4 June 1946 Juan Perón was elected president – effectively dictator – of Argentina. Perón established himself as the leader of the *decamisados* (the shirtless ones – i.e., the masses) and set in process a programme of aggressive socialism, using the tactics of 1930s fascism.

Borges, like many intellectuals, opposed 'Perónismo' and imprudently made his opposition known. On Perón's assuming office he was dismissed from his library position and reappointed 'poultry inspector for the Buenos Aires municipal market'. He resigned – as was intended. For the next eight years he and his family suffered persecution and some physical threat. On Perón's being deposed in 1955, Borges was appointed director of the National Library. It was, as he noted, a supreme irony since he was, sadly, wholly blind, and could see neither books nor chickens.

5 June

Daring novelist dies, no longer daring

1920 Rhoda Broughton, who died on this day, wrote her own wry epitaph: 'I began my career as Zola, I finish it as Miss Yonge' (the latter reference was to Charlotte M. Yonge, 1823–1901, the Tractarian

Movement spinster novelist, the embodiment of every Anglican decency).

Broughton, a Victorian bestseller, is undeservedly forgotten and unread by posterity. Born in 1840, she was the daughter of a clergyman, the granddaughter of a baronet, and distantly the niece of the Irish novelist, Joseph Sheridan Le Fanu (who encouraged her career).

Much of her childhood was spent in an Elizabethan manor house in Staffordshire, which supplied the setting for much of her fiction. Its well-stocked library, and much spare time, rendered her better-read than most of the women writers of her time.

Orphaned in her early twenties, and following a disastrous disappointment in love, Broughton went to live with relatives in Oxford. Here it was she became a favourite of Mark Pattison – the original of Casaubon in *Middlemarch* – whom she skewered, even more neatly (and more wittily) than George Eliot, with her depiction of the goaty old academic as 'Professor Forth' in *Belinda* (1883).

By this point in her career, Broughton had made her name, and her fortune, with steamy (for the time) and daring romances such as *Cometh up as a Flower* (1867), *Not Wisely but too Well* (1867), *Red as a Rose is She* (1870), and *Goodbye Sweetheart* (1872). They are everything their titles may suggest – but they were huge favourites with the three-volume, romance-addicted patrons of Mudie's and W.H. Smith's circulating libraries. She was, at this period of her life, in the elite £1,000-a-title class of Victorian writer. Six weeks, she calculated, was all that was needed for her sprightly bestsellers.

Alas the bulk of her readers died long before she did (of cancer, aged 80), and although she wrote to the end, she was regarded at best as a charming, but somewhat dusty, Victorian literary antique. Zola and even Miss Yonge (who has two very active societies dedicated to her fiction in London) have both fared better.

6 June

Wallace Stevens writes to the editor of Poetry *allowing her to change his most famous poem – for the worse*

1915 'Dear Miss Monroe', Stevens wrote to the already legendary founder editor of *Poetry* magazine, a force (usually for good) in the campaign for American modern – and modernist – poetry:

> Provided your selection of the numbers of *Sunday Morning* is printed in the following order: I, VIII, IV, V, I see no objection to cutting down. The order is necessary to the idea.
>   I was born in Reading, Pennsylvania, am thirty-five years old, a lawyer, reside in New-York [*sic*] and have published no books.

Clearly Mr Nobody from Reading, PA didn't need such careful handling as Amy Lowell and Carl Sandburg, whose work would also appear in that same issue of *Poetry*, Vol. 2, No. 7 (November 1915). In the event, Harriet Monroe accepted the forced arrangement, while disastrously allowing him a further stanza – VII in the canonical version – to end on. It's the least good segment of the poem as we know it, and certainly doesn't belong at the end, since it's a young man's exotic fantasy of what might take the place of conventional religion:

> Supple and turbulent, a ring of men
> Shall chant an orgy on a summer morn ...

'Sunday Morning' begins with a woman enjoying 'Complacencies of the peignoir, and late / Coffee and oranges in a sunny chair', musing on the 'holy hush of ancient sacrifice' that Sunday commemorates in the Christian faith. The poem is a hedonist's meditation on what lives after death, when the standard religious consolations no longer engage the imagination.

The answer, after seven stanzas – almost movements – is to relish change, the 'Passions of rain, or moods of falling snow ... Elations when the forest blooms; gusty / Emotions on wet roads on autumn nights; / All pleasures and all pain ...' – to take pleasure in the short-livedness of beauty.

The eighth 'movement' restates the predicament and its solution:

Deer walk upon our mountains, and the quail
Whistle about us their spontaneous cries;
Sweet berries ripen in the wilderness;
And in the isolation of the sky,
At evening, casual flocks of pigeons make
Ambiguous undulations as they sink,
Downward to darkness on extended wings.

Or rather, in stating the predicament it demonstrates the solution. With such a powerful complex of images – with modifiers like 'spontaneous', 'isolation' and 'ambiguous' restating the lack of a conventional 'divine' plan, and with the near-rhyme of 'make', 'sink', 'wings' reinforcing the expressive rhythm caught in those heavy stresses on 'DOWNward' and 'DARKness' – the predicament becomes a pleasurable aesthetic experience in itself, proving and *enacting* the consolation argued discursively earlier in the poem.

That's why it needed to come at the end of 'Sunday Morning', and why it was a shame that Stevens had to put it second (after the woman in her peignoir) as a way of getting the poem into print. Fortunately it reverted to its original form in his first collection, *Harmonium* (1923), and has stayed like that ever since.

7 June

Washington Irving greets his native land after seventeen years living abroad

1832 Born in Manhattan in 1783, Washington Irving was to become the first American author to be read avidly on both sides of the Atlantic. He couldn't have got there by staying at home. So he took off for Europe, where he introduced himself to Walter Scott and others, and stayed on for seventeen years. His literary speciality was turning Europe's folklore and historiography into short stories and sketches of popular history, like *The Sketch Book* (1819–20), the *History of the Life and Voyages of Christopher Columbus* (1828) and *Tales of the Alhambra* (1832).

By the time he returned to the US in 1832 he was an internationally bestselling author, and such a celebrity that he was given a formal banquet in New York on this day. In his thank-you speech after dinner he seemed anxious to allay any doubts about his willingness to return to, or remain in, his native land:

> It has been asked, 'Can I be content to live in this country?' ... What sacrifice of enjoyments have I to reconcile myself to? I come from gloomier climes to one of brilliant sunshine and inspiring purity. I come from countries lowering with doubt and danger, where the rich man trembles and the poor man frowns – where all repine at the present and dread the future. ... I am asked how long I mean to remain here? ... I answer, as long as I live.

Next day, 8 June, the speech was printed in the *New York Mirror*. By 11 June a copy had got as far west as Franklin, Michigan, just west of Detroit, where a hard-working English immigrant called John Fisher wrote to his brothers who had stayed behind in Suffolk: 'I have left England and its gloomy climes for one of brilliant sunshine and inspiring purity. I have left the country cowering with doubt and danger, where the rich man trembels and the poor man frowns' – and so on, right through Irving's speech, virtually word for word.

Irving stayed at home and turned his attention to western lore and history, like *A Tour on the Prairies* (1835; see 27 January). So persuasive (and pervasive) was Irving's rhetoric that Fisher too stuck it out, though he died soon after 1840, exhausted by clearing over 100 acres of land in eight years.

8 June

Mr Higginson gets a letter from Miss Dickinson

1862 He was the militant abolitionist and champion of women's rights, the soldier-scholar about to lead the first regiment of freed slaves to fight in the Union army. She was developing into the greatest lyric poet of the 19th century – some would say of any century.

In April 1862, Thomas Wentworth Higginson had published a 'Letter to a Young Contributor' in *The Atlantic Monthly*, offering encouragements that even then must have been wildly optimistic. 'The real interests of editor and writer are absolutely the same', he wrote, and 'the supposed editorial prejudice against new or obscure contributors' is quite without foundation in reality. 'On the contrary, every editor is always hungering and thirsting after novelties.'

Utopian or not, such blandishments were enough to encourage the 32-year-old Emily Dickinson to write to their author, enclosing four of her poems, prefaced by the shy question: 'Are you too occupied to say if my verse is alive?' Among the enclosures was one of her best, of which this is the first of two stanzas. The poem's negation of the departed townsfolk's pious hopes is devastating:

> Safe in their Alabaster Chambers—
> Untouched by Morning
> And untouched by Noon—
> Sleep the meek members of the Resurrection—
> Rafter of satin,
> And Roof of stone.

Struck by (as he would later write) this 'wholly new and original poetic genius', Higginson encouraged, offered some technical suggestions and asked for more. She wrote again, with more samples of her work, and he responded with increasing enthusiasm. On 8 June he received a third letter, this one 'in a different mood':

> DEAR FRIEND, – your letter gave no drunkenness, because I tasted rum before. Domingo comes but once, yet I have had few pleasures so deep as your opinion, and if I tried to thank you, my tears would block my tongue.

It ended: 'will you be my preceptor, Mr Higginson?' Yes, he would – military and moral campaigns allowing – and his friendship would underpin her confidence until his death.

9 June

Dickens's heroism at the Staplehurst rail accident

1865 On 9 June 1865, the 2.38 pm 'tidal' train, carrying ferry passengers from France, thundered through the Kent countryside towards London. Charles Dickens, incognito, was in a private first-class carriage with his mistress Ellen Ternan and her mother (strange, but true). In the rack above the antimacassars was Dickens's surtout (a frock coat – he was a renowned dandy). Stuffed into its pocket was the manuscript of the next instalment of *Our Mutual Friend*, currently being serialised. All England was agog for what was written on those pages (the breakfast scene between the Boffins and the Lammles, as it happened).

It was touch and go as to whether *Our Mutual Friend* would go the way of *Edwin Drood*, into eternal incompleteness. At 50mph the train hurtled into an unrepaired viaduct at Staplehurst and flew off the rails. Warning signs had not been erected. All the first-class carriages, except Dickens's, fell to the river bed far below, killing the passengers. His was suspended, precariously, between life and death. Dickens, ingeniously using workmen's planks, rescued his two Ternan ladies. Once they were safe, he returned to the dangling carriage to rescue – at the risk of his life – his coat and, most importantly, the manuscript. Greater love hath no author.

Having taken care of his own, Dickens walked among the corpses, helping the injured. Biographers assume, plausibly, that he never quite recovered from this event. His son recalls him turning pale during later journeys. At the time, his main concern was that the press should not report who his travelling companions were: which they did not.

Dickens wrote a whimsical 'postscript in lieu of a preface' to *Our Mutual Friend*, commemorating his brush with the grim reaper:

> On Friday the Ninth of June in the present year, Mr and Mrs Boffin (in their manuscript dress of receiving Mr and Mrs Lammle at breakfast) were on the South Eastern Railway with me, in a terribly destructive accident. When I had done what I could to help others, I climbed back into my carriage – nearly turned over a viaduct, and caught aslant upon the turn – to extricate the worthy couple. They were much soiled, but otherwise unhurt. The same happy result attended Miss Bella Wilfer on her wedding day, and Mr Riderhood inspecting Bradley Headstone's

red neckerchief as he lay asleep. I remember with devout thankfulness that I can never be much nearer parting company with my readers for ever, than I was then, until there shall be written against my life, the two words with which I have this day closed this book:—THE END. September 2nd, 1865.

10 June

Registering a new word every 98 minutes, the vocabulary of English reaches one million words, more than the sum of Italian, French, Spanish and German combined

2009 At least that's according to the Global Language Monitor (GLM), a website managed by a group of computer scientists using what they call an 'algorithm' to 'crawl the web' in search of new words. And the millionth English word? It was a close-run thing, with 'Web 2.0' beating 'slumdog' by a whisker.

Interviewed on BBC TV's *Newsnight* on the evening of 10 June, the English-usage expert Professor David Crystal called the GLM's 'English Language World Clock' 'the biggest pile of chicken droppings ever'. Crystal estimates that English already has around 1.5 million words, 70 per cent of them scientific or technical.

At least 1.5 billion people speak the language, whether in its standard form or one of its local dialects. This is a bit like the Latin spoken in the Roman empire, with a formal level on top and a number of variants at the spoken level, which later diverged into Portuguese, Italian, French, Spanish and so on.

Why so many words, though? Crystal says because of England's and Scotland's early lead in science. Language follows power, he says, and English was the language of an empire. That's the imperial model. But the strength of English lies also in its openness to new influences. There is no cultural resistance to neologisms – no 'academy', as in France, to rule for or against new words.

This may have as much to do with weakness as imperial might. Contrary to the mythology of an island fortress, Britain has been invaded again and again, by peoples laying down linguistic layers from the Celtic languages, through Latin, Anglo-Saxon (a form of German) and Danish, to French, which came in with the Norman conquest and quickly became the language spoken at court, while ordinary people carried on in Anglo-Saxon.

So English has a rich redundancy of vocabulary – more words than needed to get through the day – in which to express tone as well as bare content. Thanks to the Norman invasion (see 14 October), we use words derived from French for 'cooked' and cultivated things, Anglo-Saxon for 'raw' and natural. We raise pigs and cows and sheep, but eat pork and beef and mutton.

Poets too can speak plainly of shady caves or – if they want to be posh – umbrageous grots, blue sky or the azure firmament. Chaucer was the first great English writer to exploit this double vocabulary of official French and informal vernacular. Here is the beginning of 'The Knight's Tale' in *The Canterbury Tales*:

> Whilom [once], as olde stories tellen us
> Ther was a duc that highte [was called] Theseus;
> Of Atthenes he was lord and governour,
> And in his tymes swich [such] a conquerour,
> That gretter [greater] was ther noon under the sonne.

And this is the start of 'The Miller's Tale', the antimasque, or ironic companion piece, to 'The Knight's Tale':

> Whilom ther was dwellynge at Oxenford
> A rich gnof [lout] that gestes [guests] held to bord,
> And of his craft he was a carpenter.

Or even better, how about the endings of the two tales?

> And thus with alle blisse and melodye
> Hath Palamon ywedde Emelye. …
> And he hire [her] serveth so gentilly,
> That nevere was ther no word hem [them] between
> Of jalousie or any other teene [trouble].
> Thus endeth Palamon and Emelye;
> And God save all this faire compaignye!
> Amen.

> 'The Knight's Tale'

Thus swyved [fucked] was this carpenteris wyf,

For all his kepyng [caution] and his jalousie;
And Absolon hath kist her nether ye [eye];
And Nicholas is scalded in the towte [arse].
This tale is doon, and God save all the rowte [crowd]!

'The Miller's Tale'

11 June

Owen Wister sets the scene for the western movie – literally

1891 Great literature or not, Owen Wister's *The Virginian* (1902) is generally credited as the story that gave the movies their idea of the western – its protagonist, the soft-spoken cowboy who brings law and order to an American frontier town, the model for that universal hero played by Gregory Peck, James Stewart, Alan Ladd, Henry Fonda, Clint Eastwood and many others.

What's less known is that Wister may also have given Hollywood the idea for the typical frontier town – that dusty jumble of board fronts (and boardwalks) meandering between one or two more substantial stone or brick buildings like a bank.

On his visit to Wyoming and Yellowstone Park in the summer of 1891 – the journey that decided him to write about the West – he described the town of Douglas, Wyoming. And since his journal is so often fresher, more direct and less studied than *The Virginian*, it's worth quoting from the relevant entry, for 11 June:

> The Town ... is a hasty litter of flat board houses standing at all angles, with the unreal look of stage scenery. ... On a bottom bench of sand and sage above the town, a large brick school-house that will mostly be empty as long as it lasts ... The town reminds you of a card town, so aimless and insubstantial it seems ... There are no mines here. Farming is impossible. ... There was absolutely nothing that could possibly make Douglas a real place.

Wister got it right: the town is now all but abandoned. Once the terminus of a railroad, Douglas stands 'like a pillar of salt', now that the terminus has moved 50 miles west. But following the strange logic of the western, Hollywood replicates the town's physical appearance while repopulating it with children, schoolmarms, sheriffs, easy women and bartenders – without ever hinting at the economic underpinning of all this activity. It's not mining. It's not farming. It's not even ranching, since not a blade of grass grows in the desert roundabout for the cattle to nibble on.

12 June

Conrad enters the Heart of Darkness

1890 In his 'personal record', published in 1912, Joseph Conrad recalls 'imagining Africa' in his childhood (he was then Teodor Korzeniowski, living with his exiled Polish family in Russia):

> It was in 1868, when nine years or thereabouts, that while look-ing at a map of Africa of the time and putting my finger on the blank space then representing the unsolved mystery of that continent, I said to myself with absolute assurance and amazing audacity which are no longer in my character now:
> 'When I grow up I shall go *there*.'

Conrad was 33 years grown up when he finally entered the white space of the heart-shaped 'dark continent'. He had the year before received his only command as a (British) mariner and – while on shore – had begun writing his first novel, *Almayer's Folly*. In May 1890, he made his first visit to Poland in sixteen years. It was a period of multiple transitions for him. He was between careers, between countries, in the middle years of his life.

The circumstances that brought him to the Belgian Congo in June 1890 are explained in a letter to his uncle Aleksander:

> I am now more less under contract to the 'Société Belge du Haut Congo' to be master of one of its river steamers ... when [they] will send me to Africa, I do not yet know; it will probably be in May [1890].

As Zdzislaw Najder, the editor of Conrad's *Congo Diary*, records:

Conrad's stay in Congo (12 June–4 December 1890) is one of the most important periods of his life … He left Europe full of energy and thrilling expectations, with ideas about a 'civilizing mission'. He returned gravely ill, never to regain fully his good health, disillusioned, with memories to be used later in his most famous story, *Heart of Darkness*.

Conrad put it more trenchantly. Before he went to the Congo he was, he said, an 'animal'. The experience made him a human being – and, one might speculate, the novelist he later became.

Conrad's Congo experience is, thinly veiled (with careful anonymities as to employers and employees of the Société Belge du Haut Congo), transmuted into Charlie Marlow's experiences in *Heart of Darkness*, published (serially) in *Blackwood's Magazine* nine years later.

The work is, as Najder says, his most 'famous'. Arguably concentration on it has siphoned off attention to other, full-length works (such as *Nostromo*) which, literary criticism would aver, are even worthier of attention than this novella. Over the last 30 years, however, *Heart of Darkness* has become notorious as well as famous. For decades in the 20th century the work was prescribed as an exemplary text on the iniquities of racism, as filtered through Conrad's liberal sensitivity. This comfortable view was contradicted, violently, by the Nigerian novelist Chinua Achebe, initially in a lecture at Amherst College on 18 February 1975, 'An Image of Africa: Racism in Conrad's *Heart of Darkness*'. 'Conrad', Achebe observed:

was born in 1857, the very year in which the first Anglican missionaries were arriving among my own people in Nigeria. It was certainly not his fault that he lived his life at a time when the reputation of the black man was at a particularly low level. But even after due allowances have been made for all the influences of contemporary prejudice on his sensibility there remains still in Conrad's attitude a residue of antipathy to black people which his peculiar psychology alone can explain. His own account of his first encounter with a black man is very revealing:

A certain enormous buck nigger encountered in Haiti fixed my conception of blind, furious, unreasoning rage,

as manifested in the human animal to the end of my days.
Of the nigger I used to dream for years afterwards.

Certainly Conrad had a problem with niggers.

Conrad, Achebe concluded, was, on the evidence of *Heart of Darkness*,
a 'bloody racist'.

Achebe's revisionist verdict provoked critical disagreement, fierce
defences of Conrad's integrity, and, for the novel itself, an ambiguous
place in the standard 'Great Books' courses in Britain and America.
In one of the periodic outbursts of student rebellion at Stanford
University in the 1980s, one placard read: 'Read *Heart of Darkness*;
Get your Racist Education here.'

13 June

Charles A. Lindbergh receives a ticker-tape reception as he parades down 5th Avenue, New York

1927 He had become the most famous man in the world overnight,
this former airmail pilot who had flown solo and non-stop from
Long Island to Paris. Now he was getting the city's traditional welcome for conquering heroes. Fame had its dangers, though. In 1932
the Lindberghs' infant son was kidnapped and never returned alive.
The enormous publicity surrounding the crime and trial drove them
to Europe.

While there, Lindbergh was asked by the US military to assess the
strength of the Luftwaffe. He visited German aircraft factories and air-
fields, flew planes, met Göring, and generally concluded that the Nazis
were well ahead of the US in both design and production. On Hitler's
orders, Göring presented him with the Service Cross of the German
Eagle, a white cross adorned with four little swastikas.

Back in the States, Lindbergh, convinced that Jewish financiers and
the Jewish media were tricking America into a European war, became
a prominent spokesman for the America First movement. After Pearl
Harbor he worked as a private citizen, advising aircraft manufacturers
on design, and later flew over 50 combat missions in the Pacific.

This mixture of heroism and absurdity gave Philip Roth the idea for a stunning *what if* novel. What if Lindbergh had campaigned for the presidency, and won in 1940, instead of Roosevelt securing his third term? Above all, how would a Lindbergh government play in the predominantly Jewish Weequahic district of Newark, New Jersey, where Roth was brought up? *The Plot Against America* (2004) interweaves public events with the fortunes of the Roth family, and so manages to be a touching memoir of childhood as much as a political thriller.

At first the anti-Semitism is just petty and personal, however painful. The family visit Washington, where a local calls them 'loud-mouth Jews' for defending Roosevelt, and they are turned out of their hotel. Then the 'Office of American Absorption' revives the 1862 Homestead Act to disperse Jewish families from 'ghettos' like the Weequahic district to wholesome towns in Wyoming and Kentucky.

Things begin to hot up elsewhere, finally in Newark and the family home. The legendary anti-fascist radio commentator Walter Winchell decides to run for president. His speeches cause riots all over the country. Finally he is shot in the head by an American Nazi. But when Mayor Fiorella La Guardia speaks his eulogy at Temple Emanu-El, New York, the tide begins to turn. To tell how and why would spoil the suspense for the first-time reader. Let's just say that however far-fetched, the fiction is underpinned by Roth's grasp on family memories and national history.

14 June

William Brazel comes across a 'large area of bright wreckage made up of rubber strips, tinfoil, a rather tough paper and sticks' while working on the Foster homestead, near Roswell, New Mexico

1947 Shortly after the Second World War, many Americans began to see things in the sky that accelerated to greater speeds, and changed direction more suddenly, than any known aircraft could manage. By day these were silver and disc-shaped; by night they appeared as lights, often flying in formation. The majority of sightings were in the southwest of the country, but the unidentified flying objects, or UFOs for short, were seen almost everywhere, including Washington DC, where a group of lights was photographed and tracked on radar, supposedly accelerating from 100 to 7,200 miles per hour.

Thanks to the Freedom of Information Act, it's now clear that at least some of these mystery sightings came from the US military testing advanced airframes and systems, some based on designs developed in Germany during the war. But at the time, the government's reluctance to come clean bred a whole new branch of the entertainment industry feeding, and feeding on, paranoid fantasies that the authorities were covering up news of invasions from outer space.

Cack-handed military public relations tended to ratchet up the tension. Take Brazel's discovery, for example. At first intelligence officers from the Air Force base at Roswell allowed that they might be the wreck of a UFO, then quickly changed their minds to identify the remains of a weather balloon with a hexagonal radar reflector attached – which (judging by the materials) it almost certainly was.

Changing the story was a mistake. Whatever could 'they' be hiding? Before long the story got around that a complete flying saucer had been retrieved from the desert site, and even that bodies of aliens had been dug out of the wreckage, one of which was taken away for an autopsy. The government responded that they had conducted a number of high-altitude experiments using dummies to test the effect of falls and decompression. The darkest version of this theory, as set out in Nick Redfern's *Body Snatchers in the Desert*, is that the 'dummies' had been Japanese prisoners of war being used to assess the effects of radiation and decompression.*

The Roswell story was kept alive by a more-or-less unbroken stream of books, as well as documentary reports and other coverage on cable channels like Sci-Fi and Discovery. Fictional spin-offs included TV series like *Dark Skies* (1996–97) and *Roswell* (1999–2003), in which alien survivors of the crash take human form and live as teenagers in Roswell, and the evergreen *The X-Files*, which ran for just under a decade from 1993 to 2002.

---

* Nick Redfern, *Body Snatchers in the Desert: The Horrible Truth at the Heart of the Roswell Story*, New York: Paraview, 2005.

15 June

The ball before the cannon balls flew

1815 The most famous ball in literature was that thrown (histori-cally) in Brussels, on this day, the eve of what would be the Battle of Waterloo. It was given by the Duchess of Richmond for her son. The event was first immortalised in Canto III of *Childe Harold's Pilgrimage*:

> There was a sound of revelry by night,
> And Belgium's capital had gathered then
> Her Beauty and her Chivalry, and bright
> The lamps shone o'er fair women and brave men;
> A thousand hearts beat happily; and when
> Music arose with its voluptuous swell,
> Soft eyes look'd love to eyes which spake again,
> And all went merry as a marriage-bell;
> But hush! hark! a deep sound strikes like a rising knell!
> What is the deep sound? Not the wind, but the cannon's roar.

In his 1843 novel, *Charles O'Malley*, the Irish novelist Charles Lever made the ball the centre-piece of his picaresque hero's career (in which, preposterously, he ends up advising both Wellington and Napoleon on how to conduct their battle). More temperately (and deliberately aiming his account against Lever, with whom he had differences), Thackeray makes the ball (the most glamorous such event 'since the days of Darius') central to his 'Waterloo Novel', *Vanity Fair* (1847–8). Other novelists (Georgette Heyer, Bernard Cornwell, creator of 'Sharpe') have featured it.

These commemorations are well known and much cited. Less well known is the career of the young man for whom the duchess threw the ball – who was also a novelist. Lord William Lennox (1799–1881) was the fourth son of the fourth Duke of Richmond. His godfather was William Pitt and one of his cousins was Charles James Fox.

While still a thirteen-year-old boy at Westminster School, William was gazetted to a cornetcy. He then joined Wellington's staff as an aide-de-camp, remaining in that post until three years after Waterloo. He missed the battle itself, although he made the ball.

Lennox sold his commission in 1829 and served as a Whig MP over the Reform years. He was always more interested in horses than

Parliament. He went on to write extensively for the journals of the day and turned out a number of fashionable novels. There was a taste for what was called 'silver forkery' – particularly if penned by actual blue-bloods. None was bluer than that of the author of *Compton Audley* (1841), *The Tuft Hunter* (1864), *The Adventures of a Man of Family* (1864) and ten other effusions lying, undisturbed, in the vaults of the British copyright libraries. In his later life, a sadly broken-down figure, Lennox hired himself out for lectures on the theme of 'Celebrities I have known'. They, alas, no longer knew him as they had on that glorious night in June 1815.

16 June

James Joyce goes out on his first date with his future wife,
Norah Barnacle

1904 The author later memorialised this day by turning it into Bloomsday, when the action of *Ulysses* (1922) takes place. *Ulysses* spends its 265,000 words elaborating the ordinary events and thoughts during the day of Stephen Dedalus, a struggling young writer who has to teach bored children for a living, Leopold Bloom, an advertising salesman, and Bloom's wife, Molly.

Bloom's peregrinations through Dublin take him to the post office, where he receives a clandestine letter from his lover, to a funeral, to the office of a newspaper to sell advertisements, the National Museum to gaze at the beautiful rear end on a statue of Venus, the National Library, and a maternity hospital. From time to time his path intersects with that of Dedalus, but they never really interact.

Along with T.S. Eliot's *The Waste Land* and the first of Ezra Pound's *Cantos*, which also came out in that same *annus mirabilis* of modernism, 1922, *Ulysses* remains one of the paradigms of modernist literature in English. Like those other works, the novel reinvents the classics for a contemporary readership. It is revolutionary in technique – for example, in the stream of consciousness in Episode 3 and in Molly Bloom's soliloquy at the end, and in its range of tone and reference, powered by the contrast between its classical register and its vernacular events and their expression, including sexual explicitness.

Above all, *Ulysses* is modernist in its elaborate parodies, puns and other wordplay, and in making the medium part of the message. Episode 14, 'The Oxen of the Sun', in which Bloom visits the maternity hospital, enacts the whole process of gestation in terms of the evolution of the English language itself, with the conjunction of Latin and Anglo-Saxon producing the embryo, developing in skilful parodies of Middle English, the prose of the King James Bible, 18th-century essays, Dickens and Carlyle, before being born in the slang and street talk of contemporary Dublin.

17 June

The death of Joseph Addison. Bibles and brandy

1719 On his deathbed, literary legend has it, Joseph Addison summoned his dissolute stepson, Warwick, to witness how 'a Christian can die'. The cause of death was asthma, complicated by dropsy. He was 47 years old. The setting was comfortable and dignified – Holland House, Kensington.

Addison had, his biographer records, 'studied attentively the deaths of Augustus, Socrates, Petronius Arbiter, Seneca, Cato and Sir Thomas More'. In various essays he had defined the ideal exit as a dignified combination of classical stoicism and Christian humility, and like the 'winding up of a well-written play'. Addison has the hero declare, in his excessively well-written play, *Cato* (1712):

How beautiful is death, when earn'd by virtue!
Who would not be that youth? What pity is it
That we can die but once to serve our country!

Alexander Pope professed to find Addison's ostentatiously vaunted 'virtue', and his life- (and death-) long habit of gathering acolytes around him to admire that Addisonian quality, stomach-turning (nor did he much like that pompous *Cato* play). He duly satirised the other writer as 'Atticus' in the 'Epistle to Dr Arbuthnot', as a prig on a self-erected throne, who would,

Like Cato, give his little senate laws,
And sit attentive to his own applause;

It was typical that Addison would want applause as he breathed his last, expiring to the sound of sycophantic, but decently muted, clapping from his faithful claque.

The anecdote about deathbeds and dissolute stepsons is wholly Addisonian (or Atticus-like, if one is feeling catty) but, alas, 'of dubious authority', as beautiful literary anecdotes most often are. According to the sardonic Horace Walpole: 'unluckily Addison died of brandy – nothing makes a Christian die in peace like being maudlin.'

Addison's body, after lying in state, was interred in the Poets' Corner of Westminster Abbey.

Thomas Tickell (whose career in politics and poetry had benefited from Addison's patronage) felt the poetic community had been somewhat remiss in not showering Addison's passing with elegiac verse, and wrote a poem delicately censorious of his fellow versifiers:

To the Earl of Warwick, on the Death of Mr. Addison

If, dumb too long, the drooping Muse hath stay'd,
And left her debt to Addison unpaid;
Blame not her silence, Warwick, but bemoan,
And judge, oh judge, my bosom by your own.
What mourner ever felt poetic fires!
Slow comes the verse that real woe inspires:
Grief unaffected suits but ill with art,
Or flowing numbers with a bleeding heart.

Pope, who disliked Tickell as much as he did Addison, was not moved to elegise.

18 June

Crossing the country on his way to the California Gold Rush,
Edward Tomkins tries to describe the buttes and pinnacles in
the Platte Valley

1850 'The whole country seems overspread by some of the loftiest
and most magnificent pallaces that imagination of man can reach',
he wrote in his diary. 'Here lays the ruins of a lofty Pyramid, there a
splendid Castle.' Other shapes reminded him of 'our nations Capitol
at Washington' and the 'City Hall at N.Y.'. It was all too much.
'Even the ruins of Rome, Athens, Bagdad and Petria fall into perfect
insignificance.'

The Forty-Niners were not horny-handed frontiersmen. Despite
the danger, dust and fatigue of the 2,000-mile, seven-month overland
trek from Missouri to California – not to mention the poor light at
night – a great many of them kept diaries or journals. As with Sarah
Kemble Knight (see 2 October), their anxiety at being so far from
civilisation prompted them to invent daydreams of artefacts, the more
classical and old-world the better.

When that project failed the credibility test, they resorted to the
opposite mode of topographical description, scientific measurement.
Here is Joseph Warren Wood describing Chimney Rock on 9 June
1849:

> The Chimney ... stands upon a high mound of clay & is about
> 100 ft high the elevation of the whole mass is 250 or 300 ft high.
> ... The chimney is about 30 ft in Diameter at the base & 20 at
> the top ...

But this was no flight from fantasy to hard fact. With their recourse to
science they weren't getting back to basics, but following – in Wood's
case, almost literally copying out – well known reports on the same
landscape like John Charles Fremont's *Report of the Exploring Expedition
to the Rocky Mountains in the Year 1842*, published under US government auspices in 1845, and Edwin Bryant's *What I saw in California*
(1848).

The trail to California was already over-inscribed with geographical
description. The most plotless of American landscapes had been over-
plotted before the Forty-Niners arrived to see it for themselves.

19 June

*Julius and Ethel Rosenberg are executed by electric chair at
Sing Sing Prison, Ossining, New York*

1953 A decade before President Kennedy was shot in Dallas, another public killing also prompted major paranoid fiction that played with ideas of plots both sinister and fictional. It was the trial and death of the Rosenbergs, supposedly for leaking secrets of the atomic bomb to the Russians, the only time in American history when civilians were executed for espionage.

Julius and Ethel Rosenberg were certainly active communists, certainly spies. Julius had worked during the Second World War in the Army Signal Corps Laboratories, developing complex electronic systems like radar and guided missile controls; Ethel seems to have recruited her brother, David Greenglass, for the Soviets. He worked as a machinist in the Manhattan Project, developing the atomic bomb in New Mexico.

Writing later, his NKVD handler, Alexander Feklisov, claimed that Julius passed him a number of electronics secrets but knew nothing about the atomic bomb. At Los Alamos the major operator was the German-born British theoretical physicist Klaus Fuchs, who transmitted numerous secrets about the atomic – and later, hydrogen – bombs to Feklisov, using an intermediary called Harry Gold.

Arrested in 1950, Gold implicated Greenglass as one of his informants, and Greenglass, in turn, testified that he gave Julius some diagrams of the bomb, while his sister typed notes on nuclear secrets in their apartment. He later recanted his testimony about the typing. That's as close to atomic espionage as the Rosenbergs got, yet they were executed, while Gold was sentenced to 30 years, of which he served just over fifteen, Greenglass got fifteen and served ten, and Klaus Fuchs, sentenced by a British court to fourteen years, spent nine in jail before emigrating to East Germany.

There had been sporadic red scares before the war, but America's shock when the Russians tested their first nuclear bomb in 1949 still reverberates in this author's memory. The communist witch-hunts, the national paranoia – the whole Cold War mentality – dated from then. Novelists like E.L. Doctorow and Robert Coover looked back on it from two decades later as the moment when America went crazy.

Their prose followed suit. At the end of the over 500 big pages of Coover's *The Public Burning* (1977), the Rosenbergs are electrocuted in a grand spectacle in Times Square, New York. Popular values are turned upside down in a riot of excessive plotting. America's mascot, Uncle Sam, who tells part of the story, has become a foul-mouthed, garrulous old bigot, while the principal narrator, the (then) vice-president Richard Nixon, though awkward, mawkish and self-involved, emerges as not half bad. Here, at least, his cynicism is needed, to undeceive.

Where Coover uses real names for fictional characters (Jack Benny, Betty Crocker, Charlie McCarthy and the Marx Brothers are just some of the others who pop up), Doctorow does the opposite. In *The Book of Daniel* (1971) Greenglass is (substantially) Selig Mindish, the Rosenbergs are the Isaacsons, and their two children (a boy and a girl instead of two boys) are the protagonist Daniel and his disturbed New-Left sister Susan, who commits suicide at the end of the sixties. In his search for answers to why his parents died and others more guilty didn't, Daniel discovers that the law has its own reasons more to do with the logic of cause and effect than the truth – that bad things happen because plots (apocalyptically, as in the biblical book of the same name) work to complete themselves, regardless. Don DeLillo would later explore the same idea in *Libra* (see 29 November).

Doctorow's book ends with book-ends in the plot's time scheme: a horrific description of the electrocution itself, and the (anti-) climax of Daniel's search for reasons why it happened. He tracks Mindish down to conservative, suburban Orange County, California, and finally confronts him, senile and unable to explain anything, endlessly riding toy cars in Disneyland. It's the perfect irony – the failure of memory in the setting that obliterates history in sound-stage nostalgia.

20 June

After one of Anne Bradstreet's many grandchildren dies at three years and seven months, her grandmother writes a poem on the brittleness of life

1669 Was ever stable joy found below?
Or perfect bliss, without mixture of woe? ...
Farewell dear child, thou ne'er shalt come to me,
But yet a while, and I shall go to thee.

The poem is not about the child or even her grandmother's love for her. Instead it draws the stern Puritan lesson about the fickleness of this world's pleasures. By this, her 57th year, Bradstreet might be excused for feeling the strain, having settled a frontier farm in the New World, borne eight children, suffered recurrent bouts of illness and had her house burn down, devouring her library. Three years later she did, indeed, join her granddaughter in heaven.

Born into an impeccably Puritan family in England and married at sixteen to a graduate of Cambridge's most Puritan college, Anne and her family joined the Great Migration to Massachusetts Bay (Boston) in 1630. Though both her father and husband would become governors of the colony in time, Anne still had the arduous practical work of settling and running a frontier farm near Andover.

She also wrote poetry – lots of it. In bulk, her major output was a series of 'quaternians' – like 'The Four Seasons of the Yeare', and 'Of the foure Humours', inspired by the Huguenot poet Du Bartas. In 1650 her brother-in-law carried these manuscripts back to London, where they were published as *The Tenth Muse Lately Sprung up in America*, the first volume of American poetry to be published.

But it is her shorter, more personal lyrics that people read now – possibly because they can more easily be studied in practical-criticism classes. And they were not all gloomy. Many were intimate expressions of love – like 'To my Dear and loving Husband' – of thanksgiving ('For Deliverance from a Fever') and even praise for God's work in nature – as in this leaf-peeper's joy at a New England autumn:

Their leaves & fruits seem'd painted, but was true
Of green, of red, of yellow, mixéd hue,
Rapt were my senses at this delectable view.

21 June

Isaac Asimov submits his first SF story, 'The Cosmic Corkscrew',
to John W. Campbell of Astounding Science Fiction

1938 Asimov was born (the exact date is uncertain) in Petrovichi in
the USSR, in a period when it was unlucky to be a Russian Jew. His
family emigrated to the USA, where the infant Isaac was naturalised
in 1928. Asimov Sr. ran a candy store in Brooklyn. Isaac grew up a
brilliant, over-achieving high-school pupil, going on to take degrees in
chemistry at Columbia University, culminating in a PhD in 1948. A
brilliant academic career was in prospect.

An early fan of pulp SF (much to his father's disgust, although the
Asimov candy stores had a profitable sideline in the product), Isaac – a
young man imbued with a strong sense of his intellectual omnipotence
– tried his hand with a short story in the genre. The 9,000-word 'The
Cosmic Corkscrew' was written between May 1937 and June 1938. It
draws, clearly, on the last chapter of H.G. Wells's *The Time Machine*.
Asimov's 'traveller' (or 'chronic argonaut', as Wells called his hero) travels into the far future to find earth deserted. He cannot, due to the
corkscrew nature of time, return to find out what went wrong.

Asimov submitted the story on 21 June 1938 to John W. Campbell,
editor of *Astounding Science Fiction*. At that time he was the most powerful arbiter of taste in the genre. Asimov's tale was not to Campbell's
taste. Ferociously right-wing, he perhaps found it too glum. It was
rejected, the manuscript was lost, and the story has never seen the light
of print.

Much else did appear with Asimov's name on it. His first science-
fiction novel, *A Pebble in the Sky* (earth becomes radioactive following
nuclear war), was published in 1950 – a period when nuclear war was
imminently expected and middle-class America was investing in fall-
out shelters. In that same year, 1950, there appeared Asimov's most
famous volume, *I, Robot*, a collection of short stories published over
previous years, expounding the author's 'three laws of Robotics'.

The most prolific of writers, Asimov published some 60 works of SF,
fifteen crime mysteries (which he began writing in 1956), a hundred
or more popularising works of 'science fact', and scholarly treatises on
Shakespeare, the Bible, and quantum mechanics – 600 titles in all. His
collected papers, donated to his Boston University alma mater, occupy
71 metres of shelf space. Elsewhere in the library there are printed

volumes by Isaac Asimov in nine out of the ten Dewey Decimal classification categories.

22 June

The Un-American Activities Committee of the House of Representatives publishes its 'Red Channels' blacklist

1950 The American right-wing media have never liked movie actors who get involved in politics, whether it's radio shock jock Rush Limbaugh attacking Parkinson's sufferer Michael J. Fox for exaggerating his tremors to get sympathy for a campaign for stem cell research, or Fox TV's Bill O'Reilly laying into Martin Sheen for backing Jesse Jackson for president. These days the actors don't mind; they can use the publicity.

But back when the red scare followed Russia's first test nuclear bomb test (see 19 June), actors, producers and writers had the whole establishment against them – from the federal government right down to their own employers. From 1947 the House Un-American Activities Committee (HUAC), originally formed in 1938 to gather information on communists, fascists and other threats to the American way of life, turned its attentions exclusively leftwards, with the Hollywood film industry squarely in its sights.

At first the committee subpoenaed screenwriters like Alvah Bessie, Ring Lardner, Jr., Adrian Scott and Dalton Trumbo. Asked if they were, or ever had been, members of the Communist party, ten of the witnesses refused to answer, invoking the First Amendment in defence of free speech and the freedom of association. As a result they were formally charged with contempt of Congress and sentenced to a year in prison. These became known as the 'Hollywood Ten'. Instead of backing their workers, the studio bosses announced that the Ten would be fired without compensation, and would never work in Hollywood again.

Three years later, on this day, the HUAC published its 'Red Channels' blacklist, prelude to a second, more comprehensive wave of hearings. This time the victims were chosen to enhance the committee's press coverage. Now actors figured alongside writers and producers – among them José Ferrer, Sam Jaffe, Zero Mostel and Orson Welles – and in place of screenwriters of whom no one had ever heard, celebrity play-wrights like Arthur Miller (see 24 January) were subpoenaed.

Ironically, when right-wing actors go into politics, no one seems to notice. Charlton Heston was president of the very political National Rifle Association from 1998 to 2003. As president of the Screen Actors' Guild, Ronald Reagan double-crossed his own members by supporting moves to blacklist them. Thirteen years later, in a notorious letter to *Playboy* editor Hugh Hefner, he either denied – or more likely forgot – that there had ever been a blacklist. Yet he served two terms each as Governor of California and President of the United States.

23 June

Lady Mary Wortley Montagu writes a novelette of London gossip to her clinically depressed sister in Paris

1727 'I'm always pleased to hear from You (Dear Sister)', she wrote to the Countess of Mar, 'particularly when you tell me you are well … Air, Exercise and Company are the best med'cines, and Physic and Retirement good for nothing but to break Hearts and spoil Constitutions'.

Even from this shortest of extracts, it's clear that Lady Mary was a practised prose stylist, somewhat brisk in the expression of her sympathies. In fact she was the epistolary champion of her age. Her letters from Turkey, to which her husband had been posted as ambassador, offered a classic account of Muslim manners and customs. She was also skilled at portraits in paint, and an early advocate of inoculation against the smallpox, a disease that had marred her own legendary beauty.

Alexander Pope clearly adored, then loathed her, libelling her as 'Sappho' in his various verse satires – probably because he suspected she had mocked his affliction, Pott's disease or TB spine – behind his hunchback. 'Sapho enrag'd crys out your Back is round', and 'Poxed by her Love, or libell'd by her Hate', were his complaint and his revenge.

But this was a letter to cheer her sister up, and how better to do that than by relating 'the most diverting Story about Town at present'. It seems that 'a Tall, musical, silly, ugly thing … called Miss Leigh' paid an unexpected and unwelcome call on Betty Titchburne, Lady Sunderland's sister. Not long after she arrived they heard 'a violent rap at the door, and someone vehemently run up stairs'. Miss Titchburne 'seem'd much surprised and said she believ'd it was Mr Edgecombe, and was quite amaz'd how he took it into his Head to visit her'.

The moment Edgecombe entered the door, Miss T. introduced Miss L. as an accomplished keyboard player, and would she oblige the two of them?

> Miss Leigh very willingly sat to the Harpsichord, upon which her Audience decamp'd to the Bed Chamber, and left her to play … to her selfe. They return'd, and made what excuses they could, but said very frankly they had not heard her performance and begg'd her to begin again, which she comply'd with, and gave them the opertunity of a second retirement.

Again profuse apologies; again Mr Edgecombe pleaded: 'if she would play Godi ['Godi l'alma', an air from Handel's *Ottone*], it was a Tune he dy'd to hear, and it would be an Obligation he should never forget.' A furious Miss L. replied that 'she would do him a much greater Obligation by her Absence', running down the stairs and telling the story so fast that 'in 4 and twenty hours all the people in Town' had heard it.

'I send you a novell instead of a Letter', she concluded, 'but as it is in your power to shorten it when you please by reading no further than you like, I will make no Excuses for the length of it.' Whether the unhappy countess was cheered by the anecdote has not been recorded.

24 June

The day before the Battle of Little Bighorn, Jack Crabb is appointed official jester to the commander of the 7th Cavalry, George Armstrong Custer

1876 'Either the most neglected hero in history or a liar of insane proportion', to quote the publicity tagline for the movie, Thomas Berger's Jack Crabb – alias Little Big Man in the 1964 novel of that name – seems to have been present at nearly every factual (or fanciful) event in the history (or romance) of the Old West. Captured as a child when the Lakota Sioux attack his family's wagon train, he is brought up in the native language and culture until recaptured by soldiers and adopted by a childless couple in Missouri.

He marries a Swedish girl and starts a family, only to be ambushed again by the natives and reunited with his old Lakota family. Settling back into the tribe, he marries a native woman. On the very morning their child is born, Custer's 7th Cavalry attacks their camp on Washita Creek. Crabb's wife and child are killed, along with two dozen other women and children. Crabb escapes, determined to get even with George Armstrong Custer.

After a run-in with Wyatt Earp and a spell of being taught how to gamble (and shoot) by Wild Bill Hickok, Crabb winds up in Custer's camp on the eve of Little Bighorn, working as a teamster, still seeking revenge. But he finds Custer puzzling over a set of sand drawings and bones that the natives have left behind in their abandoned lodge, and can't resist helping the general interpret the signs, the 'practical combination of fact and fancy', as he calls them, left as a warning that they are there and intend to fight this time.

Custer is so amused by this teamster promoting himself as Indian expert that he appoints him his personal jester. Of course he disregards everything Crabb has said, and next day rides to his doom.

Crabb's double perspective on white and native life works to reverse many of the old clichés of western fiction. Natives turn out to be more sensitive than savage, more loyal than treacherous, while the whites are incompetent, rapacious and dishonest. Yet *Little Big Man* is not simply a satire on received notions. Wild Bill may never have been able to put ten shots through the dot of an 'i' on a sign at 200 yards, but he did get them all within the 'O' at 100 – and with a handgun, that's some shooting. Custer may have been incompetent, cruel and mad, but Crabb is moved to admire his courage – even his style – in death. *Little Big Man* redeems even the objects of its satire, which is to say that the book accepts that the romance of the Old West can hold its own against the historical actuality.

25 June

T.S. Eliot writes to his lawyer, patron and friend John Quinn that he has 'written a long poem of about 450 lines'

1922 It was done, he explained, 'mostly when I was at Lausanne for treatment last winter'. Together 'with the notes that I am adding', he thought that it 'should make a book of thirty or forty pages. I think it is the best I have ever done, and Pound thinks so too.' Originally titled 'He Do the Police in Different Voices', it would come out later that year as *The Waste Land*.

So from its beginnings three strands were woven into this terrifying modernist poem about the decay of modern times: psychiatric distress (the reason for the 'treatment'); footnotes to aid the reader in identifying the poem's many literary allusions; and the support of that other great Anglo-American modernist, Ezra Pound.

In fact, Pound had been a midwife to *The Waste Land*, not only in introducing Eliot to Quinn in the first place, promoting his work from the beginning, and even trying to raise money to buy him out from his demanding job at Lloyd's Bank in London, but also in his lively editing of the poem's manuscript. This last service has been over-emphasised in the lore that has now accumulated around the famous production. Pound's changes were mostly minor, though well-judged.

For one thing, he seems to have wanted to reduce the poem's tone of provisionality. While Eliot's typescript had 'Mr Eugenides', the gay Smyrna merchant, inviting the poet's persona 'To luncheon at the Cannon Street Hotel / And perhaps a weekend at the Metropole', Pound scribbled in the margin, 'dam per'apsey' – and the 'perhaps' was duly dropped. And when the original had the blind prophet Tiresias surmising that 'one half-formed thought *may* pass' across the abandoned typist's brain after being seduced by 'the young man carbuncular', Pound pulled Eliot up with: 'You, Tiresias if you know[,] know damn well or else you don't.'

As for those footnotes, we need them, Eliot thought, because we are part of that modern decline that no longer knows Dante's *Divine Comedy*, Shakespeare's *Antony and Cleopatra*, Webster's *The White Devil* – or dozens of other texts including the *Upanishads* – as part of an integral culture.

Yet in the comparison between traditional and modern, the irony can be read both ways. Take courtship, for example.

Elizabeth and Leicester
Beating oars
The stern was formed
A gilded shell
Red and gold
The brisk swell
Rippled both shores
Southwest wind
Carried down stream
The peal of bells
White towers

This vignette is inset into a modern Thames, one that 'sweats / Oil and tar ... Down Greenwich reach / Past the Isle of Dogs', and on which a less glamorous encounter took place:

'Trams and dusty trees.
Highbury bore me. Richmond and Kew
Undid me. By Richmond I raised my knees
Supine on the floor of a narrow canoe.'

But then, what were Elizabeth and Leicester up to, if not an adulterous dalliance of their own? Is their affair morally superior to the modern one in a boat rented by the hour, on a stagnant, colourless, polluted river – or just classier? Or is Eliot's idea that the modern decline all started with the Tudors, who came to power through a violent interruption of the 'natural' succession, and made Protestantism the national faith?

26 June

The writers' writer dies at Deauville

1939 He produced nearly 80 works of poetry, criticism, literary and cultural history, biography, travel and mould-breaking novels. He founded *The English Review* and *The Transatlantic Review*. He befriended and supported everyone from Henry James and Joseph Conrad, through Ezra Pound, D.H. Lawrence, Joyce, Hemingway and Gertrude Stein, to William Carlos Williams, Allen Tate, Caroline

Gordon and Robert Lowell. Yet though his novels have seldom been out of print, he's a stranger to university English courses, not to mention A-level syllabuses.

His name? It evolved, during the course of his long and eventful life, from Ford Hermann Hueffer and H. Ford Hueffer through Ford Madox Hueffer, finally settling (at the outbreak of the First World War, when the Saxe-Coburg and Gothas became the Windsors) on Ford Madox Ford. His life? A kaleidoscope of marriages and other alliances, two bouts of bruising service in the Great War, residence in London, Paris, Provence and Sussex – even a spell in New York – and writing, writing, writing. According to Max Saunders in the *Oxford Dictionary of National Biography*, he used to get up early and write 'a thousand words or two'.

Pound made him the subject of a famous essay in *Poetry*, 'The Prose Tradition in Verse' (1914), because he thought that Hueffer's (as he then was) poetry was grounded on 'an instinct for prose', or an ear for everyday language. He gives for example the start of Hueffer's poem, 'Finchley Road':

As we come up Baker Street
Where tubes and trains and 'buses meet
There's a touch of fog and a touch of sleet;
As we go on up Hampstead way
Toward the closing of the day ...

Today Ford is better known for his novels, especially *The Good Soldier* (1916), the one that opens with the most arresting line since 'Call me Ishmael' – 'This is the saddest story I have ever heard'. Thus John Dowell introducing the novel, but it soon becomes clear that he didn't hear the story – he was part of it, as one half of one of the two seemingly perfect couples whose lives are laid waste during the course of the action.

Dowell is not just both narrator and participant; he is unreliable in other ways too, jumping around the story (as Julian Barnes has put it) 'backwards, forwards, sideways, switching times and tenses' and even coming up with 'an "impossible tense", beginning a sentence like this: "Supposing that you should come upon us sitting together ..." – as if such a coming-upon were still possible.'* These were radical departures

---

* Julian Barnes, 'The Saddest Story', *Guardian*, 7 June 2008: http://www.guardian.co.uk/books/2008/jun/07/fiction.julianbarnes

for 1914, surpassing even Henry James in slippery narration and pre-dating Joyce by six years.

27 June

John Fowles despairs too early

1969 John Fowles's novel *The French Lieutenant's Woman* was published on 12 June of this year by Jonathan Cape. Fowles had not yet made his name and had a lot riding on the work. He was buoyed up, however, by the confidence that his charismatic editor at Cape, Tom Maschler, had in the work. 'Magnificent' was Maschler's telegraphed verdict on reading the manuscript.

The British reviewers were less enthused. *The Times* was curtly negative. The *Guardian* reviewer objected that 'symbols and allegory stain every page of this long, puzzling book'. Fowles found the pervasive lack of sympathy with the new things that he was trying to do in the novel 'mean'.

As his biographer Eileen Warburton records:

> Fowles drifted in a blue mood for weeks after the publication of *The French Lieutenant's Woman*, complaining of malaise, aches and pains, nicotine addiction, and morbid apathy ... He had a persistent sense of failure. He began, on June 27, 1969 a novel with the working title *Futility*.

It would never see the light of print. The autumn publication of the novel in the USA by Little, Brown was an unqualified triumph. Fowles was, to his astonishment, described as 'the most brilliant of stars, better than Bellow, Roth, and Updike'. On an author's tour in the US, he discovered, on campus visits, that his book was wildly popular: it had replaced *Lord of the Flies* and *The Catcher in the Rye* (novels of the 1950s) as the novel of the sixties. Along with *The French Lieutenant's Woman*, his earlier novel *The Magus* (universally scorned by British reviewers) achieved cult status.

No longer haunted by a sense of futility, the jubilant Fowles even contrived to give up smoking.

28 June

Lawrence fails an examination, disgustedly

1916 D.H. Lawrence and his wife (née Frieda von Richthofen) had an unhappy First World War. Her origins, and his bohemianism, meant that they were constantly suspected of being German spies. Lawrence's anxieties were heightened when he was summoned to a medical examination, 27–29 June, under the terms of the Conscription Act. If unfit for frontline service (C1), they might well find him serviceable for clerk's duties (C2)

On arrival at Bodmin railway station, the novelist (currently wrestling with *Women in Love*) was marched with 30 other men (all 'decent' men, Lawrence later recalled) to the centre where they spent much of the next two days trouserless, with only their shirts covering their embarrassment.

Lawrence informed the examining physicians that he was suffering from TB. So obvious was it that he was unfit, they did not require the certificate he had ready from Ernest Jones (a doctor, but better known as Sigmund Freud's biographer). He was exempted.

Lawrence elaborated his disgust at the medical examination – particularly the physical intrusion into his body by a 'chemist assistant puppy' – in Chapter 12, 'Nightmare', of his post-war novel, *Kangaroo*.

He put his hand between Somers' legs, and pressed upwards, under the genitals. Somers felt his eyes going black.

'Cough,' said the puppy. He coughed.

'Again,' said the puppy. He made a noise in his throat, then turned aside in disgust.

'Turn round,' said the puppy. 'Face the other way.'

Somers turned and faced the shameful monkey-faces at the long table. So, he had his back to the tall window: and the puppy stood plumb behind him.

'Put your feet apart.'

He put his feet apart.

'Bend forward—further—further—.'

Somers bent forward, lower, and realised that the puppy was standing aloof behind him to look into his anus. And that this was the source of the wonderful jesting that went on all the time.

After the war, Lawrence left England, never to return.

29 June

Theodore Roosevelt writes to Brander Matthews, professor of literature at Columbia: 'What a miserable little snob Henry James is! His polished, pointless, uninteresting stories about the upper classes in England make one blush to think that he was once an American'

1894 The irony behind this contempt is that both men started out much the same. Both were born in New York City, sons of wealthy parents. Both attended Harvard, though James only briefly, while Roosevelt graduated with distinction. And as Philip Horne, editor of James's letters, points out, both young men were affected by ill health, but 'James came East to Europe for his cure, while Roosevelt worked out with weights and went West'.*

It is true that Roosevelt, like Francis Parkman, saw the West as a test of American manhood, and that he approved mightily of Owen Wister's *The Virginian* (see 15 February, 11 June and 4 August). What is not so true – at least not in the sense that Roosevelt expressed it – is that James had somehow ceased to be American. First of all, technically, he had retained his American citizenship, and wouldn't give it up until 1915, one year from his death, in protest at America's refusal to join the war in Europe.

Secondly, though James was sufficiently defensive on the issue to insist that he *could* write an American novel (see 8 April), in a sense nearly all his novels were American – that is, about Americans in Europe, or (in rare cases, like *The Europeans*) Europeans in America. He was forever posing the question of what it was to be an American, by exploring the borders between American and European social behaviour and emotional responses.

And when James wanted to get inside the consciousness of his protagonists, it was more often than not the American characters he chose – from Christopher Newman in *The American* (1877), through Isabel Archer in *The Portrait of a Lady* (1881) to Maggie Verver in *The Golden Bowl* (1904).

---

* Philip Horne, 'Henry James and "the forces of violence": on the track of "big game" in "The Jolly Corner"', *Henry James Review*, 27 (2006), pp. 237–48, p. 1.

30 June

The United States passes the Pure Food and Drug Act

1906 So what has that got to do with literature? Simply that the legislation was the direct result of pressure following revelations of life and conditions in the Chicago meat-packing industry in Upton Sinclair's *The Jungle* (1906).

Sinclair was a journalist, one of the so-called 'muckrakers', like Lincoln Steffans, Ira Traubel and Jacob Riis, who flourished during the progressive presidency of Theodore Roosevelt. They believed that the public needed to know about the hidden lawlessness of American industry and politics, and about the foul living and employment conditions of many American workers.

Funded by the socialist newspaper, *The Appeal to Reason*, Sinclair went to work in the Chicago stockyards for seven weeks. What emerged was a searing *Tendenzroman* that followed the misfortunes of a family newly arrived from Lithuania in the illusory hope of well-paid work. After a number of financial disasters, including (a modern touch, this) being conned into a sub-prime loan on a house they can't afford, the whole family – men, women, children and even an ill old father – have to go to work for the meat-packers.

The world of their work is one in which the ordinary operative is underpaid, bullied, blacklisted. As an index of the company's indifference to its workforce, Sinclair included a typical practice in the industry, in which men in the rendering room regularly fell into the cooking vats, and 'would be overlooked for days, till all but the bones of them had gone out to the world as Durham's Pure Leaf Lard!'

Public outrage was immediate. Overseas sales of American meat fell by a half. The packers too recognised the danger, and lobbied the government for extra meat inspectors – to be funded by the taxpayer, of course. Within the year, the Pure Food and Drug Act was signed into law.

Sinclair, who went on to a long career as author and left-wing political campaigner, was always disappointed that *The Jungle* hadn't aroused the same degree of outrage over the workers' exploitation. 'I aimed at the public's heart', he said ruefully, 'and by accident I hit it in the stomach'.

1 July

No smoking day

2007 On this day Britain gave up cigarettes – at least in public. The event dominated the news but made little impact on literature, with one exception. In his diary (now, alas, in its fateful 'prostrate [*sic*] years') Adrian Mole, 39¼, recorded:

> A momentous day! Smoking in a public place or place of work is forbidden in England. Though if you are a lunatic, a prisoner, an MP, or a member of the Royal Family you are exempt.

Although he himself has never indulged, Adrian records that 'smoking has blighted my life':

> There is a picture of me in my mother's arms, the day I was released from the maternity hospital. She is standing in the hospital car park with me cradled in one arm, the other arm is hanging at her side and in her hand is a lit cigarette. I have been ingesting smoke since I was five days old.

Lung cancer is the malignancy that causes most deaths among British males, and Mole's creator, Sue Townsend, has made public that after seven volumes, and a 30-year chronicle of his sadly inadequate life, she wants to do away with her diarist. It seems, however, that it is the second most common mortal malignancy, prostate cancer, that is destined to carry Adrian Mole off. We take our leave of him in the toils of a chemotherapy which looks, alas, as unsuccessful as everything else in his life.

2 July

Blast *deafens philistine opposition, until the blasts of war destroy it*

1914 The announcement of an anarcho-Vorticist manifesto magazine, entitled *Blast*, edited by Wyndham Lewis, published by John

Lane (original publisher of the 1890s *Yellow Book*), was announced in April 1914. With its eye-catching pink cover, the first issue appeared on 2 July, at half a crown. Lewis and Lane hosted a launch dinner party at the Cave of the Golden Calf, a cabaret club for London's bohemians.

The first issue of *Blast* announced, in a fighting foreword ('Long Live the English Vortex'), its intention to 'deny politeness ... We will convert the King if possible ... A VORTICIST KING! WHY NOT?' No response was forthcoming from the palace. More hopefully, the magazine aimed its shot against the despised Italian futurist Marinetti. *Blast* was, if not loyal to the crown, firmly chauvinist. It would forge an English modernism.

The first issue (although the production never paid for itself, or its expensively unorthodox printing) was well enough received to warrant a grand dinner, on 15 July, at the Dieudonné Restaurant in Ryder Street to celebrate 'the great MAGENTA cover'd opusculus' (Ezra Pound's description).

A second *Blast* was published in July 1915, including among its contributors Ezra Pound (who had actually invented the term 'vorticist'), T.S. Eliot, and the artist Gaudier Brzeska. It already represented a nucleus of home-based modernism, despite the internationalism of its contributors.

Had world history not intervened, the 'men of *Blast*' (i.e. those featured in its pages, and promoted by the magazine) – Wyndham Lewis, Pound, T.E. Hulme, Eliot, and Joyce – would probably have cohered into something culturally dominant. The Great War extinguished the movement, with its louder blasts. Lewis himself enrolled (appropriately) in the artillery (his experience of these years is commemorated in the autobiography, *Blasting and Bombardiering*). Hulme and Gaudier were casualties. Modernism, in Britain at least, lost its way. The country still awaits its Vorticist monarch.

3 July

To save face, Francis Bacon asks Robert Cecil for a knighthood

1603 The old queen was dead. Bacon had served Elizabeth as the consummate politician – literally in that he had sat as Member of Parliament, first for Melcome in Dorset, then for Taunton, and also in the Shakespearean sense of turning against his benefactor the Earl of Essex when it seemed politic so to do. Now he was heavily in debt – not for the first or last time – and not so much out of royal favour as off the new king's radar altogether.

Would a letter to Robert Cecil do the trick? Cecil had been Elizabeth's secretary of state, and having smoothed James I into the system, was being retained in that august office. In less than a month, James would make him a baron – and two years later, first Earl of Salisbury. So Bacon wrote to Cecil on this day in 1603, bemoaning his debts and suggesting that, since knighthoods were now two a penny (the king had granted over 300 of them even before reaching London), maybe he could get one too, to soothe his humiliation.

> I could without charge, by your Honour's means, be content to have it, both because of this late disgrace, and because I have three new knights in my mess in Grey's Inn commons, and because I have found out an alderman's daughter, an handsome maiden, to my liking.

It worked. He got the gong and the girl (Alice Barnham), and could hold his head up once again among his lawyer friends. But better was to follow. He was soon back at court, and in such royal favour that he aroused envy in those around him. By 1613 he was attorney general, and five years later lord chancellor. Then it all unravelled. Once again he fell into debt. In 1621 a parliamentary commission found him guilty of corruption. He was fined £40,000 (over £6.5 million today) and even locked up in the Tower for a while. This time he really was out.

Not in posterity's judgement, though. He had already worked out the theory of inductive reasoning (from the natural fact to the general rule, instead of the other way round) on which all modern science rests, publishing his thesis in *Novum Organum* (1620). Next came his seductive utopian romance, *The New Atlantis* (1627). His *Essays* (1597) had long offered valuable tips for bureaucratic infighters, and still survive as models of the plain style.

4 July

Two American founding fathers die on the 50th anniversary of the United States they did so much to establish

1826 It is one of the most remarkable coincidences in history, surpassing Shakespeare's birth and death on St George's day (see 23 April). John Adams, the Massachusetts lawyer, and Thomas Jefferson, the Virginia planter – respectively the second and third American presidents – died within hours of each other, nearly 500 miles apart, on the country's national day. They had worked together for American independence from Great Britain, Adams arguing strenuously for the measure, Jefferson writing its Declaration.

They didn't always get on, representing as they did the two opposing parties, the Federalists (urban and mercantilist) and the Democratic Republicans (rural and agrarian) – not to mention such diverse strands of the continent's cultural geography. When the Federalist Adams narrowly lost to Jefferson in the presidential election of 1800, he refused to attend the latter's inauguration.

But in due course they were reconciled, and when both men were well into retirement, they began to correspond. 'You and I differ,' Jefferson wrote to Adams in October 1813, 'but we differ as rational friends, using the free exercise of our own reason.' What followed was a series of 158 letters in which they discussed everything from politics and diplomacy at home and abroad, via the question of 'natural' versus man-made aristocracy, to religion and philosophy – many of their arguments referenced in classical authors, from whose Greek and Latin they could freely translate.

Ezra Pound thought the Jefferson–Adams letters a 'shrine and monument to American culture' – not so much a monument, he added, as 'a still workable dynamo'. They wrote well. Their 'sanity and civilisation … stems from the Encyclopaedists. You find in their letters a varied culture, and an omnivorous … Curiosity.' They belong in the American literary curriculum (Pound argued), which was presently 'restricted to mostly second-rate fiction'.*

---

* Ezra Pound, 'The Jefferson–Adams Letters as a Shrine and a Monument', in *Selected Prose, 1909–1965*, ed. William Cookson, London: Faber & Faber, 1973, pp. 117–28, 124, 117.

5 July

Rebecca Butterworth writes to her father from 'The Back Woods of America' asking him to pay her way back to England

1846 Pessimistic or defeatist letters home written by emigrants to North America are extremely rare. Most are full of the New World's promise – the natural bounty or the low prices, the political freedom, the absence of taxes. That's because people are more likely to write if they make it, and their families at home more likely to keep their letters as proof of their relatives' success.

But just occasionally an expression of despair or cry for help survives this filtering. Rebecca Butterworth and her husband had emigrated from Rochdale, Lancashire to a country settlement in Arkansas sometime before 1843. Being city folk, they found it hard to cope in the country, and by 1846 things hadn't got much better. 'What little corn we had the cattle [h]as jumped the fence and eaten it', she wrote. 'John can milk one cow which makes us a little butter, but the other won't let him.'

As city people too they placed their faith in doctors rather than self-dosing with botanic remedies. So when Rebecca fell ill with 'bilious intermittent fever', she was treated with mustard plasters, 'steamed bricks' and '60 grains of calomel' (mercurous chloride, used as a powerful 'anti-bilious' laxative) – the last of which eroded her mouth so that 'I had one of my cheeks cut half way through'.

When the fever struck, Rebecca was pregnant with her fourth child. The first three had died in infancy. Either the illness (or more likely the bizarre treatment for it) brought on premature labour. Her brother-in-law 'did not like to help me as he had not studied midwifery much', so they had to wait two hours for the doctor to come. When the baby was born, 'he cried like a child at full time', but lived for only ten minutes, before taking 'his flight to heaven to join my other 3 little angels'.

'I felt when I heard him crying so if I could have him in my arms and put him to his breast I would be glad', she added, 'but the lords will be done and not ours.'

6 July

The first Nobel laureate blogs his principles

2009 José Saramago (b. 1922) won the Nobel Prize for literature in 1998, the first Portuguese writer to do so. A proclaimed communist and atheist (his *The Gospel According to Jesus Christ*, 1991, caused uproar in his native country), Saramago is not merely adversarial, but outspoken. His award of the Nobel was probably more warmly received in Stockholm than in Lisbon.

In September 2008, Saramago found a new way of speaking out when, during Barack Obama's presidential election campaign, he began writing a blog – the first Nobel laureate so to expose himself to the cyber-public. On 6 July 2009, Saramago was stung by a criticism that he was 'not a real blogger'. He took the opportunity to state his reason for using this new form of literary address, and his personal faith as a writer:

> If he is a person of his time, if he is not chained to the past, a writer must know the problems of the age in which he happens to live. And what are these problems today? That we do not live in an acceptable world; on the contrary, we live in a world that is going from bad to worse and that does not function humanely. But please note – do not confuse my complaints with any kind of moralizing; I am not saying that the purpose of literature is to tell people how they ought to behave. I am talking about something else, about the need for ethical content without the least trace of demagoguery. And – this is fundamental – a literature that never holds itself aloof when a critical point of view is needed.

It may not be 'real blogging'. But the role of the engaged writer in the modern world has rarely been more nobly expressed.

7 July

Ida L. Moore interviews the Haithcocks of West Durham, North Carolina

1938 The most comprehensive literary project undertaken by the Federal Writers' Project (see 27 July) was the life histories of ordinary Americans. Almost 3,000 of these were filed in the Library of Congress, and several thousands more in state collections. Typically the writers would approach the subjects, interview them, then write up the encounter from memory. Few had shorthand and none had recording devices.

Life stories of the south-eastern region often had the flavour of case studies, as if interrogating an underlying social problem. As assistant field supervisor for the region, Ida Moore had formulated many of the questions that the writers were to ask.

The Haithcocks, interviewed on this day in 1938, live with another family in 'a small four-room house'. The two men work in the cotton mill; the wives stay at home sewing tags on Bull-Durham tobacco sacks, and the children amuse themselves. Here is how Moore sets the scene:

> Monkey Bottoms begins with a washed-out, hilly road, flanked on one side by closely-placed and disorderly-looking houses and on the other by a jumbled growth of hedge, scrubby trees and briars. ... Freida Haithcock and Hulda Foster sit in this room hours at a time, both fortified by a generous quantity of snuff, tagging the tiny sacks and dreaming of the day when they will again have a job in the mill. Together they share a tin can spittoon which is obligingly shifted from one to the other as the need arises. Flies swarm thickly about the poorly screened house and hunt out the bread crumbs scattered by the three oldest children.

The women's avid snuff-taking could come right out of Erskine Caldwell. In this panoramic moral view of the Haithcocks' case, the decrepit landscape of Monkey Bottoms slides imperceptibly into the physical and social disorder within the house. As Freida and Hulda dream idly of a steady job, the flies are already exploiting the poorly maintained household defences and the children's slovenliness, moving in to undermine the family's health.

It's not clear how even the most independent and vigorous life story could surface through this heavy imputation of universal degeneration.

8 July

Ralph Waldo Emerson prepares to deny the miracles of Christ – sort of

1838 'We shun to say that which shocks the religious ear of the people', Emerson warned himself in his journal on this day in 1838, only a week before he was due to deliver the commencement address to the graduating class of the Harvard Divinity School. 'But this fear is an impotency to commend the moral sentiment.'

Until now Emerson had been a Unitarian, the son of a Unitarian minister. This was already a pretty radical break from the rest of Christianity – whether Catholic, Anglican, Orthodox, Protestant, or even Puritan – in that it refused to insist on the divinity of Christ. Jesus was a good man and prophet whose works and teachings were there for all to read in the New Testament. His life and example in the world were 'divinity' enough.

Now, though, Emerson was preparing to demystify the works themselves, and to deconstruct the titles traditionally applied to Christ, like our 'lord' and 'king'. 'The idioms of his language and the figures of his rhetoric have usurped the place of his truth', he would say in the address, 'and churches are not built on his principles, but on his tropes.'

Where does that leave the miracles? Christ 'spoke of miracles', Emerson would admit, but that was because 'he felt that man's life was a miracle'. What Emerson hinted at, but didn't say, was that to treat the miracles as the magical interventions of a supernatural being was to denature Christ's work, to divorce it from 'the blowing clover and the falling rain'. 'Let me admonish you', he would urge the young graduates about to embark on their ministry, 'to go alone, to refuse the good models, even those which are sacred in the imagination of men, and dare to love God without mediator or veil.'

Records differ on how many divinity students were graduating that year. Some say six, others seven. Yet so portentous were the Sage of Concord's cogitations that the Boston papers the next morning were full of alarm and denunciation. Among the Unitarians themselves opinion was divided. A few, like William Ellery Channing, welcomed the address, but most agreed with Andrews Norton, who called it 'irreverent' and 'atheistic', then published his response, *On the Latest Form of Infidelity*, a year later. It would take two decades for Emerson to be asked back to lecture at Harvard.

Though radical, however, the address was a logical enough development of New England Puritanism, which rejected the formalism and episcopacy of Anglicanism – not to mention its 'tropes' – as so many 'veils' between worshippers and their god. But would a philosophical shift of position cause such a stir today, however eminent its mouthpiece? Unlikely, though we still 'shun to say that which shocks the religious ear of the people'.

9 July

Mrs Gothic is born

1764 Although Horace Walpole invented the gothic novel (see 28 January), Anne Radcliffe was by far its most successful practitioner. Born Anne Ward in Holborn, London on this day, and married at 22 to the editor of the *English Chronicle*, Mrs Radcliffe started to write at just the point when the new circulating libraries in London and fashionable watering places like Bath were crying out for high-class romance. So once her fiction had found its audience, it attracted the highest fees in the business. *The Mysteries of Udolpho* (1794) netted her £500, and *The Italian* (1797) £800 (£300,000 and £480,000 in today's money, using book prices as the index of relative value.) At the same time £80 was the average price for a copyright.

The main elements of Radcliffe romance were exotic mountain locations that the author and most of her readers had never seen, like the Alps or the Apennines, virtuous heroines captured by scheming men – as often after their money as their bodies – castles with secret passageways and hidden rooms, supernatural apparitions or sounds of sighing and groaning, and a general air of mystery, not just in the immediate atmosphere but also in the fate and identity of the characters, some of whom go missing, while others prosper following a revelation of their true identity and the fortune attaching to it. Jane Austen would satirise the genre in *Northanger Abbey* (written 1798–99) while striking a blow for realism, when she showed Catherine Morland to be intrigued by the fanciful mysteries of the old country house, only to discover that the real horrors emanated from the vile snobbery of its present-day owner.

Typically the novels end by resolving the mysteries, but Mrs Radcliffe's innovation was to include rational explanations for even the supernatural events as part of her dénouements. So in *Udolpho*, for example, the ghosts that Emily hears and sees are really pirates hiding in the castle, entering and leaving her apartments via a secret passage-way, and a horrific figure behind a veil turns out to be a wax dummy. This was fiction in a period of scientific discovery, a sort of 'let's pretend' in the supernatural, even though the age of reason had largely discredited it.

For later, more 'serious' authors, this device of the supernatural explained led to experiments in indeterminate narratives foreground-ing the process of interpretation. Henry James exploited the gothic ambiguity in *The Turn of the Screw* (1898), when what the governess encounters can be interpreted as either demonic possession of the chil-dren in her care or her own displaced desire and jealousy. So gothic romance became a way of talking about the unconscious before Freud gave us the vocabulary for it.

10 July

Poet shoots poet

1873 Paul Verlaine's connection with Arthur Rimbaud began when the latter (at seventeen, ten years the junior of the two poets) began a correspondence in 1871.

Verlaine was the leader of the symbolist school and Rimbaud was ambitious to make his mark. He enclosed his strikingly precocious poem, 'Le Dormeur du Val' ('The Sleeper in the Valley'). The last six lines of the poem, which pictures a sleeping soldier, read:

Les pieds dans les glaïeuls, il dort. Souriant comme
Sourirait un enfant malade, il fait un somme:
Nature, berce-le chaudement: il a froid.

Les parfums ne font pas frissonner sa narine;
Il dort dans le soleil, la main sur sa poitrine,
Tranquille. Il a deux trous rouges au côté droit.*

The last line, shockingly, reverses the reader's expectation. The soldier is not sleeping, but dead, with two (bullet) holes in his side.

With war memorials to the Franco-Prussian conflict being raised throughout France, the poem had a topical resonance. On reading it, and the accompanying letters, Verlaine (married to a pregnant, seventeen-year-old wife) was instantly besotted. He sent Arthur a one-way ticket to Paris, with the instruction: 'Come, dear great soul. We await you; we desire you.' We being Paris and Paul.

Rimbaud duly came from his home in the Ardennes and the two men embarked on a violent, but from the poetic point of view, highly productive relationship. They drank absinthe to excess, experimented with hashish, made love, and wrote wildly.

By September 1872, they were together in London, Verlaine having abandoned his family. They supported themselves by Verlaine's teaching. Rimbaud passed many hours in the British Museum, which, he said, was warm.

The London experiment failed. The relationship, always volatile, became violent. The final act took place in Brussels. After a bitter argument, Verlaine bought a revolver and shot Rimbaud, on 10 July 1873. Although the wound in the younger man's wrist was slight, Verlaine was arrested for attempted murder and sentenced to two years in prison.

Disgust at the immorality of the relationship may have been a prejudicial factor. Rimbaud returned home to write what is regarded as his finest work, *Un Saison en Enfer*, while his lover was suffering in a different, penal circle of hell, in Mons prison. While there he composed his great treatise, *Art poétique*, separated from his wife, and re-converted to Catholicism.

---

* 'Feet in the gladioli, he sleeps. Smiling like / A sick child would smile, he takes a nap: / Nature, cradle him warmly: he is cold. / Fragrances do not make his nostrils quiver; / He sleeps in the sun, hand on his chest, / At peace. He has two red holes in his right side.'

11 July

To Kill a Mockingbird *is published*

1960 Within a year of coming out, the novel had been translated into ten languages. A year later it won the Pulitzer Prize for fiction. Then came the Oscar-winning movie. The story has never gone out of print. In all, it has sold over 30 million copies. Dozens of literary list-makers have voted it the best novel of the 20th century, and it's a staple of school curricula around the world. In 2007 President George W. Bush awarded its author, Harper Lee (who had written nothing further of consequence), the Presidential Medal of Freedom.

So *To Kill a Mockingbird* was – is – as much a monument as it is a book. Why? To what? Set in a small Alabama town in mid-Depression, the story is built around the imaginative adventures of the tomboy Scout Finch, her older brother Jem, and their friend Dill Harris, who stays with his auntie during the summer. Atticus, the Finch children's father, is a stern but kindly lawyer, whose conscientious decision to defend a young black man unjustly accused of rape turns the towns-people against the family, shattering the children's innocence.

The book has been classified as southern gothic – wrongly, since much of its apparent grotesquery is based on actual characters and events. Truman Capote, Lee's childhood friend and the model for Dill, remembered the original of the mysterious Boo Radley, who lives in a boarded-up house and leaves little gifts for the children in the knothole of a tree.

Stylistically, in other words, the narrative is much closer to real-ism than fantasy, told in the first person through the medium of an adult vocabulary, yet maintaining the strategic naivety of the child's vantage point – more *What Maisie Knew* (1897) than *The Heart is a Lonely Hunter* (1940). Thematically *To Kill a Mockingbird* is an open book, because Atticus preaches the lesson explicitly to his children, and enacts it in the courtroom. It is the importance of sympathy, of imagining yourself inside another's predicament.

This relative lucidity of both style and theme must have something to do with the book's popularity. So must its timing – the moment of the book's appearance, that is, not its setting. From the mid-fifties, with the Supreme Court decision against segregation in southern schools, *Brown vs. the Board of Education*, and the Montgomery, Alabama bus boycott, to the early sixties with its freedom rides and voter registration, the civil rights movement was gathering momentum.

Then there's the trial. Although (or maybe because) only 5 per cent of criminal cases are heard before a jury, Americans love courtroom drama, because it gives them back the pure image of the country's founding ideals. 'Thomas Jefferson once said that all men are created equal', Atticus tells the jury in his summing-up. Maybe not born with equal opportunities, or equal in wealth or talent, he allows. 'But there is one way in this country in which all men are created equal. ... In this country the courts are the great levelers, and in our courts all men are created equal.'

The American Film Institute ranked the movie number one on their list of courtroom dramas, and Atticus Finch, as played by Gregory Peck, the top screen hero of the past 100 years. Even the Monroe County courtroom has achieved iconic status. Though never used in the film, it was minutely copied and reproduced on a Hollywood sound stage. Now the original building is a museum – devoted to the book, the movie, to Harper Lee and the historical people behind her fictional characters.

12 July

The end of blasphemy

1977 As an instrument of literary persecution the English laws of blasphemy have traditionally pilloried the crazy. (The first blasphemy offender was John Taylor, in 1676. He claimed, *inter alia*, to be the younger brother of the whoremaster Christ.) Blasphemy prosecutions thereafter were invoked against a series of martyrs to free thought (e.g. Paine and Shelley). Free thinkers have always loathed, and resisted, theocratic laws and (after 1776) point to America where persecution on grounds of religious deviance is unconstitutional.

With the Sexual Offences Act in the UK in 1967, homosexual acts between consenting adults ceased to be criminal. They remained, however, offensive to many Britons – not least those associated with Mrs Mary Whitehouse's pressure groups and moral crusades: VALA (the Viewers' and Listeners' Association); the Festival of Light; the Responsible Society, etc.

In June 1977 a copy of the weekly newspaper *Gay News*, issue 96, was referred to Mrs Whitehouse (by an affronted probation officer, it was later reported, a member of the Responsible Society).

The paper contained a full-page poem by James Kirkup, entitled 'The Love that Dares to Speak its Name', illustrated by Tony Reeves. The illustration shows a conventional Deposition, with the difference that the body of Christ is being lowered by a Roman soldier and features what Philip Larkin, in another poem, called 'a tuberous cock and balls'. The soldier, as the poem narrates, enjoys himself with some Roman sodomy on the corpse, justifying the act by reference to Christ's sexual preferences:

I knew he'd had it off with other men –
with Herod's guards, with Pontius Pilate,
With John the Baptist, with Paul of Tarsus,
with foxy Judas, a great kisser, with
the rest of the Twelve, together and apart.
He loved all men, body, soul and spirit – even me.

Kirkup was a well known and respected poet. He made no comment in the furore subsequently whipped up by Mrs Whitehouse other than to say that he, personally, found Christians' versions of the Crucifixion 'deeply disgusting'. Whitehouse, under the aegis of VALA, ingeniously brought a private prosecution against *Gay News*, its editor Denis Lemon, and the paper's distributors not on grounds of obscenity, but blasphemy.

The offence was, most of the legal profession thought, a dead letter in the mid-1970s. Nonetheless, a trial took place at the Central Criminal Court in London, 4–12 July 1977.

Bernard Levin and Margaret Drabble were called in by the defence as expert witnesses, to testify to the literary worth of the poem. John Mortimer was the counsel for *Gay News*. The prosecution line was that the poem was self-evidently 'filthy' and its blasphemy 'too obvious for words'. Mortimer wondered whether they had, somehow, been transported back into the Middle Ages.

The jury, by a majority verdict of ten to two, agreed with Whitehouse. The judge, in passing his verdict, was not sympathetic:

I have no doubt whatever that this poem is quite appalling and is the most scurrilous profanity. It is past my comprehension that a man like James Kirkup can express himself in this way and that the paper should publish it in reckless disregard for the feelings of Christians.

It was 'touch and go' as to whether Lemon should go to prison. He was instead fined £500, with a nine-month suspended sentence. On appeal the Law Lords sided, five to three, with the court's verdict.

Despite an attempt to revive it during the *Satanic Verses* controversy fifteen years later (on the grounds that Rushdie's novel blasphemed against Islam), this was the last prosecution for literary blasphemy in the UK, although no government has taken the risk (a certain vote-loser) of revoking the law.

13 July

William Carlos Williams writes to James Laughlin at New Directions: 'Working like hell on Paterson. *It's coming too. … You'll see, it'll be a book'*

1942 Laughlin had founded New Directions with family money. Since 1936 the press had brought out work by Williams, Pound, Marianne Moore, Elizabeth Bishop and Wallace Stevens, among others, and as the leading publisher of modern American poetry, it was the obvious first choice for Williams's new project. 'Thrilling material I'm digging up every day', he added. 'It's a theme for everything I've got and more. Wish I had more.'

In the event, the poet needn't have worried about his material. He had plenty of it, which – along with his full-time medical practice – delayed the book until 1946. And that was just *Paterson*, Book One. Four further volumes would follow – in 1948, 1949, 1951, and 1958 – and there were even notes for a sixth. *Paterson* was destined to be another of those American open-ended compositions, like Whitman's *Leaves of Grass* (1855–92) and Ezra Pound's *Cantos* (1922–69) that end only when their authors do.

Like Pound's *Cantos*, *Paterson* is a great compendium of verse and prose, dialogue and description and above all quotation. Both poems are open to chance encounter. The difference is that while Pound's references are both widely scattered as between the Classics, Renaissance history and biography, Chinese philosophy and the 17th-century

English jurist Edward Coke's commentary on Magna Carta, they were also highly personal to Pound, put down more or less as he turned the pages of a recently discovered authority. *Paterson*'s quotations are mainly of the vicinity – not personal to the author but selected to pique the curiosity in local history.

'Paterson' is both a man and a city – Paterson, New Jersey, six miles from where Williams lived. It was here that Alexander Hamilton established the Society for the Establishment of Useful Manufactures in 1791, a private, state-sponsored corporation to promote industrial development that would use the water power provided by the Great Falls of the Passaic River. This was a highly political act. As a Federalist, Hamilton stood for the manipulation of credit and the concentration of capital to fund large enterprises polarising society into owners and proletariat – as against Thomas Jefferson's Anti-Federalists, who championed agrarian interests and the rights of the states over central government.

As one of the oldest industrial cities in the United States, Paterson was correspondingly old in the evils of industrialism. It had the first strike and first lock-out in American history, and when its old industries, like silk-weaving and railroad locomotive manufacture, became uneconomic, the city was left with the classic ills of high unemployment and a low tax base. By exploring this story from a hundred oblique angles, Williams makes *Paterson* a more radical analysis of history than Pound ever achieved in *The Cantos*.

14 July

La Marseillaise – *to sing, or not to sing?*

1795 The song, destined (after many vicissitudes) to become France's national anthem was originally written and composed in 1792, by the royalist Claude Joseph Rouget de Lisle in Strasbourg, under the title 'War Song for the Army of the Rhine'. It was adopted as a call to arms by regicidal street revolutionaries, particularly those fiery provincials who poured into Paris from Marseilles. Hence the second name by which it became generally known. Largely at the urging of François Mireur (later a general under Napoleon) it was adopted, by decree, as the country's national anthem on 14 July 1795. Thereafter it was banned under the regimes of Napoleon I, Louis XVIII, and Napoleon III. It became the country's permanent anthem after 1879.

In the late 20th century, however – with France now a central member of the EU – there was growing uneasiness at the 'sanguinary' nature of the lyrics, e.g.:

> Allons enfants de la Patrie,
> Le jour de gloire est arrivé!
> Contre nous de la tyrannie,
> L'étendard sanglant est levé,
> Entendez-vous dans les campagnes
> Mugir ces féroces soldats?
> Ils viennent jusque dans vos bras
> Égorger vos fils, vos compagnes!*

The uneasiness was focused by the bicentenary celebrations in 1992, when a ten-year-old girl, Severine Dupelloux, clad in white, was chosen to warble the anthem, as virtually the whole country watched on TV.

A subsequent poll revealed that 40 per cent of the population thought the *Marseillaise* 'too bloodthirsty', and that it should be toned down. The protest was resisted by traditionalists. The no-change camp strengthened itself further on 12 September 2005 when it was legislated that *La Marseillaise* should be compulsory learning for young children – this was to be particularly enforced in areas of high immigrant population, in the interest of promoting assimilation.

15 July

The fictional origins of Scott's great work of fiction

1814 It is a moot point as to whether the publication of Scott's *Waverley* on 15 July 1814, or Dickens's first instalment of *The Pickwick Papers* on 1 April 1836, was the more formative on 19th-century fiction.

---

* Come, children of the Fatherland, / The day of glory has arrived! / Against us, tyranny's / Bloody banner is raised, / Do you hear in the countryside / Those ferocious soldiers roaring? / They come up to your arms / To slit the throats of your sons and wives!

Both works had accidental origins. The young Boz would not have become the Great Inimitable had not his senior collaborator on the *Papers* committed suicide. Scott outlined the accidents that led to the publication of his epochal historical work in the introduction to the 'Magnum Opus' editions (itself an epochal venture) in 1829.

The 1829 introduction is a remarkable document, if only for its fantastic modesty. As he tells it, Scott is the Inspector Clouseau of fiction. Some ten years before 1814, he 'threw together' seven chapters of a historical romance based on the 1745 uprising, which he showed to a 'critical friend' who was discouraging. Scott flung the project aside. It would have been his first novel, but that clearly was not his metier. He would stick to verse.

The chapters were thrown into an 'old writing desk' which was itself stored in an attic when, in May 1812, Scott moved in to his baronial mansion, Abbotsford – a pile built to his own Romantic specifications. Scott forgot all about them.

Then came Byron (see 10 March), whose *Childe Harold* wholly eclipsed Scott's efforts in poetry. 'He beat me', the Scot candidly admitted. But what to do next? In autumn 1813, fate intervened. Abbotsford lay alongside the River Tweed, and Scott loved to fish. As Scott recalled:

> I happened to want some fishing tackle ... when it occurred to me to search the old writing desk already mentioned, in which I used to keep articles of that nature. I got access to it with some difficulty; and in looking for lines and flies, the long-lost manuscript presented itself. I immediately set to work to complete it, according to my original purpose.

The composition went fluently, *Waverley: Or, 'Tis Sixty Years Since* was published, and literary history was changed. J.G. Lockhart, Scott's son-in-law and biographer, piously recorded that after Scott's death, the desk was bequeathed to his steward, William Laidlaw, and that 'it is now [in 1840] a treasured possession of his grandson, Mr W.L. Carruthers, of Inverness'.

The reading public has always loved the '*Waverley* and fishing tackle' story. Recently, however, scholars (notably in this case Peter Garside) have become wary about taking Scott's and Lockhart's versions of such episodes too faithfully. Some very technical, but convincing, research (involving allusions to current events and watermarks) makes it overwhelmingly probable that the old-writing-desk genesis of *Waverley* is a myth. But a beautiful myth.

16 July

J.D. Salinger's The Catcher in the Rye *is published. It will go on to sell 60 million copies and be translated into almost all the world's languages*

1951 'If you really want to hear about it, the first thing you'll probably want to know is where I was born, and what my lousy childhood was like, and how my parents were occupied and all before they had me, and all that David Copperfield kind of crap, but I don't feel like going into it.'

From the outset of *The Catcher in the Rye* there's no risk of the reader being reminded of Dickens. Unlike *David Copperfield*, *The Catcher in the Rye* is no *Bildungsroman*, because the narrator/protagonist doesn't want to grow up. What's really being evoked here is the opening of *Huckleberry Finn* (1884), in which another first-person narrator speaks conversationally without introducing himself, as though you already knew him, before embarking on an unconventional story, in the course of which he shows himself throughout to be as alienated from the social norms around him as he is from the conventions of literary narrative.

Except that Huck is naively oppositional, while Holden Caulfield *knows* he detests all the 'phonies' he meets on his winter weekend in New York after being kicked out of Pencey Prep. And Huck's childhood really was severely disadvantaged, whereas, as we soon learn, 'lousy' is just one of Holden's routine modifiers – along with 'sort-of', 'old' (used affectionately as well as not), 'corny', 'goddam', and of course 'phony'.

Great American fiction is supposed to resemble the romance more than the novel. 'In American romance, it will not matter much what class people come from', Richard Chase has written, 'and where the novelist would arouse our interest in a character by exploring his origin, the romancer will probably do so by enveloping it in mystery.'* In the novel, character is more important than the action; in romance,

---

* Richard Chase, *The American Novel and its Tradition*, New York, 1957; reprinted Johns Hopkins University Press, 1980, p. 19.

the action is more melodramatic, less believable, than in the novel. And so on

By this definition, *The Catcher in the Rye* barely qualifies as American fiction. Holden is (most novelistically) fixed within the economic and social realities of his time and place. He has been brought up in an apartment with a live-in maid, on the Upper East Side of New York City, has been expensively educated, has had his clothes bought for him at Brooks Brothers.

Unlike in so many American novels, class is an issue here. Holden knows instantly, by a hundred details of clothing and speech, when someone is 'corny' – that is, poor – or (as his parents would no doubt put it) 'comes from a less advantaged background'. What redeems his acidic observations is that he so often feels guilty for uttering them, and sorry for their victims.

So notwithstanding objections to Holden's colloquial profanity that have rivalled the reaction to Huck Finn's (see 18 February), why have millions of corny Americans gone for *The Catcher in the Rye*, and so many English teachers set the book for required reading? Why has the book become such an iconic expression of American anxiety, not to mention an international bestseller?

It might have something to do with the perennial appeal of good-bad boy stories about disruptive, naughty boys who are good at heart: Huck Finn, of course, but before that, Thomas Bailey Aldridge's *Story of a Bad Boy* (1869) and Mark Twain's other legend, *Tom Sawyer* (1876). But the figure isn't unknown in European literature either, as the popularity of Carlo Collodi's *Pinocchio* (1882) makes clear.

But there's also the Peter Pan appeal. Tom Sawyer grows up, after all, and Pinocchio gradually becomes more human. Huck and Holden, on the other hand, refuse accommodation to the adult world. Huck lights out for the Territory rather than get re-assimilated into the stifling pieties of St Petersburg.

For Holden the problem is that the phonies (or as he would say, the people who have 'prostituted' their talent and good intentions) include his brother, the writer D.B., who now works in Hollywood, the jazz pianist 'Old Ernie', who no longer knows whether he's playing well or not, because of 'all those dopes who clap their heads off', and even his own father, who could be doing *pro bono* defences, but is a corporation lawyer instead.

'If I were a piano player, I'd play it in the goddam closet', says Holden. But who'd hear him? There may be a clue to Salinger's famous reclusiveness here, right up to his death in January 2010, at the age of

91. Holden's phonies are just people who have to earn a living, grown-ups with mortgages to pay and families to support. Boring, of course, but pretty goddam important, if you really want to know.

17 July

Alexander Pope and his doctor

1734 Pope's physician, John Arbuthnot, wrote to Pope on this day, informing the poet that he (the doctor) was dying. Arbuthnot, as famous for his wit as his medical expertise (he attended Queen Anne), was a fellow member, with Pope and Swift, of the Martin Scriblerus satirists' club. Arbuthnot is credited with inventing for it the caricature of Anglo-Saxon philistinism, 'John Bull'.

No poet was ever less like the beefy British stereotype than Alexander Pope. He was severely disabled from early childhood by bone disease that left him 'hunchbacked' (as the cruel description was) and a virtual dwarf at 4 feet 6 inches tall. Samuel Johnson, in his *Lives of the Poets*, describes Pope in 'middle life':

> He was then so weak as to stand in perpetual need of female attendance; extremely sensible of cold, so that he wore a kind of fur doublet, under a shirt of a very coarse warm linen with fine sleeves. When he rose, he was invested in bodice made of stiff canvas, being scarcely able to hold himself erect till they were laced, and he then put on a flannel waistcoat. One side was contracted. His legs were so slender, that he enlarged their bulk with three pairs of stockings, which were drawn on and off by the maid, for he was not able to dress or undress himself, and neither went to bed nor rose without help. His weakness made it very difficult for him to be clean.

Pope was of necessity physically closer to his physician than any other human being. The news of his friend's impending death (from asthmatic and kidney problems) provoked one of the poet's 'Horatian Epistles'.

In his 'Advertisement' to the poem (published 2 January 1735) Pope makes clear that it is conceived as (1) an *apologia pro vita sua*, and

(2) a response to the many attacks 'not only on my writings … but my *person, morals,* and *family*'.

The 'Epistle to Arbuthnot' is famous for its satirical portraiture of 'Sporus' (Lord John Hervey) and 'Atticus' (Addison). As remarkable are the poet's candid depiction of his own 'person'. He candidly holds the mirror up to his own disfigurement:

> There are, who to my person pay their court:
> I cough like *Horace*, and, though lean, am *short*.

According to Johnson, the caricatures of Pope (which habitually pictured him as a monkey, or a dwarfish monster) caused him great pain. But in the Epistle, while frankly anatomising himself, he revolves the central question of how deformation has formed the writer:

> Why did I write? what sin to me unknown
> Dipp'd me in ink, my parents', or my own?
> As yet a child, nor yet a fool to fame,
> I lisp'd in numbers, for the numbers came.
> I left no calling for this idle trade,
> No duty broke, no father disobey'd.
> The Muse but serv'd to ease some friend, not wife,
> To help me through this long disease, my life,
> To second, Arbuthnot! thy art and care,
> And teach the being you preserv'd, to bear.

His disease may have been long. His life, alas, was not. He died aged 66, some nine years after Arbuthnot.

18 July

Led by white officers, including Henry James's brother, the 54th Massachusetts Regiment of black soldiers attack Fort Wagner with courage and terrible loss of life

1863 It was one of the most poignant engagements of the American Civil War. 'Fort' Wagner was really just a battery on a sandy, flea-infested island at the entrance to Charleston Harbor, South Carolina.

After it had been bombarded from land and sea, General Quincey Gilmore ordered the Union infantry to attack it, with bayonets fixed, along a narrow strip of beach, mined and stockaded and bounded by marshes on one side and the Atlantic Ocean on the other. The outcome was inevitable. The bombardment had done little to weaken the battery, and there were still five cannons and over a thousand Confederate troops able to sweep the field with shells and massed musket fire. In all, over 1,500 Union troops were killed, wounded or captured, as compared to 174 Confederate casualties.

What redeems the event from the long catalogue of military blunders is the role played by the 54th Massachusetts Regiment of free African-Americans, commanded by Colonel Robert Gould Shaw, with Garth Wilkinson ('Wilky') James as his adjutant. The 54th led the assault and after bloody hand-to-hand combat actually gained a temporary foothold on the battery, where they planted the Union flag, but Shaw was killed and Wilky wounded in the side and foot. After a long convalescence in the James household, he survived, but limped and was in pain for the rest of his not very long life.

There was at least one good outcome of the fiasco. No one with any knowledge of the situation would ever doubt the fighting spirit of African-American troops again. As one of the black soldiers put it afterwards: 'It is not for us to blow our horn; but when a regiment of white men gave us three cheers as we were passing them, it shows that we did our duty as men should.'* The 54th had been 'the pride of the Massachusetts abolitionists', according to Henry James's biographer, Fred Kaplan. Old Henry James Senior had watched the regiment's proud march out of Boston, accompanied by 'great reverberations of music, of fluttering banners'. Henry Junior was 'helplessly absent'.†

Not far from the old man's vantage point now stands an arresting bronze bas-relief by the Irish-born sculptor Augustus Saint-Gaudens, showing Colonel Shaw in profile alongside his proud regiment. Or as Robert Lowell put it in 'For the Union Dead' (1960):

Two months after marching through Boston,
Half the regiment was dead;
At the dedication,

---

* Private James Henry Gooding; see: http://www.awod.com/gallery/probono/cwchas/fedwag. html

† Fred Kaplan, *Henry James: The Imagination of Genius: A Biography*, London: Hodder & Stoughton, 1992, p. 50.

William James [another brother] could almost hear the bronze
   Negroes breathe.

Their monument sticks like a fishbone
In the city's throat.
The Colonel is as lean
As a compass needle.

19 July

Jeffrey Archer goes down

2000 Unlike politicians, art collectors or policemen, British novelists
– even crime novelists – are a law-abiding lot. How many have gone
down? Defoe, the father of the English novel, heads the list of fiction's malefactors. He was fined, imprisoned and pilloried in 1703 for
sedition (see 31 July). John Cleland served some easy time in debtors'
prison, and he rewarded posterity with *Fanny Hill*, the onanist's bible.
Has any work of fiction stimulated the expenditure of more honest
English seed? Oscar Wilde got two years' hard labour for 'unnatural
practices' with his seed in 1895. Erskine Childers, the author of *The
Riddle of the Sands* (one of the progenitors of Jeffrey Archer's thrillers),
was shot by an Irish Free State firing squad in 1922.

Among his other career achievements (as politician, art collector and policeman), Lord Archer of Weston-Super-Mare is the most
famous British novelist – certainly the biggest bestselling British novelist – to have been convicted of a major felony.

The trail runs thus: on 8 or 9 September 1986, Archer was alleged
to have slept with a prostitute, Monica Coghlan. A sting was set up by
the *News of the World* in which a friend of Archer's, Michael Stacpoole,
was induced to offer Coghlan £2,000 to leave the country.

When the *News of the World* and the *Star* published their allegations
that Archer had consorted with Coghlan (the *Star* added the detail of
'perverted sex'), Archer issued libel suits. Crucial to his defence was
the testimony of another of Archer's friends, Ted Francis, that he had
dined with Archer on the night he was alleged to have had his dealings,
perverted or not, with Coghlan. A new diary was secretly procured,
and entries made to cover the relevant dates.

In a sensational trial – in which Mary Archer gave key evidence, and was complimented in his summing-up by the judge on her 'fragrance' – Archer was awarded half a million pounds compensation by the jury for the gross libel on his character.

Thirteen years later, in October 1999, Ted Francis contacted the publicist, Max Clifford, to reveal that the alibi he had provided for Archer was false. The *News of the World*, still stinging, set up a telephone conversation between the men that seemed to confirm Francis' revised version of events in September 1986.

At the time, Archer was a front-runner for the Mayor of London election (subsequently won by Ken Livingstone). On 20 November he withdrew from the mayoral race, and he was expelled (prejudicially) from the Conservative party in February 2000. After a second sensational trial, in which his wife's fragrance was ineffective, Archer was sentenced to four years' imprisonment for perjury, on 19 July.

He wrote a Dantean trilogy, recounting his time inside: *Hell: Belmarsh* (2002), *Purgatory: Wayland* (2003), *Heaven: North Sea Camp* (2004). They are regarded by discerning critics as his finest work of fiction, along with the A4 diary that was his main defence evidence in 1986.

20 July

The Modern Library proclaims the 20th century's 100 best novels in English

1998 News of the '100 Best' first broke on this day in the *New York Times*. First and third was James Joyce, with *Ulysses* and *Portrait of the Artist*. Nabokov's *Lolita* came in fourth, followed by Aldous Huxley's *Brave New World*. Of the top ten, probably only two would have been much favoured – or even read – by the general literate public: F. Scott Fitzgerald's *The Great Gatsby* (in second place), and Joseph Heller's *Catch-22* (seventh).

Publishers of affordable literary classics since 1917, the Modern Library is now a subsidiary of Random House. To re-focus attention on the venerable imprint – and incidentally sell a few more of its titles – the parent company dreamed up the '100 Best' stunt, drafting in a panel of nine historians and novelists including Daniel Boorstin,

Arthur Schlesinger, Jr., Gore Vidal and (the only woman) A.S. Byatt, to make the hard choices.

Lists are meant to provoke, and this one produced plenty of reactions – both in the public prints and on the Random House website. Only nine women's novels make it – eight if you reckon that Edith Wharton is down for two. Where were Toni Morrison, Isak Dinesen, Doris Lessing – not to mention the doyenne of all the other list-makers in the nation (see 11 July), Harper Lee? And where were the inventive, narratalogically experimental Thomas Pynchon and Don DeLillo? Or, to venture a personal opinion: welcome, Philip Roth, but where is your namesake Henry, author of *Call It Sleep*, the most imaginative novel of immigration and assimilation in English?

Regrets for those included? There were a few. Why the wordy *On the Road*? Was it any more than the talisman of a movement? Did *Brave New World* really belong at number five – or at all? And how had John O'Hara's *Appointment in Samarra* snuck in at number 22? O'Hara had long been disparaged by both academic and metropolitan critical opinion because, as a social realist, he ran counter to what the ideology taught that 'American literature' ought to do – that is to engage with the abstract universals of (as de Tocqueville put it) 'human destiny, man himself, … face to face with nature and with God'.

Still, left to itself the general public didn't do all that much better. Invited by the Modern Library panel to produce their own list, they came up with a '100 Best' whose top ten featured three novels by L. Ron Hubbard, founder of Scientology, and four by Ayn Rand – nothing short of her entire fictional oeuvre.

21 July

Pottermania is good for you – or is it?

2007 Literary manias, and concurrent sales bonanzas, are regular events; as regular nowadays as the ocean tides. The only change, it would seem, is that they get even more maniacal with the passing of centuries. At the witching hour – midnight – on 20/21 July 2007, the seventh (mystic number) and final instalment of the Harry Potter series (the 'Potteriad') was released.

Harry Potter and the Deathly Hallows had been kept under the kind of security usually reserved for high-grade plutonium. For up to three days, among the wettest on meteorological record, expectant Potter fans camped outside London bookshops. Many were wearing wizard regalia. The town of Colchester converted its town centre into a Hogwarts theme park. J.K. Rowling was the biggest thing since Boadicea laid the place waste in AD 60.

When the stores opened at the anti-social hour, it was the literary equivalent of the Oklahoma land rush. And as chaotic. Three million copies were sold in 24 hours: a record, outstripping by at least a million the sales of the book's predecessor, *Harry Potter and the Half-Blood Prince.*

Is the Potter Effect a good thing, unlike the Werther Effect, which led hundreds of young men to follow Goethe's hero into copycat suicides? The Potterian memesis, it is suggested, is quite different. Life- and limb-preserving. In a witty letter to *The Times Books Supplement,* 28 July 2007, Edward Kelly wrote:

> For those of us who have yet to read any of J.K. Rowling's Potter series there is little to be gained from the current reviews. I did, though, stumble across this statistic that may please some readers: on an average weekend, the emergency room at the John Radcliffe Hospital in Oxford treats 67 children for injuries sustained in accidents. On two weekends, however, only 36 children needed treatment: June 21, 2003 and July 16, 2005 – just after the releases of Harry Potter Five and Six. It was suggested at the time that talented writers produce high-quality books for the purpose of injury prevention.

The deduction is obvious. Pottermania is good for children. It keeps them from things that go bump against their legs. But does it? The day after Mr Kelly's letter was printed, there were alarmed accounts about a 'damning report' about the 'soaring rate of childhood obesity'. As the *Observer* put it, on its front page (29 July):

> The number of six- to ten-year olds who become obese will keep rising relentlessly until the late 2040s, with as many as half of all primary school-age boys and one in five girls dangerously over- weight by 2050, according to the document.

For the first time in recent history, Britain would breed a generation of children who could confidently expect to live less long, and less healthily, than their parents.

Those 67 children who, averagely, turn up at the Radcliffe ER would, most of them, have hurt themselves playing. Reading (particularly reading a 600-page book) is the epitome of couch-potatoism. Was the Potter Effect, insidiously, helping rob young fans of their allotted span? Reading is a good thing (hence all those honorary doctorates for services to literacy for J.K. Rowling). But would it not be an even better thing for children to be outside – actively 'doing' something, rather than passively 'reading' or 'watching' something?

22 July

Robert Graves: the War Office regrets, then doesn't

1916 The poet Robert Graves (born Robert von Ranke) was among the first to enlist in the Royal Welch Fusiliers on the outbreak of the war to end wars, in August 1914, forgoing a scholarship at Oxford to do so.

He was commissioned and promptly saw active service in France. Graves proved a good soldier (his military experience is recalled in his autobiographical *Good-bye to All That*, 1929). He was promoted captain, and company commander, in 1915.

During this period in the trenches he befriended his fellow poet, and fellow fusilier, Siegfried Sassoon. At the Somme, on 20 July 1916 (not yet 21 years old), Graves was hit by shell shrapnel, sustaining serious internal injuries (Sassoon was wounded in the same battle). The field hospital where Graves was taken reported him dead and an obituary was printed in *The Times*. His commanding officer, Lieutenant Colonel Crawshay, sent his parents the standard letter of condolence, along with their son's private possessions, on 22 July:

> I very much regret to have to write and tell you your son has died of wounds. He was very gallant, and was doing so well and is a great loss. He was hit by a shell and very badly wounded, and died on the way down to the base I believe. He was not in bad

pain, and our doctor managed to get across and attend to him at once.

We have had a very hard time, and our casualties have been large. Believe me you have all our sympathy in your loss, and we have lost a very gallant soldier. Please write to me if I can tell you or do anything.

Graves in fact survived the wounds to see his obituary corrected (on 6 August) and his first volume of poems, *Over the Brazier* (1916), published (thanks largely to the indefatigable friend to poets, Edward Marsh). He wrote a poem on the subject of his death and resurrection, 'Escape'. It records:

> ... but I was dead, an hour or more.
> I woke when I'd already passed the door
> That Cerberus guards, and half-way down the road
> To Lethe, as an old Greek signpost showed.

Although invalided out of the front line (his lungs never quite recovered), he was instrumental in getting a shell-shocked Sassoon treated at the progressive Craiglockhart War Hospital, under W.H.R. Rivers, near Edinburgh. Both Sassoon and Graves befriended Wilfred Owen (also at Craiglockhart), thus forming the most renowned nucleus of First World War poets (see also 30 July). Owen would not survive the war. Sassoon wrote little worthwhile poetry after it. Graves went on to lead a rich and fulfilling career in literature. The Craiglockhart episode is commemorated in Pat Barker's award-winning 'Regeneration' trilogy of novels (1991–95).

23 July

Henry David Thoreau spends a night in jail for refusing to pay his poll tax

1846 How to describe Thoreau? He was one of that group of American Transcendentalists who included Ralph Waldo Emerson, Bronson Alcott and Margaret Fuller. They flourished around the middle of the

19th century in Concord, Massachusetts – though only Thoreau was native to the town – just west of Boston.

But that allegiance was Thoreau's least distinctive descriptor. He was also a surveyor, a self-taught, highly observant naturalist, an amateur builder and gardener, a thinker so original as to be taken – even by Emerson – to be contrary to the point of perverseness. But he is best summed up as a man who tested his thoughts and ideas in his everyday life.

In one of these living experiments he built a shack out of second-hand boards on the shores of Walden Pond, near Concord, living there on and off for two years, in order to test the relative merits of solitude and social interaction, to collect data on the flora and fauna of his native country, and even to try his hand at gardening. In another he chose to go to jail rather than to pay his poll tax.

Thoreau didn't object to the local road tax, or other levies aimed at improvements around town. But for six years he refused to pay his poll tax, because it went to a federal government, which in 1846 had just declared an unjust war on Mexico, and under which one sixth of the population were slaves. Finally the authorities lost patience and locked him up in the local hoosegow.

That was alright by Thoreau, who would later write, in 'Resistance to Civil Government' (1849), that 'Under a government which imprisons any unjustly, the true place for a just man is also a prison'. That essay set out his thesis that consent in government must be based on the individual conscience of the citizen. 'I think that we should be men first and subjects afterwards', he wrote. 'Any man more right than his neighbors constitutes a majority of one already.' To be fair to Thoreau, these ideas were hard-won. To be fair to his fellow Americans, they would also be pretty hard to put into practice.

The prisoner spent the night chatting with his cell-mate ('a first-rate fellow and clever man', according to the jailer), hearing all about the history of former jailbreaks, and looking out of the window. The next morning he was let out because, as he put it, 'someone interfered, and paid that tax'. That was an ungenerous judgement, but then Thoreau wasn't known for his graciousness.

24 July

Sailing the Atlantic, Francis Higginson shows why there will be no room for blasphemers and sodomites in the 'new paradise of New England'

1629 The Puritan minister Francis Higginson was one of the most strenuous and ingenious boosters of settlement in the New World. Educated at Cambridge, he took up a ministry in Leicestershire before deciding to join the Massachusetts Bay Company's emigration to New England, leading an advance group, a year ahead of John Winthrop's Great Migration of 1630 (see 11 November). Higginson's account of the crossing was kept as a journal, then – dated this day – turned into a letter to be sent home. A later letter describing the country for 'his friends in Leicester' was published as *New-Englands Plantation* (1680), some time after his death.

Hoisting sail at Gravesend on 25 April 1629, the fleet made its way slowly around the south coast of England into the Atlantic. At sea one of Higginson's eight children, a little girl, died of smallpox. But since she had long been ill, he recuperated the tragedy as an expression of God's mercy, 'a blessing from the Lord to shorten her misery'.

Apart from the Puritan saints, there were labourers on board, hired to build log houses and plant crops for the larger migration still to come. One of these was a 'notorious wicked fellow that was given to swearing and boasting ... that he had got a wench with child ... railing and jesting against puritans'. He too 'fell sick of the pox and died', but this time it was God's justice operating, not his mercy. Meanwhile, the saints 'sounded and found thirty-eight fathom', showing that they were now close to land. They celebrated by pausing briefly 'to take codfish and feast ... merrily'.

Most challenging of all were 'five beastly sodomitical boys', whose

> ... wickedness not to be named ... was so foul we reserved them to be punished by the governor when we came to New England, who afterward sent them back ... to be punished in Old England, as the crime deserved.

Just two days further on, the sea was wreathed in flowers, 'which we supposed to be brought from the low meadows by the tide. ... Now fine woods and green trees by land and these yellow flowers painting the sea, made us all desirous to see our new paradise of New England.'

The argument is clear. New England is for God's elect, not for the wicked, whom God punishes either with death or the ignominious punishment fitting the crime: a passage back for those who live by the back passage. Those who pass the test of the Atlantic crossing find their ground, feast on nature's bounty and thrive. 'Whereas I have for divers years been very sickly and ready to cast up what I have eaten', Higginson claimed, 'yet from the time I came on shipboard to this day I have been strangely healthful.'

Within a year of writing this he was dead.

25 July

At the height of the Potsdam Conference, Tyrone Slothrop, disguised as Rocketman and cradling a twelve-pound bag of hashish, sees Mickey Rooney leaning over the balcony of no. 2 Kaiserstrasse

1945 Did this really happen or was it just a hilarious imaginative construct in Thomas Pynchon's *Gravity's Rainbow* (1973)? If it did, Mickey Rooney immediately suppressed the memory of the event as too improbable, the narrator assures us. Did giant industries really influence the bombing in the Second World War so as to obliterate their outdated plant, while sparing factories making the most advanced weapons for use against their 'own' side?

Or to take another Pynchon fiction (but *is* it fiction?), *The Crying of Lot 49* (1966), is Oedipa Maas really the victim of a secret, elaborate, electronic assault on her integrity, or does she just think she is? Does a secret, alternative postal system really exist, with a long history extending back into Renaissance Europe? Plausible references to actual historical events (albeit up to now given a more innocent interpretation), reinforced by scholarly footnotes, support the hypothesis. And what about Kurt Vonnegut's *Slaughterhouse-Five* (1969)? Was an American Nazi dressed up as Captain America really allowed to visit prisoners of war in Dresden, trying to recruit them to the Wehrmacht?

This is the fiction of paranoia, very fashionable in the sixties because it paralleled events in both political and critical history. On one level it was an appropriate response to covert operations in real life, like the plot to kill Kennedy (see 29 November) and the publication of the Pentagon Papers in 1971, which showed that the US had been waging a top-secret war in Vietnam from as early as 1945. On another it deconstructed distinctions between fact and fiction, posing both as plots to control the world.

As for the 'truth' behind the allegations, a popular paradigm is the so-called urban myth. Do giant albino alligators really roam the New York sewers? Remember all those baby alligators given children as toys during the 1950s? What did your mother do with yours when you got tired of it? Exactly. But lacking proof, the truth remains elusive. Who wants to go down into the sewers to find out? Well, in the case of Pynchon studies, the resourceful Tim Ware does. He runs the Thomas Pynchon Wiki (http://pynchonwiki.com/). According to him, Mickey Rooney wasn't really at Potsdam, though he came close. He was in Germany attached to an army entertainment at the time of the conference, but was unable to get away.

26 July

John Muir spends 'a day that will never end' among the trees and crystals at the top of Mount Hoffman

1869 Travellers and adventurers in the American West, from the humble Forty-Niners to the grandly educated Francis Parkman (see 15 February), kept track of their encounters in journals. This was partly to keep a record, of course, but it was also to add physical detail to an account of strange and wonderful landscapes and settings that would otherwise seem simply fantastic in retrospect.

John Muir was one of the greatest of these natural observers – a Thoreau who actually went somewhere. Born in Dunbar, Scotland, he emigrated with his family to Wisconsin, and studied botany and geology at the University of Wisconsin. His articles on Yosemite and other sites of overwhelming natural beauty in the California Sierra, published in *Harper's*, *Scribner's* and *The Century* in the 1870s and 1880s, did much to promote the American National Parks movement. He founded the Sierra Club, which remains one of the country's most effective ecological lobbying groups.

On this day, as published in *My First Summer in the Sierra* (1911), Muir 'rambled' to the top of Mount Hoffman – at 11,000 feet, 'the highest point in life's journey my feet have yet touched'. Although his account of the view is rhapsodic – 'serene, majestic, snow-laden, sun-drenched, vast domes and ridges … [with] lakes and meadows in the hollows' – it also deploys the language of scientific geology: 'a ridge or spur about fourteen miles from the axis of the main range, perhaps a remnant brought into relief and isolated by unequal denudation.'

In fact, the two descriptive modes reinforce each other. Knowing the scientific names of things enhances their brilliance – indeed, makes them visible in the first place. 'The surface of the ground, so dull and forbidding at first sight … shines and sparkles with crystals: mica, hornblende, feldspar, quartz, tourmaline … keen lance rays of every color flashing.'

But it was the trees that really got him going:

The hemlock (*Tsuga Mertensiana*) is the most beautiful conifer I have ever seen … It is now in full bloom, and the flowers, together with thousands of last season's cones still clinging to the drooping sprays, display wonderful wealth of color, brown and purple and blue. Gladly I climbed the first tree I found in the midst of it.

So full of glee is he, the serious scientist is not embarrassed to confess climbing a tree like a child. It's part of the fun – and also part of the close observation. No wonder his spirits remained high:

Toward sunset, enjoyed a fine run to camp, down the long south slopes, across ridges and ravines, gardens and avalanche gaps, through the firs and chaparral, enjoying wild excitement and excess of strength, and so ends a day that will never end.

27 July

President Franklin Delano Roosevelt signs the Federal Writers' Project into law

1935 Putting unemployed writers to work during America's Great Depression, the Federal Writers' Project (FWP) was among the most visionary pieces of legislation brought in as part of Roosevelt's reformist New Deal.

Some of the 6,600 writers employed by the FWP (up to 25 per cent, falling to 10 per cent after 1936) could be recruited from the ranks of professional writers – journalists, novelists and the like – whether or not they were out of work. The rest had to be the actual unemployed on relief. This meant teachers, librarians, bank clerks – almost anyone who could put together a coherent paragraph.

But for FWP director Henry G. Alsberg, invoking the best Popular Front spirit of collective egalitarianism, these very disadvantages could be given an ideological spin. Writers needed to get away from the idea that their art was 'sacrosanct', he thought. Instead 'cheap books, less fuss about our sacred personalities, and more service to the common cause in the fight against fascism … would bring us very much closer to the masses'.*

What did they write? Best remembered are the American Guide series, one devoted to each state in the union. Though providing itineraries for car tours, along with suggested places to eat and stay, these were far more than guide books, offering histories, cultural surveys and even the folklore of the states covered.

More useful in the long run were the FWP's oral histories, begun after the state guides were completed. 2,900 of these life stories have been filed in the Library of Congress; thousands more remain in state collections. They cover every occupation and region, from cowboys in Texas to fishermen in Maine, including tenant farmers and even ex-slaves in the South.

Among the many American authors to be given their first chance, or an early break, by the FWP were Conrad Aiken, Saul Bellow, John Cheever and Frank Yerby. Studs Terkel turned the life histories into his life's work. His *Division Street, America* (1966), *Hard Times* (1970) and

---

* Henry G. Alsberg, speaking extemporaneously at the Second American Writers' Congress, 1937, in Henry Hart, *The Writer in a Changing World*, New York: Equinox Cooperative Press, 1937, p. 245.

The Good War (1984) presented the voices of Chicagoans talking about their jobs and their city.

Black writers gained most. Zora Neale Hurston in Florida, Richard Wright in Chicago and Ralph Ellison in New York – all found their material and voices while working for the project. Hurston finished three novels, Wright wrote *Native Son* (1940), and Ellison's experience in gathering oral history in New York gave him the key to black speech in his masterpiece, *Invisible Man* (1952).

28 July

Last Exit to Brooklyn, *the censor's last throw*

1966 Segments of Hubert Selby Jr.'s *Last Exit to Brooklyn* had been printed in the US as early as 1957. One extract – recounting the gang rape of the whore Tralala – had been prosecuted, and cleared, around the period of the first *Lady Chatterley* trials, in 1959. The whole work was published in America in 1964. Selby's novel was palpably rawer than Lawrence's, and there was a nervous interval in the UK before the firm of Calder and Boyars (who specialised in avant-garde literature) took the risk of publishing *Last Exit*, on 24 January 1966. The British publishers took the precaution of sending a pre-publication copy to the director of public prosecutions (DPP), who said he could not instruct them on the legal situation, and to various professors, who were all for going ahead. The publishers took the further precaution of pricing the novel sky-high, at 30 shillings, a ruse that often mollified the censorious. Nonetheless, the book proved a bestseller, selling 11,000 copies in its first few weeks.

There were, from the first, stirrings of anger among establishment figures. A Conservative MP, Sir Charles Taylor, on 28 June, brought this 'filthy and disgusting book' to the notice of the attorney general, who declined to take action. Another Tory MP, Sir Cyril Black, using a provision in the 1959 Obscene Publications Act, moved at Bow Street on 28 July to have *Last Exit* banned. The magistrate issued a search warrant of Calder and Boyars' premises and seized three sample copies. The publishers vowed to continue publishing. By this stage, however, booksellers were distinctly anxious about handling it.

The case was heard at a magistrates' court in mid-November. Unlike the *Lady Chatterley* case (a fiasco, moral conservatives thought), the prosecution mustered persuasive witnesses – including the then respectable mogul Robert Maxwell (who declared the novel 'muck'). The magistrate, Leo Gradwell, found the book obscene and ordered the three seized copies destroyed.

Calder and Boyars appealed. On 6 February 1967 the DPP indicated that he would, after all, prosecute. A second trial was heard at the Old Bailey, 13–22 November 1967. The jury was, by direction of the judge, all male, to spare ladies possible embarrassment. Among the array of prosecution and defence expert witnesses, particular impact was made by David Sheppard, former opening batsman for England, who had given up his sporting career to work among the poor and take religious orders (he would later be appointed Bishop of Liverpool). Sheppard had been, he testified, 'not unscathed' by reading the raping-to-death of Tralala, and the violation of her corpse with a broomstick. Despite a barrage of expert defence from leading academics, cultural commentators, writers and clergymen, the jury found the book to be obscene. The publishers, somewhat bad-temperedly, accused the jury of being ignorant and suggested that in such trials in the future at least an A-level in literature should be a necessary qualification. It did not go down well.

On July 1968, an appeal was heard. Acting for Calder and Boyars was John Mortimer. The appeal judges, while not actually clearing *Last Exit to Brooklyn*, could see no reason, under the terms of the existing law, for suppressing its sale and circulation.

Effectively the exoneration of Selby's book completed the process begun with the *Lady Chatterley* trial in 1960. Henceforth censorship on grounds of sexual obscenity was a dead letter.

29 July

The USS Indianapolis *is sunk by a Japanese torpedo*

1945 The Portland-class cruiser USS *Indianapolis* was on a return voyage, having delivered critical parts for the atomic raid on Japan, 6 August. She was torpedoed and sunk in minutes by a Japanese submarine in the Philippine Sea.

For security reasons, there was strict radio silence. Three hundred men went down with the ship. Some 900 were left in the water, with no lifeboats – exposed to shark attacks – for three days. Only 316 were eventually rescued. It was the largest loss of life from a single vessel in the US Navy during the whole of the Second World War.

The disaster is memorialised in the 1975 film *Jaws*, in which Quint, in an edgy drinking scene on board the *Orca*, with Chief Brody and the marine biologist Hooper, recounts his experiences as an *Indianapolis* survivor.

Quint's monologue is, with Orson Welles' 'cuckoo clock' monologue in *The Third Man*, one of the most famous such moments in film. Both were the invention not of scriptwriters, nor the novelists (Peter Benchley, Graham Greene) from whom the film narratives were adapted, but composed by the actors themselves.

Robert Shaw's Quint monologue can be heard and seen at: http:// www.youtube.com/watch?v=5nrvMNf-HEg (It will be noted he gets the date wrong – June, not July.)

Shaw was born in Lancashire, the son of an alcoholic doctor who had married one of his nurses and killed himself with an overdose of opium when his son was twelve. Shaw taught for a while, after himself leaving school in Cornwall (whose regional accent is detectable, even under his assumed American accent), before studying at RADA. At school he excelled at sport and might – had his career gone differently – have been a professional rugby player. He would gravitate towards physical roles. He was also a novelist of great talent.

Like Richard Burton, Shaw could not afford to waste his considerable acting talent on the stage, where he made an early reputation in Shakespeare. His most commendable film role was as Aston, in the 1963 adaptation of Pinter's *The Caretaker*. Notably memorable is the character's extended monologue about the abusive effect of electroconvulsive therapy on his brain. Shaw's name was made, and his career likewise, by his performance as the psychopathic SPECTRE assassin, Grant, in the James Bond film, *From Russia with Love*, which also came out in 1963.

Like Burton, Shaw enjoyed (if that's the word) riotous sessions with fellow-drunk and screenwriter, Alistair MacLean. He died, on the set of a wholly undistinguished film, aged only 51, leaving a clutch of distinguished novels. 'I would rather', he once said, 'go down as having written one good novel than be acclaimed as a great actor.'

It is as Quint, alas, that he is destined to be remembered on the innumerable TV re-runs of Steven Spielberg's most popular film.

30 July

Better late than never?

1919 In the last year of the First World War a shell-shocked Wilfred Owen was treated at Craiglockhart Hospital in Scotland (see also 22 July). Here he met Siegfried Sassoon – something that was influential on the poetry Owen was writing. It shows a remarkable development over these months, notably his masterpiece, 'Strange Meeting'. It opens:

> It seemed that out of battle I escaped
> Down some profound dull tunnel, long since scooped
> Through granites which titanic wars had groined.
>
> Yet also there encumbered sleepers groaned,
> Too fast in thought or death to be bestirred.
> Then, as I probed them, one sprang up, and stared
> With piteous recognition in fixed eyes,
> Lifting distressful hands, as if to bless.
> And by his smile, I knew that sullen hall,—
> By his dead smile I knew we stood in Hell.

Unfortunately for Owen, the treatment at Craiglockhart, under the brilliant psychotherapist A.J. Brock (Sassoon was treated by the equally brilliant William Rivers), was the best to be had anywhere. Craiglockhart did not cure Owen, but it rehabilitated him sufficiently to be returned to the Front in September 1918. Following the ever-bloodier battles of 1917–18, there was an urgent need for men, particularly trained officers, for the 'last push'. He was, he informed Sassoon, 'in hasty retreat to the Front'. The shells, he said, 'scream at me every time: "Haven't you got the wits to keep out of this?".'

In October 1918 Owen won the Military Cross by capturing a German machine gun. He claimed, in a letter, to have killed only one of the enemy, with his revolver. The official (and witness-verified) commendation for his Military Cross reports differently:

> He personally manipulated a captured machine gun in an isolated position and inflicted considerable losses on the enemy. Throughout he behaved most gallantly.

Oddly enough, it was in the same battleground, at the Sambre-Oise Canal, that Fitzgerald's Jay Gatsby is recorded as doing heroic things with a machine gun, and winning his Montenegran medal for gallantry.

Owen was killed on 4 November, by rifle fire. His family were informed by telegram, a week later, as bells rang across England to celebrate the long-awaited Armistice, on the eleventh day of the eleventh month. He was 25 years old. If he had lived, as did his comrades Robert Graves (who rather despised Owen, and hinted at cowardice) and his fellow homosexual, Siegfried Sassoon, would he have developed as a poet (as, arguably, Graves did and Sassoon didn't)?

Almost a year after his death, on 30 July 1919, his family received his Military Cross.

31 July

Daniel Defoe is pilloried – literally – for The Shortest Way with the Dissenters

1703 To a high Tory like Alexander Pope, Daniel Defoe was just one of those innumerable hacks of Grub Street, part of that 'involuntary throng' buzzing around the throne of Dulness. In Book II of *The Dunciad* (1743) the goddess presents a tapestry picturing her most illustrious acolytes, among whom, 'Earless on high, stood unabash'd De Foe' (line 147) – that is, Defoe punished as though a 17th-century Puritan under Archbishop Laud.

Defoe irked Pope for three reasons: he was a radical dissenter, he was a political pamphleteer, and he wrote for money, rather than being supported by patrons. These very qualities might prompt a later age – imbued with Adam Smith's respect for the market and (Defoe's own) Robinson Crusoe's genius for practical solutions – to admire him the more.

As it happens, there's some substance to Pope's portrait of Defoe standing 'unabash'd' on the podium of punishment. In 1702 he published *The Shortest Way with the Dissenters*, an ironic proposal that religious dissenters should be done away with – banished from the realm if not something worse. The Church of England had been too lenient up to now, the pamphlet argued. In the reign of King James I, 'the worst they suffered was, at their own request, to let them go to New

England, and erect a new colony'. Even now, the worst they suffer is to be fined 'Five Shillings a month for not coming to the Sacrament, and One Shilling per week, for not coming to Church: this is such a way of converting people as was never known! This is selling them a liberty to transgress, for so much money!'

If any think the remedy cruel, consider that 'It is cruelty to kill a snake or a toad in cold blood, but the poison of their nature makes it a charity to our neighbours, to destroy those creatures! ... Serpents, toads, vipers, &c., are noxious to the body, and poison the sensitive life: these poison the soul! corrupt our posterity! ensnare our children! destroy the vitals of our happiness, our future felicity! and contaminate the whole mass!'

It was a satirical trick that Jonathan Swift would repeat 29 years later with *A Modest Proposal*, in which he urged that children of starving Irish beggars be cooked and eaten. The trouble with *The Shortest Way* was that many in authority took it seriously and even began to borrow its imagery. When they discovered who had written the pamphlet, the high-church establishment, tricked into making fools of themselves and thereby proving his satirical point, took their revenge. Defoe was punished on this day for seditious libel – not by having his ears cut off but by being put in the stocks for three days, fined heavily and thrown into Newgate prison.

Legend has it that instead of throwing rotten vegetables and dead rats at him, the populace bestrewed his scaffold with flowers.

1 August

Shakespeare's little helper is laid to rest in St George's church, Southwark

1715 Although an accomplished translator, satirist and dramatist (he helped Dryden with the second part of *Absalom and Achitophel* and wrote the libretto for Purcell's *Dido and Aeneas*), Nahum Tate is best remembered for his weird adaptations of Shakespeare. His version of *Richard II*, rewritten as *The Sicilian Usurper* (1681), made all references to both the person and institution of majesty respectful, even though the king was being deposed. In the same year he reworked *Coriolanus* as *The Ingratitude of a Common-Wealth* so as to 'Recommend Submission and Adherence to Establisht Lawful Power'. With all such submission gone, the unruly Roman plebs (meant to parallel Tate's contemporary Whigs) ensure that the play ends in a melodramatic explosion of violence, with Aufidius, Young Martius and Virgilia dead by the end, and Volumnia gone mad.

But it was on *King Lear* that Tate really went to town – in that same *annus mirabilis* of 1681. The mouthy Fool is cut out altogether, no doubt because he would simply confuse the new simplicities. The wicked are punished. Gloucester survives. Cordelia is spared the makeshift hanging and lives to marry Edgar. Lear is restored to his throne, and all live happily ever after. Edgar speaks the postscript:

> Our drooping Country now erects her Head,
> Peace spreads her balmy Wings, and Plenty Blooms.
> Divine *Cordelia*, all the Gods can witness
> How much thy Love to Empire I prefer!
> Thy bright Example shall convince the World
> (Whatever Storms of Fortune are decreed)
> That Truth and Vertue shall at last succeed.

Coming after even what horrors are left in Tate's version, these rhyming decasyllabics sound neat to the point of absurdity, but it's worth recalling what one of the greatest English critics, Samuel Johnson, wrote about *King Lear* in the notes to his great 1765 edition of Shakespeare's plays. What he called 'the extrusion of Gloucester's eyes' he found 'an act too horrid to be endured in dramatick exhibition'. Moreover, Shakespeare 'suffered the virtue of *Cordelia* to perish in a just cause, contrary to the natural ideas of justice, to the hope of the reader, and, what is yet more strange, to the faith of the chronicles'.

'A play in which the wicked prosper', he continued, 'and the virtuous miscarry, may doubtless be ... a just representation of the common events of human life; but since all reasonable beings naturally love justice, I cannot easily be persuaded, that the observation of justice makes a play worse.'

Aristotle would agree. His *Poetics* (ca. 335 BC) argues that the crucial distinction between art and real life, *mimesis* or imitation, plays out in the audience response. If you witness a murder on the street corner, you are terrified, disgusted. In a play or an epic poem, set in the logic of moral cause and effect, the act becomes more true than horrifying.

And it's true that the sacrifice of Cordelia takes *King Lear* a step beyond the customary dénouement of tragedy. Albany starts the sort of usual winding-up speech used to conclude the earlier tragedies, saying to Kent and Edgar, 'you twain / Rule in this realm and the gored state sustain', but Kent knows he is about to die, while Edgar thinks that (for once at the end of a tragedy) we should: 'Speak what we feel, not what we ought to say.'

2 August

Murdoch's brain

1999 It was announced on this day that John Bayley had given the brain of his late wife, Iris Murdoch, to OPTIMA (the Oxford Project To Investigate Memory and Ageing). The team's principal interest is Alzheimer's disease.

Murdoch, an Oxford philosopher and Booker Prize-winning novelist (for *The Sea, The Sea* in 1978) had requested that her body be donated to medical research.

She was diagnosed, at the age of 77, with Alzheimer's two years before her death.

The pain that she, her husband, and friends suffered during her decline (and earlier, happier times) is recorded in John Bayley's memoir, *Iris*, published in late 1998 (i.e. shortly before she died), and *Elegy for Iris* (1999). Bayley's recollections were successfully filmed in 2001 with Kate Winslet as the younger Murdoch, and Judi Dench as the older, in *Iris*, directed by Richard Eyre.

Since her death on 8 February 1999, Murdoch's brain had been preserved at Addenbrooke's Hospital in Cambridge. It was removed to the OPTIMA laboratory at the Radcliffe Hospital, Oxford. Murdoch's funerary arrangements are described by her biographer, Peter Conradi:

> At her own request, no one attended her cremation; nor the scattering of her ashes 'North of J8 flower-bed', as the undertakers vouchsafed, at Oxford Crematorium; and no memorial service followed.

The 19th century, as an aspect of their fascination with phrenology, were fascinated by novelists' brains. When Thackeray was a little boy, his favourite aunt was alarmed to discover that his uncle's hat exactly fitted William's five-year-old head. He was rushed to the doctors – water on the brain (hydrocephaly) was suspected. Aunt Ritchie was reassured to be told 'that the child indeed had a large head: but there was a great deal in it'.

Thackeray's head, as busts and portraits made during his life testify, does look unusually capacious. When he died prematurely, aged 52, Thackeray's brain was extracted and declared to be extraordinarily heavy: 'weighing no less than 58.5 oz'.

In point of literary-anatomical fact, Thackeray's brain was not, for a novelist, outstandingly big. The Russian novelist Turgenev, for example, weighed in at a jumbo 70 oz. To the disgrace of French literature, Anatole France's cranium supplied only 36 oz of grey matter.

The weight of Murdoch's brain is unrecorded.

3 August

John Rut writes the first letter home from the New World

1527 'Pleasing your Honourable Grace', the letter to Henry VIII began, 'to heare of your servant John Rut with all his company here in good health thanks be to God.' Very little is known about John Rut, and nothing further was heard from him after he returned to England.

But he emerges briefly on the world stage as author of the first known letter to be sent to Europe from North America.

A seasoned mariner, Rut was recruited by Henry VIII to look for a north-west passage, a search that would motivate voyages of exploration and settlement for the next century. Even as far south as Virginia in 1608, Captain John Smith, shortly after landing with the first permanent English settlement in America, was ordered to sail up the Chickahominy River to find the fabled route over the top of what is now Canada through to the Pacific.

The search eluded both men – Smith because the Chickahominy soon became too shallow to explore further, and Rut and his crew because they kept running into icebergs:

> We ran in our coarse to the Northward, till we came to 53 degrees; there we found many great Islands of ice and deepe water; we found no sounding, and then we durst not go no further to the Northward for feare of more ice.

But they did find St John's Harbour in Newfoundland, which provided both a welcome shelter and also (to the modern reader) a surprise, since 'there we found Eleuen Saile of Normans and one Brittaine and two Portugal barks all a fishing'. In fact, though we popularly date the discovery of America with Columbus landing in 1492, mariners from Portugal, France and even the west of England had been fishing the Grand Banks of Newfoundland since at least the second half of the 15th century, and had certainly gone ashore for supplies and provisions.

Rut and his men had gone ashore too, where they found

> … wilderness and mountains and woodes and no naturall ground but all mosse and no inhabitation nor no people in those parts; and in the woods we found footing of divers great beasts but we saw none not in ten leagues.

Failing the north-west passage they could at least fill their ship with salt cod, and sail southwards. And so to home, via the east coast of Florida, the first English ship to follow that route.

4 August

Out West for the first time, Owen Wister is underwhelmed by cowboys

1885 Owen Wister's *The Virginian* (1902) invented the western, signalling the cowboy as an American hero and establishing patterns of plot and character that would last through the 20th century in film and fiction. Yet for all its mythical dimensions, Wister would always claim that the book was based on first-hand experience, gleaned over a decade of travel in British Columbia, Washington, Oregon, California, Texas – above all (and repeatedly) Wyoming.

Wister's journal kept on the first of these excursions, to Wyoming in July and August of 1885, suggests boys camping out and doing a lot of shooting – of grouse, elk, bear, even sheep (wild, presumably). His first account of ranch life, on 4 August 1855, was a one-liner: 'At a roundup – it's very interesting, but beastly hot.' Later he expanded on his reaction. After describing their skill in cutting and bunching the cattle, he had this to say about the cowboys:

> They're a queer episode in the history of this country. Purely nomadic, and leaving no posterity, for they don't marry. I'm told they're without any moral sense whatever. Perhaps they are – but I wonder how much less they have than the poor classes in New York.

Perhaps there's just a hint of the noble savagery to come in that last sentence, but how different this first impression from Wister's preface to *The Virginian*, where the typical cowpuncher is courageous, honest, polite and well-spoken to women, 'the last romantic figure upon our soil'. As for what he portends for the country's history: 'He and his brief epoch make a complete picture, for in themselves they were as complete as the pioneers of the land or the explorers of the sea.'

Why the change? Wister was one of those well-born and well-educated easterners for whom vacations in the West were a way of discovering timeless values from which eastern civilisation had slipped. Another was his classmate at Harvard (and dedicatee of *The Virginian*), Theodore Roosevelt. Roosevelt, who had his own ranch in North Dakota, authored a series about ranch life in the *Century* magazine in

1888, in which he promoted the West as a test of American manhood, a rite of passage to full citizenship.

If Wister gave us the fiction of the West, Roosevelt provided its ideology.

5 August

Nathaniel Hawthorne and Herman Melville meet for the first time

1850 At mid-century, in mid-summer, the two classical authors of the American renaissance were in mid-career. Hawthorne's *The Scarlet Letter* had come out five months earlier. Melville had written five books on seafaring themes, starting with *Typee* (1846), the bestselling account of his adventures in the South Pacific – favourably reviewed by Hawthorne, as it happens – and was now at work on a sixth, about a whaling vessel hunting an albino whale.

Melville had just bought a house in Pittsfield, in north-western Massachusetts, where other literary notables lived, like the poet and medical professor Oliver Wendell Holmes and James Russell Lowell, poet and later editor of the *Atlantic*. Just six miles away, in Lenox, lived Nathaniel Hawthorne.

A perfect setting for a literary coterie, you might think. You'd be wrong. Nineteenth-century America didn't do literary coteries, except in New York City. Melville and Hawthorne had never met, nor even knew they were neighbours, and it's not clear that Melville had yet met Holmes and Lowell either. Café society it wasn't.

So it took a New Yorker, Melville's friend, Evert Duyckinck – editor, publisher and leading light of the Young America Group, which promoted American literature and worked for copyright reform to keep cheap British books from flooding the local market – to bring them together. At his suggestion a picnic was arranged for 5 August, to include Melville, Hawthorne and Holmes. They would climb nearby Monument Mountain, drink champagne and talk about the necessity of a distinctly American literature.

As it turned out, the excursion was surprised by a thunderstorm. While sheltering from the rain, the two novelists got to talking, and Melville's usually chilly manner thawed into a torrent. In a later letter to Hawthorne he wrote: 'I feel that the Godhead is broken up like the bread at the Supper, and that we are the pieces. Hence this infinite fraternity of feeling.'

Something else happened too. Either in preparation for the meeting, or in response to it, Melville belatedly read Hawthorne's collection of stories, *Mosses From an Old Manse* (1846). His essay on the experience, published in two parts by Duyckinck in *The Literary World* for 17 and 24 August, remains one of the most perceptive assessments of Hawthorne's deep allegories ever written. Commenting on the 'darkness' lurking in Hawthorne's tales, Melville wrote that 'this great power of blackness derives its force from its appeals to that Calvinistic sense of Innate Depravity and Original Sin, from whose visitations ... no deeply thinking mind is wholly free'.

That association between darkness and depth would, in turn, deepen the white whale tale, then in process, and turn it into *Moby-Dick*.

6 August

The poet Robert Lowell receives his letter drafting him for service in the US armed forces. He declines the invitation

1943 'Dear Mr President', Lowell wrote in answer to his draft notice, 'I very much regret that I must refuse the opportunity you offer me in your communication of August 6, 1943, for service in the Armed Forces.' Once willing to serve, he had now become a conscientious objector in protest at the Allies' policy of saturation bombing of German cities. 'I was a Roman Catholic at the time', he recalled in a 1969 BBC interview, 'and we had a very complicated idea of what was called "the unjust war". ... So I refused to go into the army and was sent to jail. I spent about five months in jail and mopped floors.'*

Before being sent to the Federal Correctional Center in Danbury, Connecticut, which specialised in COs, along with first-offence bootleggers and black marketeers, he was held a few days in New York's tough West Street jail, in a cell next door to Murder Incorporated's Louis (Lepke) Buchalter. 'I'm in for killing', said Lepke. 'What are you

---

* Robert Lowell, 'Et in America ego – The American Poet Robert Lowell Talks to Novelist V.S. Naipaul about Art, Power, and the Dramatisation of the Self', *The Listener*, 4 September 1969, pp. 302–04.

in for?' 'I'm in for refusing to kill.' Lepke laughed. Five months later he was electrocuted at Sing Sing.*

'Memories of West Street and Lepke', in *Life Studies* (1959), would tell the story more succinctly:

> I was a fire-breathing Catholic C.O.,
> and made my manic statement,
>   telling off the state and president …

That was written looking back from 'the tranquillized Fifties', as Lowell put it. But an earlier poem, one that mentions nothing of these particulars, had much more to say about the poet's mood and thought at the time. This was 'The Quaker Graveyard in Nantucket' (1946), a strenuously ambitious meditation drawing on Thoreau's description of a shipwreck in *Cape Cod* (1865), Captain Ahab's mad pursuit of the white whale and the sinking of his ship in Melville's *Moby-Dick* (1851), and other allusions to the self-destructive will.

'The Quaker Graveyard' is dedicated to 'Warren Winslow, Dead at Sea'. Winslow was Lowell's cousin, a sort-of alter ego to the poet. Both hailed from the high-minded New England Protestant establishment; both attended Harvard. But while Lowell left to study poetry with John Crowe Ransom, converted to Catholicism and got jailed for resisting the draft, Winslow joined the Navy on graduating in 1940, serving as an officer on three destroyers.

On 3 January 1944, while Lowell was 'serving' in quite another sense, the last of Winslow's postings blew up while at anchor at the entrance to New York harbour, killing 123 sailors and fifteen officers, Winslow among them. No enemy was involved; the damage was entirely self-inflicted. To the poet the accident must have seemed a perfect emblem for what he felt had changed Allied strategy. The real theatre of operations was in home waters, the real violence self-generated, the real struggle within the American soul.

---

* Ian Hamilton, *Robert Lowell*, London: Faber & Faber, 1983, p. 91.

7 August

Rumour has it the Scottish play is first performed – though not in the usual place

1606 Shakespeare probably wrote *Macbeth* early in 1606. There are allusions in the play to the Gunpowder Plot of 1605 and the trial of the conspirators early the following year – particularly in the play made by the porter in Act II, scene iii on the word 'equivocation', not just a facetious comment on the double-dealing and double-speaking going on in the play, but also the theological concept posed by one of the conspirators, the English Jesuit Henry Garnett, as a justified tactic against injustice.

But when and where was it first performed? The earliest documentary account places the play in the Globe Theatre on the South Bank in 1611, with legendary tragedian Henry Burbage in the leading role. But it's more likely that the play saw first light at Hampton Court on this day, when a number of works were presented by the King's Men before King James and his brother-in-law, King Christian IV, then visiting from Denmark.

Shakespeare seems to have been keen to flatter both parties, leaving the Danes out of the Scandinavian attack on Scotland at the beginning of the play, playing up to James's interest in witchcraft, and celebrating the long lineage of Banquo, as shown in the masque presented by the witches in Act IV, scene i, down through eight happy generations, culminating in James himself – the sixth of Scotland, and first of England. Macbeth is horrified:

Another yet! A seventh! I'll see no more.
And yet the eighth appears, who bears a glass
Which shows me many more; and some I see
That twofold balls and treble sceptres carry:
Horrible sight! Now I see 'tis true;

In this most psychological of Shakespeare's tragedies, Macbeth's soliloquies have struggled between his conscience and ambition. Now that he realises he has been shut out of history, that gap between desire and act closes down. 'From this moment', he says just after the witches depart with their dumb show, 'The very firstlings of my heart shall be / The firstlings of my hand'. Everything contracts, shuts down; in this shortest of the tragedies time seems to accelerate almost to an apocalyptic crisis.

8 August

Elizabeth rallies her mariners

1588 British monarchs, with the noble exception of Alfred and James I, do not figure high in the literary annals of their country. Highest is Elizabeth I, who wrote very creditable poetry (notably 'On Monsieur's Departure') and – assuming it is all her own work – a patriotic speech unmatched in its oratorical eloquence by any except those of Winston Churchill in the Second World War.

The occasion for her great speech was the imminent invasion by the Spanish empire. One hundred and fifty ships and 26,000 men of the Spanish Armada had set sail from Lisbon on 28 May 1588, with the aim of making England a Spanish colony and returning it to the Catholic faith. It was planned that 30,000 extra troops would join the invasion force from the Spanish Netherlands.

The Spanish were sighted off the coast of England in late July and the news communicated by beacons to London. The logistic task of mustering the combined Spanish army from the Low Countries gave the English time to organise their own forces, to harass and successfully engage the Spanish fleet – taking full advantage of the British navy's superior seamanship and more manoeuvrable vessels.

On 8 August, with the final encounter in the Channel imminent, Elizabeth came to Tilbury, as near the front line as a monarch could come, and delivered her speech to her sailors, and to her people:

> My loving people, we have been persuaded by some that we are careful of our safety, to take heed how we commit ourselves to armed multitudes for fear of treachery; but, I do assure you, I do not desire to live to distrust my faithful and loving people. Let tyrants fear, I have always so behaved myself, that under God I have placed my chiefest strength and safeguard in the loyal hearts and goodwill of my subjects; and, therefore, I am come amongst you as you see at this time, not for my recreation and disport, but being resolved, in the midst and heat of battle, to

live or die amongst you all – to lay down for my God, and for my kingdoms, and for my people, my honour and my blood even in the dust. I know I have the body of a weak and feeble woman; but I have the heart and stomach of a king – and of a King of England too, and think foul scorn that Parma or Spain, or any prince of Europe, should dare to invade the borders of my realm; to which, rather than any dishonour should grow by me, I myself will take up arms – I myself will be your general, judge, and rewarder of every one of your virtues in the field. I know already, for your forwardness, you have deserved rewards and crowns, and, we do assure you, on the word of a prince, they shall be duly paid you.

Famously, the Armada was defeated principally by a series of late summer storms that scattered their fleet and made them easy prey for the English privateers (commanded by such heroes as Sir Francis Drake and Sir John Hawkins). As the medal cast for the event recorded, *Afflavit Deus et dissipantur* – 'God sent forth His breath and they were scattered'. The speech, doubtless, helped.

9 August

Edgar Allan Poe invents the detective story, then disparages his achievement

1846 Alright, maybe Poe didn't actually invent the novel of detection – that distinction is claimed by E.T.A. Hoffman, whose *Das Fräulein von Scuderi* came out in 1819 – but he set the conventions for the genre as we know it, from Conan Doyle to Raymond Chandler. Detectives are not policemen – far from it. They may be anything from seedy private dicks to scholars of a retiring disposition, but they will work outside the police investigation, often incurring the suspicion of the flat-footed regulars. The detective will often have a sidekick who doubles as narrator of the tale. Most important – and this gives the genre its name – the process of catching the culprit depends on detection, or reasoning from evidence.

In Poe's 'The Murders in the Rue Morgue', first published in *Graham's Magazine* in 1841, Le Chevalier C. Auguste Dupin and his friend read in the papers about the horrific murder of two women, one with her throat cut and the other strangled, then stuffed half-way up a chimney. Normally retiring and asocial, Dupin is intrigued and visits the scene of the crime, and – through a series of deductions – works out that the 'murderer' was a pet orang-utan that had escaped its owner, after grabbing his straight-edge razor while he was shaving.

But in a letter to the lawyer and minor poet Philip P. Cooke written on this day, Poe played down the significance of his invention. 'These tales of ratiocination [as he called his detective stories] owe most of their popularity to being something in a new key', he wrote. 'People think them more ingenious than they are.' To take 'The Murders in the Rue Morgue', for example, 'where is the ingenuity of unravelling a web which you yourself (the author) have woven for the express purpose of unravelling? The reader is made to confound the ingenuity of the sup-positious Dupin with that of the writer of the story.'

Important as this passage seems now, it wasn't Poe's main concern in the letter. He was anxious to sign Cooke up for his planned compendium of 'Literary America' (a grand project, never completed), as the author of the essay on himself. To that end, he wanted to pass on Elizabeth Barrett's good opinion of his poem 'The Raven' – 'This vivid writing! – this power *which is felt!*' – as conveyed in a recent letter. 'Would it be bad taste to quote these words of Miss B. in your notice?' Opportunistic? Maybe, but don't forget that Poe was the first American to make his living solely through creative writing. It was never too late in one's career for a touch of log-rolling.

10 August

The Vikings defeat the Anglo-Saxons in the Battle of Maldon, early testimony to the English cult of defeat

AD 991 Now known for its sea salt, Maldon on the Blackwater estuary in Essex was once the site of a skirmish that led to one of the great works of Anglo-Saxon poetry.

Three thousand Viking raiders led by Olaf Tryggvasson were camped on Northey Island in the estuary. Against them, Byrhtnoth, a local ealdorman (or earl) loyal to King Aethelred, led a much smaller

English force, drawn up on the bank opposite the island. The Vikings offered a truce for gold, which Byrhtnoth scornfully refused.

Unable to get off the island except at low tide via a narrow causeway bordered by mud, the Vikings realised that only a few of their fighters at a time would be able to confront the English. Their numerical advantage would be cancelled out. So they asked leave to be allowed off the island before the battle began. In a gesture still debated by historians, Byrhtnoth granted this condition. In the battle that followed he was killed, along with many of his household thanes, and the militia raised locally was defeated.

The Battle of Maldon, written that same year, focuses on English values still discussed today as part of the national identity. First, there was Byrhtnoth's concession to the Viking raiders, explained in the poem as fair play prompted by his *ofermode* (literally 'over-mind'), which can mean courage as well as pride.

Then came loyalty to the liege lord even in defeat. The poem invokes the virtue of sacrificial courage, in full knowledge of the hopelessness of the cause. After Byrhtnoth is hacked down, the old retainer Byrhtwold speaks to the remaining English soldiers:

'Hige sceal the headra, heorte the cenre,
mod sceal the mare, the ure mægen lytlath,
Her lith ure ealdor eall forheawen,
god on greote; a mæg gnornian
se the nu fram this wigplegan wendan thenceth.'*

The Battle of Maldon provides early proof that the English see moral lessons in defeat, relish and remember it far more keenly than victory.

---

* 'Thought shall be harder, heart the keener, / Courage shall be greater, as our might lessens. / Here lies our elder all hewn down, / The good [man] in the dust; may he mourn [forever] / Who from this warplay thinks to turn [away].'

11 August

Enid Blyton is born in a flat above a shop in Lordship Lane, East Dulwich, London

1897 The phenomenally successful author of children's fiction was nothing if not prolific, regularly producing between 10,000 and 14,000 words of finished copy a day. In 1948 alone she brought out 28 titles under fifteen imprints. By 2007, nearly 40 years after her death, over 3,400 translations had been made of her books, almost as many as of Shakespeare's work.

She is best known now for the Famous Five and Famous Seven stories (Noddy, for very young children, was a relatively late arrival). The 'Five' tales involve four boarding-school pals home on holiday, plus their dog, going on adventures like camping, or exploring the seaside. In the 'Seven' series the companions are amateur sleuths solving mysteries that baffle the police. The bad guys are invariably working-class, sometimes foreign as well.

As the country's social climate lurched from rationing and austerity to sexual liberation in the swinging sixties, Blyton's fiction was criticised for its increasingly eccentric construction of normality. Families had mummies and daddies who sent their children away to school; everyone had access to the countryside; boys were leaders while girls played with dolls (unless, like Georgina in the Five books, they called themselves George and wanted to out-Tom the boys).

No doubt these comforting family structures compensated for the lack of them in Blyton's own life. Just before her thirteenth birthday her father left the family to live with another woman. Blyton herself married a divorced man, then divorced him in turn to marry another, making sure that the children would never see their father again.

And what is less often remembered is that before Blyton's work was assailed for classism, sexism and racism, librarians in the late forties and fifties worried that it was linguistically and stylistically too undemanding to stretch their young readers' minds – the sentences too short, the vocabulary limited, the implied authorial attitude moralising and condescending.

Of course Ernest Hemingway worked very hard to achieve short sentences and a basic vocabulary, but this was middle-class England. Anyway, as Enid Blyton said, librarians probably disliked her books because 'the hordes of children swarming into the library on Saturday morning became a nuisance'.* Or so she would have found them, anyway.

12 August

Who or what killed J.G. Farrell?

1979 It was on this day that the death of the Booker Prize-winning novelist J.G. Farrell was announced to the world. The exact nature of his death, however, remains mysterious – despite rigorous biographical investigation – to this day.

Had he been born a year later, posterity would probably never have had Farrell's fiction. When he went up to Oxford in October 1956, 'Jim' Farrell was anything but literary. Head boy at his Irish public school, 'rugger was pretty well my life', he later recalled.

On 28 November 1956 – the height of the season – Jim Farrell had a bad game. He didn't feel right in the changing room afterwards, 'cut the usual drinking session', took a bus back to college and crawled fully-clothed into bed.

He had polio. Six days later he was in an 'iron lung – that life-saving apparatus which was half Edgar Allan Poe's "Buried Alive" and half medieval torture rack'. Jonas Salk's vaccine became widely available six months later, leading to the eradication of the disease, and the iron lung would join the hook-hand in the medical museum.

When he was recovered sufficiently for 'physio' he was three stones lighter, and had shoulders that, to his mortification, he heard one girl call 'flabby'. It was like the Charles Atlas story in reverse: the husky young athlete had become a 90-pound weakling. Jim Farrell became J.G. Farrell; an 'outsider', in the term popularised by Colin Wilson that same year. No longer a player, he became a spectator. The novelist was born.

Farrell scraped a third. It did not faze him. He had already resolved to write. That was what outsiders did best. Over the next few years, he got by on various teaching jobs and travelling fellowships. He compensated for his disability by sexual athleticism, running three or four girlfriends at the same time.

---

* Quoted in Robert Druce, *This Day our Daily Fictions: An Enquiry into the Multi-Million Bestseller Status of Enid Blyton and Ian Fleming,* Amsterdam: Rodopi, 1992, p. 38.

Farrell's first three ventures in fiction did nothing to separate him from the 1,500 or so novelists every year who try their luck and get nowhere. He was, however, mining his own family background – the Anglo-Irish ascendancy, the Anglo-Indian professional classes, the army-officer caste.

Novelists, like generals, need luck. *Troubles*, Farrell's story of the Irish uprising and the battles between the IRA and the Black and Tans, came out in 1970, a few months after Ulster exploded into flames. Few novels have been more timely. *Troubles* hit the jackpot. And Farrell made it to the top with his Indian Mutiny novel, *The Siege of Krishnapur*, which won the Booker in 1973.

Farrell, only 38, was rich and famous. He fired his agent and went into tax exile in Kilcrahone, south-west Ireland. Here, living close to the land and the sea, he found, as he said for the first time, *douceur de vivre*.

There then happened the strange episode of Farrell's death, aged only 44, on 11 August 1979. He was fishing in high seas near his home and was knocked off the rock on which he was standing by a wave, falling into the water. It was the same storm that would later drown eighteen contestants in the Fastnet yacht race. What was odd, according to witnesses, was that Farrell made no effort to save himself. He did not shout for help and his body was recovered only much later.

Was it suicide? An IRA hit? Is J.G. Farrell, like Elvis, still alive? It remained a mystery for 30 years until the last person to see Farrell alive, Pauline Foley, went on record in *The Times* (7 February 2010) to recall what actually happened. Foley was walking alongside the rocks with her children:

> When Foley ... saw him, he was standing on a ledge, wearing wellington boots and holding a fishing rod. Fishing was the first sport Farrell had been able to enjoy since contracting polio. The illness had left him unable to cast the rod overhead with one hand, so instead he tucked the rod under his arm and cast by twisting his body. It made balancing tricky. 'It was very rough, splashing up on the rocks, but there weren't killer waves,' recalled Foley. 'He turned and waved to the boys. The boys waved back. He turned back, started to cast and slipped. I think it was more of a slip than the waves.' Farrell made no attempt to save himself. Foley said: 'I called to him, "I'm coming" ... I started to go down there. It was just his head in the water. There was no

waving, no call to me. He was just looking at me. All the time he looked at me. I don't even want to think what he felt.'

What killed him was the long-term debility of his polio. He was too weak to save himself. What made him a writer killed him.

13 August

The Duke of Marlborough leads an army of northern European forces against the French at Blindheim, to win a famous victory

1704 The bloody Battle of Blenheim (as the English spelled it) was fought on the banks of the Danube near the small Bavarian town. It was part of the long-running War of the Spanish Succession to prevent Philip V, grandson of Louis XIV of France, from becoming King of Spain and thus threatening a grand alliance between those two countries. The duke's army included Austrians, Prussians, Hessians, Dutch and Danes, alongside the 12,000 English. After a long day's fighting 20,000 French troops lay dead and another 14,000 had been captured, including their commander-in-chief, Marshal Tallard.

It was a famous victory. When Marlborough returned to England a grateful Queen Anne granted him extensive parkland at Woodstock, north-west of Oxford, along with £240,000 to build a country house there. That's well over 30 million in today's pounds. The result was the monumental and gargantuan Blenheim Palace, designed by Vanburgh in the mercifully short-lived style of the English baroque. It is still the seat of the Dukes of Marlborough, and the only building not connected with monarchs or bishops to be called a palace. Winston Churchill was born there in 1874.

Poetic tributes were more modest in scale, though at first no less adulatory. Joseph Addison's 'The Campaign' (1705) tells the story in 47 stanzas of decasyllabic couplets prefaced by a Latin epigram. Though not glossing over the scenes of razed villages and murderous conflict, the poem draws the national moral:

Such are th' effects of Anna's royal cares:
By her, Britannia, great in foreign wars, [...]

By her th'unfetter'd Ister's states are free,
And taste the sweets of English liberty:

Getting on for a hundred years later, when people had forgotten why the war had been fought in the first place, the literary establishment wasn't so sure – not even the Poet Laureate Robert Southey. His 'After Blenheim' (1796) imagines little Peterkin coming across a smooth, round, hard object while playing in a field, and bringing it to his grandfather to be identified. ''Tis some poor fellow's skull', says his grandfather, adding that he often ploughs them up. Prompted by Peterkin, he tells the saga of the battle, his father's house burnt to the ground, the women and children put to the sword, the bodies rotting in the sun after the battle.

'And everybody praised the Duke
Who this great fight did win'—
'But what good came of it at last?'
Quoth little Peterkin.
'Why that I cannot tell,' said he,
'But 'twas a famous victory.'

14 August

John Updike publishes his first contribution to the New Yorker.
It is a comic poem entitled 'Duet with Muffled Brake Drums'

1954 It fantasised the moment when Rolls met Royce 'where grey walks sloped through shadows shaped like lace / Down to dimpleproof ponds, a precious place', and Rolls asked:

'Ah—is there anything you'd care to make?
A day of it? A fourth at bridge? Some tea?'
Royce murmured, 'If your afternoon is free,
I'd rather, much, make engineering history.'

John Updike (1932–2009), one of America's most prolific and gifted fictional realists, wasn't best noted for his poetry – even if he did publish ten volumes of it between 1958 and 2009 – nor for his stories, critical essays and other short pieces. What made him popular with such a wide and varied readership were his novels like *Couples* (1968), his exploration of suburban adultery, *The Witches of Eastwick* (1984), popular social satire with an edge, and above all, the near-epic span of the four volumes, running from the fifties through the eighties, that filter the anxieties and satieties of each decade through the limited perception and wide emotional range of Harold C. Angstrom, better known by his nickname 'Rabbit'.

Alongside the novels, Updike wrote over 800 poems, stories and essays for the *New Yorker* alone. It made an ideal medium. Started in 1925, the (usually) weekly magazine, with over a million subscribers in the top quartile of the American incomes, has published fiction by John O'Hara, John Cheever, Philip Roth and many others, long non-fiction features like John Hersey's *Hiroshima* (1946) and Rachel Carson's *Silent Spring* (1962), biographical essays, book and film criticism, political commentary (fastidiously neutral until George W. Bush came along) – not to mention its classic cartoons by Charles Addams, Saul Steinberg, Otto Soglow and William Steig.

Updike's contributions to the *New Yorker* show the same closely observed detail and critical accuracy apparent in his longer work – whether in a patient's fear of the dentist:

> Burton's heart beat like a wasp in a jar as the dentist moved across the room, did unseeable things by the sink, and returned with a full hypodermic. A drop of fluid, by some miracle of adhesion, hung trembling to the needle's tip.' ('Dentistry and Doubt', 1955)

Or in the legendary Ted Williams hitting his last home run for the Boston Red Sox:

> From my angle, behind third base, the ball seemed less an object in flight than the tip of a towering, motionless construct, like the Eiffel Tower or the Tappan Zee Bridge. It was in the books while it was still in the sky. ('Hub Fans Bid Kid Adieu', 1960)

Or (just to show that he could also write about writing) on Herman Melville's faith, which was also his own:

> Melville is a rational man who wants God to exist. He wants Him to exist for the same reason we all do: to be our rescuer and

appreciator, to act as a confidant in our moments of crisis and to give us reassurance that, over the horizon of our deaths, we will survive. ('Herman Melville', 1982)

15 August

Disguised as a snake, the Devil invades a meeting of the Synod in Cambridge, Massachusetts, but Mr Thomson, an elder of Braintree and a man of much faith, treads it under foot

1648 American Puritan settlers in Massachusetts saw the hand of God behind everything from droughts and tempests to a snake in the meeting house. Since devout Puritans were either saved or damned from before birth, no amount of good works could save their souls. Good and evil were abstractions to which the most momentous or trivial events could be key.

This one is recorded in the journal of John Winthrop, twelve times governor of the Massachusetts Bay Colony that settled the area around Boston in 1630. At first it looked like an ordinary snake that came in through an open door during the sermon and slithered onto one of the elders' seats, causing 'diverse of the elders' to get up and move pretty smartish, until Mr Thomson stood on the intruder's head and held its body 'with a small pair of grains [barbed prongs], until it was killed'.

Only afterwards, 'nothing falling out but by divine providence', did they assign the true meaning of the occurrence: 'The serpent is the devil; the synod, the representative of the churches of Christ in New England.'

Why should everything remind these worthies that the Devil was out to get them? Because the churches of New England, as Winthrop wrote in an earlier entry, were 'such as come together into a wilderness, where are nothing but wild beasts and beastlike men, and there confederate together in civil and church estate'. To this exposed position the threats were not just the wild animals and savages of the New World, but the dissolution of the colony itself – discouraged people leaving for the West Indies, or to join the Dutch on Long Island, or even to return to England.

Throughout most of the 1640s it was this fear that the great Massachusetts experiment would fail through depopulation that fed the governor's paranoia, which anxiety was displaced, in turn, onto fantasies of diabolical snakes.

16 August

Massacre of Peterloo

1819 What is hyperbolically called the Massacre (or the 'Battle') of Peterloo took place on St Peter's Field, in Manchester, on 16 August 1819, in the wake of the profound industrial unrest that followed the Napoleonic wars. Such periods are invariably feared by authorities as potentially revolutionary.

Some 80,000 working-class Lancastrians (and 'agitators' from outside – notably the firebrand orator, Henry Hunt) massed to demand the reform of Parliament, so as to give greater representation to the unenfranchised non-householders in the country. Anger at the relaxation of the Corn Laws and widespread unemployment had further inflamed popular resentment.

The panicked magistrates mustered the local military, and instructed them to disperse the crowd and arrest Hunt. The crowd was not unruly, and the demonstration, despite radical speeches, was not violent. Organised by their chapels (i.e. trades unions) the workers in the crowd were, in point of fact, better disciplined than the nervous soldiers facing them.

Cavalry charged on the crowd, causing panic. Something under twenty people were killed (compared with 48,000 at Waterloo) and around 500 injured – more by horses' hooves and trampling than by sabres. Hunt, along with eight others, was arrested and sentenced to two years in prison for 'sedition'.

The 'Massacre' tilted political agitation in Britain towards 'physical' rather than 'moral force' solutions. And the event entered the calendar of radicalism as a holy day in the workers' struggle. It was helped there by the poet Shelley. In Italy, he got the news on 5 September and fired off his anthem to the oppressed classes of England:

Men of England, heirs of Glory,
Heroes of unwritten story,
Nurslings of one mighty Mother,
Hopes of her, and one another;

Rise like Lions after slumber
In unvanquishable number,
Shake your chains to earth like dew
Which in sleep had fallen on you—
Ye are many – they are few.

17 August

Charlotte Perkins Gilman commits suicide

1935 Charlotte Perkins was born in Hartford, Connecticut. The Perkinses were a cultivated family rooted in a cultivated community (Harriet Beecher Stowe was a distant relative – see 20 March).

Charlotte was physically vital as an adolescent: visiting a gymnasium twice a week and running a mile every day. She disdained corsets. On leaving school she studied at the Rhode School of Design, leaving without any formal qualification but with the working skills to design greeting cards and tutor young people in art. She intended to pay her way through the world.

In 1884 Charlotte married the artist Charles Walter Stetson. After the birth of their first child, a daughter, she was plunged into post-natal depression.

In 1887 the advice of S. Weir Mitchell, a specialist in 'women's disorders', was called on. A believer in the 'rest cure' (i.e. solitary confinement and sensory deprivation), Mitchell prescribed the regime described, horrifically, in Gilman's most famous story, 'The Yellow Wall-paper', in which the 'cure' is portrayed as therapeutic, patriarchal sadism.

Charlotte escaped by fleeing to Pasadena, California, from where she divorced her husband. They remained on amicable terms. He married her best friend (for whom, it is speculated, Charlotte's feelings had been overtly erotic) and took over the care of their child. In California

Charlotte (still Stetson and now genuinely 'cured') began to write and lecture on feminist subjects.

She was, by nature and intellectual conviction, utopian: believing in the possibility not merely of equality, but gynocracy; a theme pursued in her novel, *Herland: A Feminist Utopian Novel* (1915), which foresees a woman-dominated world. Androcracy, she firmly believed, could be overset. In 1900 she married a cousin, George Houghton Gilman, an attorney of passive character and seven years younger (Gilman's sexual interests, in her early Pasadena years, seem to have been principally lesbian). The Gilmans lived contentedly, by all accounts, in southern California, until his death in 1934. Gilman, afflicted with breast cancer and a believer in euthanasia, killed herself (with chloroform that she had methodically stored) a year later, leaving an autobiography, *The Living of Charlotte Perkins Gilman* (1935), and a suicide note of Roman stoicism, stating: 'When all usefulness is over, when one is assured of unavoidable and imminent death, it is the simplest of human rights to choose a quick and easy death in place of a slow and horrible one.'

18 August

Lolita *is published in the US*

1958 Five years after it was written, three after its first appearance in Paris under the imprint of the Olympia Press and the subsequent seizure by British customs of all copies entering the UK, *Lolita* finally emerged in the United States, to become an almost instant bestseller. Usually we chronicle such past repressions implying that we are all much more enlightened and liberal now, but would the 21st century greet any more warmly a novel about a middle-aged man falling in love with, then kidnapping, a twelve-year-old girl? Not likely.

Of the two films made of the book – Stanley Kubrick's in 1962 and Adrian Lyne's in 1997 – the former was the better, thanks to the script (to which Nabokov contributed) and the outstanding acting of James Mason and Shelley Winters as Humbert and Charlotte, and the ingenious improvisations of Peter Sellers as Quilty. But good as it was, the movie could only reproduce surface dialogue, whereas the heart of the prose narrative is the complex working of Humbert Humbert's consciousness as he advances then retreats, rhapsodises most subjectively over his nymphet then stands apart in objective blame of his behaviour, only to exonerate himself by appeal to irresistible passion.

The dialectics of Humbert's inner monologue open thematic debates too. Who does the seducing – the innocent American or the wily European (perhaps representing America and Europe generally)? 'Frigid gentlewomen of the Jury! … I am going to tell you something very strange: it was she who seduced me', claims Humbert. Tactically, maybe, but only within Humbert's elaborate, long-planned strategy.

Again, who is the more trapped – Lolita as she is moved around from Kumfy Kabins to Sunset Motels to U-Beam Cottages ('Children welcome, pets allowed'), always watched over by Humbert until sprung by Quilty? Or Humbert by his obsession? It is Humbert who winds up in prison, literally; but Lolita, who escapes, is betrayed by Quilty, only to be trapped again as the heavily pregnant 'Mrs Richard F. Schiller', stuck in a ramshackle cabin, unable to pay her debts or get to Alaska, where her husband has the promise of a good job. But this time it's Humbert who springs her, with the gift of four thousand dollars, out of hopeless love.

Then he sets off for his vengeful rendezvous with Clare Quilty.

19 August

The New York Herald *breaks the news of the California Gold Rush*

1848 'The gold mine discovered in December last', reported the paper's anonymous correspondent, 'is only three feet below the surface in a strata [*sic*] of soft sand rock.' The same vein, between twelve and eighteen feet deep, runs at least twelve miles to the south and five to the north, he continued, so that 'I would predict for California a Peruvian harvest of the precious metals, as soon as a sufficiency of miners, &c., can be obtained'.

Nearly right. On 24 January 1848 (not the preceding December), James Marshall was building a lumber mill for a Swiss settler called John Sutter, in the foothills of the Sierra, east of what is now Sacramento, when he came across some gold flakes in the tailrace. The two men tried to keep the discovery quiet, but the rumour spread, and by March a newspaper editor was broadcasting it in San Francisco.

Almost immediately, people in California downed tools and headed for the mountains to try their luck. But the *Herald* announcement spread the word to the rest of the country – and the world. Prospectors came by sea – around the Horn or across the isthmus of Panama – while as many again, with less to spend, crossed the country in wagon trains starting from Missouri. For these transcontinental voyagers (more like tourists than pioneers, let alone explorers), it was the journey of a lifetime, producing an explosion of vernacular writing in diaries and journals as they struggled to account for the strange physical and social landscapes on the way (see 18 June).

But the Gold Rush also attracted professional writers. If the Forty-Niners were writing for their families, journalists like Leonard Kip, J.D. Borthwick and Bayard Taylor had metropolitan readerships in their sights. For them California was just so much local colour, its details to be described and consumed *de haut en bas*.

Nothing was what it seemed. Kip in *California Sketches* (1850) told how he 'peeked into' many gambling houses 'and was surprised to see how easily French paper, fine matting, and a small chandelier, can convert the rough ribs of an old barn into an elegant hall'. They were fascinated by California's lack of scale. San Francisco had grown in under a decade from a small Mexican outpost and mission town to an American city of 50,000 inhabitants, supported by restaurants, hotels, banks and even an opera house. Yet whole tracts of it could burn down in a single night. The city's earthquake and fire of 1906 is what people remember now, but that was just the largest of a series of natural disasters to be made good in record time.

Social codes were scrambled too. On landing in San Francisco, Bayard Taylor had tried to find a porter to carry his trunk, only to be told that 'every man is his own porter here'. 'Dress was no gauge of respectability', he wrote in *Eldorado* (1850). 'Lawyers, physicians, and ex-professors dug cellars, drove ox-teams, sawed wood, and carried luggage', wrote Taylor in a sketch later collected in his book, while 'men who had been Army privates, sailors, cooks or day laborers were at the head of profitable establishments'. Comic or just democratic? Depends on your point of view.

20 August

England's finest naturalist–novelist is buried

1887 Richard Jefferies was born near Swindon in Wiltshire. His father was a farmer in a small way, with 40 acres. He was unlucky, being bankrupted in 1877, and ending up a jobbing gardener. James Luckett Jefferies (1816–96, he outlived his son by several years) is immortalised as Iden, in *Amaryllis at the Fair* (1887).

Richard was educated locally and at Sydenham, in Kent, among aunts and uncles. Aged sixteen he demonstrated his independence of spirit by running away to France with a friend. They intended to make their way to Moscow, or failing that, America.

Jefferies finally settled on Swindon, where he began to write for Wiltshire newspapers, journals and magazines – mainly on local historical and natural history topics. His views were strongly Conservative, and conservationist.

In 1867 he suffered severe illness and was never again to be in good health. Tuberculosis had, in fact, been diagnosed in his early childhood. He married Jessie Baden, a farmer's daughter, in 1874 and began writing.

It was some time before Jefferies could find a publisher for his more sensitive and introspective work, *The Dewy Morn* (eventually published in 1884). In it he found his distinctive mix of ruminative countryman essay and fictional plot. His essays on rural distress in *The Times*, in the early 1870s, were influential, and publicised his name.

In 1876 he moved to London, where his reprinted papers *The Gamekeeper at Home* (1878) and *Wild Life in a Southern County* (1879) were well received. The two strands of Jefferies' prose – descriptive essay and fiction – merged, triumphantly, in *Wood Magic* (1881). It was followed by the childhood autobiographical novel, *Bevis* (1882), and the spiritual autobiography of adolescence, *The Story of My Heart* – his masterpiece and a work that Jefferies had been meditating for seventeen years.

In 1881 Jefferies' health collapsed. Tuberculosis and a painful fistula (and numerous operations on it) made writing an agony. The remainder of his life was passed as an invalid in various health resorts, impecuniously. He nonetheless refused aid from the Royal Literary Fund, on moral principle. His last works were dictated to his wife from his death bed. He died of tuberculosis, at Goring on Sea, aged only 38, leaving his wife and three children virtually penniless. His remains were buried on 20 August 1887 at Broadwater cemetery, Worthing. Despite the wretched pauperism of his last years, Jefferies' reputation has risen steadily over the century following.

21 August

The first of two English sisters arrives in Montreal to kick-start Canadian literature

1832 She was Catharine Parr Traill, and since she would be followed in under a month by Susanna Moodie, 1832 can really be counted an *annus mirabilis* of Canadian literature. Their maiden name was Strickland, and back home other sisters were also adding to the freight on library shelves. Elizabeth Strickland was author of *Disobedience: or, Mind what Mamma Says* (1819), while Agnes, who (like Susanna) also wrote children's books, is best remembered as a historian and biographer, author of (among many other studies) the twelve-volume *Lives of the Queens of England* (1840–48). None of them had formal schooling.

Susanna and Catharine married friends from the Orkneys, both army officers. Lots of Scots were emigrating to Canada. Thomas Traill already had relatives there, while the older John Moodie, who had spent ten years in South Africa (and of course, in this literary environment, had written a book about it), was also disposed to join the flow. After landing at Montreal, where a plague of cholera was raging, Thomas and Catharine took the stage westwards for Cobourg, on the north shore of Lake Ontario, then headed north to Lakeland, in what Susanna would call 'the bush'. John and Susanna first tried working an already cleared farm near Cobourg, but soon ran out of money, sold up and joined the Traills at Lakeland.

There they lived in log cabins, learned to manage everything from a horse and plough to a birch-bark canoe, and shared hopes, fears and practical tasks with their neighbours, like clearing land, building houses, pulling teeth and assisting at childbirth. But they didn't go native. Susanna sent frequent sketches of her life in the bush to the Montreal *Literary Garland*, and Catharine wrote regular letters home to her literary family. In time these dispatches coalesced into their best-known books, Traill's *The Backwoods of Canada* (1836) and Moodie's *Roughing It in the Bush* (1852).

In these accounts and others, the sisters established a Canadian voice quite distinct from that of their contemporaries south of the border. Whereas American immigrants (especially on what they called the frontier, rather than the bush) tended to develop an ideology of initiation, in which they imagined themselves to have experienced a rite of passage into a freer, more independent way of life, the Canadians, having retained their connections with the British empire, were happy to foster a community, unashamed to ask for help, or even to admit that they were bored as often as exhilarated by the wilderness – that at times the New World felt (as Moodie would put it) like a 'green prison'.

Maybe this is why Margaret Atwood, the doyenne of Canadian writing, gave the sixth (and best) volume of her poetry the title *The Journals of Susanna Moodie* (1970), and why her imagination was so captured by the determination of those early immigrants, who:

> pretend this dirt is the future.
> And they are right. If they let go
> of that illusion solid to them as a shovel,
> open their eyes even for a moment
> to these trees, to this particular sun
> they would be surrounded, stormed, broken
> in upon by branches, roots, tendrils, the dark
> side of light
> as I am.

22 August

Jack London's Wolf House burns down

1913 Since selling his first story ('To the Man on Trail') in January 1899, Jack London had written for his living. His work ranged from socialist dystopias such as *The Iron Heel* to the perennially popular dog-and-wolf story, *The Call of the Wild* – a work that gave London his nickname, 'Wolf'. No writer in American literature wrote more profitably. In his last years (he died – by suicide, probably – in 1916, aged just 40) he was earning around $75,000 annually by his pen: in modern currency values about $2 million (and virtually tax-free).

London had taken to himself a handsome new wife (or 'mate-woman', as he called her) in 1905. He had high hopes of a Jack London Jr. by her (he had two daughters by his previous marriage). London had also in 1905 bought a property in northern California's Sonoma County – the beginnings of what he named his 'Beauty Ranch'.

London developed his ranch with an enthusiasm bordering on obsession. He was infected with the eucalyptus-planting mania that swept California in 1909 in the (false) belief that the eastern US was running out of timber and that 'Circassian walnut' (as eucalyptus wood was grotesquely called) would be commercially viable. The following year, London tore up 700 acres of vines and planted 16,000 seedlings on his ranch. Before the mania subsided some years later, London had planted around a quarter of a million trees and spent some $50,000. It was a wholly unprofitable speculation. Glen Ellen wine from London's ranch sells strongly to this day.

By 1912 Beauty Ranch had expanded to some 1,000 acres. At its centre, London began erecting a mansion to be called 'Wolf House'. The Spanish tile roof alone cost $3,500, and when finished the house would be a fit habitation for one who had shown himself so indisputably a leader of the human pack.

August 1912 was a month of disaster. On the 12th, London's wife, Charmian, had a miscarriage. There would be no son to carry on his name. On the very day that the couple intended to move into Wolf House, 22 August, it burned down. The cause – act of God or arson? – was unknown (most plausibly a disaffected workman was responsible).

The event, accompanied by chronic ill health, plunged London into the gloom that intensified over the last four years of his brief, but extraordinarily productive, life.

23 August

Unconquerable

1849 W.E. Henley was born on this day. When he died just under 54 years later, so would most of what little reputation he had built up during his lifetime. But every so often a poem, buried in the oblivion of the anthologies, takes off thanks to a wholly unpredictable celebrity boost. W.H. Auden became Beatle-famous when his lament, 'Funeral Blues', was featured in the 1994 film *Four Weddings and a Funeral.*

In January 2010, chance swung a similar spotlight on W.E. Henley and his poem 'Invictus'. It was mentioned by British prime minister Gordon Brown ('a battler', as he informed TV interviewer Andrew Marr) as his inspiration in fighting back the latest of the intra-party plots to unseat him.

On another front, Henley's poem inspired the title to the 2010 film recording Nelson Mandela's welding of the new Republic of South Africa on the rugby fields of Johannesburg. Henley's lines resound through the heart-warming film. ('Is *Invictus* based on a book?' is one of the FAQs on the IMDB website. 'Yes', is the astounding answer.)

For posterity Henley was known, if at all, as one of the more memorable of Robert Louis Stevenson's close acquaintances (they met in a hospital ward), and as the one-legged man who was a principal source for Long John Silver.

Unkindly, one commentator said that Brown's choosing Henley's poem 'is equivalent to choosing "My Way" as a Desert Island Disc … "Invictus" is the sort of poetic anthem that Hitler would have savoured in the bunker as Magda Goebbels poisoned her children and Eva bit into the capsule.'

This is too hard – although one might note that Timothy McVeigh, the Oklahoma bomber, chose the poem as his final statement to the world before his lethal injection for the murder of 168 fellow Americans in 2001.

Let the poem speak for itself:
Out of the night that covers me,
Black as the pit from pole to pole,
I thank whatever gods may be
For my unconquerable soul.

In the fell clutch of circumstance
I have not winced nor cried aloud.
Under the bludgeonings of chance
My head is bloody, but unbowed.

Beyond this place of wrath and tears
Looms but the Horror of the shade,
And yet the menace of the years
Finds and shall find me unafraid.

It matters not how strait the gate,
How charged with punishments the scroll,
I am the master of my fate:
I am the captain of my soul.

24 August

Rosencrantz and Guildenstern live again

1966 The first performance of Tom Stoppard's career-breakthrough play, *Rosencrantz and Guildenstern are Dead*, was on this day at the Edinburgh Festival 'fringe', in the dusty Cranston Street Hall off the Royal Mile.

The performance was poorly attended and even more poorly received.

The Scotsman, Edinburgh's premier paper, dismissed the play as 'a clever revue sketch which has got out of hand'. Other reviewers were similarly unimpressed. Cleverness was always in over-supply at the Edinburgh fringe and there was no reason to suppose a major theatrical career was being launched.

There was, however, one rave review – by Ronald Bryden, successor to Kenneth Tynan as the *Observer* theatre critic. Tynan, a king-maker in the stage world, was now commissioning for the National Theatre and he requested a copy of Stoppard's play. Long runs in London's West End and Broadway ensued.

The three-act text performed at Edinburgh and sent to Tynan was an expansion of a one-act *jeu d'esprit*, written by the 27-year-old Stoppard in 1964. *Rosencrantz and Guildenstern are Dead* draws on the then fashionable theatre of the absurd, specifically Samuel Beckett. Vladimir and Estragon – with Prince Hamlet as Godot – were clearly models in Stoppard's mind.

In Shakespeare's tragedy Rosencrantz and Guildenstern are what Henry James termed *ficelles* – 'strings', whose only function is to make the plot move. They are brought from Wittenberg to Elsinore by Claudius (with malign step-paternal intent) and Gertrude (with benign maternal intent) to discover what ails their melancholic fellow student, the Prince of Denmark.

Hamlet soon perceives that they are spies and later callously arranges their death. When Horatio (another Wittenberg comrade) suggests it is rather hard that they should 'go to it', Hamlet shrugs off his homicide with the comment: 'Why, man, they did make love to this employment. / They are not near my conscience.'

In Stoppard's play the two courtiers quibble between themselves, ponder deep questions of free will and probability (there is much flipping of coins) and try, desperately and futilely, to work out what is going on in a machine in which they are mere incognisant cogs.

Playing with Shakespeare 'metatheatrically' was not new. Eliot had hinted at something like Stoppard's play in 'The Love Song of J. Alfred Prufrock':

No! I am not Prince Hamlet, nor was meant to be;
Am an attendant lord, one that will do
To swell a progress, start a scene or two.

One of Brecht's exercises for his Berliner Ensemble in the 1950s was to replay the balcony scene ('Romeo, Romeo, wherefore art thou Romeo?') from the Nurse's point of view, as if she too were eager that night to get away for a tryst with her lover. 'Charles Marowitz's Hamlet', an absurdist 30-minute cut-up, had been performed at the Royal Shakespeare's Theatre of Cruelty season in 1965.

Stoppard's most likely inspiration (if there was one) was W.S. Gilbert's *Rosencrantz and Guildenstern*, a 'tragic episode: in three tabloids, founded on an old Danish legend'. Gilbert's fantasia was first published in 1874 in *Fun Magazine*. P.G. Wodehouse and George Bernard Shaw took part in subsequent amateur performances and Gilbert's playlet may well have influenced their own comedies. Gilbert's plot has Rosencrantz (very sensible, unlike the crazed prince) marrying Ophelia. She it is who comes up with the ideal solution to the Hamlet problem:

A thought!
There is a certain isle beyond the sea
Where dwell a cultured race compared with whom
We are but poor brain-blind barbarians;
'Tis known as Engle-land. Oh, send him there!
Exit Prince of Denmark.

25 August

Born in Belfast: the man who will overturn the American western film

1921 No wonder Brian (pronounced Bree-an) Moore was Graham Greene's favourite living author. He wrote thrillers, and novels about Catholic doubt, and had got 'a good grounding in shifting relativities and ambiguous loyalties' (as Bernard McGinley in the *Oxford Dictionary of National Biography* has put it) while working in Poland after the war for the United Nations Relief and Rehabilitation Administration (UNRRA).

After UNRRA he emigrated first to Canada, where he worked as a journalist, then to the United States, finally settling in Malibu, California. He wrote nineteen novels and eight screenplays, including Alfred Hitchcock's *Torn Curtain* (1966) and the script for *Black Robe* (1991), an ambitious recreation of the Jesuit mission in what is now Quebec City and the territory to the north-east of it, based on his own novel of the same name, published six years before.

To write *Black Robe*, Moore had immersed himself in the letters and reports back home of the Jesuits trying to convert the natives, a perspective that radically altered the conventions of the usual cowboys-and-Indians epic out of Hollywood – reinforced in the film, made in Canada and directed by an Australian, the seasoned Bruce Beresford.

Not that Hollywood hadn't already begun to undermine its own clichés. *Little Big Man* (1970; see 24 June) had reversed the old dichotomy between terrorised white families and predatory natives. Now the savages were the very US Cavalry that had so often ridden in at the last minute to save the beleaguered settlers, and their victims the Indian women and children camped on the Washita River. *Dances With Wolves* (1990) postulates one thoughtful man who takes the time and trouble to learn the ways of the Oglalla Sioux, only to have his good work cancelled out by unruly soldiers who come across his camp.

In *Black Robe* a party of Algonquins sets off with some Jesuits ('Black Robes' to the natives) to relieve a distant mission to the Hurons. It quickly becomes clear that the two cultures are entirely different, mutually incomprehensible, with no John Wayne out of *The Searchers* (1956) or Kevin Costner out of *Dances With Wolves* to read the natives' behaviour. Yet they have a culture if not equal to, then at least capable of confronting that of the whites. Though marvelling at writing and trying to make music from a European recorder by blowing in at the wrong end, they can shoot a partridge on the wing with a bow and arrow.

But there's nothing left of the noble savage. Indians fight their enemies just as bitterly as do the European and native white settlers. They are expert, exquisite torturers. The whites are unheroic, but they are not the murderous, rapacious cavalry out of *Little Big Man*. Though rough, they are courageous, hard-working and sincerely bent (for good or ill) on leading the Indians to Jesus.

Not that they succeed – on any level of grace. The Hurons resist the missionaries because their shamans have told them they will be destroyed if they convert. When they reluctantly accept the Gospel it's because they believe it will save them from another white import, the smallpox. The film's closing legend supplies the bleak dénouement:

Fifteen years later, the Hurons, having accepted Christianity, were routed and killed by their enemies, the Iroquois. The Jesuit mission was abandoned and the Jesuits returned to Quebec.

26 August

The last southern gentleman dies, aged 70

1744 Like Thomas Jefferson, William Byrd II of Westover was a Virginia country gentleman. Unlike Jefferson, he did not fret in the fetters of the mother country. Byrd belonged to a generation content to be British. If they lamented their distance from the court, coffee houses and other locales of wit and good conversation found in the metropolis, it was not as inhabitants of an adversarial separate country, but as provincials on the edges of a great empire. Byrd had been born in Virginia, but was schooled in Essex, went to Rotterdam to study business, then back to London to study law, before returning to Virginia to inherit his father's estate.

Back home he lived in a brick three-storey Georgian mansion on a plantation large enough to provide the land for present-day Richmond and Petersburg, as a government official (he was treasurer of Virginia), as an amateur naturalist (he was a Fellow of the Royal Society), and as the author of voluminous letters and diaries. He could read Hebrew,

Greek, Latin, Italian and French. His library of 4,000 volumes, one of the largest in the colonies, made up in books for what he lacked in good conversation.

Byrd's coded secret diary gives the flavour of his daily routine. On the last day of 1711, 'I rose about 7 o'clock and read a chapter in Hebrew and six leaves in Lucian. I said my prayers and ate boiled milk for breakfast.' On New Year's Day, 1712, 'I lay abed till 9 o'clock this morning to bring my wife into temper again and rogered her by way of reconciliation.' Later, 'Mr Mumford and I went to shoot with our bows and arrows but shot nothing, and afterwards we played at billiards.'

Private pleasures were balanced by public projects. His best known work, *The History of the Dividing Line Betwixt Virginia and North Carolina* (widely circulated but not published until 1841), followed an expedition to survey the disputed boundary. It is a mixture of science and satire: close observations of flora and fauna, of the natives' habits and the history of European settlement, spiced with sketches of the North Carolinans' gluttony, laziness and sexual excess: 'The only business here is the raising of hogs, which is managed with the least trouble and affords the diet they are most fond of' – so much so that they are beginning to look like hogs themselves.

Properly used for improving the mind and morals, leisure was a virtue, Byrd thought. This was very much a southern belief, not one shared by New England, for example. In his *Letters from an American Farmer* (1782), St John de Crèvecoeur tells the story of 'Mr Bertram, the botanist', who first cleared his land, then cultivated it, through which effort he earned the leisure to study nature in the abstract, and to take pleasure in his studies.

Susan Manning thinks that Byrd's contempt for North Carolina is displaced anxiety about his own idleness. After the Revolution, which imposed (even for Jefferson) a strict dividing line 'between virtuous industry and unpatriotic indolence', the precarious balance could no longer be maintained. Then the southern gentleman turned into a 'historical and literary myth', she argues, 'from the effete, enervated, but perfectly civilised Augustine St Clare in Stowe's *Uncle Tom's Cabin* to the atavistic heirs of Faulkner or Flannery O'Connor'.*

---

* Susan Manning, 'Industry and Idleness in Colonial Virginia: A New Approach to William Byrd II', *Journal of American Studies*, 28 (1994), pp. 190, 172.

27 August

Spain's most popular and prolific playwright dies at 73. His state funeral will attract vast crowds and last nine days

1635 He was born before Shakespeare, outlived him by nearly two decades and wrote (at the most conservative estimate) some 800 more plays. Félix Lope de Vega y Carpio, to give him his full name, invented a new drama for his time and place. He tore into the conventions of classical drama, banishing the three Aristotelian unities of time, place and action and coming up with dialogue and metre adjusted to the social and political status of the characters – formal for toffs, vernacular for peasants. He was the first dramatist to make a living from his plays.

And they came so quickly, so apparently easily. He claimed to have written some 1,500 three-act *comedias* (a term that includes tragedies as well as comedies), more than a hundred of which, he boasted, took 'only twenty-four hours to pass from the Muses to the boards of the theatre'. These totals may be exaggerated, but over 637 *comedias* are known by title, and the texts of 450 are still extant.

They ranged from explorations of conflicts between love and propriety that seem almost to presage English restoration drama – like *El perro del hortelano*, or *The Dog in the Manger* (1613), in which a countess falls in love with one of her servants – to plays of revenge, a popular Spanish genre that he began to deconstruct and ironise late in his career, as with *El castigo sin venganza*, or *Punishment Without Vengeance* (1631), in which a man kills his wife for an affair she starts in order to pay him back for his own infidelity, and winds up exposing himself, not only as a murderer but (worse) as a cuckold.

Besides his theatrical works he composed a large body of lyric poetry, pastoral novels, epic poems, autobiographical reminiscences and much else. On top of all this he was a man of action in and out of bed, with two wives and many mistresses – all of whom he seems to have loved dearly – not to mention serving with the Spanish army against Portugal, and the navy in the Azores, even joining the Armada to sail against England. He was lucky to be in one of the few ships not blasted out of the water at Gravelines or dashed against the coast of Ireland in the later attempt to escape. But he improved the six-month voyage by writing the better part of *La Hermosura de Angelica* (1602), a long verse epic in the manner of Ariosto.

28 August

Sebastopol falls, a great novelist rises

1855 During the Crimean War, Sebastopol, a Russian stronghold, was besieged by the British and French for many months. One of the Russian defenders of the city was Leo Tolstoy, a volunteer and very junior artillery officer. He wrote, as his first serious fiction, a series of short stories and descriptive pieces based on his military experience. They were published in book form as *The Sebastopol Sketches* in 1856.

Sebastopol, with its blood-drenched and battered bastions, is defended because the generals can think of nothing better to do. The besieged citadel leaks good Russian blood like a severed jugular – but not generals' or tsar's blood, of course.

Finally the position is surrendered on 28 August 1855 – for no other reason than that the generals, and their tsarist commander-in-chief, have arbitrarily decided to turn tail and run. The description of the shameful retreat forms a savagely anticlimactic conclusion to the last story of the Sebastopol series:

> The enemy saw that something incomprehensible was happening in awe-inspiring Sevastopol ... they did not yet dare to believe that their unflinching foe had disappeared ... The Sevastopol army, surging and spreading like the sea on a rough dark night, its whole mass anxiously palpitating ... away from the place where it was leaving so many brave comrades, from the place saturated with its blood, the place it had held for eleven months against a far stronger foe, but which it was now ordered to abandon without a struggle. The first effect this command had on every Russian was one of oppressive bewilderment.

And, in the case of one young officer, a lifelong scepticism about military 'strategy'. War is fog, blood and bad generalship. End of story.

During the weary months of the siege, when there was nothing to do but undergo bombardment and the occasional skirmish, Tolstoy read obsessively. His reading matter is interesting: the more so since this was largely the period in which his own authorial personality was being formed. Over 8–9 June 1855, for example, he records: 'Laziness, laziness. Health bad. Reading [Thackeray's] *Vanity Fair* all day.' The same lazy week he read, for good measure, Thackeray's *Henry Esmond* and *Pendennis* (we should all be so idle – this is about a million words of fiction). Tolstoy, as he dodged English and French shrapnel, read the English novel in French translation.

It is demonstrable (from textual echoes) that Thackeray's 'Waterloo Novel' (i.e. *Vanity Fair*) influenced Tolstoy powerfully, as did Thackeray's 'Showman of Vanity Fair' technique. It was the arch-Jamesian critic, Percy Lubbock (in *The Craft of Fiction*, 1921), who linked Tolstoy and Thackeray as the two masters of the 'panoramic' novel (in opposition to the 'dramatic' and more artistic James). It would seem they had already made the connection themselves.

29 August

As the Cuban missile crisis looms, Robert Frost leaves on a goodwill tour of the USSR

1962 Robert Frost was America's unofficial poet laureate. He was an icon, a national treasure, a bestseller compared to contemporary poets, widely consulted on cultural matters. In January 1961, he had been chosen to read a new composition at John F. Kennedy's inauguration – the first poet to be so honoured. Entitled 'Dedication', the poem prophesied a new 'Augustan age / Of a power leading from its strength and pride, / of young ambition eager to be tried'. But after a few lines the sun's glare troubled his eyes so that he could read no further, and he had to fall back instead on one prepared earlier (as the television cooks say) that he could recite by heart.

There were gaps between the public and private Frost. He was the genial poet-philosopher drawing universal truths from nature, but accused of being an uncaring father and husband. He was born and brought up in cities – San Francisco and Lawrence, Massachusetts, a textile-manufacturing centre – before spending two years at Harvard, yet his popularity owed a lot to his persona as a plain-speaking New England farmer. As the poet and critic Yvor Winters has written, 'the rural life is somehow regarded as the truly American life'; yet he adds, 'it is the poet's business to evaluate human experience, and the rural setting is no more valuable for this purpose than any other or no particular setting'.*

Another surprise is that some of his best-known poems, thought to be most typical of felt life on his New Hampshire farm – 'Mending Wall', 'After Apple-Picking', 'The Death of the Hired Man' – were written in England, where he lived from 1912 to 1915 before he moved to New Hampshire, and where he networked with other poets like Edward Thomas, Rupert Brooke and T.E. Hulme. Though now long regarded as the antithesis of modernism, his work piqued the interest of Ezra Pound, who reviewed it and got it published in *Poetry*.

So maybe it should be expected that his goodwill trip to Russia should have turned out to be less straightforward than anticipated. Secretary of the Interior Stewart Udall, a friend of Frost's, was due to go to the Soviet Union on a diplomatic mission, and suggested that Frost go along to read his work and do some general cultural interacting. Frost was keen to go, though fearful of the effect on his 88-year-old constitution. Kennedy endorsed the idea.

But Frost really wanted to meet Nikita Khrushchev, to tell the Soviet premier how much he admired his forceful denunciation of Stalin and encouragement of young writers like Yevtushenko and Solzhenitsyn, and to suggest a new relationship between the Soviet Union and the United States – not 'mutual co-existence' (Khrushchev's formulation, which Frost thought too negative) but, as Udall remembered the exchange, 'a hundred years of grand rivalry based on an Aristotelian code of conduct he called "mutual magnanimity"'.

What neither man knew was that Khrushchev had already begun to install missiles in Cuba, and was using his meeting with Frost partly to gauge how Kennedy would react to the disclosure. According to Udall, 'the only truculent outburst during our long talk' was a coarse joke Khrushchev made about some American senators talking big about invading Cuba but being unable to 'perform'.

Interviewed in New York after a long flight, unable to sleep for eighteen hours, Frost reported accurately on their hopeful exchange, but then, misremembering the joke (or misinterpreting its tone), claimed that 'Khrushchev said he feared for us because of our lot of liberals. He thought that we're too liberal to fight.' The next day the

---

* Yvor Winters, *The Function of Criticism: Problems and Exercises*, London: Routledge & Kegan Paul, 1957, p. 160.

Washington Post carried a banner headline: 'Frost Says Khrushchev Sees U.S. as "Too Liberal" to Defend Itself".*

Kennedy, who had already garnered intelligence of the missiles, was furious. Frost was sorry. If the president had been any less sure-footed, the provocation might have started the Third World War. Just under five months later the poet was dead.

30 August

The hotline between the leaders of the US and the Soviet Union goes operational

1963 It was the Cuban missile crisis that prompted the direct line between the two capitals. President Kennedy had demanded that the Russians remove their missiles from Cuba. The world waited, on the brink of the Third World War. Then at 6.00pm on 26 October 1962, the White House received a message from Soviet First Secretary Nikita Khrushchev, offering to remove the missiles if the Americans would undertake not to attack Cuba.

It took the Americans twelve hours to decode this crucial communiqué. Thinking the US was stalling, Khrushchev sent another message at 11.00 the next morning. This time the conditions were more stringent: the US to remove all its Jupiter missiles from Turkey and Italy first. Then Kennedy's advisors had a brilliant idea. Why not accept the conditions in Khrushchev's first message and ignore his second? It worked, but it was a close run thing.

So on 20 July the two countries set up a hotline between the capitals. In just a month it went into action. Phase one was just a duplex telegraph line, on the assumption that voice transmission would require simultaneous translation both ways, and lead to confusion – not to mention comic possibilities of the sort exploited in Stanley Kubrick's *Dr Strangelove* a year later.

Here's the scenario. Air Force General Jack D. Ripper, convinced that the Soviet Union has been polluting the 'bodily fluids' of the American people, has launched a nuclear strike on Russia. In the war room the American president, played by Peter Sellers to look and

---

* Stewart Udall, 'Robert Frost's Last Adventure', *New York Times*, 11 June 1972: http://www. nytimes.com/books/99/04/25/specials/frost-last.html

sound as much like Adlai Stevenson as possible, is calling Soviet premier Dmitri Kissov on the hotline:

> Hello? … Uh … Hello D– uh, hello Dmitri? Listen uh uh I can't hear too well. Do you suppose you could turn the music down just a little? … Oh-ho, that's much better … Now then, Dmitri, you know how we've always talked about the possibility of something going wrong with the Bomb … The *Bomb*, Dmitri … The *hydrogen* bomb! … Well now, what happened is … ahm … one of our base commanders, he had a sort of … well, he went a little funny in the head … you know … just a little … funny. And, ah … he went and did a silly thing … Well, I'll tell you what he did. He ordered his planes … to attack your country … Ah … Well, let me finish, Dmitri … Let me finish, Dmitri … Well listen, how do you think *I* feel about it? … Can you *imagine* how I feel about it, Dmitri? … Why do you think I'm calling you? Just to say hello? … Yes! I mean i-i-i-if we're unable to recall the planes, then … I'd say that, ah … well, ah … we're just gonna have to help you destroy them, Dmitri … All right, well listen now. Who should we call? … *Who* should we call, Dmitri? The … wha-whe, the People … you, sorry, you faded away there … The People's Central Air Defence Headquarters … Where is that, Dmitri? … In Omsk … Right … Listen, do you happen to have the phone number on you, Dmitri? … Whe-ah, what? I see, just ask for Omsk information.

Sellers ad-libbed much of this himself (it was later retro-scripted to become part of the film's official transcript). Four takes were spoiled because the actors around the war room table couldn't stop laughing.

31 August

Richard III is killed as the Tudors defeat the Plantagenets at Bosworth Field, bringing the Wars of the Roses to an end

1485 The scene is familiar from Shakespeare's *The Tragedy of Richard the Third* (written 1591, published 1597). The wicked king starts the day badly, having spent a sleepless night haunted by the ghosts of his victims, who have 'struck more terror to the soul of Richard / Than can the substance of ten thousand soldiers'. During the battle, key allies like Lord Thomas Stanley and his brother Sir William Stanley change sides. Richard is unhorsed ('My kingdom for a horse!') and killed. Henry Tudor, Earl of Richmond, is crowned Henry VII on the spot.

Did Shakespeare get it right? How would Mary McCarthy (see 7 September) assess the facts in this fiction? Richmond's claim to the throne he seized from Richard was shaky. His lineage descended through his mother, the great-granddaughter of John of Gaunt and his mistress. If he was going to be presented to the world as the founder of a great dynasty, he would need to hire some good spin doctors.

Step forward, Polydore Vergil, an Italian cleric on the make. Henry VII hired him to write the 'official' history of England up to his reign. The best way to promote the Tudors was to denigrate the man they replaced. So in Vergil's *Anglica Historia* (first edition, 1534) Richard becomes 'deformyd of body, th[e] one showlder being higher than th[e] other, a short and sowre cowntenance, which semyd to savor of mischief'.

Not only that, but he 'was woont to be ever with his right hand pulling out of the sheath to the myddest, and putting in agane, the dagger which he did alway were'. And Vergil's Richard conspires against Lord Hastings and (ultimately) the Duke of Buckingham, and has the two princes murdered in the Tower of London.

Shakespeare goes one further than Vergil by having Richard order that the Duke of Clarence be drowned in a barrel of malmsey wine, and by turning Richard into an old-fashioned villain of a medieval morality play – taking the audience into his confidence, hence co-opting them in his wicked plans, manipulating events, finally getting his just deserts.

Even the battle itself still arouses controversy. Did it really happen at Bosworth Field in Leicestershire, or eight miles away on the Warwickshire border? New archaeological finds, including part of a sword and a silver-gilt badge showing a boar (Richard's personal symbol, worn only by his closest retainers), places the climax of the battle, and probably the king's death, in a field four miles south-west of Market Bosworth, with the village of Shenton to the north and Stoke Golding to the east.

1 September

Somerset Maugham, literary travel agent

1947 No writer of modern times has been more peripatetic than Somerset Maugham. Born in Paris, he was bi-cultural. Bi-sexual as well, it was usually more convenient for him not to stay for long periods in Britain or America but in places more tolerant of diversity – famously the French Riviera.

He was, however, obliged to stay in the UK or – at a pinch – America during the Second World War. The alternative was to suffer the indignities visited on that other pre-war south of France resident, P.G. Wodehouse. The Nazis were not tolerant.

After the war, an economically devastated Britain imposed strict exchange controls. The limits on currency that the country's citizens were allowed to 'export' were minimal – £10 per annum in the late 1940s. Enforced insularity had a cramping effect, Maugham believed, on the author's mind: particularly the young author. Could he have written as he did, had he remained (as he began professional life) a doctor in Lambeth?

A world-wide bestselling author who had made other fortunes from his plays and film adaptations, the 70-year-old Maugham was well placed to set up a prize, named after himself. 'Millionaires and such like', he once sourly observed, 'are always ready to give money to universities and hospitals … but will never do anything for the arts.'

The Somerset Maugham prize was endowed to be administered by the Society of Authors. There were strict conditions attached to it. Eligible authors had to be under 35 years old and the £500 cash stipend was to be spent on at least three months' travel abroad, in places felt to be useful to the writer's future work.

The winner of the first award was announced on 1 September 1947: A.L. Barker for her collection of short stories, *Innocents*. There was universal praise for Maugham's enlightened philanthropy. There was, however, one dissenting voice – that of Evelyn Waugh, who thought it wrong to encourage the young, and tantalise the elderly, in this way. He wrote in protest to the *Daily Telegraph*:

> Does Mr Maugham realize what a huge temptation he is putting before elderly writers? To have £500 of our own – let alone of Mr Maugham's – to spend abroad is beyond our dreams …

What will we not do to qualify for Mr Maugham's munificence? What forging of birth certificates, dyeing of whiskers and lifting of faces? To what parodies of experimental styles will we not push our experienced pens?

Maugham's prize survives and has an excellent record in picking winners (Doris Lessing, Kingsley Amis, Martin Amis, V.S. Naipaul, Julian Barnes, among others). The cash amount, £12,000 currently, has risen with inflation and can still, with a little scrimping, yield a valuable foreign experience.

2 September

Pepys – eye-witness to the Great Fire of London

1666 The most vivid evocation of the fire that transformed London is that of Samuel Pepys. A narrator of genius – true always to the impression of the moment – Pepys, like other Londoners, was initially somewhat blasé (fires were commonplace in a metropolis warmed by coal and constructed out of wood).

2nd. Some of our mayds sitting up late last night to get things ready against our feast to-day, Jane called us up about three in the morning, to tell us of a great fire they saw in the City. So I rose and slipped on my nightgowne, and went to her window, and thought it to be on the backside of Marke-lane at the farthest; but, being unused to such fires as followed, I thought it far enough off; and so went to bed again and to sleep. About seven rose again to dress myself, and there looked out at the window, and saw the fire not so much as it was and further off. So to my closett to set things to rights after yesterday's cleaning. By and by Jane comes and tells me that she hears that above 300 houses have been burned down to-night by the fire we saw, and that it is now burning down all Fish-street, by London Bridge.

So I made myself ready presently, and walked to the Tower, and there got up upon one of the high places, Sir J. Robinson's little son going up with me; and there I did see the houses at that end of the bridge all on fire, and an infinite great fire on this and the other side the end of the bridge; which, among other people, did trouble me for poor little Michell and our Sarah on the bridge. So down, with my heart full of trouble, to the Lieutenant of the Tower, who tells me that it begun this morning in the King's baker's house in Pudding-lane, and that it hath burned St Magnus's Church and most part of Fish-street already. So I down to the water-side, and there got a boat and through bridge, and there saw a lamentable fire. Poor Michell's house, as far as the Old Swan, already burned that way, and the fire running further, that in a very little time it got as far as the Steeleyard, while I was there. Everybody endeavouring to remove their goods, and flinging into the river or bringing them into lighters that layoff; poor people staying in their houses as long as till the very fire touched them, and then running into boats, or clambering from one pair of stairs by the water-side to another. And among other things, the poor pigeons, I perceive, were loth to leave their houses, but hovered about the windows and balconys till they were, some of them burned, their wings, and fell down.

The pigeons are a touch of genius. Pepys, a trusted functionary, hurried off to advise the authorities (the king and the Duke of York, no less) that houses must be pulled down to create firebreaks. When he hastened back to the fire, Pepys was told by the frantic Lord Mayor that the fire was moving faster than houses could be demolished (or owners prepared to let them be demolished), and the oil and tar warehouses alongside the river were in flames. 'Firedrops' were showering all over the city.

Pepys realised that his own house was in danger. His entry for 3 September notes: 'About four o'clock in the morning, my Lady Batten sent me a cart to carry away all my money, and plate, and best things, to Sir W. Rider's at Bed[th]nall-greene.' On the next day the authorities began blowing up houses. After supping on a cold shoulder of mutton ('without napkins, or anything'), he and his wife went out into the garden 'and saw how horridly the sky looks, all on a fire in the night, was enough to put us out of our wits; and, indeed, it was extremely dreadful, for it looks just as if it was at us; and the whole heaven on fire.' Genuinely alarmed, Pepys now made arrangements about his £2,000-odd worth of gold. It was not until the 7th that the fire ('thank God!') finally burned out.

3 September

William Wordsworth has to kill London in order to love it

1802 This is the date the poet assigns to an inspired Petrarchan sonnet bearing what may be the least inspired title in English literature: 'Composed upon Westminster Bridge, September 3, 1802'. The two quatrains go like this:

> Earth has not anything to show more fair:
> Dull would he be of soul who could pass by
> A sight so touching in its majesty:
> This City now doth like a garment wear
>
> The beauty of the morning: silent, bare,
> Ships, towers, domes, theatres, and temples lie
> Open unto the fields, and to the sky,
> All bright and glittering in the smokeless air.

What was Wordsworth, so famously associated with the wild landscapes of the Lake District, doing in London? Accompanied by his sister Dorothy, he was on his way to France, there to meet his former French mistress Annette Vallon, to try to agree an arrangement for her support and that of their illegitimate daughter Caroline. They crossed the Thames by Westminster Bridge because it offered the most direct route south, without their having to thread their way through the crowded City to reach London Bridge.

But they crossed on 31 July. It was on this date that the poem was at least begun. It was the date of their return crossing that Wordsworth chose to affix to the poem's title.

Either way, what would they have seen? Obviously not the present Houses of Parliament, Charles Barry's neo-gothic monstrosity not substantially complete until the 1860s, but Westminster Abbey and the lower-level buildings associated with it, like St Stephen's Chapel, where the House of Commons sat. Dorothy's diary mentions St Paul's, which would have loomed over the City to the right of their view.

The poem itself refers to 'Ships, towers, domes, theatres and temples … / Open unto the fields, and to the sky', which brings two further points of difference between their time and ours: lots of shipping in the Thames, including smaller sailing ships and barges servicing the larger vessels, and a much lower density of building to the west of the City, allowing fields and gardens between the houses.

Was it this Canaletto-like vision that melted Wordsworth's hardness of heart towards the great wen? Because he wasn't above using the capital city as an emblem for all that had gone wrong with the country, as the title of another of his famous Petrarchan sonnets written that year makes clear:

'London, 1802'

Milton! thou shouldst be living at this hour:
England hath need of thee: she is a fen
Of stagnant waters: altar, sword, and pen, ...

The answer, as so often, lies within the poem itself. In the first place, the first line of 'Westminster Bridge' is oddly phrased. Alright, so he needs 'not anything' (as opposed to nothing) to fill out the iambic line, but what lies behind that curiously negative construction, as though disputing many 'fairer' sights commonly claimed? And why 'Earth' and not 'the earth'? Is the planet being personified? If so, to what purpose? And 'Dull would he be of soul who could pass by / A sight so touching in its majesty'? Is the nature poet reproving himself for taking too little notice of the city's beauty?

Maybe, but it's worth noticing that he has to de-citify London in order to like it. First, there are no people here – no stinking crowds throwing their sweaty nightcaps in the air to greet the morning. Second, there is no smoke. It's the early morning, you see, so for once 'The Smoke' isn't smoky. Third (those negatives just go on and on), the usual noise and clutter of the big city is absent; the scene is 'silent, bare'.

Wordsworth's most triumphant negative amounts to an admission, almost a rebuke to himself. He has gained from this scene an emotion to match his more usual landscapes:

Never did sun more beautifully steep
In his first splendour valley, rock, or hill;
Ne'er saw I, never felt, a calm so deep!

But to gain the revelation he has, in a sense, to kill London off:
Dear God! the very houses seem asleep;
And all that mighty heart is lying still!

Still hearts don't beat, don't sustain life.

4 September

Dame Shirley, writing from the California gold mines, entertains the local blacksmith

1852

'Who writ this 'ere?' is his first remark, taking up one of my most precious books, and leaving the marks of his irreverent fingers upon the clean page. 'Shakespeare', I answer as politely as possible. 'Did Spokeshave write it? He was an almighty smart fellow, that Spokeshave, I've hear'n tell', replies my visitor. 'I must write hum [home] and tell our folks that this 'ere is the first carpet I've seen sin I came to Californy, four year come next month.'

When Dr Fayette Clapp decided to practise in the mining camps of the California Gold Rush, his wife went along with him, rather than repine at home. Louise Amelia Knapp Smith Clappe (she added the terminal 'e' for style), a tolerably well-educated woman from Massachusetts, relished the adventure. Her letters, purporting to be written to her sister back home, were later published in San Francisco's fledgling (and short-lived) literary monthly, *The Pioneer*, under the pseudonym 'Dame Shirley'.

Dame Shirley was really one of those traveller-journalists like Leonard Kip, J.D. Borthwick and Bayard Taylor (see 19 August) who 'wrote up' the Gold Rush for readers further east. Like her, they thought the western vernacular was both demotic and inventive. In *Three Years in California* (1857) Borthwick recalled a man being described as '"strapped", "dead broke" – *Anglicé*, without a cent in his pocket'. Quote marks and Latin serve to separate the observers writing for their cultural equals back home from the specimen under observation. There's lots of defensive over-production of diction and rhetoric.

Dame Shirley begins her letter of 4 September with an elaborate inability *topos*: 'If only I … could weave my stupid nothings into one of those airy fabrics, the value of which depends entirely upon the skillful work … which distinguishes it' – and so on for over a page. Just under half-way through the letter she constructs an elaborate *occupatio*, or list of topics she won't discuss while actually doing so:

I will not tell you, how sometimes we were stepping lightly over immense rocks, which a few months since, lay fathoms deep below the foaming Plumas … nor shall I say a single word about the dizziness we felt, as we crept by the deep excavations lying along the road …

But at least she conveys a sense of the mine workings and their environment. And she doesn't shrink from the darker truths of the Forty-Niner experience. Forget any notions about the romance of crossing the plains:

The poor women, looking as haggard as so many Endorean witches, burnt to the color of a hazel-nut, with their hair cut short, and its gloss entirely destroyed by the alkali, whole plains of which they are compelled to cross on the way.

Details like these go well beyond local colour, and set Dame Shirley apart from the other Gold Rush journalists.

5 September

Born: father of the Edinburgh Festival

1903 Henry Harvey Wood's remarkable career probably couldn't happen today. It took easier access to university employment, a more relaxed approach to academic specialism, plus a world war, to bring his talents into full play. Born on this day in Edinburgh, Harvey Wood sailed through the Royal High School and the Edinburgh College of Art, where he won a prize for his draughtsmanship, before entering Edinburgh University to study English literature. Following more prizes and a first-class honours degree, he joined the faculty as a lecturer. In those more innocent times his promise was enough; no publications, not even a research degree were required.

At the outset of the Second World War he tried to enlist, but was turned down on medical grounds. Still wishing to serve, he joined the British Council, which was looking to set up an Edinburgh branch. In the national emergency, cultural diplomacy was needed at home more than abroad, as thousands of Allied servicemen – Americans, Poles,

Czechs and Norwegians – not to mention refugees from the various theatres of war, fetched up in Scotland. Wood catered for them all, with activities ranging from basic English classes to readings and performances given by poets, musicians and artists brought to Edinburgh, and culminating in a series of exhibitions of 'The Art of our Allies' in the National Gallery of Scotland.

When he heard that the opera impresario Rudolph Bing, a refugee from Nazi Germany, was thinking of setting up a music festival in Britain, Harvey Wood persuaded him that Edinburgh had the resident audience and local backing to underpin the event. When politicians and bureaucrats dragged their feet, Wood's tact, experience and persistent lobbying carried the scheme through, and in August 1947 the first Edinburgh International Festival was launched. From the start, Wood intended that it be a festival of the written and spoken word as well as music, and one of his first projects was to revive the mid-Scots morality play, *Ane Pleasant Satyre of the Thrie Estaitis* (1540), an earthy survey of Edinburgh society, politics and the law.

Also present from the beginning was what later came to be called the 'Fringe'. While the official festival kept to formal theatre and opera, dance and concert music – whether classical or modern – the fringe went in for small, often experimental theatrical productions (including musicals), satire and stand-up comedy, dance and children's shows. Then as now, performance in the official festival was by invitation only, whereas the Fringe is open to anyone who pays the exhibition fee.

From Harvey Wood's modest start, the Edinburgh Festival has now grown into the largest arts festival in the world, with funding (in 2009) approaching £10 million. As an index of its range of support, half that sum is raised by ticket sales, sponsorship and donations, and half by grants from central government and other public-sector grants.

6 September

Thus perish all heretics

1536 What is the most *read* work of English literature over the fifteen centuries we've had such a thing as English literature? The answer will be found in the drawer alongside every hotel and motel bed in the US

– the authorised, or King James version of the Holy Bible, published in the seventh year of his reign (1611).

It may have been authorised by the monarch, via some five committees and 50 scholars (most Oxbridge-based), but the authorship of central sections, as any modern copyright court would adjudicate, belongs to William Tyndale, 80 years earlier. Eighty per cent of the 'King James' New Testament, it is estimated, is verbally unaltered from Tyndale's earlier translation. To stretch a point, we could entitle him the most read author in English literary history.

Who was he? His dates, as best we can determine his birth, are 1494–1536. His death, which was very painful and very public, we know about. Little is known of Tyndale's early life: even his surname is not certain. He sometimes appears in documents as 'Hichens'. But it is known that Tyndale/Hichens was a student at Oxford. On graduation in 1512, he enrolled to do what we would call research, or advanced study, into theology. He was evidently a brilliant linguist.

He went on to become a tutor in a noble household, but young Tyndale was soon in trouble for heresy. He was the most pugnacious of clerics. Early on, he developed two very dangerous aspirations: (1) to defy Rome, and (2) to translate the scriptures into English. His aim, as he put it, was that 'even the ploughmen of England' should know the scriptures: and know them as well as they knew their plough handles.

It was a perilous doctrine, and he decided to leave England for Germany in the 1520s, where he may have met Martin Luther. Tyndale was on the Continent when Luther's own vernacular Bible was published. Over the years, Tyndale himself worked on his great translation, abroad.

He fell out with Henry VIII on the issue of the king's flagrantly multiple divorces. He was captured in Belgium, tried for heresy, strangled and burned at the stake in Brussels on the above date. His final words reportedly were: 'O Lord, open the King of England's eyes.'

7 September

French and Russian armies clash at the Battle of Borodino

1812 Nearly a century and a half later, the battle produced another, quieter clash when the novelist and critic Mary McCarthy declared the centrality of fact in fiction. 'Dante can be wrong in *The Divine Comedy*', she said. 'It does not matter, with Shakespeare, that Bohemia has no seacoast, but if Tolstoy was all wrong about the Battle of Borodino or the character of Napoleon, *War and Peace* would suffer.'

'We not only make believe we believe a novel, but we do substantially believe it, as being continuous [contiguous?] with real life, made of the same stuff, and the presence of fact in fiction, of dates and times and distances, is a kind of reassurance – a guarantee of credibility.' She liked Melville's *Moby-Dick* (1851) because, along with its other strengths, it was 'a compendium of everything that was to be known about whaling'.

The critic Frank Kermode, who (along with the present author) heard McCarthy's lecture in Manchester in February 1960, remembered being told by an expert on whaling that Melville's knowledge of the subject was inaccurate and unprofessional. 'I mentioned this to McCarthy', Kermode recalled, 'asking whether ... she would feel obliged to think ill of "Moby-Dick." She replied that she certainly would. I called this attitude extreme.'*

It's not clear where this leaves those readers of *War and Peace* who like to skip the war bits and cut straight to the love interest. In any case, Tolstoy's treatment of the Battle of Borodino is more of an essay set out to refute the conventional wisdom of (especially Russian) historians than a historical event incorporated into fiction.

Was he right or wrong about it? Contrary to the official version, he writes in Book 10, Chapter 19 of *War and Peace*: 'The battle of Borodino was not fought on a chosen and entrenched position with forces only slightly weaker than those of the enemy, but ... on an open and almost unentrenched position, with forces only half as numerous as the French.' Consequently, 'its immediate result for the Russians was that we were brought nearer to the destruction of Moscow – which we feared more than anything in the world; and for the French its immediate result was ... that they were brought nearer to the destruction of their whole army – which they feared more than anything in the world.'

So the French won the battle, but lost the war. That seems to get the balance about right.

---

* Frank Kermode, 'Bookend; Wilson and McCarthy: Still Entangled', *New York Times*, 23 November 1997.

8 September

Edward Bellamy's cousin reveres the flag

1892 For all Edward Bellamy's success in making his name, fortune and a whole political movement out of his anti-capitalist utopian bestseller, *Looking Backward: 2000–1887* (1886), the political impact of a 22-word affirmation penned by his cousin Francis was literally national in scope. The irony is that Francis Bellamy was a Christian socialist, a political designation that would be incomprehensible in America today.

He created the oath to the nation that all children in public (state) schools have to swear before lessons, all congressmen and other government officials at the start of their legislative sessions, all meetings of the Freemasons, the Boy Scouts, and many sporting events. It was on this day that he published his 'Pledge of Allegiance' in a popular children's magazine, *The Youth's Companion*.

In its first version the pledge said: 'I pledge allegiance to my Flag and the Republic for which it stands, one nation indivisible with liberty and justice for all.' 'Republic' because not kingdom or empire; 'indivisible' because we weren't about to revisit the traumas of the Civil War. And that was it.

There were later additions and emendations, like 'the flag of the United States of America' in case immigrants thought they were still addressing their old national banners, and 'under God' inserted after 'one nation' – this last a tribute to Lincoln's Gettysburg Address, which promised 'this nation, under God, shall have a new birth in freedom'.

In other words, Americans revere the flag – not just respect it, fly it and wear it in their lapels. The British have a head of state, to whom peers in the House of Lords bow even on the 364 days in which she is *in absentia*. The American head of state is 'The People', the first two words of the Constitution.

The British national anthem 'Send[s] her victorious / Happy and glorious / Long to reign over us'. And the American national anthem? Well, that's about the flag, of course, the 'Star Spangled Banner' that continued to wave over the ramparts of Fort McHenry after a day and long night's bombardment by British ships in Chesapeake Bay during the War of 1812:

And the rockets' red glare, the bombs bursting in air,
Gave proof through the night that our flag was still there:

O say, does that star-spangled banner yet wave
O'er the land of the free and the home of the brave?

9 September

In Cologne, William Caxton completes his translation of
The Recuyell of the Histories of Troye; *three years later he will
produce it as the first printed book in English*

1471 'And for as moche as in the wrytyng of the same', he wrote when
he had finished, 'my penne is worn, myn hande wery and not sted-
fast, myn eyen dimmed with overmoche lokyng on the white paper.'
Caxton, a prosperous mercer (fine cloth merchant) and diplomat,
had started the work in Bruges with the encouragement of Margaret,
Duchess of Burgundy, sister of Edward IV of England, and when she
approved the result, her courtiers wanted copies too. Clearly if Caxton
was going to oblige them – not to mention sell further copies – he was
going to have to make use of the new technology of printing (see 23
February).

The *Recueil des histoires de Troye* by Raoul le Fèvre was one of those
medieval romance versions of ancient myth, like *Le Roman de Thèbes*
(1150–55) or *Le Roman de Troie* (1155–60) by Benoît de Sainte-
Maure. A 'recueil' is a compilation, and the *Receuil* scooped up Greek
mythology along with the Fall of Troy, strictly speaking considered a
part of the Roman story, in which the Duchy of Burgundy itself – like
Britain – was supposed to have followed on that cataclysmic event.

To acquire a press, and hire the artisans who knew how to run it,
Caxton went to Cologne in Germany, where he finished his translation. Back to Bruges, he set up the press, and by late 1473 or early
the following year he had completed production of the *Recuyell*, the
first book to be printed in English. But he was more a publisher than
a printer; which meant that he was constantly on the lookout for new
titles (some of which he translated himself) and new markets to sell
them in. As publishing claimed more and more of his time and interest, he realised that books in English would sell best in London; so
there he moved in 1475 or early 1476, setting up his press in the pre-
cincts of Westminster Abbey.

Once in England, Caxton imported printed books from France and Flanders, but he also produced more chivalric and historical romances, as well as religious tracts and pamphlets. But for modern readers his masterpiece was the first edition of Chaucer's *The Canterbury Tales* (1478, second edition, 1483).

Caxton's Chaucer was as crucial to the development of English literature as Dante's *Divine Comedy* was to Italian: it allowed literature to be in the language people actually spoke and heard around them, rather than in some official lingo. In a period when French was still the conventional language of literature in England, Caxton's Chaucer proved that the full range of high and low styles – serious and comic, ironic and straight – could be achieved only in that glorious mixture of French, Latin and Anglo-Saxon that make up the English language.

And it's important not to miss the connection between the merchant adventurer, his sense of the demand (even Margaret of Burgundy preferred to read her stories in English) and the technology he mastered in order to bring the product to market. It was no accident that modern English literature was born along with the printing press.

10 September

The death of Amy Levy

1889 Few literary careers, or literary deaths, are more poignant than Amy Levy's. She was born at Clapham in 1861, into a cultured and orthodox Jewish family, generally relaxed on matters of religion, who actively encouraged her literary talents. Her father was a stockbroker. She was educated at Brighton and at Newnham College, Cambridge, where she was the first Jewish woman to matriculate. At university her first volume of poems, *Xantippe* (1881), was named after Socrates' fabled shrew of a wife – famously supposed to have been in the habit of emptying chamber pots over her luckless husband's head.

The details of Levy's subsequent life are tantalisingly mysterious. She may have taught, or worked (out of motives of socialist solidarity) in a factory. She published poetry and fiction including one novel, *Reuben Sachs* (1888), which caused a furore among Britain's Jews for its satire on their community's materialism. Levy was not devout and her poetry suggests she may have been lesbian.

A prey to melancholy, Levy committed suicide in her parents' London home after correcting the proofs of her fifth volume of verse. She had foreseen this end for herself in a verse monologue, 'A Minor Poet', published a few years earlier. It opens with the speaker making preparations to end it all:

> *What should such fellows as I do,*
> *Crawling between earth and heaven?*
>
> Here is the phial; here I turn the key
> Sharp in the lock. Click! – there's no doubt it turned.
> This is the third time; there is luck in threes—
> Queen Luck, that rules the world, befriend me now
> And freely I'll forgive you many wrongs!
> Just as the draught began to work, first time,
> Tom Leigh, my friend (as friends go in the world),
> Burst in, and drew the phial from my hand,
> (Ah, Tom! ah, Tom! that was a sorry turn!)

There was no Tom for Miss Levy. She was 28 years old when she died. She is recorded as the first Jewish woman to be legally cremated in England.

11 September

Fateful date in fiction – fatal in real life

2077 On this date the science-fiction writer Arthur C. Clarke imagined an asteroid striking Italy, causing huge devastation – *arrivederci* Padua, Verona, Venice – leading to the launch of Spaceguard, a NASA early-warning programme to watch for threats from space. In June 2130 Spaceguard detects a strange space vehicle in the shape of a sausage 20 kilometres round by 54 long. This is the scenario for *Rendezvous with Rama* (1972), which scooped all the sci-fi prizes for that year.

Told of the 'real' 9/11, Tom Clancy commented: 'Four planes? That many people willing to die for the same cause at the same time? If any writer turned in a story like this, the publisher would have just handed it back and said, "No way. Not believable."' His own final scene in

Debt of Honor (1994) has an embittered Japanese pilot of the 'lone nut' persuasion, following a not awfully believable war with the United States in which his son and brother have been killed, crash his 747 into the US Capitol building in Washington, killing the president, most of the Congress and cabinet, the joint chiefs of staff and all nine justices of the Supreme Court – all convened for a celebratory joint session of Congress.

Clancy claims he foretold the attack on the Twin Towers, and that NORAD, the North American Aerospace Defense Command, should have been in the air over New York to shoot the hijacked planes out of the sky on that sunny September morning. More up-market authors thought fiction might never rise to the occasion, now that it had actually happened. Within a fortnight the *New Yorker*'s 'Talk of the Town' department had got together a symposium of first (non-fictional) impressions, including John Updike's on the abstract fury of the perpetrators, Amitrav Ghosh's on how hard it was for a victim's children to take in the enormity of his sudden death, and Susan Sontag's that this was not another Pearl Harbor, but revenge for America throwing its weight around in the Middle East.

But the end of fiction? Not a bit of it. By mid-decade the fictions were positively gushing out: Jonathan Safran Foer's *Extremely Loud and Incredibly Close* (2005), Claire Messud's *The Emperor's Children* (2006), Jess Walter's *The Zero* (2006). Martin Amis's short story 'The Last Days of Muhammad Atta' (2006) imagined the interior mental framework of a fanatical personality. So did Updike's *Terrorist* (2006), only now the fanatic was an American-born Muslim high school senior in New Jersey, both attracted to and repulsed by the girls who 'sway and sneer and expose their soft bodies and alluring hair'. Then Don DeLillo explored modes of union and isolation in *Falling Man* (2007). Reviews were mixed.

No one departed from Clancy's paranoid vision of an embattled America. Clarke's very different projection remained unshared. When the Americans finally gain entrance to the spaceship *Rama*, the aliens are too busy preparing their ship for a crucial manoeuvre to pay them any attention. They have no interest in earth, let alone the United States. They are just passing through the solar system – not visiting it (let alone assaulting it) – in order to use the sun's gravity to sling-shot them into a faster trajectory for another destination altogether.

12 September

Death of a literary louse

1908 On this day John Churton Collins died, aged 60. His was the lot of the worthy scholar, outshone by what F.R. Leavis and his stern disciples liked to call 'facile journalists'. They usually win.

A career swot, Collins made it with difficulty to Balliol College, Oxford (a benevolent uncle paid his way, under the misapprehension – encouraged by his nephew – that a career in the church was in prospect). At university (Oxford was currently going through the period that Gladstone called its 'agony' of religious doubt) Collins read deeply and widely.

He aimed already to be a man of letters based in Oxford, the only thing he is recorded in his life as ever having passionately loved. Alas, he was awarded a second-class degree: a handicap that hung, for the rest of his career, like an albatross round his neck. It precluded any academic post and his kind uncle, on learning of the fraud perpetrated on him, was kind no more.

Collins took up hack work in Fleet Street and, when his fortunes ran low, menial clerical work. It is recorded that he was superhumanly fast at addressing envelopes, for which he received a pound every thousand he did. Eventually he found a steady post as a 'crammer' for students entering the universities or the Civil Service (the Northcote Trevelyan Report of 1854 had recommended entry examinations – much to the disgust of old hands like Anthony Trollope).

What he really wanted to do was to write about literature, and by the end of the 1870s he had made a small reputation for himself as a higher journalist and could marry the lawyer's daughter who had already borne the first of his seven children.

In 1880 Collins was taken up by Henry Morley, the indefatigable founder of adult education in England, and head of the English department at the University College of London. Collins followed Morley's example as an industrious university extension lecturer. He is estimated to have given some 10,000 lectures. It was not, however, Oxford where, in the few days allowed him, he took his annual vacation.

Collins' enduring quality was that of making himself royally unloved by the literary great. An uncomplimentary, but solidly researched, article on Tennyson's poetic derivativeness earned him the description from the laureate that has immortalised him. Collins, Tennyson declared, was 'the louse on the locks of literature'.

Collins buried his vengeful hatchet into the work of other literary grandees – always with sound scholarly warrant, which made him even less loved. His attempt to get himself elected professor of literature at Merton College, Oxford in 1885 provoked a powerful critique of the feeble way the subject was taught in the universities. He was right, but it won him no friends in high places.

His greatest offence, in the eyes of the London literary world, was his devastating satire on the (admittedly lax) scholarship of Edmund Gosse's Clark lectures at Cambridge in 1886. A 'mass of error and inaccuracy', he called it. Collins' hatchet was razor-edged, delicately aimed and transparently a shriek of (egotistic) scholarly pain:

> That such a book as this should have been permitted to go forth into the world with the imprimatur of the University of Cambridge, affords matter for very grave reflection. But it is a confirmation of what we have long suspected. It is one more proof that those rapid and reckless innovations, which have during the last few years completely changed the faces of our Universities, have not been made with impunity.

Gosse's reputation never recovered. On 12 September 1908, Collins' body was found in a dyke at Oulton Broad in Suffolk, with a bottle of sedatives nearby. Despite the court's verdict of accidental death, suicide seems more likely.

13 September

On reaching its 1,998th performance, Agatha Christie's The Mousetrap *becomes Britain's longest-running straight play*

1957 It's amazing to think that the record set way back in 1957 should have been surpassed by another 58 years and still counting; that both the Queen and the play should have celebrated their silver jubilees together, and that the production is still running in 2010 – well into the 21st century. By now, of course, it has set many more records: it is now the longest-running show of any kind in the universe, having gone through many changes of cast, a shift of venue (from The Ambassadors to St Martin's, where it has played since 1974), and of course props and stage furniture – though not design. Only an old armchair and a clock on the wall date from the first production.

Not that the critics were all that excited about the play when it opened. Quoting Tallulah Bankhead that 'there is less to it than meets the eye', the *Guardian* objected that: 'Coincidence is stretched unreasonably to assemble in one place a group of characters, each of whom may reasonably be suspected of murder in series.' Still, the critic liked Richard Attenborough's performance as Detective Sergeant Trotter, 'an unconventional police sergeant on skis', and thought 'the whole thing whizzes along as though driven by some real dramatic force'.

It all started out as a 30-minute radio play broadcast in 1947. The scene is a country hotel in which a number of people are stranded by a snow storm. Christie's adaptation for the stage allowed her more time to develop character and prolong suspense. All the characters have a secret, though only one of them a murderous one. There's a twist in the ending – two, actually – which the audience are asked to swear they won't divulge. Since the play has now been seen by well over ten million people in more than 40 countries, it's not clear how much of the world's population still doesn't know the secret.

So how to account for the play's evergreenery? Clever plotting, certainly, along with deft portrayal of character. A scenario, the country house murder mystery, so timeless that it's still being used, or – in the case of Robert Altman's superb film, *Gosford Park* (2001) – deconstructed. But by now it's probably simply the fact that its longevity has turned the play into a phenomenon, a station on the tourist itinerary. In other words, *The Mousetrap* is famous for being famous.

14 September

After speculating on ring-ousel migration, Gilbert White comes down on the side of local natural history

1770 'From whence, then, do our ring-ousels migrate so regularly every September, and make their appearance again, as if in their return, every April?' he wrote to his friend Thomas Pennant, Fellow of the

Royal Society. 'They are more early this year than common, for some were seen at the usual hill on the fourth of this month.'

This combination of curiosity and close observation typifies Gilbert White's method. While Captain James Cook was off collecting exotic specimens in the South Seas, this country clergyman in the Hampshire village of Selborne studied what went on around him through the seasons, making careful notes on plants, birds, bees – even earthworms, which he properly valued for their effect on the soil.

His letters to Pennant, and another Academician, Daines Barrington, were published as *The Natural History of Selborne* in 1788. Admired by writers as distant as Wordsworth and Virginia Woolf, the book has gone through 200 editions and translations, and has never been out of print.

In the same letter he informs Pennant that he had just got hold of a copy of Giovanni Scopoli's recent work on natural history, in which 'he advances some false facts', such as that 'the hirundo urbica ... pullos extra nidum non nutrit' ('the house martin doesn't feed its chicks outside the nest'). This White 'knew to be wrong' because he had seen them feeding their young on the wing, but 'the feat is done in so quick a manner as not to be perceptible to indifferent observers'.

To prevent this sort of careless scrutiny, White urged what he called 'parochial history', in which observers stick to what they know and can verify, for (as he went on to say in this letter):

> [A]s no man can alone investigate all the works of nature, these partial writers may, each in their department, be more accurate in their discoveries, and freer from errors, than more general writers; and so by degrees may pave the way to an universal correct natural history.

The local is all very well, but it would be hard to sustain if it weren't for that often overlooked infrastructure of Romantic nature writing, the *Systema Naturae* (1735) of Carl Linnaeus. White, who had tried and failed to find a permanent position at Oxford, knew that Linnaeus' universal system of binary classification into family and species (like 'hirundo urbica') would still connect his 'parochial' observations to the rest of the world. Like his admirer Henry David Thoreau over half a century after him, who also felt himself to be on the cultural margins, Gilbert White had found in Linnaeus a language for the universal oversoul.

15 September

Stephen King is honoured, but not respected

2003 The clash between low- and highbrow is one of the never-ending, and more entertaining, literary wars. One side, typically, has the money; the other side the prestige.

Few authors have had more money than Stephen King. In 2003 the author of *Carrie*, *The Shining*, and *It* made #14 on the *Forbes* wealthiest celebrity list, with an estimated income of $50 million-plus. Only novelist Michael Crichton ranked higher among writers. And Crichton was, by contrast with King, a child of privilege. He had written best-selling novels while a Dean's List medical student at Harvard.

Stevie King had had no such advantages and always believed that he was denied the respect he deserved. Unlike Crichton, he had pulled himself up by his bootstraps, from mobile home to mansion.

It rankled. Even in the years of his triumph. On 15 September 2003 the National Book Foundation announced that King would be the recipient of 'lifetime award'. In his acceptance speech at the public ceremony on 19 November that year, King recalled how he and his wife Tabitha lived in a trailer …

> … and she made a writing space for me in the tiny laundry room with a desk and her Olivetti portable between the washer and dryer … When I gave up on *Carrie*, it was Tabby who rescued the first few pages of single-spaced manuscript from the wastebasket, told me it was good, said I ought to go on.

The main thrust of his November speech was *Carrie*-style payback. They hadn't emptied a bucket of pig's blood over his head, but the literary establishment was guilty of 'tokenism' – treating him like a house negro with their lifetime award. It was an awkward occasion.

Nonetheless, the literary establishment declined to be cowed by some hack who had struck it rich with a reading public even less cultivated than himself. Harold Bloom, who is to literary criticism what Einstein was to physics, declared that the NBA's decision to give an award to King was:

> … another low in the shocking process of dumbing down our cultural life. I've described King in the past as a writer of penny

350

dreadfuls, but perhaps even that is too kind. He shares nothing with Edgar Allan Poe. What he is is an immensely inadequate writer on a sentence-by-sentence, paragraph-by-paragraph, book-by-book basis.

The war goes on.

16 September

The Great Preston Lockout

1853 There are few topics on which one can find Karl Marx, Charles Dickens, and Mrs Gaskell engaged in discussing the same event. The Great Preston Lockout was one.

For years, workers in the (immensely profitable) cotton mills of Lancashire had agitated and unionised for higher wages: 'ten percent' was the slogan. The masters resisted and, on 16 September 1853 – in the face of a threatened walkout by the labour force, or 'operatives' as Victorians called them – closed the factory doors. The intention was to starve their workforce into docile submission. As many as 20,000 workers were involved. Karl Marx was quick to perceive the episode as potentially revolutionary, following a street riot in late October. In the *York Daily Tribune*, 1 November 1853, he declared:

> While the first cannon bullets have been exchanged in the war of the Russians against Europe, the first blood has been spilt in the war now raging in the manufacturing districts, of capital against labor.

The days of the 'millocrats' were, Marx believed, numbered (ironically his own income came, substantially, in the form of handouts from the millocrat Engels). 'Our St Petersburg is at Preston!' was the communists' rallying cry.

Dickens was less sure. Now the proprietor of a weekly newspaper, *Household Words*, he made a personal trip to Preston in early February 1854 and wrote an article, 'On Strike', based on what he saw there. Declaring himself a friend to both employers and employees, Dickens reserved his criticism for the trade union organisers – particularly the rabble-rouser, 'Gruffshaw', from London (in historical fact the rela-tively unradical George Cowell, further satirised as 'Slackbridge' in *Hard Times*). Dickens' conclusion was that:

> This strike and lock-out is a deplorable calamity. In its waste of time, in its waste of a great people's energy, in its waste of wages, in its waste of wealth that seeks to be employed, in its encroach-ment on the means of many thousands who are labouring from day to day it is a great national affliction.

The first-hand experience, and the long continuation of the dispute, inspired Dickens to write his only novel set outside London, *Hard Times*, serialised in *Household Words* from April to August 1854. In the novel, Dickens moved round to a more direct attack on the masters – in the form of the odious hypocrite Bounderby. But his conclusion is that of the saintly mill-worker, Stephen Blackpool: 'A muddle! Aw a muddle!'

The union funds were less ample than those of the masters, who recruited 'knobsticks' (i.e. scabs) from Ireland to break the Lancashire workers' resolve. 'Hands' began to trickle back in spring 1854 and on May Day, at a rally of 10,000 men, it was decided to sanction a return to work.

Dickens was still exercised by the upheaval, and he commissioned an after-the-event serial from the Lancashire novelist Mrs Gaskell, *North and South*, serialised in *Household Words* from September 1854 to January 1855. In her novel, Gaskell is at pains to be scrupulously fair to the mill-owners (whom she had earlier criticised in *Mary Barton*). Margaret Hale is transplanted from a comfortable life in Hampshire to 'Milton-Northern' (i.e. Manchester) when her clergyman father's 'doubts' force him to leave the Anglican Church. Initially appalled, Margaret is gradually won over by the rough northern community and its tough (but moral) textile workers. Her southern softness tempers the hardness of the factory-owner Thornton and helps bring about an acceptable end to a savage strike.

Marx, equally hopefully, foresaw less happy endings.

17 September

Maggie Joy Blunt follows a woman hoarding salt

1946 If the Mass Observation archive is a famous resource for British social history, its value as a repository of vernacular literature is less celebrated than it ought to be. From 1937 Mass Observation surveyed ordinary people's feelings about what was going on around them. Its founders were not sociologists, but an eclectic mix of the poet Charles Madge, the documentary film-maker Humphrey Jennings, and the polymath Tom Harrisson, newly returned from studying cannibals in the New Hebrides, who decided it was time for 'an anthropology of ourselves'. Others involved included the literary critic William Empson, poet and critic Kathleen Raine, and the *Picture Post* photographer Humphrey Spender, brother of the poet.

The survey's managers started out a bit like the American Federal Writers' Project (see 27 July), paying journalists, civil servants and the like to note down conversations overheard in pubs and workplaces. Later they realised they could get a broader response for less money by recruiting volunteers to answer questionnaires or just keep diaries to note down their feelings and opinions about day-by-day occurrences.

The returns were especially illuminating for the immediate post-war period, which was supposed to bring peace and prosperity, instead of austerity, the fear of nuclear war, a balance of payments crisis, the continuation of domestic rationing, and a shortage of coal during the coldest winter on record, 1946–47. Where were those sunny uplands promised by Winston Churchill? Who won the bloody war, anyway? The vernacular voices of Mass Observation offered a sobering counterbalance to the official optimism about a great technological future in a new Elizabethan age.

Maggie Joy Blunt was a freelance writer and publicity officer in a metal factory living near Slough. On this day she noticed:

> ... a woman [going] from shop to shop in the village today. She was buying cooking salt. One block from the greengrocer which she concealed in her basket and then another from the grocer. Expect she is salting beans.

Not that salt was rationed. The woman wasn't on the fiddle; she was just hoarding. But with shortages still a public issue, Maggie couldn't help noticing – and yet a kind of communal feeling for a fellow victim prevented her judging:

> I wonder how many of us do this sort of scrounging for a quantity of something, with and without feelings of guilt? I do it for cigarettes and do have a twinge of conscience.*

18 September

Edie Rutherford supports the communist squatters

1946 The day after Maggie Joy Blunt noticed the salt hoarder (see 17 September), a much more serious post-war shortage caught the attention of the Mass Observation diarists. This time it was housing. With so many of the country's houses destroyed by bombing, and over three million servicemen being demobbed in the middle of a baby boom, there just weren't enough houses to go round – at any price.

The great 1946 summer squat began in empty Nissen huts on abandoned army camps, a movement that quickly spread across the country. The government responded leniently, even offering to reconnect gas and electricity, providing the squatters would register as council tenants. Then in September some communist councillors led an occupation of five blocks of luxury apartments in Kensington, originally requisitioned for the war effort and not yet re-let. To this invasion of private property the government reacted furiously, blockading the buildings, arresting the five (elected) councillors and charging them with 'conspiracy to trespass'. These events were widely reported, picked up by papers even in Australia and the US.

But the public backed the squatters. On this day Edie Rutherford, a South African-born housewife living in Sheffield, noted in her diary kept for Mass Observation:

> How cautiously Bow Street [Magistrates' Court] has dealt with the Communist squatters today. I should jolly well think so. Public opinion does count for something, and not all the

---

* Simon Garfield, ed., *Our Hidden Lives: The Remarkable Diaries of Post-War Britain*, London: Ebury Press, 2005, p. 275.

populace are against the squatters. It is mostly the haves who are. The disclosure at court by the woman who had to take her child to hospital fifty times for rat bite was more than enough for everyone I should think.

Maggie Joy Blunt, while sceptical of their motives, could still approve of the communists' campaign:

> I think the Communists were right, whatever their ulterior motives may have been, to draw attention to the shocking housing conditions that many of the flat-squatters have had to put up with. Rat bites! Just think of it. It seems to me scandalous that a Labour Government couldn't have done better for their own people in this last year.*

Housing minister Nye Bevan was also busy getting the NHS up and running – and this was just over a year after Labour won its landslide general election – so maybe it was a bit early to blame the government for letting down its supporters. Still, these diaries testify to a humane common judgement that can rise above prejudices of class or politics.

19 September

Amiri Baraka is de-laureated

2001 Eight days after 9/11, Amiri Baraka (the African-American writer formerly known as Leroi Jones) appeared at a poetry festival in Stanhope, New Jersey. Baraka had been appointed the poet laureate of his native New Jersey a couple of years before and had penned, in some haste, a poem to read aloud at Stanhope on the recent outrage in Manhattan. It was entitled, quizzically, 'Somebody Blew Up America?' His outrage, it was clear, was not directed at Al Qaida, or any other US-hating terrorists. It was equally clear, from a central stanza, who the 'somebody' in the title was:

---

* Simon Garfield, ed., *Our Hidden Lives: The Remarkable Diaries of Post-War Britain*, London: Ebury Press, 2005, pp. 275–6.

Who knew the World Trade Center
was gonna get bombed
Who told 4,000 Israeli workers
at the Twin Towers
To stay home that day
Why did Sharon stay away?

There was some angry response and protest. But so distracted were the months after 9/11 that no great publicity was given to the laureate's allegation that Zionists had been privy to the imminent destruction of the Twin Towers. Finally, in July 2002, the Jewish Anti Defamation League complained. They would, they threatened, launch a law suit against Amiri Baraka for inciting 'global anti-Semitism'.

Pressure was put on Baraka to resign and save the NJ authorities public embarrassment. He posted on his website a defiant refusal:

I WILL NOT 'APOLOGIZE', I WILL NOT 'RESIGN!'

The recent dishonest, consciously distorted and insulting non-interpretation of my poem, 'Somebody Blew up America' [*sic*] by the 'Anti-Defamation' League, is fundamentally an attempt to defame me. And with that, an attempt to repress and stigmatize independent thinkers everywhere. This trashy propaganda is characteristic of right-wing zealots who are interested only in slander and character assassination of those whose views or philosophies differ from or are in contradiction to theirs. First, the poem's underlying theme focuses on how Black Americans have suffered from domestic terrorism since being kidnapped into US chattel slavery, e.g., by Slave Owners, US & State Laws, Klan, Skin Heads, Domestic Nazis, Lynching, denial of rights, national oppression, racism, character assassination, historically, and at this very minute throughout the US.

The governor of New Jersey was not inclined to support his state's appointed poet. But legal advice suggested that First Amendment Rights might cover Baraka's poem, and he could have grounds, if dismissed, for a lawsuit of his own. Hemlock was not available.

Finally a way through was found. The New Jersey State Assembly voted 69 to 2 on 7 July 2002 to abolish the post of poet laureate. In the language of the business world, Baraka was 'let go'. In the annals of literature he is the only poet laureate to have been de-laureated.

20 September

Born: the midwife of the modern American novel

1884 Maxwell Perkins – or Max to everyone who knew him – who worked at the august publishers Charles Scribner's Sons from 1910 until his death in 1947, was one of those editors who exist today only in the dreams of aspiring authors. He actually went out looking for unknown writers, and when he found them, he made up his own mind about their work, brought it on and nurtured it. When he joined the firm, Scribner's was a distinguished, if somewhat staid publishing house. Its authors included Edith Wharton, then in mid-career, and Henry James, his major fiction behind him, now into his autobiography.

On the lookout for younger writers, Perkins came across the 23-year-old F. Scott Fitzgerald, who had been trying, and failing, to interest publishers in a blushful *Bildungsroman* about doomed youth that he called *The Romantic Egoist*. Perkins took it on, suggested radical revisions and a new title (never Fitzgerald's strong point – see 7 November), and forced it through his colleagues' resistance. *This Side of Paradise* came out in March 1920, selling out its first print run of 3,000 copies in three days. The next day Scott felt enough confidence in his future to marry his sweetheart Zelda Sayre. By the end of 1921 the novel had gone through twelve printings, selling nearly 50,000 copies.

In other words, Perkins could pick them. Through Fitzgerald he met Ernest Hemingway, snaffling up his first novel, *The Sun Also Rises*, and publishing it in 1926. Together with Fitzgerald's *The Great Gatsby* (1925) it set the themes and (more important) the tone of a literary decade. Among other authors Perkins discovered or got into print were Erskine Caldwell, James Jones, J.P. Marquand and Alan Paton.

But he wasn't just an astute talent scout. Once he got them on board, Perkins would cosset his authors like a broody hen, coping with their drunkenness and self-doubt, forever encouraging them, even lending them money from time to time. When they panicked about their prose, he would say: 'Just get it down on paper, and then we'll see what to do with it.'

In the editorial process itself he wasn't very hot on the details, but he was a genius when it came to the larger structure. After a long struggle he persuaded Thomas Wolfe to cut 66,000 words (not 90,000, as is commonly reported) from *O Lost*, another disastrously titled first novel that no one else wanted to publish, to turn it into *Look Homeward Angel* (1929), still a healthy first-born weighing in at 233,000 words on 626 pages.

21 September

Publius Vergilius Maro dies, his Aeneid *not quite finished*

19 BC If its homeland is a tribe's identity, how devastating it must be to lose one, and how like rebirth to find (found) another. That's the plot of Vergil's epic. In twelve books, each of around 800 hexameter lines, the *Aeneid* tells the story of how a party of Trojans escapes the Greeks' destruction of their city and wanders the Mediterranean for six years until fetching up, first in Carthage, then on the coast of Latium to establish a new home. Some of those lines are curtailed, as though awaiting their endings, and the whole comes to an abrupt end – suggesting that Vergil didn't quite finish his masterpiece.

Unlike Homer's *Iliad* and *Odyssey* on which it draws, the *Aeneid* is written to a nationalist agenda, explicitly to provide a myth for the founding of Rome – and specifically the empire under the Julio-Claudian dynasty. Buttressing the myth is the theme of continuity and rebirth: the religious beliefs and moral virtues of the archaic age refreshed in the vigour of the Latin peoples.

To reinforce this theme, Vergil adapts a device used in the *Odyssey*. Exactly in the middle of both epics, the heroes visit the underworld for advice on how to get home. While Odysseus wants to get back to his literal home, Aeneas needs to find out where his tribal identity will finally be 'at home'.

The shade of his father, Anchises, answers his question with a prophecy detailing the Trojans' founding of Rome, from Romulus through the age of kings, the Republic, the defeat of Carthage and Gaul, right down to the establishment of the empire under Caesar Augustus.

Aeneas and his followers marvel at such news, but the prophecy device exerted a powerfully authenticating effect on Vergil's contemporary readers, who experienced the poem's fictional action as verifiable history. They were in the position of the gods, knowing as fact what the poem's characters can only glimpse as improbable guesses about the future.

In *The Divine Comedy*, Vergil takes Anchises' place as Dante's guide to the underworld. The *Aeneid* has been the same to European and American foundation stories as a whole.

22 September

Death of the worthiest knight that ever lived

1586 Sir Philip Sidney lives in the annals of English literature as the author of what is often taken to be the first novel in the language (*Arcadia*), the author of the first serious literary-critical treatise in the language (*An Apology for Poetry*), and the author of the first notable sonnet sequence in the language (*Astrophil and Stella*).

Sidney was also one of Queen Elizabeth's favoured courtiers and a soldier. In 1586 she appointed him governor of Flushing in the Netherlands – a region where England was then in conflict with the other major imperial power of the age, Spain.

In a skirmish with the Spanish near Zutphen on 22 September 1586, Sidney was wounded in the upper leg by a musket ball (he had, recklessly, left off his 'cuisses', or thigh protectors). Three weeks later he died of the wound (or, more precisely, the poor medical treatment he received), aged only 32.

His body was brought back to London and transported in honour through the streets. Reportedly, citizens shouted: 'Farewell, the worthiest knight that lived.' Sidney's worthiness is immortalised by the account given of the poet-warrior's nobility by his friend (and fellow poet) Fulke Greville, as he was being carried away with his fatal wound from the field of battle at Zutphen:

[P]assing along by the rest of the Army ... and being thirstie with excess of bleeding, he called for drink, which was presently brought him; but as he was putting the bottle to his mouth, he saw a poor Souldier carried along, who had eaten his last at the same Feast, gastly casting up his eyes at the bottle. Which Sir Philip perceiving, took it from his head, before he drank, and delivered it to the poor man, with these words, 'Thy necessity is greater than mine.

Greville's anecdote is usually believed to be invented, although in character. It is less often recorded that the Spanish won at Zutphen and in the larger war in which it featured.

23 September

'An important Jew dies in exile'

1939 Sigmund Freud died in exile in Hampstead, England, where he had lived after fleeing Vienna the previous year. War had been declared on his persecutor, Nazi Germany, a fortnight earlier. Freud did not wait to see the outcome. He doubtless feared the worst. Suffering from terminal cancer (brought on by his habitual cigar), he prevailed on a doctor friend, Max Schur, to overdose him with morphine. 'It is nothing but torture and makes no sense any more', he stoically explained.

There were many obituaries, none finer than that from W.H. Auden, in his poem 'In Memory of Sigmund Freud'. Over the 28 verses Auden does not over-praise Freud, but shrewdly sees him as less a psychotherapist than a prophet who has changed humanity's vision of itself for, at least, a generation:

> for one who'd lived among enemies so long:
> if often he was wrong and, at times, absurd,
>   to us he is no more a person
> now but a whole climate of opinion.

Auden had been introduced to Freud early in life by his doctor father. At university, he spread the Freudian gospel to acolytes such as Stephen Spender and Christopher Isherwood – the poet, he insisted, must be 'clinical'. In 2001 a collection of unpublished (and later deemed unpublishable by the poet) 'case poems' came to light. They were written in the late 1920s and early 1930s by Auden on Freudian themes.

It was in his visits to his friends Isherwood and Spender in Weimar Berlin that Auden came into closest contact with Freudianism, via the teachings of Homer Lane, to whom he was introduced by John Layard.

Auden was a convert – although a sceptical one. After Layard's bungled suicide attempt, Auden referred to him as 'loony Layard' (Freud gets away with a mere 'absurd'). Less benevolent than Max Schur, when Layard – who had shot himself in the mouth – asked Wystan to 'finish him off', Auden refused, saying: 'I'm terribly sorry, I know you want this, but I can't do it, because I might be hanged if I did.'

Ten years later, when he wrote his elegy for Freud, Auden was himself a refugee. He and Isherwood had sailed for the USA, fearing the outbreak of war in Europe, in January 1939. He died in 1973, after a peripatetic life, in Freud's Vienna, alone in a hotel room.

24 September

60 Minutes *gets its first showing on CBS television*

1968 Created by veteran CBS producer Don Hewitt, who had directed Edward R. Murrow's *See it Now* show – not to mention the debates between presidential candidates John F. Kennedy and Richard Nixon – *60 Minutes* (actually 42 minutes without the adverts) has offered high-quality investigative reporting in the format of a television news magazine for 42 years. It's the longest-running prime time programme still in production in the United States.

Its popularity has been staggering for a news review in prime time. Always in the top twenty, it actually topped out the Neilson audience measurement ratings in 1976. It has won getting on for 80 Emmy awards, swung major policy decisions, even got into the movies, when the network's struggle with the tobacco industry was dramatised in *The Insider* (Michael Mann, 1999).

Inevitably in that long run there have been pratfalls. One very embarrassing one also says a lot about what's been happening to the American media recently. On 6 September 2004, Dan Rather, the seasoned anchor man for the CBS Evening News, did a *60 Minutes* piece alleging that President George W. Bush had gone absent without leave from the Texas Air National Guard during the Vietnam War of the 1970s. This was a serious charge, right in the middle of a presidential election, and the liberals loved it. Bush was already under fire for using family influence to get himself posted to the National Guard as a safe alternative to combat in Vietnam. But Rather seemed to seal the accusation by showing a series of letters and memos from Bush's National Guard commander 'grounding' him – that is, withdrawing his flight status (and extra pay) – for failure to report for a physical examination, and for other absences from duty.

Within hours, bloggers began to post doubts about the documents shown on *60 Minutes*. The letterheads and signature blocks were wrong. Above all, the body type of the letters and memos themselves could never have been produced in the early 1970s, when hard-type typewriters printed letters all of the same width, and could not 'kern', or fold letters like 'f' and 'l' into one another. The documents shown on *60 Minutes* all had letter spaces of variable widths, with those kerned where appropriate. They had been produced on a word-processor, using Microsoft Word with default settings, some 30 years after their purported dates.

After some huffing and puffing, CBS admitted its mistake. Rather apologised too, then lost his job. *60 Minutes* soldiered on, and ultimately recovered. But the wider lesson was that a new force had entered the world of news broadcasting. Following the tsunami disaster later that year, a significant number of Americans turned to blogs for breaking news. Increasingly, the internet began to look like the news medium of choice for the new millennium.

25 September

Queen Victoria delays her diamond jubilee. Rudyard Kipling delays publication of his celebratory poem

1896 On this day Victoria outlasted George III as the longest-reigning monarch in English history. A diamond jubilee was in prospect. It was held on 22 September 1897, to commemorate the queen's coronation some 60 years earlier (the precise date of that event was 28 June 1837). The whole British empire, then at its furthest reach across the globe, was instructed to rejoice, and given a public holiday for the occasion. There was a Naval Review and a regal procession through London, to cheering crowds, the queen escorted by soldiers from all her many domains. Royalty flooded in from those quarters of the globe not already under Victoria's dominion.

Shortly after ten o'clock, with a loyal Indian servant in close attendance, the queen and empress descended the stairs at Buckingham Palace and pressed an electric button that (courtesy of Associated Press) flashed across the world the message: 'From my heart I thank my beloved people. May God bless them.'

The poet of empire, Rudyard Kipling, composed a celebratory verse. His first idea was an early version of the poem later known as 'The White Man's Burden'. This, however, was held back for two years and dedicated to America, then (in 1899) embroiled in its bloody campaign of suppression in the Philippine Islands. Its theme (that the US must now assume the weary burden of racial superiority and the bloodletting that goes with it) would not have been entirely suitable for the earlier event:

> Take up the White Man's burden—
> Send forth the best ye breed—
> Go bind your sons to exile
> To serve your captives' need;
> To wait in heavy harness,
> On fluttered folk and wild—
> Your new-caught, sullen peoples,
> Half-devil and half-child

Kipling offered as his jubilee tribute instead the poem 'Recessional' (dated 22 June 1897). It too expresses a sombre conviction that the high-point of imperial greatness, like all the greatnesses before it, has passed.

> Far-called our navies melt away—
> On dune and headland sinks the fire—
> Lo, all our pomp of yesterday
> Is one with Nineveh and Tyre!
> Judge of the Nations, spare us yet,
> Lest we forget – lest we forget!

Kipling's gloom rings truer than the cheers in Pall Mall that June, with the Boer War looming. The inexorable shrinkage of the British empire would continue for the next 60 years until the last winds of change, in the 1950s, blew it away for ever.

26 September

Stage censorship finally ends in Britain

1968 Oppression of the stage in Britain has almost as long a history as Britain itself. The church has traditionally conceived theatrical performance as more dangerous than literature. Audiences (unlike solitary readers) are 'crowds' and crowds easily become rebellious mobs.

The Puritans, after their victory in the Civil War, put down all public drama as work of the devil. Even after the Restoration, Charles II (an inveterate lover of the theatre and its orange girls) extended 'Patents' (i.e. licences) to only two theatres: Sir Thomas Killigrew's Theatre Royal, Drury Lane and Sir William Davenant's Theatre Royal, Covent Garden. Unroyal theatres did not qualify.

In the 18th century, licensing of the national theatre came officially into the domain of the Lord Chamberlain, a dignitary in the royal household charged with matters of protocol, civil order and state occasions. The Chamberlain delegated theatrical matters to his deputy – 'the examiner of plays'. That such an office existed chilled creativity. Early plays to be banned were *Gustavus Vasa* (1739) by Henry Brooke, and *Edward and Eleonora* (1739) by James Thomson – both on grounds of their political content – innocuous though it was. For theatre managers and proprietors it was enough, as with the Inquisition, to 'show the instruments'. Self-censorship did the Lord Chamberlain's work for him.

Censorship was refined by the Theatre Regulation Act of 1843. As 'licenser' of plays, and theatres, the Lord Chamberlain now required every script to be physically deposited with him, scrutinised, corrected (if necessary) and cleared before performance.

As the 19th century progressed – particularly with the arrival of 'Ibsenism' – friction rose. It reached a head in 1894 when the Lord Chamberlain declined to license (even with modifications) George Bernard Shaw's third play, *Mrs Warren's Profession*.

In this drama of ideas, Shaw wittily portrayed prostitution and brothel-keeping (neither word features in the text) as 'rational' alternatives to marriage that enabled women to make economic use of their sexuality. Women, Shaw wrote, were driven to the streets for the same reason that prize-fighters were driven to the ring. The playwright was an admirer of pugilism (he conducted, later in life, an interesting cor-

respondence with the world heavyweight champion – and intellectual
– Gene Tunney).

In Shaw's play the young heroine, Viv Warren, a Girton Girl, has
grown up in ignorance of her mother's 'profession'. After the initial
shock, she disowns the family, discards her lover, and becomes a wholly
independent woman. The last image the audience has of her is methodically doing her accounts.

The 'King's Reader' (as Shaw called him) argued that the play
offended by not depicting the 'loathsomeness' of prostitution. Shaw
assumed that his more serious offence was failing to render the subject
at all 'aphrodisiac'. Perversely, if *Mrs Warren's Profession* had been either
more horrific or more erotic it would have been more presentable. It
was the naked analysis (sex is as saleable a commodity as cabbage) that
was objectionable.

Shaw's larger contention (as in his first play, *Widowers' Houses*) was
that the British middle classes all live on immoral earnings – the more
immoral since they blind themselves to the fact.

After the ban, Shaw promptly published *Mrs Warren's Profession*
(with a lengthy introduction and voluminous stage directions) as one
of his 'Plays Unpleasant'. The play was eventually staged on 5 January
1902, at London's New Lyric Club. Such 'closed' events, with member-
only audiences, were immune from the Lord Chamberlain's authority.

It was a victory of sorts. But Shaw, the greatest British playwright
of the 20th century, would be destined to work out his half-century
career under the Lord Chamberlain's censorship: duelling all the way.

Mrs Warren's Profession was finally permitted public performance on
27 July 1925, at the Prince of Wales Theatre in Birmingham. Shaw
surmised that the authorities had been shamed into letting it through
by their own exploitation of women's labour in factories during the
First World War. He was not triumphant. The 1925 performance was,
he felt, too late. *Mrs Warren's Profession* was now historically irrelevant.

The play had a similarly fraught passage to acceptability in the
US. On 27 October 1905 its American premiere in New Haven,
Connecticut (one of the routine preludes to Broadway production) was
shut down by the local mayor after its first night. The same thing happened three days later when the play opened in New York. The whole
cast, crew and management of the Garrick Theater were charged with
'offences against public decency'. It was not until 9 March 1907 that
Mrs Warren's Profession was permitted unhindered public performance.

The club loophole was increasingly used as the 20th century progressed, and British drama chafed under the nonsense of state control.

The play that is credited with finally abolishing 'royal' censorship of the stage was Edward Bond's *Saved*, featuring as it did the stoning to death of a baby on stage. The Lord Chamberlain banned public performance. The Royal Court (the theatre that had pioneered 'new' British drama) promptly reconfigured itself as a club and staged a performance on 3 November 1965. The play provoked furious discussion in the press and media. Following Roy Jenkins' Obscene Publications Act five years earlier (and the ground-breaking *Lady Chatterley* acquittal), the interference on the creative arts of Britain by this ermined flunkey appeared absurd. The Lord Chamberlain's power of censorship was abolished by the Theatres Act, which came into force on 26 September 1968.

Interestingly, however, the act retained a clause requiring that every play, publicly performed in the UK, should have its pre-production script deposited at the British Library. This archive survives as the shadow of centuries-long censorship of the stage.

27 September

Midwich survives

1957 It was Brian Aldiss who coined the term 'cosy catastrophe', specifically for the novels of his fellow science-fiction practitioner, John Wyndham (one of the pen names of John Wyndham Parkes Lucas Benyon Harris). No catastrophe is cosier than that depicted in Wyndham's novel, *The Midwich Cuckoos* (1957).

The action is set in Miss Marples-land. The fictional Midwich is located in fictional Winshire – 'an ordinary little village where nothing ever happened'. It has a Norman church, some 60 houses, a pub called the Scythe and Stone, and an aura of time-in, time-out unchangeability.

Something, however, does happen. On 26 September (in an unspecified 1950s year) two Midwich residents, Richard Gayford and his wife, spend the night in London, celebrating his birthday. On their return on the 27th, they discover that for 24 hours, the village has been sealed off under an invisible and wholly impenetrable bubble. The authorities are impotent and have no explanation. The bubble mysteriously lifts and life returns to normal – as the village fondly but mistakenly thinks.

Some months after the 'Dayout', as it is called, every one of the 65 or so fertile women in Midwich – including young maids and middle-aged spinsters – find themselves with child. It emerges that they have been impregnated by aliens – xenogenesis.

Nine months to the day, a crop of clone-like, golden-eyed *Wunderkinder* are born. The children have extra-human powers, telepathic communication among themselves, and mature at a terrifyingly precocious rate. It becomes clear that they have no great love for their hosts – any more than does the nestling cuckoo for any young birds alongside it. Anyone who crosses the Midwich children dies.

Other nests of these ominous children have implanted themselves in various parts of the world. The Russians ruthlessly nuke theirs. Midwich requires a more humanely English genocide. Gordon Zellaby, a man of great learning and a terminal cardiac condition, has befriended (insofar as it is possible) the Midwich cuckoos. He straps explosive to himself and, while discussing classical history, blows them, and himself, to smithereens. The world (more specifically rural England) is saved. For now.

Zellaby leaves a bleak farewell note for his wife:

[W]e have lived so long in a garden that we have all but forgotten the commonplaces of survival. It was said: *Si fueris Romae, Romano vivito more* ['If you are in Rome, live in the Roman way'], and quite sensibly, too. But it is a more fundamental expression of the same sentiment to say: If you want to keep alive in the jungle, you must live as the jungle does.

Uncosiness (Zellaby's bomb) is the only key to survival.

It is tempting to tie Wyndham's novel, and his other catastrophic scenarios (*The Kraken Wakes, The Day of the Triffids, The Chrysalids*), with the 1950s 'Age of Anxiety' when nuclear destruction was expected, with only four minutes' warning, from the skies at any moment. The nervousness of the decade is similarly caught in Nigel Kneale's 1953 TV series, *The Quatermass Experiment* – which may well have influenced Wyndham.

The Midwich Cuckoos has itself been adapted for TV and has been twice filmed (in 1960 and 1995) under the fatuously gothic title, *Village of the Damned*.

28 September

*Juan Rodríguez Cabrillo lands near what is now San Diego,
to become the first European to set foot in California*

1542 As it would prove so often in the future – to the Forty-Niners
looking for gold, the Okies for jobs, and electronics engineers for cut-
ting-edge opportunities in Silicon Valley – people imagined California
as their promised land before they experienced its actuality. In fact,
California had existed in literature for some time before it was discovered – in *Las Sergas de Esplandián* (*The Adventures of Esplandián*) by the
15th-century Spanish author of *Amadís de Gaula*, Garci Rodríguez de
Montalvo:

> [A] la diestra mano de las Indias existe una isla llamada California
> muy cerca de un costado del Paraíso Terrenal; y estaba poblada
> por mujeres negras ... de bellos y robustos cuerpos, fogoso valor
> y gran fuerza. ... Sus armas eran todas de oro ... porque en toda
> la isla no había otro metal que el oro.*

At almost the same time as *Las Sergas* appeared, Columbus was entering into the diary of his first voyage in 1492 another story – this one
told by the natives – of an island inhabited by women. Just 32 years
later, the *conquistador* Hernán Cortés reported to the king of Spain
that one of his captains had heard yet another tale of a paradisal island
'rich in gold and pearls', inhabited only by women.

Another of Cortés' captains, Juan Rodríguez Cabrillo, fought as the
head of a crossbow detachment in the conquest of Mexico, before settling in what is now Guatemala. Brought up as a shipwright, he was
unusual among explorers in being able to build his own ships. He was
also a canny adventurer and a hard employer, using the Indians virtually as slaves to carry supplies to his Guatemalan gold mine, and pitch
from the mountains to waterproof his ships.

In 1542 Cabrillo was charged by Pedro de Alvara, then Captain
General of Guatemala, to explore the west coast of what is now the
United States, not least to settle those old rumours of golden islands and
dusky beauties. Arriving at Ensenada, Baja California on 17 September

---

* 'To the right of the Indies there is an island called California, very close to the coast of
the earthly paradise; and it was inhabited by black women ... with strong, beautiful bodies,
fiercely brave and very strong. ... Their armaments were made completely of gold ... because
in all the island there was no metal other than gold.'

1542, they sailed north until they entered San Diego Bay on the 28th, which Cabrillo named San Miguel and described as 'a closed and very good harbour', landing at Ballast Point and claiming the area for Spain. They then coasted what is now California as far north as the Russian River in present-day Sonoma County, north of San Francisco, before coming back south. Cabrillo died of infection following a leg wound sustained while scrambling ashore at Catalina Island, off Los Angeles.

But no Amazons, alas – and no gold either; it would take a foreman working a watermill for a German-Swiss immigrant in 1848 to start up the California Gold Rush.

29 September

The Greek fleet swamps the Persians in the Battle of Salamis;
Aeschylus writes it up

480 BC The Greeks were up against it. The Athenians had evacuated their city for the island of Salamis off the coast of Attica, close enough to watch in agony and fury as the invading Persians sacked their city, setting fire to the sacred temples on the Acropolis. Offshore, the Persian fleet threatened with 700 or 800 triremes and support vessels. Within the straits between the island and the mainland some 360 allied Greek warships lay waiting.

But only for a while. Some of the allies were growing edgy, thinking they had better get their ships back to defend their own city states. Themistocles, the senior tactician of the battle, hit upon a way of turning this hazard into an advantage. If he could tip off Xerxes, the Persian commander, that certain of the Greek triremes were about to escape, he could lure the Persians into the straits, where limited room to manoeuvre would cancel their superior numbers. Sure enough, the Persians swallowed the bait, rowing all night to reach and then patrol the southern exit to the straits, leaving them exhausted the next morning.

As the Persians entered from the south, thinking to pursue some allied ships that appeared to be fleeing the scene, the main body of Greek triremes fell on their flank from the west, using their heavy rams to stove in the ships' sides, then sending their marines to board and fight hand-to-hand. In the confusion more than 200 Persian ships ran aground, or into each other, or turned turtle and sank. The Greek allies lost fewer than 30. The Persians retreated, taking their occupying army with them. Historians still consider Salamis to have been the most important sea battle ever.

Taking part in the battle was Aeschylus, the Athenians' greatest dramatist. It's as though Shakespeare had fought in the Battle of Agincourt. Naturally the playwright wanted to use his experience, but there were two problems. First, he was a tragedian and this victory was anything but a tragedy for the Athenians. Second, the plots of tragedies were conventionally based on myths or legends, and this was near-contemporary history.

As for the second difficulty, he may have thought the sea battle so important – deciding as it did the fate of Greek, and especially Athenian, civilisation – as almost to have reached mythic significance. The solution to the first was to set the play in Persia, at the court of King Xerxes, where Salamis really was felt as a tragedy – though more in the modern newspaper-headline sense than the Aristotelian. As a result, *The Persians* (472 BC) was not packed with action; the climax (from the vantage point of its vast Greek audiences) was a long speech by a messenger reporting the battle to a shocked Queen Atossa, mother of Xerxes. It is one of the most powerful descriptive passages in all Greek drama, full of details like blood-bespattered shipwrecks and corpses rolled by the waves onto rocky shores. You could tell that Aeschylus had seen it for himself.

30 September

The first part of Little Women *comes out – to instant and lasting acclaim*

1868 Loved by every generation of women since its first appearance, *Little Women* has inspired – or spawned, according to your point of view – no fewer than fourteen movies from 1917 to 2001. The book spans exactly a year in the lives of the poor but genteel March girls, Meg, Jo, Beth and Amy, as they make do with their mother in a large but ramshackle house in Massachusetts. Short of money ever since their father 'lost his property in trying to help an unfortunate friend', and now left behind while he's away serving as an army chaplain in the Civil War, the girls do their best to support their 'Marmee', while all engage in various charitable and caring works at home and in the neighbourhood.

Though based loosely on the author's own childhood, it's not the sort of book that Louisa May Alcott might have been expected to write. Her father and mother were part of that Concord, Massachusetts circle of Transcendentalists that included Emerson and Thoreau (see 23 July). They were feminists and anti-slavery activists who had welcomed the widow and daughters of the violent abolitionist John Brown into their home, and sheltered an escaped slave on his way to Canada.

Louisa was no less adventurous. At 30 she signed up as an army nurse in a chaotic Washington hospital. Some of her earliest writings were gritty sketches of her work among the Civil War wounded, offering vivid details of the men's wounds, their words and their callous treatment by the surgeons (they can be seen at: http://digital.library. upenn.edu/women/alcott/sketches/sketches.html). After that she wrote a series of sensationalist stories for *Frank Leslie's Magazine* under the pseudonym of 'A.M. Barnard'. 'Dealing with masquerade, mesmerism, rebellion, desire, anger, revenge, and incest', Elaine Showalter writes, 'these thrillers allowed her to express the volcanic side of her personality.'*

In moving to write *Little Women*, did Alcott abandon frankness for sweetness and light? After all, this is a novel about adolescent girls in which there are no – not even coded – references to sexual maturation, and where love between the sexes is represented mainly by good fellowship. In exploiting the enormous popularity of *Jane Eyre* (first American edition, 1848) and America's first bestseller, Susan Warner's *The Wide Wild World* (1850), did Alcott sell her birthright to the market? Not necessarily. Showalter points out the thematic links between these popular works, with their isolated heroines who ultimately triumph through patience, and the rebellious Jo in *Little Women*, and her ambition – a clear reflection of her creator's – to become an author. With the father erased and the military hospital (of which the author had first-hand experience) marginalised, 'Alcott suppresses her own anger and ambition' even as Jo masters her quick temper. But in volume two, *Good Wives* (1869), Jo achieves her ambition. She becomes the author of sensational stories for the *Weekly Volcano*. Maybe that's why Gertrude Stein and Simone de Beauvoir so admired her example of aspiring womanhood.

---

* Elaine Showalter, *A Jury of Her Peers: American Women Writers from Anne Bradstreet to Annie Proulx*, London: Virago Press, 2009, pp. 140, 142.

1 October

Wuthering Heights *and the long journey of the four-letter word*

1848 The least successful governess of the three novel-writing Brontë sisters (but arguably the greatest novelist), Emily was the most attached to the Yorkshire moors where she was brought up, and largely educated, in her father Patrick Brontë's Haworth parsonage. It was, ironically, the bitter weather of her beloved moors that killed her. On 1 October she left Haworth to attend her wayward brother Branwell's funeral service. Drink, drugs (laudanum), and moral dissipation had doomed him, the only son and the great hope of the family.

Branwell's self-destruction is pictured in the downfall of Hindley, Heathcliff's predecessor as master of Wuthering Heights. None of the owners of that ominous property, in the three generations covered by the novel, comes to a happy end. The curious inscription over the door, which no one can read, may plausibly be a curse.

Branwell died, as did all of his siblings, of pulmonary weakness, principally. He was buried on 28 September 1848 in Haworth church-yard. His father (who would outlive all his children) was too upset to officiate. Three days later, at the funeral service, Emily developed the chill that exacerbated her consumption and killed her, on 19 December. Six months later, her sister Anne joined her in the Haworth vault.

Brontë's one complete novel had been published, the year before, by the most dubious publisher in London, Thomas Cautley Newby. Newby (who the same year did his best to ruin the early career of Anthony Trollope by his shoddy and dishonest practices) printed *Wuthering Heights* as a three-decker (by 'Ellis Bell') along with Anne Brontë's *Agnes Grey* (by 'Acton Bell'). The reviews were few and indifferent. The general opinion was that *Wuthering Heights* was 'coarse'. There was too much damning and blasting in Yorkshire for genteel metropolitan ears.

Charlotte Brontë, in a posthumous reissue of *Wuthering Heights* (which began that novel's progress to its huge fame) was apologetic, but made a prophetic plea for frankness:

A large class of readers, likewise, will suffer greatly from the introduction into the pages of this work of words printed with all their letters, which it has become the custom to represent by the initial and final letter only – a blank line filling the interval.

I may as well say at once that, for this circumstance, it is out of my power to apologise; deeming it, myself, a rational plan to write words at full length. The practice of hinting by single letters those expletives with which profane and violent persons are wont to garnish their discourse, strikes me as a proceeding which, however well meant, is weak and futile. I cannot tell what good it does – what feeling it spares – what horror it conceals.

It would, however, be a long time until the four-letter word – with Kenneth Tynan's primal fuff-fuff-fuff-uck (see 13 November) and Lady Chatterley's legalised 'effing' – would be reached.

2 October

Sarah Kemble Knight begins her epic journey from Boston to New York

1704 In those days you weren't spoilt for choice when it came to ways of moving about the American colonies. There were no roads to speak of, so no stage coaches. East-coast cities were best served by ship. That's how Benjamin Franklin made his career-building move from Boston to Philadelphia 1725.

But 21 years before that, Sarah Kemble Knight, a Boston business-woman, legal scrivener and schoolteacher who may have taught the young Ben, decided to risk the trip on horseback, possibly because her legal business required that she go by way of New Haven, Connecticut. She was gone for five months, arriving home on 3 March 1705.

She made her way along barely marked tracks, usually assisted by a local guide. Where rivers were shallow enough to ford, they rode across them. Where not, they might cross by canoe, the water almost up to the gunwales. Details like these she recorded in her journal, along with acute observations of the manners and mores of tobacco-chewing country 'bumpkins' (her word), native Americans little more than animals, and frontier settlers living in huts with bare dirt floors, with no

furniture but a Bedd wth a glass Bottle hanging at ye head on't; an earthan cupp, a small pewter Bason, A Bord wth sticks to stand on, instead of a table, and a block or two in ye corner instead of chairs.

It was 'the picture of poverty', yet 'both the Hutt and its Inhabitance were very clean and tydee: to the crossing the Old Proverb, that bare walls make giddy hows-wifes'.

In places this reads like *Domestic Manners of the Americans* (1832), but Madame Knight wasn't just Frances Trollope *avant la lettre*. What really distinguishes the journal from the travel book is the former's sense of irony, its grip on reality. One night as they made their way along a dark, narrow track, 'Going I knew not whither, and encompassed wth Terrifying darkness', they breasted the top of a hill to suddenly see the full moon. Or as she put it, 'the Kind Conductress of the night'.

My tho'ts on the sight of the moon were to this purpose:

> Fair Cynthia, all the Homage that I may
> Unto a Creature, unto thee I pay;
> In Lonesome woods to meet so kind a guide,
> To Mee's more worth than all the world beside …

And the Tall and thick Trees at a distance, expecially w^n the moon glar'd light through the branches, fill'd my Imagination wth the pleasant delusion of a Sumpteous citty, fill'd wth famous Buildings and churches, wth their spiring steeples, Balconies, Galleries and I know not what: Grandeurs wch I had heard of, and wch the stories of foreign countries had given me the Idea of.

> Here stood a Lofty church – there a steeple,
> And there the Grand Parade – O see the people!
> That Famous Castle there, were I but nigh,
> To see the mote and Bridg and walls so high –
> They're very fine! Sais my deluded eye.

What is it about the occasion that causes her to burst into poetry, the most formal manner of discourse? What prompts her rhetorically heightened references to the moon, like the elegant periphrasis 'Kind conductress of the night' and the classical allusion to the goddess Cynthia? Why do her most 'pleasant delusions' consist of famous buildings and churches got from stories of foreign countries'?

The obvious answer is that these elaborate forms were the author's compensation, the fantasies of civilisation that came to her in the wilderness. True, but the point is, she knows it; she realises her 'eye' is 'deluded'. And in case we miss that point, here is how she concludes the episode:

> Being thus greatly entertain'd without a thou't of any thing but thoughts themselves, I on a suden was Rous'd from these pleasing Imaginations, by the Post's sounding his horn, which assured mee hee was arrived at the Stage, where we were to Lodg.

'Without a thou't of anything but thoughts themselves'? Can it be that an American first theorised deconstruction some two and a half centuries before the French?

3 October

Poet meets leech-gatherer; poem ensues

1800 In her journal for 3 October, Dorothy Wordsworth records an encounter, while out walking with her brother William, in the Lake District around Grasmere:

> We met an old man almost double. He had on a coat, thrown over his shoulders, above his waistcoat and coat. Under this he carried a bundle, and had an apron on and a night-cap. His face was interesting. He had dark eyes and a long nose ... He was of Scotch parents, but had been born in the army. He had had a wife, and 'a good woman, and it pleased God to bless us with ten children'. All these were dead but one, of whom he had not heard for many years, a sailor. His trade was to gather leeches, but now leeches are scarce, and he had not the strength for it. He lived by begging, and was making his way to Carlisle, where he should buy a few goodly books to sell. He said leeches were very scarce, partly owing to this dry season, but many years they had been scarce – he supposed it owing to their being much sought after, that they did not breed fast, and were of slow growth. Leeches were formerly 2s 6d. [per] 100; they are now 30s.

It was a striking enough experience for Dorothy to inscribe it at length in her journal. In William it inspired one of his finest poems, and his noblest reflection on the rigours of the poetic career, 'Resolution and Independence'. In the poem (in which, rather unkindly, he pictures himself walking around Grasmere by himself) Wordsworth first experiences 'joy' at a gorgeous morning, then a sudden decline into melancholy – thinking, specifically, of poets who have died young or wretched or both (principally Burns and 'the marvellous boy', Chatterton).

Suddenly, he encounters an old man. How is it you live, and what do you do? Wordsworth asks:

> [He] said, that, gathering leeches, far and wide
> He travelled; stirring thus about his feet
> The waters of the pools where they abide.
> 'Once I could meet with them on every side;
> But they have dwindled long by slow decay;
> Yet still I persevere, and find them where I may.'

The leech-gatherer's courtesy, courage, and stoicism correct his own self-indulgence, and he concludes that when in the future melancholy strikes: 'I'll think of the leech-gatherer on the lonely moor!'

The poem has some ecological and medical interest. Leeches were in great demand in the 18th and 19th centuries for 'bleeding' or phlebotomy – a treatment for a whole range of conditions. The species, due to over-harvesting, was exhausted in Britain by the 1830s and the bulk of leeches (which travel well) were imported from France and Germany. By the beginning of the 20th century the medicinal leech was virtually extinct across the whole of Europe.

4 October

Printing of the Coverdale Bible is finished, the first complete Bible to be published in English

1535 At the heart of the Protestant Reformation was the devout worshippers' desire for direct access to God through Jesus Christ. People wanted to work out their own salvation, not have it decided by a parish priest working the gates of confession and absolution. So they needed to know God's word directly, not filtered through someone's loose paraphrase of the Latin scriptures.

Needless to say, the established Roman Catholic Church was strenuously opposed to translations. The Bible was so complexly figurative; ordinary people would just get confused if they tried to read it for themselves. Besides, they might discover that there was no scriptural authority for purgatory, let alone the profitable indulgences sold to curtail the loved one's time there.

Only ten years earlier, the reformist English priest William Tyndale had published his English version of the New Testament, only to have it denounced by the Catholic Church and himself be charged with heresy, for which he was strangled at the stake in Vilvoorde castle near Brussels, after which his body was burned (see 6 September).

Thanks to a certain Ms Boleyn, Yorkshireman Myles Coverdale was luckier. Although he too had to have his Bible printed abroad, that's because the funding and printing expertise were there, rather than for fear of persecution. Newly divorced and remarried, split from Rome, and in 1534 officially designated head of the Church of England, Henry VIII had plenty of use for English translations of the Bible.

He ordered a Coverdale Bible to be supplied to every church in England, chained to a lectern so that parishioners could read it for themselves. If they couldn't read, here was an added incentive to learn. Over time, the Bible's effect on literacy in English – not to mention its influence on the imaginative use of the language – has been incalculable.

Coverdale wasn't a great Bible scholar. He had little Greek and less Hebrew, using (among others) Tyndale's work and Martin Luther's great German translation for cribs. But his translations of the Psalms lived on in the Anglican *Book of Common Prayer*, which means that to churchgoers of a certain age it's they that are the Psalms, not those in the Authorised Version.

For Handel too, Coverdale was the proper psalmist. In *The Messiah* (1742), Psalm 22 is exploited for its prophetic bearing on Christ's crucifixion:

> All they that see me laugh me to scorn: they shoot out their
>   lips, and shake their heads, saying,
> He trusted in God, that he would deliver him: let him deliver
>   him, if he will have him.

And a whole chorus is built around the lead line of Psalm 2: 'Why do the heathen so furiously rage together: and why do the people imagine a vain thing?'

5 October

Steinbeck begins a series of articles in a San Francisco paper; they will change his life

1936 It's often forgotten that *The Grapes of Wrath* (1939) was not John Steinbeck's first novel about migrant farm workers in California's Central Valley. That was called *In Dubious Battle* (1936), and it wasn't very good. It was about a strike. To gather information on it, Steinbeck had relied on a few second-hand accounts. He wanted his plot to prove a theory he had heard from his friend, the marine biologist Ed Ricketts, that men in a group behave like cells in the body, not thinking or acting for themselves but for the greater organism.

As a result, *In Dubious Battle* didn't work, either as fiction or documentary – hazy on concrete detail, its characters mouthing set philosophical and political positions. Though the migrant workers had won the actual strike on which the story was based, they had to lose it in the novel, in order to conform to the pre-existent theory.

Never mind, *In Dubious Battle* made Steinbeck look as though he knew something about conditions down on the farm, so when the *San Francisco News*, a liberal evening daily, wanted to cover the residential camps set up by Roosevelt's New Deal to keep the migrant 'Okies' and their families out of the drainage ditches where they were washing and going to the toilet, they asked the novelist to investigate.

This was journalism, not fiction, so it was going to require some real fact-finding about local people and conditions, rather than half-baked biologistic theories. So Steinbeck travelled down the Central Valley, finally winding up at Weedpatch, the leading government camp near Arvin, where he found out about the systems for welcoming migrant families, keeping them dry, clean and happily occupied between jobs, and fending off the landowners' vigilantes. Meeting the migrants face to face, hearing them speak, sitting in on their meetings, Steinbeck quickly came to recognise them as something more than cells in a larger organism.

'The Harvest Gypsies', as his articles were called, appeared as seven full-page pieces in the *News*, from 5 to 12 October 1936, illustrated by the government documentary photographer Dorothea Lange (see 26 May). A survey of the migrants' living conditions outside the government camps began with the material facts as experienced on the ground:

The dirt floor is swept clean, and along the irrigation ditch or in the muddy river, the wife of the family scrubs clothes without soap and tries to rinse out the mud in muddy water. The spirit of this family is not quite broken, for the children, three of them, still have clothes, and the family possesses three old quilts and a soggy, lumpy mattress.

THEN COME THE RAINS
With the first rain the carefully built house will slop down into a brown, pulpy mush; in a few months the clothes will fray off the children's bodies while the lack of nourishing food will subject the whole family to pneumonia when the first cold comes.

Families barely subsist; they are terrified of starvation, the children too weak to go to school. Medical attention hardly exists.

Shock details were reinforced by analysis. Steinbeck went back into history, explaining how California farms had evolved, not through thousands of individual settlements, but through a few large landholdings subdivided again and again. Then he explained how many of the big farms were owned by absentee landlords, banks and corporations, and managed by supervisors, before showing how the new government camps were working.

Besides being one of the best pieces of investigative journalism to come out of the Depression, 'The Harvest Gypsies' opened the door to *The Grapes of Wrath*, awakening in Steinbeck a genuine sympathy for the Okies and their political struggle, and teaching him the value of minutely-observed particulars as a way of setting a scene and piquing the reader's participation in bringing the picture to life.

6 October

William Golding's sour-tasting Nobel Prize

1983 As his biographer, John Carey, records, William Golding (a Grand Old Man of English fiction, at 72) received the first intimation that he was to be 1983 Nobel laureate by phone, at ten o'clock on the morning of 6 October. He was so informed by a Swedish journalist who said, tantalisingly, that he had a '50–50 chance'. The award was confirmed by lunchtime.

The 50 per cent adverse possibility was, despite the notorious secretiveness of the Stockholm literary committee, made public in the days thereafter. One of the judges, 77-year-old poet Artur Lindkvist, had single-handedly tried to blackball Golding's nomination in favour of a Senegalese poet, Léopold Senghor (he was also the first president of his country after its independence). Senghor (five years older than Golding) was well known in the francophone literary world. He had been elected a member of l'Académie française on 2 June 1983, the first African writer to be so honoured.

Lindkvist explained: 'I simply didn't consider Golding to possess the international weight needed to win the prize … I admire Anthony Burgess very much. He is of far greater worth than Golding and is much more controversial.' The author of *Lord of the Flies* was, he concluded, 'too nice'.

Golding was chronically self-doubting. Lindkvist's spiteful criticisms soured what should have been the crowning moment of his literary career.

7 October

As Allen Ginsberg first reads Howl *aloud at the Six Gallery, San Francisco, the Beat Generation comes of age*

1955 'I saw the best minds of my generation destroyed by madness, starving, hysterical, naked', he intoned,

dragging themselves through the negro streets at dawn looking
for an angry fix,

angelheaded hipsters burning for the ancient heavenly
   connection to the starry dynamo in the machinery of night,
who poverty and tatters and hollow-eyed and high sat up
   smoking in the supernatural darkness of cold-water flats
   floating across the tops of cities contemplating jazz ...

These are just the first four verse paragraphs in a total of 88 in Part I alone. Most reiterate that parallel construction beginning with 'who ...', so are about those 'best minds' 'who studied Plotinus Poe St John of the Cross telepathy and bop kaballa' and 'let themselves be fucked in the ass by saintly motorcyclists, and screamed with joy'.

Howl took over from where Ginsberg's fellow New Jerseyian Walt Whitman left off – not just in that conversational rhythm and versification based on breath, but also in those frank vignettes of urban low-life, and of the gay scene generally.

Howl came out in 1956 in a now legendary 'Pocket Poets' edition published by the poet Lawrence Ferlinghetti under the imprint of the City Lights Bookshop, 261 Columbus Avenue, San Francisco. The book's format was nearly square – 6½ inches high by just under 5 wide – and it cost 75¢.

As a result of its sexual explicitness, the San Francisco police prosecuted Ferlinghetti for publishing obscene material after the local district attorney declined to act. In the trial that followed in 1957, the book was defended by the American Civil Liberties Union, calling on artists and academics as expert witnesses. Ferlinghetti won when Judge Clayton Horn ruled that the work was of 'redeeming social importance'. The trial was as widely publicised in the US as was the *Lady Chatterley* case in Britain (see 10 November).

But for all the book's notoriety, who were the Beats, after all? Was their 'generation' anything more than one of those convenient clichés of literary classification, like the so-called 'lost generation' between the wars, an epithet actually based on a disparaging remark made by Gertrude Stein to her French garage mechanic? Were they a literary movement, or just a public relations gesture, a bunch of guys, their women seldom mentioned, famous for making themselves famous?

Take Neal Cassady. Did anyone ever read anything by him, or just *about* him in Jack Kerouac's defining narrative of the Beat moment, *On the Road* (1957)? The (rather more conventional) poet Gary Snyder, who also read that night at the Six, denies that the movement had much coherence, other than as a 'circle of friends'.

Yet the reading at the Six Gallery remains a monument in American poetry. By its 50th anniversary, *Howl* had reached its 53rd printing, and nearly a million copies remained in print.

8 October

Herta Müller wins the Nobel. Handkerchiefs flutter in celebration

2009 One of the things that hobbles the Nobel Literature Prize is its founder's instruction that it should be awarded to the author of 'the most outstanding work in an ideal direction'. There is argument about how *idealisk* (in the old dynamitard's original Swedish) should be translated. But the basic instruction is clear – the laureate should be on the side of the angels.

The 'idealisk' criterion probably also explains why Philip Roth (many things – but no angel) has never been honoured. It also explains why, lest some bombshell is dropped later, the committee usually aim to get in just ahead of the undertaker (the two of them practically got jammed in the door with poor Harold Pinter, the 2005 honoree).

'I am very near the end', said V.S. Naipaul in his winner's lecture. He wasn't. But had his nomination come up after, rather than before, Patrick French's 2008 warts-and-all biography the odd black ball might have been cast.

It must have been painful when, with the laurel leaves still fresh on his brow, Günter Grass disclosed that he had a Waffen-SS uniform in his skeleton's closet (Grass may, perhaps, have slyly forecast that Stockholm would regret it by giving his lecture on the subject of rats).

Herta Müller, the 2009 laureate (announced to the world on this day), was, by Nobel standards, young – in her mid-fifties. She was also the daughter of a Waffen-SS soldier. Not that it should be held against her any more than the paternity of Nicholas Mosley (son of Oswald, and one of Britain's most underrated novelists) should affect critical judgement. But it must have been mulled over in Stockholm.

Brought up in a German-ethnic-minority family in Ceauşescu's horrid Romania, Müller falls into a favourite category with the committee – writers who express human freedoms while suffering under totalitarian regimes (Pinter under Blair, for example). Müller chose to give her winner's lecture not on the subject of liberty but of snot (beats rats). This is how it opens:

> 'Do you have a handkerchief?' was the question my mother asked me every morning, standing by the gate to our house, before I went out onto the street.

The same maternal query came up the day the Securitate came to haul Herta's mother off to a Gulag. The whole of Müller's lecture revolves around the big things that little things mean. It's very touching, and like no other Nobel lecture on record. Even a hankie can be idealistic.

9 October

Dario Fo wins the Nobel for Literature

1997 Aged 71 when he received the honour and still going strong, Dario Fo, the Italian dramatist, screenwriter, composer, librettist, theatre manager, television game show author and political activist, has used his art and wit to ridicule political corruption, the Catholic Church, fascism, the Communist party, the Mafia, Israel, Lyndon B. Johnson and the US in general, the Carabinieri (Italian state police) – and many other persons and institutions not at all good at taking jokes. The wonder is not that he got the Nobel Prize, but that he lived long enough to take delivery of it.

Against the limits of frequent censorship and worse, Fo's greatest achievement in strictly literary terms has been to make theatre popular. While in most other countries it's a small segment of the middle classes who patronise the live theatre (where they can find it), Fo and his wife Franca Rame have brought theatre to the people – touring the country first with the company bearing their names, then with the Associazione Nuova Scena with its portable stages, and finally their Collettivo Teatrale La Commune.

Among their most popular productions were *Mistero Buffo* (*Slapstick Mystery*) (1969), seen by up to three million Italians, in which Fo drew on the tradition of medieval travelling performances often held in town squares, and *Accidental Death of an Anarchist* (1970), his most often performed work outside Italy – staged in over 40 countries.

Based on a real-life case in which an anarchist, suspected of having bombed a bank in Milan, mysteriously fell or was thrown from a fourth-floor window in a police station (at first the police said he jumped in remorse for his part in the atrocity), the play draws on the popular tradition of the *commedia dell'arte*, posing a Harlequin-like trickster, 'the Maniac', to infiltrate the judicial system and get the police to deconstruct the official account in their own words.

Dario Fo 'emulates the jesters of the Middle Ages', his Nobel citation read, 'in scourging authority and upholding the dignity of the downtrodden'. On receiving his award, Fo paid tribute to Ruzzante Beolco – 'the true father of the *commedia dell'arte*', he called him – who, along with Molière, 'was despised for bringing onto the stage the everyday life, joys and desperation of the common people; the hypocrisy and the arrogance of the high and mighty; and the incessant injustice. And their major, unforgivable fault was this: in telling these things, they made people laugh. Laughter does not please the mighty.'

10 October

A True Leveller is baptised somewhere in the parish of Wigan

1609 His origins are obscure (where in the large parish was he born? Who was his mother?), but he was well enough known in his day, with over twenty books and pamphlets to his name – all but one of them reprinted. After that his fame was eclipsed again, until revived by left-wing historians like D.W. Petegorsky and Christopher Hill. What his published work proves is that Gerrard Winstanley was one of the most original political thinkers in English history. Why? He took Christianity seriously as a political programme. Hill put it well: 'Winstanley's relation to traditional theology is like Karl Marx's relation to Hegelianism: he found it standing on its head and set it the right way up.'*

Take the Apostles, for example – as Winstanley himself did. In the Book of Acts (2: 43–5) they and those they converted to Christianity 'had all things in common; / And sold their possessions and parted them to all men, as every man had need'. So in *The New Law of*

---

* Christopher Hill (ed.), *Winstanley: The Law of Freedom and other Writings*, Harmondsworth: Penguin Books, 1973, p. 53.

Righteousness, published in 1649 just four days before Charles I's execution, Winstanley plotted England's predicament against the grand narrative of the Bible itself, tracing unequal distribution of property back to the original Fall of mankind, and proposed a new socialist dispensation based on the New Testament.

When that didn't catch on, Winstanley and his followers acted out their ideals in real time and space. Occupying a piece of common land near Cobham, Surrey, on the first Sunday in April 1649, they proceeded to dig it over and sow beans, carrots and parsnips in it. Their enemies called them 'Diggers'. They didn't mind. Their own name for the movement was the 'True Levellers', as distinct from the 'Levellers', those agitators for political reform under John Lillbourne, who pressed for the right of all to own property. The True Levellers wanted to abolish the ownership of property altogether.

But then, property is violence, as Proudhon might have said, but didn't, and as the local landowners proved, when two yeomen led a group of men dressed as women to assault and beat four Diggers sowing a winter crop. Following this setback, Winstanley went silent for a while, before producing the book for which he is best known today.

In *The Law of Freedom in a Platform, or True Magistracy Restored* (1652), to give it its full title, Winstanley continued to analyse the recent history of England in terms of the Bible, but now he was turning increasingly to the apocalyptic books, Daniel and Revelations, for his terminology. Thus 'kingly government or monarchy' is 'the government of the Beast' and 'the very city of Babylon, full of confusion'; while 'commonwealth's government', 'whereby there is a provision for livelihood in the earth, both for elder and younger brother', is 'the ancient of days' (an old man in Daniel, chapter 7, who prefigures Christ), 'the true restorer of all long-lost freedoms'.

We're still waiting.

11 October

Where's Charley? *opens a long run on Broadway*

1948 *Charley's Aunt*, by Brandon Thomas, was the prototype London West End farce – the inspiration for a hugely profitable and popular theatrical genre.

The play ran for 1,466 performances from 21 December 1892, with Thomas (now in his mid-forties) playing one of the fathers in the action. On Broadway *Charley's Aunt* ran for an even longer four years.

The central element in the plot – as often in farce – is cross-dressing. Two young undergrads at Oxford, and lads around town, Charley Wykeham and Jack Chesney, are in dire need of a chaperone, so they can decently entertain the two young ladies they are sweet on. Charley's aunt (whom he has never met, and who is coming from Brazil, 'where the nuts grow') will serve, they decide, perfectly. But she is delayed and a friend, Lord Fancourt Babberly, is prevailed on to impersonate her. Complications ensue.

Charley's Aunt became folkloric, thanks to repertory company performances over the years and film adaptations. Astonishingly, there was enough life left in this Victorian fun-piece for a musical adaptation, *Where's Charley?* (music by Frank Loesser, 'book' by George Abbott), to break box-office records half a century later.

Where's Charley? (which adheres more or less faithfully to the original 1892 plot) opened on 11 October 1948 and ran for an astonishing 792 performances. It greatly enhanced the stardom of Ray Bolger, as Charley. He went on to reprise the part in the 1952 film version.

Bolger (born in 1904, famous as the Scarecrow in *The Wizard of Oz*) would have seemed somewhat too old to play an Oxford undergraduate, and the part was changed to 'graduate', to make him more plausible.

The London version (which ran for 404 performances) starred Norman Wisdom as Charley. He, like Bolger, is one of the less-likely actors one would (if plausibility were a factor) have cast as an Oxonian gilded youth. But in farce, anything goes.

12 October

Tennyson crosses the bar

1892 As Samantha Matthews notes in her study of Victorian literary funerals, Tennyson's was the biggest of them all in a century that revered its authors as never before or since.

Alfred, Lord Tennyson, the poet laureate for almost half a century, died at dawn on 6 October 1892 in Haslemere, Surrey, aged 83. He was suffering from gout and influenza. The news that the queen's favourite poet had died was telegraphed to the newspapers. They already had reporters in place outside the poet's residence, Aldworth House.

Victoria herself sent a telegram of condolence (how far the communication systems had advanced since 1837, when there was not even a penny post). It was, the nation agreed, an event of truly national – not merely literary – importance. Something important was passing away: a whole era.

Tennyson's physician, Dr Dabbs, posted a bulletin recording the death to the gates of Aldworth House, vividly picturing the poet's last hours:

> Nothing could have been more striking than the scene during the last few hours. On the bed a figure of breathing marble, flooded and bathed in the light of the full moon streaming through the oriel window; his hand clasping the Shakespeare which he had asked for but recently, and which he had kept by him to the end; the moonlight, the majestic figure as he lay there, 'drawing thicker breath,' irresistibly brought to our minds his own 'Passing of Arthur'.

All poets should have such a physician at their deathbed.

The actual marble statue would, of course, be raised in Poet's Corner. The interment in the Abbey was arranged for 12 October. It was decided that he should lie for eternity (or until the final judgement) alongside Browning. The coffin (cased in lead, as regulations on intramural burial required) was closed on 8 October. A copy of Shakespeare's *Cymbeline*, with its funerary lines, was slipped into it by a well-meaning house servant:

> Fear no more the heat o' the sun,
> Nor the furious winter's rages;
> Thou thy worldly task hast done,
> Home art gone, and ta'en thy wages:
> Golden lads and girls all must,
> As chimney-sweepers, come to dust.

The grave was dug in the Abbey at night, by gaslight. The coffin, draped in a Union Jack, was brought to London, also at night, by special train to Waterloo station, where a small crowd awaited. It was then taken by hearse to the Abbey, where it lay among a mass of floral tributes.

There were insufficient tickets available for those wishing to view the coffin, lying in poetic state, and crowds massed outside the Abbey. Tennyson's son, Hallam, noted that many attending could be seen reading the poet's 'In Memoriam' before the service.

The papers printed handy maps, indicating where the dignitaries would be sitting. The queen herself was not present but 'represented' during the short service, during which the coffin rested on a purple-clothed trestle. The service itself was dominated by the musical version of the poem that Tennyson had composed three years earlier for his own death, 'Crossing the Bar' (inspired, in fact, by a bout of seasickness on the trip to his holiday home in the Isle of Wight). Its last stanza forecasts what was currently happening in the Abbey:

> For tho' from out our bourne of Time and Place
> The flood may bear me far,
> I hope to see my Pilot face to face
> When I have crossed the bar.

The national flag was removed, and the body was lowered into the earth, sacred to God and English literature, decked with a few 'wreaths of honour' – foremost that of Queen Victoria: laurels, with an inscription 'in the monarch's own hand'.

13 October

Sonia Brownell marries George Orwell in his room in University College Hospital, London, the hospital chaplain officiating

1949 The author of *Animal Farm* (1945) and *Nineteen Eighty-four* (1948) was critically ill with tuberculosis but his doctor, the distinguished chest specialist Andrew Morland, thought the disease might be damped down to a chronic state, allowing the author to work quietly.

Orwell himself was full of hope and ideas for future projects, including a book on Joseph Conrad's political fiction. He was happy at his marriage to his beautiful young wife, and now for the first time well-off, thanks to the success – in the United States as well as Britain – of *Nineteen Eighty-four*.

At first the book's popularity in the West owed something to the accelerating Cold War, since its dystopian satire was so apparently aimed at the Soviet Union, what with the manipulation of information through constant erasure and rewriting of the newspaper of record, and with 'Big Brother' and Goldstein (the regime's fantasy hate figure) so obviously resembling Stalin and Trotsky.

But Orwell insisted that his target was not socialism or communism, but the totalitarianism into which parties of either left or right could harden. He set the book in England to suggest that 'the English-speaking races are not innately better than anyone else and that totalitarianism, *if not fought against*, could triumph anywhere'.* Another reminder that the book was not just about Russia lay in the totalitarian regime's practice of turning allies into enemies overnight, just as Britain and America had done with the Soviet Union.

By 1989 *Nineteen Eighty-four* would be translated into more than 65 languages, and phrases like 'newspeak', 'doublethink', 'thought crime' – not to mention 'Orwellian' (to suggest the insidious control of a whole population) – have entered the language.

Not that Orwell himself would live to see any of this. He never left the hospital. Just three months after his wedding there, on 21 January 1950, he died of a massive lung haemorrhage. The editor of the *Observer* and long-time supporter David Astor found him a grave plot in an Oxfordshire village. Another friend, Malcolm Muggeridge, noted in his diary that Orwell dying on Lenin's birthday and being buried by the Astors, 'seems to me to cover the full range of his life'.†

14 October

The Normans defeat the English at the Battle of Hastings, changing the English language for ever

1066 The newly married couple were lucky. In their first two months together they'd known an *endlessness* of new feelings, and felt the bliss of being *enoughly happy*. What *hearthotness* (mania)! What

---

* Letter to Francis A. Henson of the United Automobile Workers, dated 16 June 1949; *The Collected Essays, Journalism and Letters of George Orwell, Volume 4: In Front of Your Nose, 1945–1950*, London: Secker & Warburg, 1968, p. 502.
† D.J. Taylor, 'Last Days of Orwell', *Guardian*, 15 January 2000.

fleshbesmittingness (carnal attraction)! Now, after a summer that was *beweepingly* (lamentably) short, they were in a *sound* house, had *sound* friends, and a *sound* working life.

According to a recent book on the subject, this is how we might talk if the Battle of Hastings had gone the other way – as it nearly did.* After the Norman Conquest, ordinary people continued to speak English, since *begengness* of *wordhoard* (the application of vocabulary) is down to folk, but the governmental and social elites spoke French, while contracts and the courts were conducted in Latin.

In time this official vocabulary infiltrated the vernacular, in some places displacing perfectly good English words, but in others settling alongside them, so that eventually 'English' had almost as many loan words drawn from French and Latin as it had words originating in Old English. This is one reason why English has such a huge wordhoard (the other is the need for new words to accommodate the science done predominantly in English-speaking countries – see 10 June).

Where French- or Latin-derived words have survived alongside English words meaning at least roughly the same, what's the result – pointless redundancy or expressive enrichment? Guides to good style often favour English over 'French', because since 1066 the latter has been the voice of officialdom. So (to take an actual example from the Plain English Campaign's website): 'High-quality learning environments are a necessary precondition for facilitation and enhancement of the ongoing learning process' could be stated more simply in English as: 'Children need good schools if they are to learn properly'.

The limit to this argument is that where the English word has survived alongside, and not been displaced by the French or Latin loan word, it's usually for a reason. 'Sight' and 'vision', for example, don't have exactly the same meaning; the latter often implies moral, intellectual or aesthetic values – invisible things that (on one level) are out of sight. The same goes for 'till' and 'cultivate', 'win back' and 'redeem', 'beginning' and 'origin', and thousands of other such binaries in the expanded language.

In 'Politics and the English Language' (1946) George Orwell offered five rules for clear composition, among which was: 'Never use a foreign phrase, a scientific word or a jargon word if you can think of an everyday English equivalent.' Yet who recognised the limits of plainness better than he? In *Nineteen Eighty-four* (1949) the Party is working

---

* David Cowley, *How We'd Talk If the English had Won in 1066*, Sandy, Bedfordshire: Bright Pen Books, 2009.

on a form of English in which synonyms are being erased in order to extinguish ambiguity and make 'crimethink' impossible. Push plain English too far, and you may wind up with Newspeak.

15 October

Winston Churchill, novelist

1953 On this date Winston Churchill, serving prime minister of England, was elected winner of the annual Prize for Literature by the Nobel committee. The practice of giving warmongers (such as Henry Kissinger) the Peace Prize had not yet been established: and he was no scientist. The committee was, of course, stretching a point in their rather desperate desire to honour the greatest Englishman of the century. Their 'rationale' for awarding the literary prize to Churchill was 'for his mastery of historical and biographical descriptions as well as for brilliant oratory in defending exalted human values'.

Oddly, Churchill did indeed have a work of literary fiction to his name, though it was never mentioned either in the award speech or the acceptance speech at a banquet given in his honour in Stockholm (Churchill was unable to be present, and the speech was read by his wife: it was a somewhat deflated occasion).

Savrola, a Ruritanian romance, was serialised in *Macmillan's Magazine*, May–December 1899. It was a scrappy period in the 25-year-old Churchill's life. He had failed to win a seat in parliament and was not yet fully engaged (as he soon would be) in the South African war, where his exploits (notably his capture and escape from the Boers) would make his name.

He was, in the late 1890s, picking up journalistic commissions and whatever other bits and pieces of remunerative work he could (Macmillan paid a handsome £100 for the serial rights to the novel). The action of *Savrola* opens on the day of a great parade in the capital of 'Laurania'. An old republic, the country has been a dictatorship under the presidency of Antonio Molara since the civil war of five years earlier (1883, we are told). Savrola, a brilliant philosophical soldier in his thirties (clearly based on Disraeli's omnicompetent Sidonia in *Coningsby*), has formed a radically conservative party to restore

Laurania's 'ancient liberties'. Romance, revolution, and the overthrow of international socialism follow.

The fascination with supreme power clearly took root in Churchill early. The novel earned handsomely and, had public life not opened a path for him, he could well have gone on to be a novelist in the Anthony Hope and, conceivably, even in the Conan Doyle class. He would certainly have made a better novelist than Hitler would have made a landscape painter, had both stuck to their respective lines of early work.

16 October

Abraham Lincoln deconstructs 'the sacred right of self-government'

1854 As more and more conquests or frontier settlements added to the American dominion, their inhabitants pressed to be admitted to the Union – first as territories, then in time, if they progressed and prospered, as states. In the years leading up to the Civil War this business grew more and more politically charged over whether slavery was to be allowed in the new territory or state. In 1820 and again in 1850, southern and northern congressmen reached compromises that drew a northern limit to slave-holding – the 36°30' parallel, the boundary between Arkansas and Missouri.

Then in 1854 the chairman of the Senate Committee on Territories, the prominent Democrat Stephen Douglas, introduced the Kansas–Nebraska Act to admit those two territories to the Union. All very uncontroversial, so far as slavery went, since both territories were above the 36°30' waterline. But there was a sting in the tail. Under southern pressure, Douglas drafted the Act so as to allow the inhabitants of the new territories to choose for themselves whether or not to hold slaves. Though practically speaking, the climate and terrain of the territories made them unsuitable for plantations, Douglas thought, he argued that 'the sacred right of self-government' ought to prevail in principle.

Abraham Lincoln, already a rising star in the Republican party, saw this for what it was – an attempt to repeal the hard-fought compromises that had so far preserved the Union. So he fought Douglas and the Act in a series of speeches, of which the longest and best-remembered was given at Peoria, Illinois, on this day. As for 'the sacred right', etc., 'The doctrine of self-government is right – absolutely and eternally right', he said, 'but it has no just application' here, because those claiming that right are also denying it to their slaves. 'When the white man governs himself, that is self-government; but when he governs himself, and also governs *another* man, that is *more* than self-government – that is despotism.'

Then, citing the Declaration of Independence almost as scripture (our 'ancient faith', he called it), he reminded his audience that:

> The just powers of governments are derived from the consent of the governed. Now, the relation of masters is, PRO TANTO, a total violation of this principle. The master not only governs the slave without his consent; but he governs him by a set of rules altogether different from those which he prescribes for himself. Allow ALL the governed an equal voice in the government, and that, and that only, is self-government.

The Act passed, despite Lincoln's oratory. But Lincoln would confront Douglas again – in their great campaign debates over the Illinois seat in the US Senate in 1858, and in the struggle for the presidency in 1860. In electoral terms Lincoln lost the first and won the second. In terms of great American rhetoric he won both, and a great deal more.

17 October

A St Louis newspaper interviews Walt Whitman on the future of American literature

1879 America's most expansive, most inclusive poet was prone to prophesy about a literature that would somehow embody the whole country. In his Preface to *Leaves of Grass* (1855) he went as far as to say that 'The United States themselves are essentially the greatest poem.'

This may have been cribbed from Ralph Waldo Emerson's famous remark – in 'The Poet' (1844) – that 'America is a poem in our eyes', but its meaning is quite different. Emerson was talking about contemporary, native raw materials for the creative imagination that might equal the impact of the fall of Troy and the Delphic oracle on classical literature – things like 'our logrolling, our stumps and their politics, our fisheries, our Negroes, and Indians'.

As he writes in the Preface, by 'The United States' Whitman means the sum total of the country's progressive institutions and its common people:

> [T]heir manners speech dress friendships – the freshness and candor of their physiognomy – the picturesque looseness of their carriage … their deathless attachment to freedom … the fluency of their speech … their good temper and openhandedness – the terrible significance of their elections – the President's taking off his hat to them not they to him – these too are unrhymed poetry.

Nearly a quarter century on, his interview on the subject published on this day suggested that the literary millennium might be delayed. The country had endured a horrific civil war, yet no American *War and Peace* had emerged. Asked, 'Do you think we are to have a distinctively American literature?', he answered, in the version reprinted in his prose collection, *Specimen Days* (1892):

> It seems to me that our work at present is to lay the foundations of a great nation in products, in agriculture, in commerce, in networks of intercommunication … materialistic prosperity in all its varied forms … are first to be attended to. When those have their results and get settled, then a literature worthy of us will be defined.

This reason for the delayed development of American literature had been advanced for over a century. But Whitman still had his hopes for the power of the demotic. 'Our American superiority and vitality are in the bulk of our people, not in a gentry like the old world.' And this was true. Trouble was, America needed to find a way to allow its citizens the security and leisure to write without encouraging the snooty elitism of the Old World gentry. But wouldn't that mean letting some people take a holiday from agriculture and commerce? Not easy.

18 October

Bosavern Penlez hangs, for being in the wrong place at the wrong time

1749 The legal control of brothels was a matter of some contention for London magistrates, such as Henry Fielding (the novelist). A particularly contentious case arose during Fielding's period on the bench. As Dan Cruikshank records, in *The Secret History of Georgian London*:

> Bosavern Penlez was executed on October 18, 1749, for having been involved in an assault on, and theft from, a building in the Strand during a period of rioting caused by the mistreatment of sailors at a bawdy house. Three sailors had been robbed of their watches and over £50 in cash and, when they demanded their possessions back were ejected from the house by the bawd's gang of bullies.

The *Newgate Calendar* offered some colourful details as to what happened next:

> [W]hereupon they went away, denouncing vengeance; and, having collected a number of their companions in the neighbourhood of Wapping, they returned at night, broke open the house, turned the women almost naked into the streets, ripped up the beds, threw the feathers out of the window, broke the furniture in pieces, and made a bonfire of it.
>
> Having proceeded to behave in a similar manner at another house of ill fame, a party of the guards was sent for, and the mob for the present dispersed.

As Cruikshank records, this 'bold attack against private property ... sent a chill through the London middle classes'. Henry Fielding shared the shock. On the evidence of the brothel-keeper, he committed to Newgate a peruke-maker, Bosavern Penlez, on charges of rioting – a crime that carried capital punishment. The luckless Penlez was duly hanged.

It seems certain that Penlez was nothing more than an innocent bystander who lived and worked in the area, and happened to be drunk that night. But, the sailors having absconded, an example was required so that London houses – even houses of ill-repute – should not be at risk of violence. Fielding was attacked by newspapers as a paid protector of bawdy houses. He responded with a self-serving treatise, *A True State of the Case of Bosavern Penlez.*

The *Newgate Calendar* is more sympathetic in its account of Penlez's unhappy fate:

> When the day of execution arrived he prepared to meet his fate with the consciousness of an innocent man, and the courage of a Christian. The late Sir Stephen Theodore Janssen, Chamberlain of London, was at that time sheriff; and a number of soldiers being placed at Holborn Bars, to conduct Penlez to Tyburn (as a rescue was apprehended), the sheriff politely dismissed them, asserting that the civil power was sufficient to carry the edicts of the law into effectual execution.
>
> This unhappy youth was executed at Tyburn on the 18th of October, 1749.
>
> The worthy inhabitants of St Clement Danes, who had been among the foremost in soliciting a pardon for Penlez, finding all their efforts ineffectual, did all possible honour to his memory, by burying him in a distinguished manner in a churchyard of their parish, on the evening after his unfortunate exit, which happened in the twenty-third year of his age.

19 October

Dylan Thomas leaves on his fourth trip to the US – his second that year – a voyage from which he will never return

1953 What British poet has ever claimed such celebrity in America as Dylan Thomas? Certainly not his contemporaries Stephen Spender or W.H. Auden, or any other would-be traveller or settler in the States. Celebrities are sought out for who they are as much as for what they do. So that lets out even Famous Seamus Heaney, whose outstanding work overshadows his amiable and self-depreciating personality.

It was the poet and critic John Malcolm Brinnin who first brought Thomas to America. An admirer of Thomas's poems, he raised $500 – the equivalent of around $4,500 today – plus his air fare, for him to read his work at a poetry centre he ran in New York, and with his good contacts he was able to arrange for the poet to read at over 40 schools and colleges across the country.

Audiences loved his Byronic exuberance, his sonorous voice, his 'Welsh lilt', not knowing that between them Thomas and his school-master father had managed to expunge all traces of his native Swansea from his plummy accent. Byron by day, maybe, more like Borat the Kazakh by night. Exhilarated by his reception, invited to endless drinks parties, he would get drunk and foul-mouthed, playing up to his persona of the troubled romantic, leering at the college girls and offering to suckle their breasts.

Breasts also came into a well-reported incident in Hollywood. Introduced to Shelley Winters, Thomas told the actress that his two ambitions in Hollywood were to 'touch the titties of a beautiful blonde starlet and to meet Charlie Chaplin'. Winters, then sharing a flat with Marilyn Monroe, invited the poet to dinner. They drank dry martinis out of milk bottles. Winters cooked and Monroe washed up (Marilyn's idea of making a salad was first to brush each lettuce leaf with a Brillo pad, Winters recalled in her autobiography), then Thomas did indeed get to touch the starlet's titties, but only with a single finger, one at a time.

Afterwards they drove over to one of Chaplin's weekly open house parties. With the drunken Thomas fatally at the wheel, they crashed onto Chaplin's tennis court, into the net. When his hero deprecated his bad behaviour, Thomas strolled out into the solarium and urinated on a large specimen plant.

The truth is, his offended hosts, so smitten by the notion that he was a great creative talent, colluded in the mischief and enjoyed the fun. In all, Thomas visited the US four times between 1950 and 1953 – for 'flattery, idleness and infidelity', according to the sour but accurate judgement of his long-suffering wife Caitlin. Besides, the money was good – not least for Brinnin, who, as Thomas's agent, took a hefty 25 per cent of the poet's earnings.

Then, just as he was on the verge of signing a contract for future readings and lecture tours for $12,000 a week, the fun ran out. In October 1953, suffering from a chest complaint, he arrived at New York's Idlewild airport, to be met by Brinnin's assistant, Liz Reitell, with whom he had started an affair on his third visit. Fatigue and drink exacerbated his condition. Doctors injected him with steroids, then morphine. He fell into a coma. Reitell called an ambulance, which took him to St Vincent's Hospital. There he died without regaining consciousness.

20 October

John Florio's translation of Montaigne's Essais is entered in the Stationer's Register in London

1595 John (or Giovanni) Florio is best remembered now as the man behind Gonzago's vision of a reformed commonwealth in *The Tempest* (1610–11). He was born in London around 1553, the son of a fugitive Franciscan friar who had converted to Protestantism and, for his linguistic skills and Protestant sympathies, been taken up by Queen Elizabeth's chief advisor, William Cecil, Lord Burghley. With John, the family would continue to enjoy royal and aristocratic patronage.

Michel Eyquem de Montaigne (1553–1625) more or less invented the short prose exploration of a topic or event that he called the *essai* (French for 'trial' or 'attempt'). In 1580 he published a collection of 107 of them, ranging from topics of general interest, such as the nature of sadness, virtue and vanity, to more specific political and social observations, like the Battle of Dreux (between Catholics and Huguenots in 1562) and suggestions for moderating the excess show and consumption of the French aristocracy. Montaigne's tone was easy-going, often ironic; his beliefs were broadly humanistic, his angle of approach surprisingly modern in its moral relativism.

Typical of the *Essais* is Montaigne's take on what he had read (in Peter Martyr's *De Orbe Novo* (1511)), about the 'cannibals' of the Caribbean. OK, so they take the occasional bit out of each other, but is that any worse than the vicious religious wars that were ravaging Europe? Besides, they live in a world in which food is abundant, illness unknown, social and political rank non-existent. The very words for lying, greed and envy are unknown to them.

'Of the Caniballes', Florio's translation of this essay, puts it like this:

> It is a nation ... that hath no kind of Trafficke, no knowledge of Letters, no intelligence of numbers, no name of magistrate, nor of politicke superiority, no contracts, successions, no partitions,

no successions, ... no manuring of lands, no use of wine, corne,
or mettle.

Though he may well have read Montaigne's source, Peter Martyr,
there's little doubt that Shakespeare drew on his friend John Florio for
the vision of the ideal commonwealth that Gonzago projects in Act 2,
scene 1 of *The Tempest*:

> No kind of traffic
> Would I admit; no name of magistrate;
> Letters should not be known; riches, poverty,
> And use of service, none; contract, succession,
> Bourn, bound of land, tilth, vineyard, none;
> No use of metal, corn, or wine, or oil ...

He is mocked for it in the play (by the bad guys), but Gonzago's vision
endures.

21 October

Poststructuralism comes to America

1966 The academic 'discipline' of literary criticism, and the depart-
ments in which it finds its traditional home, are generational in their
doctrines. That is to say critical orthodoxies tend to rule for the average
length of a full academic career – 40 years.

After its emergence as a respectable subject in American universities
in the 1890s, the dominant orthodoxy was 'Philology' (i.e. applying to
native literature the same kind of analysis that was applied to ancient
Greek and Latin). This was replaced (after fierce quarrelling between
old and new guards) by 'New Criticism' – strenuous analysis of 'words
on the page'. Leading figures were Cleanth Brooks and Robert Penn
Warren in the US and, with a slightly different accent, I.A. Richards
and F.R. Leavis in the UK.

By the 1960s another generational turn was due. The New Criticism
was Old Hat. It happened on 21 October 1966, when Jacques Derrida
gave his lecture 'La Structure, le signe et le jeu dans le discours des sci-

ences humaines' at the International Colloquium on Critical Languages and the Sciences of Man, at Johns Hopkins University in Baltimore.

Derrida had travelled from France with Roland Barthes and Jacques Lacan, two other foundational figures in what would be called (misleadingly) 'Theory'. Initially derided as 'higher Froggy nonsense', the new approach took off like wildfire among the younger American faculty. As they progressed upwards through the academic ranks, it became orthodoxy.

'Theory' redefined not just critical procedure but a new, expanded terrain. It was international and cross-disciplinary. Its branches – semiology, poststructuralism, deconstruction – drew on the work of Swiss linguists such as Saussure, Italians such as Umberto Eco (virtuoso in what Derrida called *jeu*, or 'play'), German New-Marxists (such as Hans Magnus Enzensberger), social scientists such as the Bulgarian Tzvetan Todorov, and psychoanalysts such as Lacan. Barthes and Derrida were as engaged with philosophical problems as traditional *explication de texte*.

Essentially 'Theory' represented a turn back to what Aristotle called 'Poetics' – the question of how meaning is generated by permutations of small black marks on a white surface. Theory (particularly 'deconstruction') tended to lose itself in the problem of how fixed, or arbitrary, or limitlessly 'decentred' those meanings might be.

The proceedings of the 1966 event were printed up as *The Structuralist Controversy*. Theory would certainly be controversial, but it soon became the main item on the academic literary agenda. J. Hillis Miller was teaching at Johns Hopkins in 1966 and recorded that his first encounter with Derrida at the conference was 'a decisive moment in my life'. Paul de Man (Belgian by origin, and a comparatist by training) was also at the conference, where he too met Derrida for the first time. He and Miller (along with Geoffrey Hartman) set up their base at Yale, which became, after 1970, the HQ of American Theory.

Forty years on, the Academy is due for its next critical revolution.

22 October

Sartre wins the Nobel Prize, rejects it, then thinks – 'Well, why not? It's a lot of money'

1964 A hundred or so writers have won the Nobel Prize for Literature; thousands plausibly think themselves robbed for not having won it. Only one writer, however, can be said to have won it, rejected it, then, some years later, decided he would, after all, accept.

On this day in 1964 the Nobel committee resolved to give the prize to Jean Paul Sartre. He was not principally known as a novelist or play-wright – although his works in that field are distinguished. It was more his record of wartime resistance and his current vanguard position in the radical movements of the 1960s that predisposed the Stockholm Academicians: that, and Sartre's proclaimed anti-Americanism.

His rejecting the prize was not seen as any kind of humiliation by the Nobel committee, but rather a validation of the rightness of their choice. Sartre had forewarned them, on 14 October, that he would not accept the award; nevertheless, academy members felt that 'he was the only possible recipient this year'. They went ahead and gave it to him, knowing it would be turned down. The chairman of the eight-een-strong panel, Anders Oesterling, saluted Sartre as the 'father of the existentialist doctrine, which became this generation's intellectual self-defence'. Defence against what? (Something draped in stars and stripes, one deduced.) In the same year, Martin Luther King won the Peace Prize. He accepted.

Sartre's published explanation was expressed as a defence of inviola-ble individual freedom:

> It is not the same thing if I sign 'Jean Paul Sartre' or if I sign 'Jean Paul Sartre, Nobel Prize Winner'. A writer must refuse to allow himself to be transformed into an institution, even if it takes place in the most honourable form.

In his autobiography, the distinguished Swedish novelist Lars Gyllensten (who was elected to the Academy in 1966) claimed that Sartre, in 1975, indicated privately that he would now accept the money for the prize that he had briefly, but legitimately, held (the 1964 prize money had been returned to the Foundation and reinvested). The application was, according to Gyllensten, turned down. The story has never been confirmed – although there must, if it is true, be correspondence in the Nobel archive.

Gyllensten resigned from the committee in the late 1980s for what he saw as its weakness in not awarding the Prize to Salman Rushdie, after the *fatwa* brought down on him for *The Satanic Verses*. Gyllensten died in 2006.

23 October

Beowulf *escapes incineration*

1731 There was an English literature before there was an England. Most of that literature, alas, is forever lost.

Only fragments have survived – principally the first text on which the mighty structure of English literature rests.

That we have *Beowulf* is the result of an almost miraculous series of accidents. It was composed – for recitation – probably in the 6th century, by pagan newcomers from north-eastern Europe. The epic was handed down, through generations of minstrels, or 'scops' – until, at the point when it would certainly have disappeared, a monk (or monks) transcribed it. We don't know who, or where their monastery might have been. He/they evidently took the text down faithfully, but could not resist interpolating some pious Christian doctrine at various places. It's easy to see where.

The 3,000-line (incomplete) narrative is divided into two parts, the first twice as long as the second. Beowulf is a Geat, a tribe in what we call Sweden. He is a mighty warrior. Not yet a king, but destined to be one. He comes to Denmark, to help Hrothgar, King of the Scyldings, whose great hall has been terrorised by Grendel, a monster from the nearby marshes, for twelve years.

Beowulf defeats Grendel in single combat. Then, when Grendel's mother comes to take revenge, he drives her back to her watery lair and dives in to kill her underwater. There follows feasting, drinking, and treasure-giving before Beowulf sails back to his own people. In the second part of the epic, many years later, Beowulf is now King of the Geats, and his kingdom is terrorised by a great dragon. Beowulf slays the dragon, but is himself mortally wounded. The poem ends with his ceremonial burial.

The history of the sole *Beowulf* manuscript is, in its early career, mysterious. By the 16th century, however, it is known to have been in the possession of the antiquarian Laurence Nowell. As the British Library (the manuscript's current custodian) records:

> It was acquired in the 17th century by Sir Robert Cotton, a keen collector of old manuscripts whose library was presented to the nation by his grandson in 1700. However, the dilapidated state of Cotton's house gave cause for concern over the collection's safety. The library was moved first to Essex House in the Strand, then to Ashburnham House in Westminster ... on 23 October, 1731, Ashburnham House was ravaged by a fire that destroyed or damaged a quarter of Cotton's library. *Beowulf* was saved with other priceless manuscripts, but not before its edges were badly scorched.

In 1753 it came into the care of the more fire-proof British Museum. The hand that saved *Beowulf* is unknown.

Had English Literature, as a university-based discipline, not had an 'epic' on which to base itself, and an Anglo-Saxon literature to study, its academic respectability and evolution would have been very different. To speculate further, English literature itself would have been very different. J.R.R. Tolkien, to take an obvious example, was the greatest *Beowulf* scholar of the 20th century. And Tolkien's view on the poem was uncompromising. It was the fantasy – the monsters, dragons, and epic battles – that made *Beowulf* great. And that, of course, inspired *The Lord of the Rings*. Had the manuscript burned in 1731, Tolkien's saga would have burned with it.

The British Library has put the manuscript beyond the reach of any flames in its 1993 electronic/DVD facsimile version.

24 October

Martin Amis joins the ranks of the literary breast-men

2009 One of the phenomena bemoaned by the literary establishment in this generally gloomy year was the vast popularity, among the British Reading Public, of the 'celebrity' novel. Typically this was a 'ghosted' product – the nominal author blithely admitting the fact that the only pen they had put to paper was on the contract. 'They' wrote her novels, Katie Price (famous as the glamour model Jordan) said in one of her innumerable interviews (most of which concentrated on her F-cup, surgically enhanced, frontal features).

One novel of Price's (or at least, a novel with her name on the title page and her full-on picture on the dust flap), *Crystal*, sold more – the literary commentator David Sexton wryly noted – than all the Booker shortlist for that year (2007) combined. These, as Richard Hoggart would have said, were the 'uses of literacy', 2009-style. Tabloid newspapers had always known: 'tits sell'. 'Lit', notoriously, doesn't sell.

Jordan, wrote the author Lynda La Plante, was 'killing publishing' – which seemed a little perverse, at least for Price's publisher who was in the best of financial health. Jordan's success had also irritated Martin Amis mightily. At a lecture on this evening, 24 October 2009, for the 'Hay in London' literary festival, he informed his audience that Price/Jordan 'has no waist, no arse … an interesting face … but all we are really worshipping is two bags of silicone'. Her (so to call it) fiction he regarded as beneath notice. Nonetheless, he had introduced a character ('Threnody') obliquely based on her in his forthcoming work of fiction, *State of England*.

The giveaway word 'worship' aligns Amis with male authors similarly attracted. It's an impressive crew. Fielding's overdone jokes about Lady Booby betray a fascination with what he elsewhere more reverently calls 'beauteous orbs'. Hardy makes similarly revealing references to Tess Durbeyfield's frontal development. The 'luxuriance of her figure' is what first catches seducer Alec's eye. The sage of Wessex, we deduce, also had an eye for them.

J.G. Ballard adored Elizabeth Taylor, and wrote a great novel about her – *Crash*. But Ballard had to concede that Marlon Brando was the better actor and, in his later years, had the bigger breasts.

Lawrence complains bitterly, in *Lady Chatterley's Lover*, about the flat-chested flapper. He despised what he called 'little iron breasts' and women who wanted the vote. Connie, like Frieda, was, we apprehend, generously endowed. Lawrence lyricised on the ample breast in his poem, 'Look, we Have Come Through':

Between her breasts is my home, between her breasts.
Three sides set on me space and fear, but the fourth side rests,
Warm in a city of strength, between her breasts.

He loved, Lawrence said in another poem ('Song of the Man who is Loved'), to get his 'hands full of breasts'. Groping some call it.

Leading the mammalian crew among the moderns is Philip Roth, who published a novel in 1972 in which the hero, David Kapesh, in a pathological recycling of Kafka, is metamorphosed into a 155-lb breast. No prizes for guessing the title.

Norman Mailer is hot on Roth's heels as a breast-worshipper. In *Marilyn: A Biography* he ponders, at immense length, the power of Marilyn's 'popped buds and burgeons of flesh'. She was, Mailer enthused, 'a cornucopia. She excited dreams of honey for the horn'. Mailer's encomium, in *Esquire*, on the 40DD breast picture (nothing else, just the breasts) that took (male) America by storm in 1999 is rather slangier:

> These breasts really hit home for a nation eager to stare at a huge honkin' set of big ol' whoppers. The reassuring presence of this enormous pair of mamajamas is something all Americans, from every walk of life, can relate to.

Why is it, Susan Seligson (the author of *Stacked*) recently enquired, that 'big breasts never fail to render men instantly stupid?'

25 October

St Crispin's Day: two kinds of glory in British military history

1415, 1854 The battles of Agincourt and Balaclava appealed mightily to William Shakespeare and Alfred, Lord Tennyson – but in very different ways. At Agincourt Henry V really did lead his outnumbered forces into battle, unlike Charles VI of France, who had been kept at home because he was mad. Thanks to their highly trained longbow archers, the English won overwhelmingly, killing an average of between six and ten French soldiers each. After the battle Henry wooed and won the hand of the French king's daughter. How romantic is that?

Balaclava, the second major engagement of the Crimean War, produced romance of another sort. A scramble of badly articulated orders from Lord Raglan through Lord Lucan down to Lord Cardigan resulted in the last of these temperamental toffs first refusing to send the Light Brigade cavalry to attack the left flank of the Russian cavalry, then leading it down a valley bristling with Russian cannon on both sides and at the far end. The outcome was inevitable.

Shakespeare's Henry starts off with ambiguous motives for going to war, but grows into the responsibility of leading his compatriots into and through the conflict. In Shakespeare the war makes the man, but it also makes the nation. During the Second World War, Laurence Olivier was released from the navy to make the movie of *Henry V* that came out in 1944, just in time – not so much to stiffen backbones as already to celebrate the impending Allied victory.

So when Henry speaks to his troops before the battle, he lays down rhetorical tracks for the later conflict too. The first line alone provided Churchill's epithet for heroic Battle of Britain pilots and the title of a TV mini-series of 2001 following a company of parachutists from the Normandy landings to the end of the war in Europe. But more important is Henry's conceit of social levelling through the shared danger of combat. That may well have fed into the tremendous Labour victory in the 'Khaki Election' of 1945.

> We few, we happy few, we band of brothers;
> For he to-day that sheds his blood with me
> Shall be my brother; be he ne'er so vile,
> This day shall gentle his condition;
> And gentlemen in England now-a-bed
> Shall think themselves accurs'd they were not here,
> And hold their manhoods cheap whiles any speaks
> That fought with us upon Saint Crispin's day.

The Crimean War was remembered more for its victims than its victors. Florence Nightingale famously looked after the wounded, while Tennyson's 'The Charge of the Light Brigade', written in that same year, dramatised the quandary of those troopers sacrificed in the fatal charge:

> 'Forward, the Light Brigade!'
> Was there a man dismay'd?
> Not tho' the soldier knew
> Some one had blunder'd:
> Theirs not to make reply,
> Theirs not to reason why,
> Theirs but to do & die,

Into the valley of Death
Rode the six hundred.

Cannon to right of them,
Cannon to left of them,
Cannon in front of them
Volley'd & thunder'd;
Storm'd at with shot and shell,
Boldly they rode and well,
Into the jaws of Death,
Into the mouth of Hell
Rode the six hundred.

'Do & die', so often misremembered as 'do *or* die', is the key: here the dying is in the doing, and the romance is not in the battle won through the fellowship of leaders and led, but in the courageous pursuit of the impossible. As the French Marshal Pierre Bosquet put it, while witnessing the massacre: 'C'est magnifique, mais ce n'est pas la guerre.' Or to quote a less friendly comment by a contemporary Russian general: 'Lions led by asses.'

26 October

A gunfight breaks out at the O.K. Corral in Tombstone, Arizona, when Marshal Virgil Earp, his brothers Wyatt and Morgan and Doc Holliday try to disarm Billy Clanton and Frank McLaury

1881 It took place in nowheresville between two buildings (not in the O.K. Corral), yet it went down in the popular memory as the most famous gunfight in the Old West. On one side were the 'cowboys' who came into town to raise hell from time to time. On the other were the federal marshal, Virgil Earp, his brothers Morgan and Wyatt, and a gambler called Doc Holliday. After 30 seconds it was all over. Three of the cowboys lay dead in the dust, Frank and Tom McLaury and the hot-headed Billy Clanton. Morgan, Virgil and Doc Holliday were wounded, Wyatt unscathed. From that his reputation as a gunslinger took its start.

Who shot first? Who, apart from the marshal and his 'deputies', was armed? Billy Clanton and Frank McLaury had been seen flaunting revolver belts, but others of the cowboys had been disarmed in pursuance of a town ordinance requiring everyone entering the area to check their guns and bowie knives at the hotel or livery stable – wherever they first dismounted.

Despite these lingering doubts, the gunfight became the stuff of legend, revisited in over 25 books, movies, TV series and documentaries. The popular culture, while maintaining a hint of Wyatt's moral ambivalence, posed it as the paradigm conflict between civilisation and barbarism, law 'n' order as against unruly 'thugs and cattle thieves' (to quote one movie's plot summary).

The pattern was set by the classic film *Gunfight at the O.K. Corral* (Hal Wallis, 1957). 'Here the outlaw band / Made their final stand', as the tuneful soundtrack had it, and Burt Lancaster and Kirk Douglas, as Wyatt and the Doc, were there to meet them. In *Tombstone* (1993), the costumes were period, the shooting balletic, and everyone nasty. A year later, Lawrence Kasdan's *Wyatt Earp* cast Kevin Costner as the romantic hero caught in the tragic dilemma of having to fight dirty to defeat evil.

It took a lot longer for the myth to get deconstructed, and it took the print medium – in the hands of probably the best novelist to come out of the West – to do it. Larry McMurtry's *Telegraph Days* (2006) only brushes past the O.K. Corral as one of Nellie Courtright's many picaresque adventures. She's a sort of Jack Crabb (see 24 June) who doesn't just meet and interact with all the legendary figures of the Old West, but goes to bed with them too.

What all these versions of the story leave out – whether inflating or deflating – are the economics behind the fight. The cowboys weren't just thugs raising hell in the town's saloons; they were ranchers come in to sell their stock and get supplies. The Earps and their like were city people, easterners, Yankee capitalists, congenitally hostile (ever since the Civil War) to the ranchers' values and way of living. In Tombstone the conflict wasn't metaphysical; it was political.

27 October

Maxine Ting Ting Hong is born in Stockton, California

1940 She sold her first prose at the age of fifteen. It was called 'I am an American', and it appeared in *The American Girl*, the official Girl Scout magazine. She got $15 for it. 'I worked out the idea that you don't have to be white to be an American', she told Michael Martin of National Public Radio 57 years later, after she had become the cynosure of gender and ethnic studies: Maxine Hong Kingston. 'But all the time I was aware that both my parents were illegals and I had to be very careful to write in such a way that I can insist on our being American without giving away their illegal status.'*

Status is woven into better recognised themes of gender, migration and the succession of generations in Kingston's first and best-known book, *The Woman Warrior: Memoirs of a Girlhood Among Ghosts* (1977). The 'ghosts' are figures in Chinese folk tales, but also the white Americans around them, whose habits and manners the older Chinese find so difficult to fathom.

A challenging read, *The Woman Warrior* rewards close attention. Composed of five sections, written in styles ranging from 'magical' to conventional realism, it explores aspects of ethnicity, gender and the relationship between generations through the recurrent image of voice. 'No Name Woman' and 'White Tigers' are 'talking stories' – about a disgraced aunt of whom the family never speaks and the mythical woman warrior of the title. By taking on the personae of both characters, Kingston's narrator restores the aunt's voice and internalises the heroic role of the female avenger.

The last three parts develop the relationship between the narrator and her mother. 'Shaman' shows that her mother has had her own cultural struggles, fighting village convention in training as a midwife. From a limited-consciousness point of view (because she still knows very little of her mother's past) the narrator in 'At the Western Palace' explores the stresses and dislocations of emigration. In 'A song for a Barbarian Reed Pipe' the narrative breaks out into the American demotic, importing a modern scepticism along with the accent.

---

* 'Maxine Hong Kingston Takes Pride in Mixed Heritage', *Tell me More*, National Public Radio, 4 July 2007.

Now the issue of voice becomes explicit, even literal. Her mother tells her that she cut her fraenum (the little vertical membrane under the tongue) when she was a child.

'Why did you do that to me, Mother?'
'I told you.'
'Tell me again.'
'I cut it so that you would not be tongue-tied. Your tongue
    would be able to move in any language ...'
'But isn't "a ready tongue an evil"?'
'Things are different in this ghost country.'

Now the narrator is caught on the knife-edge between the two communities. 'Sometimes I hated the ghosts [Americans] for not letting us talk', she comments; 'sometimes I hated the secrecy of the Chinese'. As for Chinese 'tradition', 'even the good things are unspeakable'. Keeping silent about their culture:

the adults get mad, evasive, and shut you up if you ask. You get no warning that you shouldn't wear a white ribbon in your hair until they hit you ... They hit you if you wave brooms around or drop chopsticks or drum them.

It's a brilliant demystification, leaving both narrator and reader mystified. 'I don't see how they kept up a continuous culture for five thousand years. Maybe they didn't. Maybe everyone makes it up as they go along.'

28 October

Henry David Thoreau reclaims from his publisher 703 unsold copies of his first book, out of 1,000 printed

1853 The book, printed at the author's own expense by Ralph Waldo Emerson's publisher in 1849 after failing to interest a commercial publisher, was *A Week on the Concord and Merrimack Rivers*. 'I now have a library of nearly nine hundred volumes', Thoreau noted ruefully in his journal after taking the books home, 'over seven hundred of which I wrote myself'.

A Week purported to be a travel journal of a trip that Henry made in 1839 with his brother John, in a sort of camping dinghy. From their home in Concord, Massachusetts, they sailed and paddled down the Concord River to the Middlesex Canal, thence up the Merrimack River to Concord, New Hampshire – and back.

Only three years later John died of lockjaw at the age of 27. Henry, devastated, decided to retire for a spell to a piece of land that Emerson owned on Walden Pond, just a mile and a half from Concord. There he built a hut out of surplus lumber and lived – on and off – for two years (see also 23 July).

While there, Thoreau set about completing his loving tribute to his brother. The problem with *A Week* is that it really had very little to say of John, or their relationship – and not even much about the particulars of the river trip. Or rather, a concrete observation, like 'We passed a large and densely wooded island this forenoon', would shift gears to a slightly whimsical abstraction – 'An island always pleases my imagination, even the smallest, as a small continent and integral portion of the globe' – after which he moves the reader on to Pindar's account of the island of Thera, and how the sun god Helios felt when he first looked down on Rhodes – all embellished by eighteen lines of poetry. Learned? You bet. But no one could wish it longer.

As he wrote *A Week* at Walden, Thoreau continued to keep his journal. Over time, what emerged was his masterpiece, *Walden or, Life in the Woods* (1854) – equally meditative as *A Week*, equally allusive, and still quoting the ancients, but this time more within the gravity of the natural world around him. The sight of a striped snake, still in its 'torpid state' in the March cold, tempts him to a very New-England moralisation (see 15 August):

> It appeared to me that for a like reason men remain in their present low and primitive condition, but if they could feel the influence of the spring of springs arousing them, they would of necessity rise to a higher and more ethereal life.

But that's not the end of the snake, as it would be in a conventional sermon. Instead Thoreau returns to the concrete scene:

> I had previously seen the snakes in frosty mornings in my path with portions of their bodies numb and inflexible, waiting for

the sun to thaw them. On the first of April it rained and melted the ice, and in the early part of the day, which was very foggy, I heard a stray goose groping about over the pond and cackling as if lost, or like the spirit of the fog.

That movement in and out between the specific and general, that apparently haphazard plotting by the motions of nature rather than the preacher's agenda, is what sets *Walden* apart from *A Week*. At Walden Pond Thoreau wrote one bad book while learning how to write a much better one.

29 October

Sir Walter Raleigh's sharp medicine

1618 No Renaissance man was more dazzling in his accomplishments than Sir Walter Raleigh (the name, incidentally, is spelled 70 different ways in documents of the time). Aged fifteen he was already a military hero, fighting for the French Huguenots. In his early thirties he was a renowned explorer of the New World. Now Sir Walter, when the Spanish Armada sailed, as commander of the *Ark Royal* he led the successful maritime defence of his country in 1588 and was rewarded with a huge slice of Irish real estate. Legends accumulated around him (most famously, and apocryphally, that of him throwing down his velvet cloak to spare the footwear of his monarch, Elizabeth I, from a spot or two of mud).

Less salubrious anecdotes also attached themselves to him, as that recorded by Aubrey in his *Brief Lives*:

He [Sir Walter Raleigh] loved a wench well; and one time getting one of the Maids of Honour up against a tree in a wood ('twas his first lady) who seemed at first boarding to be something fearful of her honour, and modest, she cried, 'Sweet Sir Walter, what do you me ask? Will you undo me? Nay, sweet Sir Walter! Sweet Sir Walter! Sir Walter!'

At last, as the danger and the pleasure at the same time grew higher, she cried in the ecstasy, 'Swisser Swatter, Swisser Swatter!' She proved with child, and I doubt not but this hero took care of them both, as also that the product was more than an ordinary mortal.

On the death of Elizabeth and with the accession of James I, Raleigh was accused of rebellion and sentenced to be executed as a traitor. It was commuted to life imprisonment in the Tower, during which period (some twelve years) he wrote his *History of the World*, and some distinguished poetry. He was released in 1616, to undertake a voyage to discover the fabled Eldorado in South America. He failed, unsurprisingly, and on his return to England, under Spanish pressure (the country was indignant at his bloody incursion into their colonial territory) the death sentence was re-invoked. He was executed on 29 October 1618. As a courtesy, the former punishment of disembowelling was commuted. As a further courtesy, he was allowed to feel the axe that would remove his head. He commented, wryly: 'This is a sharp Medicine, but it is a Physician for all diseases and miseries.' The removed head was embalmed and preserved by his wife for the 29 years of life that remained to her. It never, supposedly, left her presence.

30 October

The abolitionist and suffragette Amy Post authenticates Incidents in the Life of a Slave Girl, *and vouches for its author, Linda Brent*

1859 Amy Post's comments, so dated, appear as an appendix to *Incidents in the Life of a Slave Girl* (1861), by 'Linda Brent'. In it, Post writes that 'Brent' had lived in her house, during which time 'her deportment indicated remarkable delicacy of feeling and purity of thought', even though the life events she had to relate were horrific. Though 'she passed through a baptism of suffering, even in recounting her trials to me', Post urged her to write about her life, and publish the result.

'Linda Brent' was really Harriet Jacobs, and her story – of repeated sexual harassment by her master, her liaison with another white man, her hiding for seven years above her grandmother's store-room, and her eventual flight to the North – is the fullest and frankest of all the women's slave narratives. Her styles range from that of the sentimental novel, to the camera obscura effect of her outlook from her hiding place, to cool irony out of Dickens via *Uncle Tom's Cabin* (see 20 March):

> Mrs Flint [her mistress] … was totally deficient in energy. She had not strength to superintend her household affairs, but her nerves were so strong, that she could sit in her easy chair and see a woman whipped till the blood trickled from every stroke of the lash.

These literary powers made the book's provenance suspect. How could an unlettered slave write like this? Had it been ghost-written by abolitionists? Or maybe it was an anonymous novel written to mimic a slave story? It wasn't until 1981 that Jean Fagan Yellin, Jacobs' biographer with access to all her papers, proved by acute literary detective work that *Incidents* was indeed the work of Harriet Jacobs.

31 October

Brecht, having baffled HUAC, leaves the USA

1947 Bertolt Brecht gave evidence to the House Un-American Activities Committee (HUAC) on the morning of 30 October 1947. He was, by definition, un-American. Although he had passed the first stage of the naturalisation process, and had expressed his intention to move to America as early as 1941, he was still a foreigner. He testified as one of the so-called 'Hollywood 19' – voluntary witnesses who aimed to oppose the witch-hunt against supposed 'Reds' in the American movie industry. They had agreed they would not give a direct answer to the key question: 'Are you, or have you ever been, a member of the Communist Party?'

Brecht's connection with Hollywood was slight and he was, as he informed the Committee, a 'guest' in the country. He is said to have rehearsed for his appearance with his friend Hermann Budzislawski, in order to give the most evasive and slippery answers. He had been, of course, deeply involved with the communist movement.

As the *Los Angeles Times* reported, 'Brecht spoke with a heavy accent and puffed at a long cigar with easy poise' (his responses can be sampled at: http://www.archive.org/details/BrechtAndTheHuac).

The chaotic nature of the proceedings is evident from the following excerpt ('Stripling' is the HUAC Chief Investigator Robert E. Stripling):

Stripling: Uh, Mr Brecht ... is it true that you have written a number of very revolutionary poems, plays, and other writings?

Brecht: I am uh written a number of poems, songs, and plays, in the fight against Hitler, and, of course, they can be considered, therefore, as revolutionary, cause, I, of course, was for the overthrow, of that government.

Unidentified voice: Mr Stripling, we're not interested in ...

Stripling: Yeah ...

Unidentified voice: ... any works that he might have written, uh, going for the overthrow of Germany.

Stripling: Yes, I ...

Unidentified voice: The government there ...

Stripling: Uh well, from the examination of the works which Mr Brecht has written, particularly in collaboration with Mr Hanns Eisler, uh, he seems to be a person of international importance to the, Communist revolutionary movement. Now Mr Brecht, uh, is it true, do you know whether or not you have written articles, for ...

[Gavel bangs three times]

Thomas: There's gonna be another fall here pretty soon so will you boys just, sit down quietly please, while we're ... [murmur from audience] ... Go ahead.

HUAC was totally baffled by their German witness and made no request that he hang around to make them look even more clumsy. Brecht left the country for Europe on an Air France flight on 31 October 1947. He would never return.

1 November

W.H. Smith open their first bookstall at Euston station

1848 The leading British wholesaler and retailer of printed materials, the Smith ('first with the news') dynasty began in 1792, when Henry Walton Smith set up as a newsvendor in Grosvenor Street, London. By 1817 the firm was also a leading bookseller and purveyor of news materials (by horse-drawn coach) to the provinces.

Smith's grandson W.H. Smith II (nicknamed 'Old Morality') originally hoped for a career in the church. It was under him that the firm gained its dominating position as a railway newsvendor and (linked, via station-stall) bookshop chain, selling and lending volumes. Between 1840 and 1870 nearly 15,000 miles of rail track were laid, effectively connecting the nation in a communication network for the first time.

The first W.H. Smith's bookstall was opened on the Northwestern Line terminus at Euston, on 1 November 1848. The station was, with its famous Doric Arch, a temple to British world supremacy. Smith's were given the monopolistic concession (for which they paid rent) on the understanding that they clean up the quality of reading material ('purify the sources of instruction and entertainment') for the travelling public. This they did.

By the 1860s the firm had bookstalls on all the main lines and main stations in the country. Smith's not only sold fiction from their outlets (notably Routledge's 'Railway Library') but they also went into production of so-called 'yellowbacks' (cheap volumes of fiction with illustrated board covers). In 1860 they set up a 'circulating library' that enabled subscribers to borrow a book at one station and return it at another.

Their library activities enlarged when they moved, in the late 19th and early 20th century, into High Street outlets. With the similarly censorious Mudie's 'Leviathan' circulating library in London, W.H. Smith became what the novelist Wilkie Collins called one of the 'twin tyrants of literature'. Smith's continued their moralistic line to the late 20th century – banning, for example, the satirical magazine *Private Eye* (who returned the compliment by labelling their boycotter 'W.H. Smut'). W.H. Smith's lending libraries flourished until 1961 when they were finally killed off by the newly energised post-war public libraries.

2 November

Spenser's tomb is dug up

1938 When Edmund Spenser died on 13 January 1599 he was laid to rest, as the author of the greatest epic in the English language, *The Faerie Queene*, in the Poets' Corner of Westminster Abbey, alongside Geoffrey Chaucer (the first to be so honoured).

Spenser might well – given the extraordinary amount of achievement he crammed into his 47 years of life – have been entered in the annals of his country as a statesman, colonial governor, and soldier.

In Ireland, under the leadership of his patron, the Earl of Essex, Spenser proved one of the most efficient (and occasionally brutal) administrators of Elizabeth's dominion over the restless Celtic colony.

Insoluble mystery surrounds the circumstances of Spenser's final days. There had been an outbreak of rebellion in Ireland. Spenser had, since September 1598, occupied the post of Sheriff of Cork. His castle at Kilcolman was sacked the following month, obliging him and his family to take refuge in Cork. In December he left for London, with messages for the Privy Council.

Arriving in London at the turn of the year, he took up residence in King's Street and, according to Ben Jonson, died there alone, 'for lake of bread', early on a Saturday. It seems strange that a nobleman, on state business – a man with many friends in high places – should have starved to death a few hundred yards from the seat of government.

Three days later, on 16 January 1599, he was interred in the abbey, the expenses (lead coffins were expensive) being supplied by the Earl of Essex.

Many poets die poor. But as pauper's burials go, Spenser's was glorious. According to the normally reliable historian, Camden (writing in Latin), Spenser had:

> scarcely secured the means of retirement and leisure to write when he was ejected by the rebels (in Ireland), spoiled of his goods, and returned to England in poverty, where he died immediately afterwards, and was interred at Westminster near to Chaucer; his hearse being attended by poets, and mournful elegies, and the pens they wrote them with, being thrown into the grave.

Legend has identified the poets assembled round his coffin as it was lowered to its resting place; they were the leading playwrights of the time: Jonson, Beaumont, Fletcher, and Shakespeare.

Camden's account (which did not identify the exact location of the coffin) was tantalising. On 2 November 1938 the Dean of the abbey was persuaded to allow the earth under Spenser's (notionally) located memorial tablet to be dug up, in the hope of finding, inter alia, that unicorn among literary relics, the holograph manuscript of a Shakespeare work.

Alas, 'all that was discovered was a collapsed lead coffin surrounded by dry soil'. In the coffin were some loose, disarranged bones and a skull. The coffin (which had been plundered by grave robbers – presumably immediately after inhumation) was dated by funerary experts at least a hundred years later than 1599. The identification was, plausibly, that of Matthew Prior (who died in 1721).

The manuscripts, if they are indeed beneath the flags of the abbey, still await a luckier dip – or a more adventurously exhuming Dean.

3 November

Boris Pasternak is offered the chance to leave the Soviet Union and refuses

1958 Russia has a long history of censorship and the persecution of writers – never more so than under the USSR regime. This was the harsh environment in which Boris Pasternak (1890–1960) prosecuted his literary career. By a mixture of cunning, silence (on public matters) and inner exile, Pasternak contrived to produce an enduring masterpiece of Russian literature chronicling the Revolution – this despite the Stalinist purges and the coercion of the Writers' Union propaganda machine. He was not permitted to collect the Nobel Prize awarded him in 1958 for *Dr Zhivago* (whose publication in the West had been financed by the CIA). And there was a strong sentiment among diehards in Moscow that he should be expelled for a work so clearly dissident from the party line. In the mild warmth of the so-called 'thaw', on this day in 1958, Khrushchev actually offered him the opportunity to leave – without dishonour. Pasternak refused. 'I am linked to Russia by my birth, my life, and my work … To leave my country would be for me the equivalent of death', he wrote in a letter to the premier. He died barely a year later. His passing was hardly noticed by the Soviet-controlled press, but thousands attended his funeral at Peredelkino. Over his grave the poet Andrey Voznesensky defiantly recited Pasternak's banned poem, 'Hamlet':

> But the order of the acts is planned,
> The end of the road already revealed.
> Alone among the Pharisees I stand.
> Life is not a stroll across a field.

4 November

Anthony Trollope's mother emigrates to America – temporarily

1827 Frances Trollope arrived in the United States on this day, not through the usual portals of Boston, New York or Philadelphia but via the Mississippi Delta. She could tell they were approaching their landfall, as she was later to write in *Domestic Manners of the Americans* (1832), when 'the deep blue of the Mexican Gulf' began to be sullied by the Mississippi's 'muddy mass of waters'.

As they made their way upstream, she 'never beheld a scene so utterly desolate', relieved only by huge crocodiles 'luxuriating in the slime' and a tree that had been dislodged by a hurricane, 'with its roots mocking the heavens while the dishonoured branches lash[ed] the tide in idle vengeance', like 'the fragment of a world in ruins'. In short, it was the world turned upside down, as the old radical anthem had it, nature's emblem for the 'I'm-as-good-as-you' politics of the young republic.

But this was written after her disappointing return from her American venture. The New World hadn't always presented such a vision of chaos. It was to be the way of mending the family's hopes and fortunes after her husband failed at the bar because of his bad temper. Taking her three youngest children (Anthony, now at school, stayed behind with his father), she made her way to Cincinnati, Ohio, where she decided to open an 'emporium' offering the latest European fashions.

Twenty years on, after canal and railroad connections had brought increasing trade, the investment might have paid off. As it was, the settlement was only eleven years old as a 'city' when the Trollopes moved in, and the residents were mostly preoccupied with more practical matters. Disappointed and more or less destitute, Mrs Trollope had one last card to play.

Returning home by way of the more established cities of the east coast, she turned herself into a tourist, just as other disappointed and failed English emigrants had before her – William Clark, Richard Weston, Francis Wyse, and many others – their sights fixed on the avid home market for books that satirised or otherwise deprecated the upstart offspring that had dared to break away from its maternal roots. Titles like Clark's *The Mania of Emigrating to the United States* (1820) set both scene and tone. *Domestic Manners of the Americans* was Frances Trollope's own variant of the sub-genre. It sold like hot cakes.

5 November

William of Orange arrives in England to take up the offer of the throne, and Dryden loses his job

1688 Appointed by Charles II, John Dryden was the first official Poet Laureate, and the only one – so far – to be sacked. His pay was a pension of £300 (£34,322 or $55,603 in today's money), plus one butt of Canary wine per year. A butt is a barrel big enough to drown a man in, as is clear from *Richard III*. It holds 476 litres, or 210 imperial (252 US) gallons. This was a lot more than later emoluments. Alfred, Lord Tennyson (laureate from 1843–50) got £72 a year in cash and another £27 'in lieu of the butt of sack'. Andrew Motion (1999–2009) started on £5,000, but claimed the fortified wine, now refined as 600 bottles of sherry.

Poets Laureate are a bit like Nobel Prize-winners in literature (see 10 December). With political and literary criteria always so intermixed, official approval has seldom coincided with critical opinion. The poetic standard has ranged from Tennyson and Wordsworth to forgotten nonentities like Henry James Pye (see 21 May) and others whose work even their contemporaries thought worthy only of parody.

Some live on only in these jokes at their expense. 'The Old Man's Comforts and How He Gained Them' (1799), by Robert Southey (1790–1813), has long been displaced by Lewis Carroll's 'You are Old,

Father William'; and the hapless Alfred Austin (1850–92) didn't pen the following lines on the illness of Edward VII:

> Across the wires the electric message came,
> He is no better, he is much the same
> … but might as well have, judging from the quality of his other work.

But the first Poet Laureate was also one of the best. Dryden was an immensely practised versifier, committed to his craft, and not afraid to use his invention and skill to tackle big, public issues, as well as the more private topics of the traditional lyric, as in these words set to Purcell's music in *The Indian Queen* (1695), his own late echo of the Petrarchans and the Metaphysicals:

> I attempt from love's sickness to fly – in vain,
> Since I am myself my own fever,
> Since I am myself my own fever and pain.

Today Dryden is often remembered for his feud with another poet and playwright, Thomas Shadwell. They were divided by party as well as religion: Shadwell was a Whig and a Protestant, Dryden very much the other thing. The two poets had got along well enough, and even collaborated, but Dryden's verse satires on populist Whig manoeuvres following the so-called Popish Plot of 1678, 'Absalom and Achitophel' (1681) and 'The Medal' (1682), brought Shadwell out in opposition. His 'The Medal of John Bayes' (1682) attacked Dryden, not for his politics, but for the quality of his satire:

> He quite defiles the *Satyr's* dignity.
> For Libel and true *Satyr* different be;
> This must have *Truth*, and *Salt*, with *Modesty*.
> Sparing the Persons, this doth tax the Crimes,
> Galls not great Men, but Vices of the Times.

Of course, all satirists high-mindedly aspired to attack the sin, not the sinner, but sometimes it was hard to dissect out the two, as Shadwell himself found when he went on to reveal an idle joke Dryden shared with a few friends one lazy afternoon:

Thou [Dryden] never mak'st, but art a standing Jest;
Thy Mirth by foolish Bawdy is expresst;
As —
Let's Bugger one another now by G-d.
(When ask'd how they should spend the Afternoon
This was the smart reply of the Heroick Clown.)

Dryden was too clever to respond with a counter-libel. In fact, he side-stepped lampoon altogether, and went instead for a tone of comic seriousness that has since been styled the mock heroic. 'MacFlecknoe' (1682) imagines the Prince of Dullness trying to decide 'which of his Sons was fit / To Reign, and wage immortal War with Wit'. Before long the obvious choice presents himself:

S[*hadwell*] alone my perfect image bears,
Mature in dullness from his tender years.
S[*hadwell*] alone, of all my Sons, is he
Who stands confirmed in full stupidity.
The rest to some faint meaning make pretence,
But S[*hadwell*] never deviates into sense.

Dryden's sly inversions of expectation ('Mature … dullness' and 'deviates … sense') are part of that measured tone that severs the head from the body while leaving it in place. At first, you could mistake the attack for praise.

Dullness isn't just being boring; it is the absence of wit. It includes bad political and critical judgement, of course, but it's also present in the snobbery that considers profanity to be the more serious because uttered 'in the company of persons of Quality'. Alexander Pope was quick to see the possibilities of the trope. He would create an entire mock epic of dullness, in his monumental *The Dunciad* (1728, 1729, 1743).

Who remembers 'The Medal of John Bayes' today? About all we have left of Shadwell's is that old chestnut of girl-guide outings, 'Nymphs and shepherds, come away. / In the groves let's sport and play, / For this is Flora's holy day'. But who now understands those callow classical references? Who was Flora, anyway, and why was she on holiday?

But royal favour and poetic achievement don't always coincide. In 1688, when the Protestant monarchs William and Mary were invited to succeed the deposed Catholic James II, Dryden lost his job. And who took his place? Step forward, Thomas Shadwell, who would hold the post until his death in 1692. Or as Dryden himself would put it in another context (his attack on the Earl of Shaftesbury in 'Absalom and Achitophel'), 'He had his jest, and they had his Estate'.

6 November

The first (but by no means the last) death of Count Dracula

1897 Bram Stoker's novel, which along with *Frankenstein* has inspired more movies than any other work of 19th-century fiction, is narrated as a series of breathless, as-it-happens, journal entries from Jonathan Harker's first arrival in Transylvania (3 May) to the vampire-count's decapitation, six months later, on 6 November.

Using Mina Harker's partially-vampirised, radar-like ability to track the 'King Vampire', Dr Van Helsing leads the hunt. Dracula is finally cornered trying to escape, at nightfall, his coffin being carried away in a cart by his faithful band of gypsies, guarded by a pack of wolves, subservient to his will. He must be destroyed before night falls and he regains his awful powers. The last act is described in Mina's journal entry:

> I saw the Count lying within the box upon the earth, some of which the rude falling from the cart had scattered over him. He was deathly pale, just like a waxen image, and the red eyes glared with the horrible vindictive look which I knew so well.
>
> As I looked, the eyes saw the sinking sun, and the look of hate in them turned to triumph. But, on the instant, came the sweep and flash of Jonathan's great knife. I shrieked as I saw it shear through the throat. Whilst at the same moment Mr Morris's bowie knife plunged into the heart.
>
> It was like a miracle, but before our very eyes, and almost in the drawing of a breath, the whole body crumbled into dust and passed from our sight.

The American, Quincey Morris, is killed in the fray. Jonathan and Mina (purified from her vampire taint) live happily ever after. Dracula (never was the term 'undead' more appropriate) would rise again to suck blood in innumerable sequels. Oddly, Bram Stoker never wrote one.

7 November

F. Scott Fitzgerald writes to his publisher with the definitive title of his new novel. It is to be called Trimalchio in West Egg

1924 You can see a sort of logic behind the title. The new story concerned a wealthy man who loved to give parties. In the *Satyricon*, the 1st-century Latin work of poetry and prose fiction by Petronius, Trimalchio was a man of self-made riches who loved to show off by throwing lavish feasts featuring such exotic dishes as live birds sewn up in the bellies of roast pigs.

In Fitzgerald's novel West Egg is the fictional stand-in for Great Neck, a peninsula on Long Island where the new money built their mansions in the 1920s. Its counterpart, East Egg (Manhasset Neck), had already been colonised by old money. The two small communities faced each other across a narrow body of water.

Max Perkins, Fitzgerald's editor at Scribner's (see 20 September), was uneasy with the author's choice of title. How many potential readers would understand the allusion to the Latin classic? What did 'West Egg' mean to someone who hadn't already read the novel?

Other ideas Fitzgerald came up with at various times included *Among Ash-Heaps and Millionaires, On the Road to West Egg, The High-Bouncing Lover* and – even after he had read the proofs – *Under the Red White and Blue*. 'Fatal' was the editor's reaction to the last offering. Finally, Fitzgerald would settle for a title he never grew to like, *The Great Gatsby*.

Like other American novels (*Look Homeward, Angel* being the most famous), *The Great Gatsby* benefited from Perkins's surgery. That evocative last chapter ('So we beat on, boats against the current …') came at the beginning in the original manuscript. Fitzgerald had concentrated Gatsby's biography into a solid, indigestible block. Perkins persuaded him to break it up into segments, to be revealed piece by piece, to make the protagonist more mysterious. He was right about that title too.

8 November

Theodore Dreiser's Sister Carrie *is published but not publicised*

1900 Wisconsin farm girl Carrie Meeber comes to Chicago to find work. On the train she meets Charles Druet, a slick travelling salesman, with whom she eventually moves in after a debilitating bout of factory work. Druet introduces Carrie to George Hurstwood, manager of Fitzgerald and Moy's bar, 'the finest resort in town' and a 'way-up, swell place', according to Druet.

Before long, impressed by his savoir faire and elegant clothes, Carrie has started an affair with Hurstwood. One night while closing the bar, the manager is tempted by the cash in the safe. He picks it up, but when he tries to return it, finds that the safe door has closed.

He and Carrie have to flee, first to Montreal, then to New York, where Hurstwood takes up various unsatisfactory jobs and Carrie gets increasingly bored and restless. As a successful actress she meets wealthy patrons of the arts, including Robert Ames, a handsome young scholar who lectures her on the futility of material possessions, while having plenty himself. Hurstwood, meanwhile, loses his job, can't pay his rent, lives on the streets, and finally commits suicide in a flophouse.

As the men in her life fall away, are ruined or worse, Carrie ascends the ranks of fortune, sophistication and success. She isn't happy, but unlike other fictional fallen heroines – Flaubert's Madame Bovary, Tolstoy's Anna Karenina and Dickens's Lady Deadlock – she at least comes out alive.

Submitted to the prestigious New York publishers Doubleday and Page, the manuscript of *Sister Carrie* was strongly backed by the firm's reader, the California naturalist Frank Norris. Walter Page agreed to publish, but when Frank Doubleday got back from a trip to Europe he was much less keen on the project. Rumour has it, though it has never been documented, that it was his wife who found the book especially repugnant.

In the event, the publishers honoured their verbal agreement, came to contract and brought the book out after the author had made a few adjustments to assuage middle-class respectability – but he kept to his chief innovation, that Carrie was the first fallen heroine in the history of the novel whom the author didn't feel compelled to kill off by having her die of consumption in a graveyard or jump in front of a train.

The first-edition print run of 1,000 copies sold only about half. Doubleday and Page didn't push the marketing.

9 November

Hitler's beer hall putsch

1923 Adolf Hitler has rarely been glorified in British or American literature. There is, however, one notable exception – the 'underground bestseller', *The Turner Diaries*.

The novel was written by Dr William Luther Pierce. Pierce was born in Atlanta, Georgia (KKK territory) in 1933. He was educated at a Texas military academy, and graduated BA from Rice University in 1955. He spent a year at Caltech as a graduate studying physics. At this point he fell in with, and then fell out with, the radical right-wing John Birch Society, whose HQ was just down the road from his lab. He evidently read, with attention, the Birchites' favourite novel-cum-tract, *The Franklin Papers*.

Caltech was too demanding – or his political activities too distracting – and Pierce moved on to Colorado, where he acquired a PhD in physics. Now a 'rocket scientist' (a breed few and far between among neo-Nazis), he taught at college level for a while, before sacrificing his academic career 'to devote himself to the service of his people'.

More specifically he entered the service of the 'American Führer', George Lincoln Rockwell. When Rockwell was assassinated in 1967, Pierce went independent with his 'National Alliance', later 'National Vanguard' movement, based in Virginia. In his neo-Nazi fastness he ran a publishing business, a radio station, and a clearing house for co-ideologues – spreading his word.

He spread it most effectively as 'Andrew MacDonald', under which pen-name Pierce wrote *The Turner Diaries* (1976). The plot derives, transparently, from Jack London's 'Revolutionary Memoir', *The Iron Heel* (Pierce impudently claimed that London was 'a National Socialist before his time').

The Turner Diaries became what the FBI called the 'Bible of the Racist Right'. Pierce used the FBI warning as a shoutline on self-published reprints. The diaries are those of Earl Turner, the martyr who crowns a career of race vigilantism with a suicide bombing assault on the 'Jewish capital', Washington DC (Tom Clancy wasn't the first to anticipate 9/11 in fiction, as Pierce indignantly claimed after the outrage). He does so 'on November 9 – our traditional Day of the Martyrs … in the year 1999, according to the chronology of the Old Era – just 110 years after the birth of the Great One' (i.e. Hitler).

9 November 1923 was, of course, the day of the 'Beer Hall Revolution' when Hitler and his band of stormtroopers marched on the Bavarian War Ministry with the ultimate aim of starting a Nazi revolution in Berlin. They failed ignominiously – but success was to follow.

In *The Turner Diaries* the heroic American Nazis nuke Tel Aviv as well, and clean up the west coast, their HQ, with 'the Day of the Rope'. At every intersection in Los Angeles, there dangles a corpse bearing one of two placards: 'I betrayed my race' (for traitors) or 'I defiled my race' (for women 'who were married to or living with blacks, with Jews, or other non-white males'). National Vanguard actually created a 'Day of the Rope' musical that outdoes 'Springtime for Hitler' in surrealist excess.

There were many reprints of *The Turner Diaries*. Skinheads pored laboriously over its pages, their lips moving as they struggled with the occasional polysyllable such as 'Hebrew' or 'miscegenation'. It sold, over the years, over half a million copies: mainly through non-bookstore outlets.

Famously, Timothy McVeigh (who sold the *Diaries*, cut-price, at gun shows) had seven strategically highlighted pages of the novel in his getaway car from the Murrah Building bombing in Oklahoma City in 1995. The novel was plausibly linked to many other acts of domestic terrorism. Pierce blandly disowned them. It was 'only a novel', as Jane Austen would have said.

10 November

Lady Chat acquitted

1960 The term 'sea change' is frequently used but seldom justified. A genuine change of the literary weather (to vary metaphors) occurred in Britain and America in November 1960.

D.H. Lawrence wrote three versions of *Lady Chatterley's Lover*, the last of which was the freest with the awkwardly-termed 'four-letter words'. The final draft could not, in 1928, be published in Britain (nor easily printed: printers are notoriously strait-laced and nervous, as the easiest targets for prosecution). *Lady Chatterley's Lover* was printed – like other subversively obscene works of literature (notably *Ulysses*) – offshore, principally in France, where it sold massively over the years.

Various expurgated versions of the novel were published in the English-speaking world. Lawrence, who died in 1930, would have disapproved. His novels 'bled', he complained, if they were cut.

Times changed in the late 1950s in the US, with the liberating Roth changes to the law of obscenity and the decline of censorious lobbies such as The Society for the Suppression of Vice. In 1959, after a series of trials, Lawrence's novel was deemed mailable and publishable. It was not, at that point, covered in the US by copyright protection and there was a flood of pirated versions. At one point, in 1960, the novel was being sold, as a newspaper supplement, on street corners in Boston for 25¢.

In the UK, the home secretary, Roy Jenkins – who complacently declared that 'the permissive society is the civilised society' – got into UK law an amended obscenity statute that allowed publication of an 'offensive' work if it could be shown to be of literary or social 'merit'. Bad books could, in the right circumstances, be good books.

Penguin, to celebrate the 30th anniversary of Lawrence's death, brought out a collective ten-volume set of his work – including *Lady Chatterley's Lover*. They prudently kept the stock in a warehouse, sending a dozen copies to the director of public prosecutions, daring him to act: which he duly did.

In November 1960 the publishers were tried at the Old Bailey. They mustered an impressive corps of witnesses to testify to the novel's merit (tactfully, they did not draw the prosecution's attention to the act of anal rape, late in the narrative, nor had the prosecution read the novel carefully enough themselves to notice it). Among other fatuities on the witness stand, the Bishop of Woolwich averred that the adultery of the gamekeeper and the aristocrat was equivalent to an 'act of communion'.

By general agreement, the case for censorship was lost by the prosecutor, Mervyn Griffith Jones, instructing the jury, in his opening address

to ask yourselves the question, when you have read it through, would you approve of your young sons, young daughters

– because girls can read as well as boys – reading this book? Is it a book that you would have lying around in your own house? Is it a book that you would even wish your wife or your servants to read?

He had forgotten it was the 1960s. Or perhaps he never knew.

11 November

The Pilgrim Fathers land in America. Ten years later, William Bradford will turn the event into New England's founding myth

1620 On this day the Scrooby Separatists, a group of Puritans who had separated from the Church of England, dropped anchor just inside the hook of Cape Cod, offshore of present-day Providence, Massachusetts. Three days later they would begin to explore the New World (see 15 November) before finally settling at Plymouth, and to write up their adventures almost as soon as they lived them.

But though William Bradford may well have written some or all of that earlier account, ten years after the event he was engaged in something much more serious. Up the coast, the Massachusetts Bay colony was beginning to settle the area around Boston. This was a much bigger enterprise than Plymouth's, better-funded, better-educated, and – being Congregationalist rather than Separatist – better-connected with the London establishment. Would Plymouth's population and business begin to leak away to the prosperous new colony?

Bradford's book *Of Plymouth Plantation*, begun in 1630, was an attempt to establish Plymouth's primacy – at least in the settlement of Massachusetts, and hence in the history of New England. Whereas in *Mourt's Relation*, their contemporary account of exploration, he and his colleagues had been writing for potential backers in England, now he was writing for posterity.

So everything changes. Instead of running away, as they had in the earlier account, the natives are 'savage barbarians ... [who were] readier to fill their [i.e. our] sides with arrows than otherwise'. The weather was 'sharp and violent, and subject to fierce storms'. Gone are the deer, the vines and the springs of fresh water that so delighted the early explorers; now all is 'a hideous and desolate wilderness, full of wild beasts and wild men'.

Not only that, but the settlers' coming was a portent. Though Puritans were not supposed to draw connections between the Bible and their everyday life, Bradford begs an exception. 'May not and ought not' their posterity boast that 'Our fathers were Englishmen which came over this great ocean, and were ready to perish in this wilderness, but they cried unto the Lord, and He heard their voice, and looked on their adversity'? This is Deuteronomy 26:7, almost word for word. In other words, the Scrooby Separatists had now become Pilgrim Fathers, the chosen people brought out of captivity in Europe to found the Promised Land.

12 November

John Bunyan is arrested for preaching outside the established church. 'Not so much a prison as an office'

1660 When the monarchy was restored that year, it became illegal once again for a preacher to conduct a divine service outside the ritual of the Anglican Church. Those not in Episcopal orders were forbidden even from preaching.

John Bunyan was an itinerant tinker by trade, and a lay preacher by calling. This meant that he would gather congregations to pray and hear him preach the word of God – by the side of a road, under a tree, or wherever else people wanted to convene.

Just six months after Charles II returned to England, Bunyan was arrested in a village near Bedford as he was about to conduct a service in a private house. He was imprisoned for twelve years. Though he could preach in prison, his quarters were very uncomfortable. He had to sleep on straw; he was held in a room without a chimney. Worst of all, he was separated from his wife and children, for whom he was always anxious. Occasionally the authorities would offer to release him, provided he undertook not to preach. Despite his privations, he always refused these offers.

While in prison Bunyan wrote the most complete spiritual auto-biography in English, *Grace Abounding to the Chief of Sinners* (1666) and – scholars now think – most of his masterpiece, *Pilgrim's Progress*

(1678). *Pilgrim's Progress* blends the language of the King James Bible with evangelical theology and English 17th-century vernacular speech and geography to form the greatest Christian allegory of salvation in the language. The book was and remains a bestseller. In Bunyan's lifetime the first, most substantial part went through eleven editions, and it has never been out of print since.

Bunyan was let out of jail in 1672, when Charles II, preparing the ground for toleration of Roman Catholics, issued his Declaration of Religious Indulgence. Under the new law Bunyan was granted one of the first licences allowing non-conformist pastors to preach wherever they could gather a congregation. He built a new meeting-house in Bedford and even set up new congregations.

In March 1675, after Parliament had forced Charles to withdraw the Declaration of Indulgence, Bunyan's fortunes changed once again for the worse, and the devout preacher found himself back in jail. 'Maybe this is not so much a prison as an office from which I can reach the world with Christ's message', he wrote.

13 November

Kenneth Tynan ejaculates the word 'fuck' ('fuff-fuff-fuff-uck') on BBC TV: a first – for TV, not Tynan

1965 Asked during the course of a live debate whether he would allow sex to be represented on stage, the theatre critic and producer replied: 'Well, I think so, certainly. I doubt if there are any rational people to whom the word "fuck" would be particularly diabolical, revolting or totally forbidden. I think that anything which can be printed or said can also be seen.' Hard to imagine a time when 'fuck' could cause such a furore, now that it's become a commonplace in every 'reality' TV show from *Big Brother* to *Come Dine With Me*, and a celebrity chef even has a programme named after it. But this was the first time the word had been spoken on British television, and for a time Tynan became the most infamous man in public life – exactly his intention.

The satirical magazine *Private Eye*'s hilarity was unbounded. Pointing out that Tynan's stammer had created the first thirteen-syllable four-letter word in history, they lampooned the original debate in their 26 November issue:

Millions of viewers were surprised last night … when in the course of a discussion of the nature of charity between the Lord Chamberlain, the Bishop of Hampstead and dramaturg Kenneth Tynan, Mr Tynan was seen to make a certain gesture involving in no small measure the glans penis.

He then said, 'In this day and age a quick flash is in no way shocking or offensive. If it has been done in a book, there's no reason why it shouldn't be brought to life on the screen'.

The dramaturg was as good as his word – as soon as the law allowed. Four and a half years later, after the Theatres Act had abolished the Lord Chamberlain's power of stage censorship (see 26 September), he produced *Oh! Calcutta!* This was not (as some bemused subcontinental tourists supposed) about the problems of India's most overcrowded city. The title punned on the French for 'Oh what a lovely arse!' ('O quel cul t'as!') 'Mr Tynan's Nude Review' (*The Times*'s frosty description) gathered together sketches from different hands – some crude, some subtle – mixed up with song and dance. John Lennon, Joe Orton, and Samuel Beckett were among Tynan's best-known contributors. Lennon's piece featured a masturbation rite, each member (members dangling) calling out women's names to stimulate fantasy. Suddenly one interjects 'Frank Sinatra'. Members droop catastrophically.

Oh! Calcutta! opened at London's Roundhouse Theatre, a converted railway shed, on 20 July 1970. Since the theatre was Arts Council-supported, feathers were predictably ruffled by 'state handouts for filth'. Tynan revelled in such controversy and did his utmost to whip up pre-event publicity by having a series of packed 'previews' in advance of opening night. The (anonymous) *Times* staff reporter who attended one such event was typically disapproving:

It will prove of interest to those excited by the prospect of unclothed ladies and gentlemen cavorting in a stuffy former engine shed … it will bore most adults … If it was for this that the battle against the censor was fought and won, then the struggle was barely worth it.

There ensued a fevered correspondence in the paper. Tynan's contribution to it was sublimely insolent.

Sir,

Lord Drogheda joins several of your other correspondents in ascribing to me the phrase 'tasteful pornography'. What ever his lordship may have read, I have never used this expression to describe *Oh! Calcutta!* or anything else. I have a horror of the word 'tasteful'.

Yours etc.
Kenneth Tynan

14 November

Lawrence's Rainbow *goes up in flames*

1915 Wartime, with the emergency powers assumed by the state, invariably brings in censorship. On 30 September 1915, D.H. Lawrence's fourth novel *The Rainbow* (the work that posterity generally applauds as his masterpiece) was published. It drew a chorus of disparagement from the London reviewers, as 'worse than Zola' and a filthy exhortation to unbridled sexual licence. Obscurely, it was also felt to be unpatriotic (the oblique criticism of the Boer War, in the narrative's later section, was found fault with on this score). Two reviewers roundly called on the authorities to take action against the publisher, Methuen.

A search warrant was duly procured on 3 November and a thousand warehoused copies were seized. The publishers were prosecuted that same month. None of Lawrence's literary friends were prepared – such was the vindictive mood of the time – to offer themselves as witnesses for the defence. The pusillanimous publisher offered no defence, merely stating (to avoid a punitive fine) that they 'regretted having published it'. They piously testified to the court that they 'wished they had scrutinised the manuscript more carefully'. They did not trouble to inform Lawrence about the prosecution, possibly to protect his feelings – more likely to get the embarrassing affair out of the way with as little publicity as possible. Methuen escaped with a mere ten guineas costs.

On 13 November 1915 the Bow Street magistrate, Sir John Dickinson (under the 1857 Obscene Publications Act), solemnly determined *The Rainbow* to be 'a mass of obscenity' and ordered all copies, in shops, warehouses, and libraries to be seized and burned to protect the British population. Lawrence's patron, Lady Ottoline Morrell, attempted vainly to have the matter raised in Parliament. The home secretary had more important things to worry about.

The bonfires were stocked on 14 November for incineration the next day. The shameful conflagration was completed, by legal order, within the week. Lawrence and his wife Frieda (née von Richthofen) attempted, unsuccessfully, to get passports and exit visas for America. Lawrence, chronically unhealthy, was called up for medical examination by the War Office in December; a horrific experience vividly recalled in the 'Nightmare' section of *Kangaroo* (see 28 June).

The Lawrences, denied emigration, found refuge in a cottage in Cornwall for the duration of the war, where they were suspected of being spies and ostracised. *The Rainbow* did not see unexpurgated publication until 1926.

In later life, invoking the suffering of Christ, Lawrence declared: 'The War finished me: it was the spear through the side of all sorrows and hopes.' His battles with the 'censor morons' would continue until his last novel, *Lady Chatterley's Lover*. That too was banned.

By a nice coincidence, Kenneth Tynan took the battle to the censor morons of his own day with his epochal ejaculation of 'fuck' on the BBC on 13 November 1965. Fifty years to the day of *The Rainbow*'s prosecution.

15 November

The Scrooby Separatists set off to explore the New World

1620 Once ashore, they 'espied five or six people with a dog … who were savages', but they ran away, 'whistl[ing] the dog after them'. That night they camped out. 'Some kindled a fire, and others fetched wood, and there held our rendezvous.' The next morning they 'saw a deer, and found springs of fresh water … and sat us down and drank our first New England water with as much delight as ever we drunk drink in all our lives'.

These were the Scrooby Separatists, so called because they had come from that village in Nottinghamshire, though by way of a twelve-year sojourn in the Netherlands, and had formed a Puritan church entirely separate from the Church of England. In this they differed from the Congregationalist Puritans who would settle around Boston ten years later, and who kept communion with the C of E, while dissenting from some aspects of its ceremony and governance.

The settlers' first encounter with New England is told in *Mourt's Relation*, a short account of their first year, published in London in 1622 – less than a year after the last events (including the first Thanksgiving) covered in the narrative. It was a booster's tract, an attempt to attract further settlement and financial backing for the settlement.

No doubt that's one reason why, despite the season and their exposure to the wilderness, they manage to make their first steps sound like a delightful adventure, in a land where 'grew … many fine vines, and [where] fowl and deer haunted', and where the natives, far from threatening them, had run away, leaving behind curious artefacts, like a 'basket … round, and narrow at the top … very handsomely and cunningly made'.

Ten years later, when William Bradford re-told the story (see 11 November), the discourse would be aimed not at potential backers in London, but at posterity. The Scrooby Settlers would be promoted to Pilgrim Fathers, and their story nothing less than the founding myth of America.

16 November

Britain's pioneer lesbian novel is judged obscene

1928 (Marguerite) Radclyffe Hall (1883–1943), author of the first English novel to deal explicitly with lesbianism, was already notorious when *The Well of Loneliness* came to trial in November 1928. She dressed in an ostentatiously male style, insisted on being addressed as 'John', wore a monocle, smoked in public, and made no secret of her sexual preferences.

Hall – who started fiction late, in 1924 – had written four novels before *The Well of Loneliness*. That immediately previous, *Adam's Breed* (1926), was intermittently autobiographical. So too (with a lot of wish-fulfilling romanticism) was *The Well of Loneliness* – with the difference that Hall took the plunge and made the heroine, 'Stephen' Gordon, female.

Stephen is the only child of Sir Philip and Lady Anna Gordon, who desperately wanted a son. The novel implies that their excessive desire for a male heir has tainted the foetus. Stephen is born with broad shoulders, narrow hips, and the invert's tendency to neurasthenia.

The Gordons have a magnificent estate, Morton Hall in Worcestershire. Stephen has an idyllic childhood (Hall's was actually rather pinched, and passed in unlovely places like Bournemouth). She grows up loving horses, cultivating her biceps with dumb-bells, and falling in love with the female servants.

Sir Philip is killed by a falling cedar tree, his last words a desperate attempt to warn his wife about Stephen, who subsequently falls in love with the wife of a local businessman, Angela Crossby. Angela, to save herself, betrays Stephen, who is denounced by the infuriated husband as 'a sin against creation'. She is cast out by her mother with only a faithful housekeeper, 'Puddle', and the fortune her father has thoughtfully left her for just such an emergency.

Stephen becomes a novelist, and resides in Paris with her 'kind'. On the outbreak of war, Stephen serves in an all-woman ambulance unit. Here she meets the great love of her life, Mary Llewellyn, a sweet, simple girl from the Welsh valleys. In Italy, after the war, they consummate their love ('that night they were not divided'). Stephen eventually realises that the degenerate life of the lesbian will corrupt her lover, and forces her to leave. The novel ends with the hero(ine) Stephen and her lament: 'Acknowledge us, oh God, before the whole world. Give us also the right to our existence.'

The Well of Loneliness promulgates Havelock Ellis's (since discredited) view, expressed in *Sexual Inversion* (1897), that lesbians are males trapped in female bodies. The first edition of the novel was published by Jonathan Cape, with an afterword by Ellis, on 27 July 1928.

On 19 August, the *Sunday Express's* editor, James Douglas, attacked the novel ('I would rather give a healthy boy or a healthy girl a phial of prussic acid') and demanded that it be prosecuted. A moral panic ensued, with virtually all the British press joining in. The novel's publishers, Jonathan Cape, lost their nerve and dispatched stereo plates to Paris, so that *The Well of Loneliness* could be published there, under the imprint of their subsidiary Pegasus Press.

The home secretary was reassured that no further copies were printed in England. In America, Knopf also withdrew the novel – Alfred Knopf's wife, Blanche, was influential in the suppression.

Despite Cape's craven unwillingness to offend, imported copies from Paris were seized by HM Customs, and a magistrate's prosecution ensued in November 1928.

Radclyffe Hall was a Conservative, a Catholic, and at best a mawkishly middlebrow author. Nonetheless, sections of the literary establishment (including Bloomsbury) supported her. Inevitably the book was found to be obscene under the terms of the 1857 ('tends to deprave and corrupt') legal criterion, and the distributors fined. *The Well of Loneliness* remained unpublishable in Britain or America until after the liberating 1959–60 *Lady Chatterley* trials (see 10 November).

17 November

Sir Walter Raleigh goes on trial for treason

1603 Walter Raleigh probably never laid his cloak down over a muddy puddle so Queen Elizabeth I could walk over dry-shod. It probably wasn't he who brought tobacco and the potato back from the New World to England. Even so, his actual life was crammed with near-legendary action. In turn soldier, explorer, member of parliament and (unsuccessful) settler of colonies, he was the queen's favourite – contending with the Earls of Leicester and Essex – until he secretly married one of her ladies-in-waiting and got thrown in the Tower at her majesty's displeasure. Incurring not wrath but cold revenge from Elizabeth's successor, he went on trial for treason on this day, suspected of taking part in a plot against the life of James I, but the sentence was commuted.

Less often remembered, or even mentioned, is his writing: his narratives of exploration, his monumental *A History of the World* (1614) – above all, his verse. In the nearly 700 pages of his *English Literature in the Sixteenth Century*, C.S. Lewis can spare just under two to Raleigh, whom he dismisses as 'an amateur' with 'no style of his own'. He is usually classified as one of the 'silver' – or even 'drab' – poets. By this they mean that he eschewed the polysyllabic, Latinate diction of the high Renaissance (as in Daniel Drayton's 'the almes of thy superfluous prayse') and also the strenuous ingenuity of Donne and the other metaphysicals.

Raleigh's style (yes, he did have one) was anti-romantic, deploying an Anglo-Saxon vocabulary to challenge the more optimistic clichés of romantic love. He focused more on love lost than sought or enjoyed, more on the end of life than its prime, more on actual conditions in the countryside than on its pastoral idealisation. His response to Marlowe's 'The Shepherd's Plea' is typical. Here is Marlowe:

> Come live with me, and be my love, …
> And we will sit upon the rocks,
> And see the shepherds feed their flocks.
> And here is Raleigh's 'The Nymph's Reply':
> If all the world and love were young,
> And truth in every shepherd's tongue,
> These pretty pleasures might me move …
> But time drives flocks from field to fold,
> When rivers rage and rocks grow cold.

If Raleigh had treated fantasies of New World riches as sceptically as he had literary conventions, he might have died in his bed. As it was, he made not one but two fruitless voyages to Venezuela in search of El Dorado, the golden city. On the second he laid waste to a Spanish settlement on the Orinoco. Buckling under Spanish pressure, James I reinstated the death sentence handed down in 1603.

The condemned man kept his *sang froid* to the end (see 29 October). The executioner's axe was 'a sharp Medicine', he said, but 'a Physician for all diseases and miseries'. As he lay ready for the blow, he cried out: 'Strike, Man, strike!' So Raleigh died as he lived: bravely, sardonically.

18 November

Walt Disney launches Steamboat Willie

1928 The third to feature Mickey Mouse, *Steamboat Willie* was the first Disney cartoon with a soundtrack synchronised to its action. Setting a long precedent for the animated cartoon to be shown before the newsreel and main feature, the sound linked to the action favoured music over words, since elaborate dialogue would detract from the slapstick humour.

Mickey is a junior officer on a river steamer, bullied by a bruising cat of a captain. Minnie Mouse comes aboard, with a guitar and the sheet music of 'Turkey in the Straw', both of which are swallowed by a goat. No problem. Minnie produces the tune by turning the goat's tail like the crank of a hurdy-gurdy, while Mickey 'plays' (in turn) a row of suckling pigs, the sow's teats and even a goose as a bagpipe. (Some of this was later cut out on a cruelty-to-animals basis; if you Google it, make sure to watch the eight-minute version.)

In less than a decade Disney had taken a step change in animation, producing ambitious feature-length literary adaptations in full colour. These started with *Snow White and the Seven Dwarfs* (1937), and by the 21st century had morphed into computer-generated films like *Finding Nemo* (2004) and *WALL-E* (2008). With *Snow White* they could hardly dispense with words, yet the intended audience forced certain simplicities on the originals.

The Brothers Grimm *Snow White*, with the heroine's three 'deaths' and 'rebirths' and the wicked stepmother's three symbolic gifts of girdle, comb and apple, is a tale of initiation. Central to Snow White's dilemma is the contrast between her natural mother and stepmother, who is finally punished by being forced to walk in hot shoes to her death. Disney deletes the natural mother, gives the seven dwarfs childlike names and temperaments, invents forest creatures to minister to Snow White, and blunts the moral logic of the tale by having the wicked stepmother killed through a natural accident – a lightning strike – not through human agency.

Disney's *Bambi* (1942) burnished even more hard edges. The original, Felix Salten's *Bambi: A Life in the Woods* (1926), traces the life of a deer from childhood to old age as he escapes the threat of hunters and finally learns, when he comes across a dead human body, that his persecutors can turn against themselves, and are not omnipotent. The Nazis burned the book in 1936 as an allegory of anti-Semitism. Salten, whose real name was Siegmund Salzmann, fled to Hollywood, where Disney bought the rights for the knock-down price (measly even in the late 1930s) of $5,000, then set about changing both tone and content.

Though in the film the hunters still threaten, out goes the grim lesson in man's fallibility. Bambi gets a chum in the woods, a rabbit called Thumper. The movie ends happily ever after, with Bambi and his sweetheart Faline starting a family, whereas in the book he leaves Faline to manage her fawns, just as his father did his mother. It all comes down to audience. Target just the adults, and you exclude the children. But adjust the approach to the young, and you get both.

19 November

After a sound night's sleep at the Willard Hotel, Washington, DC,
Julia Ward Howe wakes early in the dawn with the words of
'The Battle Hymn of the Republic' in her head

1861 'I scrawled the verses almost without looking at the paper', the fervent abolitionist remembered, fearing to use a light 'lest I should wake the baby'. Then she returned to bed and fell asleep, 'saying to myself, "I like this better than most things I have written"'.*

Though she was already a published poet, Howe was right to guess that 'The Battle Hymn of the Republic' would eclipse her other work. It came just in the nick of time to galvanise the Union's moral fervour. Since April of that year America had been embroiled in a civil war, and since July the first Battle of Bull Run (or Manassas, as the victorious South had the right to call it) had made it clear that the war was going to be bloody and prolonged.

On her way back from visiting an army camp, Howe heard soldiers along the road singing the ballad 'John Brown's Body'. Brown was the militant abolitionist who tried to start a slave revolution at Harper's Ferry, Virginia in 1859, and was hanged for his troubles. 'John Brown's body lies a-mouldering in the grave', the song went, 'but his soul goes marching on'. It's not recorded whether she also heard the soldiers' favourite pastiche of the ditty, 'John Brown's bollocks are a-dangling in the air', but in any case Howe was persuaded she could find more seemly and patriotic words to the same tune.

Her version contains six verses, each followed by the chorus 'Glory, Glory, Halleluja' thrice, followed by a variant of 'His truth is marching on'. The God invoked is one of vengeance, not mercy. He is 'trampling out the vintage where the grapes of wrath are stored' and has already 'loosed the fateful lightning of His terrible swift sword'. Here even Jesus, though born 'in the beauty of the lilies', is not forgiving, but an incitement to violent sacrifice: 'As He died to make men holy, let us die to make men free.'

Howe's lyrics really do sound as though they were 'got twixt sleeping and waking'. It's grapes that are trampled, not their vintage; Christ was born in a stable in winter, not 'in the beauty of the lilies'. Maybe their oddity is why they have been such a rich source of American

---

* Quoted in Elaine Showalter, *A Jury of her Peers: American Women Writers from Anne Bradstreet to Annie Proulx*, London: Virago Press, 2009, p. 134.

titles, like *The Grapes of Wrath* (1939; the first edition had the whole anthem printed on its end-papers) and John Updike's *In the Beauty of the Lilies* (1996), and Martin Luther King, Jr., used 'Mine eyes have seen the coming' in numerous speeches.

20 November

Melville and Hawthorne meet for (nearly) the last time, and take a walk in the sand dunes of Southport, Lancashire

1856 It was only just over six years after they first met on that picnic in the Berkshire Mountains (see 5 August). In return for his campaign biography of President Franklin Pierce, Hawthorne had been awarded the American consulship at Liverpool, then the chief port through which American goods and travellers entered the UK. Seeking a break from his work and family, Melville was on his way to the Holy Land.

Since their first meeting their literary fortunes had diverged. Contemporary critics actually preferred Hawthorne's *The House of the Seven Gables* (1851) to *The Scarlet Letter* (1850), and much admired *The Blithedale Romance* (1852), his satire on an idealistic farming commune. Melville's monumental *Moby-Dick* (dedicated to Hawthorne) had appeared in 1851 to mixed reviews, while *Pierre* (1852), his next novel – and his last conventional one – was a disaster, both critically and financially.

On first seeing Melville at the Consulate, Hawthorne noted in his journal of 20 November that his old friend looked 'a little paler, and perhaps a little sadder', perhaps because he had 'suffered from constant literary occupation, pursued without much success latterly'. So he invited him to stay for a few days in the family residence at Southport, to get a breath of sea air.

On a long walk, sitting down 'in a hollow among the sand hills', Melville announced 'that he had "pretty much made up his mind to be annihilated"'. He seems to have meant this in the metaphysical sense, not referring to his critical reputation, for Hawthorne reports that he had always lacked a 'definite belief' and seemed doomed to wander over these deserts of doubt 'as dismal and monotonous as the sand hills amid which we were sitting'.

They did meet just once again, when Melville returned from his voyage and passed through Liverpool on 4 May 1857. But this time Hawthorne's journal is silent on the occasion. As for Melville's critical standing, that would have to wait nearly a century to be justly valued.

21 November

Jane Welsh Carlyle confronts the taxman on behalf of her husband

1855 Jane Baillie Welsh wrote her first novel at thirteen. At 25 she married the then unknown essayist, Thomas Carlyle. Her letters have long been admired for their vivacity, warmth and wit, their prose often compared favourably with that of her husband. Their London house in Cheyne Walk, Chelsea was the hub of a lively social and intellectual scene – at a rare period in English life when 'intellectual' wasn't used ironically, or as a term of abuse.

But this anecdote comes not from her letters, but from a journal she kept between October 1855 and the following July. The Tax Commissioners had summoned Carlyle to explain why he had paid no income tax for the past few years. 'Mr C. said "the voice of honour *seemed* to call on him to go himself"', she wrote, 'but either it did not call loud enough, or he would not listen to that charmer'. In any case he would probably 'run his head against some post in his impatience'.

Arriving at 'a dirty, private-like house only with Tax Office painted on the door', she was shown into 'a dim room where three men sat round a large table spread with papers'. The chairman of the panel seemed to be impersonating Rhadamanthus, the judge and prosecutor of the dead in the underworld:

'Ha!' cried Rhadamanthus … 'What is this? Why is Mr Carlyle not come himself?' … 'I was told … that Mr Carlyle's personal appearance was not indispensable.' '*Huffgh! Huffgh!* What does Mr Carlyle mean by saying he has no income from his writings …?' 'It means, sir, that in ceasing to write, one ceases to be paid for writing, and Mr Carlyle has published nothing for several years.' 'Huffgh! Huffgh! I understand nothing about that.'

The spirited, articulate Jane finally faced Rhadamanthus down, who, with a good deal of further huffing and puffing, split the difference on the disputed sum. On leaving, her 'first thought was, what a mercy Carlyle didn't come himself.'

22 November

Norman Mailer, uxoricide

1960 New Yorkers awoke on Monday morning, 22 November, to read in the *New York Times* that the city's most famous novelist might be writing his future works from Sing Sing. He had been arrested a few hours earlier, charged with stabbing his 37-year-old wife Adele in the abdomen, chest and back. She was in critical condition at University Hospital, having been driven there in a private car.

It was fascinating stuff, but there was much confusion about what had happened. As the *Times* reported:

> According to the police of the West 100th Street station, where the 37-year-old writer was being held, Mrs Mailer told physicians at the hospital that she had fallen on glass in her apartment at 250 West 94th Street. The physicians were suspicious and notified the police.

It had not been a good week for Mailer, as regards the law. He had been arrested a few days before on a disorderly conduct charge after an argument over a $7.60 bill at the Birdland jazz nightclub (he attempted to pay by credit card, illegal where liquor was purchased, and became violent with the waiter).

When detectives went to question Mrs Mailer, she was reluctant to talk to them, claiming to be too ill. She finally conceded that Norman had stabbed her at a party on Sunday around 5.00am, for 'no reason that she could offer'.

He had 'suddenly walked up to her, looked at her, stabbed her with what she thought was a penknife or clasp knife, and left the apartment'. He returned and drove her to the hospital, some ten hours later. He was arrested when he came to visit her, late on Sunday night. He denied everything and was paroled on Monday morning.

It all blew over, thanks to Adele's refusing to press charges (had she done so, the novelist would certainly have served time in prison). Mailer, six times married, kept none of his wives long (although in the other cases his divorce procedures were more orthodox).

Adele, after separation, went on to pursue a successful career as an alternative healer. She wrote a late-life memoir, in which she recalled her version of the stabbing episode. The weapon in question had been 'a dirty three-inch penknife'. In those hours in the apartment before she went to hospital he had gone down tearfully on his knees, she recalled, begging her not to prosecute. It would ruin him. Mailer (in imagination, at least) went through with the uxoricide more manfully, in his novel published later in the year, *An American Dream*. The narrative opens with the hero, Rojack, strangling his wife before proceeding to anally rape her German maid. All in the Mailerian day, one apprehends.

23 November

Berger spurns Booker

1972 For writers other than the austerely Marxist John Berger this would have been an *annus mirabilis*. His TV series – *Ways of Seeing* – had revolutionised art history, and how it was taught, doing for the discipline what 'Theory' was currently doing for literary criticism (see 21 October). Later in the year, his novel *G.* won the country's premier literary prize, the Booker (Booker-McConnell, to give it its full title).

There were three judges for the prize (now in its third year). The most influential was Dr George Steiner, a very advanced thinker and literary critic. The chair was the sadly decrepit lion of London's (1940s) literary world, Cyril Connolly: no longer an advanced thinker, constitutionally lazy, and chronically ill. It was Steiner's authority, everyone assumed, that tilted the choice towards Berger's extravagantly literary work (submitted by his publisher, Weidenfeld and Nicolson, not himself, as it later became clear). The publisher's blurb played down the elliptical, enigmatic, epistolary nature of the narrative.

'G.' is a young man forging an energetic sexual career in Europe during the early years of this century. With profound compassion, Berger explores the hearts and minds of both men and women, and what happens during sex, to reveal the conditions of Don Juan's success: his essential loneliness, the quiet culmination in each of his sexual experiences of all those that precede it, the tenderness that infuses even the briefest of his encounters, and the way women experience their own extraordinariness through their moments with him. All of this Berger sets against the turbulent backdrop of Garibaldi and the failed revolution of Milanese workers in 1889, the Boer War, and the first flight across the Alps, making *G.* a brilliant novel about the search for intimacy in history's private moments.

The award ceremony at the Café Royal (not, as it proved, the ideal location) did not go to anyone's plan, except Berger's. His winner's speech opened with a critique of cash prizes for art and the pernicious (capitalistic) competition they represented:

> Since you have awarded me this prize, you may like to know, briefly, what it means to me. The competitiveness of prizes I find distasteful. And in the case of the prize, the publication of the shortlist, the deliberately publicised suspense, the speculation of writers concerned as though they were horses, the whole emphasis on winners and losers is false and out of place in the context of literature.
>
> Nevertheless prizes act as a stimulus – not to writers themselves but to publishers, readers and booksellers. And so the basic cultural value of a prize depends upon what it is a stimulus to. To the conformity of the market and the consensus of the average opinion; or to imaginative independence on the part of both reader and writer.

This was bad, but worse was to come. Berger turned on the sponsors, Booker-McConnell, whose commercial wealth, he contemptuously noted, had largely come from 130 years of cultivating sugar, with indentured black labour, in the West Indies. He would no more accept their laurels than a handout from Simon Legree (the vicious slaveowner in *Uncle Tom's Cabin*). Half the £5,000 award he would donate to the Black Panthers (alas, their British chapter no longer existed: but, as they say about gifts, it's the thought that counts).

The evening was a disaster. Not least because *G.* went on to be a flop in the bookshops. The reading public did not share Steiner's enthusiasm for fiction they found baffling. The events of 23 November led to material changes in the way the prize was subsequently run. The panels were expanded to five – with a majority of lay (and, occasionally, 'celebrity') judges. The apparatus, paradoxically, increasingly conformed to Berger's stinging remark about 'stimuli' to book sales and the welfare of the British book trade.

Berger himself left Britain for good eighteen months later, to live in a village in the French Alps, and write a novel on the plight of foreign migrant workers.

24 November

James Boswell conquers in armour

1762 Boswell records in his *London Journal* for 24 November a lusty adventure of the previous evening:

> I picked up a girl in the Strand; went into court with intention to enjoy her in armour. But she had none. I toyed with her. She wondered at my size, and said if I ever took a girl's maidenhead, I would make her squeal. I gave her a shilling, and had command enough of myself to go without touching her. I afterwards trembled at the danger I escaped.

By 'danger', of course, Boswell means venereal disease. No member, whatever its size, could hold out against the clap in those pre-antibiotic times. What, however, was the 'armour' that the whore neglected to carry with her? Rubber condoms would not be available for a century and galvanised rubber condoms for two centuries. The condoms that Boswell would have used were made of washable sheep-gut. One, long retired from battle, is on display at the Johnson House in London. It was fastened at the top by tape, to prevent mid-coitus slippage.

These contraceptive sacks dried out between use and needed to be moistened. Boswell elsewhere in his journal recalls dipping his 'machine' (as they were called) in the (filthy) water of the lake in St James's Park before dipping his wick with another lady of the London night.

25 November

Yukio Mishima's good career move

1970 Mishima (birth name 'Kimitake Hiraoka') was born in Tokyo in 1925. He suffered, while under the custody of a relative, childhood disciplines that verged on the sadistic and that are plausibly credited with the morbid obsessions of his later life.

He had the education and military indoctrination typical of a young Japanese male of his upper class in the nationalist-imperialistic 1930s. But, while absorbing samurai codes he was also fascinated by the writings of European 'decadents', such as Wilde and Rilke. His sexuality was ambiguous and his narcissism pronounced from his earliest years. He published his first book in 1944, and adopted the pen name by which he was later famous (it was initially a nickname given him by schoolmates). He was obliged to write in secret – being forbidden by his father to follow such an effeminate career.

Mishima was called up for military service in the final desperate years of the war, when boys were being recruited. He dodged the draft by faking TB (he had a bad cold at the time of the medical). He went on to graduate from university in 1947 and entered the civil service. After a year he resigned and devoted himself thereafter to literature.

Fame, in Japan, came with *Confessions of a Mask* (1948), in which Mishima explored the delicate subterfuges required to be homosexual in a homophobic society such as Japan's. He was, as his career progressed, regarded as the country's strongest candidate for the Nobel Prize (in fact it went in 1968 to his mentor, the novelist Yasunari Kawabata).

A flamboyant figure, dedicated to body-building, Mishima appeared in films and modelled. In the last decade of his life he became increasingly obsessed with bushido codes and ultra-nationalism (at a period of general westernisation in his country). He formed a martial cult around himself, the Tatenokai (Shield Society), fanatically dedicated to the imperial traditions of ancient Japan.

On 25 November 1970, Mishima and four of his followers invaded a military camp in Tokyo, taking its commander hostage. He apparently aimed to trigger a coup d'état, although he may also have intended self-immolation on the world stage.

After an address to the soldiers below from the camp balcony (who jeered), Mishima retired to commit the act of seppuku

– self-disembowelling – curtailed by beheading by one of his followers (the designated attendant botched the job, horribly).

It was, as Gore Vidal cattily pronounced on the death of Truman, 'a good career move'. Better, in point of fact, than a Nobel would have been.

One response in the West was amusement at the strange ways of the Japanese. *Private Eye* had a spoof headline, 'Famous British Novelist Commits Public Suicide By Drinking Himself To Death', over a picture of Kingsley Amis (who did indeed drink himself to death in 1995).

More significantly, Mishima's headline-reported suicide provoked a wave of interest in his fiction. Particularly successful in its translated form was his 1963 novel, *The Sailor Who Fell from Grace with the Sea*, the story of a widow with a son who schemes hideous violence against his prospective stepfather (the sailor of the title). *The Sailor Who Fell from Grace with the Sea* was adapted in 1976 as a film, its setting moved to England, starring Kris Kristofferson.

More successfully, the distinguished director Paul Schrader did a biopic, *Mishima: A Life in Four Chapters*, in 1985. It is, Schrader claims, the best film he ever made (judges at the Cannes Festival agreed with him, audiences less so). Mishima remains the only Japanese novelist with high name recognition outside his country – less, alas, for his works than his spectacular death.

26 November

The great(est) storm

1703 'It was a dark and stormy night' begins Edward Bulwer-Lytton's 'best-worst' novel, *Paul Clifford* (1830). It has inspired (along with the *Literary Review*'s 'Bad Sex in Fiction' award) the most famous spoof prize in Anglo-American fiction for the worst opening paragraph of the year in new fiction.

Few actual dark and stormy nights have, however, been commemorated in fiction. An exception is the 'Great Storm' of 1703 – often judged to be the worst ever to hit mainland England. 'No pen could describe it, nor tongue express it, nor thought conceive it unless by one in the extremity of it', wrote Defoe, its most famous chronicler, in *The Storm*.

Gales had battered Britain from 19 November. Barometer readings had sunk below 870, and were continuing to fall. Trees, even oaks that had stood centuries, were blown over and Defoe himself nearly killed by a falling chimney in London.

The gales reached hurricane force a week later, most devastatingly on the night of the 26th. On that night not just chimneys, but whole houses were destroyed. The newly constructed wooden Eddystone lighthouse was blown away, with not a timber remaining where it had once stood. Westminster Abbey lost its lead roof, lesser churches their spires. Queen Anne and her family were obliged to cower in the cellars of St James's Palace as the roofs above her royal head collapsed.

Bristol was flooded to a depth of three feet by water driven by the storm from the sea into the city. Some 1,500 sheep, 800 houses and many human lives were lost in the inundation. There was terrible destruction in the country's shipyards. Defoe claimed to have seen with his own eyes 700 ships wrecked in the upper Thames estuary. Some 1,500 sailors were estimated to have perished. It was a serious loss of men and matériel – Britain was currently engaged abroad in the War of the Spanish Succession.

The queen proclaimed a national 'day of fast' on 19 January 1704 to commemorate the loss of life and property sustained by her realm. The Great Storm itself became folkloric and was remembered long after those, like Defoe, who had witnessed it were dead. It figures centrally in W.M. Thackeray's 'Queen Anne' novel, *Henry Esmond* (1852). It is also the backdrop to the first ten chapters of W.H. Ainsworth's historical bestseller, *Jack Sheppard* (1840). Drawing heavily on Defoe, Ainsworth paints a gothic picture of that dreadful night of Friday, 26 November 1703, from the ominous stillness of the eye of the storm to the terrible assault of its full force on London:

> During the foregoing occurrences a dead calm prevailed. But as Rowland sprang to the helm ... a roar like a volley of ordnance was heard aloft, and the wind again burst its bondage. A moment before, the surface of the stream was black as ink. It was now whitening, hissing, and seething like an enormous cauldron. The blast once more swept over the agitated river: whirled off the sheets of foam, scattered them far and wide in rain-drops, and left the raging torrent blacker than before. The gale had become a hurricane: that hurricane was the most terrible that ever laid waste our city. Destruction everywhere marked its course. Steeples toppled, and towers reeled beneath its fury.

Trees were torn up by the roots; many houses were levelled to the ground; others were unroofed; the leads on the churches were ripped off, and 'shrivelled up like scrolls of parchment.' Nothing on land or water was spared by the remorseless gale. Most of the vessels lying in the river were driven from their moorings, dashed tumultuously against each other, or blown ashore. All was darkness, horror, confusion, ruin. Men fled from their tottering habitations, and returned to them scared by greater dangers. The end of the world seemed at hand.

27 November

Heine's credo

1823 Most literary people expire as unmemorably as unliterary people. The death of the poet Heinrich Heine is an exception on two counts.

The first is his last words – the wittiest on record and among the most authentically attested-to. Heine was born in Düsseldorf (then under French occupation) in 1797, a German-speaking Jew. He converted to Lutheranism in 1825, taking on the ultra-German forename 'Heinrich' – largely to avoid impediments put in the way of ambitious young intellectuals of Jewish origin in Germany. For the same reason he emigrated to France in 1831, spending the next 25 years in Paris. In 1835 his works were banned in Germany, on the grounds of his association with the radical 'Young Germany' movement (the forerunner of Disraeli's 'Young England' movement).

Heine died in Paris in 1856. He is buried in the Cimetière de Montmartre, among predominantly Catholic graves. His famous last words similarly allude to the Last Rites: 'Dieu me pardonnera. C'est son métier.' ('God will forgive me, it's his line of business.')

A letter that Heine wrote on 27 November 1823 suggests that his religious views were never anything but extremely relaxed:

There is nothing new to tell you, my dear Robert, except that I am still alive and still love you. The last will endure as long as the first, for the duration of my life is very uncertain. Beyond life I promise nothing. With the last breath all is done: joy, love, sorrow, macaroni, the normal theatre, lime-trees, raspberry drops, the power of human relations, gossip, the barking of dogs, champagne.

Born a Jew, converted to Lutheranism, a death-bed flirt with Rome, and a constitutional disbeliever, Heine has been disowned by every one of the nations that might lay claim to him. His books were burned by the Nazis (unaware, presumably, of the fact that he was the author, in *Almansor*, of the proverb 'Where Books are Burned, Men are Burned'). Düsseldorf has always been nervous about owning him with commemorative street or place names. In Israel his religious defections are often held against him.

The other aspect of Heine's death that has provoked speculation is what actually brought him to his 'last breath' (breath he employed so wittily). He was a long time dying, and lay on his death-bed ('the mattress coffin') for eight years. It was traditionally suspected that the cause of death may have been syphilis, or multiple sclerosis ('creeping paralysis'). Or it may have been precipitated by his abuse of opium. In 1997, analysis of one of his hairs (left as a souvenir) revealed that it was chronic lead poisoning. How he ingested the toxin is not clear. God only knows.

28 November

Edward Taylor loses his way en route to the town on the Massachusetts frontier where he will spend the rest of his life

1671 They had set out from Cambridge, Massachusetts the day before, 'not without much apprehension of a tedious and hazardous journey', as Taylor wrote in his diary, 'the snow being about Mid-leg deepe, the way unbeaten … over rocks and mountains'. Now, on day two of the 100-mile trek, 'we lost our way in the snow and woods, which hindered us some 3 or 4 miles: but finding it again by the markt trees, on we went', until they 'came in, through mercy, in health, to our Lodgen [lodging]'.

And so America's most gifted and prolific poet until Emily Dickinson came along nearly 200 years later made his arduous winter way to Westfield, a small farming town in the Connecticut River

Valley, where he would serve as the community's pastor and physician until his retirement in 1725, four years before his death.

The decision to go can't have been easy. Born the son of a Leicestershire yeoman farmer, and grammar school-educated, Taylor may even have matriculated at the English Cambridge before emigrating to New England following the Act of Uniformity of 1662. At Harvard College he entered with advanced status and graduated with distinction, after which he was offered a college fellowship. Yet when the call came from the beleaguered community on the frontier, he saw it as his Christian duty to answer it.

Every three months or so, Taylor's congregation would celebrate Holy Communion – or what they called the Lord's Supper. This called for a special sermon and – the night before – a meditation on the text to be preached on. Taylor's 'sacrificial meditations' were in verse, following the model of George Herbert, whose work he had known and loved since his school days. So America's only metaphysical poet was still writing in the 1720s, when England had moved on into the age of wit and elegance, of Dryden and Shadwell, and verse satire in decasyllabic couplets. There's something very New England about Taylor's story.

29 November

President Lyndon B. Johnson sets up the Warren Commission to investigate the assassination of John F. Kennedy

1963 Established just a week after those terrible events in Dallas, headed by the chief justice of the Supreme Court and including a former head of the CIA, the Warren Commission took evidence from 552 witnesses and reviewed over 3,100 exhibits. After ten months the report came out in 888 pages. As a character comments in *Libra* (1988), Don DeLillo's masterpiece on the plot to kill Kennedy, the Warren report was the book James Joyce would have written if he'd moved to Iowa City and lived to be a hundred.

The report's findings, that Lee Harvey Oswald had acted alone and without assistance when he shot the president from the sixth floor of the Texas School Book Depository, quickly came to be disbelieved. What about the persistent reports that shots had also come from the 'grassy knoll' to the right of the motorcade track? How could Oswald have got three shots spot on the target in the documented time, using an old bolt-action rifle? And how convenient that Jack Ruby, with his Mafia connections, should have been allowed into the Dallas police headquarters just two days later, only to draw a revolver and shoot Oswald dead.

To keep him from talking? Who was covering up what? That black underground river of paranoia, so abundant in America, soon boiled to the surface. A whole library of books following the assassination and its aftermath tried to implicate Cuban exiles (following the failure of the Bay of Pigs 'invasion'), the CIA, the Mafia (in retaliation for the heat being put on the Mob by the president's brother, Attorney General Robert Kennedy), J. Edgar Hoover, Lyndon B. Johnson, the Russians, even the Israelis.

As for creative writers, the problem was, as Philip Roth had argued only three years earlier, reality in mid-century America was outpacing the imagination of the most ambitious fictioneer. 'The actuality is constantly outdoing our talents', he wrote, 'and the culture tosses up figures almost daily that are the envy of any novelist.'*

So Norman Mailer abandoned fiction altogether for his *Oswald's Tale* (1995), as he had for *The Executioner's Song* (1980), his massive treatment of the Gary Gilmore story (see 17 January). James Ellroy's *American Tabloid* (1995) mixes fictional characters and real-life-figures in an intricate plot involving the CIA, the FBI and the Mafia colluding over a six-year period leading up to the assassination.

The best so far has been *Libra* – like *American Tabloid* a fact-fiction, but one that deepens in seriousness because it explores paranoia within the context of plots both conspiratorial and fictional. DeLillo's imaginative hypothesis is that the CIA made the plot to kill Kennedy look as though it came from Cuba – not to succeed but only to push him into declaring all-out war on that country. Coincidence and intention interact to turn the plan lethal, but then it is the nature of plots to run their course, and all plots lead to death.

If that were all it had to say, *Libra* would be a poor abstraction. Its real strength lies in old-fashioned novelistic attention to detail: what people eat and wear, the contents of their refrigerators and car boots – above all, how they speak. Marguerite, Oswald's mother, drifts through

---

* Philip Roth, 'Writing American Fiction', in *Reading Myself and Others,* New York: Farrar, Straus and Giroux, 1975.

the novel in fragments of an unstoppable address to an imagined judge ('I am the mother in the case, your honor'). She's strong on her dignity:

> I was sitting pretty in our American slang, managing Princess Hosiery, when Mr Ekdahl proposed in the car. I made him wait a year and he was a Harvard man.

And on Lee's care for his mother:

> I have a story to tell. He came home with a birdcage that had a stand with a planter. It had ivy in the planter, it had the cage, it had the parakeet, it had a complete set of food for the parakeet. This boy bought gifts for his mother.

DeLillo used the transcripts of the Warren hearings as a contemporary reinvention of the Federal Writers' Project life histories (see 7 July and 27 July). What he shows is that the true dialogue of the underdog is monologue, because no one cares enough to listen – let alone reply.

30 November

A comet blazes, Mark Twain is born. It blazes again at his death

1835 Two days after Samuel L. Clemens's (i.e. Mark Twain's) death, a reader wrote to the *New York Times* to draw the editor's attention 'to a peculiar coincidence'.

> Mark Twain, born Nov. 30, 1835.
> Last perihelion of Halley's comet, Nov. 10, 1835.
> Mark Twain died, April 21, 1910.
> Perihelion of Halley's comet, April 20, 1910.

'It so appears', the paper's correspondent pointed out, 'that the lifetime of the great humorist was nearly identical (the difference being exactly fifteen days) with the last long "year" of the great comet'.

In fact the coincidence was noted, and actually predicted, by the writer himself, recollecting, doubtless, with some justified self-importance the line from Shakespeare's *Julius Caesar*: 'When beggars die, then are no comets seen / The heavens themselves blaze forth the death of princes.'

Thirty years before he died, an 1881 interview with Twain was published under the title 'Mark Twain's Preparations for a Possible Encounter With the Comet'. In 1909, as his angina worsened, he made the much quoted remark:

> I came in with Halley's Comet in 1835. It is coming again next year [1910], and I expect to go out with it. It will be the greatest disappointment of my life if I don't go out with Halley's Comet. The Almighty has said, no doubt: 'Now here are these two unaccountable freaks; they came in together, they must go out together'. Oh, I am looking forward to that.

That Twain came into this world and left it along with Halley's comet is universally noted as one of the pleasing symmetries of literature. Astrology and literary history rarely concur so neatly.

But is it neat? A spoilsport article by Louis J. Budd, 'Overbooking Halley's Comet' (in the *Mark Twain Circular*, January 2000), modifies and – arguably – overturns the coincidence of birth, death, and comet. According to Budd, Twain's Halleyan entrance and exit works 'only if we arrange the facts loosely'. He goes on:

> Astronomers use perihelion as one of the pivotal (no pun) dates of its schedule. That's when its orbit comes closest to the sun. However, rubberneck fans of the comet date its fly-bys by its visibility without a telescope ... In 1835 such visibility began in very late September, peaked on 9 October in England, and faded out before the end of that month (track 'Comet' through the precisely indexed London *Times*). An astronomer in New England calculated that visibility would peak there on 16 October ... Perihelion occurred on 15 November, and the next Clemens baby [i.e. Twain] arrived on the 30th.
>
> In 1910 the earliest, dim sighting without telescope was claimed for 29 April. Visibility in New York City – at a commuting distance from Redding, Connecticut [where Twain died] – peaked on 18 May. Twain had died on 21 April, the day after perihelion.

Budd's observations about observation seem irrefutable. But literary history will always prefer to 'arrange the facts loosely'.

1 December

American Declaration of Independence (e-text version) proclaimed

1971 Johannes Gutenberg, pioneer of the Western printing press, chose the Bible as his first major text in c. 1455. Some 180 copies were run off and the history of the world changed by an apparatus that, to the untutored eye, looked like a cider press. Copies of the first Gutenberg Bibles sold at 30 florins in Gutenberg's native Mainz – which restricted circulation to wealthy or institutional purchasers. The Latin text was no more universally readable than the earlier manuscript codex versions, whose layout and script Gutenberg simulated exactly. But the technology was infinitely liberating.

Five hundred and sixteen years after Gutenberg's Bible, Michael S. Hart launched 'Project Gutenberg'. At the time, Hart was a graduate student at the University of Illinois. The mainframe computer he had access to was stone-age, technologically, but he managed to wangle virtually unlimited time and space on it.

Hart mobilised a team of volunteers to archive, digitally, the great books of the English language. Until 1990 they were manually key-boarded and mostly transliterated into basic 256-character ASCII computer script (some HTML versions were also available). Optical recognition apparatus made later transcription more efficient.

Hart's all-volunteer army (a genuine 'point of light') was dependent principally on graduate labour, which by the early 21st century had compiled an e-textual library of 120,000 titles, growing all the time.

In 2000, the project was institutionalised as a non-profit organisa-tion and, as such, was able to attract tax-deductible charitable dona-tions. The texts (almost all in the public domain) were offered, free of charge, to any reader with computer access to them.

Educationally, Project Gutenberg was a godsend. Prescribed read-ing for advanced courses (hitherto impeded by the high cost of printed textbooks) could expand hugely. Despite some rough edges, erroneous transcription, and imperfect bibliographical accompanying data, PG texts were adequate to most teaching purposes. The project remains true to Hart's original belief that getting the material out takes prec-edence over scholarly punctilios and that free texts make for better learning.

Johannes Gutenberg launched his medieval project with the Bible. In as grand, and as democratic a gesture ('let the people read'), Michael Hart chose, as his primal text, the American Declaration of Independence, released on 1 December 1971. 4 July might, perhaps, have been too neat.

2 December

Would Jane Bigg-Wither have written better, or worse, or not at all?

1802 Jane Austen went to the grave a virgin, leaving six full-length novels behind her. Would those novels have been better had Miss Austen had as lively a sex-life as, say, slutty Lydia Bennet? Does a writer's carnal experience matter? D.H. Lawrence, the most unzipped of British novelists, believed it did. His chauvinist sneer at Austen as a 'narrow gutted spinster' indicates that some sexual intercourse would have improved her fiction no end.

One can only wonder, and focus that wonder on this day, in winter 1802, when the 20-year-old Harris Bigg-Wither proposed marriage to the 27-year-old Jane Austen. He did so in the impressive surroundings of his family home, Manydown Park in Hampshire. Harris was the heir to the estate and could expect to be very well provided-for. He was eminently eligible and a catch for a well brought-up, but not well-dowered, parson's daughter who – like Anne Elliot at 27 – might be thought to have lost her youthful 'bloom'. Harris was accepted. The fact was known to the families, who rejoiced. Then, after what one must suppose was a sleepless night, Jane rejected her young fiancé the following day. One of the shortest engagements in literature was at an end. The Austen company fled in a coach the same day.

It is not known why Miss Austen changed her mind. It might be that she was put off by Harris's recorded clumsiness of person and manner. She may also have been put off by the prospect of children – something one can suspect from hints in Emma Woodhouse's distaste for marriage, having seen her sister Isabella's child-a-year ordeal after her marriage to John Knightley. Harris Bigg-Wither, on the rebound, married two years later. His wife bore him ten children.

Austen's greatest fiction – at least in its final, canonical form – was still to come. The biographer Claire Tomalin has little doubt that the world has reason to be grateful for that doubt-tossed night in December 1802. 'We would naturally rather have *Mansfield Park* and *Emma* than the Bigg-Wither baby Jane Austen might have given the world.' Or ten Bigg-Wither babies, come to that.

3 December

A Streetcar Named Desire *opens at the Ethel Barrymore Theater on Broadway, launching the career of 23-year-old Marlon Brando*

1947 'They told me to take a streetcar named Desire, and then transfer to one called Cemeteries and ride six blocks and get off at – Elysian Fields.' These are the first lines spoken by Blanche Dubois, 'daintily dressed', according to the stage directions, 'in a white suit with a fluffy bodice, necklace and earrings of pearl, white gloves and a hat', in Tennessee Williams's classic melodrama, set in the working-class Faubourg Marigny of New Orleans.

Arriving to stay with her sister Stella, Blanche is perplexed. Can this slum with the L&M Railroad tracks running through it really be the 'Elysian Fields'? Blanche commiserates with her sister, but has her own grief to tell, in a powerful speech about relatives seen through their dying moments, and their gracious southern mansion in ruins. When Stella's husband Stanley Kowalski comes in from a night of bowling, the explosive triangle is complete: the faded beauty living in the past, the robust, rough-hewn working-class son of Polish immigrants, and his submissive wife.

Playing Stanley Kowalski, Marlon Brando method-acted his way to stardom, scowling, snarling, bullying, slamming doors, and finally drunkenly forcing himself on Blanche, saying: 'We've had this date from the beginning.' Elia Kazan, who directed the first production, later took him to the film version (1951), in which Vivien Leigh supplanted Jessica Tandy as Blanche, then on to *Viva Zapata* (1952) and *On the Waterfront* (1954).

Meanwhile, Brando brought the method to Mark Antony's 'Friends, Romans, countrymen' speech in Joseph Manciewicz's film production of *Julius Caesar* (1953), before donning the gear and a menacing air as leader of a motorcycle gang in *The Wild One* (1953), directed by Laslo Benedek. The film started a world-wide craze for leathers and 'cycle boots' – not to mention widespread anxiety about where 'the youth of today' were heading.

All of these have lasted better than *Streetcar*, which now seems a little dated in posing the illusions of the past against the vibrant realities of the present, when the lively culture of the white working class itself now seems to belong to the past.

4 December

Currer Bell meets Michaelangelo Titmarsh

1849 The composition and publication of Charlotte Brontë's *Jane Eyre* is the stuff of book trade legend. The parson's daughter in Yorkshire had sent an unsolicited manuscript, under androgynous pseudonym ('Currer Bell') to the eminent London publisher, Smith, Elder & Co., in early 1847. The work (later published as *The Professor*) was judged unpublishable, but Smith, Elder asked if he/she might like to think about submitting a longer, three-volume work for the circulating library market. Brontë set to and produced *Jane Eyre* in a few weeks. Published late in 1847, it was one of the literary sensations of the year (a year that also saw the publication of *Vanity Fair*, *Dombey and Son*, and *Wuthering Heights* – by 'Ellis Bell').

A second edition was called for, and was published in February 1848. To it Brontë (still pseudonymous) attached an extraordinarily eulogistic preface (dated 27 December 1847) dedicating her novel to Thackeray, whom she had never met:

> There is a man in our own days whose words are not framed to tickle delicate ears: who, to my thinking, comes before the great ones of society, much as the son of Imlah came before the throned Kings of Judah and Israel; and who speaks truth as deep, with a power as prophet-like and as vital – a mien as dauntless and as daring. Is the satirist of *Vanity Fair* admired in high places? I cannot tell; but I think if some of those amongst whom he hurls the Greek fire of his sarcasm, and over whom he flashes

the levin-brand of his denunciation, were to take his warnings in time – they or their seed might yet escape a fatal Rimoth-Gilead.

The 'son of Imlah' had, like the rest of literary London, devoured *Jane Eyre* in a single delighted sitting. Thackeray also perceived, as did everyone else, that the author must be a woman, and a remarkable one. As it happened, the dedication was profoundly embarrassing to him. Thackeray's wife, Isabella, had lost her mind three years earlier and, after several suicide attempts, was currently in care. It was suspiciously like the situation of Rochester and Bertha Mason. Rumours swept around London, in the wake of Brontë's preface, that 'Currer Bell' was a former governess (Thackeray had two young daughters) and lover of the author of *Vanity Fair*. It did not help that 'Laura Bell' (acoustically very similar) was the name of the most famous, and highly paid, courtesan in London (Thackeray mischievously used the name for the indomitably virtuous heroine of his next novel, *Pendennis*).

The two novelists did not meet in person until Brontë made a daring trip to London, at the invitation of Smith, Elder (who had recently recruited Thackeray to their list) in December 1849. Charlotte described the encounter with Thackeray, on the fourth of the month, to her father, in a letter:

> As to being happy, I am under scenes and circumstances of excitement; but I suffer acute pain sometimes, – mental pain, I mean. At the moment Mr Thackeray presented himself, I was thoroughly faint from inanition, having eaten nothing since a very slight breakfast, and it was then seven o'clock in the evening. Excitement and exhaustion made savage work of me that evening. What he thought of me I cannot tell.

He found her tiny and amusing. Charlotte confided other details to her friend, and biographer, Elizabeth Gaskell. Thackeray, she quickly apprehended, was not the Old Testament, lightning-bolt-bearing prophet she had pictured in her preface: 'She told me how difficult she found it, this first time of meeting Mr Thackeray, to decide whether he was speaking in jest or in earnest.'

A few days later the novelists met for a second time. Thackeray had written for ten years disguised under pseudonyms, such as 'Michaelangelo Titmarsh', before, with *Vanity Fair*, actually putting his name on a title page. He advised 'Currer Bell' to drop the pseudonymous mask, and appear to her readers in her own person. If nothing else it would inhibit gossip and nasty rumours.

5 December

Burton concludes his great work (not for the only time)

1620 In the epilogue to the manuscript of his great work, Robert Burton inscribed, with a terseness atypical of his usual style: 'From my Studie in *Christ Church Oxon*. Decemb. 5 1620.' The work he had finished was: *The Anatomy of Melancholy, What it is: With all the Kinds, Causes, Symptomes, Prognostickes, and Several Cures of it. In Three Maine Partitions with their several Sections, Members, and Subsections. Philosophically, Historically, Opened and Cut up.*

The contents are as sprawling and ambitiously wide-ranging as the title. Burton published a first version in 1621 that ran to 353,369 words. Three years later he published an enlarged version comprising 423,983 words. Four more editions followed. No classic text is more fluid and, until computer typesetting (as superintended by Thomas Faulkner – a scholarly life's work), no complete *Anatomy* has been compiled.

The *Anatomy* has always posed insoluble problems for the Dewey Decimal Library Classification system. What exactly is it? It purports to be a work of psychology. But its contents are a compendium of learned knowledge and reference – an anatomy less of medicine than of the well-stored, not to say over-stuffed, Renaissance mind. Librarians usually shelve it in 'English Literature'. Arguably it is itself the condensation of a whole library. It was, Samuel Johnson (a notorious slugabed) recorded, the only book which ever inspired him to get up early. The style – which modulates between the Ciceronian (expansive) and Senecan (epigrammatic) models – qualifies *The Anatomy* as a genuine, if eccentric, work of literature.

Burton describes his titular subject in the third paragraph of his first 'Partition', or section:

> Great travail is created for all men, and an heavy yoke on the sons of Adam, from the day that they go out of their mother's womb, unto that day they return to the mother of all things.

Namely, their thoughts, and fear of their hearts, and their imagination of things they wait for, and the day of death. From him that sitteth in the glorious throne, to him that sitteth beneath in the earth and ashes; from him that is clothed in blue silk and weareth a crown, to him that is clothed in simple linen. Wrath, envy, trouble, and unquietness, and fear of death, and rigour, and strife, and such things come to both man and beast, but sevenfold to the ungodly. All this befalls him in this life, and peradventure eternal misery in the life to come.

A number of contemporary admirers have seen Burton's world-weariness, and his fascination with what subsequent medicine labels 'depression', as psychotherapeutically perceptive and ahead of its time. It is not impossible to align *The Anatomy* with the arguments in Freud's essay 'Civilisation and its Discontents'. The more we know, the more comfortable our circumstances become (Burton's condition of life as an Oxford vicar and 'student' – i.e. fellow – of Christ Church was eminently comfortable), the unhappier we become. There are virtually no events recorded in his long, scholarly life.

It is, however, the sheer eccentricity of *The Anatomy* that perennially beguiles. The prescription, for example, for the cure of 'Love-Melancholy' in ladies:

Those opposite meats which ought to be used are cucumbers, melons, purslane, water-lilies, rue, woodbine, ammi, lettuce, which Lemnius so much commends, lib. 2, cap. 42. and Mizaldus hort. med. to this purpose; vitex, or agnus castus before the rest, which, saith Magninus, hath a wonderful virtue in it. Those Athenian women, in their solemn feasts called Thesmopheries, were to abstain nine days from the company of men, during which time, saith Aelian, they laid a certain herb, named hanea, in their beds, which assuaged those ardent flames of love, and freed them from the torments of that violent passion. See more in Porta, Matthiolus, Crescentius lib. 5. &c., and what every herbalist almost and physician hath written, cap. de Satyriasi et Priapismo; Rhasis amongst the rest.

Preferable, perhaps, to the modern cold shower.

6 December

Hopkins's 'great dragon'

1875 Gerard Manley Hopkins is, with T.S. Eliot, the most influential poet of the 20th century. Had his career in literature been his primary vocation he might have been the most influential poet of the 19th century, in which he lived and died.

A Jesuit priest, Hopkins wrote quantities of verse, a small fragment of which was entrusted, by letter, to his friend Robert Bridges. That fragment is, alas, all that has survived. Hopkins, under instruction from his superiors and his own sense of religious duty, destroyed the bulk of his work. Ironically, Bridges – a Poet Laureate and immensely popular in his own day for bestselling works such as *The Testament of Beauty* – is remembered, today, for one thing only. He saved some of the poetry of Hopkins.

Hopkins died in 1889: wholly unknown to the reading public. Bridges belatedly published the surviving corpus of his friend's poems in 1918. The opening poem in the collection, 'The Wreck of the *Deutschland*', Hopkins's longest, was what Bridges called 'a great dragon folded in the gate to forbid all entrance'. The opening stanza indicates clearly enough what Bridges meant:

> THOU mastering me
> God! giver of breath and bread;
> World's strand, sway of the sea;
> Lord of living and dead;
> Thou hast bound bones and veins in me, fastened me flesh,
> And after it almost unmade, what with dread,
> Thy doing: and dost thou touch me afresh?
> Over again I feel thy finger and find thee.

The dragonish difficulty of the poem lies principally in Hopkins's innovative prosody ('sprung rhythm') and the complexity of his literary expression – something alien both to the norms of Victorian poetry (when it was written) and Georgian poetry (when it was published).

The poem has an explanatory dedication:

> *To the*
> *happy memory of five Franciscan nuns*

> *exiles by the Falk Laws*
> *drowned between midnight and morning of*
> *Dec. 7th, 1875*

On 4 December 1875 the steamship *Deutschland* left Bremerhaven in Germany for New York, via Southampton. Among the passengers were five Franciscan nuns, fleeing Bismarck's anti-Catholic Falk Laws, part of a programmatic campaign (the so-called *Kulturkampf*) to secularise – more specifically de-Catholicise – the country. They intended to resettle in a religious community in Illinois.

The vessel ran into a storm and ran aground on a shoal (the Kentish Knock). This was 5 December. Distress rockets attracted no attention from passing ships. The next day the order was given to abandon ship. The lifeboats were inadequate, and one sank. Of the 213 souls on board the *Deutschland*, only 135 made it to safety (embarrassingly, the captain was one of them – prompting a high-profile court of enquiry: which exonerated him).

Among those drowned were the five Franciscan nuns. Why, Hopkins's poem ponders, would God persecute the already persecuted in this way? They are, the poem concludes, martyrs. Their suffering is an extreme form of the discipline ('mastering') they had chosen as their life with their vows.

Hopkins was, unusually, encouraged to write the poem by his religious superior; but, in the event, it was deemed unpublishable. Bridges, normally sympathetic, concurred. He would not, he told his friend, read it again 'for any money'. Then read it for love, Hopkins (good-naturedly) replied.

7 December

Harold Pinter hurls his stick of Nobel dynamite at America and Britain

2005 Harold Pinter was too weakened by the oesophageal cancer that would kill him three years later to accept in person his Nobel Prize for Literature in 2005. In a departure from tradition, he prepared a video to be shown at the ceremony at the Swedish Academy in Stockholm on 7 December.

The award was made eighteen months after the invasion of Iraq by coalition forces. The event had provoked the largest street protest ever witnessed in London, on 15 February 2003 (the event is commemorated in one of the novels of the period, Ian McEwan's *Saturday*).

It was widely suspected that the award to Pinter was double-edged. He was Britain's greatest living playwright. But he had also taken a public stance against the Iraq war and for the Palestinian people's struggle – formally linked with Iraq in the 15 February demonstration.

If there were a political motive, Pinter rose to it in his video address. His theme was that current political administrations – notably those of Bush and Blair – used language 'to keep thought at bay'. It was the responsibility of the writer to protect language from this political degradation, to keep words open as a channel for honest thought.

Pinter's linguistic plea made less impact than his furious *j'accuse* against the warmongering leaders of the so-called 'Free World'.

> We have brought torture, cluster bombs, depleted uranium, innumerable acts of random murder, misery, degradation and death to the Iraqi people and call it 'bringing freedom and democracy to the Middle East'.
>
> How many people do you have to kill before you qualify to be described as a mass murderer and a war criminal? One hundred thousand? More than enough, I would have thought. Therefore it is just that Bush and Blair be arraigned before the International Criminal Court of Justice.

They weren't.

8 December

The Saturday Evening Post *publishes Zora Neale Hurston's* 'A Negro Voter Sizes up Taft'

1951 The disconnect between the talent and politics of one of the best African-American writers of the 20th century has posed a puzzle, if not a problem, for her admirers. Senator Robert A. Taft was a principled conservative. He had opposed the New Deal and America's involvement in the Second World War (at least until Pearl Harbor), and – over

Harry Truman's veto – written and steered through Congress the Taft–Hartley Act banning closed shops and enforcing an 80-day 'cooling off' period when an impending strike threatened the national interest. Now he was seeking the Republican nomination for president, which in seven months' time he would lose narrowly to Dwight D. Eisenhower.

Hurston, who had also opposed the New Deal and Roosevelt's interventionist foreign policy, and would go on to argue against the de-segregation of southern schools in 1954, saw Taft as the reincarnation of Thomas Jefferson. Liberals may not see it that way, she wrote, but that was because 'the word "liberal" is now an unstable and devious thing in connotation' and has come to be associated with 'a person who desires greater Government control and Federal handouts'.

Was this another case, like John Steinbeck, of the early radical's political arteries hardening in middle age? After all, Hurston was a central figure in the Harlem Renaissance, energetically promoting the work of black writers, and in 1938 even went to work for the New Deal's Federal Writers' Project (see 27 July), editing the state guidebook for Florida.

Not necessarily. Things in her youth and training contributed to her conservatism. She grew up in the first all-black town to be incorporated in America, where she could live free of the constraints of white society. Her later education at Barnard College, New York (where she was on a scholarship, the only black in the student body) pointed her increasingly towards anthropology and ethnography. In 1937 she was granted a Guggenheim Fellowship to conduct ethnographic research in Haiti and Jamaica.

Hurston wrote her greatest work, *Their Eyes Were Watching God* (1937), while doing that field work, and it shows. It's not that the characters in the novel talk like Haitians or Jamaicans – they don't, of course – but that the author's ear was so trained to register accents and speech rhythms that she could do the sound of southern black dialogue with complete assurance:

> 'Wid you heah [says Jody to Janie in *Their Eyes*], Ah oughtn't ta hafta do all dat lookin' and searchin'. Ah done told you time and time agin tuh stick all dem papers on dat nail! All you got tuh do is mind me. How come you can't do lak Ah tell yuh?'

Apparently confusing this for something out of *Uncle Remus*, Richard Wright thought it amounted to a 'quaint' exhibit put on for a

condescrisy white audience. Other old Harlem Renaissance associ-
ates deplored her lack of political subject matter, her apparent indifference to the struggle for black advancement. But Hurston felt secure
in her blackness, didn't feel it needed to be 'advanced', and suspected
– as Wright himself would come to realise (see 7 May) – that her left-
wing friends had been slotting 'the Negro', as an undifferentiated bloc,
into that gap left by the missing American proletariat so necessary to
European communist theory.

Her work forgotten, Hurston died a pauper and was buried in
an unmarked grave in 1960. By the mid-1970s a new generation of
black novelists began to notice her work – women like Alice Walker,
Maya Angelou and Toni Morrison, who were proving that the African-
American experience was not confined to issues of racial and political
struggle. Walker's 'In Search of Zora Neale Hurston', published in the
March 1975 issue of *Ms* magazine, brought her work to life again.

9 December

Peanuts *gets its first of many outings on television*

1965 With *A Charlie Brown Christmas*, America's most popular cartoon strip took to the air. Over half of the country's television sets were
tuned to the half-hour cartoon produced and directed by the former
Warner Brothers animator Bill Menéndez. The theme was the discovery of the true meaning of Christmas beneath the tinsel, the buying
and selling, and the highly organised secular festivities.

Though Snoopy the Beagle enters wholeheartedly into festooning
his doghouse as part of a competition for best Christmas decorations,
the girls in the story – always the iconoclasts – have already faced down
the hypocrisy behind the season's gift-giving. Lucy van Pelt doesn't
want a 'lot of stupid toys' for Christmas; she wants real estate. Sally
Brown dictates a letter to Santa asking him to 'just send money', pref-
erably in tens and twenties.

It's left to Sally's older brother Charlie, always the worrier, to puzzle over the meaning of Christmas, to roll back both the cynicism
and the commercialised sentiment. After he buys a tiny tree, the only
living thing in a lot featuring plastic and aluminium imitations, the
other kids join in the search for authenticity, borrowing from Snoopy's

prize-winning decorations to adorn the vulnerable plant, after Lucy's brother Linus recites the gospel account of Christ's birth.

The fact that *A Charlie Brown Christmas* was itself a species of commercialised sentiment didn't prevent its winning an Emmy and a Peabody Award for excellence in radio and television – and probably ensured that it would go on being shown and seen as a perennial Christmas favourite. But the real story behind the programme's success was the enduring popularity of the strip itself, Charles Schultz's *Peanuts*, which appeared over half a century in (at its peak) over 2,600 newspapers, read by 3.5 million people in 75 countries.

Peanuts started back in 1950, when American Sunday papers all had their cartoon strips set apart in brightly coloured comic sections. Popular strips included the very different humour of *The Captain and the Kids* and *Li'l Abner*, but not all were funny. Some, like *Dick Tracy* and *Flash Gordon*, followed detective or adventure plots. *The Captain* was a comedy of situation, while *Dick Tracy* and *Li'l Abner* told a serial story, to be continued the next week.

Peanuts was both comic and serial, which meant that, in the words of Robert Thompson, professor of popular culture at Syracuse University, it grew into 'arguably the longest story ever told by one human being'. It also carried the plot into four-panel monochrome strips in the daily papers, which widened its social and economic readership beyond the usual 'funny pages' audience.

What made it so popular? Partly the way it reversed expectations. The characters were drawn as children, but their dialogue was adult. Or rather, they interacted as kids but moved into adult concerns. Girls were mean to boys rather than the other way round. They didn't always succeed – the strip was very un-American in that way, and quite unlike the usual English children's story too. Charlie Brown managed a Little League baseball team that never won a game – except when for some reason he couldn't play.

Why did *Peanuts* endure? Its longevity must have had a lot to do with its running gags: Lucy's sidewalk booth selling not lemonade – the usual kids' venture – but psychiatric advice, for 5¢ a throw; Linus's security blanket; Schroeder playing Beethoven on his toy piano; Snoopy on top of his doghouse, forever fantasising about being a First World War flying ace; Lucy holding a football for Charlie Brown to kick, then pulling it away at the last minute, causing him to cartwheel backwards and land on his head – and Charlie Brown falling for the trick again and again.

10 December

Mikhail Sholokhov collects his Nobel Prize for Literature in Stockholm: how an apparatchik became an unperson

1965 The Nobel for Literature has frequently proved controversial, for which read curious, at best. So many criteria, whether diplomatic, political or whatever, have to be considered along with literary quality that the judges' choice often diverges from that of posterity.

Among those never awarded the prize were Leo Tolstoy, Henry James, Emile Zola, Franz Kafka, Graham Greene, Jorge Luis Borges and Norman Mailer. Meanwhile, the winners included Henryk Sienkiewicz, Romain Rolland, Sinclair Lewis, Pearl Buck, Harry Martinson and Selma Ottilia Lovisa Lagerlöf.

Is Sholokhov another of those now forgotten literary laureates? Yes, but not because of literary quality. His *And Quiet Flows the Don* (1934), an epic sweep across Russian life during a time of fundamental change, has often been compared to *War and Peace* – with some claim to justice.

The book has also been cited repeatedly as a masterpiece of Soviet realism, which isn't the same kind of praise, of course, but at least meant that he wouldn't lack for home-grown accolades. As well as the Nobel, Sholokhov won the Stalin Prize in 1941, and was much rewarded by the Stalinist state in other ways. He was elected to the Supreme Soviet, to the Central Committee of the Soviet Communist party, made an Academician of the USSR Academy of Sciences, a Hero of Socialist Labour (twice), and elected Vice President of the Association of Soviet Writers.

As an establishment figure, Sholokhov also seems to have played a dubious role in the country's cultural struggles. For example, he supported the sentences of seven and five years respectively handed down to dissident writers Andrey Sinyavsky and Yuli Daniel for 'anti-Soviet activity', and approved the persecution of Alexandr Solzhenitsyn.

Solzhenitsyn himself (Nobel, 1970) in turn accused Sholokhov of plagiarising most of *And Quiet Flows the Don*. His evidence was circumstantial, but Sholokhov had lost his notes and early drafts, so couldn't prove his authorship conclusively. In 1984 two Norwegian scholars demonstrated through statistical analyses that Sholokhov was indeed the likely author of the book, and in 1987 the lost notes and drafts – several thousand pages of them – were discovered and authenticated.

But the world didn't relent: *And Quiet Flows the Don* has long been out of print. Orlando Figes, in his monumental cultural history of Russia, *Natasha's Dance* (2002), devotes not one word to Sholokhov.

11 December

Damon Runyon tells it as it is as he takes off for the poker game in the sky

1946 If Damon Runyon is remembered at all, it is primarily as the author of the short story (in fact two of them) later adapted as the movie and stage musical *Guys and Dolls*.

Runyon (1880–1946), the laureate of Manhattan, was, ironically, born in Manhattan: the difference being that it was Manhattan, Kansas. The Runyons were a newspaper family and, after some service in the Spanish–American War, Damon moved to New York, where he became a sports journalist, specialising in boxing and baseball. His chosen friends – outside the newsroom and the sports arena – were mobsters, bootleggers and what were euphemistically called 'colourful' metropolitan types.

In addition to his reportage, Runyon wrote short stories for the papers, centred around characters such as Harry the Horse, Liverlips Louie, the Lemon Drop Kid and Nick the Greek (Runyon was masterfully creative with nicknames – it was he who gave heavyweight champion James J. Braddock the label 'Cinderella Man'). Runyon's narratives, invariably comic in tone, were rich in slang and comically romanticised criminality.

Runyon died of throat cancer. The obituaries were instructed to say so. As his son, Damon Runyon Jr., records: 'As far as I know my father was the first person of note whose death was attributed publicly and bluntly to cancer.' Runyon Sr. hated the common euphemism 'lingering illness'.

On 11 December 1946, to the family's distress ('a shocking breach of trust'), Runyon's comrade in the newspaper world, Walter Winchell, could not resist the scoop of releasing – the day after Runyon's death – his final wishes as to the disposition of his body. He wanted to be cremated, and his ashes thrown from an aeroplane over Manhattan.

It involved the family in vexing disputes with the authorities, who had strict sanitary rules against the dumping of dirt (however distinguished). On 18 December the First World War ace, Eddie Rickenbacker (about whom Runyon had written a book in 1942), arranged for Eastern Airlines, of which he was CEO, to do as Runyon had wished. Rickenbacker himself tipped the ashes from the urn as the plane wheeled around the Statue of Liberty.

Runyon, shortly before he died, said that he when he 'woke up dead' he hoped to find himself with a good hand in an infernal poker game.

12 December

Edgar Wallace sees Hollywood and dies

1931 Richard Horatio Edgar Wallace was born in 1874 on April Fools' Day, spectacularly illegitimate. He was the child of a touring actress: a second-line performer in a third-rate troupe, Mary Jane 'Polly' Richards. A young widow at the time of her son's conception, she surrendered her virtue at a drunken party to the company's romantic lead, Richard Horatio Edgar.

Edgar claimed not to remember the encounter. Polly sneaked away to bear her shameful offspring in secret in Greenwich. Barely hours after birth, the boy-child was farmed out to the family of an amenable Billingsgate fishmonger who brought him up as 'Richard Freeman'.

Smart as paint, young Dick earned an honest penny as a printer's devil, a newspaper vendor, and – as an early photograph indicates – a villainous-looking milk van boy. He was dismissed from the last position for lifting a few dishonest pennies from the coin bag. Cash was always his great weakness.

Aged eighteen, Edgar enrolled in the army under the name Wallace. Trained in the infantry, he was shipped to South Africa, in 1896, and wangled a transfer into the Medical Corps. It was a cushy berth. In 1899, as the war with the Boers broke out, Wallace (no fool) married a local girl and bought himself out.

By this point Wallace had cultivated contacts in the press. On his return to Britain he took up work with the *Daily Mail*. In 1905 he produced his first novel, *The Four Just Men*. The idea was ingenious. Four cosmopolitan vigilantes, of impeccable breeding, set out to overthrow Britain's xenophobic 'Aliens Act' (Wallace was always a champion of the underdog). The narrative pivots on a locked room mystery. The home secretary is warned that unless he liberalises the legislation, he will die. The minister ensconces himself in his Portland Place office, surrounded by guards. He is assassinated. But how?

Wallace, still slaving as a hack and a racing tipster (his preferred occupation), picked a winner in 1911 with his next serious foray into fiction: 'Sanders of the River'. Before being sacked by *Daily Mail* owner Lord Northcliffe (furious at the never-ending libel suits his star reporter incited) he had been dispatched to the Belgian Congo – the heart of darkness. He span out of this experience a series of adventure tales, chronicling Mr Commissioner Sanders' mission to bring 'civilisation' to 'half a million cannibal folk' with his Maxim machine gun and Houssa storm-troopers.

Wallace came into his own as a mass producer of fiction in 1920. His agent, A.P. Watt, negotiated a sweet deal with the publisher Hodder and Stoughton for what was, effectively, a fiction assembly line. H&S would pay him £250 advance (around the national annual wage at the time for people born in Wallace's station of life) for any and every title. Wallace rose to the challenge, with 150 novels over the next 25 years. All he needed was his Dictaphone (he hated the labour of actually writing), pyjamas, a freshly brewed pot of tea every half hour (heavily sugared), and his cigarette holder, nearly a foot long, to keep the smoke from his 80-odd cigarettes a day out of his eyes.

He boasted he never walked more than four miles a year (and then only between bookies at the track). He feared draughts and went to extreme measures to protect himself against them. He travelled habitually in a closed Rolls Royce; his windows were kept shut in all but the warmest weather, and he wore two sets of underwear.

In financial difficulty, despite his vast income, Wallace accepted Hollywood's lucre in 1931 and arrived there on 12 December. RKO loved him. A new career, even more splendid, was in prospect. He set to work on a story about a giant ape he had devised, *King Kong*.

He was never to finish. On 10 February as he waited, impatiently, for the Hollywood starlet who would warm his bed that night, Wallace fell into a terminal diabetic coma (sweet tea did for him – he was teetotal). He left huge debts, and some grieving turf accountants. The bells tolled and flags in Fleet Street were lowered when his body returned. His personal verdict on his life's achievement was blunt: 'The good stuff may be all right for posterity. But I'm not writing for posterity.'

King Kong, nonetheless, has found considerable favour with later generations – miniscule as Edgar Wallace's credits are on the various film versions.

13 December

E.M. Forster finds salvation

1913 The most important event in the personal life of E.M. Forster was his meeting with Edward Carpenter – the early evangelist for gay (or, as he called it, 'Uranian') emancipation – in 1913. The 35-year-old Forster discovered Carpenter to be his 'saviour'. It was, however, another of the 'Carpenterians', as Forster later recalled, George Merrill (Carpenter's lover), who worked the saving miracle on him:

> Carpenter … was a socialist who ignored industrialism and a simple-lifer with an independent income and a … believer in the love of comrades, whom he sometimes called Uranians. It was this last aspect of him that attracted me in my loneliness. … I approached him … as one approaches a saviour. It must have been on my second or third visit to the shrine that the spark was kindled as he and his comrade George Merrill combined to make a profound impression on me and to touch a creative spring. George Merrill also touched my backside – gently and just above the buttocks. … The sensation was unusual and I still remember it as I remember the position of a long-vanished tooth. It was as much psychological as physical. It seemed to go straight through the small of my back into my ideas, without involving my thoughts.

As Sheila Rowbotham recounts (in her 2009 biography of Carpenter), Merrill's touch triggered a creative release in the novelist. On 13 December 1913 he commemorated it in his diary, with the jubilant entry: 'Forward rather than back, Edward Carpenter! Edward Carpenter! Edward Carpenter!'

One result of this new forward-looking mood was his *Bildungsroman* about growing up gay in Edwardian England, *Maurice*. The novel transcribes much of Forster's experiences growing up, and at Cambridge.

As obviously, Maurice's proletarian lover, Alec Scudder, is based on George Merrill.

Maurice was completed at high speed and the manuscript sent to Carpenter in August 1914 (when, as history records, even more important things were happening). It could not, of course, be published. Forster tinkered with the manuscript over the subsequent years. He had particular problems with the conclusion (that published, in which Maurice and Scudder live together in a happy ever after, is extravagantly optimistic, a mere two decades after the martyrisation of Oscar Wilde).

Maurice was not published until after Forster's death in 1971, after the 1960 acquittal of D.H. Lawrence's *Lady Chatterley's Lover* (in which Forster was a witness for the defence) had made its theme inoffensive and the 1967 Sexual Offences Act had made the love it describes between consenting males legal.

In a 1960 postscript, inscribed on the cover of the manuscript, Forster noted that the novel was now 'publishable' but asked himself, quizzically, whether it was 'worth it'? It had 'dated' sadly over the years. The world had moved on far beyond any relevance it might have. *Maurice* belonged, he thought, 'to an England where it was still possible to get lost. It belongs to the last moment of the greenwood' – the England, that is, destroyed in the First and Second World Wars.

Maurice finally saw print in the authoritative 'Abinger Edition' of Forster's work, and a successful film was made by Merchant and Ivory in 1987.

14 December

Two giants of modernism meet

1956 The two great modernists, Stravinsky and Eliot, first met, face to face, on this day in the winter of 1956. The influence of the composer's *Le sacre du printemps* (1911) on *The Waste Land* (1922) was frankly acknowledged by the poet, who hailed Stravinsky, in 1921, as 'our lion' – 'our' referring to their international artistic movement.

The first personal encounter of these by now grizzled lions was arranged by their mutual friend, Stephen Spender – still something of a literary cub. A nervous Spender drove Eliot to the Savoy Hotel, where the composer was staying. Their subsequent conversation was conducted 'mostly in English, though some of it was in French, which Eliot talks slowly and meticulously'.

As Spender recorded, the opening topic was unlikely:

> Stravinsky complained that ... he suffered from an excessive thickness of the blood. Moving his hands as though mould-ing an extremely rich substance, he said: '[The doctors] said my blood is so thick, so rich, so very rich, it might turn into crystals, like rubies, if I didn't drink beer, plenty of beer, and occasionally whisky, all the time' ... Eliot said meditatively: 'I remember in Heidelberg when I was in Heidelberg when I was young I went to a doctor and was examined and the doctor said: "Mr Eliot, you have the thinnest blood I've ever tested."'

This strangely allegorical conversation, although Spender does not mention it, was precipitated by an opening inquiry by Eliot about the composer's health. Stravinsky had suffered a cerebral aneurism in Berlin, in October. He was still disabled and had to delegate the con-ducting of a new composition in St Martin-in-the-Fields church, on 11 December, to his long-time companion Robert Craft.

Despite his illness, and although being the older man by six years, Stravinsky outlived Eliot by six years. Perhaps the beer and whisky (which, following medical advice, he consumed in heroic quantities) helped. Following their meeting he composed a brief *a capella* setting of lines from 'Little Gidding' ('the dove descending breaks the air') as a gift to the poet. On Eliot's death, on 4 January 1965, he did a more substantial 'Introitus: T.S. Eliot In Memoriam'. Ever sly, Eliot may have been making a self-depreciating joke about his thin blood. It was emphysema that killed him.

15 December

Fanny Hill *seized – still banned*

1964 John Cleland – the first recorded author of a work indicted as 'obscene' – described his pioneer work as: 'A Book I disdain to defend, and wish, from my Soul, buried and forgot.' No novel has been less so than *Fanny Hill; or, Memoirs of a Woman of Pleasure*.

Cleland (1709–89) was well born. His father, a former army officer of distinguished Scottish lineage, later a civil servant, was a friend of Alexander Pope's. His mother's family were wealthy anglicised Dutch Jewish merchants, and well in with high literary and political circles.

Young John spent two years at Westminster School before being expelled. Offence unknown; delinquency suspected. There may well have been some disgrace. Aged 21 he was packed off to India to serve for twelve years as a soldier, and later an administrator, in the East India Company. He returned to London in 1741, as his father was dying. In 1748 he was arrested for debts of almost £1,000, and spent a year in the Fleet Prison.

Debt drives the pen. In jail he wrote *Fanny Hill*. The first volume was published in November 1748, the second in February 1749. The author was paid £20 for the copyright. Legend has it that the publisher, Fenton, gained as much as £10,000 by the bargain. Who enabled Cleland's release from prison is not known.

The composition of *Fanny Hill* behind bars, as a kind of extended masturbation fantasy by a man denied his doxies, is a pretty anecdote. It may be prettier than true. Twenty years later, Cleland boasted to James Boswell that he had actually written the work in Bombay, in his twenties, as a wager to prove that one could write erotica without ever using a single item of foul language.

In late 1749 Cleland was arrested along with his publisher and charged with 'corrupting the King's subjects' with his novel. In court, Cleland, 'from my soul' wished the work 'buried and forgot'. He got off.

According to his obituary in the *Gentleman's Magazine*, Cleland was awarded a pension of £100 a year from the public purse, on condition that he write no more corrupting works. This is unlikely – although he may well have received financial assistance from his friends in high places.

Cleland was, for the remainder of his life, a productive, unpornographic, and consistently unsuccessful Grub Street author. Cleland grew quarrelsome in later life, falling out with friends. He lived by himself, never married, and had the reputation of being a 'Sodomite'.

Fanny Hill; or, Memoirs of a Woman of Pleasure, as published in 1748–9, takes the form of a confessional letter describing the heroine's 'progress', and was clearly designed to contradict the joyless moralism of Hogarth's 'The Harlot's Progress' (1732) and to show up the timidly parsimonious reference to sex in Defoe's 'whore's autobiography' *Moll Flanders* (1722), both of which aims *Fanny Hill* achieves triumphantly. The name is a somewhat laboured pun on 'Veneris mons' – Venus's hill. It is not clear whether 'fanny' was, then as now, street slang for 'quim'.

Following the acquittal of *Lady Chatterley's Lover* in 1960, the paperback publisher, Mayflower, announced an above-ground edition of *Fanny Hill* in November 1963. Copies were seized from a London retailer (a joke shop in Tottenham Court Road) on 15 December. It went on trial at Bow Street Magistrates' Court in February 1964. Cannily, it was the West End retailer – not the publisher (as in the *Lady Chatterley* case) – who was hauled into the dock. The book was deemed (locally) offensive and the seized stock ordered destroyed.

Oddly, no successful defence of *Fanny Hill* has ever been mounted. It crept back into print, and now has a learnedly annotated existence as one of the Oxford World's Classics. A BBC TV version, adapted by Andrew Davies in 2007, attracted an audience of seven million. It remains, technically, a banned book: at least, in Tottenham Court Road and environs.

16 December

A literal hatchet job

1943 One of the stranger coincidences of the First World War is Erich Maria Remark (as he then was) and Adolf Hitler serving alongside each other in the trenches at the Third Battle of Ypres (Passchendaele) in July 1917. Some have fantasised that the two men may have rubbed shoulders, unconscious of each other's identities.

Remark was badly wounded by a British shell and invalided out. The injuries ended his hoped-for career in music. A week before the end of hostilities, in November 1918, he was returned to the trenches in Belgium where, again, he was serving close to Corporal Adolf Hitler (who, in the intervening months, had won an Iron Cross First Class).

After the war the two ex-soldiers' careers went in opposite directions. On his return home, Remark (who was a non-commissioned conscript) was arrested for impersonating a lieutenant, decorated with two Iron Crosses (he was already displaying a talent for fiction

– or perhaps, as sympathisers have suggested, he was suffering from post-traumatic stress disorder: 'shell-shock').

Remarque (as he renamed himself) went on to publish in 1929 *Im Westen Nichts Neues – All Quiet on the Western Front*, routinely voted the best anti-war novel ever. It became an international bestseller after its blockbusting 1933 film tie-in. The story tracks the fortunes of six classmates swept up in the Great War, as narrated by Paul Bäumer. The soldiers reserve their hatred not for the 'enemy' but the armchair warriors on the home front. On the day that the Armistice is signed, Paul, realising that he can never readjust to civilian life, walks into no man's land, and is shot.

In the same year, 1929, Hitler published his own bestseller, *Mein Kampf*. His hatred was reserved for the Jews who, he believed, were responsible for Germany's defeat in 1918. His book was pro-war: fanatically so.

The Nazis banned Remarque's detestably 'pacifist' novel and, on coming to power in 1933, stripped him of his German citizenship. Remarque, now rich (thanks to his book sales and film adaptation), fled to America where he continued his career as a novelist. He had a passionate affair with a fellow exile, Marlene Dietrich, and later married another Hollywood star, Paulette Goddard. German propaganda suppressed his works, alleging that he was actually a French Jew named 'Kramer' ('Remark' backwards).

Unable to lay hands on him, the Nazi party arrested Remarque's sister, Elfriede Scholz, in 1943, on a trumped-up charge of 'undermining the war effort'. The judge at the 'Peoples' Court' frankly admitted: 'Your brother is beyond our reach, but you will not escape us!' She was sentenced to beheading on 16 December 1943.

Erich Maria Remarque was sent a bill by the party for the 90 marks executioner's fee.

17 December

Dr Martin Luther King attends the world premiere of Gone with the Wind *(in a sense)*

1939 The world premiere of the MGM adaptation of *Gone with the Wind* was held at Loew's Grand Theater in Atlanta (the town so memorably burned in Margaret Mitchell's novel and the David O. Selznick film) on 17 December 1939. 'The South' – it was said – would be mortally offended if it were held anywhere else. The New York and Los Angeles opening showings were duly postponed to 19 December.

The stars and their spouses (Clark Gable and Carole Lombard; Vivien Leigh and Laurence Olivier), together with the author and a host of film dignitaries, attended a grand reception at the Georgian Terrace Hotel; while, opposite on Peachtree Street, spotlights played over the cinema and the crowds massed to catch a glimpse of their screen idols.

Guests at the celebration in the hotel were entertained by the all-negro Ebenezer Church Choir, under choir-mistress Alberta Williams King. They were dressed in slave costume and sang negro spirituals. Among the choir was the leader's son, ten-year-old Martin Luther King, dressed as a handsome little pickaninny.

Loew's was a white-only theatre and the choir would not have been able to join the ecstatic audience that night – or any night until 1940, when *GWTW* (as enthusiasts called it) was shown to segregated audiences.

Although MGM tempered the unreconstructed elements in Mitchell's text (Rhett, for example, does not ride with the Klan), it is unlikely that the future leader of the civil rights movement would have found much to entertain him in the film, other than the spirited performance of Butterfly McQueen as Scarlett's maid, Prissy.

18 December

Dryden mugged

1679 Poet laureateship was a riskier office in the 18th century. The first writer formally to be appointed to the position in 1670, John Dryden, was thought to have had a hand in *The Essay on Satire*, nominally the sole work of John Sheffield, Earl of Mulgrave (later Duke of Buckingham) – one of Dryden's principal patrons, and not renowned as a poet of the first class.

The work, circulated in manuscript (and anonymously), contained smart sarcasms against the Earl of Rochester – the most wicked poet of his age – not for the earl's wickedness (which would have amused the author of *Sodom*) but his 'want of wit'. In the Restoration period such an accusation, between versifiers, was blood libel.

On the night of 18 December 1679, in Rose Alley (a dank corner off Covent Garden, still to this day used as a convenient public toilet), Dryden was set on by three bullies (one of whom was later identified as 'Black Will') and brutally beaten up. It was never decisively proved, although widely suspected, that Rochester organised the assault. It ranks as one of his lesser outrages.

The 'Rose Alley Ambuscade' (uncommemorated to London's metropolitan shame by any blood-red plaque) has become allegorical of the woes of authorship. The event is annually re-enacted. In 1995 David D. Horowitz founded the 'Rose Alley Press' in Seattle, whose list specialises in 'rhymed and metered poetry, cultural commentary, and an annually updated booklet about writing and publication'.

19 December

The first Poor Richard's Almanack *is printed*

1732 Almanacs were popular in colonial America. They offered a calendar, long-term weather predictions and astrological tables for the coming year, along with jokes, puzzles and practical household hints. Benjamin Franklin's *Poor Richard's Almanack*, which he wrote and published for sixteen years, also included aphorisms and proverbs, like 'He that falls in love with himself will have no rivals', 'Wise men learn by others' harms, fools by their own', and (inevitably) 'God helps them that help themselves'.

In his autobiography, written from 1771 to 1790, over the period straddling the country's fight for independence, Franklin tried so hard to present himself as a representative American that it's hard not to read *Poor Richard's Almanack* as a uniquely American production. After all, it seems to have suited a democratic readership so well, being practical, written in a demotic style and immensely popular, selling 10,000 copies a year at a time when the literate population of the British colonies in America probably numbered under 625,000.

But in all respects of literary and publishing history, *Poor Richard's* was less original than it has since been seen to be. For one thing, not all the aphorisms were freshly minted; many, by Franklin's own admission, were gathered from the 'wisdom of the ages and nations'. As he has often been quoted as saying: 'Originality is the art of concealing your sources.'

Poor Richard's is a parodic almanac; it pokes fun at conventional almanacs, often for satiric purposes. The parodic form goes back almost as far as its 'straight' counterpart, to François Rabelais's *Pantagrueline Prognostications* (1532), which Franklin knew. Popular English predecessors included Jonathan Swift's *Isaac Bickerstaff's Predictions* (from 1708), and before that, two almanacs from which Franklin took the name of his own: *Poor Robin's* (from 1663) and Richard Saunders' *Apollo Anglicanus, or English Apollo* (from 1694).

Frank Palmieri shows that *Poor Robin's*, though conservative in its politics (upholding the values of the Restoration, for example), also debunked 'the pieties generally accepted by the serious almanacs', and so 'had an implicitly irreverent and deflating effect on the form and the culture that was at odds with its overt allegiance'.

Facing each other across the Atlantic, the satiric almanacs began to diverge in their politics as the 18th century advanced, the British remaining 'staunchly royalist' while *Poor Richard's* became 'more radical, Whiggish, and contrarian'. For all that, though, 'both address the reader as a member of the nation, defining him as an Englishman in one case and an American in the other'.* Or maybe it would be more accurate to say, two Englishmen of differing political persuasions. For the lesson implicit in *Poor Richard's* lack of originality is that Franklin and his readers were not yet thinking of themselves as part of an exceptional, distinct nationality, but as part of a wider British community allowing diverse political viewpoints. This is a perspective often obscured by the 'American Studies' industry.

20 December

Phileas Fogg arrives on the right day, but does not know it

1872 Jules Verne's *Around the World in Eighty Days* is a novel with a calendar at its narrative heart. The novel's hero is Phileas Fogg, the

---

* Frank Palmieri, 'History, nation, and the satirical almanac, 1660–1760', *Criticism*, Summer 1998: http://findarticles.com/p/articles/mi_m2220/is_n3_v40/ai_21182130/pg_2/?tag=content;col1, *passim.*

incarnation of Anglo-Saxon *sang-froid* (his surname, however, indicates a lingering Gallic anglophobia – we may admire the *rosbifs*, but who would want to live there?).

Phileas lays a bet with his fellow Reform Club members that he can – using the latest transport systems (as advertised in the *Daily Telegraph*) – circumnavigate the globe 'in eighty days or less; in nineteen hundred and twenty hours, or a hundred and fifteen thousand two hundred minutes'. He will leave England on 2 October, and return on – or before – 'Saturday the 21st of December 1872', at a quarter to nine. This narrative idea was supposedly inspired by Thomas Cook, catering for the first generation of world 'tourists'.

There follows Verne's extravagant travelogue of Fogg's worldwide peregrinations, assisted by his omnicompetent 'man', Passepartout (ancestor of Jeeves). Alas, despite heroic efforts, they miss the return deadline of Saturday, 21 December by minutes. Disconsolate, they do not go to the club but slink home.

The following day (Sunday, as the two men think) – again with minutes only to spare – Passepartout rushes into his master's mansion in Savile Row. It is, he breathlessly announces, a day earlier than they thought. They have forgotten, in all the excitement of their travels, crossing the date line. The two men scamper the 576 yards to the Reform Club, arriving breathless but just under the wire, as the club clock pendulum beats the 60th second.

Verne tells his tale with such verve that the reader generously overlooks the unlikelihood of Fogg not looking at his *Daily Telegraph*, or not noticing the difference between lively Saturday and gloomy Sunday in foggy London Town.

21 December

Dostoyevsky's last night on earth

1849 Fyodor Dostoyevsky came to literary fame precociously, at the age of 24, with his first novel, *Poor Folk* (1845). As the title indicates, the work was what contemporary Britons called a 'social problem novel', or 'political fiction'. It was politics that almost ended the young writer's career before it had properly got going, four years later. The experience – arguably – made him the novelist he became.

In early 1849, secret police in St Petersburg uncovered an underground socialist cell, 'the Petrashevsky Group'. Tsar Nicholas I demanded exemplary punishment. The ringleaders, among them Dostoyevsky, were arrested on 23 April, and peremptorily sentenced to death.

On 22 December 1849, twenty of the Petrashevsky Group were publicly executed, by firing squad, in St Petersburg's Semenovsky Plaza. Dostoyevsky, stripped to his underclothes and freezing in the sub-zero morning temperature, heard his sentence read out. But before he was blindfolded and led to be bound to the execution post, the event was stopped. An arbitrary amnesty was announced for certain of the convicted. Dostoyevsky was sentenced to four years of penal servitude in Siberia and another four years of service as a soldier, also in Siberia.

Later that day he wrote to his brother to say: 'I did not whimper, complain and lose courage. Life, life is everywhere, life is inside us.' The traumatic event is directly recalled in *Notes from the Underground*, where the narrator recalls:

> [A] man I met last year ... was led out along with others on to a scaffold and had his sentence of death by shooting read out to him, for political offences. About twenty minutes later a reprieve was read out and a milder punishment substituted ... he was dying at 27, healthy and strong ... he says that nothing was more terrible at that moment than the nagging thought: 'What if I didn't have to die! ... I would turn every minute into an age, nothing would be wasted, every minute would be accounted for.'

The experience is also clearly evoked in the crisis of *Crime and Punishment*, when Raskolnikov finally confronts the consequences of his guilt (like the author, he escapes execution and undergoes exile to a Siberian camp). When the hero resolves to confess, he is described as having 'a feeling akin to that of a dead man upon suddenly receiving his pardon'.

It's hard to think of a more personally painful but artistically rewarding apprenticeship for an author than Dostoyevsky's trial by fire (and, of course, 'hold your fire').

22 December

Nathanael West dies

1940 It has been argued that West (author of *Miss Lonelyhearts* and *A Cool Million*) is one of the very greatest writers of his time. Few would dispute that he was one of the worst drivers.

The Ancient Mariner of 20th-century literature, West's career had been dogged by bad luck. His first published novel, *The Dream Life of Balso Snell* (1931), was still-born when the publisher handling it went down in the post-1929 Crash. Mysteriously, although review copies of *Miss Lonelyhearts* went out in 1933, and the novel was glowingly reviewed, no copies were delivered to bookshops. *A Cool Million* (1936) was deemed too depressing by readers in the depths of the Depression. West, who wrote fiction with great difficulty, reckoned in the year before his death that he had made less than $1,000 from his three major novels.

He had been obliged, like other writers of the time, to indenture himself to Hollywood. He hated the work, but could do it easily. And in the two years leading up to his death he was, at last, on Easy Street, earning up to $500 a week writing scripts for RKO. He married and bought himself a handsome Ford station wagon.

On the way back from a hunting trip in Mexicali with his wife, Eileen, his liver-coloured pointer bitch, Julie, and a trunk full of dead duck, West was driving along the highway to El Centro. Normally his wife refused to drive with him, regarding him as 'murderous' behind the wheel. Many of his friends were similarly disinclined to be Nate's passenger. He had a bad habit of turning his head to whomever he was talking to – and he talked animatedly.

Blithely shooting a boulevard turn (at which he should have stopped) onto Route 80, West ploughed into an oncoming Pontiac truck driven (entirely legally) by a farmer. The Wests were killed (the fate of Julie is unrecorded). West was 37 years old.

It was a season of literary death. Over the winter months of 1940–41 Sherwood Anderson, Virginia Woolf, and James Joyce died. It is sometimes surmised that West was preoccupied on the fateful afternoon of 22 December by news that his friend, and idol, Scott Fitzgerald had died on the evening of the 21st – news that he had received by telephone.

23 December

Scientists at AT&T's Bell Laboratories first demonstrate the transistor

1947 Before transistors, the sort of electric currents used in audio systems, radio and television receivers and the like were managed by thermionic valves (or vacuum tubes in American usage). They looked a bit like old-fashioned light bulbs. Depending on the wiring and where the signal was put in, tubes/valves could act as amplifiers or switches or detectors, enlarging the signal or shutting it off, or separating it out from the high-frequency carrier wave needed to send it from broadcaster to receiver. But they used a lot of power, generated a lot of heat, and often blew out – just like light bulbs.

At the Bell labs, William Shockley and his team found that crystals of silicon or germanium 'doped' (grown) with impurities like boron or phosphorus would become semiconductors – that is, materials that neither conducted electrical currents nor insulated against them, but performed something in between these functions. When they sandwiched the semiconductor in between two conducting plates, they found that small variations of current applied to the sandwich 'filling' would control large flows across the device as a whole. So the transistor could act as a valve, amplifying current or switching it on and off.

That's the simplest model. Transistors soon grew into a bewildering variety of design and function. But their ability either to amplify or switch meant that they could be used in binary computer processors and memory, in place of those banks of valves that used to occupy floor after floor of old mainframe computers – back in the days when 'mainframe' was a literal description.

The final stage was the integrated circuit. Transistors and other components could be assembled, not by soldering but by being layered on to circuit boards, then assembled as microchips so tiny that it takes a microscope to see the connections.

So what has this got to do with literature? Simply that the microchips underpin the way modern books, newspapers and magazines are written and produced – and increasingly read. In its impact on literacy, the invention of the transistor may not yet rank alongside that of the printing press, but it's catching up fast.

24 December

Booth Tarkington makes the cover of Time

1925 Booth Tarkington (1869–1946) is a famous novelist whose actual name is everywhere forgotten. Echoes of his grandiloquent prose (in Orson Welles's fruity baritone) have – via a classic film adaptation of *The Magnificent Ambersons* – kept his work, if not its author, fresh and alive while contemporaries like Winston Churchill (the other one, the American who wrote novels) – judged greater in their time – have faded utterly.

Booth Tarkington was Indiana-born (a 'Hoosier') and a lifelong booster of the region, particularly his native Indianapolis. It changed during Tarkington's lifetime from quiet rural town to an industrial powerhouse (this is the background to George Minafer's 'comeuppance', and his family's decay, in the last scenes of *The Magnificent Ambersons*). Tarkington's first novel – not his best, but his most characteristic – was *The Gentleman from Indiana* (1919). His pedigree was locally 'magnificent' – like the Ambersons, the Tarkingtons were among Indianapolis's 'top 500'. Booth's middle name (Newton) honoured an uncle, then governor of California. His father was a lawyer (later a judge).

Tarkington attended Princeton, where he enjoyed king-of-the-campus success. He was voted most popular man in his 1893 class. A fellow student recalled him as 'the only Princeton man who had ever been known to play poker (with his left hand), write a story for the *Nassau Lit* (with his right hand), and lead the singing in a crowded room, performing these three acts simultaneously'. Such ambidexterity rarely makes for academic magnificence. Tarkington did not graduate (although in the years of his fame Princeton would award him two honorary degrees).

Tarkington tried public life, unsuccessfully. He was, for one term in 1902, an Indiana State Representative in the Indiana government. He married twice. The only child from his marriages died early – nonetheless, the vicissitudes of childhood would be a principal theme in his best-known and bestselling fiction.

Tarkington had his first bestseller with *Monsieur Beaucaire* (1900), a 'no man is a hero to his valet' spoof on the current American rage for historical fiction. Tarkington had even greater success with his comic epics about the trials of youth. Adolescence was a psycho-genetic category invented in America at this period by G. Stanley Hall. Tarkington popularised it in *Penrod* (1914). Penrod Schofield – invariably accompanied by his dog Duke; and latterly by his gang, Sam Williams, Maurice Levy, Georgie Bassett, and Herman (the second Jewish and the last black) – is an eleven-year-old rebel against the middle-class values of his Midwest family and community. His little battles are narrated in arch-ironic style by Tarkington.

Penrod clearly draws on *Tom Sawyer* and just as clearly inspired Richmal Crompton's *Just William* (1922). Addressed principally to adult readers, both depictions of juvenile machismo exude tolerant adult amusement at the barbarism of the young male child in Western civilisation. *Penrod* inspired the sequels *Penrod and Sam* (1916) and *Penrod Jashber* (1929).

Tarkington continued this bestselling vein with *Seventeen* (1916). With eighteen-year-olds (and, after 1917, American boys) dying by the hundred thousand in France in 1914–18, Tarkington's idylls offered escape to a safer, if imaginary, world. Adolescence agonistes of a more tragic kind is portrayed in Georgie Minafer of *The Magnificent Ambersons* (1923). This novel made up a trilogy with *The Turmoil* (1915) and *The Midlander* (1923). These socially troubled novels earned Tarkington two Pulitzers and a front page on *Time* magazine on this day in 1925. Like everyone else, the young Orson Welles read them admiringly.

Around this period Tarkington was losing his sight, and his later novels – none of which enjoyed the success of the earlier – were dictated. Royalties and film rights (his work adapted smoothly onto the screen) enriched him and allowed him to indulge a taste for English 18th-century painting and fine furniture for his mansion in Indianapolis.

Tarkington was increasingly right-wing in later years, conceiving a violent distaste for President Roosevelt, the New Deal, and virtually everything that happened after 1929 (not least to his beloved Indianapolis).

25 December

Bing Crosby first sings 'White Christmas' on his NBC radio show,
'The Kraft Music Hall'

1941 With words and music by Irving Berlin, Crosby's recording of
'White Christmas' would go on to be the best-selling single of all time.
Originally penned in Beverley Hills, California, in a fit of nostalgia for
the old-fashioned winters of the American east coast ('Where the tree-
tops glisten, / And children listen / To hear sleigh bells in the snow'),
the song was soon standing in for home – with nearly unbearable
poignancy – for thousands of GIs in Guadalcanal, North Africa and
other hot, dangerous places where they didn't want to be.

There are at least three stories here. The first is about Berlin himself, who lived to be 101, his career running from the ragtime to the
Kennedy eras (he wrote 'Alexander's Ragtime Band' and the score for
the musical *Mr President*, which premiered in 1962 with the young
president in the audience). He was the Jew who wrote the classic
Christmas song; the immigrant who composed the country's unofficial
national anthem, 'God Bless America'. So the second story is about
America.

The third is about musical comedies, the usual vehicle for Berlin's
songs (even 'White Christmas' found its setting a year later in *Holiday
Inn*). Possibly out of a lingering Puritanism, American intellectuals
don't treat musical comedy as seriously as they do the 'straight' theatre.
And while literature courses will spend hours analysing Donne's

> Sweetest love, I do not goe,
> For weariness of thee,
> Nor in hope the world can show
> A fitter Love for me ...

... they will pay scant attention to the lyrics of musical comedies, like
Berlin's own comic context between male and female sharpshooters in
Annie Get Your Gun (1944):

> Anything you can be
> I can be greater.
> Sooner or later,
> I'm greater than you.

No, you're not. Yes, I am.
No, you're not. Yes, I am.
No, you're NOT! Yes, I am.
Yes, I am!

I can shoot a partridge
With a single cartridge.
I can get a sparrow
With a bow and arrow.
I can live on bread and cheese.
And only on that?
Yes.
So can a rat!

The joke lies in how the war of the sexes infantilises the combatants. Or what about Cole Porter's words to 'You're the Top' in *Anything Goes* (1934)?

You're the top!
You're Mahatma Gandhi.
You're the top!
You're Napoleon Brandy.
You're the purple light
Of a summer night in Spain,
You're the National Gallery
You're Garbo's salary,
You're cellophane.

And so on, through 53 other supposed superlatives. It's inventive (because it could go on for ever); it's witty (because the references are comically scrambled between high and low commodities of travel and the market). Above all, like hundreds of show-tune lyrics, it's in the plain style: accessible and memorable. Not as easy as it looks.

26 December

*Just three weeks after Pearl Harbor, President Roosevelt sets
the day for Thanksgiving*

1941 Newly plunged into the Second World War, the President of
the United States could still take time off to decide when the nation
should celebrate its annual day of thanksgiving. This wasn't the first
time that war had turned the thoughts of the country's leaders in
that direction. In the middle of America's War of Independence the
Continental Congress proclaimed Thursday, 18 December to be a
day of 'SOLEMN THANKSGIVING and PRAISE', and Abraham
Lincoln took time off from the Civil War in 1863 to set the day on the
last Thursday in November.

Roosevelt settled on the penultimate Thursday of November, a
month that sometimes stretches to five. His reason, he said, was to add
an extra week to the pre-Christmas shopping spree, thus increasing
spending and profits in the most serious depression in the country's
history.

But even that motive tells a story. Whereas in Britain adverts men-
tioning Christmas begin to dribble out around the middle of September,
America keeps its Christmas spending strictly post-Thanksgiving.
And Thanksgiving itself is non-commercial: no presents, no decorations (apart from a few paper table favours shaped like pumpkins or
Puritans), no hoopla. More even than Christmas, Thanksgiving is the
one day in the year when American families, however far apart, try
their best to get back together – think *Planes, Trains and Automobiles*
(1987). More even than the 4th of July, it is America's national holiday.

Why? There was nothing very auspicious national in its beginnings. 'Our harvest being gotten in', wrote Plymouth settler Edward
Winslow to 'A loving and old friend' in the autumn of 1621, 'our governor sent four men on fowling, that so we might … rejoice together
after we had gathered the fruit of our labors.'

The 'fowl' were probably wild turkeys. There is no mention of
pumpkins. The 'fruit of their labors' amounted to maize or Indian corn
and an 'indifferent' crop of barley. They invited the natives, too, who
after all had shown them how to plant corn by putting a small fish in
with each kernel. 'Many of the Indians [came] amongst us, and among

the rest their greatest King Massasoit, with some ninety men, whom for three days we entertained and feasted.'*

Ever since then, even as immigrants arrived from southern and central Europe, the Far East, and the country's Spanish-speaking neighbours to the south, the United States has continued to picture its origins in those steeple-hatted, white English men and women sitting down to celebrate their first harvest. How did so much glamour and prestige come to be attached to this tiny movement of peoples to Massachusetts? Because William Bradford, governor of Plymouth Plantation, told the story of the colony's settlement so as to re-enact the Israelites' trek to the Promised Land, the very paradigm of the immigrant experience shared by all (see 11 November).

27 December

Alfred Nobel's last will and testament

1895 The most prestigious prize in literature has its home not in one of the imperial capitals of the world, but in Stockholm. And, even more ironically, it is funded by the revenue from the world's most popular explosive.

The story behind the setting up of the Nobel Prizes is legendary. *Time* magazine (16 October 2000) offers one chatty version. In 1888, Alfred's brother Ludwig Nobel had died while visiting Cannes:

> Alfred, a pacifist who liked to write poetry, had intended his explosive to be used mostly for peaceful purposes and was dismayed that it became so powerful an instrument of war. A French newspaper – thinking it was Alfred and not his brother who had passed on – ran his obituary in 1888 under the cutting headline 'Le marchand de la mort est mort' (the merchant of death is dead). With the family name obviously in need of some burnishing, Nobel hit on the idea of his golden prize.

---

* Edward Winslow, 'A Letter Sent From New England to a friend in these parts [i.e. England]', *Mourt's Relation: A Journal of the Pilgrims at Plymouth*, 1622, Part VI: http://etext.lib.virginia. edu/users/deetz/Plymouth/mourt6.html

Seven years later, on 27 December 1895, Nobel (who was childless) drew up his last will and testament. In it he decreed that the bulk of his wealth, derived from his deadly invention, should be invested to establish a foundation that should superintend the annual award of monetary prizes for physics, chemistry, medicine, literature and peace (economics came later).

The criterion for science was clear-cut. It should go to whomever was judged to have made 'the most important discovery'. That for literature was fuzzier. It instructed that the Literature Prize be given 'to the person who shall have produced in the field of literature the most outstanding work in an ideal direction'. The epithet 'ideal' – which is both moral and aesthetic, and extremely slippery – has been the cause of much controversy over the century the prize has been awarded.

Nobel died less than a year after drawing up his will, in December 1896. When the document was read out to the family it was violently objected to, and legally challenged by two nephews. The King of Sweden, Oskar II, declared the disposition of Nobel's vast treasure 'unpatriotic'. It took three years of difficult negotiation to get the literary prize running, under the auspices of the Swedish Academy, in 1901. The first laureate was the French author Sully Prudhomme. It was given, the judges declared, 'in special recognition of his poetic composition, which gives evidence of lofty idealism, artistic perfection and a rare combination of the qualities of both heart and intellect'. Whatever his lofty idealism, Prudhomme, alas, remains one of the less read Nobellists by posterity. In their wisdom, the judges had decided against Leo Tolstoy (as they did in 1902) because of his anarchism and eccentric religious views. The Russian claimed to be glad 'because it saved me from the painful necessity of dealing in some way with money – generally regarded as very necessary and useful, but which I regard as the source of every kind of evil'.

28 December

The Tay Bridge collapses in a violent storm, dashing a trainload of passengers to their deaths

1879 Two estuaries form barriers to travel along the east coast of Scotland – the Firths of Forth and Tay. Trains from Edinburgh to

Dundee and Aberdeen had to cross both, so the early railway companies were keen to bridge them. The Tay Bridge was the first to be built. Of lattice-grid design, resting on cast iron piers, it was – at two and a quarter miles – the longest bridge in the world on its opening in June 1878.

It lasted a year and a half, until one stormy night the combined stresses of load and winds brought the mid-section down with a train on it, killing 75 passengers and crew.

> So the train mov'd slowly along the Bridge of Tay,
> Until it was about midway,
> Then the central girders with a crash gave way,
> And down went the train and passengers into the Tay!

The Tay Bridge disaster was celebrated or mourned (it's hard to tell which) by the lines above, from what is commonly considered to be the worst poem in the English language, by William Topaz McGonagall. What makes the poem's tone so unstable is partly those unruly metrics, with lines varying randomly from eight to thirteen syllables – or as long as it takes them to arrive at those obsessive rhymes. Even in his time and place McGonagall was a popular figure of fun, something of a town treasure, but since then his fame has spread, and he has never been out of print.

By contrast, the disaster was also marked by a much better poem, now almost forgotten. This was 'Die Brück' am Tay', which the German novelist and poet Theodor Fontane managed to get into print just thirteen days after reading of the tragedy.

With scant regard to Scottish priorities, Fontane re-schedules the accident for Christmas Eve in order to underscore the human tragedy. On the north shore the bridge-keeper and his wife scan the south anxiously for a light, the sign that the Edinburgh train is crossing the bridge with their son Johnnie on board, bringing the Christmas tree for the family celebrations.

The point of view then shifts to Johnnie, who laughs to recall all those earlier Christmases when the old ferryboat failed to get him home in time. Granted, a storm is brewing up, but now they have the bridge, and the train, pulled by

> Ein fester Kessel, ein doppelter Dampf,
> Die bleiben Sieger in solchem Kampf.

Und wie's auch rast und ringt und rennt,
Wir kriegen es unter, das Element.*

It was not to be. The elements, conjured up by those elemental forces, the three witches from *Macbeth*, who open and close the poem, bring the pride of Victorian engineering crashing down. '"Tand, Tand / Ist das Gebilde von Menschenhand"', say the weird sisters. '"Trash, trash / Is everything built by man's hand".'

29 December

The destruction of Paternoster Row

1940 Book-burning has huge significance – from the library of Alexandria, through Savonarola and Goebbels to the incineration of *The Satanic Verses* by enraged Muslims in Bradford.

The biggest book bonfire in England occurred in the early stages of the German Blitz in 1940. Since the introduction of the craft of printing in the 15th century, the heart of the British book trade had been located in the small area around St Paul's in London – Paternoster Row.

Between the 20th-century wars it was still the centre point, dominated by Longman's (the oldest surviving commercial firm in the country) and Simpkin and Marshall's huge wholesale warehouse, which distributed books to all parts of the British isles.

St Paul's Cathedral survived the Sunday raid (as its predecessor, in the Great Fire of London, had not).

But over a million books went up in flames on that awful night. Seventeen publishers' premises were totally destroyed. As George Bernard Shaw noted drily: 'The Germans have done what Constable's [his publisher] have never succeeded in doing. They have disposed of 86,701 sheets of my work in less than twenty-four hours.'

One of Simpkin and Marshall's warehousemen recalled his impressions next morning:

---

* 'A strong boiler and a double head of steam, / Bound to win such a battle, / And as it races and wrestles and runs, / We'll beat it down, the element.'

I went up on the Monday morning and all the Simpkin Marshall staff were standing in Ludgate Hill, surveying the ruins. We had heard there'd been a heavy raid, and set out not knowing what we would find. But what we saw was indescribable. I had never seen such desolation in my life. Paternoster Row, Ave Maria Land and bordering onto Ludgate Hill was a scene of smouldering ruins, and what had been Simpkin Marshall's was just a heap of rubble.

Paternoster Row, and its adjoining streets, was now – as one observer put it – 'the crematory of the City's book world'.

But it wasn't. The raid demonstrated the extraordinary resilience of the British book trade (which, amazingly, contrived to export more product in wartime 1941 than it had in peacetime 1939).

Longman's catalogue was reduced overnight from 6,000 titles to twelve available to the retail trade. But within a month (using trestle tables and improvised lighting) they contrived to rebuild their backlist.

Organisationally, the 29 December raid had long-lasting and benign results. No 'Leviathan' wholesaler replaced Simpkin and Marshall (only very recently have the Amazon and Barnes & Noble electronic catalogues rivalled its stock range). Instead publishers came to rely on 'sales reps', who built up personal connections with bookshops, creating an immensely sensitive feedback mechanism (the British book trade, unlike its American counterpart, has never – until recently – believed in 'sale or return', itself a kind of Blitzkrieg technique). The 'organic' nature of the British book trade owes much to the sales-rep system.

The other benign effect of the Luftwaffe's malignity was the diaspora of the book trade to more spacious areas (Harlow in Longman's case) where it could expand to become a 20th-century industry.

30 December

Betwixt 'Yol and Nwe Yer' a green knight rides into King Arthur's court

c. 1350 The guests at Camelot have just sat down to their dainty dishes served up in such abundance that there is scarcely room for them on the table, when in at the door of the feasting hall there bursts a frightening spectacle, a huge knight dressed all in green, with green skin and hair and riding a green horse. He is looking not for a fight, but for 'a Christmas gomen [game], / For it is Yol and Nwe Yer [Yule and New Year]', the season of games.

The game is an odd one. The Green Knight will allow one of the king's young knights to strike off his head, providing he can return the blow in a year's time in his own Green Chapel. Gawain, Arthur's youngest knight, accepting the challenge, severs the head, which the Green Knight picks up again, departing with the reminder not to forget their rendezvous.

A year later, after an arduous journey through woods and wilderness, Gawain comes across the castle of Bertilak de Hautdesert, who tells him the Green Chapel is only two miles away, so he can stay for three days before his fateful encounter. Three times over the three days, as Bertilak goes out hunting, Gawain is tempted by Bertilak's beautiful wife entering his bedroom and asking for the usual courtly favours. Three times Gawain resists, only a little less so on each occasion. Finally she gives the young knight a green girdle, which she promises will keep him from harm.

Come the meeting at the Green Chapel, and Bertilak reveals that he is none other than the Green Knight. His axe swings three times at Gawain's neck; only the third blow causes a wound – a slight one. Gawain returns to Camelot, where his fellow knights take to wearing green girdles as light-hearted memorials of his peccadillo.

The 14th-century *Sir Gawain and the Green Knight* is the best-plotted of medieval romances, and one of the most intriguing works of English literature. It poses and doesn't quite resolve so many tensions: sex and hunting (the word 'venery' means both); the exchange of gifts and blows; games and serious combat; chastity and courtly love; even the relative modernity of Middle English against the old alliterative Anglo-Saxon verse. The Knight of the title is a version of the old green man, the pagan god of rebirth at the year's turning (he even carries a branch of holly – 'That is greatest in green when greves [groves] are bare'), yet the stress on redemption is certainly Christian. It really does belong between Yule and New Year.

31 December

Richard Yates's Revolutionary Road *is published, his classic novel
of a doomed marriage in American 1950s suburbia*

1961 The career of Richard Yates is one of the great mysteries of
20th-century American literature. His work was acclaimed by, among
others, Tennessee Williams, Dorothy Parker, Kurt Vonnegut, Joyce
Carol Oates, Tobias Woolf and Andre Dubus. *Revolutionary Road*, his
first novel, was enthusiastically reviewed and entered as a finalist for
the 1962 National Book Award for fiction, alongside Joseph Heller's
Catch-22 and (the winner) Walker Percy's *The Moviegoer*. And Yates
wasn't a one-book wonder, either. In all, he produced seven novels and
two collections of short stories. Yet none of them sold over 12,000 in
hardback. By his death in 1992, they were out of print, and he was
forgotten.

Then, at the turn of the millennium, the novel was reissued, fronted
by an admiring and perceptive introduction by Richard Ford, by
Vintage in the US (2000) and Methuen in the UK (2001), and the
critics fell in love all over again – especially the British. 'The literary
discovery of the year', enthused popular novelist Nick Hornby. The
playwright David Hare handed out copies to anyone who would take
them. 'It is one of the most moving and exact portraits of suburbia in
all of American literature', he said.

The movie rights languished for four decades – then, when the
AMC TV series *Mad Men* was making the world of 1950s commuters
smart again, they were bought up by BBC Films. Justin Haythe wrote
a meticulous screenplay, and in 2008 Sam Mendes (*American Beauty*,
1999; *The Road to Perdition*, 2002) directed his wife Kate Winslet and
her old *Titanic* lover, Leonardo di Caprio, in the lead roles. Suddenly
on TV and in the cinema everybody was smoking again – even pregnant women. The soundtracks were electric with the zing and snap of
Zippo lighters.

Set in 1955, the novel follows Frank and April Wheeler through
the dissolution of their marriage. They live on Revolutionary Road in
a decidedly un-revolutionary west Connecticut exurb. He commutes
to a dull job writing advertising copy for an adding machine firm, and
she waits at home with his dinner ready when he gets back. Tragically,
they know the limitations of their neighbours and of their own lifestyle
but don't have the courage or concentration – or frankly, the talent – to

escape them. Her dream of getting away to an alternative life in Paris, where she will support them while he sort-of 'finds himself' in some vaguely defined career, falls apart when he gets promoted and begins to take his job seriously, and she gets pregnant for the third time.

Through closely observed details of speech and behaviour, much of it comic without being mocking, Yates sucks his readers into this downward vortex, leaving them without comfort – not even the deeper truth of more classical tragedy – just the stark confrontation of failure. 'It's his insistence on the blunt reality of failure that drew me to Yates', Stewart O'Nan has written. 'In the world I knew … Fortunes didn't change, they just followed a track into a dead end and left you there. To find a writer who understood that and didn't gussy it up with tough-guy irony or drown it in sentimental tears was a revelation.'* But then maybe that very honesty is what limited the book's appeal in its first incarnation.

---

* Stewart O'Nan, 'The Lost World of Richard Yates: How the great writer of the Age of Anxiety disappeared from print', *Boston Review of Books*, October/November 1999.

Text acknowledgements

Extract from *A Question of Upbringing* by Anthony Powell, published by William Heinemann/Arrow, reprinted by permission of The Random House Group Ltd.

Extract from 'For John F. Kennedy His Inauguration' from *The Poetry of Robert Frost* edited by Edward Connery Lathem, published by Jonathan Cape, reprinted by permission of The Random House Group Ltd.

Extract from 'To Brooklyn Bridge', from *Complete Poems of Hart Crane* by Hart Crane, edited by Marc Simon. Copyright 1933, 1958, 1966 by Liveright Publishing Corporation. Copyright © 1986 by Marc Simon. Used by permission of Liveright Publishing Corporation.

Extract from Frank O'Hara, *Lunch Poems*, copyright 1964 by Frank O'Hara. Reprinted by permission of City Lights Books.

Extract from *The Letters of Evelyn Waugh* (1942), edited by Mark Amory, reproduced by permission of Weidenfeld & Nicolson, an imprint of The Orion Publishing Group, London.

Extract from Susan Howe, 'Hope Atherton's Wanderings', from *Singularities* © 1990 by Susan Howe. Reprinted with permission of Wesleyan University Press.

Extract from Michael Holroyd, *Lytton Strachey: The New Biography* (Vintage, 1995) reproduced by permission of AP Watt Ltd on behalf of Michael Holroyd.

Every effort has been made to contact copyright holders for works quoted in this book. If notified, the publisher will be pleased to acknowledge the use of copyright material in future editions.

Index

9/11 11 September 2077; 19 September 2001

60 Minutes (TV programme) 24 September 1968

2001: A Space Odyssey 13 April 1970

Abelard, Peter 17 May 1164

Accidental Death of an Anarchist 9 October 1997

Achebe, Chinua 12 June 1890

Adam and Eve (public house) 14 January 2001

Adams, John 4 July 1826

Addison, Joseph 17 June 1719; 13 August 1704

Aeschylus 29 September 480 BC

Aeneid 21 September 19 BC

Age of Innocence, The 7 April 1908

Alcott, Louisa May 30 September 1868

Aldiss, Brian 27 September 1957

All Quiet on the Western Front 16 December 1943

Amaryllis at the Fair 20 August 1887

Amazing Stories 1 April 1926

Amazon (electronic bookseller) 15 May 1997

American Civil War 12 April 1861

American Declaration of Independence 1 December 1971

American Dream, An 22 November 1960

American Gold Rush 19 August 1848

Amiel, Henri-Frédéric 20 April 1848

Amiri Baraka (Leroi Jones) 18 September 2001

Amis, Kingsley 2 March 1948

Amis, Martin 24 October 2009

Anatomy of Melancholy, The 5 December 1620

And Quiet Flows the Don 10 December 1965

Appointment in Samarra 20 July 1998

Arbuthnot, Dr John 17 July 1734

Archer, Jeffrey 19 July 2000

Archer, Mary 19 July 2000

Armstrong, Neil 13 April 1970

Arnold, Matthew 20 April 1848

Around the World in Eighty Days 20 December 1872

Asa-Asa, Louis 31 January 1831

Ashford, Daisy 15 January 1972

Asimov, Isaac 21 June 1938

Astounding Science Fiction 21 June 1938

Atlas Shrugged 9 March 1982

Atwood, Margaret 21 August 1832

Auden, W.H. 16 February 2009; 20 May 1946; 24 May 1951; 23 September 1939

Austen, Jane 9 July 1764; 2 December 1802

Autobiography of Alice B. Toklas 7 March 1967

Bacon, Francis 3 July 1603

Bad Blood 11 January 2001

Bainbridge, Beryl 2 July 2010 (Preface)

'Ballad of the Gibbet' 8 January 1463

Bambi 18 November 1928

Banville, John 23 May 2005

Barker, A.L. 1 September 1947

Barker, Pat 22 July 1916

Barnacle, Norah 16 June 1904

Barrie, J.M. 1 January 1988; 15 January 1972

Barthes, Roland 21 October 1966

'Battle Hymn of the Republic, The' 19 November 1861

Battle of Maldon 10 August AD 991

Beerbohm, Max 3 June 1997

Beethoven, Ludwig van 17 January 1972

Beeton, Mrs Isabella Mary 14 March 1836; 4 May 1891

Beggar's Opera, The 29 February 1728

Behn, Aphra 16 April 1689

Bell Jar, The 11 February 1963
Bellamy, Edward 8 September 1892
Bellow, Saul 22 February 2007
Bennett, Alan 2 July 2010 (Preface)
Beowulf 23 October 1731
Berger, John 23 November 1972
Berger, Thomas 24 June 1876
Berlin, Irving 25 December 1941
Berryman, John 7 January 1972
bestseller lists 28 April 1974
Betjeman, John 25 May 1895
Bezos, Jeff 23 February 1455; 15 May 1997
Bierce, Ambrose 12 April 1861
Big Sleep, The 6 February 1939
Bigg-Wither, Harris 2 December 1802
Birth of a Nation, The 3 March 1915
Black and White 25 February 1985
Black Mask (**magazine**) 6 February 1939
Black Robe 25 August 1921
Blake, William 17 April 1794
Blast (**magazine**) 20 February 1909; 2 July 1914
Blasting and Bombardiering 2 July 1914
Blindheim (Blenheim), Battle of 13 August 1704
Bloom, Harold 15 December 2003
Bloom, Mary 17 January 1972
Blunt, Maggie Joy 17 September 1946
Blunt, Wilfred Scawen 18 January 1914
Blyton, Enid 11 August 1897
Bolger, Ray 11 October 1948
Bollingen Prize 19 February 1949
Book of Common Prayer 21 March 1556
Book of Daniel, The 19 June 1953
Booker Prize 2 July 2010 (Preface); 23 November 1972
Borges, Jorge Luis 4 June 1946
Borodino, Battle of 7 September 1812
Bostonians, The 8 April 1883
Boswell, James 24 November 1762
Bosworth Field, Battle of 31 August 1485
Bradford, William 11 November 1620
Bradstreet, Anne 20 June 1669
Brando, Marlon 3 December 1947
Brave New World 29 March 1933

Brazel, William 14 June 1947
Breast, The 24 October 2009
Brecht, Bertolt 29 February 1728; 31 October 1947
Brent, Linda 30 October 1859
Bridge, The 3 January 1870
Brinnin, John Malcolm 19 October 1953
Britten, Benjamin 3 February 1832
Brodsky, Josef 4 January 1965
Brontë, Charlotte 1 October 1848; 4 December 1849
Brontë, Emily 1 October 1848
Brooke, Rupert 4 February 1915
Brooklyn Bridge 3 January 1870
Broughton, Rhoda 5 June 1920
Brownell, Sonia 13 October 1949
Bulwer-Lytton, Edward 26 November 1703
Bunyan, John 12 November 1660
Burgess, Anthony 16 May 1963
Burgess, Guy 24 May 1951
Burns, Robert 25 January 1759
Burton, Richard 27 February 1972
Burton, Robert 5 December 1620
Butterworth, Rebecca 5 July 1846
Byatt, A.S. 14 January 2001
Byrd II, William 26 August 1744
Byron, Lord George 29 January 1819; 10 March 1812; 11 April 1815; 15 June 1815; 15 July 1814

Cabrillo, Juan Rodríguez 28 September 1542
Calder and Boyars (publishers) 28 July 1966
Caleb Williams 6 March 1842
California Gold Rush 19 August 1848
Call of the Wild, The 22 August 1913
Campbell, John W. 21 June 1938
Campbell, Roy 14 April 1949
Campaign, The 13 August 1704
Carlyle, Jane Welsh 21 April 1866; 21 November 1855
Carlyle, Thomas 21 April 1866
Carpenter, Edward 12 December 1913
Carretta, Vincent 29 April 1789
Castle of Otranto, The 28 January 1754
Castro, Fidel 21 February 2005
Catcher in the Rye, The 16 July 1951

Dreiser, Theodore 8 November 1900
Dresden (bombing of) 13 February
1945
Dreyfus, Alfred, Captain 13 January
1898
Dryden, John 5 November 1688;
18 December 1679
Dublin Uprising 24 April 1916
'Duet with Muffled Brake Drums'
14 August 1954
Dumas, Alexandre 5 January 1825
Dust Bowl 15 April 1935
Dylan, Bob 9 April 2008

Earp, Marshal Virgil 26 October 1881
'Easter 1916' 24 April 1916
Eckermann, Johann Peter 22 March
1832
Eco, Umberto 21 October 1966
Edinburgh Festival 5 September 1903
Edinburgh Review, The 1 June 1820
Eikon Basilike 30 January 1649
Eliot, George 5 June 1920
Eliot, T.S. 4 January 1965; 19 February
1949; 4 April 1984; 25 June 1922;
24 August 1966; 14 December 1956
Elizabeth I of England 3 July 1603;
8 August 1588
Ellis, Havelock 16 November 1928
Emerson, Ralph Waldo 8 July 1838
Encounter 27 April 1966
Enoch Soames 3 June 1997
'Epistle to Dr Arbuthnot' 17 June
1719; 17 July 1734
Epstein, Barbara 1 February 1963
Equiano, Olaudah 29 April 1789
Esterhazy, Major Ferdinand 13 January
1898
Eugene Onegin 10 February 1837
European Union 20 January 1972
Evans, Harold 28 April 1974
Everyman Books 9 May 1926
Executioner's Song, The 17 January
1977; 29 November 1963
Exit Ghost 19 March 2007

Falconer 29 March 1933
Fanny Hill 15 December 1964
Farrell, J.G. 12 August 1979
Faulkner, William 11 May 1942

Feast of Fools 6 January 1482
Federal Writers' Project 6 May 1937;
27 July 1935
Ferlinghetti, Lawrence 7 October 1955
Fielding, Henry 18 October 1749
Fitzgerald, F. Scott 20 September 1884;
7 November 1924
Flaubert, Gustave 7 February 1857
Fletcher, John 18 March 1640
Fleurs du Mal, Les 7 February 1857
Florence, Peter 28 May 1988
Florio, John 20 October 1595
Fo, Dario 9 October 1997
'For the Union Dead' 18 July 1863
Ford, Ford Madox (Hueffer) 26 June
1939
Ford, Henry 29 March 1933
Forster, E.M. 12 December 1913
Foster, Professor E. Gordon 2 May
1966
Foucault, Michel 21 October 1966
Four Just Men, The 12 December 1931
Fowles, John 27 June 1969
Foxe's Book of Martyrs 21 March 1556
Francis, Dick 8 May 1962
Frankenstein 11 April 1815
Franklin, Benjamin 19 December 1732
French Lieutenant's Woman, The
27 June 1969
Freud, Sigmund 23 September 1939
Frey, James 26 January 2006
Friedan, Betty 23 March 1963
Frost, Robert 29 August 1962
Fullerton, Morton 7 April 1908
Futurist Manifesto 20 February 1909

G 23 November 1972
Gaskell, Mrs Elizabeth 16 September
1853
Gawain and the Green Knight
30 December c. 1350
Gay, John 29 February 1728
Gay News 12 July 1977
George III of Great Britain 29 January
1819
Gernsback, Hugo 1 April 1926
Ghosts 13 March 1891
Gilman, Charlotte Perkins 17 August
1935
Gilmore, Gary 17 January 1977

Howe, Susan 19 May 1676
Howl 7 October 1955
Huckleberry Finn 18 February 1885;
    16 July 1951
Hughes, Ted 4 January 1965;
    11 February 1963
Hugo, Victor 6 January 1482
Hunchback of Notre Dame, The
    6 January 1482
Hurston, Zora Neale 8 December 1951
Huxley, Aldous 29 March 1933
Huxley, T.H. 29 May 1895
Hyperion 31 March 1909

I, Robot 21 June 1938
Ibsen, Henrik 13 March 1891
Ides of March 15 March 44 BC
Importance of Being Earnest, The
    22 May 1935; 25 May 1895
In Dubious Battle 5 October 1936
In Our Time 26 February 1925
Incidents in the Life of a Slave Girl
    30 October 1859
Indian Removal Bill 27 January 1825
Infante, Guillermo Cabrera
    21 February 2005
Inherit the Wind 5 May 1925
Inside Mr Enderby 16 May 1963
*Interesting Narrative of the Life of
    Olaudah Equiano, The* 29 April
    1789
'Invictus' 23 August 1849
Iris 2 August 1999
Irving, David 13 February 1945
Irving, Washington 27 January 1825;
    7 June 1832
ISBN (International Standard Book
    Number) 2 May 1966
Isherwood, Christopher 20 May 1946

'J'accuse' 13 January 1898
James I of England 7 August 1606
James, Garth Wilkinson 18 July 1863
James, Henry 23 January 1895; 7 April
    1908; 8 April 1883; 29 June 1894;
    18 July 1863
James, William 18 July 1863
Jarrell, Randall 22 February 2007
Jaws 29 July 1945

Jefferson, President Thomas 30 April
    1803; 4 July 1826
Jefferies, Richard 20 August 1887
Jenkins, Roy 10 November 1960
Jewsbury, Geraldine 21 April 1866
Johns Hopkins University 21 October
    1966
Johnson, Samuel 27 March 1766;
    19 April 1759; 1 August 1715
Joyce, James 24 April 1916; 18 May
    1922; 16 June 1904
Julius Caesar 15 March 44 BC
Jungle, The 30 June 1906

Kafka, Franz 26 March 1911;
    24 October 2009
Keats, John 31 March 1909
Kell, Joseph (pseudonym) 16 May 1963
Kennedy, President John F.
    29 November 1963
Kermode, Frank 27 April 1966;
    7 September 1812
Kerouac, Jack 7 October 1955
Khomeini, Ayatollah 14 February 1989
King James Bible 6 September 1536
King Kong 12 December 1931
King Lear 1 August 1715
King, Dr Martin Luther 17 December
    1939
King, Stephen 15 September 2003
King, Tabitha 15 September 2003
Kingston, Maxine Hong 27 October
    1940
Kipling, Rudyard 25 September 1896
Kirkup, James 12 July 1977
Knight, Sarah Kemble 2 October 1704
Khrushchev, Nikita 12 February 1974;
    29 August 1962; 3 November 1958
Kubrick, Stanley 13 April 1970;
    30 August 1963

La Marseillaise 14 July 1795
Lacan, Jacques 21 October 1966
Lady Chatterley's Lover 23 March
    1963; 10 November 1960
Lane, Allen 22 May 1935
Lane, John 22 May 1935
Lange, Dorothea 26 May 1895
Larkin, Philip 2 March 1948; 23 March
    1963

Miller, J. Hillis 21 October 1966
Million Little Pieces, A 26 January
  2006
Milton, John 30 January 1649
'Minor Poet, A' 10 September 1889
Mishima, Yukio 25 November 1970
Mitchell, Margaret 17 December 1939
Moby-Dick 20 November 1856
Modern Library 20 July 1998
Modest Proposal, A 31 July 1703
Mole, Adrian 1 July 2007
Monroe, Harriet 6 June 1915
Monroe, Marilyn 24 January 1961;
  24 October 2009
Montagu, Lady Mary Wortley 23 June
  1727
Montaigne, Michel 20 October 1595
Moodie, Susanna 21 August 1832
Moore, Brian 25 August 1921
Moore, George 21 January 1933
Moore, Ida L. 7 July 1938
Mortimer, John 28 July 1966
Motion, Andrew 5 November 1688
Mount Tambora 11 April 1815
Mousetrap, The 13 September 1957
Mrs Warren's Profession 26 September
  1968
Mudie's Circulating Library
  1 November 1848
Muir, John 26 July 1869
Müller, Herta 8 October 2009
'Murders in the Rue Morgue, The'
  9 August 1846
Murdoch, Iris 2 August 1999
Mysteries of Udolpho, The 9 July 1764
Mystery of Edwin Drood, The 6 March
  1842

Nabokov, Vladimir 18 August 1958
Naipaul, Shiva 25 February 1985
Naipaul, V.S. 25 February 1985
Napoleon I of France 14 July 1795;
  7 September 1812
Native Son 7 May 1945
NBA (National Book Awards)
  15 September 2003
Natural History of Selborne, The
  14 September 1770
'Negro Boy's Narrative, The' 31 January
  1831

'Negro Voter Sizes up Taft, A'
  8 December 1951
New Atlantis, The 3 July 1603
New Directions 13 July 1942
New York Review of Books 1 February
  1963; 23 May 2005
New Yorker, The 14 August 1954
Newby, Thomas Cautley 1 October
  1848
Nietzsche, Friedrich 24 March 1882
Nineteen Eighty-four 4 April 1984
Nobel, Alfred 27 December 1891
Nobel Prize 6 July 2009; 6 October
  1983; 8 October 2009; 9 October
  1997; 22 October 1964; 7 December
  2005; 10 December 1965
Nolan, Christopher 19 January 1988
North and South 16 September 1853
Northanger Abbey 9 July 1764
Notes from the Underground
  21 December 1849

O'Connor, Feargus 10 April 1848
O'Hara, Frank 9 February 1962
O'Hara, John 20 July 1998
O'Keefe, Georgia 15 April 1935
O'Neill, Eugene 2 February 1956
'Ode to Joy' 17 January 1972
On the Road 7 October 1955
One Day in the Life of Ivan Denisovich
  12 February 1974
'Open Boat, The' 2 January 1897
Oregon Trail, The 15 February 1849
Oroonoko 16 April 1689
Orwell, George 4 April 1984;
  13 October 1949
Osborne, John 12 May 1946
Our Mutual Friend 9 June 1865
Owen, Wilfred 22 July 1916; 30 July
  1919

Paine, Thomas 10 January 1776
Paltrow, Gwyneth 14 January 2001
Parkman, Francis 15 February 1849
Pasternak, Boris 3 November 1958
Paternoster Row 5 February 1797;
  29 December 1940
Paterson 13 July 1942
Pattison, Mark 5 June 1920
Paul Clifford 26 November 1703

Rosenberg, Isaac 28 March 1918
Rosenberg, Julius 19 June 1953
Rosencrantz and Guildenstern are Dead 24 August 1966
Rosetta Stone 11 March 1802
Rossetti, Dante Gabriel 8 January 1463
Roswell, New Mexico 14 June 1947
Roth, Philip 19 March 2007; 13 June 1927
Routledge Railway Library 1 November 1848
Rowlandson, Mary 4 March 1676
Rowling, J.K. 21 July 2007
Royal Court (theatre) 12 May 1956
'Rule Britannia' 12 March 1710
Runyon, Damon 11 December 1946
Rushdie, Salman 14 February 1989
Rutherford, Edie 18 September 1946
Rut, John 3 August 1527

Sadleir, John 17 February 1857
Sage, Lorna 11 January 2001
St Crispin's Day 25 October 1415
Saison en Enfer, Un 10 July 1873
Salamis, Battle of 29 September 480 BC
Salem witch trials 1 March 1692
Salinger, J.D. 16 July 1951
Salt Lake City 17 January
Salten, Felix 18 November 1928
Saramago, José 6 July 2009
Sartre, Jean-Paul 22 October 1964
Sassoon, Siegfried 22 July 1916
Satanic Verses, The 14 February 1989
Saturday 23 May 2005
Savrola 15 October 1953
Schiller, Friedrich 20 January 1972
School for Scandal, The 24 February 1809
Schrader, Paul 25 November 1970
Schultz, Charles 9 December 1965
Scopes, John 5 May 1925
Scott, Walter 10 March 1812; 15 July 1814
Scrooby Separatists 15 November 1620
Sea, The 23 May 2005
Sebastopol, Siege of 28 August 1855
Seeger, Pete 1 March 1692
Selby Jr, Hubert 28 July 1966
Seligson, Susan 24 October 2009

Sellers, Peter 30 August 1963
'serendipity' 28 January 1754
Seymour, Robert 8 February 1836
Shadwell, Thomas 5 November 1688
Shakespeare, William 5 March 1750; 15 March 44 BC; 1 August 1715; 7 August 1606; 31 August 1485; 25 October 1415, 1854
Shaw, George Bernard 13 March 1891; 26 September 1968
Shaw, Robert 29 July 1945
Shelley, Mary 11 April 1815
Shelley, Percy Bysshe 11 April 1815; 16 August 1819
Sheridan, Richard Brinsley 24 February 1809
Sherlock Holmes 4 May 1891
Sholokhov, Mikhail 10 December 1965
Shortest Way with the Dissenters, The 31 July 1703
Sidney, Sir Philip 22 September 1586
Sinclair, Upton 30 June 1906
Singularities 19 May 1676
Sister Carrie 8 November 1900
Slaughterhouse-Five 13 February 1945
Smith, George 4 December 1849
Smith, Captain John 5 April 1614; 14 May 1607
Smith, Reverend Sydney 1 June 1820
Smith, Winston 4 April 1984
Snow, C.P. 28 February 1962
Society of Antiquaries 11 March
Solzhenitsyn, Alexander 12 February 1974
'Somebody Blew up America?' 19 September 2001
Southey, Robert 29 January 1819
Southwark Cathedral 18 March 1640
Spender, Stephen 16 February 2009; 27 February 1972; 14 April 1949; 27 April 1966; 24 May 1951; 14 December 1956
Spenser, Edmund 2 November 1938
Spielberg, Steven 29 July 1945
Staplehurst rail accident 9 June 1865
Starr, Ringo 27 February 1972
Steamboat Willie 18 November 1928
Stein, Gertrude 7 March 1967
Steinbeck, John 15 April 1935; 5 October 1936

Steiner, George 23 November 1972
Steiner, Rudolf 26 March 1911
Stevens, Wallace 6 June 1915
Stevenson, Robert Louis 23 August 1849
Stoker, Bram 6 November 1897
Stoppard, Tom 24 August 1966
Stowe, Harriet Beecher 20 March 1852
Strachey, Lytton 16 March 1916
'Strange Meeting' 30 July 1919
Stravinsky, Igor 18 May 1922; 14 December 1956
Streetcar Named Desire, A 3 December 1947
Strickland, Susanna 31 January 1831; 21 August 1832
Striphas, Ted 2 May 1966
'Sunday Morning' 6 June 1915
Swift, Jonathan 31 July 1703
Swinnerton, Frank 15 January 1972

Tarkington, Booth 24 December 1925
Tate, Allen 4 January 1965
Tate, Nahum 1 August 1715
Tay Bridge disaster 28 December 1879
Taylor, Sir Charles 28 July 1966
Taylor, Edward 28 November 1671
Taylor, Elizabeth 27 February 1972
Taylor, John 12 July 1977
Tennyson, Alfred Lord 3 June; 12 September 1908; 12 October 1892
Ternan, Ellen 9 June 1865
Thackeray, William Makepeace 15 June 1815; 2 August 1999; 28 August 1855; 4 December 1849
Theatre Royal, Drury Lane 24 February 1809
Thomas, Brandon 11 October 1948
Thomas, Caitlin 19 October 1953
Thomas, Dylan 19 October 1953
Thomson, James 12 March 1710
Thoreau, Henry David 23 July 1846; 27 October 1853
Threepenny Opera, The 29 February 1728
Time Machine, The 29 May 1895
Time 30 March 1964; 24 December 1925
Timebends 24 January 1961

RMS *Titanic* 31 March 1909
To Kill a Mockingbird 11 July 1960
Tocqueville, Alexis de 2 April 1831
Toklas, Alice B. 7 March 1967
Tolkien, J.R.R. 23 October 1731
Tolstoy, Leo 28 August 1855
Tomalin, Nicholas 27 February 1972
Tomkins, Edward 18 June 1850
Townsend, Sue 1 July 2007
Traill, Catharine Parr 21 August 1832
Tres tristes tigres 21 February 2005
Tristram Shandy 19 April 1759
Trollope, Anthony 17 February 1857; 4 November 1827
Trollope, Mrs Frances Milton 4 November 1827
Troubles 12 August 1997
Turner Diaries, The 9 November 1923
Turner, Lana 9 February 1962
Twain, Mark 16 January 1851; 18 February 1885; 24 March 1882; 30 November 1835
Two Cultures, The 28 February 1962
Tynan, Kenneth 12 May 1956; 1 October 1848; 13 November 1965
Tyndale, William 6 September 1536

Ulysses 16 June 1904
Un-American Activities Committee 1 March 1692; 22 June 1950; 31 October 1947
Uncle Tom's Cabin 3 March 1915; 14 March 1836; 20 March 1852
Under the Eye of the Clock 19 January 1988
Updike, John 14 August 1954
Upward, Edward 16 February 2009
USS *Indianapolis* 29 July 1945

Vampyre, The 11 April 1815
Vanity Fair 15 June 1815; 28 August 1855
Vega y Carpio, Félix Lope de 27 August 1635
Vergil (Publius Vergilius Maro) 21 September 19 BC
Verlaine, Paul 10 July 1873
Verne, Jules 20 December 1872
Vicar of Wakefield, The 27 March 1766

Victoria of Great Britain 25 September 1896

Vidal, Gore 25 November 1970

Vidocq, Eugène François 6 March 1842

Villa Diodati 11 April 1815

Villon, François 8 January 1463

Virginian, The 11 June 1891; 4 August 1885

'Vision of Judgement, A' 29 January 1819

Vizetelly, Henry 21 January 1933; 7 February 1857

Vonnegut, Kurt 13 February 1945

W.H. Smith (stationer) 1 November 1848

Walden 28 October 1853

Wallace, Edgar 12 December 1931

Walpole, Horace 28 January 1754; 9 July 1764

Walpole, Robert 29 February 1728

War and Peace 28 August 1855; 7 September 1812

Warren Commission 29 November

Waste Land, The 25 June 1922

Waterloo, Battle of 15 June 1815

Waugh, Evelyn 20 May 1946; 31 May 1942; 1 September 1947

Waverley 10 March 1812; 15 July 1814

Way We Live Now, The 17 February 1857

Week on the Concord and Merrimack Rivers, A 28 October 1853

Weill, Kurt 29 February 1728

Well of Loneliness, The 16 November 1928

Wellington, Duke of 15 June 1815

Wells, H.G. 29 May 1895

West, Nathanael 22 December 1940

Wevill, Assia 11 February 1963

Wharton, Edith 7 April 1908

Where's Charley? 11 October 1948

Whitbread Prize 19 January 1988; 25 February 1985

White, Gilbert 14 September 1770

'White Christmas' 25 December 1941

'White Man's Burden, The' 25 September 1896

Whitehouse, Mrs Mary 12 July 1977

Whitman, Walt 3 January 1870; 17 October 1879

Wiener, Jon 9 January 1988

Wilde, Oscar 8 March 1859; 22 May 1935; 25 May 1895

William of Orange 5 November 1688

Williams, Tennessee 3 December 1947

Williams, William Carlos 13 July 1942

Wind in the Willows, The 8 March 1859

Winfrey, Oprah 26 January 2006

Wings of the Dove, The 7 April 1908

Winstanley, Gerrard 10 January 1776; 10 October 1609

Winters, Shelley 19 October 1953

Wister, Owen 11 June 1891; 4 August 1885

Wodehouse, P.G. 1 September 1947

Wolfe, Thomas 20 September 1884

Woman Warrior, The 27 October 1940

Wood, Henry Harvey 5 September 1903

Wordsworth, Dorothy 3 October 1800

Wordsworth, William 13 May 1803; 3 September 1802; 3 October 1800

'Wreck of the *Deutschland*, The' 6 December 1875

Wright, Richard 7 May 1945

Wuthering Heights 1 October 1848

Wyndham, John 27 September 1957

X-Files, The 14 June 1947

Yates, Richard 31 December 1961

Yeats, W.B. 18 January 1914; 24 April 1916

Yellow Book, The 8 March 1859

'Yellow Wallpaper, The' 17 August 1935

Yonge, Charlotte 5 June 1920

Young, Graham 12 January 1976

Young Poisoner's Handbook, The 12 January 1976

Young Visiters, The 15 January 1972

Zola, Emile 13 January 1898; 21 January 1933; 5 June 1920